JOHN MONASH

Sir John Monash by John Longstaff, 1918-19

JOHN MONASH

A Biography

GEOFFREY SERLE

MELBOURNE UNIVERSITY PRESS
IN ASSOCIATION WITH MONASH UNIVERSITY

North Suburban Synagogue Beth El
Library

First Published 1982
Reprinted 1982, 1983, 1985, 1990

Typeset by Dovatype, Melbourne
Printed in Australia at
Griffin Press Limited, Netley, South Australia for
Melbourne University Press, Carlton, Victoria 3053
U.S.A. and Canada: International Specialized Book Services, Inc.,
5602 N.E. Hassalo Street, Portland, Oregon 97213-3640

This book is copyright. Apart from any fair dealing for the purposes of private study, research, criticism or review, as permitted under the Copyright Act, no part may be reproduced by any process without written permission. Enquiries should be made to the publisher.

© Alan Geoffrey Serle 1982

National Library of Australia Cataloguing in Publication data

Serle, Geoffrey, 1922–.
  John Monash.
  Bibliography.
  Includes index.
  ISBN 0 522 84239 9.

  1. Monash, Sir John, 1865–1931. 2. Australia. Army — Biography. 3. Generals — Australia — Biography. 4. Engineers — Australia — Biography. I. Title.

355'.0092'4

Contents

Preface	ix
Acknowledgements	xiii
A Note on the Name and its Pronunciation	xv
The Family Tree	xvi
1 The Focus of his family 1865–1881	1
2 University Student 1882–1885	25
3 To What End? 1885–1890	51
4 The Course of True Love 1888–1891	87
5 A Rough Passage 1891–1896	106
6 Little Accomplished 1897–1906	126
7 Pillar of Society 1906–1914	163
8 Gallipoli 1914–1915	201
9 Egypt and Salisbury Plain 1916	255
10 3rd Division in Action 1917	277
11 Something to have lived for 1918	305
12 Feeding the Troops on Victory 1918	329
13 The Best Man in France?	375
14 The Blare and Blaze of Fame 1918–1920	404
15 The State Electricity Commission 1920–1931	435
16 A National Possession 1920–1929	463
17 A Very Tired Man 1929-1931	512

APPENDIXES
  I   John Monash post–1931   531
  II Major Allanson and Robert Rhodes James   534
  III Portraits   536

Notes   538

Select Bibliography   583

Index   591

Illustrations

John Monash, by John Longstaff, 1918–19		*frontispiece*
Bertha and Louis Monash, 1863	*facing*	24
Bertha and John, November 1865		24
John Monash in 1868 and 1878		25
The post-matriculation class, Scotch College, 1881		56
John Monash, late 1881		56
Examples of handwriting		57
Germania Cottage, Richmond		88
Yarra Street, Hawthorn		88
In camp at Queenscliff, 1887		89
At work on the Outer Circle railway, c. 1889		89
Annie Gabriel, 1888		120
John Monash, c. 1888		120
George Farlow		120
Will Steele		120
Vic and John, 1890		121
Three generations, c. 1895		121
Mathilde, 1908		152
Lou and Walter Rosenhain		152
Monash with his wife and daughter, 1908		153
Iona, c. 1914		184
The library		184
Monash in 1912		185
Leaving Port Melbourne		248

ILLUSTRATIONS

4th Brigade headquarters	*facing* 249
3rd Division Headquarters staff, November 1916	280
General Sir Hubert Plumer, drawn by John Monash	281
Monash in May 1918	*between* 360 *and* 361
Presenting a decoration	360 *and* 361
Bertangles chateau and the 'dubbing'	360 *and* 361
Monash at Menton	360 *and* 361
Senior officers, Corps staff, late 1918	360 *and* 361
Keith Murdoch and W. M. Hughes, 1918	*between* 424 *and* 425
Hughes and Monash	424 *and* 425
James Quinn at work	424 *and* 425
Monash and Bertha in France, 1919	424 *and* 425
With Birdwood and Murray, V.C.	424 *and* 425
John and Vic at St Kilda	424 *and* 425
Monash and Lizzie Bentwitch at the Melbourne Cup	424 *and* 425
Leading the Anzac Day march in 1927	*facing* 472
Inspecting New South Wales ex-servicemen police	472
Monash and his S.E.C. secretary	473
With J. G. Latham at a University garden party in 1930	504
Planting a tree near the Shrine in 1930	504
A photographic portrait by Spencer Shier	505
Leaving Iona for the office	505

Maps

	page
Victoria and the Riverina	4–5
Inner Melbourne	17
Gallipoli	215
The Anzac Perimeter	217
The August Offensive	235
The Road to Passchendaele, 1917	288
March–June 1918	312
The July–October 1918 Offensive	345

Preface

It is rare in Australia for a comprehensive collection of private papers, which makes a real biography possible, to become available. When it does, it is usually irresistible to a historian.

Sir John Monash's daughter, the late Mrs Gershon Bennett, and her children David, Elizabeth and Colin, in 1975 offered me access to the Monash Papers in order to write a biography. This book which has resulted is not an 'official' biography. Monash's descendants were determined that the eventual biographer making full use of the Papers should have entire freedom to tell the truth, as he saw it, about his subject. I thank them for believing in me, for their determination that nothing should be concealed, and for their delight in the project as it developed. It has been a rare example of an ideal collaboration between family and biographer.

Monash himself, when he considered the possibility of a future biographer, was neither demanding nor vain. 'I have no wish', he told his son-in-law, 'that you should preserve *indefinitely* my large collection of correspondence, diaries, letter books, press-cutting books, pilot files etc etc. But if there should be any suggestion to have my biography written, much of this material would be useful'. His modesty is not so surprising when it is remembered that it was very unusual at the time for biographies of distinguished Australians to be written, except, for example, in rare cases like Higinbotham, Parkes and Deakin. I remain convinced that, having carefully destroyed a very little of his more intimate records, Monash was sure that his personal papers made up a remarkable detailed record of a life and that he was content to expose himself, in his strengths and failings, to any biographer of integrity. Although vain in some respects, Monash was as ruthlessly clear-sighted about himself as about others, and I believe he would take exception to little that I have written. I have possibly been too generous to him: it is more likely that I have been too hard on him. One cannot be sure: one can only strive to be fair-minded. I make no comment on the remark in 1889 by one of Monash's close friends, Will Steele, that he 'had often thought of the improved life the biographer would lead while engaged in giving an account of your mental activity as shown by your journal'.

Another of my great debts is to the late Charles Bean, the Official Historian for the 1914-18 war and one of Australia's outstanding historians. It happens that Bean's relations with Monash were inharmonious (and Bean found them highly disconcerting). I have had to write of him in critical vein, but my admiration for him as a man and as a historian remains. I have relied primarily on his *Official History* for the general context of the war and for his accounts of the A.I.F. in battle. I am no military historian and, while I am aware that radical reinterpretations of the military conduct of the war, especially of British generalship, are possible, it would have been foolhardy for me to diverge markedly from standard accounts. Technical military history of the First A.I.F. in battle, apart from the *Official History*, hardly exists. Bean remains our guide and inspiration.

I have many more debts to acknowledge — notably to the few remaining veterans of the First A.I.F. whom I could consult. I hope that nothing that I have written offends them. Friends and colleagues at Monash University, especially Leslie Bodi, David Bradley, Ross Day, John Legge and Andy Spaull, contributed valuable insights and spurred me on when I sometimes needed a cheer during the marathon run. So did many others elsewhere, including Alec Hill, John Levi, Robert O'Neill, Warren Perry, Peter Ryan, Barry Smith and my brother Bob. I had many valuable discussions with Captain Peter Pedersen who is also writing on Monash. In England, Susan Scammell, Jack Smithers and others were wonderfully helpful and hospitable. I remember fondly Hüseyin Uluarslan, my guide on Gallipoli. Patsy Hardy and Geoff Browne, my successive research assistants, have been enthusiastic participants. I thank Sir Louis Matheson and Professor Ray Martin for their support. My colleagues in Canberra on the *Australian Dictionary of Biography* have contributed more than they know. And, among many others, I recall the help given by Marie Bodi, Alan Davies, Edgar French, Bill Gammage, Angus McLachlan, Gerry Noble, John Rickard, Ron Taft, Denis Winter, and Val Chapman and Ian Gilbert at Jerilderie.

I remain immensely fortunate in my publishers. I pay tribute to the many officers of the Australian War Memorial, the National Library of Australia, the La Trobe Library, the Monash University Library, the Baillieu Library and the Archives of the University of Melbourne, the State Electricity Commission of Victoria, and of other repositories at home and abroad, for whom nothing was too much trouble. I owe a particular debt to those who translated for me from the German, Dymphna Clark especially, Albrecht Briedenhahn, Danielle Charak and Gisela Tiemann Kaplan. I thank Raie Goller and the others in the Monash History Department who typed the manuscript so expertly. I gratefully acknowledge the assistance given by the Australian Research Grants Committee.

And few writers can be so blessèd in their wife and children.

G. S.

Monash University

Acknowledgements

For permission to use and quote from documents I thank particularly Lord Haig and the Trustees of the National Library of Scotland; the Trustees of the Liddell Hart Centre for Military Archives, University of London King's College; the Trustees of the Australian War Memorial; Mrs C. E. W. Bean (for the Bean correspondence in the Australian War Memorial); and the Council of the National Library of Australia.

The frontispiece and photographs facing pages 248, 249, 424 (top) and on the left and top right pages of the double-page spread between pages 360 and 361 are from the Australian War Memorial collection; all others are from the Monash Papers.

Wendy Gorton drew the six military maps and Sue Tomlin the other two.

G. S.

Conversions

1d (penny)	0.83 cent
1s (shilling)	10 cents
£1 (pound)	$2
£1 1s (guinea)	$2.10
1 inch	2.54 centimetres
1 foot	0.30 metre
1 yard	0.91 metre
1 mile	1.60 kilometres
1 acre	0.40 hectare

A Note on the Name and its Pronunciation

The name Monash (Monasch) probably derives from Manasseh, one of the twelve tribes of Israel.

The normal German pronunciation is MOHnaash; occasionally it is MohNAASH. At some stage the Australian family adopted MOHnash. The natural popular Australian pronunciation has been MONash. Sir John Monash does not seem to have made a point of correcting mispronunciation, but his sister Mathilde was very particular. Most of those who knew Monash, especially military men, used MOHnash; however, the children and grandchildren of some of his close associates are certain that they said MONash. In the 1930s, after Monash's death, his daughter Bertha Bennett and her husband decided to accept MONash. When consulted at the time of the foundation of Monash University, she and her children confirmed this pronunciation.

Abraham Monasch (1710–59)
Joseph Monasch (1745–98)
Loebel Herz Monasch (1770–1831)
Baer-Loebel Monasch (1801–76) = Mathilde Wiener (1804–64)

Julie	Marie	Isidor	Louis	Charlotte	Julius	Rosa	Ulrike	Max	Adolf
1824–91	1826–(?)	1829–1912	1831–94	1833–99	1835–87	1840–1923	184(?)–1928	1845–1920	1847–1921
m. B. Behrend	H. Graetz	P. Wolfsohn	B. Manasse	N. Goldschmidt	E. Manasse	H. Goldschmidt	M. Roth	H. Behrend	M. Monasch
(Krotoschin)	(Breslau)	(Minneapolis)	(Melbourne)	(Newark, N.J.)	(Melbourne–Berlin)	(Krotoschin)	(Melbourne)	(Melbourne–Vienna)	(Muhlhausen)
9 ch.	5 ch.	7 ch.		1 ch.	3 ch.	4 ch.	5 ch.	3 ch.	3 ch.
Albert (1845–1917)		Leo			Berthold		Karl	Bruno	
m. M. Blaschki							Mathilde		
Hilda							Louis		
m. M. Brandt							Herman		
							Sophie		

Mathilde (1869–1939)
Louise (1873–1942)
m. Walter Rosenhain (1875–1934)

Mona Nancy Peggy

John (1865–1931)
m. Hannah Victoria Moss (1869–1920)

Bertha (1893–1979)
m. Gershon Bennett (1892–1955)

John M. (1922–29) David M. (1924–) Elizabeth M. (1926–) John Colin M. (1929–)
                   2 ch.   3 ch.   2 ch.

1

The Focus of his Family
1865–1881

JOHN MONASH, destined to become Australia's most famous soldier, was born on 27 June 1865 at West Melbourne. His parents, Louis and Bertha, were recent migrants to Victoria from Prussia. Louis registered the birth at the East Melbourne synagogue as well as with the government registrar; the official certificate was wrongly dated 23 June.

Several generations of John's paternal ancestors had lived in the town of Krotoschin, Posen province, Prussia (Krotoszyn, Poznán, in modern Poland), some forty miles from Breslau (Wroclaw). Since the fourteenth century Krotoschin had had a Jewish community, which survived mass slaughter in 1656 and fires in 1774 and 1827 which destroyed their quarter. After the absorption of Posen into Prussia in 1793 the community, largely of small craftsmen, continued to prosper modestly and, while broadly identifying itself with German culture, maintained its reputation as a centre of Jewish scholarship. In 1850 almost one-third of the town of about 7500 people were Jewish.

John's grandfather, Baer-Loebel Monasch, was a learned publisher and printer. Baer-Loebel's father, Loebel Herz (Louis), had been a schoolmaster and teacher of the Talmud. In 1855 Baer-Loebel began to compile the story of his turbulent life, labours, joys and sorrows. He wrote these reminiscences in stylistically poor German. He preferred to write and speak Yiddish, was learned in Hebrew and probably had only a smattering of Polish, the language of the aristocracy and the peasants. Born in 1801, he had been a delicate child and never became robust. Despite his parents' determination to make him a rabbi, he trained and was licensed as a bookbinder. The 'thread of misfortune' which wound through his life began when, at eighteen, he was swindled out of his savings. When he was twenty-two he married his first ardent love, Mathilde Wiener, of the Südfeld family which had arrived in Posen in 1684 after banishment from Vienna. Three of her ancestors had been scholar-rabbis and officials of the Krotoschin Jewish community; Max Nordau, the sociologist, was her first cousin once removed. Baer-Loebel was one of thirteen children, all but three of whom died in infancy, and he and Mathilde had another thirteen. Their descendants in Australia were to be much less prolific.

By the early 1830s Baer-Loebel was established as a printer. He acquired a variety of fine Hebrew types, and proceeded to publish famous scholarly editions, in Hebrew and German, of the Pentateuch, a twelve-volume Bible, prayer books, a standard Hebrew edition of the Jerusalem Talmud, and the Torah in eighteen volumes with German and Yiddish translations. He took the lead in rebuilding the Krotoschin synagogue about 1845 and often acted as cantor. Although at one stage he had thirty-six employees his finances were constantly precarious: about 1847 he became insolvent and, in order to save his business, opened an inn. He struggled to survive the chaos of the 1848 revolution, the 1852 cholera epidemic and the mental illness of his wife. His cousin Moritz Monasch, a Breslau bookseller, helped him through. He was continually preoccupied with the problem of providing dowries for his five daughters. The eldest married Benzion Behrend, a scholar-translator and communal activist whom Baer-Loebel took into the business—disastrously. The next married the eminent scholar, Heinrich Graetz (1817–91), of Breslau University; his eleven-volume history of the Jews (1853–75) is a classic pioneer work.

Baer-Loebel employed a tutor for two years to instruct his elder sons in religion, Jewish learning and Hebrew, but they showed little inclination to become scholars. Nevertheless he retained some hopes for his second son, Louis, born on 5 April 1831. For a year he sent him to the high school at Glogau, Silesia, but when the cost proved too much he brought him back to the local high school. Louis eventually found work as a clerk in a Berlin trading-house, and resolved to make the family's fortune by migrating to the Australian goldfields; he may also have been escaping from his family's orthodoxy. He arrived in Melbourne on the *Johan Caesar*, travelling cabin class, on 31 January 1854. His Berlin employers had allowed him 2000 marks worth of goods on credit. Although by now, more than two years after the gold rush began, the colony was glutted with speculative imports which had to be sold at sacrificial prices, Louis managed to make a start in partnership with Louis Martin, also from Germany. He remained in Melbourne and did not get to the goldfields. Like most of the gold-rush migrants he had intended to return home after a few years—yet, as early as 25 April 1856, 'Louis Monasch, merchant, native of Prussia' was naturalized in the presence of Mr Justice Sir Redmond Barry, his stated purpose being 'to establish himself for life' in Victoria. Soon he anglicized his name by dropping the c, as later did two brothers in Australia and some of his American relatives.

Martin & Monash traded as commission agents and general merchants in Flinders Lane west from 1854 to 1858, moving then to Little Collins Street west. Louis lived on the premises in company with Emil Todt, a capable sculptor, until early in 1862 when they all took a villa at St Kilda. For some time from 1858 Louis was secretary to the Deutscher Verein (German Association) and his office became a clearing-house for communication and gossip among German migrants. The business prospered. In 1861 he wrote home to ask for his sixteen-year-old brother Max to help him, sending the passage money; Max arrived in December with Albert Behrend, Louis' eldest nephew. The business dealt in 'wholesale fancy goods and toys', mostly from Nuremberg and Frankfurt, 'combs, brushes, paper and envelopes, Bohemian glassware, cutlery, concertinas, flutinas, Berlin embroideries, tobacco pipes, snuff-boxes, playing cards, all kinds of beads'.

Louis returned to Europe early in 1863 to buy goods, to see his family again, and to find a wife. He was shocked to learn the full extent of his father's financial troubles: Baer-Loebel had had to pay off many of the debts of his sons Isidor and Julius, the latter having been imprisoned for debt. Louis promised to continue supporting his father and was loyally to do so, but Baer-Loebel's troubles were by no means over. His beloved wife died in 1864. Rumours of the wealth of his rich son from Australia inflamed his creditors and he had to sell his house. But he managed to marry off his remaining daughters; the youngest inherited his printing works and her husband carried on the business. Well before his death in 1876 Baer-Loebel had proudly paid off all his debts. Only two of his children remained in Posen: four had migrated to Australia and two to the United States. Other Monasch relatives also migrated to Australia, America, Holland and France. Krotoschin and its environs became an economic backwater and by the close of the century its Jewish community had almost entirely dispersed.

Louis was soon courting Bertha, the twenty-one-year-old sister of his brother Julius's wife, youngest of six children of the late Jacob Manasse, merchant, and Charlotte Benjamin, from Dramburg, near Stettin (Szczecin) in northern Prussia. Louis and Bertha were probably distant relatives, the Manasses having retained the Hebrew and biblical form of the name. Louis was charmed especially by Bertha's piano-playing, as well as by her figure and enchanting eyes—'my black-eyed Xanthippe', he called her. It was a love-match, but the Manasse family did not make him welcome, resenting the threat of this 'odd Australian' to remove their sister to the end of the earth. Moreover, the Manasses were far out of the ghetto, lived in a town with few Jewish neighbours and no synagogue and, in contrast to the Monasches, were culturally assimilated; they may also have felt some sense of class superiority.

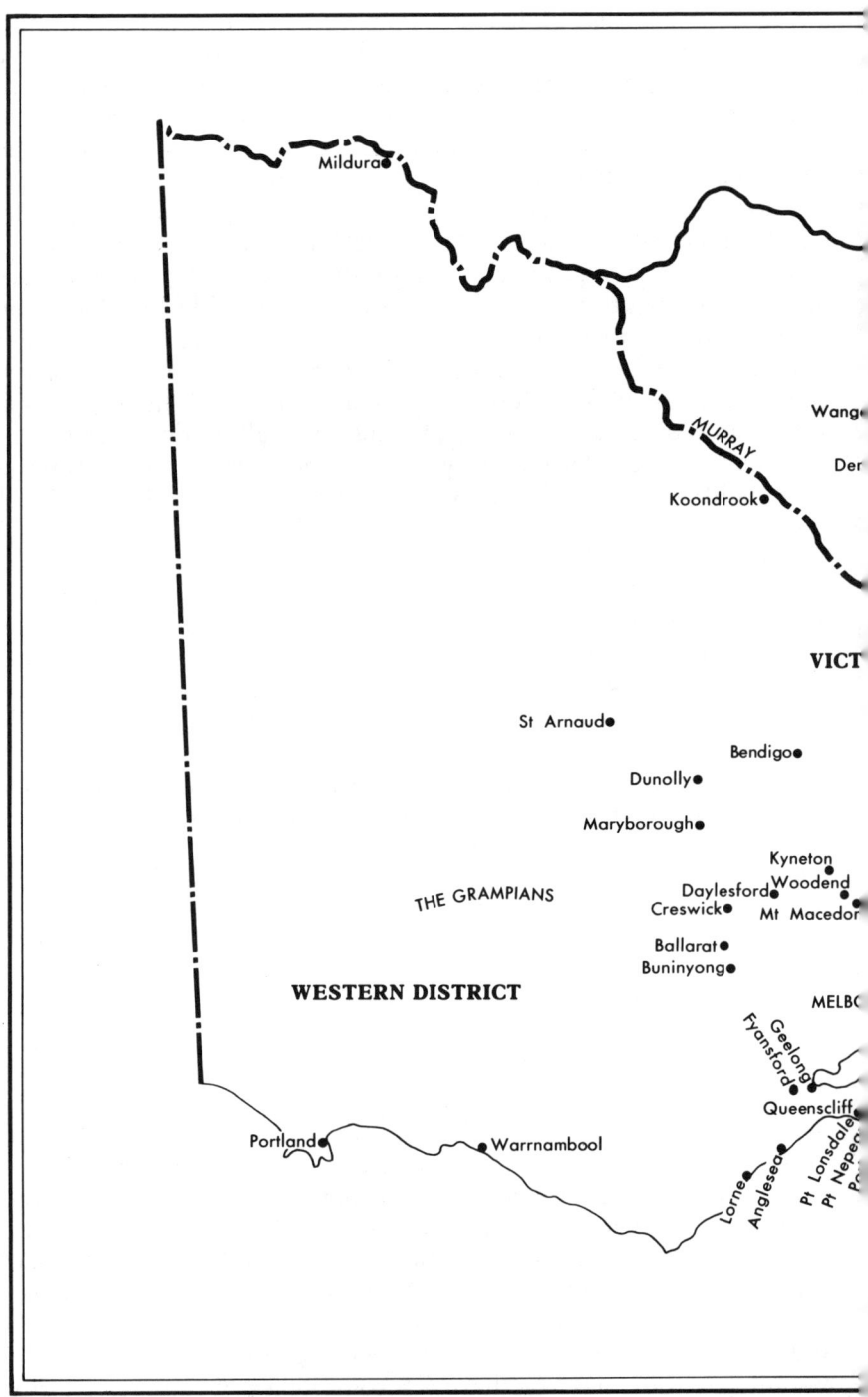

Victoria and the Riverina

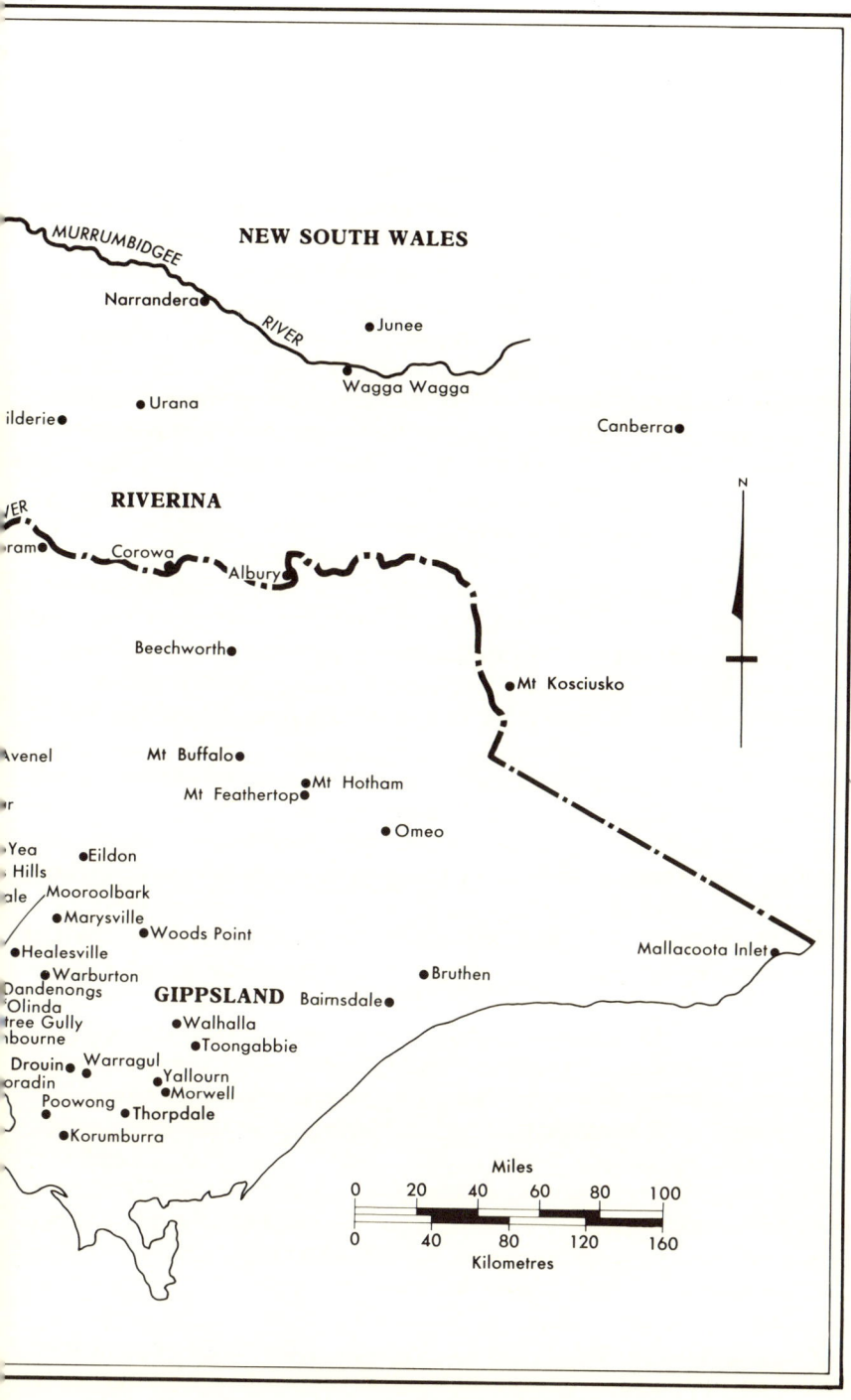

Permission to marry was refused: Bertha and Louis were forbidden to write to each other while he was away on business, but his brothers and sisters conspired to pass messages. His sister Ulrike told him: 'You may feel *quite* sure of her. . . . She commissioned me to send you a multitude of greetings and kisses . . . be of good cheer, for all will come right, when you once come back again'. Bertha wept herself into illness and when she made it clear that she was prepared to break with the family, her mother lifted the ban. Louis and Bertha met briefly again and, when he had to leave once more on business, began a passionate correspondence. In it he is seen as a charming confident man of the world: Bertha writes coyly, in a flowery elaborate style, with perfect command of German. 'What do I care', she wrote, 'if they believe Australia is a desert, where I am in danger of being eaten for dinner one day by savages'. Engrossed with each other, they had no time for the affairs of the world. Religious convictions, if any, seemingly did not intrude on their idyll; Bertha even wrote to Louis on the Day of Atonement, taking care to conceal the transgression from her mother.

They had both a civil marriage and a Jewish wedding on 15 November 1863 at Stettin, and honeymooned in Paris and London before sailing from Liverpool for Melbourne on 11 February. Bertha had promised her family to come back within five years. She was never to return.

The voyage was unpleasant and took 124 days: Louis had confused the *Empire of Peace*, a 'miserable tub', with the fine clipper the *Star of Peace*. They found the eight other cabin passengers and the 259 in the steerage bad company: Bertha felt she was imprisoned and set herself to improve her English. When they arrived at Port Melbourne, Max and Albert went out by boat to their anchorage and 'on our calling out their names they were let down in big baskets amid derisive screams from those on board'.

They went to live in St Kilda where, according to Albert, Bertha made conquests among the local Jews 'not so much by her good looks as by her splendid play[ing] and charming manner and powers of conversation'. The household and the business were broken up when Martin, who had had a stroke, left for Europe to seek medical advice. Louis and Bertha moved to Richhill Terrace, Dudley Street, West Melbourne, on the north side of the Flagstaff Gardens, where John was born.

The English first name illustrates Louis and Bertha's intention of permanent settlement. Louis had begun a chain of migration which soon extended beyond Max and Albert, who continued to live with them on and off. Louis financed the emigration of his disgraced brother Julius and their sister Ulrike who arrived late in 1865. So Bertha was supported in her motherhood by a favourite sister-in-law. Ulrike lived with them for two or three years before marrying Max Roth from Berlin, who was doing well as a storekeeper at Deniliquin in the Riverina. Some time later Albert Behrend's sister Hilda arrived with her husband Moritz Brandt. Young John grew up in an extended family of paternal relatives, who made much of him as the first-born male of a new generation in a new land, but as with so many colonial children his grandparents were on the other side of the world. The Roths and their children were to remain in Australia, but Uncle Julius and his wife stayed only about seven years, and Uncle Max Monash went home in 1879. Albert returned to Europe twice, but brought up an Australian family. Moritz Brandt became a state-school teacher and was briefly head of the Hebrew school at Ballarat about 1880, but died in 1889 and his family returned to Europe. John Monash was to have some thirty-five first cousins on the paternal side alone, in three continents though mostly in Prussia. As a family, they were emotionally highly charged, sensitive to supposed slights, and prone to misunderstandings but quick to make up.

Few anecdotes have survived to show how infallibly the child was the father of the man. Tante Ulrike used often to speak of John drawing railway engines at the age of two. His young nurse and Bertha's maid of all work, Emma Arnott, wheeled him in his pram daily in the Flagstaff Gardens and took him as a toddler down the hill to see the trains in the West Melbourne yards. They remained at Richhill Terrace for about three years and then moved to a succession of modest cottages—in Victoria Parade, East Melbourne, in 1868; Church Street, Richmond, in 1869; and Clifton Street, Richmond, probably in 1871. They bought this last house and named it, significantly perhaps, Germania Cottage. Richmond Hill was a fashionable area, surrounded by humble housing.

Early in 1869 Bertha and John lived for three months with the Roths and Uncle Max at Deniliquin. Mathilde Monash was born in the Church Street cottage on 18 October 1869. Two hundred yards up the hill the Jesuits were building the huge bluestone St Ignatius Church; presumably his mother or the maid often took John to watch. Next year Bertha began to teach him the piano and to take him to Liedertafel concerts; before John was six he played a short piece as a surprise for his father on his birthday. Louise was born in Germania Cottage on 5 August 1873.

John was brought up bilingually. Louis and Bertha spoke good English and used it with the children; Bertha read to John in English. But John also became fluent in German and it may have predominated before he went to school.* His spoken English had a slight accent,

---

* Louis had been brought up to speak Yiddish and his father wrote to him in Yiddish, but Bertha did not know it. None of their children acquired even a smattering of it.

which he ultimately took pains to rid himself of; when he was nineteen he was still conscious of 'pronouncing the gutturals in a distinctly Teutonic accent'. After he went to school and his English developed, his parents insisted that he keep up his German. His first letter to survive was written when he was about seven:

> My beloved Mamachen,
> Papa went with me to the ferry and kept watching me till I reached the other side and I found the house without problem where Aunty ... expected me at the door. ... Then I played a lot with Karl in the sand. ... At 10 o'clock I went to bed [and] in the morning I got up at a quarter past seven and had a bath.
> I hope that you and Mathilde are quite well. Kiss Papa and Mathilde for me.
> Your loving son,
> Johnny

Already Louis and Bertha were proudly writing home to their families of their 'wunderkind'. Since the age of six John had attended St Stephen's Church of England School, close to home. A fellow pupil, George Dethridge, later chief judge of the Arbitration Court, eventually recalled 'how young John delighted the other boys with the pictures he used to draw for them'. He won his first prize in the second form. When he left after three years, the headmaster wrote of him as a 'boy of much present intelligence and gives promise of success in his future school career. ... Industry seems to be his chief characteristic. ... Conduct excellent'.

So far as we know, it was a fairly undisturbed and unremarkable childhood: not unhappy, not oppressive, no evidence of slights and taunts, no conspicuous tensions or deprivations which might implant driving ambition and an implacable will to succeed. Yet his unknown fears, loves and hates in these years are the key to his subsequent career. We do not know how often he was spanked or cuddled, or the degree to which he was allowed to roam or ordered to keep off the street and shun neighbourhood children, or given responsibilities such as a small shopping excursion. Photographs of him as a child show an arresting, determined face, with bottom lip protruding and a 'born old' expression.

When John was nine the family moved to Jerilderie in the Riverina. At some stage Louis had suffered 'terrible losses' and was never again to be well off. From 1870 his business activities are obscure. His brothers Max and Julius, like so many migrant Jews without craft-training, had established themselves as storekeepers, at Narrandera and Wanganella in New South Wales. Louis eventually decided to launch out similarly at Jerilderie and the family joined him early in 1875.

The Riverina was developing as a farming area, and frontier townships like Jerilderie had prospects of quick growth. It was a crossroads on the Billabong Creek on a flat plain, like a station on the transcontinental railway, John remembered late in life. Narrandera was 71 miles to the north-east, Deniliquin 57 to the south-west, Tocumwal 36 to the south on the Murray River. Some 250 settlers inhabited about fifty mostly ramshackle wooden houses. Louis had his store on one of the crossroads corners with a rival opposite. He was active in the progress association and on the school board and, in the interests of town development, supported the selectors in the Farmers and Traders' Association whose chief concern was to break down the pastoralists' near-monopoly of water frontages. The 1876 Jerilderie Show was a failure because of the selectors' hostility. Although they were almost the only German or Jewish family in the area, the friendly Louis and Bertha were popular. But the township's growth was disappointing and Louis did not prosper much.

William Elliott, in his early twenties, was in sole charge of about seventy pupils at the recently opened public school. Johnny was a delight to him: he taught him all the mathematics he knew and 'many things outside the school curriculum'. His precocious pupil lent a hand with some of the younger and more backward children. They were a roughish and mixed lot of bush barbarians, but the bookish and musical boy may have benefited from the rough-and-tumble, democratizing state-school process. His frequent requests to Elliott over the years for news of his contemporaries indicate that the experience was not unhappy. Elliott told of boys on the land, pastoral employees, railwaymen, post office clerks, miners and blacksmiths. A couple were in gaol, one was a larrikin brawler, another was frequently had up for drunkenness and obscene language, another was 'adept at billiards and blackguardism'. On the whole 'they reflected no credit on my tuition', said Elliott; 'I did my best but was not backed up by the parents'. John was later convinced that a critical part of his education was his fascination in his Jerilderie years with the Miscellany pages of the *Australasian* and *Town and Country Journal*; encouraged by his parents, he spent much of his spare time 'composing acrostics and arithmetical puzzles'.

The mid-1870s were drought years in the Riverina, with dead cattle and sheep littering the paddocks. But the area teemed with parrots and cockatoos, and with wallabies and kangaroos which hop-hopped away whenever a vehicle entered the bush around the township. Occasionally John got out to nearby stations and farms and begged many a ride on bullock- and horse-wagons. Often, in the evenings, he would ride with his mother, 'he on his little bay mare and she on her tall chestnut'. His memories of Jerilderie were to be vivid: when he was twenty-six he wrote to Elliott of the 'happy recollections that cling about every corner of the place, every bend of the creek'. He longed to return—but when he eventually did 'the simply tremendous paddock' at the back of their store seemed tiny. Fifty years after he left the town he drew a map for the benefit of his daughter making a visit. He marked ' "The Bend of the Creek" (where the Bunyip lived and where the old man lived in the haunted hut)', the spot 'where Mat and I used to build Mia Mias', and another where 'I used to see the blacks spearing Murray Cod'. The blacks, a 'miserable set of wretches', were in and out of the township; he acquired a waddy from one of them.

His sharpest memory of Jerilderie was of the goats:

> Every farm kept goats, and the duty of driving those gregarious creatures in from the plains at milking-time . . . devolved upon us youngsters. We loved doing it—aping our seniors all the time, of course! . . . We copied the drivers of bullock-teams, swimming our charges across the waist-deep river. We rejoiced over the birth of any kids to the flock. We organised goat races. And sometimes, we made goat-carts, decking the harnessed goats with red ribbons, and driving proud little brothers and sisters down the main street.

For a time John and friends collected bottles, offering a penny a dozen, but the business closed abruptly when horrified parents discovered what was going on. John and Mathilde used to manufacture toy sets of clothes for sale. Mat recalled that in those years 'the foundations of the companionship of brother and sister were set'; she was six or seven and able to tag along. John was already demonstrating his great gifts of imparting knowledge and organizing. When he was ten he began to teach her to read, write and reckon—and even some French—and to carry out 'most carefully, numerous clever and original mischievous pranks'. Despite all legends, John Monash was not in Jerilderie in February 1878 when the Kelly gang called in, although he had possibly held Ned's horse on an earlier visit.

Probably because of dissatisfaction with the school and the company Johnny was keeping—was he using bad language?—Bertha and the children after a year retreated to Melbourne. There, for about six weeks early in 1876, ten-year-old John attended the South Yarra College, conducted by the Reverend Henry Plow Kane. On 20 March he wrote to Bertha saying he was 'very sorry to lose your boy as he is one of our most promising scholars. In every way he has given me satisfaction, and has gained the good will of all—masters and pupils alike—I only wish you could make arrangements for him to remain'. For whatever reason, Bertha and the children returned to Jerilderie.

Encouraged by Elliott, eighteen months later Louis and Bertha decided in anguish that John must go to the best possible school in

Melbourne: the Jewish and Prussian reverence towards learned men which they shared made the move inevitable, sooner or later. Louis and his family would have to part for an indefinite period. Presumably he still had high hopes for his business and saw little prospect in starting afresh in Melbourne; presumably to board John at school and partially lose him was seen by Bertha as more drastic than splitting the family home. They may also have considered the bush school to be unsuitable for Mathilde. And Bertha herself probably was unhappy in Jerilderie.

Elliott was well aware of the pressure imposed on the boy:

> I had always grave fears that you were having too much study when you were with me what with German French Hebrew and Music at home in addition to the school work. I thought it was too great a strain on your mind and that your health would suffer.

Elliott became the local newspaper proprietor-editor. He was to gain lifelong satisfaction from the success of his star pupil, who always acknowledged him with affection and his contribution to laying 'the foundation of my career'.

John entered Scotch College, East Melbourne, on 9 October 1877; he was placed in the Upper Third and given the number 162. Scotch was probably the largest church school in Australia; its 300 to 350 pupils included about thirty Jews for whom classes in Hebrew were provided and who joined in Old Testament studies but were excused from prayers. Dr Alexander Morrison, a classicist from the University of Aberdeen—tall, bearded, top-hatted, ramrod-straight, and awesome pillar of the kirk—was a firm disciplinarian who used the tawse freely. He seemed to be everywhere and knew every boy in the school. He stood for academic excellence, manliness, and development of character for which he found innumerable models in ancient history. Boys must be trained for gentlemanly deportment, habits of order, submission to authority, self-control and self-reliance. His brother Robert, the vice-principal, was greatly loved and slightly ineffectual. Of those whom John had as teachers, 'The Doctor' himself taught mainly history and geography; Robert Morrison took mathematics and science; Frank Shew taught English and classics; and the 'learned and gentle' orthodox Jew Moses Moses conducted the post-matriculation class.

Monash was fortunate in that his aptitudes and interests were suited by Morrison's innovatory breadth. He had modelled Scotch on his own school, the Elgin Academy, and followed the tradition of the Scottish academies and of English Dissent as opposed to the concentration on the classics of the traditional English grammar school. Classics and mathematics were still central, but Scotch was the first school in Australia to teach English literature as such and to introduce a science laboratory; drawing and music were regular subjects. Morrison had recently returned from a year abroad, and had expanded the teaching of science and encouraged the study of German. He also intensified testing, which was placed on an almost weekly basis in order 'to secure uniformly steady application'. Scotch had no cadets as yet, but there were regular drill periods and some elementary gymnastics—sport was not yet glorified. At the speech days in 1878 and 1879 Sir James McCulloch, wealthy merchant and former premier, gave tedious exhortations on moral endeavour.

It was a school oriented to preparation for the professions as well as for business. Of the dozen in the post-matriculation class of Monash's year, four became lawyers, two engineers, two doctors, two ministers, one a teacher, and one a librarian.* It was not conspicuously a school for the sons of the wealthy and there was little snobbery of class, wealth or ethnic origin—the tone was overwhelmingly Scottish migrant. The grey granite Gothic buildings were cramped in two acres and the boys crowded in the gravel yard; but over Lansdowne Street were the Fitzroy Gardens.

About New Year 1878 John visited his father in Jerilderie, making part at least of the return journey on his own. He then dutifully wrote regularly to Louis (in German, as always) to tell him of the family's doings. That summer they were often in company with the Roths and Uncle Max. There were picnics in the Botanic Gardens and Royal Park; visits to the Troedel and Wischer families; outings to the circus, an organ concert in the Town Hall, a pantomime (John caught a bag of lollies thrown by the clown), and to the beach. He had taken up Hebrew lessons again and could 'translate already several things'; and he asked his father to be sure to keep for him any New South Wales sixpenny stamps. The highlight of his holidays was seeing the famous *Struck Oil*: he 'was so enthralled by it that for a very long time afterwards he used to play scenes from it with his sister whom he had carefully drilled in the words she had to say'; they acted all the parts again and again. J. C. Williamson's had won a lifelong addict.

Bertha trained her children 'to regard it as a privilege to be allowed to read to her'. John's early favourites were *Tales of the Arabian Nights*, *The World of Wonders*, *Chambers Miscellany*, Jules Verne and Dumas. Leach's illustrations to London *Punch* were 'a never-failing source of entertainment and amusement'. Now and later he read and re-read

---

* Close contemporaries included in the *Australian Dictionary of Biography* are J. W. McCay (soldier and politician), Lionel Robinson (financier), E. La T. Armstrong (librarian), W. Cattanach and Ebenezer Shaw (engineers), F. J. Clendinnen and F. Hobill Cole (doctors), A. Colquhoun (artist), H. E. Oliphant (journalist and scholar), Norman Bayles (businessman and politician), G. L. Aitken (businessman), and J. A. Andrews (anarchist).

most of the novels by Dickens, Scott, Bulwer Lytton, George Eliot and Thackeray, and many works in German and French. He continued throughout his life to talk of the characters as of people he had met. He was also encouraged to keep up his drawing: one of the earliest paste-ins in his albums of souvenirs was his 'first painting'—a copy of a flower-painting, on a card.

About March 1878 John reported his 'daily occupation' to his father.

> Monday, getting up 7, practising till 8, breakfast till 8.30 walk to school, school and walk back home till 1 o'clock dinner, walk to school, school til 4 o'clock, 4.30 to 6 at Mr. Meiers', till 6.30 walk back home, tea till 7, homework till 9.30 and then to bed. Tuesday is the same only from 7 to 8.30 I am at the choir and back home at 9.30. Wednesday morning I do my home-work and have my piano-lesson at night, Thursdays are the same as Wednesdays, on Friday I do not go to Mr. Meiers' and come home at 4.30 then I do my school-work before tea and after tea I have German lessons... Saturday morning I go into the synagogue and come back at 12 noon and then I have the afternoon to myself, perhaps we are going out or I read something to Mama. Sunday mornings I go to the choir again and come home at 1 o'clock. In the afternoon I have my piano lesson... so you see that I only have Saturday afternoons to myself.

The Reverend Isadore Myers was preparing him for his bar mitzvah. John possibly did not continue daily to trudge almost a mile and a half home and then back at midday for his dinner, though it was the main meal and there was an hour and a half break. Choir practice twice a week as well as synagogue on Saturday mornings was to continue for two years.*

A few days after his thirteenth birthday John celebrated his bar mitzvah at the East Melbourne synagogue. His father was not present: it is extraordinary for a Jewish father to be absent from this formal conferring of responsibility on a youth. John's cousin Albert Behrend, some twenty years his senior, Moritz Brandt and Uncle Max probably all attended. John's mother and sisters were in the gallery. His presents thrilled him—the table was 'full of things I had wanted for a very long time': from his parents a microscope, a Shakespeare and Uncle Graetz's History of the Jews in a French translation, autographed; a gold watch from Uncle Max and gold studs from Aunt Ulrike; a chemical set from Albert; Haydn's sonatas, a stamp album, a knife. All the relations and his friends Victor Wischer and Arthur Hyde passed the day with him.

---

* John probably knew by sight at least the other famous Richmond product, Nellie Melba, who was four years older. She lived a mile away in Burnley and attended the Presbyterian Ladies' College near Scotch College across the Fitzroy Gardens. Her father, David Mitchell, played a big role in Monash's life. Sixty years later D. B. W. Sladen said Monash had told him he detested her.

In his letter to his father John did not mention any formal banquet or speech he had to make. The ceremony and the familial celebrations impressed him, like any Jewish child, deeply; the 'thoughts and ideas on that occasion' flooded back to him four years later at cousin Karl Roth's bar mitzvah.

Louis seems not to have written to reinforce the lessons of the day beyond rather cursorily reminding Johnny that, now he was of an age when he was answerable to his God, he had to take even more pains to satisfy his parents who worked so hard on his behalf; and that the remarkable care he had received reflected the belief that some day he might be 'something extraordinary'. Cousin Albert, however, wrote a long epistle of moral guidance. Traditionally, for 3000 years, he affirmed, Jewish children after their bar mitzvah were accepted as citizens and undertook consequent duties, swore to serve God and follow the Holy Laws, and had to differentiate right from wrong on the basis of inexperienced judgement, while praying for guidance and obeying parents and religious teachers. The time of useless play and laziness was over. Obedience, truth and patience were the guiding rules. Obedience led to self-control. Truth was a peaceful harbour, deceit the dangerous sea; a lie was usually cowardice, was evil even as a joke; admitting mistakes made a better human being. Be patient, of even temper and good spirits; bear misfortune with resignation; keep passions under control; only weaklings lose their tempers; practise forgiveness. Albert returned to Europe in 1879 for six years and kept up an exhortatory correspondence with John whose replies became increasingly strained. He also later recalled how he 'used to hate those uncles and aunts whom I had never seen and to whom I was compelled to write'.

John had become a member of the choir at the synagogue under Louis Pulver, a young and able musician. He probably instructed the choir in the faith; moreover he was a family friend, who was in and out of the house playing music with Bertha. Even when John was twenty and emancipated, he remained respectful to Pulver: 'Our old relationship will ever be sufficient guarantee of the consideration I will give and the weight that I will attach to what you have to say to me'. And he recalled one morning on the way to the synagogue, asking him his 'opinion of the saying about the influence of little things on the shaping of character. Your answer was very emphatic to the effect that the smallest occurrence is lasting in its effects'.

About 1880 there were some three thousand Jews in Melbourne of whom about half had migrated from England and a large part of the remainder from Germany. Ten years later their numbers had almost doubled: many of the newcomers were from eastern Europe, some of them refugees from the appalling Russian pogroms, and they included many Yiddish speakers. The Melbourne Jews remained too few and too diverse in origin for anything like a Jewish district to develop yet. Moreover the community was highly assimilated: Jewish visitors were impressed by its prestige. Jewish historians stress how rarely the virus of anti-Semitism flared; representation in parliament by men like Edward Cohen and E. L. Zox, and in local government and civic bodies, was far greater than their numerical proportion. The community's dignified campaign in the 1850s for religious equality had been irresistible, given the growing dominance of liberal assumptions; superficially it was a minor grievance, but it reflected the worldwide struggle for recognition of civil rights. Occupationally they tended to concentrate in general mercantile activity, the clothing business, and skilled trades; many like the Monash brothers became rural storekeepers. The Melbourne community was by no means united. Its origins were diverse and there were also terrible rows on doctrinal matters between and within the three main congregations at Bourke Street, East Melbourne and St Kilda. Religious orthodoxy was in steady decline, especially among German Jews who tended to pursue liberal tendencies or to lapse. Only a minority of the community regularly attended synagogue; because of the disparity of the sexes about one-quarter of the males were 'marrying out'; many businessmen were not prepared to observe the Saturday Sabbath strictly; observance of dietary laws was lax and the struggle to educate the young in Hebrew generally unavailing. Of those who slipped away from religious practice, many of course continued to regard themselves as Jews ethnically and culturally.

The East Melbourne congregation was largely non-British in membership with a strong Polish core. The new synagogue in Albert Street had been completed in 1877; during a monster bazaar around New Year's Day 1880 John participated in a concert by Jewish children under Pulver in the Town Hall. Louis and Bertha Monash were no longer orthodox, although they were still prepared to send their children to synagogue. They could not have been devout or they would not have moved up-country away from a synagogue; their names do not appear in the Jewish press as members of a congregation or as subscribers to religious funds; the inscriptions on Bertha's grave, presumably arranged by Louis, are in German as well as Hebrew; at some stage in Prussia the Monasches cut off social relations with the Manasses because they had abandoned the faith. The indications are that Louis and Bertha were 'enlightened', 'liberated' Jews. Few of Bertha's Melbourne friends seem to have been Jewish, though many were German, such as Herman Püttmann junior, the printer-littérateur, W. A. Brahe the lawyer-consul, Charles Troedel the lithographic printer, and their wives and families. This group had more than a trace of the radical German Enlightenment. Those of German birth in Victoria outnumbered all other Continental Europeans, but there were only some 2500 in Melbourne.

John Monash was to be very much a Melbourne man. By 1880 it was no mean city, already almost the largest in the Southern Hemisphere. The gold rushes of the 1850s had permanently attracted hundreds of thousands of young migrants like Louis Monash, who swamped the existing pastoral settlement and made Victoria almost the most populous and famous British colony. This generation of migrants was to remain dominant till the end of the century when some of their children like John became prominent. Gold provided the basis for one of the most prosperous communities in the world in which a liberal, egalitarian and democratic political and social framework allowed full play to men of enterprise competitively on the make. It was a predominantly English society, but with strong Scottish-Presbyterian and Irish-Catholic minorities, which became fervently imperialistic rather than Australian nationalist, and extremely puritanical in outlook. Melbourne was a true metropolis which closely reflected English, Continental and American intellectual currents, and maintained educational institutions, libraries, and a daily, weekly and quarterly press of high world standard. Physically the city had an American tone deriving from its gridiron pattern, but it was reminiscent also of London, Liverpool and Edinburgh. It was raw-looking still in its combination of noble stone and humble weatherboard: John was to spend much time in the grand classical Public Library and the bluestone Barracks. It was widespread and open because of the low density of housing and the broad belt of parklands. During the boom 1880s, while the population grew towards 500 000, the city was to be largely rebuilt (to look like 'a Renaissance gone wrong') and extensive public works programmes were carried out.

As a boy and youth, John had plenty of walking. His almost daily route from Clifton Street to Scotch College on the eastern rim of the city was by lanes to Punt Road, through the park above the Melbourne Cricket Ground, then across Wellington Parade to the wild and untailored Fitzroy Gardens. Or possibly, while escorting his sisters to Yarra Park State School, he would make for the Bridge and Punt Roads corner, then along Wellington Parade. The synagogue was a quarter-mile beyond Scotch, past St Patrick's and St Peter's, at the side of Parliament House. It was nearly two miles on Sundays to the Roths in South Yarra across the Chapel Street bridge or by the ferry at Punt Road. Local shopping was nearby in Swan Street. For travel to and from the city itself, Richmond station was only three hundred yards away and the fare was one penny; or occasionally he might use the horse-bus between Bridge Road and Flinders Street. Friends in

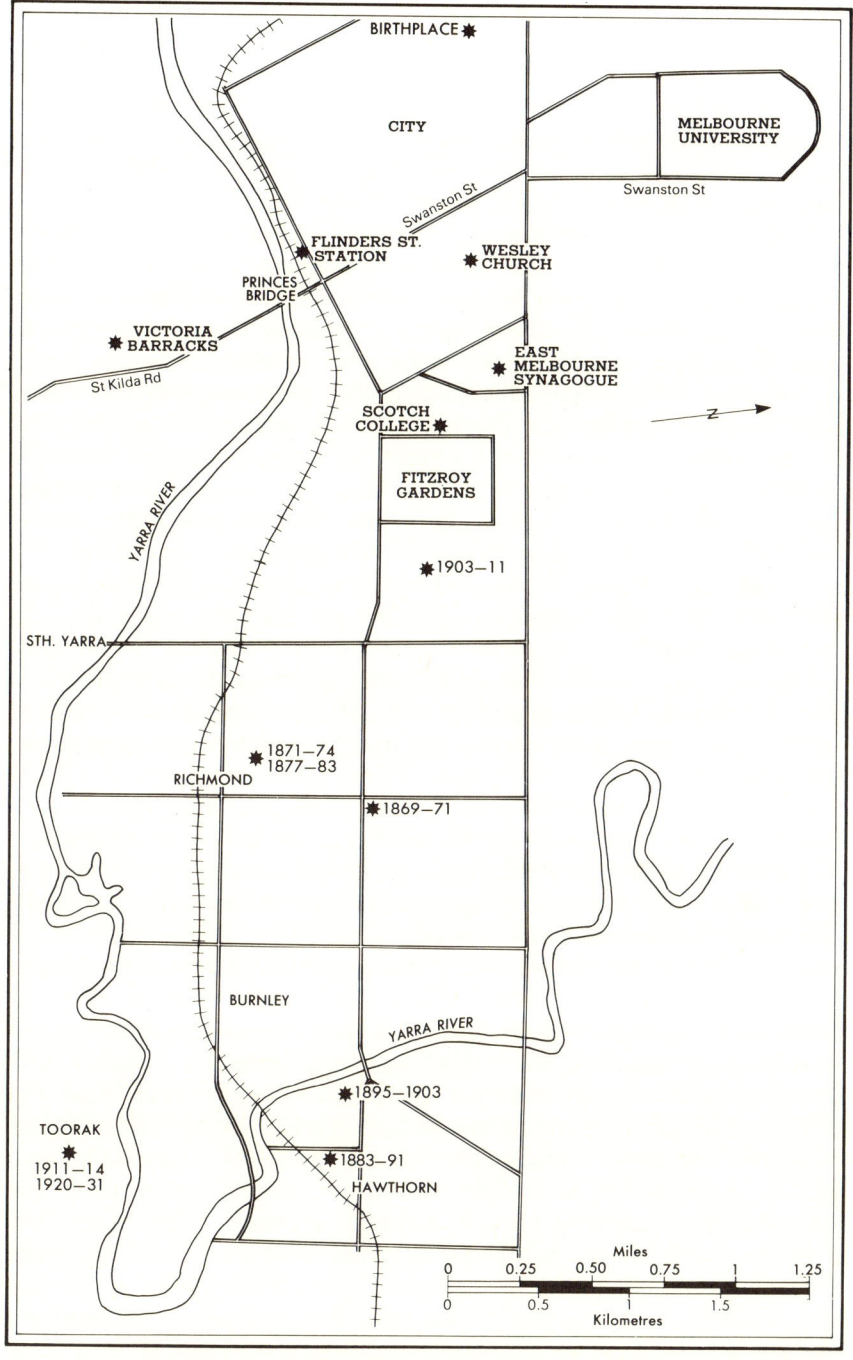

Inner Melbourne

west Hawthorn, two miles away, were handy to the station there, though John would often walk for economy and exercise. When he went to the University in 1882 he took the train to Flinders Street and walked the mile and a quarter, usually up Swanston Street, and back. When the family moved to Hawthorn and the elegant cable-trams came in from 1885, movements were much easier. Cabs were a luxury, only for family or dance-parties.

Louis' letters from Jerilderie, written to John when he was thirteen, are heavy-handed and unimaginative and display little intimacy with the boy. Johnny was again and again reminded to be industrious, well-behaved, obedient. His school reports showed deficiencies in English, Latin, Geography and History: in view of his intelligence, was he doing well enough? Did he feel advanced enough yet to enter for the school essay prizes? His talent for the piano would bring advantages one day; he had had the opportunity to learn without cost because of his mother's devotion; he *must* practise regularly. Louis encouraged John to take part in sport, for the sake of his health. He gave him little tasks—exercises in German, measuring the temperature twice daily. His occasional praise was almost lost in the exhortatory barrage. Again and again John was reminded of all his parents were doing for him and of his duty to love them and give them joy through his success. If Louis and Bertha were classically Jewish in their willingness to make sacrifices for their first-born son, they also pointed it out to him at wearisome length. John always felt that his father was slightly cold towards him.

From twelve to seventeen, apart from occasional brief visits to and from his father, John lived with his mother and small sisters—and Louis had earlier been away for long periods. His children remembered him as a mild and gentle man, 'of advanced ideas and thought'. Although scanty, the information about Bertha is sufficient to indicate that she was the dominant parent. Her daughters vividly remembered her conviction that Johnny was destined to be a great man, as she told her husband again and again. She had fully accepted the consequences of migration, mastered the English language herself, and made sure that her son would grow up as an Australian within the British cultural context, with German influences and contacts secondary. At the same time she consciously strove to provide for him the very broad Prussian type of middle-class education. Within two years of her arrival she had worked vigorously for a Melbourne Hospital bazaar, and had received the formal compliment of a life governorship. Her young maid, who nursed John, 'loved and honoured' her and thought her 'a noble lady'. After the prosperous 1860s they could not always afford to keep a servant, let alone a horse and buggy, but John remembered his mother's tireless energy and competence in managing the household.

Bertha was a gifted hostess who took pride in building up a circle of pleasant friends; she left cards conscientiously and had many callers on her days 'at home'. She looked forward eagerly to a new house as an elegant centre for hospitality. Her friends were by no means exclusively German; many were English migrants or Australian such as the Hodgsons, whose eldest son Richard left for Cambridge University in 1878 to begin a world-famous career as an investigator of the supernatural, and Catherine, elder sister of Alfred Deakin, the brilliant young politician. These friendships speak volumes for her capacity for assimilation. Catherine Deakin, though ten years younger, became a close friend. When John was fifteen and Catherine thirty, he worked out the deductions for Books 1 and 2 of Euclid, to help her in her teaching at the Presbyterian Ladies' College. Catherine and Bertha were both talented pianists. Chopin was Bertha's favourite composer. Several times a week someone would visit Germania Cottage to play and sing— her nephew Albert, Pulver, members of the musical German community.

The family considered that John resembled his mother and was not particularly Jewish in looks, manner or speech. Two letters from Bertha to him, written when he was sixteen, survive. They are long, fluent, chatty and intimate. She is eager for further news of him on holiday; she calls him Johnnychen, reminds him about several letters he should write, and concludes: 'Now, dear son, fare well; stay happy and good, take care with your riding; you know how dear your life is to your parents. Keep loving your mother Bertha'. She remarks on the good progress at school of his sisters: 'You just wait and see, dear Johnny, you will eventually be just as proud of your sisters as they are of their brother. May God keep you all in good health and make good people of you!!' Her love is evident and though there is little to suggest that her possessiveness was smothering, she was a driving, striving parent. It is likely that she and her friends had lavishly praised and caressed the eager child, marvelled at his cleverness and discussed his future as a genius. In her husband's absence, Bertha in the daily round had talked much with her son who developed a precocious articulateness and ease in adult company. Like most great men and most great soldiers, John Monash was a mother's boy, a favourite child, an only son with adoring younger sisters, who eventually would stride confidently through life and be highly attractive to women.

In 1878 John took Mathematics, in which he came top, Elementary Physics and Bible studies in the Lower Fifth form, English and Electricity and Magnetism in the Upper Fourth, and Latin and French in the Lower Fourth. His earliest surviving notebook, probably of 1878–79, includes arithmetical workings, exercises in Latin translation, a start on the traditional essay on 'How I spent my Holidays', notes on Nelson and Wellington, and notations in Pitman's shorthand—which he quickly mastered. 'About this time', he wrote in some autobiographical notes made when a university student, 'I first formed the resolve of studying in the University and so in 1879 (by good luck) was placed in the Matriculation Class'—the Upper Fifth. In June that year he started his first diary and made brief entries for a couple of weeks. It includes his planned time-tables for after-school and weekend work: for example,

> home at 4.30, rest till 4.45. Practise piano 4.45-5.45. Get tea ready 5.45-6.15. Tea till 6.45. Collect books together till 7 o'clock. Euclid etc. till 7.30. English till 8.30. Latin till 9 o'clock. Maps etc. for Wednesday till 10. Bed at 10 or after.

At the Matriculation and Civil Service examination that year, aged fourteen, he passed in Arithmetic (well), Algebra (well), Euclid, English, Latin, French, German, History and Geography. Only five candidates passed nine subjects, three of them from Scotch. In his form he was placed first in German, fourth in Mathematics and seventh in French. He also won a prize for an essay on Australian explorers. At the end of the year he looked up the University Calendar in order to find out what was involved in a B.A. course.

In 1880 in the post-matriculation sixth form John was placed second in Mathematics and Logic, fifth in French and sixth in Latin. James Whiteside McCay topped all these subjects; the rivalry with McCay, a son of the manse seven months his senior, was to continue for forty years. Early in the year at least, Monash was also taking German and Greek. He wrote to his father in March: 'in German I read Lessing's works, in French Telemaque by Fenelon, in Latin—Horace, and in Greek, Euripides and Plato; I also translate Macaulay's essays into German'. He was runner-up for the Sir James McCulloch prize for English composition for his substantial 4000-word essay on 'The Life, Time, and Works of John Milton'—a high-toned eulogy, grossly overwritten but with an incipient sense of style.

John's friend George Farlow recalled him as being at Scotch 'a studious quiet boy. . . . If ever he got into a quarrel he could always easily get out of it by ridiculing his opponent and disarming him with ridicule or argument'. How much did he share the common fear of Jewish schoolchildren of being made a butt for being different? Did one part of him long to be like other boys and regret being one of the chosen? To what extent was his English imperfect and his accent foreign-sounding? Might Farlow (with whom he carved his name in the bluestone)—a scholarship-boy from Brunswick and a mighty scrapper—have been something of a protector? Joe Miller was another from Brunswick (the three of them were to be fellow-officers in the Garrison Artillery a few years later)—were they to any extent outsiders? Schoolboys were no more gentle to each other in the nineteenth than in the twentieth century. Yet bullying was not common at Scotch and Jews were usually quite at home there. Farlow recalled that John 'took no part in games or appeared to be in any way athletic'. He was not blessed with ball-sense or eye-hand co-ordination. As a boy, he did not box, shoot, camp, or play football, but his years in the country had given him some knockabout experience which the ordinary urban child entirely lacked. He later became a reasonably good runner, a mediocre horseman and a fair shot. The impression remains that John was a gentle child, physically unassertive though possibly quick-tempered, and not unpopular. His later affection for the school, its masters, and the boys with whom he shared the benches indicates that he was not unhappy there.

His closest friends, however, were not schoolfellows, nor were any of them Jewish. One was Victor Wischer, who when Johnny was twelve quarrelled because he did not have a cricket bat; but on a return visit to the Wischers' John played cricket and draughts with Victor and they watched an eclipse of the sun. When a little older, they went on long walks together to Ivanhoe, Doncaster and other outlying villages. They were to remain lifelong friends, Victor eventually acting as John's solicitor. About 1879–80 John saw much of George Jackson who lived nearby and eventually became a teacher. But his closest friend by far from thirteen to seventeen was another neighbour, Arthur Hyde, who was a little older. Arthur had quite uncommon literary knowledge; the two boys dreamed of founding a literary magazine, confided their ambitions and sharpened each other's minds. When John was ill in 1880, possibly with mumps, Arthur visited him nearly every day. He later prided himself on having 'had some trifling share . . . in waking your talents'.

John attempted his first writing when about thirteen: 'the first scribbling I ever did, was a critique or report of a concert' at the local church hall. He sketched the outline of a story set in England during the Civil War, and wrote two unpromising pages of a play. He was first published at sixteen, when for a short-lived weekly *Town Talk* he strung together for a competition more than fifty words beginning with the letter f: 'for four flimsy farthings . . . furnishes fun for fascinating females', etc. He may also have submitted contributions to the Richmond paper, but does not seem to have written for the school journal *Young Victoria*. His tastes were by no means exclusively high-minded: when thirteen or fourteen he used to revel in the Jack Harkaway adventure stories which he sometimes read in Cole's Book Arcade in Bourke Street; he even recalled 'wagging' school for that purpose. He retained interest in his stamp collection until he was at least sixteen and he also practised some elementary carpentry.

As well as constantly helping Mathilde with her lessons, he was often left in charge of his sisters. Mat retained grateful memories all her life of the way in which John organized games at their parties—especially the fireworks displays in the back garden and the charades, *tableaux vivants*, play-acting and recitations with which he frequently entertained them. He was 'full of pranks and energy', would often get up stealthily at night to turn the lights on again so that he and Mat could read. 'He was a born teacher. He could explain everything.'

John believed he was leaving school at the end of 1880, expecting to go on to the University; fifteen-and-a-half was not an unusual age of entry. On speech-day he received prizes for Mathematics and his Milton essay; one of them was Adam Smith's *Wealth of Nations*. His first suit was tailored by Goldberg Brothers. In mid-December he was already working at Greek and Latin at night with Arthur Hyde. Early in January, however, a startling letter arrived from Dr Morrison:

> My dear Monash,
> I write to ask you to return to the College for another year in order that you may compete for the exhibitions . . . . I am making special arrangements for working up a few boys for December and I am sure you could carry one of them. At all events come and see me when I return to town on the 7th February.

Morrison, being anxious to regain ground lost to Wesley College, was eager to hold every boy who might win an exhibition. Though fully deferring to his father, John made up his own mind: he wanted to accept the challenge. Louis, who was inclined anyway to think John was too young to go to the University, was persuaded that another year at school would make the University course easier and that the chance of winning a valuable exhibition outweighed the cost of continued school fees. Meanwhile John visited the International Exhibition more than once; an exhibitor showed him over the wool factory, and he examined ice-machines, printing-machines, envelope-makers and rock-borers. And he enjoyed immensely a week at Sorrento with his aunt and cousins, after being badly seasick on the steamer down Port Phillip Bay. He 'had a lot of fun and went for a swim twice or three times each day; daily I took little walks to Portsea, the Quarantine Station, the Back-beach and Dromana and was positively delighted with the environment'.

Back at school, John took Mathematics, French, German and Logic. He made out a time-table for nightly work, 7 to midnight, Monday to Saturday, which he could not possibly have maintained. It was a time of change: the matriculation standard was being raised to lower the step up to first-year University requirements, and honours classifications were introduced. He could afford to drop Latin and Greek for a year. Moses, whom John regarded as a teacher of great ability, coached him in Mathematics; A. C. Aucher and Otto Mueller had him for French and German, as a sole pupil. With his teachers, family and the Jewish and German communities expecting much of him, he braced himself for a tremendous effort.

Macbeth was one set topic for the school essay prize, which John won. He spent many weeks' work on it and produced a highly intelligent and ingenious piece of rhetorical prose—a remarkable schoolboy essay. The greater part of it was concerned to refute the then novel suggestion that the Third Murderer was Macbeth himself. He borrowed the discussion, without acknowledgement, from the notes and critical material in an 1873 American edition of *Macbeth*, of which there were few copies in Melbourne. He selected the essentials of the argument, stated them more sharply than in the original, reworked a complex mass of material, knitted together diverse comments—paraphrasing often but sometimes copying verbatim, covering his tracks and passing off as original much that was not. It would be condemned today as, in part, plagiarism. But a century ago scholarly attribution of sources was not customary—and young scholars have to learn the ethics of their trade. It seems that no one in Melbourne was familiar with the source, even Professor E. E. Morris who some years later read the paper to the University Shakespeare Society. To anyone familiar with the source John could reply, reasonably, that he had given it a gloss and made some original points. Remarkably, however, he did have two or three novel insights and critical comments. For example, his assertion that Shakespeare 'knew better than to sacrifice the consistency, the unity, or in other words the poetry of his plays to any forced or unnatural desire for characterization' is a fairly radical opinion, even today. His approach may also have benefited from reading Lessing's critical works. If he had made proper acknowledgement of sources, the essay would still have been excellent—evidence of a first-rate precocious mind at work. At all events, for years to come, his *Macbeth* essay was convincing evidence to his contemporaries of his striking talent.

He concluded the year triumphantly: top in Logic, French and German, and Mathematics, massive improvement on the previous year. He was equal dux of the school and shared the *Argus* prize with James S. Thomson, later a physician—the only time in fifty years there was no outright winner. He spent his book prizes on sets of Froude's *History of England*, Gibbon's *Decline and Fall of the Roman Empire* and

Scott's Waverley novels. More important, at the public examinations he won the Mathematics exhibition with a first-class honour and gained a first in French and German, being fourth in the class list.

While holidaying at Portsea, John heard from his mother that he had taken his objective. Scotch had done better than any other school, a fact which Morrison immediately set about publicizing. John now spent three weeks with his father at Narrandera; Louis had moved there to take over Max's store. Bertha wrote excitedly to her Johnny-chen:

> from everywhere they congratulate me. I have to tell you from Miss Deakin: you realised fully and entirely her expectations. Mrs. Bourke wants to let you know that . . . she loves you for being such a good son and she respects you for being such a clever boy. Mr. and Mrs Koch send their kindest congratulations, so do Saul and Louis Pulver.

And the Brandts and the Püttmanns and the gasman and the postman added their plaudits.

John described a country-town store—surely his father's—to his American cousin Leo: 'a most curious conglomeration of all that appertains to man . . . a shelf with Scott's novels under which is placed a barrel of tar, a heap of moleskin trousers piled on top of a sugarbin etc.' In Narrandera he began to keep a diary. Almost the first entry, on 27 January, was: 'First time that I ever reported to a paper. Sent in a report of the entertainment last night also of the fire at Junee. First tasted whiskey today'. On 8 February he started home on the coach to Wagga and Albury, and summed up his trip with worldly sixteen-year-old wisdom:

> This was the first time in my life that I have been left to go on my own "hook" and I enjoyed it thoroughly. . . . But such short stays are always unsatisfactory. You make a few acquaintances, chum with everybody you meet, then leave the place, and probably never meet them again in your life.

Bertha and Louis Monash, 1863

Bertha and John, November 1865

John Monash, June 1868

John Monash, 1878

2

University Student
1882–1885

JOHN HAD intended for some years to go on to the University of Melbourne. He would follow his mathematical strength and enrol for Arts, then take Engineering. The exhibition, worth £25, covered fees and books and left a little over. His father was in no position to provide more than £1 a month pocket money, so he would largely have to support himself through his course. He began to keep careful accounts and was heartened when his friend Tom Hodgson passed on a student requiring coaching in French for matriculation.

There had been some domestic friction. The previous July Bertha had complained to his father of John's behaviour. Louis sternly rebuked him by letter for not contributing to harmony in the home and for lacking love and respect for his mother. Again in February he warned him to be more patient in teaching Mathilde, to control his temper and watch his manners with his mother. He insisted that he go to the gymnasium at the Turnverein twice a week and was foolish enough to make his allowance dependent on good behaviour and regular piano practice. John was careful not to reply to his strictures but began to complain of having to keep writing in German. When Louis discussed issues he raised, he seemed often to miss the point. John was ripe for revolt in some form.

He commenced at the University in a wavering frame of mind. The lecturers in Classics, Mathematics and Logic, Professors H. A. Strong, E. J. Nanson and Alexander Laurie, did not excite him in the least; towards the close of first term he had largely abandoned lectures. However, to his lasting benefit he mastered W. S. Jevons's *Elementary Lessons in Logic*.

He had begun his own courses of enthusiastic study. He had already started to keep diaries: one, brief notations of doings, and another more reflective one which we shall call his Intimate Diary. He opened a Commonplace Book in which to note wise words from his reading. One of the first entries was his lifelong slogan from Ecclesiastes: 'Whatever thy hand findeth to do, do it with thy whole might'. He began systematically to file the letters he received, and from January 1883 to keep copies of those he wrote. His 'Routine System', as he came to call it, of keeping records was to be a satisfying Sunday chore for most of the rest of his life and was to result ultimately in a collection of private papers for posterity, almost unparalleled in Australia. He recorded his intention to begin forming a library (he had seventy-one volumes) and collections of old coins, minerals and stones, and photographs of famous men. He began buying cheap copies of the classics and penny biographies of the great.

He started concentrated reading, mainly at the Public Library, of literature and history: Congreve (*Love for Love*), Ford ('*Tis Pity She's a Whore*), Goldsmith (*She Stoops to Conquer*); Fielding, Dickens, Bulwer Lytton; Herbert Spencer; Lessing, Mme de Stael, Voltaire; Poe. John fixed on a plan 'of studying closely through English Literature, not by any fixed routine, but as I am casually referred by one author to another'. He had run across the advice of an Oxford sage: 'Always verify your references'. He determined to follow Gibbon's methods of keeping journals and commonplace books, 'always reading with a pen in his hand'. He followed Macaulay's practice of shutting the book, after he had read a page, to test his memory. He transcribed extracts from Pope's 'Essay on Man' and from Gibbon's *Autobiography* and *Decline and Fall*, including the famous passage: 'It was at Rome ... as I sat musing. ...' He noted Carlyle on the idiocy of thirty men each from an English and a French village blowing 'the souls out of one another; and in place of sixty brisk useful craftsmen, the world has sixty dead carcases, which it must bury, and anew shed tears for'. He began to intersperse critical comments: Dr Johnson's life of Milton was 'a strange mixture of sarcasm, irony, censure, criticism, spite, praise and enthusiasm'. He wrote a note on the identity of 'Junius' and marked the death of Longfellow. He was aware of the powerful effect Macaulay might have on his own style. He noted how authors misquote and misinterpret each other. His own courses were at least as weighty and valuable as the University's. Just seventeen, he was teaching himself elementary scholarship.

John was also regularly attending the weekly meetings of the Wesley Church Mutual Improvement Society, which he had joined early in 1881, probably through the Hodgsons. During 1882, usually with his family present, he read his *Macbeth* essay, a paper on Robin Hood (of whom he approved), and another on the Saracen, Caliph Haroun Al Raschid, largely derived from Gibbon and from Sale's introduction to his 1734 translation of the Koran. John was so impressed by the Koran that he resolved to read a section every day. He repeated his paper on Haroun Al Raschid in the next few months to the Scots Church

Literary Society and to the Victoria Parade Young Men's Association. Having read Pitman's *Plea for Spelling Reform* he debated and won the cause, and often spoke from the floor on Joan of Arc, Shakespeare, electric light, fire insurance, and other topics. He 'caused a great sensation' by exposing a prominent Methodist layman who had read a plagiarized essay. His former choirmaster, Pulver, who was also a member, corrected him on this or another occasion for loss of manners in the heat of debate, but also encouraged him to disregard those who might laugh at him for his earnestness or doubt his sincerity. John was indeed doggedly gaining experience in public speaking to overcome his nervousness and fear of making a fool of himself.

The Wesleyans were harbouring a sceptic in their midst.

> 1 May: Yesterday (Sunday) I attended one of Mr. Thomas Walker's lectures, the subject being 'Miracles' . . . he put into words and speech my very thoughts which I had long had, but was never able to reduce and simplify. I can safely say that these opinions of mine have sprung from mere commonsense meditation and have not received the slightest influence from without; for which I do and ever shall heartily thank those who have had the care of my education.

Walker had been a precocious young spiritualist lecturer, had just proclaimed himself a materialist, and was about to found the Australasian Secular Association. Monash attended at least ten of his crowded Sunday evening lectures featuring crude and witty attacks on Christianity, and bought and read his pamphlet, *Orthodoxy Unmasked*. Walker's lecture on the philosophy of life set him 'thinking a great deal'. For the moment he kept to himself his racing thoughts on religion.

He was spending most evenings in the city, at Wesley Church, at the Public Library, exercising at a gymnasium, and two nights a week at the theatre. Usually standing in the gods, often with Victor Wischer, he saw the dramas, melodramas, comic opera and burlesques of a lively though not very refined period of Melbourne's stage. Among the leading performers were George Rignold, Alfred Dampier and Jennie Lee—John was thrilled to glimpse her out driving one day. He went five times to the comic opera *Boccaccio*, and twice to *Patience*, Gilbert and Sullivan's latest work. He was deceiving his mother, leading her to assume that he was elsewhere: his diary references to the theatre are in shorthand. Occasionally he attended Parliament: on 30 June 'at 11.24 I started from Parliament House and ran the whole way to the station catching the 11.30 Hawthorn train. Read a short biography of Earl of Beaconsfield. To bed at 1.30'. He was engrossed in the bustle and drama of the city, but his interest was not entirely sociological.

On 31 July he noted, 'I was never in my life nearer being drunk' than today, and he made cryptic entries in late September and early October:

> saw many wonderful sights in town.
> avoid temptation lest you may not be able to resist it.
> my guardian angel was busy tonight.
> the anticipation of a pleasure is better than the enjoyment thereof.
> strolled about streets, without success, till 11.30.

Was he accosting girls, or only trying to summon the courage? He once heard the leading barristers, J. L. Purves and John Madden, address a criminal court jury. He lingered round building-sites and harbour-works, studied the paintings in the National Gallery, browsed in Robertson's and Cole's bookshops, and was excited when he identified public figures like Mueller, the botanist, or the journalist 'Julian Thomas' ('The Vagabond').

John occasionally accompanied his mother to concerts; in March 'at one of the most beautiful evenings I have ever spent', he 'first spoke to Mr. Deakin MLA who kindly promised his assistance and advice whenever required'. John was closely involved in his mother's circle of friends—the Hodgson, Huntsman, Wischer, Püttmann, Sander, Meier and other families—and their regular exchanges of visits. Bertha very likely expected him to meet them and later to escort them to Richmond station or the bus in Swan Street or Bridge Road. The Deakins were frequent visitors—Mrs Deakin senior, Catherine and nineteen-year-old Pattie, Alfred's bride, whom John described as 'the most beautiful woman I know'. In May he went to his first ball, at Püttmanns' in Lisson Grove, Hawthorn—there were nine Püttmann sisters. In June he helped the Sanders prepare for their ball and made his '*debût* in the dancing line and also in after dinner speaking ... danced and danced ... walked home with three girls'. His seventeenth birthday was 'the most pleasant day that I have spent as long as I can remember'. On 26 July he saw snow—in Melbourne!—for the first time. He was helping Mat with her schoolwork and went walking with her quite often, as far as Doncaster and back. On 6 October they were up at 4 a.m. in the Burnley paddock to view the largest comet in fifty years: 1882 was a great year for local astronomers who also watched the transit of Venus and an annular eclipse of the sun. He saw much of Tom Hodgson and with him went walking and digging for fossils at Brighton Beach, sailing on Albert Park lake ('which I enjoyed exceedingly'), and fishing ('cannot conceive where the enjoyment lies').

For some weeks in second term John did not set foot in the University. When he did attempt to attend lectures he was frequently late, even for those at 10 o'clock, because of the hours he was keeping. In August he was writing in his diary:

I cannot understand *myself* at all, though I am ever the subject of my reflections.... They say Youth is hopeful and this may account for the peculiar condition of mind in which I find myself. Is such a condition common to all and will it last? My whole time is taken up in dreams of the future, that is the distant future, and then I feel generally happy and buoyant; but when I reflect on the near future—a restlessness comes over me.... I *cannot* submit to settle down to drudgery like my fellow students—my mind is too much engaged on other things. I am never in the same state of mind for two consecutive days. Once it is an overmastering desire for literary studies, then it is philosophical discussions, then a roving restless, unsettled feeling, then an ardour for living with the world, but most often a fitful, self-extinguishing, self-expiring eagerness in the pursuit of "fame". Is not life one great longing, yearning, hoping and desiring?

He did no work in the vacation, but by late September was studying fairly regularly. However he was continually side-tracking himself: 'Heard today subject for Bowen prize, to wit Federation and commenced to meditate on the subject'—he made out a list of a dozen references and worked at it for at least two days. He began chemical experiments at home, tried to place journalistic scribblings in country newspapers, started to write 'a short yarn of Australia'. He was disturbed late in October when his father finally came home, after selling out at Narrandera, and the family began planning to build a new house. He veered between confidence and desperation about his work. Four days before his exams, the Roths returned from overseas. Next day he was 'tired and miserable after yesterday's excitement', and for the following two days unwell and 'quite unable to work'.

He failed miserably in Latin, Greek and Upper Mathematics, passing Lower Mathematics, Logic, and Chemistry, Mineralogy and Botany; thus he failed the entire year. When the results appeared, he and others drank 'to better success next time—began to feel very unwell—trying to philosophise myself into peace'. He could not bring himself to tell his family until next day when 'there was great mourning and I soon felt fit to drown myself'. He grimly pledged himself to 'putting forth all my energies to redeem the time and opportunities lost by my present failure. Witness my hand this 28th day of November 1882 John Monash'. Years later he admitted that his infatuation with the theatre had caused his failure. Over the next month he visited Scotch several times, and talked with the Morrison brothers and other masters. On 30 December he wrote in his diary: 'Tomorrow I will give up to reflection and penitence for the deeds of the year'. The entry for next day in his Intimate Diary runs:

... it was during the past year only that were born in me, those sentiments and passions, which enabled me to form such opinions of my own as were in former [years] only guided by those of others. Upon the whole, I candidly think that my character leans to virtue's side. I believe I have the shrewdest and strictest sense of what is right, and though I do not always act up to my principles I am not so foolish as to condemn myself as irresolute; I feel that, if I once set myself a task, I can accomplish it; that I could conquer the world;— many have thought so before, and sadly did experience teach them different. I presume that this is my lot also—but why spoil the illusion while it lasts? Nobody is hurt by the downfall of air-built castles. Is it true that Ambition is a vice? Surely then it is a vice common to all mankind; for how can a man live without ambition? I have read, heard and seen enough to know that there is no true happiness in life, and the sole thing that bears up my failing spirits is this *ambition*. . . . I feel I have the power and say, as one great man has said before—'It is in me, and by Heaven, it shall come out'. And so it shall. Oh! how I should like to tear away the veil which hides the next ten years—to know the best or worst. I have been unfortunate in the past year,—have after years of childish toiling and hoping, realised at least one of my dreams, and risen to a position [which] however empty and petty it may seem to me, is at least regarded by the outer world as a rung in the ladder of life. How mournful is the reflection that, in the same way as I now despise and disdain the dignity of a University career, which I once regarded with such longing, I will some day despise the higher positions in life which I may in my turn be called upon to assume. I have spent one year as a student, am told that I thought too lightly of the work attendant thereon and so, as I failed to comply with a ridiculous condition of passing what is called an "examination", I am doomed to atone for my lost time by sacrificing my recreations. But was it "lost time"; most emphatically *no*; never was my time so well spent. I flatter myself that I have acquired a knowledge of both written and unwritten learning, in the past ten months, which exceeds all that I have ever known before. . . . And now I lay my pen and close my book, and making not one single resolution for the guidance of my future conduct, will again appear before myself when next the year draws to its close.

He could not bring himself to work for the supplementary exams. He took up the piano and drawing again, and continued to haunt the theatre. He resumed voracious reading. George Eliot's *Middlemarch, Adam Bede* and *Felix Holt* were 'all beautiful', but no novel had 'so affected' him as Bulwer Lytton's *Kenelm Chillingly*. He re-read Scott, Dickens, Pascal and Tennyson and 'again read "Maud" and "Enoch Arden" aloud'. He was disappointed that the *Narandera Argus* rejected his offer to contribute a regular column of Melbourne news, but Elliott, now editor-proprietor of the *Jerilderie Herald*, printed two 'Melbourne Gossip' items and paid him a few shillings for glib mixtures of political gossip, police scandal and mediocre anecdotes. On 2 December, however, he seized his opportunity when he 'suddenly heard a crash and soon ascertained there had been a fearful [railway] collision in Hawthorn [Burnley], hurried to the spot [near Swan Street], and saw a most horrible sight, stayed rendering all the assistance I could ... went home, repeating accounts of the occurrence many times on the way', and sent a 'Statement of an Eye-Witness' which was published in the Bendigo *Independent* for which Arthur Hyde was now working. John managed to capture roughly the contemporary manner of reporting disasters, but sensationalized what was a serious accident rather than a disaster. Like all young red-blooded colonials he had exulted in Australia's victory by seven runs in the 'Ashes' test match at the Oval in August, pasted two accounts of it in his cuttings book, and took his sisters to see the torchlight procession to welcome the heroes home to the Melbourne Cricket Ground. He reported to the *Jerilderie Herald* that they were bringing back 'the championship of the world in the manliest of British games'. After Christmas he spent two days at the match between Victoria and New South Wales.

He resumed the story he had begun in October, a 'sensational love and murder tale', and wrote several thousand words. Set in a country town like Jerilderie it had some realistic description, but reflected the conventional language and social assumptions of English models. Many a future *Bulletin* writer was similarly starting his apprenticeship. Another story set in a country town, concerning a telegraph operator and a criminal, did not get going. He was also experimenting with adaptations of French and German tales which he hoped to contribute to the newspapers.

His father had bought a block of land in Yarra Street, Hawthorn, over the river two miles east of their Richmond house, only a couple of minutes from the Hawthorn station. The Wischers, Püttmanns, Sanders and Brahes all lived nearby; another German, J. A. B. Koch, a leading architect, designed a modest brick house. John spent some time on suggested revisions—'my first venture in the engineering craft'—and early in February was discussing alterations, measuring the block and witnessing the contract with the builder. On 29 January he played a duet with Mat at a Wesley concert; next day he was 'tired and done up', so it was presumably a strain. Twelve days later he noted inadequately that after a 'stormy and exciting committee meeting' he was elected secretary of the mutual improvement society; he now had weekly committee as well as ordinary meetings. He attended some of Walker's election meetings in Richmond and on election night joined the crowd outside the *Argus* office; he hoped to take a more active part in future contests.

Early in January 1883 he told Hyde that he was 'generally miserable ... decidedly suicidal ... stagnating'. By late January, however, he had settled down and began to work 'harder than I can ever remember'. He detested it: 'sitting in front of a pile of the driest and most uninteresting books that could be printed . . . suffering from the combined attacks of headaches, overwork, and . . . ennui'. He considered he did fairly well at the exams, but there had been 'a beastly piece of prose' in Latin—'if it goes hard I'll fail'.

He *was* failed—and most cruelly. He passed five subjects but failed in Latin—the year's work was all for nought. To add to the injury, the regulations were changed within two months, so that any four subjects would constitute a pass for the year, while the compulsory Latin and Greek could be passed at any time. In later days, possibly even then, a friend at court or exercise of a bush lawyer's skills would surely have brought 'special consideration'. John's diary is silent concerning any plea he may have made, or about the domestic distress which ensued. From now on there was to be little joy in his academic work and he regarded exams as a capricious routine which had to be suffered. He defended his outside activities and inattention to university work by claiming that

> in these days of high pressure one [must] not only be able to do two, but three . . . nay a hundred things at a time or he will be left far behind in the race of life. . . . I consider myself to have spent the time devoted to romance reading . . . as well if not better than that [devoted] to turning nonsensical bits of English into bad Latin and Greek.

Passing Latin was to prove his greatest academic ordeal: the difficulty is strange—he must have suffered unusually bad teaching or had some disturbing conflict in the process. Yet the language was not entirely killed for him.

The immediate effects were shattering:

> I have seldom felt so disconsolate and hopeless. . . . I can settle down to nothing, not even reading. . . . If I could only get something definite to do, I would set about it with a right good will. . . . Nothing to do is one of the worst things that can happen to a man.

He had been consulting Hyde about the chances of a post in journalism. Hyde, who had failed first year Arts himself and whose carping resentment had contributed to leading John astray, now advised him to 'send the University to the devil and take up the press'. Late in April he asked him to join in establishing a press agency to supply country and intercolonial papers. But John had quickly resolved to continue at the University; however laborious, it was a better prospect than launching out afresh. A bad start was not irretrievable, and it would be moral cowardice to give up: 'every day I am beginning to be more and more impressed with the fact that I am doing nothing but being a burden to those around me'. On 28 March he wrote in his Intimate Diary: 'Tomorrow I am going to make a fresh start—I might say—in life. I have become a wiser and let me hope a better man'. Clumsy feelers for part-time journalism came to nothing. He found another pupil. In May he sat the exam for a clerkship at the Mint, where George Farlow worked, but was not offered a post—and he had spent three guineas for the exam. In June and July he taught some classes at Mrs Howe's West Melbourne College.

Following the appointment of Professor W. C. Kernot, the Bachelor of Engineering degree was introduced in 1883 in place of the existing certificate. The first three years of the four-year course consisted of an Arts degree with a large mathematics and physics content. Monash set out on this slightly different tack and began Natural Philosophy (physics) with Professor H. M. Andrew whom he was soon describing as 'the most brilliant lecturer in the Shop'. He was repeating most of his other subjects and gave up attending the same old lectures. He was very unhappy:

> If ever I needed strength of purpose and hopefulness it is now.... I am just beginning to realise that I am wasting my days in accomplishing nothing, and as "luck" has been hard against me of late, I have not much encouragement of hope for better prospects. I am still rapidly storing up experience—the only true means of acquiring knowledge.

About this time he drew up several time-tables of work, which included twelve hours a week teaching Mat, his cousin Karl and his two pupils. One of these time-tables, which covered 9 a.m. to midnight for the seven days of the week, he obviously could not have carried out. He also set out for 1883–86 the subjects to be passed and the possible prizes to be won.

John's periodical letters to his cousin Leo in Minnesota were not merely an exercise in family piety but deliberate practice in writing. He already had the trick of good manners by which almost every letter finished at the bottom of the page. As yet he was prolix and 'literary' but was beginning to harness his fluency. Arthur Hyde protested that 'I get a letter sometimes in the argumentative, sometimes in the elephantine-jocular style, sometimes hyper-facetious, sometimes reproachful, sometimes abusive, sometimes gushing, sometimes critical'. In February 1883 John began a correspondence with Will Steele, who was three years older, had also just failed first year Arts and was teaching at Warrnambool. With common interests in philosophy, religion, music and chess, they were to remain close friends for many years and John continued regularly to write long and revealing letters.

He had already learned to write very speedily, but habitually had dictionary and thesaurus at hand. In his later business and military writings he was systematically to practise and enjoy simplifying and sharpening his drafts. His private letters remained fluently verbose; his spelling was almost perfect—'wholely' remained an error and he never later got Villers-Bretonneux right; and his punctuation continued to be a little eccentric. But the lucid style was the man, as was the clear round handwriting.

John disagreed strongly with Cousin Leo's pan-Germanism:

> *Your* "mother-tongue" is not *mine*. . . . I do not exactly perceive the great desirability of preserving . . . this *"mother-tongue"*, by those to whom it is such no longer. Of course I mean this quite apart from the desirability of studying German *as a language*, but unless there is any distinct intention on the part of yourself or other German youth in *foreign* (!) lands, of ultimately returning to a German country . . . I should consider it not only natural but advisable and expedient to make the study of German quite a secondary matter altogether. . . . I see no great reason . . . for preferring German to French or Italian. . . . What, beyond the fact that correspondence with my relatives must be carried on in German— what, beyond this, is there to induce me to cling to the German language and German customs, or to saturate myself with a German spirit? To what country and people do I owe the most? To that which I have never seen, with which I have no connection, but that it is the home of some of my relatives?; or to that in which and among whom I was born, have grown up, where I have learned all that I know, to which I owe all the happiness that I have experienced? . . . Shall I in return for this look upon it as a foreign land, to be deserted at the first convenient opportunity? No, it is my native land; I have contracted from it a heavy debt, and it will ever be to me a prominent object, in some measure to repay that debt.

Thirty years later, Leo was supporting the Germans in World War I. But John's was the standard position among the children of migrant German Jews who usually felt no political, as distinct from cultural, loyalty to a Germany which had only very recently been united as a nation. And migrant Jews from such a background could cultivate a loyalty to Australia uncomplicated by sentiment for Great Britain.

John indeed wrote as a callow Australian patriot, presenting a garbled version of Victorian history which revealed how lamentably ill-informed a well-educated youth could be. His domestic politics were crude and conventional. Graham Berry's radical government had been a blight; O'Loghlen's was a great improvement; he approved of the Service–Berry coalition. Despite his associations with the Deakin family, he had acquired no radical tinge, although by 1887 he was expressing some standard nationalist views:

We have often been twitted with our special loyalty to the British crown and to the person of the Queen ... the Rule Britannia sentiment [is] an absurd affectation with no foundation in anything else but simply sentiment. ... We are celebrating not her jubilee alone, but that of our native country; yet very few of us give any prominence in our minds to this significant fact.

Like those of many Victorians, these opinions were but a passing phase and he did not join the Australian Natives' Association.

Early in 1883 Leo announced himself as a free thinker. John wrote in reply that he had laughed and laughed when he had read it:

Know then you of all men that I am an Infidel of the very blackest type, an atheist and a materialist, that I have been so as long as I have been able to reason, and that I shall continue to be so as long as I remain in my senses. ... the only soul about whose existence I have no doubt is Inger*soll* at which you will probably (Brad) laugh.

'I extend to you', replied Leo, 'the hand of fellowship in the grand battle ... against superstition, bigotry and the tyranny of the priesthood'. John gleefully told Will Steele: 'We are both grandsons of one of the devoutest followers of Judaism that ever lived'. He promised Will he would help him in his plan to write a critical commentary on the Bible.

Rely on my help in everything. I may be of great help to you in revising, collecting data and the like, but I have little originality. [I] have held my views for so long, that I can hardly help looking upon the falsity of the Bible in the same light as others do its truth viz as an axiom.

He told Leo proudly of the spread of free thought in Melbourne and of the great campaign to open the Public Library, National Gallery and Museums on Sundays for the benefit of the working classes. When the fight had been won he was one of the thousands who went to the first Sunday opening. But he had soon 'quite cooled down on the subject of religious beliefs (having no one with whom I cared to converse thereon)'. Nevertheless later in 1883 he eagerly followed the controversies over Bishop Moorhouse's lectures, George Higinbotham's address on science and religion and the alleged heresies of the Reverend Charles Strong of Scots Church.

'I was left to myself to choose my own mode of thinking, to reach my own beliefs in my own way', Monash wrote. As we have seen, his parents were almost certainly agnostic, but there is no specific evidence of anyone in his childhood encouraging him to think radically, though there were unorthodox thinkers close to the family circle. Although three of his teachers—Myers, Pulver and Moses—were the best and brightest of orthodox Jews he had turned violently against them and his cousin Albert by the age of sixteen. His wide reading had helped to inoculate him against dogma. Perhaps his famous uncle Graetz, the orthodox Jewish scholar and intellectual focus of his family, had been held up too often for John's admiration. About 1880 fundamental challenges to religion first became a matter of widespread intellectual excitement in Melbourne. Monash grew up in the thick of it. He claimed, when first he studied the Bible, to have jotted down more than a hundred 'glaring errors'. He had read Renan's *Vie de Jésus* and transcribed the introduction (in French) into his Commonplace Book; he had Ingersoll's *Mistakes of Moses*. He had possibly read Winwood Reade's *Martyrdom of Man* (1872); late in life he recommended it as a remarkable work which had influenced him greatly, as it did so many of his generation. Now at seventeen he was asserting that

> a man can live happily and well in this world without troubling himself about what he is, what he is here for and what will become of him.
>
> Everything that I see and hear confirms me in my impression that it were far better for the peace of mankind, to completely disassociate itself from researches after truth in the direction of superstitious beliefs, in short that there be added to the present infinite creeds, the creed of having no belief whatever not even the Belief of Unbelief.

He froze intellectually in this respect, though not with regard to problems of morality or his interest in comparative religion—nor was he any the less proudly Jewish—and probably did not reconsider his basic position or modify it until late in life. He soon lost most of his interest and had little contact with the thriving secularist movement.

John was still reading greedily: Hume, Bright, Carlyle; Tennyson, Victor Hugo and his favourite Bulwer Lytton. In April he gained a 'magnificent addition' to his library: an uncle in Prussia sent him the complete works of Goethe (thirty volumes) and Lessing (sixteen). He wrote to Leo: 'I find myself unconsciously criticising everything I read, and above all can now read very fast'. He had abandoned the piano, but Annie Hodgson had been giving him lessons in painting; at the Public Library he made copy-sketches of men from *Vanity Fair* and of women from Alexander Walker's *Beauty*. He was visiting the theatre secretly only occasionally; the family went together to George Darrell's melodrama, *The Sunny South*. His social life was fairly quiet. In May he met nearly all his German acquaintances at a party at the Brahes', and he enjoyed himself extremely at the Püttmanns' ball and at the Hodgsons' 'as I can invariably do, wherever I go'. There are only a few mentions of girls in the diaries. Much of the winter was taken up by preparations to move to the new house in July and in settling in. John must have spent the equivalent of at least three weeks in carpentering a kitchen dresser and a bookcase, packing, painting, and laying out a garden. Just after the move he was 'discouraged from the practice of Diary Keeping by the unwarranted inspection of my diary by my parents'. It was a mortifying intrusion: he was probably reprimanded for certain aspects of his conduct and embarrassed by having either to answer awkward inquiries or to refuse to. As a consequence, he kept up his diary only for six weeks in the next twelve months.

The Wesley Church Mutual Improvement Society kept John busy as secretary for most of 1883. He gave a paper on Tennyson in May, played a duet with Mathilde again at a concert night, and accompanied singers. After careful preparation he continued to speak from the floor in debates, but in August, when he attempted an impromptu speech, he

> had a complete breakdown, which if not apparent to the audience, was none the less real. I noticed the strange fact that it takes very little to damp one's ardour or overthrow a fancy, for I sat down with the conviction that oratory will never be the line in which I am destined to shine. I was the more disappointed in my failure, as I had looked forward to the occasion for a long time. The very recollection makes me feel sick at heart.

But he had outgrown the society. By September he was disgusted with it, though he feared that his own 'administration had a deal to do with its decline'. 'I have drawn all the good for myself that I could from the Association and now think it wise to throw it up altogether.'

At the University Professor Andrew held his interest in Natural Philosophy; John had most difficulty with dynamics and hydrodynamics but found the study of heat fairly easy. He went beyond the few set texts to read Tyndall's *Heat considered as a Mode of Motion* ('a masterpiece of scientific wording and splendid English'), Balfour Stewart's *Conservation of Energy* and Besant's *Hydrostatics*. Late in August he was intending to start work in earnest but read Scott's *Fair Maid of Perth* all one day, and re-read most of the *Ingoldsby Legends* ('splendid rhyming power and sparkling wit ... the best remedy for mental lassitude or *ennui*'). But he had knuckled down by the start of third term, even got to the University by 9 o'clock, felt some of his 'old mathematical vein returning', and was working with zest—'in fact from reading Tyndall and others, I am beginning to feel like a specialist in scientific learning'. He had high hopes of first-class honours. He passed in five subjects, but collapsed in the honours exams and received only a third-class for the year. This result might have been affected by his dropping

Latin, which he still did not attempt in February. The note he made in his Intimate Diary at the close of 1883 was gloomy:

> I despair of the realisation of the smallest of my dreams. My mental equilibrium is rapidly becoming disorganised and I am becoming indifferent of everything. A little longer and I will be lost for good and all. Yet another effort will I make to regain the Hope which I have lost.

His salvation was to come through student politics.

The University, in Monash's time, was undergoing rapid change amid noisy dissension. The number of students was quickly growing and in the mid-1880s passed five hundred, of whom about one-third were medical. The usual age of entry was sixteen, often fifteen, but there was a leavening of older students from impecunious families who in effect were part time, working their way; competition for valuable exhibitions was intense. The professorial performance had been patchy and remained so; fortunate appointments about 1890 were greatly to raise overall quality. The mid-1870s had seen the first great generation of students, which included H. B. Higgins, Isaac Isaacs, Alfred Deakin, Samuel Alexander and Alexander and William Sutherland; Monash's contemporaries included few, perhaps, who were so brilliant, but many of quality.* Basic reforms were being made, largely by a group of schoolmasters on the council; the 'classicists' were being overcome by the 'utilitarians' fighting for development of professional and technical education. Science was not to come fully into its own until the later 1880s, but in 1882 new chairs had been established in Natural Philosophy, Chemistry, Engineering, and English, French and German. Kernot militantly bore the standard of the academic engineer against the philistine army of 'practical men'. The first women had been admitted in 1881 and the noble Wilson Hall was opened the following year. The University as a whole, however, was demeaned by the struggle for power between factions within council, senate (of graduates) and professorial board, by squabbling professors who sometimes came to blows and some of whom were often the worse for liquor, by rivalry between the colleges, by bitter contests for the chancellorship, and by personal and religious quarrels—all of which were gleefully reported by the press.

The currents of conflict and reform invigorated the students. John Monash was one of the Arts students who formed the body which led to the foundation of the University Union. Thirty years later he recalled that 'the Union took its birth in the Classical lecture room

---

* For example, the engineers J. H. Michell, Professor Sir Robert Chapman, Arthur Lynch, Lee Murray, Lindesay C. Clark, Herbert Brookes; clergymen A. E. Albiston, E. S. Hughes, H. F. Tucker; teachers C. R. Long, C. N. Morrison; the librarian E. La T. Armstrong; the scientist T. S. Hall; and Mr Justice Sir Leo Cussen.

in the middle of 1883 by a note passed from hand to hand during lectures. I think the actual originator was the Rev. J. Mathew or G. Alec Thomson or both'. He was one of the committee which arranged an Arts Students' Conversazione at Gunsler's Café on 14 August. In the most important speech he had yet made, Monash seconded Mathew's founding motion, stiltedly but adequately. Melbourne students lacked the esprit de corps of English and Continental universities; an association of students and graduates was needed to promote good fellowship. He was elected to the committee, though he was 'somewhat disappointed at missing the secretaryship which Thomson's superior tact gained for him' and wrote the reports for the morning newspapers.

The interim body launched the Union on 2 June 1884 at the Athenaeum Hall in the presence of the Governor and with Professor J. S. Elkington as chairman; 150 members were gathered on the spot. The objects, modelled on the Oxford Union's, were debating, acquisition of the art of public speaking and, as an immediate cause, 'providing rooms in which men of every grade and school may meet together on common ground and get their angles rubbed off by coming together in social intercourse'. The council agreed to make available a professorial dwelling in the quadrangle. On 22 September Elkington opened the 'clubhouse', with a cheerful fire, notice-board, newspapers, library, simple food, a bath, chess and draughts. The Union committee began a vigorous programme of 'socials', which proved popular, but two general meetings did not attract a quorum.

John's exhilarating activity in 1884-85, however, was the *Melbourne University Review*. The Union committee had elected him as first choice to a committee to produce a journal whose objects were, he wrote ponderously in the first editorial,

> to offer some encouragement to the exercise and expression of original thought ... and to provide a field for the attainment of efficiency in the use of the pen.... Since it is from its Universities that a nation's leaders emanate, and there also that its greatest thinkers are produced—no available means should be spared for affording every opportunity for the exercise of the literary abilities and mental faculties of the individual members of such a powerful institution.

The model was the *Cambridge Review*. The committee brought out the first issue on 26 July and went on to produce four of five envisaged for 1884 and the eight planned for 1885.

The engineering students had collaborated willingly in forming the Union, and the lawyers half-heartedly. The medicals, who had formed their own society in 1879, were predominantly opposed and delighted in producing the first issue of their *Speculum* a few days before the first of the *Review*. John had medical friends and joined with them in a rag on 9 August:

> Yesterday I spent an evening in a novel and highly interesting manner. The occasion and place—the performance of "Lady Macbeth" by Geneviève Ward, at the Theatre Royal. A party of 200 students... congregated in the gallery, which had been reserved for us, and 'made a night of it'. I contributed more than my share in the shape of vociferous bawling, and as a consequence lost my voice. My efforts were duly appreciated, and I had a little advertisement, a thing I 'go for' uniformly.

A round of the pubs ended the evening. But John fell out with the Meds: the second issue of the *Review* contained a scathingly sarcastic review of *Speculum*, attacking them for their disunity. The Meds believed Monash was the author and plotted to throw him in the University lake. According to the actual author, J. B. Lewis, Monash

> respected the secrecy of the press, and was prepared to undergo this unpleasant treatment. When he told me that this was to happen I asked him to let me know when it would be convenient for him, and I would come to see the fun, and, if necessary, assist.

But enough doubt remained to save him from the fate of many subsequent notorious student politicians. In future issues of the *Review* Monash endeavoured in vain to mollify the Meds.

Jim Lewis, also a Scotch Collegian, who was to find Monash 'the staunchest, most reliable and generous of friends' over a lifetime, wrote of him as he knew him in 1884:

> a dark youth who always carried a knobby walking-stick.... He had a manner that attracted me. It was hardly aggressive, you could not describe it as pushing, it was not altogether self-assertive. To me it indicated a character sure of itself, one of strength and energy, one that must come to the front in spite of all obstacles. It will be understood that it did not make him generally popular, though when he offered himself for anything requiring ability and hard work, those even who were a little critical, felt that he was just the man for such a position.

He made other lasting friends in the student movement like C. J. Zichy-Woinarski (later a judge), J. B. O'Hara (poet and schoolmaster), John Mackey (compositor, lawyer and politician), and others who were working their way through university—like Monash effectively part-time students who missed many lectures and aided each other by swapping notes.

On 18 August 1884 John confided to his Intimate Diary:

> Oh what a change since last I wrote. Oh pen, speak out my thoughts.

Again do I find myself on the upward path, gaining in social position, moral and physical character, and most of all in self-esteem. Oh, this is the secret of mental tranquillity—despise not thyself—and do nothing to give thyself cause to do so. I have entered upon a life of turbulent activity. My stores of energy are unlimited and now at last am I finding a field for their application. I have taken up an important position in my University, one of its leaders in actual fact, known to each and all, and one of the fountain heads of the largest movement of Union that ever manifested itself within our walls, the mainstay and practical conductor of the first genuine Students Paper, ... gaining access whithersoever I wish—rising rapidly through exertion of a little push, through tier after tier of the strata of society. Withal most successful at home and in private life. Earning with but slight exertion, in spare hours, what is to many a competency, extending my acquaintanceship in advantageous directions, taking part in all movements likely to benefit myself in time to come. There is now no aimless indolence day and night.... Oh that I could continue so throughout my time. Truly not contented, but light of head and heart, no cares and nought but pleasing anxiety.

He had just found another exciting pursuit. He was one of the first eleven to apply to join the new University company, D Company, 4th Battalion, Victorian Rifles. Sworn in on 8 July, he had his first drill on the 11th; his service formally dated from the 27th. The Victorian government, sensitive to danger to the Empire, had adopted a vigorous defence policy. The Victorian Navy was expanded, Port Phillip Heads fortified, permanent forces of artillery and engineers formed, a numerous militia recruited, and rifle-clubs and cadet corps encouraged, all supervised by a small core of Imperial officers. University students rallied to the call. 'In the storm of enthusiasm I too was carried away', John told his cousin Leo. Sergeant Sullivan, a veteran of the Maori Wars, drilled them daily. The raw recruit was of soldierly build: 5 feet, 8¾ inches, well-built but slim and agile. At the first rifle drill 'the labour was so arduous' that his neighbour fainted from exhaustion. John immediately threw himself into the class-work, passed his exam for corporal with special mention, and was promoted on 14 October. If a thing was worth doing, it should be done with all one's might.

On 12 October, writing to Will Steele, he was still at a high pitch of euphoria:

You can really have no idea how terribly busy I actually am.... the combined engagements of University Union, "Review", Militia and Pupils constitute a strain upon my mental and physical powers which I can scarcely bear. But of a consequence I am enjoying the most perfect content and peace of mind, nor ever can spare a moment for pessimistic speculations. Everything is prospering with me.... The connections which I am making now, in my various official positions, will be of inestimable value to me in after life. You fear perhaps that my own work will suffer. I trust not, but if it does, what matter? The appearance of one's name in the Calendar is not the only thing to be proud of.... I wish I could share with you some of my buoyancy of spirits. I think I have a recipe for melancholy. Find something to do, and stick to it with what energy you may—activity is the antidote of despondency.... Give up philosophising for a time.... Throw yourself with energy into something. Get chockful of all sorts of employment.... I am willing to confess that the terrible strain is beginning to tell on my health, though slightly. Thank Heaven! in 5 weeks it will be all over.

That year it was a matter of a last-minute cram. He passed in Advanced Mathematics, Natural Philosophy II, French, German and Practical Chemistry—but after the subsequent honours exams was placed low in the second class, equal 14th in second year Arts. He also passed in Surveying and Levelling and Practical Mensuration which were prerequisites for Engineering. His friends wrote to commiserate on not doing better. Lewis was grieved that he had not won the exhibitions in French and German; Zichy-Woinarski was 'certain you would have got 1st class and several Exhibs had not yr time been so thoroughly taken up'. O'Hara urged him to enter for the Ormond College scholarship exams in February-March 1885; he did so, sat for French and German and was awarded a non-residential exhibition. The Master, J. H. MacFarland, expected him to work for honours in languages early in 1886, but Monash abandoned the Ormond connection. There is little evidence on what he thought of his teachers, but he did leave one serious statement about his work:

Our University has made great strides in Mathematics in the last 5 or 6 years and with such men as Profs Nanson, Andrew, and Kernot at our head, we are second to few Universities in the world in this respect.... I am essentially a mathematical student.... anyone who devotes himself for three or four years to Mathematics undergoes a complete mental reconstruction. A new system of thinking is slowly developed. While never for a moment departing from the logical fundamental laws of *all* modes of thought, there are added many peculiar axioms and elementary principles, which, inexplicable at first, soon become as firmly established in the mind as the principle that "whatever is, is" and "whatever is not, is not". Take as examples the conception of infinity and the treatment of infinite magnitudes as finite ... the peculiar method of proof known as mathematical induction ... the wonderful process of summing an infinitely large number of infinitely small magnitudes ... the various processes of approximation where absolute exactness is impossible. ... Next in the matter of treatment—the continual habit of analysis ..., the necessity for a strict logical sequence of a proof or investigation, for a painfully exact statement of every proposition so as neither to include nor exclude more than it should. . . . I would refer you to Clerk Maxwell's "Matter and Motion".

The Union committee began to take up student grievances, which were reported in the *Review*—we may sometimes detect Monash's firm, reasonable and polite style. The library was inadequate, especially in French and German books; why were the law exams held at the Law Courts?; birds in Wilson Hall were distracting examinees; results were far too slow in coming out; the University had relatively few scholarships, a situation which the 'wealthier members of society' should remedy; a lecturer in Mathematics was unsatisfactory; evening classes should be introduced. The main issue between university administration and students remained the annual Commencement and Conferring of Degrees which for several years had verged on bedlam. In 1885 the singing, screaming, hooting, whistling and cheering of the undergraduates reduced the proceedings almost to dumb show. The *Review* had correctly predicted an attempt to suppress 'what the public call rowdyism but the students "nature". The open declaration of war against the undergraduates will not, it is to be feared, assist much towards the object'. The *Review* temperately admitted the display was 'more noisy than amusing', and advised encouragement of student participation, as in Edinburgh. One feature of the day had been the singing of the forty-odd verses, some of them ribald, of the recently composed University Anthem ('We're Varsity Students all'), of which John was a part-author.

The Union was doing encouragingly well: by early 1885 most of the students had joined. Monash was active in arranging fortnightly debates, socials and concerts. A winter lecture series was his idea. He provided the *Argus* with a shorthand report of Andrew Harper's 'How to Make a University Famous'. At J. E. Taylor's talk on 'The Atmosphere', as a committeeman he 'had to be everywhere, in the reception of the lecturer and Governor, in the conduct of the ceremonies, and in the subsequent clearing up'. He considered Charles Pearson's lecture on 'The Pursuit of Learning' 'good, its delivery execrable', and he published in the *Review* 'The Muses in Australia' by Henry Bournes Higgins (later a famous arbitration judge).

Control of the journal had fallen into Monash's hands and remained there for the first ten issues over fifteen months. Zichy-Woinarski shared much of the work and Lewis was a prolific contributor. As well as editorials and news paragraphs, Monash himself contributed some of his old papers on *Macbeth*, spelling reform and other subjects. He backed Professor Kernot in his battle to impose professional engineering standards on public authorities. It was a worthy journal but lacking in verve. From July 1885 the format was changed to a smaller page and Monash set out to attract more original literary work—and largely failed. The *Review* was soon in deep financial trouble. They had hoped for 500 subscriptions and got 250, of which only fifty were from the University; advertisers were hard to snare. The Union committee bitterly deplored the lack of student support. After twelve months only one-third of the printing bill had been paid. The Union carried the loss until the publisher, William Inglis & Co., misguidedly took over the journal. Monash had been less culpable than his colleagues in ignoring the growing debt; he it was who drew up the settlement of accounts and was 'complimented and thanked over and over again for the great trouble I had taken. [It] really only took an hour'. Inglis went out of business early in 1886, after Monash had left the University; the *Review* did not appear that year and was revived briefly from 1887.

The young editor had some happy moments and won a little glory. There were celebratory dinners at which compliments were paid to him. He got to know and had 'gorgeous lunches' at the home of Dr J. W. Springthorpe, vice-president of the Union. He was asked as a representative of 'the monthly press' to a book-launching. Deakin, now a senior minister in the Victorian government, sent him a congratulatory note on the 'sustained quality' and 'improved appearance' of the *Review* and assured him that 'all things are possible to the young and earnest'.

Monash was beginning to take his military career seriously. The University Company eventually received its red infantry uniforms in January 1885. Corporal Monash (some of the men nicknamed him Corporal Potash) was delighted:

> Certainly the acquisition of one's first official dress, and the assertion of the right to wear it, is an occasion to be noted. My joining of the company I consider a good day's work; for it is affording me an infinite amount of gratification. My appearance in this gaudy outrig has caused no little astonishment and some amount of admiration among my friends.

Suddenly the business of being a volunteer soldier became much more serious. On 14 February he wrote in his diary:

> Since the terrible news of Gordon's death and the offer of the Australian Governments to assist with troops, our lives have been made a burden to us. Our appearance in the streets in uniform seems to be the signal for the display of all the wit of which unwashed Melbourne seems possessed. . . . Clearly my circumstances render it impossible for me to go, and in view of this impossibility my inclination does not seem to lean in that direction either. I am fully aware that remaining behind will be far from pleasant, much less will be the comparison with the returned troops; further I consider the

whole movement a mistake of misdirected enthusiasm. I should much prefer to see it displayed in the formation of a national army ... and in any case the colonies will derive no material advantage from the business.

A rumour circulated that Monash was off to the war. But Victoria's offer to help avenge General Gordon in the Sudan was not accepted.

The situation seemed much more serious in April, when war with Russia was believed to be imminent. Monash attended his first Easter camp at Frankston and savoured the novelty of camp-fires and jollity in the evenings; but overall it was 'a rough and vulgar time... a paragon of mismanagement'. He had enjoyed his first sham fight in February and sometimes found drill interesting and instructive. But he was frequently critical: of the officers at a review in Albert Park, of a battalion drill when 'every movement was a scramble', of the 'childish misbehaviour of some of the men who seem to have nothing beyond schoolboy impulses'. He was not a good shot and disliked the 'utter bleakness and heathlike ghastliness' of the Williamstown range. Early in July he was the first in the company to pass the exam for sergeant. After being rejected for a commission with the Engineers, late in August he, George Farlow and Tom Hodgson, the only ones qualified, applied to Captain (Professor) Andrew for promotion. Monash was made colour-sergeant on 4 September:

> I have scored a great triumph, and the fact gives me unlimited and unalloyed satisfaction. . . . It is a source of much gratification to see one's efforts rewarded and now I feel that all my self-sacrifice in the interests, ostensibly of the company, but really of myself have been repaid in full—a lesson to the crowd of weak-headed fellows who are fond of ridiculing me. In my military capacity I am what I am of my unaided making. A rise from a recruit to absolute seniority is not a bad year's work. With so much accomplished in one direction, and so much gained, I feel encouraged and instigated to a fresh start in the race for a position in the world.

He could not get his 'new decorations' out of his head and hung them up 'in full view of my pillow, so much do they represent my accomplished labours'.

Monash soon earned a reputation as an 'inconveniently sharp-eyed and efficient sergeant'. He took classes in signalling, quickly mastered the subject, but found it monotonous. He was seeing much of non-commissioned officers in other units, some of them 'very decent and agreeable fellows'. At a meeting at the Port Phillip Club Hotel to form a club, he found the men were

> of a low intellectual standard and so I had pretty much my own way. They were unacquainted with committee procedure, and I had

to set them right. . . . I met an old army Major . . . who displayed a soldier-like propensity for beer and 'baccy'. As a consequence I came home *very* late.

One evening at the Barracks mess, 'the conversation though instructive was none of the most enlightened. . . . The beer had a most uncomfortable effect. . . . I never felt so bad before'. They sometimes adjourned to 'the Cathedral Hotel and its pretty barmaid'.

When sixteen John had been excited by a tramp to the Dandenongs, twenty miles east of Melbourne, and up Ferntree Gully. In March 1884 he immensely enjoyed a two-day walking trip there, and next summer he picnicked with seven girls and stayed for three days with Mat and her friend Selina Hooper. One day, with his student Fyffe, he walked from Box Hill station over Mount Dandenong and back—forty-five miles, he reckoned—and 'got well drunk on the way home'. That 1884–85 summer was notable for his developing close friendship with the Lewis family in Carlton; Jim and he began to work together at each other's homes. On 17 January he wrote:

> I will ever remember today as being one of the most enjoyable I have ever spent. The occasion was the celebration of the German picnic, and the conditions the most favourable for rapturous enjoyment. The recollection of the day's events and the tumult of emotions wakened by them, I would fain ever keep preserved. . . . I believe to have detracted nothing and added much to my reputation today. Besides succeeding in rendering myself universally pleasant, without any maladvertence to overshadow it, I also triumphantly carried off some athletic prizes, and made a successful attempt at dancing. The chiefest pleasure (and as this diary is as a confession stool I am not ashamed to confess it) was the long ramble I took with Hermina [and] Francisca [Püttmann] . . . along the beach.

He again won races, carrying off three hundred cigars, at the German picnic two years later.

Chess and the piano were his enthusiasms of 1885; he was not reading much.

> I should much like to perfect myself in the art of chess playing, but I am much afraid that I am endeavouring to push forward in too many directions. One occasionally does hear, however, of men who have many irons in the fire at once, and yet do not dissipate their energies. I cannot help wishing that the hours of a day might be doubled; yet I find that much can be done by due economy of time.

He watched an exhibition of twenty simultaneous games by Blackburne, the visiting English champion. He took the lead in organizing the University Chess Club, earned a B handicap in an A–E range, represented Arts against Medicine, and by September was playing for the club against the Turnverein and the Victoria Club. Early in 1885 John spent much time at the piano: 'I want to give the *penchant* for music its fullest scope while it lasts. . . . am plunging deeply into classical music and am making many rich discoveries'. In Lewis's opinion his vigorous playing had a character of its own. By June he was regularly practising on Sunday mornings with his cousin Albert, who had recently returned from Vienna. By July he was performing regularly: Chopin's 'Polonaise' and 'Poet and Peasant' at Union socials, 'a sparkling pianoforte solo' at a Medical Students' Society social, and the 'now famous Polonaise' at a Union concert in the Temperance Hall—'with what success I have been unable to gather. Nervousness or perturbation was not an element'. He also played often at private houses: 'I was kept at the piano almost continuously, and had to listen to endless compliments and expressions of appreciation, which though undeserved and of little value, I feel intense gratification in hearing'. He regularly went to the Liedertafel and attended the three violin concerts by John Kruse, the local boy-prodigy returning in triumph. Kruse was assisted by, the advertisement had it, 'Mrs. Armstrong, the Charming Soprano' (Nellie Melba).

According to George Farlow, at the University,

> if any nice looking girls came our way we were glad to be their escort round the Museum. . . . if Monash once got into the conversation it was a foregone conclusion that all the young ladies became more interested in his conversation and escort than all the others of us put together.

Kate Lewis, Jim's young sister, recalled how at a cadet-camp John

> smilingly stopped, and spoke to a group of young girls [visiting their brothers]. He was simplicity itself. . . . [He had an] innate love of teasing, but in such a kindly way, that most children enjoyed it. [After a University Engineers' boating picnic and dance] on the return to town, a number of us were too nervous to face the dark, winding, snaggy river trip. . . . His word was enough! . . . as he led us down the slippery, dark track to the landing, by an arm each, we felt perfectly safe. . . . he seemed such a tower of strength and resourcefulness.

Yet despite numerous encounters, he did not make a close friendship with any girl until he was almost twenty. In August 1884 he had taken Mat and her friend Clara Stockfeld, then fifteen or sixteen, into the city one night. 'Clara has been somewhat excited about me since last Saturday, and told Mat so in confidence. Poor little thing. What experiences will she not have to pass through yet.' Some days later, when visiting, 'she gave me two little flowers. Oh the innocence of it'. He attached the flowers to a page of his Intimate Diary. Some time later he wrote out in his Commonplace Book 'Life's Crossways', thirty-five lines of doggerel signed J. M. and C. S. A young man considers and rejects the roads to Wisdom, Riches and Fame, and chooses the road to Love: 'A maiden came, and her eyes were so true/And tender and loving....' Clara went off to the country, governessing, and John began the first of his many long correspondences with girls: she addressed him as Jack'o and signed herself Queen of Hearts. For his twentieth birthday she sent him a 'neat piece of handwork. This is an attention and kindness which I do not well know how to meet'. Some time later he 'wrote to Clara and took a load off my mind'. He had over-committed himself and was careful now not to lead her on. Although she was clearly enraptured by him and although he sometimes confided his worries to her, he kept his letters to a merely friendly level—though he filed hers apart from his general correspondence, with those from other favourite girls.

From early 1885 comments in his diary on girls become frequent. About this time he developed card and conjuring tricks to help him be the life of every party. After his 'first semi-public exhibition' he confided to his diary: 'At any rate I did not take a back seat in the company, which is all that I care for'. At the German picnic he had found Franzchen Püttmann 'a tender, good-hearted, contemplative-minded girl who shewed an amount of passive appreciation of my attentions to her, as to lead me to flatter myself that I am held in considerable favour by her. Time will show how much I am deceived'. In July he joined a crowd at Steele's lodgings: 'some music, some recitation, some beer-drinking, and some tomfoolery with some girls'—an unchaperoned, almost Bohemian gathering. At a party at Püttmanns', when music and card-playing flagged, 'I rendered myself prominent by proposing and setting in motion some round games, which caused considerable amusement'. In August he took a nervous Matty to Hermina Püttmann's birthday dance

> and found much pleasure and no little pride in bringing her out. The affair was most enjoyable and left nothing to be desired. I met my old lady friends and danced in all but waltzes with them—the Straubels, Miss Anderson, Dora Sander and Olga Arnold, which latter's offered advances I readily accepted.

Early in October he escorted the Blashki sisters to a Union lecture, and again to the University Sports in which he ran in the office-bearers' race. At one party

> the choice of the company was all that could be desired, and the interesting part of it—the girls—was excellent. Owing perhaps to my terrible reputation I was made M.C. and as such had my hands full. I made several new acquaintances and met again some old ones.

...Lily Damman is a lively girl but knows how to take care of herself. We broke up at 3.30 and I suffered correspondingly the next day.

There is much evidence here of mashing and lady-killing, but none of lechery.

1885 was a highly disturbed year for John Monash for his mother had been gravely ill since February. There was an element of frantic self-distraction in his constant involvement in University and private social activity. He virtually abandoned his third year academic work: he confessed to 'absolute neglect' in first term and did not attend one lecture in the second. From mid-year he became progressively more unsettled.

> 15 June: Ever on the upward path. . . . Not quite so happy now, as when I entered active life, for activity brings unpopularity, and popularity is the object of my life, pursuit of it my greatest vice. Experiences many and varied I have gained, some at a dear price.
>
> 27 June: My 20th birthday. . . . I feel that it makes a difference of years. . . . Mixing much with my elders has I suppose given me adult ideas and manners, and this makes me feel much older than I am.
>
> 8 August: I am heartily sick of knocking about, and pushing myself into everything. I have allowed myself to be carried along with the stream for some time now and have gained as much advantage therefrom in the way of experience as I could have expected. I feel the time has come when I must pause and return again to serious things, attend to my further educational development, and work hard for name and position in other directions. As part of this intention, I am about to resume my much neglected University work, and set down this my intention to test my strength of determination.
>
> 12 August: Everything is beginning to indicate to me the utter absence of public spirit among University men—a deplorable want of individual solidity, each and all actuated directly by self-interest.
>
> 6 September: I have begun to taste of the bitterness and monotony of existence and of the vanity of human hopes. In my own interests I am working myself into a system of philosophy, which will contribute to render me proof against disappointments. . . . I shall set down my system when I have more matured it. The end of my university career is near at hand. I am sick at heart for mankind when I reflect what kind of men, such as I have met, will become leaders among men. I feel it almost ignoble to associate with them.

The Union's social functions were not proving to be popular and the *Review* was not attracting readers—but what could have induced the extreme pessimism of the last two entries? Moreover, the last was only a few days after his ecstatic cry of triumph on his military promotion. He began to attend lectures in third term but could not settle down. He was also short of money and had decided he must seek a full-time engineering job. He was finding the grind of private coaching 'sickening'; it had brought him in at least £50 in the previous year, but he had still been forced to pawn and not redeem his watch. He finally decided at the end of September not to sit until February at least, as he could not pay the exam fees. His systematic plan—completing Arts in 1885 and taking the scholarship exams in Maths and Modern Languages in February, completing Engineering in 1886 and then sitting honours, going for the Cobden Club Medal and the Shakespeare Scholarship—was in total ruin. Early in October he resumed the social whirl and went in for some dissipation.

The determined ambition to contest for the 'glittering prizes' had been naked. 'You'll get on!', the diggers of several wars were to rebuke the too eager aspirant for promotion. Monash regarded it as normal behaviour, however, unlike many upholders of 'good form' who concealed their devious determination. Writing later to Cousin Leo, he attributed his early professional success to his 'University standing and to a certain position of prominence which I worked hard to obtain. . . . This all meant hard work, much ridicule, many enemies, but withal a splendid advertisement'. His awareness of his talents—of being predestined or chosen—the high expectations of his parents, his relative poverty, and the consciousness of being an outsider—doubly an outsider as a Jew of Prussian parentage—all drove him on and made for an unusual determined assertiveness. Yet he had a genuine consciousness of the common weal, as a student had a rare ideal of what a university and what a university student ought to be, and was well aware of how ambition and reforming idealism often go hand in hand. His ingratiating and yet combative manner, his craving for popularity and to be the centre of attention, his sensitivity to slights, his vanity, were all obvious (as much to himself as others) and made him slightly notorious and an object of some ridicule. But he had many good friends and he exaggerated his unpopularity, not realizing how much respect his intellect and achievements had earned. Moreover, he was sometimes far too hard on himself in his diaries, our main source of evidence, which, while sometimes both self-justificatory and self-condemning, generally strove for objectivity. His occasional expression of blatant self-interest, while condemning the self-interest of others, is not so much inconsistent as expressive of his own moral conflicts. The similarity with the young Disraeli is uncannily close. In Robert Blake's words, Disraeli was 'a precocious, moody, sensitive and somewhat affected youth, conscious of great powers, but uncertain how or where to use them, vaguely dissatisfied with his mode of life, much given to solitary reading and imaginative flights of fancy'. And Disraeli, too, gave the impression of being a foreigner.

3

To What End?
1885–1890

BERTHA MONASH died, aged forty-four, on 18 October 1885 of abdominal cancer. Early in the year she had had an operation, but soon relapsed and 'lingered in great pain'; the family knew for months that the disease was terminal. John had nursed her, cooked for her, played the piano for her. He mentioned the subject only once in his diary during the year: 'the darkest recollection of all . . . too omnipresent to need more than a reference'. Her last words were to demand of him that he 'watch over and cherish my sisters through all my days'. 'Terrible' and 'horrible' were the words he used to describe the previous months in replying to letters of condolence and in writing to relatives overseas. He abandoned his diaries for nine months.

He occasionally gave way in letters to girl-friends—craving solace and dramatizing, but honest:

> I have lost the dearest and most sympathetic friend I ever had. My mother was *far* more than that—and now I feel utterly utterly alone. Outwardly I may seem no different . . . but I have great self-control, and were I not to tell you, you might not believe how much of the brightness of life has been taken away. I feel like a wandering unit with no place in the world, and no duty but to fill out the position in which circumstances may thrust me, and take my place in the long race, and so on and on until the winning post is reached, a piece of white marble standing erect from the green turf.

Young men who lose their mothers usually do not understand their own reactions, nor try to verbalize them. When in 1888 Will Steele tactfully inquired how much Monash's occasional wretchedness might be due to this cause, the question was evaded.

Before and after his mother's death, John spent much time with the Lewis family. Mrs Lewis was an indomitable woman: deserted by her husband, she was bringing up eight children, running a boarding-house in Carlton. She gave John staunch support and was to retain a special place in his affections: he was to call on her on the very day he returned from the war, thirty-four years later.

For the next four years John Monash's behaviour was decidedly erratic: he was questioning all his ideals and constantly trying to pull himself on to an even keel. The loss of his mother and the guilt he felt about his academic failures coincided with the awakening of a powerful sexual drive. He had to assume leadership of the family, for his father was stricken and ageing rapidly. His business of financing—little more than money-lending—in partnership with his brother-in-law Roth yielded little income. John had for some time been financially self-reliant but his decision to take full-time employment from the end of 1885 was caused partly by the need to contribute to support of the family. Mathilde, although she won two first classes at matriculation in 1885, and the exhibition in modern languages in 1886 when she was dux of the Presbyterian Ladies' College, did not go on to university because she had to run the household and look after her young sister. Her abilities were to remain sadly unfulfilled.

John's inability to face sitting for his exams in February 1886 and his weak attempt to complete his B.A. later that year and in February 1887—what was now the point of it all?—indicate his disoriented state. His relations with the four pretty Blashki sisters—Minnie, Jeanette, Rose and Eva—for eighteen months are also closely related to his mother's death. The girls were daughters of a watchmaker and jeweller in the city; their youngest brother Myer, under the name of Miles Evergood, was to become a distinguished painter.

Late in May or early June 1885 John first visited the Blashkis 'as a sort of lion', performed on the piano and wrote a verse for seventeen-year-old Eva's album.

> Eva I find is a bright, intelligent, fairly-read, warmhearted, sympathetic girl—the sort of girl a fellow could lose himself to. She flattered me by an urgent wish to read my famous prize essay on "Macbeth", which I duly left for her today, together with her returned album, a few copies of the Review, and a volume of Gibbon, more a test to her depth of knowledge and tastes than anything else. I look forward with expectation to my closer acquaintance with these girls.

From now on he was in and out of the Blashki home (often in uniform). With Minnie, the eldest, 'prettiest and most amiable', he was quickly on terms of flirting badinage. But it was Eva with whom he began a long correspondence, initially about Gibbon, in which with full propriety they ponderously circled round each other—he seeking permission to carry on the exchange between, for several months, 'Miss Blashki' and 'Mr. Monash'.

> Eva I find to be a remarkably susceptible girl and wonderfully

impressionable. I made good use of the opportunity to make the impressions favorable and powerful, for the second time I wrote in her album and descanted upon deep and personal subjects, much to the disturbance of her mental stability.

The girls, I can perceive, are already beginning to draw conclusions in certain directions. It is a pity that modern society forbids young people to [meet without] reserving for itself and exercising the right of superintendence and making inferences.

This evening I paid a visit to Blashkis in their new house. Their strictness in religious observance greatly amused me. . . . Matters are beginning to assume altogether too definite a shape for my liking.

Eva was attracting him greatly, but he kept a level head and summed up in his Intimate Diary in September:

I am now of an age when questions of heart and home are of importance if not ever present. [Eva Blashki] . . . is in aspect, demeanour, mental constitution and comportment, much in accord with my indefinite and unexpressed inclination. But I ask myself to pause, before I do harm to her or myself. Her character is after all the question on which everything turns, and incidents, which I cannot easily forget . . . have warned me of the possible existence of grave anomalies and unamendable deficiencies.

The comedy is, I think, for the present played out. . . . She is as raw as possible and quite uneducated as to feelings and sentiments . . . the defects of her nature seem radical.

Poor Eva! struggling to pass the tests of this exacting examiner.

But he did not abandon her. For about three weeks before his mother died and for several weeks after, for about ten weeks in all, he wrote voluminously to Eva and to Rosie on religion and philosophy—'Why *are* we? Why *is* the universe?'—the basis of morality, the purpose of life; the need to know oneself and cultivate one's intellect; the virtues of study, books as the repository of the world's wisdom—'the thousand tongued chorus of everything that *has been* great and good in humanity'; the uses of a diary; understanding music. He implored Eva to allow him to be her mentor or mental physician, and persuaded her to start a diary. With Rosie—it was Jack and Rosie from the first, and it was she who had invited the correspondence—he strove for much more intimacy.

He was distracting himself in his grief, writing far into the night; he was seeking to elevate intelligent girls with inadequate education; he was clarifying his thinking under the pressure of disaster; and he was seeking a replacement for the love he had lost. How intimately had he talked to his mother?—there are only inconclusive hints that he had confided much.

Writing to the Blashki girls was his chief occupation at the close of 1885. The self-indulgent habit was broken by his taking a job, then by a holiday with Mat with the Steele family at Goldsbrough, a mining town near Dunolly. Here he had a brisk encounter with one Jennie Walls who subsequently concluded that he had led her on unduly and had dallied with other girls on the side; she returned his letters and demanded hers back. The Blashki correspondence died away, and some coolness followed: the girls had grave worries about his irreligion, Rosie was far less susceptible than Eva to his overwhelming intellectual force, and inevitably he caused jealous tensions between the sisters. Nevertheless he remained a constant visitor and was on affectionate terms with Minnie, who soon, however, became engaged to Albert Behrend.

From about March 1886 John became closely involved with Jeanette Blashki—almost the first real love of his life. She was a year older than he and less inhibited than her sisters and they were soon on close terms: 'I have told you often you are just made to be petted and cuddled', and she replied to her 'Dearest Jack'. The tensions in the Blashki household grew. In August Eva 'practically declared herself. Heaven knows where this will end! I am beginning to have my doubts'. Well he might have, for his infatuation with Jeanette was waning. He admitted his foolishness on 30 August:

> No further good can come of a continuance of this little drama, a comedy for me, a bitter tragedy for the poor girl. . . . for months past I have been causing wanton infliction of pain on a sensitive being who has deserved better at my hands. . . . I have been strangely led on herein by my vanity and impulsiveness, and scarcely contemplated the tornado which I have raised. I have sought Jeanette's love and admiration, have obtained both unreservedly and had not the courage to sacrifice both in her interests often when the opportunity offered. That social ghost "other people" in the form of her parents, sisters, and the all wise Albert have prepared for her a hell upon earth. A true friendship, solely platonic, between marriageable people, is a thing not admissible in our present social system. Who knows what has passed out of my sight and hearing? I have not the curiosity to investigate but can conjecture comprehensively enough. Henceforth it is my intention that outwardly all show of a continuance of our mutual position shall cease. Under other conditions, and were I ever so little different to what I am, Jeanette might be my wife. This simple assertion speaks eloquently. . . . Will the lesson I have learnt lead to reform? Not at all. Another acute angle in the mould of my better nature has been blunted down—that is all, and my ideal of absolute good has changed in form accordingly. . . . Misery, woe, wretchedness! cries my sickened inner soul. Courage and to it again! my practical daylight spirit. I wonder how many souls now pursuing their destiny through finite time are troubled

in this intense way like my own. Perhaps few—suggests vanity, perhaps all—is the after thought.
   Eva asked for her letters today. What shall I say or do, or leave undone? In truth I don't care at what pace, or in what direction I will run the rest of the race.

Constant embarrassment followed for three years. As Mat reminded him thirty years later, every one of the Blashki girls had hoped to marry him. He tried to let Jeanette down lightly and told her that he was in no position to marry for many years. When he helped to arrange the wedding ceremonies for Minnie and Albert and was told he was interfering and officious, she took his part. The relationship ended disastrously at Christmas. According to John's version, Mrs Blashki let

   it be very clearly understood that she would not object to me as a son in law. My father, ... an open but shrewd man, ... told her frequently he was sure I had no intention of marrying for many years. The same happened with my aunt. When Mrs. Blashki saw her fishing was no good, she very spitefully turned matters round and Jeanette came to me the other night with these words "What did you mean by getting your father and aunt to tell my mother it was no use her trying to get you for one of her daughters as you had better prospects elsewhere". I grew very hot tempered, said some very warm things, she told me that I and all of us were liars, I told her she was no better and I have not seen, spoken or written to her since.

At the Behrends next April

   Jeanette was there, but we completely ignored each other. With Eva I exchanged but two words—"good evening" and to Rosie I had little more to say. I felt tempted to cry "*pax*", but perhaps it is better I did not. Minnie is the incarnation of selfishness and ingratitude—first impressions are often follies.

On the anniversary of his parting from Jeanette, he ruefully recorded: 'I would know now how better to behave myself'. In October 1888 he was reconciled with her, but she made 'most indiscreet' advances and told him: ' "Jack, your only fault is that you make people like you, without thinking of the consequences." How very true!' She remained his victim: when he was courting his wife-to-be, Jeanette was 'spiteful, tearful, reproachful, and hinted all sorts of things'. Eva was never reconciled. Minnie Behrend remained to torment him for the rest of their lives.
   When in July 1886 the orthodox Eva asked John what were his beliefs and whether he believed in God, he took several thousand words to reply with what purported to be a religious self-history. He claimed to have begun without beliefs: 'my fellow creatures have many

"religions" and codes of morals . . . among which I am free to choose, if I choose at all'. Some 'in all humility and honesty . . . strive to live up to their ideals of Right and Duty', but most wear their religions 'only outwardly as a cloak' to hide what lay behind. All religions centred on belief in 'a Deity or *Superior Existence*'; all had a 'Book or written manifestation of this Deity . . . through the mouths of patriarchs, prophets or seers'; all had 'a code of religious observances, and a system of duty, resolving itself into ways of worship'. The Book was 'an account of the world's history from the time of the Creation'; the age of the world was commonly 'set down at about six thousand years' which was irreconcilable with the 'teachings of modern Science'— archaeology, geography, geology, astronomy; all included sundry miraculous events contrary to the laws of nature and the 'promptings of ordinary reason'. The Bible, for example, was a collection of folklore, legends and ancient traditions dating back to before the invention of writing, and collected and written by later prophets. Religious observances were partly rules for rest, food and cleanliness which had become recognized as scientific and sanitary necessities; and partly a moral code which, as in the case of the ten commandments, was 'a succinct and complete basis for all systems of ethics'.

Did he then not believe in God? Not any of the Supreme Beings of the various religions which were all products of the histories of the various peoples. The God depicted in the Bible was 'no more than a terrible being in human shape, and activated by purely human feelings, and guilty of the meanest of motives, revengeful, deceitful, cunning and cruel, and *sanctioning every crime under the sun'*.

> Shall I then throw aside my birthright of enlightenment, ignore my privilege of free thought, do my reason violence, and lower myself to the moral standpoint of the people of thirty centuries ago? Emphatically NO. The ancient conception of God I will and do cast aside once and for all.
>
> Am I then without faith, without belief in the Supreme? Still more emphatically NO.

God was to be found in Nature:

> It breathes of the Spirit, of the ineffable Essence of Absolute Right, Truth and Good [but] when I come to define and describe Himself, both language and thought desert me and I am helpless as any fool. . . . I cannot define Him for He is "Everything". I cannot locate Him for He exists everywhere. . . .
>
> I *accept* wholly and unreservedly the moral teaching of the Bible, as part of the Universal Good which permeates all things, as expressed through the minds of the best men of past ages—so far as they apply to moral and spiritual self-preservation. I accept wholly and unreservedly the code of observances, so far as they

The post-matriculation class, Scotch College, 1881
Moses Moses is sitting left centre with Monash on his right

John Monash,
late 1881

Examples of handwriting:

a letter to his father

> Richmond 3 October
> 1880.
>
> Lieber Papa.
>
> [German letter text, handwritten]

... and a diary entry

> 1845.
> Sep. 6.
> . I have begun to taste of the bitterness & monotony of existence & of the vanity of human hopes. – In my own interest I am working myself into a system of philosophy, which will contribute to render me proof against disappointments. The extent of their after influence is dependant solely on their reception. I shall set down my system when I have more matured it. – The end of my University career is near at hand. I am sick at heart for mankind when I reflect what kind of men, such as I have met, will become leaders among men. I feel it almost ignoble to associate with them.

apply to all necessary attention to health and physical preservation and so far as they are possible under the altered social conditions of life. I reject wholly and unreservedly the historical portions.

'No sane man can believe in *nothing*', he wrote elsewhere to the Blashki girls. But he could not believe in immortality:

> People are born into the world under the most diverse circumstances of education or external influences, and each, when the time comes to return again into non-existence, each one has travelled along the path which he has chosen or which has been chosen for him and has approached more or less closely to the goal of his reasoning. . . .
>
> Generations after generations take to themselves human forms and *appear*. What force is in each he expends, one grinding at the mills of industry, another climbing the giddy heights of fame, another dashed to pieces on the rocks of strife. . . . a brief space, and he is recalled, his earthly vesture falls away, and soon he becomes a vanished shadow. Thus we emerge from the Unknown, rush across the astonished earth, then plunge again into the Unknown.

There is little indication that he revised his affirmation of deistic pantheism, which probably derived from Goethe, Lessing and Spinoza as well as more obvious secularist sources, or that in later years he spent much time in contemplation of eternal matters. He had been struck by Oliver Wendell Holmes's frequent comments on 'the nothingness and inutility of existence', but concluded that 'such speculations are after all an occupation for our leisure moments only'. He very likely became an apathetic agnostic, strongly tinged with anti-clericalism. When he attended Christian and Jewish funerals in the later 1880s he remarked on the 'meaningless form' and 'bitter farce' of the ceremonies.

He saw his 'religion' as private. One had to take the world as one found it—man was irreclaimable: 'Withdraw yourself in spirit', he advised Eva, 'from all the folly, the vanity, the littleness of man, since you cannot hope to reform it'. He had small interest in theories of society: apart from an elementary Australian patriotism and some scepticism about imperialist jingoism, his politics were received, orthodox free trade–conservative. He convinced himself—temporarily at least—of the virtues of enlightened selfishness:

> Hence I may take *self* as the basis of all reasoning. Now see how this fits in with the daily teachings of religion and morality. The fundamental principle of all morality is to *do no wrong* to man or beast. A wrong action bears its own fruit; for sooner or later it will cause pain or grief to a fellow creature, and to a fine-strung and higher nature . . . this causation of pain will have such a reacting

effect as to sufficiently avenge the wrong. If then you have regard for your own peace of mind and happiness you will (i) do no wrong for the punishment it brings (ii) do good for the gratification it produces.

What purpose then could there be in life? Man's 'first duty' was 'to take our "mind" or intellect and cultivate it to the fullest extent of which we are capable'. But to what end? Wisdom was unattainable. Wealth involved stealing for 'oneself the goods of the earth ... by the superior cunning and deceit which men call business'. Fame was empty and hollow: though he himself would seek it, he predicted that if he was 'honoured among men surrounded by applauding society', he would 'stand aside mentally and look with contempt at all this masquerading and petty contention'. 'Take any road I will—there is the same emptiness of purpose....' He envied 'the happiness of ignorance and the bliss of a mere physical existence of the lowest men'. Achievement of ambitions would bring no worldly happiness. 'Youth is all a hope, age is all a regret, and we must be content to take the few moments of supreme joy as a counterpoise to years of trouble and sorrow.'

Such precocious pessimism indicates too wide reading at an early age. It also again displays a loss of direction following the death of his mother. Monash acquired very early a sense of being far older than his years and of having been tempered by the fires of experience. 'I have had much of the sentiment and poetry of life knocked out of me though barely at its threshold', he told Cousin Leo. Certainly in 1886 he was far more subdued than in his university days; his driving ambition was quietened.

Throughout 1885, assuming that he would almost complete his B.A. that year and increasingly fretful about shortage of money and the irksomeness of coaching, Monash had been putting out feelers for engineering employment, largely through Jim Lewis. There were abundant opportunities for young engineers in a boom period of public works expenditure, especially in government departments and municipalities. But he found the prospect of moderate pay, slow promotion and the security of a government job unappealing and was delighted when Lewis suggested eventually setting up together as contracting engineers. Lewis was employed by the contractor David Munro on the new Princes Bridge, and persuaded him to take on Monash at the end of the year. His pay was to be thirty shillings a week (less than a navvy earned and no more than he had been getting from coaching) but he could not bargain, as others would be willing to take even less for the experience.

Munro was a contractor and a machinery manufacturer employing several thousand men; his engineering workshops were possibly the largest in Australia. He owned granite, basalt and other quarries, sawmills and steamers. Princes Bridge, linking Swanston Street and St Kilda Road, was on a scale—100 feet wide—in keeping with Melbourne's years of magnificence. The works were in the charge of George Higgins (brother of Henry Bournes Higgins). Monash confessed to being

> in great fear of my applicability to the new order of things, and troubled Lewis extremely by persistent applications to him for advice and assistance. The first work which was given me ... is usually entrusted to men of great experience and requires both time and care. It was the drawing out of a complete set of courses for the masonry. ... After a few weeks I was able to hand over to the foreman mason this work complete and correct, and upon my drawings the whole of the masonry has been cut and will finally stand.

Lewis recalled that Monash's

> restless energy egged me on to greater endeavour than I had been accustomed to. He was most enthusiastic and embarrassingly curious. He always wanted to know the reason of things and I was not always able to satisfy his curiosity. ... he always found out anything he wished to learn and when I set him some task he would invariably carry it out successfully.

For the next two years Monash assisted in elaborating the details and working drawings of the abutments, piers and retaining walls, which sometimes involved interviewing government officials and once even the minister: 'You may be sure that I tried to make the most of myself on these occasions'. He planned excavations for the foundations of the machinery used to set the stone; he opened a quarry ten miles out; he ran a supply yard: after fieldwork at the south abutment, he felt he was 'gaining by experience much of the instinct of accuracy'.

There were fillips to his pride. The *Age* published his name as one of four 'competent and able engineers' engaged on the bridge; Sir Henry Loch, the governor, and his aides had to be shown over the works; Professor Kernot and his class and the Engineers' Association came to inspect. But after long looking forward to the setting of the foundation stone, his feelings were 'deeply hurt by being excluded altogether from the list of recognized guests'. However, on request, Munro raised his salary after twelve months to £2 a week. Early in 1887 Monash was prominent in planning the employees' picnic with artisan delegates: at the first meeting he 'spoke a good deal, felt very much at home on my legs, had all my proposals adopted ... and was elected treasurer. The gathering impressed me'. After a finance committee meeting at Young and Jackson's Hotel, however, he noted, perhaps ironically, that 'these fellows do not seem to appreciate my fraternization with them as much as they ought'. The picnic went off well, he proposed the health of the ladies, and altogether enjoyed himself.

Monash enthusiastically pushed himself into each new stage of the works—the setting of the granite columns, the laying of the Malmsbury bluestone, the carving work on the masonry—and craved attention for his contributions. When the coffer dam failed 'under my feet' and had to be rebuilt, then proved difficult to pump out, he absorbed every detail of the operation, while recognizing that he was the typical willing volunteer who only got in the way. He made a serious mismeasurement—fortunately soon discovered. When eventually the dam was ready for the masonry, he immersed himself 'in mud and calculations. I am vain enough to feel myself indispensable'. He was brought up short by fatal accidents—'yesterday another unfortunate fellow was mangled by a stone. I took him to the hospital, and the business has considerably affected me—simple minded slave that he was'. He had a nasty fall himself. Monash did not easily brook control—his friendship with Lewis cooled temporarily. Higgins confided in him about his problems: 'Somehow I fancy I could get on more smoothly. ... I fancy that when I have reached his standing, and age I shall be quite as good an engineer as he and much else besides'. Higgins unsettled him, however: despite his frequent friendliness he was sometimes

> strangely unsympathetic to my interests; I shall try to make him be afraid of me, which I think it not difficult to do.... I spoke strongly to him about Blair, who has been taking to himself a lot of credit for my work. I hope Blair won't hear of this treachery—but after all each for himself.... It is a genuine pleasure to me to perceive my *savoir faire* in these matters rapidly growing.

At this time—January 1888—Monash was particularly anxious and combative. On the other hand he had struck up warm relationships with junior colleagues.

Late in 1887 work on the bridge was almost complete, but Munro had so many contracts that future interesting employment seemed to be assured. One was construction of Queen's Bridge over the Yarra and it was rumoured that Monash might have charge of it; he was 'so elated by the idea that I have perhaps spoken rather too freely about it'. He began work on plans for its masonry (which were eventually used), and had other work at Footscray, Moonee Ponds, Coburg, and the Flemington Road railway bridge where he intended 'to work myself into control'. He became edgy about his future with Munro, but was pleased when in January 1888 he extracted another ten shillings a week in pay.

In July 1886, although he had done no study that year and little the year before, Monash foresaw no difficulty in finishing his course. Early in September, with the helpful advice of O'Hara especially, he buckled down to Advanced and Mixed Mathematics, Natural Philosophy III, and Geology and Palaeontology, all of which he had to pass to gain third year Arts. He worked spasmodically at nights, but at the exams had a

> most miserable time. I did not know my work and hoped to scrape through. All went fairly up to the last when I broke down.... During the whole time that I hung about the place many pangs of regret at my severance from its associations went through me and I felt deeply my complete failure as a student.

He passed the two mathematics, but failed the other two subjects. He decided to sit a fifth subject at the supplementaries in February and took up Political Economy with the help of Farlow's lecture notes; from December he was reading Adam Smith, J. S. Mill, W. E. Hearn and Herbert Spencer. But he flagged again, was distracted by an amorous adventure, and decided not to attempt Natural Philosophy. He sat in a comparatively calm frame of mind, though he was not 'any better prepared and [had] no better chance of success'. He 'ended ignominiously'—passing three subjects and failing in Geology, which could only have been from lack of work, and so failed the year.

All allowances must be made for the difficulty of a part-time student passing a full year's work. Yet this double fiasco again indicates overconfident misjudgement of his capacity and lack of concentration reflecting an unsettled state of mind. He resolved to start work earlier in 1887. He attended Commencement in April and 'at the spree which followed at the Clyde [Hotel], I was flattered by the cordial reception I got'. In July he attended a Union social: 'I am well received at these meetings and my old unpopularity seems gone'. That week he got his 'books together for a fresh start at studying. I mean to do it this time'. He settled down well:

> 2 Sept: I am after the lapse of years, beginning to feel again the promptings of studious habits and aspirations.
> 7 Sept: Mathematical problems, which I used to shun, I now court and fight with successfully [I have] no fear of the coming exams and hence a heavy load that has been on my mind for months is removed.
> 11 Sept: ... new hopes begin to rise within me, and a strong inclination has come to me to work for the Mathematical scholarship in February—a thing I would give 5 years of my life to gain honorably. There is no reason why I should not try.

Will Steele was working with him on Political Economy and on Jurisprudence, which Monash had decided to substitute for Geology. Most of October was lost because of attention to girls and military exams, but he settled down in the last few weeks to work to a rigorous timetable, and had leave from his job to take the exams. This time all went well:

> As if by inspiration, all the difficulties of conception of the higher mathematical work vanish before a little steady application. . . . I find myself well received by all my old friends, and my ears are dinned by pleasant greetings. . . . All the trouble, worry and anxiety is over at last. . . . I have been already turning over the idea of competing for Maths Honors. Oh if I only could!!

He did indeed pass in all five subjects including Natural Philosophy, and the two mathematics—for the third time. On 1 December Farlow brought the news that he and Steele too had passed: 'Thus three old friends finish together. For me it is not quite the finish, for some trouble still awaits me in February; after which I go for my final in Engineering and enter my profession with full éclat'. The trouble awaiting him, in February 1888 and after, was that he had still to pass first year Latin to complete B.A., and Geology to qualify for fourth year Engineering.

Higgins was encouraging him to sit for final honours in Maths in February, but Monash judged his hopes for the exhibition were ill founded. Yet honours in Maths would mean an automatic M.A. after the effluxion of two years; he asked O'Hara for advice on his chances, given the little work he would be able to do, of a minor place in the class-list. Despite his early success at school and although he never worked for long enough with sufficient concentration to make the most of his talent, there is little evidence that he was potentially a brilliant mathematician, any more than an able student. He had the cast of mind, as his lifelong delight in arithmetical and algebraical problems shows, but he never won any formal university distinction in the subject. Nonetheless he loved

> the wonderful process of analysis, of the sense of law, order and sequence in all things physical—of the powerful and far reaching generalisations embracing all things that are; all things that may be—indeed all that can possibly be—grand generalisations built up by faultless processes on the simple and fundamental laws of thought—a study besides which speculative philosophy . . . seems to me but passing and incomplete.

At all events he now decided not to sit for honours in Maths and settled for the 'sickening task' of tackling his bugbear Latin. In early February, with only three weeks to go, he was 'slowly reinsinuating himself' into the subject and, to his surprise, found he had reached in a few hours the point at which he had stopped five years before; the work was 'pleasing rather than irksome, and Catullus I greatly admire'. But once again it was too little, too late. A military accident cost him several days' work; then he allowed himself to be whirled away to stay with a friend for a couple of days at Dandenong—and decided not to sit. He attended the melodrama *Drink* and found a lesson for himself in its 'severe admonition against infirmity of purpose and weakness of character'. He was humiliated. Two and a half years were to pass before he resumed his university courses.

Monash's military career had been checked. The University company was disbanded, largely because of irregular attendance, on 23 July 1886; his service formally ended on 30 June. In May he had again applied unsuccessfully for a commission in the Engineers. He was disgusted with the 'wretched business': 'The militia is a fraud and bristles with ill-management. I have little heart to bother about it further'. Many of the University men transferred to the North Melbourne Battery of the Metropolitan Brigade of the Garrison Artillery whose fixed guns defended the Victorian ports. Monash's school friend, the medical student Joe Miller, was a senior subaltern and George Farlow immediately gained a commission in the unit. Monash's hesitation for the moment cost him dear. By mid-August he had changed his mind:

> The matter which is now uppermost in my mind is the prospect of a near fulfilment of my long-cherished hoped for military advancement. I can scarcely understand why this wish is so intense within me. . . . Nevertheless the gorgeous uniforms and all the pomp of officership bear for me sufficient attraction to make their attainment a matter of fierce desire. My good prospect consists in my approach through Farlow and Miller of Major Goldstein. . . . I am feverishly awaiting the outcome of his recommendation.

Although he brought himself several times to Goldstein's attention, nothing happened for six months: it seems there was some prejudice against him for there was a vacancy. Eventually, however, his friends' lobbying bore fruit: when he received his application papers, he was rendered 'unfit for work for the rest of the day'.

He was formally attached to the battery on 3 March 1887. A descendant of Johann Sebastian Bach put him through his first drill. After passing an exam, he was appointed as a probationary lieutenant on 5 April.

> The undercurrent of my thought has been running strongly on military matters . . . a combination of military and engineering professions is a possibility that is before me. At any rate this commission will give me [an entrée where] I would have had to seek it and this is pleasing to me, for the sake of myself and my sisters.

> At last after many a weary and anxious day, the fulfillment of one of my most ardent hopes has been consummated. I may look

back upon this longing as very absurd, but for itself mainly and not alone for what it may lead me to, have I coveted this commission. I was gazetted today, and go down in full regalia.

One of his fantasies was that he might have charge of the seaward guns at Point Nepean and be the first to fire on a hostile fleet.

Monash thus took a decisive step towards ultimate glory. He had recognized his natural talent in this calling. Military theory had begun to excite him, he enjoyed the control of men in a hierarchical disciplined structure, and military precision appealed to a man who detested untidiness and disorder. He was well aware that a commission carried much more social status than the professions of engineering and teaching and would largely wipe out his handicaps of origin. His peacock-vain impulse to dress up and cut a dash with the girls would be satisfied. The pay, which barely covered cost of uniforms and equipment, was hardly a factor. He was sufficiently a product of Victoria's dominant ideology to believe in a duty to prepare to defend Australia's threatened destiny in the Pacific, and to disregard the 'sneers and reproaches' of those of his acquaintance who mocked the 'silly game of soldiering'. He even had it in mind, if engineering went badly for him, to take up a professional military career.

He got off to a bad start at the Easter camp at Queenscliff.

I displayed an utter want of tact . . . by resuming my military career at the point where I left off. I made no allowances for altered conditions and hence was sat upon by my seniors, and displeased my juniors. These fellows are not like our old boys, and when I took up my work with manifested zeal, they saw only a desire to put myself forward, and assume unnecessary officiousness. [I] gained little of that additional entrée among the higher men which I expected. . . . If I am allowed to retain my position, I do not propose to amend or alter my conduct or bearing; I have fought down much opposition in the past, and feel able to do so again.

Farlow advised him in June: 'You are not yet popular with the battery men . . . the first aim is to be firm even to severity so as to make your men *jump* at an order. Cultivate your popularity afterwards'. Monash 'began to realise what a sorry game the junior Sub has to play—walking about and kicking my heels for warmth for two solid hours afraid to open my mouth. I will be even with them yet'. Then, 'partly deservedly' he admitted, he 'incurred the serious anger of Colonel Brownrigg who specially complained of me to the Major'. But he became optimistic: 'All my fears about my future position are gone—I have a clear field before me to take my mark if I can'. He began to get on much better with the officers, and noted: 'Amongst most men the first impressions I make are the very worst'.

Monash was uneasy in his relations with his commanding officer,

Major Jacob Goldstein, and with Captain John Stanley. Goldstein, at forty-eight, was an unusual liberal-minded man, son of a Polish patriot of Jewish origin, a Unitarian and shortly to make his mark in charity organization. He handled his prickly recruit skilfully as Monash's successive diary entries indicate. After he had got into 'a frequent muddle at drill ... the Major was confidential and not aggressive'; the Major hospitably treated him to oysters; he accompanied him to the Government House fancy-dress ball; the Major had grown wondrous kind and even sought his opinion. Goldstein was obviously a model which Monash might follow—a man of non-British, Jewish origins who had won prominence in an open society. Stanley, aged thirty-five, was alternately sadistic and kind in Monash's eyes. His first impression was that he seemed to be 'a brainless idiot, but probably has a good deal of real worth'; then, Stanley 'as usual sat on me. ... I hate the man more and more'; 'as has often happened he took me and Joe to spend half an hour at the Yorick Club'; he 'is beginning to patronise me a little, and I try to flatter him'; 'Stanley seems strangely antipathetic to me. . . . A time will come though, some day'. Monash continued to try to be 'very circumspect' in conduct towards both of them.

He gradually worked into his duties. On the Major's request he prepared illustrated charts for the drill room; he took on the secretaryship of the battery ball. In June he took a parade by himself and boosted his confidence; he usually tried to make his drill 'a little sensational'. His shooting was unsatisfactory with rifle and revolver. He began lecturing to the men, and was proud and happy after one talk but floundered in another. Late in October he sat and passed exams, while also working at University subjects; early next month his commission was confirmed.

> At last I may feel safe in the possession of a magnificent prize—the reward of many years of aspiration and hard struggle. I can yet scarcely realise it, and already in its accomplishment begin to undervalue it. Very little more effort will now be required to ensure my easy advancement in my military function. Most of my brother officers delighted me by their demonstrative congratulations on my success; only that brute Stanley superciliously ignored it.

Goldstein now impressed him as 'a very smart man, with a justifiable amount of humbug'; they talked together now 'as very good friends'. Monash was pleased when he met Major G. B. Appleton, who promised him success in the militia and became a lifelong crony.

On 15 February 1888 a marker was shot at the Williamstown Rifle Range, and subsequently died. Stanley was officially in command of the North Melbourne men but had departed, leaving Monash in charge.

A sergeant was supervising the shooting; Monash was engaged elsewhere when the accident occurred. 'I came in for some bullying at the hands of Major Fellowes, and did not altogether preserve my presence of mind'; there was no way he could defend his men though he 'fought very hard'. 'So far reaching is my responsibility as an officer', he accurately wrote to Steele, 'that I *may* be put upon my defence in the matter'. Monash considered Stanley 'behaved in a cowardly and unfriendly way': he had immediately reported to him, fearful of damage to their reputations and to the battery's; moreover he had tried to avoid revealing Stanley's absence. Stanley refused to accept any responsibility and it was on his advice that Monash did not attend the first day of the inquest. He was summoned to appear the next day and the evening papers commented on his absence. 'I had expected a severe examination and had prepared myself', but the coroner was gentle. Monash even believed that the publicity had 'been a good thing for me'.

Late in March 1888 he looked forward 'to the time when I shall be commanding officer, with everything in my own way. . . . Tomorrow I go to camp, with good health, high spirits and great expectations'. This Easter camp provided 'much pleasure and a fair proportion of pain'. He put on a splendid show at 9-inch detail drill; an 80-pounder practice was very instructive; he commanded a guard for the first time; and he was vividly impressed by a mock gunboat attack at night. 'The mess tent was always lively and the meals enjoyable. The evenings were spent in story telling and some very good ones there were.' But he 'fell foul of one or two brother officers . . . Lowe and I had a silly quarrel. . . ·. I was told I was not wanted among the other officers, so I went home in company with the Torpedo men like last year'. He wrote a dignified letter to Lowe offering a 'circumstantial apology'.

> I tried to make it clear to you twice already that any offensive expression I made use of was made in the purest spirit of jest and raillery. . . . If however you really wish to quarrel with me, I cannot help it having done all on my part that I honourably can.

Lowe replied handsomely. By July Monash was telling Farlow that he now had 'a very firm footing in the battery, both with juniors and seniors. The Major and I are the best of friends, and I have at last gained that passive influence over him, which you will remember I set myself as an aim to acquire'.

No longer a full-time student at the University, Monash made his social centre the Deutscher Verein von Victoria which he joined in January 1886; a sizeable minority of the club was Jewish and his cousin Albert had become its secretary. Before he tired of it after about three years, he annually attended dozens of the German Club's social functions. All proceedings were in German and conversation normally so. Conduct was highly decorous, but occasionally a smoke-night concluded with 'drinking and sousing' until 3 a.m. He also regularly attended Metropolitan Liedertafel smoke-nights. John was occasionally M.C. at a club dance and was on the annual picnic committee; in 1887 he started the races and in 1888, living up to his 'terrible reputation as an athlete', won a prize 'as usual'. But the picnics year by year became duller and he found one Kaiser's birthday dinner 'unpalatable and slow'. He confessed in 1889 that he had 'not much influence at the German Club, because my sympathies are too English'. The pan-Germanic movement developing at this very time alienated him from the club. He spent much time in 1888 with the Rosenhain and Huntsman families, who held regular literary evenings; he could both appreciate and deplore their tendency to Teutonic earnestness.

In 1886 he attended dancing classes—a 'necessary evil'—in order to master the difficult waltz, and on 31 July 'with Ethel Jones ... had the very first waltz of my life—that is outside of a dancing class, and as a finished dancer'. At the South Yarra Assembly in September, 'I came out strongly in the dancing line, and aspire to achieve my customary superficial excellence'. Over the next couple of years, at the peak of boom extravagance, he went to scores of private, military, University, German Club, bicycle club and other balls and dances. He took his full part in making up parties, for unaffianced men did not invite single partners, and shepherded his fellow-guests to arrive promptly so that they might advantageously fill out their dance programmes. On 22 June 1887, as an officer, he attended a Government House ball, a 'great and wonderful occasion—never to be forgotten. Intense fun'. Subsequent vice-regal hospitality was never quite so exciting, partly because so few of his female friends were present, but he confessed himself 'toady enough to like to boast that I was there'.

In 1886 and 1887 Monash reached his peak as a pianist; never again could he afford adequate time. Mendelssohn, Weber, Beethoven and Chopin were his staple fare. In July 1886 he 'made a choice of some dozen pieces in which to perfect myself. ... Mendelssohn's great concerto is my present hobby'. Haydn's and Beethoven's symphonies in piano-duet versions were other favourites which he often played with a family friend Max Joseph, Albert Behrend, members of the Levy family, the Püttmann and Krakowski sisters, and Herr Kohler who gave him useful advice and incentive. John began to surprise himself with his facile sight-reading and flexibility of touch. He continued to entertain often at private gatherings and won many compliments: 'I am often reaping this reward of a steady purpose'. He took his music seriously—as with literature and the theatre he believed in its educative power: 'When once you have mastered the principle of high class music, the effect upon the character is wonderful. You can raise yourself to the supreme heights of soulful joy, or plunge into the deepest moral misery by listening to a grand sonata or symphony'.

In December-January 1886–87 he attended Martin Simonsen's Opera Company's season of Italian opera nearly a dozen times, astonishing his friends by appearing in a tall hat. He delighted in the operetta *Dorothy* by the Englishman Alfred Cellier who was conducting, bought the score and began practising it. *Princess Ida* was the new Gilbert and Sullivan work of 1887. Although he went several times to *The Tempest* and relished Essie Jenyns in *Much Ado about Nothing*, he was going to plays less often, but noted: 'I often feel elevated morally by a night in the theatre'. Nevertheless his tastes were broad: 'I have fortunate capacity for great risibility and can enjoy even the broadest fun'. 'I can find enjoyment in sensational trash even.'

He was also reading much less, although he was very impressed with Oliver Wendell Holmes's Breakfast Table series, was arguing at length in 1886 with Will Steele about George Eliot's *Romola* and Savonarola's Florence, and was an early reader of Fergus Hume's detective story set in Melbourne, *The Mystery of a Hansom Cab*. He still painted occasionally: 'Another showy accomplishment!' He viewed the visiting Grosvenor Gallery exhibition: 'I am no judge of art, and don't care to pretend to much critical taste—yet some of these paintings delighted me'.

His cousins were becoming a burden. A few months close reacquaintance with his mentor Albert Behrend was enough: 'That man can be an iceberg to his nearest and dearest and has an overmastering will'. He had to attend the circumcision ceremony of Albert's and Minnie's first-born—'my initiation into this mystery. Albert in his speech made me figure prominently—but otherwise I kept myself inactive in a corner'. The regular family visits to the Roths were 'very distressing'; once he was 'thoroughly disgusted with what I saw and heard. Perhaps unworthily but none the less truly am I ashamed of my relatives. It is a man's connections that keep him down'. He gave the eldest son Karl, a pharmacist, a piece of his mind when he 'ran amuck', and later described him as 'a roué of the first water'. He continued to see much of his friends Hyde and Steele. Their fervent political and philosophical discussions—Steele reading 'some of the best passages of Henry George', Hyde cynically man-of-the-world—were excellent training, especially as he admitted unwillingly they often bettered him in argument. New family friends were the Card family—boisterous, practical-joking good company, fond of charades. The O'Haras, Lewises, Püttmanns and others were regular visitors. His range of friends and associates—school, University, military, engineering, musical; German, Jewish and Anglo-Saxon—was wide.

His sense of Jewishness, however, although divorced from religion, remained unshaken. He had serious conversations with Joel Fredman of the West Melbourne Hebrew School on Jewish history and characteristics. He began attending meetings of the Jewish Literary Society and was tempted to speak, but did not, in the discussion of a provocative lecture on 'Jewish Talents and their Application' by the young lawyer Theodore Fink. 'Perhaps some day I will give these good folk something worth talking about. The thought, and the poor chance of its accomplishment often give me cause for mental pain.' He was disgusted by the 'miserable failure' of a symposium on the works of his uncle Graetz. He dropped away from the society but in 1889 Isidore Myers impressed him with

> the great desirability of speedy action on the part of the younger Jews of Melbourne to prevent the extinction of purely Jewish feeling. His remarks were so well in accord with my general conclusions that I feel I could enter very heartily for a very long way into his proposals, without any ... abandonment of deep grounded convictions. Perhaps this very matter may open up for me a field of enthusiastic work in the future.

He was persuaded to work up his former study of Mohammedanism into a lecture.

> Nothing more than my own manner could have better impressed me with the great change that a few years have wrought in the nervous boy of former times. To my military life I owe much of the change. I got through my subject, listened with gratification to the flattering comments, made my brief reply and all was over. I was the gainer in the esteem of many people, and gained an advertisement by brief reports (written by myself at the German Club in company with Isidore Myers and the secretary Marks) in the morning papers. I was half led to promise a second lecture on a future occasion, but I think I had better leave well alone.

Later that year he followed with interest the violent controversy following Goldstein's attack on Jewish orthodoxy in a lecture to the society.

George Farlow was a lasting friend, who was struggling with a part-time law course. He was a good companion who had mildly bawdy leanings similar to Monash's; they would indulge in gunners' bragging about besieging citadels and firing their 9-inch guns, and pursuing 'ye innocente countrie maide'—far more talk than action. At Christmas 1886 they made the first of their annual trips, always on the understanding that Monash would issue the marching-orders. This first time the route was Warragul–Drouin–Poowong in Gippsland. We 'strolled thru the country... as wandering minstrels, I playing and he singing whenever we came across a piano. The whole trip cost us about 15/- as the people were glad to give us tucker and a shakedown in return for our entertainment'. According to Farlow,

> On all our trips Monash was keen to observe the lie of the land, its water resources, the lives of the people and any engineering possibilities that suggested themselves. He was a very good bushman as far as regards finding his way and knowing the best way to reach any point.

Next year they walked from Lilydale through Healesville to Fernshaw and back. At Christmas 1888 the route was Healesville–Marysville–Warburton—they were out of condition and became very footsore—but it was 'an effective brushing away of the accumulated cobwebs of a twelve-month'. Monash was a sturdy walker, but he claimed when in his 'very best walking trim' to do no more than a mile in seventeen and a half minutes, and he could not keep it up for more than three miles.

In the following years John and George made major walking tours. The first, taking six days, was from Toongabbie in Gippsland via Walhalla—the most beautiful place John had ever seen—to Healesville, more than 100 miles of mountainous country. Next Christmas they took nine days, starting from Beechworth. They had a day on Mt Buffalo, which inspired John with 'feelings of awe, and admiration of nature. . . . the Alps are full of mystery, beauty and wonder'. They climbed Feathertop and walked through to Omeo via Hotham—all told some 125 miles—coached to Bairnsdale and took the train thence, John making his 'usual interesting study of travellers' faces'. Next year he and George could manage only a rushed trip to Buffalo for four days, taking a tent up for two nights. George used to be mildly amused at John's tendency to exaggerate distances covered and dramatic incidents.

He did not take up any sports or games. When he tried tennis he quickly realized he 'was not much of a hand at that sort of thing'. Roller-skating was a fashionable craze but he was 'too timid to make an attempt'. He had no interest in football and did not continue to follow cricket, but began to attend the Melbourne Cup each November, though he did not bet. Early in 1888 he improved his workshop and acquired a good set of tools.

After his apprenticeship with the Blashki sisters, John soon became an accomplished flirt with the innumerable girls he met at balls and dances. Berrie Rennick listened 'with an eager ear to amorous whisperings, and is not easily offended by too much boldness of speech'. Nellie Daley was 'a bright little flirt . . . a nicer ball room companion, bristling with sparkly fun and mischief I have never met'. However, he appreciated a girl of intellectual quality like Agnes Murphy (later a capable journalist) and was always glad to meet her at Government House. At Bendigo, where he stood as best man for his workmate Blair, driving back from the church the two bridesmaids accepted his 'caressing advances as a matter of course', and he was pleased with his success as M.C. He was utterly susceptible to the pretty face and lively manner and was slow to be disillusioned, but his combativeness and sense of male superiority would not tolerate any challenge to intellectual dominance.

> I was all "knocked of a heap" by the smart attacks and really first class wit of Miss Robinson, and determined to lower her flag. I succeeded in so far that I reduced her to silence and gained her sympathetic attention. I am conceited enough to think she feels she has found her match. We had a few dances together and became very good friends.

When, 'having long looked forward to such an opportunity', he met Major Goldstein's daughter Vida,

> I was much disappointed for I found her all too self-possessed and affected, and she plainly did not like me, but if I can get an uninterrupted half-hour with her, I doubt not I can put myself on a satisfactory footing with her.

An encounter in September 1886 illustrates his technique:

> [at dances I] devote myself solely to the cultivation of the esteem and, be it admitted, admiration of the lady guests. I endeavour to gauge rapidly the character of my partners and act accordingly. Sometimes this bears me flattering satisfaction and sometimes it is mere waste of energy, but in most cases my immediate aim is accomplished. ... Nell Stoddard, Con Willdridge, and Pop Cavanagh ... seem from my present knowledge of them to be more vigorous-minded and pleasanter ball room companions than any girls I have yet met of their age and circumstances and I have ascertained beyond a doubt that I have made a considerable impression. It is my aim to convince each in turn of my own great personal importance, wonderful depth of knowledge and outstanding versatility of acquirements—a task very easy to the most shallow character. In all earnestness I find I can easily take up any possible line of conversation, and approach skilfully any possible topic, though I lack altogether the faculty of gauging distinctly and rapidly the immediate effect of what I say. This faculty if I can acquire it might considerably lighten the task I set myself.

More than fifty girls are mentioned in his diaries for 1886 and 1887.

By early 1887, rising twenty-two, John was ready for adventure and fulfilment, but he was experienced enough to guard 'against any false slip which might ruin my career'. He was practised in romantic dallying and snatched kisses: his experiences demonstrate that chaperonage was not the common rule and that, in so far as it was practised, it was ineffective. He also illustrates the convention of the day that, beyond a well-understood point of flirtation and amorous display, no hand could be laid intrusively on a respectable girl unless with matrimonial intent.

In February 1887 he

> had an interesting flirtation with a pretty but mysterious girl from Adelaide. If her own account of herself is true, she is a kaleidoscope of excellence, accomplishment, and wealth; if not she is a clever adventuress. In either case she is the smartest, sharpest girl I ever met, and she very nearly deceived me; but I played my hand boldly, and I think she found her match.

He had spoken to 'Dolly' all the languages he knew, 'including love', and was 'amused to think how easily she thought to gull me and how readily she accepted my amorous advances'. John recorded their trivial sparring in detail in his diary and seemingly never solved the mystery.

A few days later, at a huge torchlight procession of the fire brigade in the city,

> Standing in the crowd, I by slow degrees found a pretty girl in my arms; I don't know and scarcely can recollect her, but the attraction was mutual and perfectly strong—awakened thoughts of natural selection and so forth.

Three weeks later opportunity knocked again:

> Returning to my office after dinner, I found two females there who sought the pay of the husband of one of them. They had made havoc within. One of them Miss Ricardo Josephine Burt was a wild girl with unbridled behaviour. I escorted them home, and she went back with me to the office where we remained locked in each others arms for nearly two hours. She left as a keepsake some verses, which I could not have believed any woman capable of writing. I shall meet her again.
>
> I did meet her again on the 16th. . . . She appears to be the unmarried wife of a bigamist and has had a child which died.

He took her to the works picnic: 'I don't intend to give her up yet awhile as I may get what I want from her yet. At any rate her acquaintance will be an amusing episode'. They went to the theatre and he visited her in St Kilda where, once, when she received him in her nightdress he admired his 'self-control and calmness', and noted: 'I honestly think that I may do her a little moral good—she needs it'. He had been balking at the jump, but

> I took her to lunch, and in the evening . . . to the theatre ("The

Magistrate"). I had prepared myself to see her home and return myself late, and made provision to do so. In the necessity for this I was not disappointed. I shall never forget May 5—1887. I am not sorry for what has happened.

In the next week he visited her again twice, but 'something occurred that forced me to the conclusion that I had been a fool'. He called on her again several times—to 'sit by your fireside and enjoy your merry voice and hear your snatches of song'. Eventually, however,

> I paid a visit to Ric ... and found there a gigantic young fellow of about 25 whom she called Gilchrist. . . . He left at her wish, and then she melted into extravagant fondness ... and wept a good deal. I took this very coldly. . . .

She eventually told him she had married Gilchrist. Meanwhile, 'my father astonished me by informing me of his cognizance of certain facts, and forthwith he told me many of his early experiences which still more astonished me'.

In winter 1887 John was briefly enchanted by Ada Krakowski, but the one girl he took very seriously that year was Rosie Schild, sister of a fellow-artilleryman of a fairly well-to-do Footscray family. He had met her the previous year at a dance when he found her 'outrageously flirty'. In July her brother took him home for a romantic reunion; John played Chopin and showed off his astonishing card tricks.

> Rosie is not a *very* pretty girl, but when she tries to be pleasant, does not fail. Perhaps she is only very slightly differentiated from others of her sex, yet she has some peculiarities of her own. She has, for one thing, my old peculiar habit of talking to the air in front of her, and while her lips utter many a quaint thought or pretty phrase, her eyes lack all expression. . . . An introspection of my feelings towards her satisfies me that I have outlived what baser instincts ever existed in my mind.

He joined her at her family house at Mooroolbark, chaperoned only by two young boys whose 'presence was a wholesome check'.

> We nestled by the fire, and I gave free vent to my sentiment. She was very easily touched and I very soon learned how to play upon the delicate keyboard of her soul. Some lingering doubts of my sincerity were soon swept away. "If I thought you were only playing with my feelings, I should never trust another man." That was more than enough to pull me up, and make her sacred to me. Even the thought of doing her wrong never dared to show itself.

Next night,

> Wandering down the beautiful fern gorge, hand in hand, in the dull,

calm moonlight, ankle deep in mud was far and away the most romantic experience I have had. "I loved you from the moment I set eyes on you" was delightful to hear, but how mean it made me feel—for what *must* be the end of it all.

Next morning they parted 'satisfied with each other, and how glad am I that not anything happened for which I could be sorry'. He boldly stepped it out for Ringwood but missed the train and had to march on to Box Hill, 'but the day was glorious, and the walk delightful'. 'How long can this last I wonder?'

Rosie was distracting him from work for exams. 'I feel very flattered at the conquest I and my belongings have made of her, but vanity, vanity what a curse you are. . . . These women are strange cattle—without exception.' A tiff followed, he began to find Rosie 'irritatingly volatile', but feared he had treated her too roughly. Soon, however, she was signing herself in her letters 'Little Tempter' or 'Little Black Devil', and referring to sand on the back of her dress. He spent Christmas at Mooroolbark with the Schilds as one of a large house-party. Rosie and John were irritable with each other, partly because of his determination to organize regimented walks. He consoled himself with Jess Robinson: on Christmas morning they 'strolled down to the creek, and there an incident took place such as one often hears of, but not often realises; the monogram J_R^M calls back to me the memory of it'. Two days later he and Rosie were on good terms again and on his return home he wrote:

> I spent with you the happiest time that I can remember. As I write your merry voice is ringing in my ears. . . . Rosie, I do believe you are about the best dose I would recommend to a fellow down in the dumps, your bright spirits are simply irresistible. I . . . hope you will forgive any ill behaviour or disagreeableness that I have been guilty of. I know I am one of the most unreasonable, selfish wretches on the face of this fair earth.

He was very fond of her, 'even to the extent of thinking foolish things'. But he drifted away—once she exploded like a 'barrel of gunpowder' for his not writing—and by April he had noted: 'I feel tired of her, as of all the rest of her sex'.

He was weary of being a social lion, of flaunting his sexual attractiveness, of distracting and involving himself too deeply with respectable girls. He was infuriated by and yet largely bound by the sexual ethic which forbade him pursuing natural inclinations. He was almost penniless and in no position to marry. He was confused by the necessity of making a Jewish marriage—and Rosie and most of those he dallied with were not Jewish.

On these and many other aspects of his life Monash's diaries are often the only source. He claimed from time to time that they were a scrupulously 'honest account of my doings sayings and feelings'. We should take him at his word: the self-criticism is patently honest, and occasional inconsistencies and self-deceptions reinforce the impression of veracity. He was reserved, however, about his sexual experiences; he was slightly afflicted with the contemporary prudery. From July 1886 he kept up consistent weekly entries—sometimes missing a week, occasionally two, sometimes making two or three entries in a week. Whereas in two and a quarter years from August 1883 he entered about fifteen thousand words with several stops and starts, in the three years 1886–89 he wrote about eighty thousand words. He had a strong sense of the need to preserve his own past and to delineate his intellectual and moral development for future contemplation, but his chief motives were to know himself better and to clarify his thinking.

Not only is my diary (and ever will be) of greatest interest to me, but it has been to me a most trusty and confidential friend, a sort of living conscience, a second self to which I could turn for consolation when I was broken down with disappointment, for reproof when I was about to break my resolutions, and for encouragement and fresh vigour, when I was dispirited by failure.

A diary is just whatever its writer makes it: it is not necessarily a confession book (though better so), it may be (and even so of *infinite* value) merely a record of daily impressions upon you of men and things, of your views and opinions on all the miscellaneous matters that come in your way. It is not sufficient to have connected and independent thoughts, you must be able to express them rapidly, store them up, and find them when you want them again. To make a habit of . . . writing to yourself as to a dear friend, . . . as to one from whom you do not withhold your smallest thought, however wrong, however 'stupid', however insignificant.

Every Sunday now he partly devoted to his diary, correspondence (with its routine of press-copying in letter-books), and sorting and storing his papers.

. . . somehow I have never yet destroyed anything but that I have some day come to regret it. As a mere matter of sentiment, it is pleasant sometimes to look upon old relics of things the memory of which has already quite faded. I have a rare collection of odds and ends and scraps that most people would laugh at me for keeping. But sometimes . . . I busy myself among them for an hour and can at will call up the vivid recollection of bygone joys and sorrows, struggles, triumphs and failures. A crowd of associations sometimes centre in a dirty scrap of paper. This habit has grown upon me, and . . . by its means I can carry the past along with me, and defy the erasing effect of time.

But he was nearly always conscious of the 'weight of arrears':

> I feel it like a burden which is strapped to me, which I cannot lay down and which I cannot shake off. And whenever I set to with determination and face the irksome task, I always get more than my reward in the feeling of lightheartedness and freedom from an incubus.

Oddly, he failed to adopt an innovation which appealed to him: in 1889 he bought a typewriter, but could not master it.

His Intimate Diary, written largely on his birthday or at the New Year, was an attempt 'to sum up for myself my whole nature as I was, all my hopes and tendencies and my reflections on the past'. At 12.15 a.m. on 1 January 1887 he reported himself as 'tolerably happy' following the 'sobering down process' of his year's employment.

> I am very satisfied with the past year. . . . My vanity has been flattered by the clear demonstration that I possess the capabilities of rising above my surroundings. Repeated successes have implanted in me a feeling of superiority present or future over those with whom I come in contact. . . . In the militia, I left many behind me, and I have made a magnificent start in my profession. . . . I do not hope for great things, nor do I wish for them as I used to, but I feel that I will always possess the self confidence engendered by actual success over other men, or the consciousness of my power.

In May he noted:

> I have . . . developed a growing tendency to habits of restraint in conduct which have led me to better results than I have yet experienced. I propose to pursue this conduct in greater detail. I have been attended with much success in my little ambitions and have gained largely in self-respect, while my confidence in myself is in no way shaken. . . . My growing repute in my profession, my reception in many places, my military advancement and my pleasant domestic circumstances all make up the essentials for my present complete peace of mind.

However, his supposed unpopularity still tortured him: 'I am mostly disliked and personally ridiculed, but I have often compelled submission, have been talked of and admired, and have thus had my greatest weakness pandered to'. He was well aware that this weakness misled him into ingratiating flattery and exaggerated response to those who expressed respect for him. He prided himself on conquering dislike—his ability to make friends with those girls especially who had initially repulsed him. But he remained unsure: 'Sam Ewing cordially met me. He was one of my detractors once. Either he, like some others, has seen the error of his ways, or I have been deceived by supersensitiveness'. In January 1888 he concluded to Steele that it had been his 'bustling activity, and many sided meddlesomeness which have earned for me the admiration of a very few and the envy, spite and unfriendliness of (alas!) the majority of those with whom I come into contact'.

His tendency to approach life as a race, or as a jungle in which it was essential to assert dominance over one's fellow-beasts, chiefly aroused antipathy. He was indeed something of a social Darwinist, a product of a University and a city in which Herbert Spencer was a leading intellectual influence. Professor W. E. Hearn and the historians G. W. Rusden and H. G. Turner were among those who explained social development in biological terms, 'the doctrine of beneficial struggle' attuned to conservative *laissez-faire* principles. In reply to Albert Behrend who believed that man should 'devote himself to the good of humanity irrespective of his own happiness', Monash argued that 'a man in pursuit of his own happiness of necessity fulfils [that] object'. Even with his close associates he had to assert his superiority: he made it his 'especial business to show [Farlow] that I still held the upper hand'.

In mid-1887 he had rallied himself into a burst of activity sufficient to take him through his exams late in the year:

> 2 June: A sudden train of thought ... has led me to an important conclusion ... having given up the pursuit of great things as an ardent ambition—I need not at all deny myself the pleasure of that pursuit merely as a mental exercise and pastime. I have been living at very low pressure, and feel an immense amount of force in reserve. Why not work up to the full limits of my potentialities and await the result?
>
> 15 July: I am slowly inaugurating a new order of things. I am daily gaining in strength and purpose, and circumspection of conduct. I am working hard to confirm a habit of punctuality of action and system in all my affairs.... I am slowly regaining my old ambitions and the faculty of working for remote advantages.
>
> 2 Sept: I have become very saving in habits, and moderate in desires. This is the capital I am storing up for the future.
>
> 10 Sept: I mark hereby a rekindling of all my highest ambitions, a birth of new activity towards their fulfilment, and of the highest hopes therefor.
>
> 5 Dec: A continuously contented frame of mind betokens a pleasant state of things. Success, and promise of further success attend me. My military position is secure, my University degree within reach, and my confidence in my ability and powers of self-restraint is greater than ever before. My daily life is becoming regular, and I have grown economic of time and money. Daily my vanity is pandered to on all sides. I am quite content.
>
> 8 Jan: The past year has been for me one of material advancement in some directions, of none at all in others, but of a complete moral

regeneration in all. . . . Materially I have gained by my reentrance into the militia with a commission. This with its responsibilities and emoluments, has made me feel quite a man. I have at least got on another step towards the end of my student days, with not a very extraordinary effort, though I had to put myself under a very severe discipline. . . . The daily strife to outdo others and make my way, is at times full of interest and at the end of a busy and eventful year I can at least set down the flattering reflection, that I have almost entirely eliminated such tendencies from my character as will be inimical to my material success or peace of mind. My present depression is a feeling of loneliness, and indistinctness of the ultimate goal of all my earnest strivings.

These entries from his Intimate Diary bear the mark of making the best of things and they run counter to the trend of his weekly diary comments. In August 1887 he had noted a 'fit of depression' lasting a few days. In October he was in an 'unsettled and gloomy frame of mind' and in January in 'almost perpetual depression'. There were reasons enough for these moods—tiffs with Rosie Schild, annoyance with the Behrends, worry about work, poverty, exams and many other tensions. His conclusive statement is in a letter to Steele of 15 January 1888:

I must correct you though in the idea that I am buoyant of spirits. [There is] no advantage in showing the world a sour face or importuning it with one's troubles. Truthfully, my outward demeanour is habitually very unreal; and my inward communings tend generally very much in the direction of moroseness, depression, and the blackest pessimism. . . . My thoughts are eternally pervaded by a sense of incompleteness of my life, of the ultimate aimlessness of all my strivings, and of disgust for my own egotistic . . . self. My manifested activity, buoyancy, or whatever you like to call it, is not a contradiction to all this, but in a practical spirit I [have] first adopted it and soon made it habitual, as the best discovered antidote to my normal (or abnormal—who shall say?) state of mind. . . . I can only sigh, as you do, for a state of mental peace and happiness.

He was indeed in a disturbed state. He was unhappy at work, did not sit for his Latin exam, was weary of chasing girls, and was avoiding company. On 8 March he noted:

I have not been in the best of health, nor have my spirits been good; . . . the recollection of the time lost, and the effect of that loss on my present circumstances have obtruded themselves much on my mind. . . . I realise the futility of regret, and make up for the past by all round self-denial and close attention to work both at home and at business. . . . With all this, I half fear that I am losing some of the faculties on which I used to pride myself. My music has gone by the wall, nor have I the same address in social gatherings as formerly.

Later that month he was drinking heavily, usually whisky, for almost the only time in his life. Carousing with engineers after their exams, he got home 'fuddled' and next night spent three hours at the City Club Hotel 'getting drunk'. (He prided himself on holding liquor well.) He was anxious about his application for a new job, on the Outer Circle railway. He was appointed—and immediately found new zest and resolution to reform himself. On 6 May he was brutally frank:

> I have reached a point where I feel disposed to take a new stand. What is the course of my life leading me to? My absurd vanity and brutal self assertion, give me growing cause for anxiety. I feel that ... the occasion has come when I must check those tendencies of character which lead to those frequent outward manifestations which make me ashamed of and disgusted with myself. I want to try to give the best qualities of my nature the very best opportunities for emphatic development.

He continued to examine himself ruthlessly in his Intimate Diary. He was also now fully recognizing the value of work as his 'salvation from much misery and wretchedness'. 'I am developing a faculty for energetic work which is beginning to know no bounds. But to what end? Oh dear!' He wrote to Steele:

> I have got myself into the belief that there is really no positive necessity for anyone ever to be unhappy. Of course you know there is such a thing as the pleasures of unhappiness—an exaggerated state of mind, but against positive and complete wretchedness it behoves each of us to provide an antidote—each according to his disposition. You know mine—it has till now been all sufficient for me.

Work was the sovereign remedy.

His correspondence of 1888 with Steele, now tutoring in the Riverina, was highly intimate. Will, who knew John was going to be a great man while he himself was already wistful and defeated, sensitively tried to help him through his bad patches. John was at his best in these letters—treating Will entirely as an equal, keeping him in touch with news, replying honestly to his tentative ministering. Will recognized the efficacy of John's antidote to depression, but continued to marvel at how he could fit the range of his activities into the hours of a day and keep up his diary-journal as well. Eventually on 20 May Will took a deep plunge:

> The powerful way in which you represented your necessity for work by reference to increasing doses of an opiate gave me food for much thought. . . . both my love for you and my intellect force

me to ask "Is it necessary?". . . . Are you flying from yourself? Can you then succeed? And if alas you do succeed and free yourself from these "obstinate questionings", is not the last stage worse than the first? . . . Suppose that one were to succeed in engrossing himself with matters of passing interest, suppose that in pursuing wealth and the various forms of pleasure and of fame, he make these worthy means his sole ends—what profit if he lose his soul!

He proposed an honest correspondence to attempt to answer the question, 'To what end?':

> I am satisfied . . . that you cannot live without an ideal—your very flight from contemplation proves it. . . . I shall think of you seated in that cosy working chair of yours at the table near the window—I shall be with you in thought.

Monash agreed to pursue the question, though he wondered whether he was currently in a suitable frame of mind and could entirely bare himself. Steele replied enthusiastically—'The question is "What are we living for?" '—but pressure of work and an all-absorbing love-interest prevented Monash from proceeding.

Jim Lewis had 'half-jokingly suggested' in March that Monash apply for the responsible job in charge of the Outer Circle railway works. He did so, and waited in 'intense anxiety'. 'I have been so indiscreet as to confide the fact of my application to most of whom I have come in contact. I wish I could break myself of the habit of promiscuous confidence.' He was exultant when appointed—it 'at one leap puts me years ahead of most of my former colleagues', he told Farlow—but he was also fearful of the test. The terms were three months probation, then twelve months, and £7 a week salary from which he would have to provide his own instruments and employ clerical assistance; it boiled down to little more than £4 a week. His parting with Munro was bitter. In his letter of resignation he could not resist expressing resentment: 'I should have hesitated to take the step, had I had any prospect of speedily bettering myself with you—a prospect which I have patiently looked forward to'. Munro exploded in wrath: 'I am so much struck with the ungratefulness of your behaviour that I . . . require you forthwith to leave my employ'.

Monash had indeed been fortunate, with his limited experience, to be given charge of a large contract. His lack of an engineering degree did not matter—it was a positive advantage in an age when the 'practical' businessmen with whom Professor Kernot was battling believed an ounce of practice was preferable to tons of theory. In a period of vast public works there was little competition from experienced engineers, but he could not help wondering how much his military commission and his own assertive self-promotion had helped to single him out from the ruck of young men. He was rather taken aback when Kernot, who had his eye on him and asked why he was not attending lectures, cast doubt on the wisdom of 'going into business':

> if you aim at becoming a scientific authority, an expert referee whose advice will be sought in difficult and intricate problems of public importance, who will sit on royal commissions and enjoy the confidence of public bodies I fear that the course you are taking will lead you further and further away from your goal.

Monash reassured him that he was determined to complete his course, but he was forced to think hard by the well-timed advice.

His employers were Graham and Wadick, large contractors who had recently been constructing several railway extensions. The Outer Circle eastern suburban line from Oakleigh to Fairfield via Camberwell, though it was to prove a white elephant and has been regarded as one of the most extravagant excesses of the boom years, seemed at the time the most sensible route for traffic from Gippsland to Spencer Street, for there was then no link between Flinders and Spencer Street stations. Residents of the eastern and northern suburbs mounted strong political pressure in its favour, and it was commonly believed that suburban extensions would spring up along its length.

Over the next three years Monash was responsible for 640 000 cubic feet of earthworks, 11 miles of mostly single-track railway, 15 miles of roadworks, a 550-foot four-span steel viaduct over the Yarra at Fairfield, 16 iron and timber bridges and many culverts, drains and sewers, to the value of £170 000. There was nothing of exceptional difficulty; the main problems arose from carrying out works through a populated area. His duties, in his own words, were to perform 'all the strictly professional work of setting out, preparation of working plans, ... taking out quantities of material to be ordered, designing of temporary structures and stagings, purchase of plant and machinery and its disposal, all dealings with sub-contractors, making up periodical certificates of work done, etc.'

He began nervously, feeling his way 'with much hesitation and many misgivings'. Graham and Wadick, like most contractors, lacked technical knowledge and were in no position to control him closely, but he had to convince them of his ability. He was careful to assert himself over his immediate associates and subordinates and to see that they did not take any credit which was really his. He quickly struck up a friendship with the government engineer-inspector: 'I appear to have well impressed him, this being still my first anxiety with regard to each new acquaintance, though not nearly so strong as of old'. He took on a young assistant without pay in return for coaching for exams.

Graham and Wadick were soon so well satisfied that they confirmed his responsibility for full charge of the works, not just of the engineering supervision. Though he revelled in 'the dignity of my responsibility and position of administrative power', he was worried that, he came quickly to realize, there was little prospect of his employers making any profit from the contract.

Monash attributed his quick mastery of administration to his military experience in 'the arts of organization and management of bodies of men':

> The engineer in charge does not often come into personal contact with the workmen; he deputes all the duties of direct and detailed supervision to the different gangers and foremen—which answer to the non-commissioned officers of the military service and it is in close supervision of these gangers that lies the chief part of my duties.

For the first time in his life he felt he was working 'at the greatest pressure that I am capable of'. The work was 'a perfect delight.... My life is like a perpetual holiday now', although 'the necessity of continually asserting myself has developed an irritability of temper'. An evening's drill was the best of relaxations. There had been

> some cause for gratification latterly at the manner in which some of my old 'Varsity acquaintances, who used to affect ridicule of me and my efforts, now come forward with apparently sincere congratulations and envious recognition of my success. Pardon the vanity which prompts these expressions.

> So you are having your triumph now? [Steele replied]. The blockheads and the envious are at last paying that tribute to success which they denied to ability. You enjoy it. I don't blame you, still be gentle.

Monash began to observe and analyse his own growing efficiency:

> In the old days when I used madly to take up and make business of mine anything that came in my way I was comparatively a paltry dabbler.... Nothing that I did was well done, but latterly with the narrowing of my sphere and the concentration of energies I feel I am doing each thing better of its kind. But one benefit my former proceedings left me—the faculty of rapidly passing from one thing to another, with little loss of time or delay in getting a fresh focus.

He had now adopted his lifelong working practice of making out a daily agenda, striking out each item when disposed of and finally drawing a vertical line through the whole. In August–September, writing to Steele, he was still exultant:

> the exercise of all my faculties to their fullest extent is a sincere delight and brings with it a state of mental balance and goodness of spirits which makes these days the happiest I have ever known.

The possession of absolute administrative power, and the conscientious attempt to make each administrative action, however insignificant, depend on a sound and logical analysis of the particular set of circumstances which rendered it necessary—just as the moves in a chess game—this all is a new and delightful experience, and one which I believe will not grow dull by habit. As I sit in my office issuing my letters of instructions and other papers, all the results of careful comparison and deliberation, I feel a new sense of dignity and importance as a tangible factor in the production of wealth. . . . Well, this feeling of living a useful life is to me a great satisfaction. Yet do not think that I am in danger of making these things an end, and of forgetting that they are but a means to attain a standpoint from which I shall some day be enabled to turn to higher exertions and higher levels of action.

The year proceeded happily and was enriched by a passionate love-affair. His Intimate Diary enshrined his conviction of professional and moral self-improvement:

1 July: I feel . . . that I am doing my duty at all points. My conquest over my tendencies to evil, has been complete, and this conquest has brought with it a mental calm and proud self respect which makes me altogether happy, and allows me to feel that I am living a full life.

7 Oct: Much has changed within me in the last few months. Firmly established and content in my professional position, successful in my work, secure in my military rank, and with gradually improving financial condition I have little cause for anxiety. Morally I have made a greater advance in the few months than in all the years that preceded. With every evil tendency allayed or checked, with the thirst for applause gone . . . I am living through happy days of work and love.

31 Dec: A happy close to a happy year. My material advancement has been rapid, and I can look back with ecstatic self satisfaction on exceptional difficulties and obstacles overcome. My new employment has taught me in a few short months an immense amount of valuable experience in the art of dealing with my fellow man, and in every sphere of action I have found myself able to hold my own. It has also been one of the benefits of the old year, that I have learned to bear worry and anxiety more easily, and to look boldly into the face of a difficulty. In my moral nature too, I have gained much that is worth gaining—increased self-respect and consciousness of power, increased strength of will, and ease of self denial—and have lost much that was harmful—much of my old brutal selfishness of purpose, and personal egotism.

Late in November the navvies on the works unsuccessfully struck for higher pay. Monash was scathing in his account of it to Steele and insensitive to any possible genuine grievance: the workman

> goes on the false doctrine that there is strength in numbers only. Thus he collects himself into a crowd and says—"We don't like work, we prefer to loaf, let us have a strike there is some variety in that". So he throws down his shovel, and rages about the country, clamouring, getting drunk, and fighting, and when all his money is gone ... he begins to feel what a fool he has made of himself, he gets sober ... and humbly begs to be allowed to work again.

Steele protested, and received a considered answer. 'Your reference to our side ... by the opprobrious title of "capitalists" is eminently unfair.' Graham and Wadick's capital had been amassed 'by a long life of hard work and self-denial. . . . It is nonsense to talk in this country of capital living on the lives of other men. . . . There is a recognised price for all kinds of labour'—and at that time the supply of navvies was such that wages, in market terms, should go down rather than up. The hard facts made it difficult to sympathize with them.

> Today I stopped one of the cuttings at noon owing to the blinding dust. By 4 o'clock the place was strewn with drunken beasts, lying in the hotels and public roads. You lose all respect for them as men. If you tried any reforming influences they would only laugh at you. Take my word for it ... there are a good many things which would shock you and still further deepen your anxiety at the hard issues of reconciling things as they are with things as they ought to be. But it is a very depressing thought. . . . For myself I want to widen the scope and extent of my experience and observation before I shall attempt to formulate a theory on so complex a subject.

Over the three years of his employment Monash had half a dozen more or less serious conflicts with Graham and Wadick, but persuaded them almost every time of his superior judgement by 'a little emphatic expression of opinion'. In general he reigned contentedly supreme. He made close friends of two enthusiastic junior assistants, Jack Grey and W. B. Shaw, a first cousin of George Bernard Shaw. From mid-1889 the pressure of work fell sharply.

He had one frightening escape. He was supervising the lifting of heavy stones on the Fairfield bridgeworks, a rope snapped, and a huge stone fell within inches of his head: 'I seemed to live over all my life in a flash. . . . By good luck I was paralysed with a moment's hesitation; had I moved a step it would have been all over with me'. A mason had his hand crushed: it took nearly an hour to stop the bleeding, after which Monash drove him to hospital.

The last months of the contract in 1890 ran smoothly. The Oakleigh–Camberwell section of the line was opened in June. The work remained sufficiently varied for Monash to regret the approach of completion, but in November he was delighted with the testing of the Fairfield bridge in pouring rain: 'the sight of the heavy engines galloping along was a magnificent one'. The contract had taken much longer to complete than originally planned, not through any fault of his but because of alterations. The final paper-work took him well into 1891; he had no regrets about his three years' 'enormous and extensive experience'.

On 22 August 1890 'Mr. J. Monash, C.E. [Civil Engineer]', read a paper on 'The Superintendence of Contracts' to the Engineering Students' Society at the University. It was lucid, practical, unpretentious advice to final-year students. He described the duties and functions of a contractor's engineer: it was essential, first, to have those duties precisely defined, to insist on absolute administrative control. If he was wise, he would 'allow himself to be guided by expert foremen, without any sacrifice of dignity or loss of prestige'. But he 'must never forget that he is the first person to place foot on the site to be operated on, and he will be the last person to leave it after the final certificate has been signed, and that the disgrace of a mismanaged contract will be carried off by him, and by him alone'. He outlined the functions of the outdoor manager, the engineer's mouthpiece, of the accountant, paymaster and timekeeper, storekeeper, foremen, gangers, messengers, grooms and watchmen. He described the daily occupational hazards: the frequent false reports of trouble far away on the works; the critical government inspector, guardian of the taxpayer, whose 'especial delight' was to 'point out that some bridge or culvert five miles away is being built upside down'; the conflicts with ignorant employers who had to be handled with tact to be saved from folly. At this point Monash gave his favourite homily on the need to keep a full and accurate work-diary, date every paper, keep a press-copy of every letter, always to carry and use a notebook, docket and pigeon-hole all papers and fold them to a uniform size, and not to destroy any paper till the contract was finished—so that there was always precise evidence available for inevitable disputes. He moved on to the techniques of ordering material—the need to have ready at hand

> the number of bricks, bags of lime and casks of cement in a dray load or lorry load, the carrying capacity of railway trucks of the K, I or Q pattern, the quantity of lime, cement or sand required per yard of brickwork, or per yard of concrete, and innumerable similar constants.

He discussed the major problem of the order of operations, precautions against changes in weather, and the need to test the comparative efficiency of gangs of workmen. The young engineer had to learn the language of building artisans, for example when to speak of quoins rather than angles. He next tackled the problems of setting out, and the need for early preparation of plans and sketches, and finally 'the important duty of making measurements and preparing certificates of completed work [when] the personal acumen, business ability and general smartness of the engineer come into full play'. He concluded by asserting that there was no reason why a well-trained engineering graduate could not successfully assume such responsibilities.

It was a remarkable performance by a student yet to graduate, carried off with no-nonsense aplomb, exact in its limited claim for respect due to experience. Its very understatement reflected his great good fortune in having, at the age of twenty-five, had such superb experience in a major professional task. When late in 1891 he left Graham and Wadick they properly gave him a glowing reference. He now knew that he was capable of fulfilling his promise.

4

The Course of True Love
1888–1891

A FEW DAYS after Monash was appointed to the Outer Circle railway in April 1888 he engaged as his assistant twenty-four-year-old Fred Gabriel whom he found to be handy, though self-assertive. Gabriel and his wife and two-year-old son Gordon took a house at Hartwell and Monash arranged to use a room as his office. The Gabriels had married in 1884 at Ballarat, with Wesleyan rites. Annie Gabriel was the daughter of John Hill of Clemenston, near Allendale, an engine-driver in a gold-mine. She was, within a few weeks, the same age as John Monash.

As so often, propinquity did it. Monash set out to charm as usual, and assiduously to cultivate the good opinion of the 'pleasant, plucky little woman. [She] seems to have grown very fond of me. . . . I bring her books to read and pay her homage'. It is a question of who, precisely, was charming whom. Early in June he wrote: 'I have been drawn imperceptibly into an altogether novel and embarrassing relationship with Annie Gabriel. . . . I have done more than I intended'. Some 'impressive scenes' and 'pleasant passages' followed: within a fortnight she had led him on 'in her simple way to a declaration which evidently made her happy'. Through July Gabriel became increasingly suspicious; when he tracked them on the first of their assignations—on the river-bank at Hawthorn—he was loath to accept their 'innocent explanation'. Annie sat by while the two of them worked in the evenings at Hartwell. She and John exchanged signs and slipped notes to each other; in August John began to write passionate love-letters. He delighted in the game of outwitting Fred, and reassured himself that he had done nothing to be ashamed of and that the romance was doing him 'much good'.

Annie was small and dainty, pretty rather than beautiful, with clear-cut features and light brown hair. She was also sexually experienced, not well educated but no fool, submissive, a patient comforter—womanly in John's eyes.

The domestic drama heightened. The lovers took full advantage one night when Fred was drunk and comatose. Then he intercepted a fully compromising letter, gave Annie a fearful time, and determined to 'send her adrift' without her infant.

> Bitterly I repented to her my wrong towards her. But 'My happiness in your love was worth it all', was ever her answer. . . . I had to humble myself deeply before him—for her sake. I stand before him on the evidence which we concerted between us, as less than a rogue, as a fool and brainless idiot. Well, at last the tension was over, and he said she might stay. . . . Shall I repel her for her own good, or shall I risk worse hereafter?

Relations between Monash and Gabriel briefly improved and they agreed to share the expenses of taking over Hartwell House as their headquarters and to rent out a paddock for agistment and run poultry for market. But Fred began to maltreat Annie, who determined to abandon both of them and fly to her parents. John bore her down: 'I spoke perhaps for the first time from my heart, and expressed determinations which I would not be surprised if I shall keep. For I have won from her all that I ever desire in my life'. His protective instincts fully aroused, he regarded Fred now as a 'bully and coward', and the 'perfect mutual understanding' with Annie was re-established. Surprisingly, Gabriel agreed to go to Ballarat to purchase poultry and they 'revelled in . . . two happy days—and nights'.

Annie briefly feared that she was pregnant: John consulted his old friend Dr Joe Miller and passed on certain advice. When in late October Fred left for Sydney for a week, John and Annie reached 'a point of mutual confidence . . . beyond anything that even I had dreamt of'. One evening they 'took a tram-ride to Brunswick under circumstances which I shall remember as long as I live'—and he was in uniform! When Fred returned he became violent and threatened to 'do for' John. Annie then became gravely ill and John feared for her life. For some six weeks he hardly saw her: her mother was staying with her and then took her home.

> I little realized how my love had grown upon me. . . . No amount of philosophy could quench the sense of loss. . . . perhaps I shall never see her again. It may be best if I never do. Hers has been a great and good influence upon me, and I could never have believed that the grief of parting would be so bitter. . . . I feel much inclined to throw aside for good and all, all this dangerous dabbling in love; it has brought me unspeakable grief in the past—but my fear is—what will my life become without the instigation of pleasing some one or other woman who loves me?

But a little later,

ermania Cottage, Clifton Street, Richmond

arra Street, Hawthorn, 1884: Bertha and John

In camp at Queenscliff, 1887: Monash is sitting nearest camera; Goldstein is second from left

At work on the Outer Circle railway, c. 1889

An interesting phase of my life and character have manifested themselves during this week. I have allowed myself to be carried away fully and completely by an imaginary grief. . . . I struggled a little, just enough to convince that my harsh and bitter stoicism was not proof against all things. A settled gloom has pervaded each waking hour. . . . A sense of personal loss, a loss of companionship, a feeling of loneliness, and withal the feeling of anxiety for her in her country house. . . . I set myself to write to her and produced a letter which *per se* is a truthful and exact representation of my state of feeling, and is the best record I can have thereof. . . . I am loth to tear myself away from . . . the greatest happiness I have known, a happiness so great that I cannot hope ever to meet the like again.

His letter was a total commitment:

What have I to live for if your love is gone? . . . Night after night, I have lain awake thinking, thinking—calling up one by one all the moments of happiness you have brought me—speaking to you again in thought—hearing the sound of your voice, feeling the touch of your lips—the thrill of your deep and loving looks—and my whole soul went out to you, as it used to do. But when the sickening reality comes back to me—I have called in agony—'Annie, my love, my darling—come back to me—be mine again'.

He regularly rode home the three miles from Hartwell to Hawthorn at midday in hope of a letter; and once, driving his buggy, 'thinking absent mindedly of the letter I was expecting . . . collided with a dray and fell over the front'.

Annie returned in mid-December. Elaborate postal arrangements, cipher-notes, secret hiding-places, trusted messengers, lantern-signals enabled the lovers to snatch minutes or half-hours together, but they were hardly ever again sexually united. The watchful Fred—'He can see and hear through stone walls, and makes the shrewdest guesses'— remained on terms of forced amiability. John maintained his torrent of letters—passionate, self-absorbed, humourless, with little or no reference to the outside world or even to common interests. This is surely the most lengthily documented *affaire* in Australian history—115 letters, nearly 200 000 words in addition to his diary. Their verbosity alone vitiates any quality as love-letters. From time to time Annie wavered—unable to remain defiant to Fred, fearful of scandal and ultimate disgrace and of the effects on her boy—but no more able than her Jack to put an end to it. She had taken on more than she bargained for perhaps. He rode down her doubts with tempestuous fervour:

You have made me a better man than ever I hoped to be, and by the tie that binds us, I love you, I honour you, I adore you. . . .

What Laura was to Petrarch, Beatrice to Dante, Lesbia to Horace— that is my Annie to me. . . .

> If ever Annie, the stores of energy that are within me, the great ambitions which are taking birth in my soul, shall burst forth, and it shall be my lot to assist in great and noble deeds, so that my name shall be in men's mouths, as one of the leaders among men, then may *you* say to yourself, that it was through the inspiration of your love and sympathy that I have become what I am. . . .
>
> If I lost your love . . . I would die morally—go downhill and be utterly lost. . . . *the sole object of my life* . . . my love, my mate, my wife in all but name. . . .

He informed her of pending divorce legislation, but they had to assume they would have to start afresh somewhere outside Victoria. He sometimes wavered: 'My reason is beginning to conquer over my sentiment. . . . Annie has given me all I can hope for. Nothing but separation remains to us—sooner or later. . . .' Farlow and Steele were in his confidence. George did not discourage him but Will gave him stern warnings which John acknowledged to be a 'useful check'. In February 1889 there are hints that he was not entirely in control of himself: 'strangely overwrought. I have not been very well'. He believed Fred had 'some deep plot maturing, but we are a match for him'.

The inevitable crisis came on 16 March. John and Annie were trysting in Studley Park, Kew. Fred, the little gamecock, rushed over the brow of the hill, seized John's stick and umbrella which were broken in their struggle, John fell over. Fred dragged Annie down to the tram at the Johnston Street bridge. John did not attack him, he explained to Annie later, for fear of worsening the scandal; Fred was already threatening legal action. Arguing the while, they all boarded a tram and got off at Smith Street, Collingwood. John departed. Annie managed to elude Fred but he recaptured her within twenty-four hours and for some days John had no news. Her father, appealed to by Fred, sent John an indignant letter. Annie eventually left for her parents' home, seen off by Fred, with John hiding on the platform. He rushed by cab, he said, to North Melbourne where in desperation he tried to board the non-stop train but, fortunately, stumbled and fell. He comforted himself that Fred and Annie were parted, and implored her by letter to pursue a legal separation. Fred at last left the job and, through John's father, requested money to leave the colony without his wife: John ignored him.

He was miserable in Annie's absence. He

> would sooner abandon the pursuit of a great position, and make a bold plunge, call her to me, and defy the world. . . . I *cannot* be active in giving her up. . . . Her love has been a great and wonderful inspiration. I have grown in all respects kinder, gentler, less self-assertive, more unselfish, more upright. . . .

His first love would 'surely leave its mark on me for the rest of my life'. In a letter to Annie on 14 April John made a fanciful formulation of what she meant to him:

> When as a young man I entered the struggle ... I was brimful of ambitions.... At every step I met with obstacles, with opposition, and many and many a time had all the courage sickened out of me. ... But I stuck to it. ... In my school life, in my University career, in my military work, in social affairs, as I passed by others in the race, I found I left behind me "friends"? No, *enemies* whose envy and spite were turned to the purpose of dragging me back, tripping me up, and stopping me. In the University, in the militia, in my social atmosphere I was the most unpopular man of all. And at last ... I gave up ..., settled down to a lonely life. ... When I took my engagement with my present employer it was with the wish ... to bury myself in a life of hard work, to become a machine like all the rest of men, and go on puffing and pulling until something gave way and was worn out. And then came to me a new experience ... a woman who looked into my soul and understood me. There came into my life—old while yet young—a love which I soon knew was to be the great passion of my life, and then ... came back with a rush, all my old ambitions, all my old incentives and motives, and with them all a new motive greater than all the rest—the motive to try to be a good man worthy of the love and the trust of a good woman—I learned to be kindly in word and deed, to be pure in thought, unselfish in action. ... Annie, my own Annie, I *have* chosen, long, long ago. ... I want to be allowed to care for you, support you, help you bring up your boy, help you always to have a comfortable home and want for nothing.

Annie replied enthusiastically and they arranged to spend a day together in Ballarat and Buninyong on 30 April: 'all passed off splendidly'—but he was not to see her again for nine weeks.

Throughout this torrid time, John had been attending the customary balls and dances, often with Amy and Evie Corrie, who accompanied him at three successive Melbourne Cups. He had first met the young Evie in September 1886:

> a poem in white muslin, with fine expressive eyes, and a frank innocent manner amused and delighted me. I won her favor and compliments by a judicious display of bragging modesty. ... I danced a good deal with her, and strove to make the occasion, which was the first of the kind for her, a memorable one.

From mid-1888 he had seen much of them, though more as a family friend than with amorous intent. But John's reconciliation with Jeanette Blashki late in 1888 and his flirtatiousness with her at dances made Evie jealous, and he grieved at her distress. He was on almost equally close terms with the elder sister Amy who—presumably on the grounds that as a Jew he could not develop their friendship towards marriage—

insisted on breaking off the relationship; he regretfully concurred. At least he was not writing to anyone but Annie.

After Annie's departure in March 1889, John took up again with the Corrie sisters. He told them more than he meant to about his relations with Annie. Amy was not surprised: 'No one can see much of you without loving you', she told him—Jeanette had recently said much the same. John wryly commented: 'I am led to wonder if this love is called up by me as I really am or as I profess to be'. Both Corrie girls were infatuated. The lively and naive Evie was indeed throwing herself at him and offered a compact—'a love affair to which both of us should set a voluntary limit; while it lasted we should throw aside all constraint, and enjoy a passionate love making'. It was all very innocent on her part: John accepted 'more for her sake than my own, for though the touch of a beautiful girl's lips is enticing to a young man, yet I cannot love two women at once. . . . Poor devil I to talk so coldly of a woman's love'. Soon at a ball, 'hidden away for hours in a dark staircase we enjoyed ourselves fully. The girl was a complete conquest—yet there was always the image of Annie before me. Now is Evie really an innocent baby, or is she deliberately seeking to sin?' But he soon paid the penalty for his trifling: 'Through you I have learned to regard all men as generous and noble, and now you have dashed all this idealism down and made me loathe and despise all mankind'. He managed to extricate himself briefly: 'I cannot deny myself the pleasure of her adoration, yet what harm may I not be doing her'. Early in June, too, Rosie Schild called at home and they were quickly 'at the same point' as before. They spent a happy evening in his Camberwell office:

> At last we approached in precise language the subject of our mutual relations, and while letting her clearly understand my racial disability to marry her, yet hinted at the slightness of my personal objection. . . . I am not afraid of harming Rosie—she is well scorched and a woman of the world.

He remained an insatiable conqueror of hearts: Lizzie Smith 'fell in love at once—visibly' at a ball, and he chased her too.

Fred captured Annie again and brought her back to Melbourne at the end of May. John was distraught: he established contact by letter again in mid-June, but Annie had resolved to give him up. Once again he persuaded her to meet him; Rosie was a willing accomplice in running messages and waylaying Fred. When John and Annie then fell out briefly, he won her back with a 'touching, mournful letter' in which he spuriously described how he had come close to shooting himself. All's fair in love: John several times strayed from the truth in his letters to Annie. She could not withstand him. From mid-July they began again to meet clandestinely, usually driving in the suburbs—to Studley Park, Brighton Beach, or the fields beyond Toorak.

Meanwhile, on 22 June at a German Club dance, John had met the beautiful twenty-year-old Jewess, Hannah Victoria (Victory) Moss:

> my attention was particularly engrossed by Vic. Moss, whom and whose sisters I met in 1882 at Portsea. I sought an introduction—a thing I seldom do—and found my name was very familiar to her. In a very few moments we were excellent friends. . . . she made a striking impression on me, and I am longing to meet her again.

They next met at a German Club social: 'I attached myself for the rest of the evening to Vic and her chaperone, and made much advance in their good graces'. At another dance at the Town Hall,

> I bespoke her for several dances, and she signalized her pleasure in my company by stealing a few more. I thus had an opportunity for studying her more carefully. But she is almost too clever for me, and nearly turned the tables completely on me, by making me disclose myself to no purpose. She is a woman far beyond her years—and has a disposition startlingly akin to my own. If she showed the least disposition to sentiment—I should very soon warm to her.

By early August he was noting:

> Vic. is clearly very much in love—yet she has shewn me little of her inner nature—I doubt if she has much softness, or any of that womanliness, which Annie possesses in such a degree. Our conversation was mainly by way of fencing—each waiting for the other.

John was carefully observing the proprieties and, having gained permission, began writing to Miss Moss. He noted in his diary that 'my affair with Annie is beginning to be a little oppressive since Vic appeared on the horizon, and with her all the gossip of my acquaintance'. John and Mat visited Vic's household by invitation: 'I found the party amusing themselves with card tricks, and this of course was playing into my hands, so I went through with my performance, but with a most peculiar and unusual nervousness'. He astonished Vic with his skill on the piano and 'she was strangely quiet and undemonstrative. She is evidently deeply puzzled, and cannot understand the full force of my character'.

This week, toward the close of August 1889, was one of the great crises in Monash's life. He had been under heavy strain. On 14 July he had confided to his Intimate Diary:

> I control my surroundings as a matter of course, and a thing fit and proper. But there has come a growing tendency to aimlessness in my immediate future, brought on by a total collapse of my close companionship with my Annie, and the consequent rude shattering

of many a dream and plan for the future. For weeks I have simply existed, living on in the hope of some change to better things, applying myself half mechanically to my duties, in business, official, and private.... I have no wish to die, yet no wish to live. No hopes, no fears.

On 29 July he had lectured to the Jewish Literary Society, having been very nervous about the outcome. In mid-August, while he had a heavy cold, his father was seriously ill and he had to nurse him and administer a catheter; during this trouble Mat had not stood up well. Annie, Vic, Evie, Jeanette and Rosie were making their various demands. From mid-August

> there came to me for several days a most despondent listless spirit. I gave way under the strain, and have passed an idle useless week. My mind lost its concentration, and I allowed myself to drivel away time in idle brooding.

In his letters fending off Evie he wrote:

> I have been in a very miserable discontented state of mind.... things are not going well with me.... illness in our house revives vividly the misery and anxious suspense and trouble that clouded our house four years ago.... I have had a mental illness of a kind I have never before experienced—loss of memory—absence of mind—inability to grasp facts or to think.

A letter to Annie on the 20th displays him as weary and rattled; he admitted he was ill.

In that very week Annie submitted, and agreed to run away with him:

> her sudden offer of willingness to come to me staggered me, and like a coward I pretended not to understand. Yet the idea has taken root, and although I know that such a step means for me the ruin of my whole future, yet I would sooner take it with all its terrible risks and dangers than break my faith with Annie. Now recently since meeting Vic—who fulfills in my estimation all the requirements of a suitable wife to me—dim visions of a home life, and a finality to all my present struggles have been assuming a prominent place in my thoughts—and the two possibilities that are before me I have been vainly trying to reconcile. This hesitation in my mind as to which I shall dismiss is causing me now the most real, and harmful mental agony that I have ever known.

Next day Vic, most unconventionally, sent him a telegram asking to meet him again. She visited him with her elder sister Belle on the 25th:

> I cannot gauge her nature yet, beyond knowing that she is anxious to please. I doubt if she could subjugate herself to me sufficiently

to suit my temperament. So the days go on, one ideal stepping off to give place to another; but with none do I feel even a touch of emotion except with Annie, who has been my first love, my true love, and who I think will be the only love of my life.

The following day he wrote to Steele,

> If there is such a thing as love in my cold, calculating, material and unidyllic temperament, [Annie] has it all [but] I have met frequently of late—a young girl—of surpassing beauty ... a girl altogether to my liking—and deeply in love with me to boot. All my nearer relatives are urging upon me to take the tide at its flood. And there comes to me the choice, "Annie and infamy" or—"a reputable home of my own". And I will not choose. I have consulted my intuitive judgment of which I have often spoken boastfully to you—and for once it fails me.

He met Annie again on the 28th:

> Her final decision to come is now taken for granted between us; but I am fearfully agitated about it; for the real risks and dangers have never been so plain to me as they are now, when I have been brought face to face with the idea. My difficulty lies not in the present, but in the distant future. I am prepared to plunge now—but perhaps I shall sink for ever.

Next evening he committed himself:

> I sat down to an important consideration, and at length coming to the conclusion that I should make the plunge, I wrote to Annie at great length, broaching to her my preliminary suggestions. Yet I did it in only a half-hearted manner; and I half hope that my warnings of danger may affect the strength of her determination.

Meanwhile John found Steele 'weak and unconvincing in his attempts to warn me about my intentions'.

Next, Annie in great distress announced that she was pregnant to Fred.

> I went forth armed with drugs and money—warm in sympathy, but with some feelings of reproach at heart. I resolved to be kind and tender—to help her over her trouble, and then—to put an end to all, on the excuse of what had happened.

But he ran into Fred on guard, and had to retreat. His letter later that night to Annie contradicts his diary entry above, for he wrote:

> This is the crisis of our lives; if you are prepared to trust yourself and your child to me for the rest of your life, come now *at once* to Hawthorn.... Decide now once for all. Everything depends on your present decision.

However, Fred had solved the mystery of their postal channels, Annie did not get the letter, and Fred took her away. When John eventually ascertained the situation on 6 September he summed up:

> The end, or what is very near it has come at last; there has been a great collapse, and a complete downfall of my pretty castle of cards. ... If she does return, I have perfected plans to help her to whatever extent she chooses; if she does not choose, then she can go for good and all, and I can feel I have come out with unbroken faith, and much the injured party. If she *does* choose, the long expected climax will be precipitated, and deliberately I will for her sake go to my ruin.

He sought out Vic next evening and they went to the theatre.

> So ended this tumultuous week. Surely I am undergoing a good training. I should soon have an extensive knowledge of the world and human nature. I feel I have some already, for in every legitimate undertaking, I sweep along with resistless force. Yet Annie, oh for Annie.

Dreading while he hoped, John had to wait another five days. Then a message came: Annie was back and promised to 'come unreservedly'. Next day, Friday the 13th, he resolved to abscond with a non-Jewish married woman and to abandon his cultural heritage.

> At last I was face to face with a great crisis in my life. Never for a moment did I think of drawing back from the position into which I had half walked half been drawn. But the more I dwelt on the details of what was before me, the more I realised the ruin it would mean to my future, and the more I feared my constancy of purpose. Yet I faced the position, and made all my arrangements with care. I spent nearly the whole of Friday, in going about from place to place providing for immediate contingencies.

That night he took his trap to Annie's Abbotsford lodgings, and they went on to pick up her child. We do not know where they proposed to go—presumably to another colony.

> At last we reached the South Yarra station, and dismounted. We were just in the act of crossing the road ... when like a thunderbolt the ubiquitous Fred rushed at me. The attack was sudden and I was straightway robbed of every resource. Before I could collect my senses, he had dragged Annie away, and forced her into a cab, and though I tried to delay matters—they drove off. Never as long as I live will I forget Annie's entreaties to me to save her, and her frightened white face. That is the last I have seen of her. My last words were 'All will be right, Annie. You know what to do,' and she answered 'Yes Jack.' As soon as they were out of sight, and the crowd dispersed, I realized that I was badly hurt, so I walked up and down the road in aimless despair. My first feelings were those of intense

relief, and of a sudden came the resolve, there and then to dismiss all from my mind.

He had a frightful black eye and had to face the amused gossip of the world. Rosie spent the next afternoon gentling him on the river bank; he arrived home to find a houseful of visitors. Within a couple of days, however, he was noting: 'Steele was right. It was an *incubus* . . .'. He soon learned that the Gabriels were in Sydney under an assumed name: 'My great longing for her is gone, and though if she came before me now I would open my arms to her, yet I care not if I never see her again'. But a letter from Annie, reproaching him for silence, 'awakened all the old grief' and he wrote agonizedly to apologize for the wretched failure of his plans (and invented an accident which had confined him to bed for several days). He arranged with Karl Roth in Sydney to help her escape to her parents or elsewhere if she wanted to, and to settle on a method of safe correspondence. When eventually he heard from her in December she seemed resigned to her fate; he implored her to keep in touch.

He had seen Vic only once in the previous three and a half weeks, and had been writing to make excuses. He was soon caught up in the normal swing: 'No time to think back. Rush on, rush on again'. At Eva Blashki's wedding he took Vic by storm: 'A thorough sympathetic understanding has grown up between us, and I like her better each time I see her'. Next night they played duet piano arrangements of Haydn symphonies together and 'were pleased with each other'. He went to *The Doll's House* and was 'fascinated'—well he might have been, in view of what Ibsen had to say about the status of wives. He was recuperating fast: on 24 September, lecturing to the assembled metropolitan batteries, he had a triumph.

Three weeks later he and Vic were engaged. It was an impulsive plunge by both of them. She had been puzzling him:

> You do not seem to me like other girls. I must confess that gallantry to women, considered as a fine art, is a thing to the culture of which I have tried to devote myself. But there is something about you that banishes from my manner the least attempt at artificiality, and I only appear to you as my own clumsy natural self.

He sought out Evie again, who was 'completely unreserved. How great a temptation there is for me here'. Vic upset him by 'utter lack of interest' when he showed her Princes Bridge, then charged him with 'concealed amours' which he had vehemently to disclaim as they walked on to South Yarra:

> I am not yet very sure if Vic has any great or refined sense of high motives and purposes, or if after all she is only a clever woman with a mind for little things. She manages to keep her disposition

concealed. At last we reached her gate, and I lingered for another half hour. Then she grew very tender, and the touch of her fingers playing caressingly about me made my blood go a little faster. . . . If she can awaken a real live spark of love, it will soon blaze into a flame that will astonish her.

Next day for the first time she addressed him in a note as 'Jack'. An awkward evening at a German Club ball—especially the pressing attention of a vulgar rival suitor—precipitated matters.

I made up my mind there and then how to act—that I would throw myself entirely on her mercy—tell her my position and leave her to judge for herself. So a night of much mental confusion came to an end.

He wrote next morning, 9 October: a declaration, not a proposal, for he had no guaranteed prospects. He had Vic's reply next day and in the evening they

strolled towards the Yarra. Her manner was more distant than I expected from her letter, and made what I had to say more difficult. Even under these unnerving circumstances I found my habit strong upon me, of listening well, and reviewing the situation before I spoke. She gave me less assistance than I had a right to expect, but at last all that was necessary was said and we understood each other. . . . Vic showed little emotion of any kind; her frigidity laid chains on my tongue, and I felt full of all kinds of doubts and misgivings.

It was as unromantic and unsatisfactory a betrothal as can be imagined. John fared well with Vic's elder sister Sarah and her husband Max Simonson. His father was pleased but Mat, disgusted at his fickleness, remarked that he had better 'keep it secret for at least twelve months'. Indeed John had terrible embarrassments:

The forthcoming round of amusements compelled me to resort to all sorts of devices and subterfuges to prevent the wrong people meeting together, and all in all I suffered so much anxiety that I was not able to throw myself with any zest into my new affairs.

Following earlier arrangements, he did not take Vic to the North Melbourne Battery ball, so that she would not clash with the Corries. To the delight of any fair-minded reader, Evie staggered him there by telling him of her own engagement: 'I impulsively told her too, and she spoke thereupon a few home truths'.* Unfortunately, two days later Vic happened to see that night's dance programme with Evie's

---

* The delightful Evie, according to a descendant, lived happily ever after in Western Australia. In 1893 she wrote: 'I shall never forget you. You are my ideal and always will be'. In 1907 they met for a 'chin-wag' and exchanged photographs.

frequent name. Jeanette, when she ran into John, 'was very rude' and was met with 'severe retaliation'.

It was high time for John Monash to retire from circulation. He was a public menace: more than most young men in their ingenuous salad days, he had made a floundering ass of himself.

Victory (as she called herself) was the youngest child of Moton Moss (1800–79) a provision merchant with hotel and other interests, and Rebecca Alexander (1829–82); both of them were London-born. By the time she was thirteen both her parents had died and she was brought up by her sisters. She was tall, dark, statuesque, graceful and musically accomplished. John knew that she had been 'one of the queens of Melbourne drawing rooms for the past year' and that she was a noted promenader of 'The Block' in Collins Street—but hardly yet what a 'giddy butterfly' she was or how conspicuous among 'the *jeunesse dorée*' and the racing fraternity. He was confident that he could remedy her educational deficiencies and mould her original but uncultured mind, and her character, to his satisfaction. This aspiration was standard in the German tradition but also a common assumption of fiancés in an age when few girls had advanced education.

The engagement began uneasily. Vic was worried by the gossip about John's recent past and by his attempts to explain it. He struggled to get on closer terms but, day by day, found her cold and imperious. At last, after a day at the Cup, 'she became of a sudden her natural self, and from that moment we stood upon a footing of the closest intimacy.... In the new light of passionate love ..., my whole nature warmed towards her in an altogether new degree'. However, they were to remain continent throughout their eighteen months engagement. Annie had been so dismissed from mind that she was not even mentioned in John's diary—although he was soon to note that over a similar period he had written forty-one letters to Vic compared with fifty-one to Annie.

John began his educational campaign:

> I took occasion ... to broach the subject of Vic's mental culture, and tried to let her feel, in a gentle way, that much was wanting in her nature. She is very unskilful in putting her thoughts into words, and hence prefers silence; but she enunciated to me the theory of self-education by observation and inspection, rather than by reading, which was original (for her) and ingenious. But this is only the first attack. I shall persevere until I wake up in her the thirst for light.

He tried to tutor her morally too: 'I am not a saint. But I have set myself high ideals. I want to be a good man, above untruth and error. Try and make a great aim for yourself also. ... change yourself within'.

But Vic displayed 'an awkward habit of ruthless faultfinding' and they began to squabble. Early in the New Year John was fairly desperate:

> I have again fallen on evil days.... In Vic I see the outward embodiment of my physical ideal. But in her moral nature I have been bitterly deceived and disappointed. These feelings lie in the great and perhaps irredeemable deficiencies in her nature. She is no mental companion for me, and has just so much knowledge of the world that she is most difficult to lead and instruct, and repels all my attempts to do so. I have battled with her now for 3 months, and nightly leave her side, disappointed, defeated, miserable. Her praise, applause, and subjugation to my will, which my soul craves for, she does not give me, nor seems to have the power to give. Yet I love her sincerely.

With a disastrously unstrategic sense he had been following up every disagreement with exculpatory pleading and insistence on total frankness. Unable to rival his epistolary force, Vic continued to write sweet loving letters, thinking it best to ignore his protests as often as possible.

Tempestuous rows and periods of coldness alternated with fervent reconciliations and warm spells of mutual submission. John was trying to save, but Vic insisted on 'frivolous dissipation'. By mid-April 1890 he had given up:

> I told her my plans plainly, that I would leave her to seek her better pleasure alone, that I would see less of her, and spend my spare time in pursuits more congenial to me than gadding about, or listening to her rebukes, in short to devote myself to study.

Try as she might she could not satisfy his craving for her admiration. In mid-July he shocked her by offering to release her from their engagement—yet once again they became intensely happy with each other.

But they were approaching a crisis. Early in August Vic insisted on going to the theatre without him.

> You seek *any* form of distraction rather than incur the tediousness of a few hours alone with me.... I fear much that my life and character are too humdrum for you, I cannot reconcile my thoughts of you to a quiet home life at my own fireside.

A fortnight later,

> I was irritable and we got quarrelling over a trifle, and I was disgusted with myself at my hardness and apathy to her. What has become of my soft nature? How selfish I have grown. I saw her writhe under my sneers without a pang. How I hate myself for it.

On 5 September, after 'a hot and bitter letter' from John, Vic broke: 'Let me go out of your life ... take your freedom.... The quarrelling of the last few months has told on me more than you think'. John rushed to see her: 'I could not help admiring her calm dignity and firmness. She practically gave me my congé, stating conditions for our further association which I cannot accept'. But he caved in, promising not again to 'assert any rights or claims against you nor place any restrictions whatever on your conduct, actions or words', and not to 'utter to you a word of reproach or complaint'. Alternatively he offered, if Vic still wanted to break the engagement, to 'leave Melbourne for ever, and take with me all the blame'. In her answer,

> She did not flinch, nor sacrifice an inch. This girl then is to be my wife. So after all my years of toil my life is to be ruined. The course of events will no doubt be that in the end I will lose all my better parts, and for her sake abandon all I held most dear.

In fact Vic's letter had been conciliatory and largely ignored the issue:

> Your promises show me how thoroughly you misunderstand my wishes and prove what I have often said, that you look at everything from an extreme point. My wishes were simple, merely to let me feel more confidence in myself, and to let us both endeavour to live a peaceful life.

Their relations did not improve. There was a storm when Vic went to the Caulfield Cup on the anniversary of his mother's death. They fell out over the attentions to be paid to each other's sisters. She ruined the Naval and Military ball for him by avoiding dancing with him—and he resolved never again to take her to a dance: '. . . were it not for the disgrace and scandal of the thing [I] would send her about her business at once'. At the Melbourne Cup 'he trotted like a little dog by her side all day'. Early in December, to his 'utter dismay and despair', John ran into her in town with another man after she had refused to go out with him. Albert Behrend took it upon himself to warn him that she was the subject of gossip. John so despaired that he again offered to return her ring—and again within a day was beside himself with remorse:

> If ever I needed your help and love I need it now. Oh Vic—pity me. Help me to be a man, help me to be great and win fame and fortune. Help me against myself. You have conquered, Vic. Make of me what you wish.

Once again they promised to let bygones be bygones.

The prospect of marriage was all the more attractive as John felt the family home was falling apart. His father was rather aloof—'too absorbed in his own broken-hearted nature to care much for my doings'—and resented John's criticism of his financial speculations. Twice in 1889 Louis was seriously ill. Mathilde had backed John staunchly in the guerilla war with Gabriel, and he composed for her the letter in which she rejected the proposal of an unwelcome suitor. But they fell out from time to time, partly because Mat did not get on with Vic, and sometimes John virtually confined himself to his room at home. His relations with Albert and Minnie Behrend were cool; Albert once rebuked him for ingratitude. Uncle Roth was struggling: John had lent him £100 and had to 'kick up an awful row' to get it back in order to meet his marriage expenses. John and young Karl had borrowed from each other occasionally, but when five weeks before John's wedding Karl asked for a loan John refused for he was in need of every penny. The feckless Karl was greatly insulted and wrote cutting off all relations: John turned the other cheek and sent him £3, but ultimately turned the lawyers on to him for repayment. John's stabilizing influence on the unfortunate Will Steele remained much to his credit; he continued to write regularly.

No longer distracted by pursuit of girls, John resolved to complete his degrees. When he addressed the Engineering Students' Society in August 1890, Kernot challenged him again about his unfinished course: it was a timely spur. In mid-September Jim Lewis and others were called on to lend their Applied Mechanics, Civil Engineering and Geology notes. John reported to Vic that he was

> very confident . . . never better prepared . . . this time I have worked systematically . . . of course my studying has been merely a case of cram, not the sort of study that gives a man much after benefit. . . . I almost feel like shaking myself by the hand . . . there is a special art of cramming for exams.

He squeezed in the last practical work the day before the final paper but had to 'give in for once in my life' and not consult a single note in preparation for it. Nevertheless he passed it and the other subjects to complete his engineering degree. In the midst of his exams he had written eagerly in response to a suggestion by Lewis that he take over as drama critic for the *Australasian Critic*—but it came to nothing. It was the end of January, which left only three weeks, before he settled down to cram for final honours. Lewis again advised, and Kernot gave some useful hints. John worked as hard perhaps as he ever did: on 9 February he was all day in the University library, had a 'counter-feed in town', then went to the Public Library, and finished 'quite dazed and stupid with work'. On the 14th he noted he was 'almost overpowered by the great strain of my studies, the military, the contract, my own finances, and my unhappy state of mind about Vic'. After the first day of exams he felt he had done well. The night before the last paper, however, he gave way, went to a military dinner and got home intoxicated at 2 a.m. Nevertheless:

> Attended my last subject in a very seedy condition—but did extremely well. This ends my course at last, and an anxiety which has been pursuing me for years is set aside at last. I can now look to the future with a clear conscience, for I have done all I can for my future success.

His diary records, however, that for days he was ill and miserable. On 24 March he learned that he had defeated his three competitors and had won the *Argus* scholarship with a high second-class honour. 'Surrounded by admiring friends' he took out his B.C.E., his first degree, on 4 April, just before his wedding.

Monash had 'long ago cast aside the idea of being a premature genius', but the fire of ambition still burned strongly. He once told Annie:

> the best efforts of my life will be devoted to doing what I can for my native land and its people. Just wait a few years, till my early struggles are over, and see what I will do if power is left me. I have a tremendous stock of energy in reserve—and it shall come out some day.

But in his diaries his confidence oscillated wildly. He still worried about his supposed unpopularity. 'Sometimes', he wrote to Annie, 'I sit brooding for hours what there is in me and my outward demeanour that inspires people with such mistrust and wrong judgment of me'. 'I have a strange knack of repelling people', he told Vic. He listed the dozens of acquaintances he met at a University Commencement Day, and made a 'catalogue' of his 'pre-nuptial friends', naming about 450. About a quarter of them were Jewish, few were German; school, university, militia and engineering friends made up the great majority. He still, like any good intellectual, despised the 'selfish pursuit of wealth'; 'I don't want *money*', he told Annie. But on another occasion he noted in his diary: 'The accumulation of money is in danger of becoming a passion with me, and this I must resist strenuously'. He sued a horse-thief but

> I had not the heart to be hard on him, and clumsily and half ashamed of my meanness I let him off with the payment of bare expenses. Yet were it not for very shame at my softness before [my] subordinates, I should have let him off altogether.

When one of his cows strayed from Hartwell and was pounded, he fought the case, unsuccessfully, partly for the fun of seeing Farlow perform in court.

Three months before the wedding in April 1891, John was at a low ebb again:

> I have lost my buoyancy of spirits and developed a tendency to

deep despondency and irritating anxiety as to my future. All things before me are uncertain. I am haunted by the feeling that my past successes have been the results of exceptional good luck and that now at last my good fortune is to leave me. Very shortly I shall be married to Vic, and I have the secret fear that I am entering upon years of toil and anxiety.

They were still quarrelling. Early in March he relented in his resolve never again to take her to a dance and basked in her prowess as a hostess at a battery social. He pleaded with her to subordinate herself to him as 'absolutely necessary to our success and happiness', but promised 'to make you rich, so that you can surround yourself with a home and all those things that will make you happy. Not until I have done that will I seek any fulfilment of my own special ambitions'. They argued about the details of the wedding and Vic had her way. There was no dowry: Vic appointed her brother-in-law, Max Simonson, trustee of her property. With a week to go John was wallowing in despair and self-pity. Vic implored him to forget the past and begin anew, and on their wedding eve sent him a loving note.

As our grandparents used to say, long engagements are a bad thing. But John and Vic were very nearly incompatible. Though Vic was not at all like his mother he expected her to re-enact Bertha's supportive role. John expected obedience and subordination, but also a merging of personality and a total intimacy which he came to admit was unrealizable. They had common interests in music and theatre, but otherwise could not meet in seriousness of mind. Vic had force of character and intellectual capacity but, while she could express herself with straightforward clarity—and dignity when he tried her too far—her education had been narrowly limited. She was wilful and inconsiderate, materialistic, engrossed in superficial social life, flirtatious, slightly coarsened by her past associations, lacking in moral concern. She tried desperately to meet John's expectations, but could not satisfy his craving for adulation, or understand his need for her to bolster his confidence, and constantly offended her thin-skinned and hypercritical lover. He was often hectoring and self-righteous, could never restrain himself from correcting her. Both were hasty-tempered and generally incapable either of admitting wrong or of discreet silence. Yet, despite their mutual unhappiness, she wavered only once in her love and determination to marry him. He could not face the disgrace and humiliation of a broken engagement and had a fatalistic inclination to accept the turn of circumstance, but despite all his gloomy prognostications, and in spite of everything, he loved his Vic dearly.

They were quietly married on 8 April by Rabbi Abrahams at the Freemasons' Hall, Collins Street East. George Farlow stood as best man and Vic had six bridesmaids. John gave Vic a gold watch. After a night at the Federal Hotel they took the train for Sydney; Vic, on departure, had a happy beaming face. In Sydney they stayed at the 'gorgeous' Grosvenor Hotel; people were 'full of kindness and courtesy to strangers'. They went several times to the theatre, 'where you bet I cut a dash with my beautiful wife' (John told Mat), for ferry and tram rides, to the Art Gallery, the Bondi Aquarium and the Cyclorama. A week followed in the Blue Mountains and at the Jenolan Caves. Fred Gabriel had been keeping an eye out: John glimpsed him at Central Station, both on arrival and departure. On return the happy couple moved into a rented house in Lennox Street, Richmond.

5

A Rough Passage
1891–1896

CONSTRUCTION of the Outer Circle railway had ended in January 1891 but Monash continued until September in Graham and Wadick's employ, calculating the final costs with railway officials. The boom had long since collapsed, and contractors had no attractive offers to make. Assumptions of rewarding work and a satisfactory salary by a young man who had grown up during a period of unparalleled prosperity had to be abandoned. Monash had happily assured Jim Lewis that they would join in private practice when he was free. They now agreed to work together on the new Spencer Street bridge competition, but John came to realize that Jim was less businesslike than he had thought. In any case a partnership was now out of the question in view of their entire lack of capital and developing hard times, though they continued to discuss possibilities—even of working together on a flying-machine.

Vic's brother Dave, a well-to-do senior officer of an American life assurance company, offered a loan of several hundred pounds. John courteously refused it for the moment as the times were so against profitable investment. He intended to wait on 'the general revival of business for one of the many big public positions which are sure to offer by and bye'. He tried to explain his limited prospects to Vic:

> I want you to understand how it is that though I was perfectly justified in saying I could command £1000 a year two years ago I would now have to be content with ⅓ that amount, because any amount of other men are willing to do so. . . . perhaps you will be content after all to share a life with me on a lesser scale than we at first hoped for. . . . after all things may improve and our first idea of a rapid social rise and a brilliant career *in our youths* may yet be realized.

Monash determined to make a demonstration: buoyed up by his success with the Outer Circle contract and by his recent academic honours, he applied for the plum job of superintending engineer of the sewerage works for the newly established Melbourne and Metropolitan Board of Works. He knew he had little chance, but to show he was 'out for big things' he called on Alfred Deakin to redeem a promise to assist him, asked Goldstein, Kernot, Graham and Wadick and Higgins to write on his behalf, and lobbied members of the Board of Works. Indeed he got into 'a fever of excitement over it' and cursed his vivid imagination. He submitted a competitive design for a bridge at Pyrmont, Sydney. He seriously considered trying his luck in Western Australia. He applied unsuccessfully to the local committee for associate membership of the Institution of Civil Engineers, London; Higgins fought for him and succeeded the following year when Monash had to pay the high admission fee.

Meanwhile he picked up one or two tiny jobs for a few days. He entered for a lectureship at the University in hydraulic engineering, submitted schemes for the Benalla water supply and the East Boort Irrigation and Water Trust works, applied to be shire engineer of Seymour and of Camberwell. He was nowhere successful. In September, however, Kernot tipped him off about a possible vacancy with the Harbor Trust, and in November he was grateful to accept a modest post there. Though he hated 'the dead level inaction of departmental service', the Harbor Trust was to be a haven for two and a half years during the worst of the depression.

Monash had had little spare cash to invest during the high boom years when 'everybody' bought land—nor had he much inclination. Yet he came to like an occasional flutter and, even when saving for marriage, had put £100—a large proportion of his savings—into supporting one of the Outer Circle employees who was working on improved sheep-shearing appliances. Monash's was a quarter-share: 'The risk is great but the prize a fortune'. He eventually recognized that the enterprise was hopeless.

John and Vic had resumed hostilities almost immediately. Indeed, after only two months of marriage, he 'told her she would either have to recognise my authority or leave me. She readily and greedily accepted the latter alternative. . . . I am determined therefore that as soon as such a step is financially possible we shall separate'. Soon, however, they were again 'very happy together'. They often went to the theatre—three times to see Sarah Bernhardt—and to concerts; Professor Marshall-Hall became one of John's heroes. They joined and attended meetings of the Austral Salon. He even persuaded Vic to read *Ivanhoe* to him for three nights, but she would not go on; several months later, however, she read *Our Mutual Friend* right through and began on *Arabian Nights*.

In July Vic was diagnosed by Joe Miller as possibly tubercular. She was packed off, with her sister Belle as companion, for a month in the hills at Beechworth, where she was a sensation. Vic and John wrote very lovingly to each other. He was appallingly lonely and could not settle down: 'I try first a little writing, then reading, then drawing, then half an hour in my workshop'. She was in much better health on her return, but became involved in 'fast goings on' with Beechworth acquaintances and made John despair when she insisted on supper with them 'in truly demimondaine fashion at the Café Anglais in a "private den" forsooth!' He told her he would 'insist on her giving up this "gadding" about town and running after men'. It was his 'right and duty to discipline her'. She was even reading his diary!—which could not have encouraged her about their future. But a fortnight later things were going on very happily and three months' relative peace followed.

1892 was no better. Their straitened finances were another cause of tension: Vic's income (among other things she had an interest in the International Hotel in Victoria Street) had almost disappeared and his father was so in debt that his furniture was seized—John had to pay out nearly £100. When he was promoted at the Harbor Trust, however, they moved to a better house in Caroline Street, South Yarra. They had survived one major crisis. John had been so enraged by Vic's defiance and goading that he threatened to spank her: she 'pretended to think I had really struck her, and swore and raged', and rushed off to her brother-in-law Max Simonson. Max tactfully talked to John like an elder brother; Vic returned after two days. She was at last pregnant and their relations improved in mid-year. At New Year 1893 John could bravely sum up: 'I am settled in my home life and am at heart happy with it. I am proud of my wife, and in time I think I will feel we could not have done better each for the other'. Their daughter Bertha was born on 22 January. Vic had a reasonably easy time of it; next Saturday morning many friends shouted for John in town. He refused to attend the synagogue for the ceremony of naming his daughter.

In August 1891 when Vic was away at Beechworth he had tackled the notoriously difficult municipal surveyors' course, and crammed himself through the eighteen hours of exams. The following January he started to read for the water supply engineers' exams under the guidance of J. T. Noble Anderson, a Dublin graduate who had migrated in 1889. The tutor was so efficient that he supplied the text of the exam papers: consequently Monash scored 100 per cent in three papers and 95 per cent in the fourth, not without feeling 'a severe moral twinge'. What *should* a student do if his tutor tells him what is on the exam paper? Perhaps the papers were notoriously similar from year to year.

Monash went straight on under Steele's and Farlow's guidance to some steady reading in Law: on 30 November 1891 he had enrolled as a student at the Supreme Court. Frequent disputes between contractors and government departments over final settlements, which went to arbitration, and his knowledge of the success of English legal engineers, had enabled him to identify a possible lucrative monopoly. What other engineer was likely to have the energy to take a Law degree, especially when the Legal Profession Practice Act of 1891 had made the course much more demanding for future students? He expected to 'be for many years at least absolutely without competition as legal engineer'—five years later there was only one other graduate in Law and Engineering in Australia—and the study would further stretch his mind. He worked sporadically early in 1892, abandoned his plan temporarily, but in September was persuaded, mainly by his legal friend Leo Cussen, to have a go. So, once again, in four weeks he 'got up' and passed Property,Obligations and Roman Law. When he had begun, he had immediately felt ill, 'owing probably to overstrain', and had given up for one or two days. He had crammed Roman Law in three days, including eighteen hours at a stretch, remembering his Gibbon well. He completed the year in December by passing Constitutional and Legal History, which merely required reading of Hearn's *Government of England*, Blackstone's *Commentaries* and Jenks's *Government of Victoria*. Again, in September the following year, six weeks before the exams, he suddenly determined 'to make a rush', probably without having attended a single lecture. Farlow lent him £10 towards the fees, Steele transcribed old exam papers, Edmund Armstrong and J. S. Battye (two future State Librarians) provided lecture notes, Jack Mackey advised and lent books. By 4 October he had worked himself into a 'nervous overwrought state' and felt 'quite ill'; next evening he went at it 'more slowly and steadily'. Wrongs, and Equity and Procedure he found 'the same old simple hash', but International Law, set by the new professor, Harrison Moore, was 'a splendid, cleverly drawn but very fair paper': he passed them all. He then charged his old bugbear Latin in December and conquered it, thus completing his B.A. at last. He had taken out the master's degree in Engineering, to which his final honours entitled him, early in 1893 and eventually, when he could better afford the fees, formally graduated in Arts and Law in 1895.

It had been an astonishing part-time programme over three years. In his earlier university career he had never done himself justice: he might have won high honours in Mathematics, Modern Languages and Literature, Philosophy or English Literature, though perhaps not in Science and certainly not in Classics. His disastrous first year, his preoccupation with student affairs and his mother's death had wrecked his intention of sustained study. Five years later, when he was stable enough to work methodically, he might surely, had there been more time, have gained a first-class honour in Engineering. For the rest, he had developed remarkable powers of concentration and machine-like efficiency in cramming, though not without indications of marked stress. 'Strange isn't it', he told Vic, 'that I can't work well unless I am very busy and hard pressed for time'.

'The commission is a pleasant and most enviable possession', Monash had told Farlow. 'It gives a man social position and tone and is an excellent advertisement. It is the very thing a man starting in his profession wants to differentiate him from and elevate him out of the ranks of the army of beginners.' Many pleasant occasions raised self-esteem: processing at the opening of the Centennial Exhibition, marching the Battery down Collins Street to a Town Hall function, in charge of a detachment helping the police control the crowd at a city fire, the joy of wearing his resplendent mess uniform at a dinner to the visiting General Edwards, even acting as senior officer of the Garrison Artillery at church parade. In January 1889 he had been elected to the Naval and Military Club.

In June 1889 Monash had passed his captain's exams and began to hope desperately for promotion. Probably with Goldstein's encouragement, he made a formal submission on the organization and discipline of the Garrison Artillery, arguing that a slight increase in expenditure might make a large difference. Many more drills were needed, lasting a half or a whole day, as often as possible under war conditions in the forts themselves rather than in drill halls at night; musketry practice could be reduced; there should be pay incentives to encourage gunners to reach first-class classification; and non-commissioned officers should have more status. Seemingly, there was no response from on high. His lecturing skill was improving: '[I] am beginning to be recognised now as a master of my subject, yet how ill-deserved this is. Among Lilliputians a little makes a great difference'. Late in 1889 he had a triumph, lecturing at the North Melbourne orderly room on the theory of laying, to the three metropolitan batteries.

> The moment when I stepped forward and commenced to speak was a supreme one in my life. I was buoyed up into full power by the importance of the occasion, and felt a perfect rapture in the sense of perfect self-possession. I spoke almost entirely without preparation, and proceeded without any stumbling with the subject—one with which I was thoroughly saturated. The time—¾ of an hour—passed as quickly to me as it is said to have done to my audience. Stanley gave me the sign to stop, and as I was replacing my sword, Col. Pitt came to me and said "It was one of the best lectures on Elementary Artillery I have ever heard".

He boasted to Vic: 'They came to scoff but remained to praise'.

He was also getting on well with the other ranks. He supported the N.C.O.s' request that officers and men should not sup separately at the Battery ball: 'the *amour propre* of the men was very much hurt by last year's arrangements'. Early in 1891 there was spontaneous applause when it was announced that he would have charge at the annual competition between batteries—but 'the men behaved execrably. Many things went wrong, and I felt sorely disappointed and ashamed'.

After a miserable first couple of years, Monash at last came to good terms with his fellow-officers, after 'the hardest fight I have yet had'; 'a little circumspection of manner' had helped. At Easter 1889 'among my brother officers I assumed for the first time a position of social equality. I was guilty of no faux pas, and was subjected to no harsh or unkindly treatment'. The journey home was very different from his previous humiliating experiences. Easter 1890 was very happy: he was 'one of the inner circle among the senior officers' and now had the task 'of playing off one against the other for my advantage'. By Easter 1891 he was beginning to feel very senior among recently recruited subalterns.

He had even won over Captain Stanley, his tormentor. When Stanley was gravely ill, Monash remarked: 'I have never liked him nor he me, yet I am very sorry for him'. Subsequently Stanley 'suddenly opened his heart to me, deeply apologized for his share in our past misunderstandings and spared no pains to make me understand that I am "One of us" '. Even more extraordinarily, a little later:

> On the way home I began to speak of my own troubles, not so much to enlist his sympathies but to gather some guidance from his comments. And then he astonished me by a most appalling and extensive confidence of his own domestic unhappiness, and overstrained marital circumstances—which evoked my genuine and fervent pity. . . . Here again is another household with a skeleton.

In July 1889 Stanley succeeded Goldstein as major and commanding officer of the Battery; 'dear old inoffensive' Joe Miller was promoted captain, so Monash became senior subaltern. By now he believed Stanley would be a 'rattling good CO'.

Just before Stanley was given command, he suggested to Monash that they construct a wooden-based and wooden-barrelled dummy model of a 5-inch breech-loading gun for practice drilling. Most of the artillerymen had been trained on muzzle-loading guns which were becoming obsolete. Stanley's open reason 'was the desire to make use of this affair as an argument to affect the promotions which were on the board'. Monash quickly produced a working specification, estimate of cost and an elaborate drawing: 'Intrinsically there is no merit in it except the simultaneous satisfying of mechanical and military requirements. . . . As a drawing however—and as my first piece of mechanical design—I was proud enough of it'. Stanley, who throughout was canvasser and advertiser and contributed nothing to the design, lost most of his interest once he was promoted. They were forced, after all, to proceed at their own expense and Monash was alarmed, when eventually he looked carefully at the breech-fittings of the 5-inch gun, at their 'extreme complication'. He called in a mechanic and a fitter to assist. Meanwhile Stanley introduced him to Colonel F. T. Sargood, the former minister of defence, 'who was very interested'. The dummy gun was not ready for inspection early in November, and a demonstration had to be abandoned; five months passed before Monash was satisfied with a revised product. Then the commandant, minister and the press failed to turn up to his demonstration and, when another was arranged, he had influenza and could not attend. However, the authorities were satisfied and a laudatory account of the Stanley–Monash practice gun appeared in the newspapers. The Defence Department did not treat them generously: Monash's expenses of £140 were paid, but no rights to any royalty or bonus were recognized. 'Such is the gratitude of the paternal state', he lamented. But the episode had helped to build his military reputation and the practice gun served for several years as a useful training device. Stanley had moved on from the battery to become a staff officer. Monash urged Miller to go for the command so that he might step up with him, but Major Outtrim, a senior postal official, was appointed. Monash found him 'an indulgent kindly man . . . quite unfit for military command' and, later, 'a bad and careless O.C.'.

In his early married and Harbor Trust years when he was also finishing off his courses, Monash gave much less attention to his military career and often missed drills. Much of the spirit had gone out of the volunteer defence movement in this period of economic crisis when governments cut down on military expenditure as on everything else. Monash's lecturing—on modern weapons, modern artillery, military explosives, mechanized science as applied to warfare, practical mechanics—continued to be very successful, whether given to artillerymen, the United Service Institution or suburban debating societies. An *Argus* report described him as having 'a first-rate style and a capacity for prompt and appropriate illustration that most public lecturers would have envied, and he carries the course through without notes'. In August 1893 he made very careful preparation, especially of the lantern-slides, for a lecture to the University Science Club on 'Implements of War'; about one hundred people, including Major-General Tulloch, the Victorian commandant, heard him speak 'with ease and aplomb'. His revolver-shooting so improved that he sometimes topped the score.

The future corps commander still was not promoted. He was no favourite of the English regular commandant of artillery, Lieut-Colonel Dean-Pitt who at the 1892 Easter Camp 'continually abused, and frequently insulted' him. Yet Dean-Pitt often acknowledged his obvious talents. Perhaps there was prejudice against Monash; perhaps there was simply no vacancy. By 1893 he was the senior active subaltern in the Garrison Artillery. He could not help hoping Miller would soon retire to clear the way. In July Outtrim made a strong recommendation on his behalf, and Monash wrote fulsomely to thank him. Lieut-Colonel Goldstein (whom Monash now addressed as Jacob) also talked flatteringly about early promotion. Early in 1894 Monash was elated when the General asked him if he would like to go to Shoeburyness in England for an artillery course, but the proposal fell through when the government refused to pay more than the sea-passage.

Monash took much pride in the task of designing a swing-bridge, the first in Victoria, over the Saltwater (Maribyrnong) River. His other work was largely on the recently excavated Victoria Dock for which he designed transit sheds, roads and drainage schemes. Though he felt 'content at weathering the storm of disaster which is raging over the whole community', in March 1892 he applied unsuccessfully for a vacancy in the Water Supply Department—Kernot put in a word for him. He began coaching again for the water supply exams, for several years continuing to take the few students he could get, and applied to the University for appointment as examiner in civil and hydraulic engineering. In May 1892 he won 'permanent' appointment at the Harbor Trust as chief draughtsman on £260 a year.

In 1892, also, he began to make his mark, to his great financial relief, in the courts. Graham and Wadick had been disappointed at the Railways' offers on their final claims, took the department to arbitration, and employed Monash as advocate. On leave from the Trust between April and July, he fought the case through successfully and won the admiration of the arbitrators. He charged Graham and Wadick five guineas a day and his lost pay, but he noted in his diary the strain and anxiety from which he once sought an adjournment. Under the pseudonym 'Equity' in the *Argus* he defended the system of settling disputes between contractors and the Railways by public arbitration. Next year he was approached to give evidence in defence of David Syme, proprietor of the radical *Age*, against an unsuccessful charge of libel brought by Richard Speight, who had been dismissed as chief commissioner of railways after sustained attack by the *Age*. Monash prepared himself by walking the Glen Iris and Outer Circle lines. Public opinion ran high, for this was a vicious confrontation between conservative and radical groupings at a time of great social stress. Monash's sympathies were with Speight—he privately referred to

Speight v. Slime—but he took the opportunity to build his professional reputation and earn much-needed fees. He knew that railway construction—cuttings, embankments, stations, ballast, fencing—had been 'highly extravagant', calculating that there had been 127 000 cubic yards of excess earthworks on the Outer Circle line and that 28 per cent of the cost had been unnecessary. Alfred Deakin took him through his evidence successfully and he stood up well to cross-examination, but there were jokes in court about the expert's youth. Both sides of the press reported him well and he escaped any satirical comment by the conservative *Argus*—which he had feared enough to ask a friend to try to prevent. His meetings with Deakin to plan his evidence meant much to him. He gave evidence again when the case was reheard and gathered some £40 for his two appearances. Thenceforward he was often in demand as an advocate in arbitrations of contracts and as an expert witness.

These were the years of the total collapse of the proud Colony of Victoria. In June 1891 Monash had realistically predicted 'very very hard times. . . . Soon it will be a hard struggle to live at all'. On that terrible 1 May 1893 when most of the banks suspended payment, he described Melbourne as 'in a panic of unbelief . . . in a tumult'. That day also, he was warned to expect the worst with regard to his job. Monash's two banks were among those which suspended, but he had little in his accounts. Public works had almost closed down, there was virtually no building construction of any kind. Most engineers were unemployed and pounced on any opening; young engineers were accepting posts without pay, for experience and a future reference. Lewis, who had earned £700 a year on Princes Bridge, was in dire poverty; Monash managed to arrange a few days' work for him at ten shillings a day. He saw Victoria's salvation in the revival of farming and mining and in reversing its traditional protectionist policy:

> when each individual has again started off on the road to his personal support and enrichment, the progress of the state as a whole cannot be far distant. . . . I have not lost faith in this land; the wealth is there; but instead of garnering it we have been living for the last ten years on artificial and speculative enterprises.

In that month of May, also, he had to handle, as executor, the affairs of the Roth family. Max Roth had died in debt; his young boys had to support Ulrike and their sisters.

The Harbor Trust was under constant attack for extravagance, though it had been ruthlessly retrenching employees, reducing salaries and cutting activities to the bone. Monash survived for the time being. By August his only remaining professional colleagues were the chief engineer and two inspectors. He had had to withstand one bitter campaign against him by a dismissed engineer, and appealed to his fellow-Jew, Commissioner E. L. Zox, to protect him. He applied unsuccessfully to the contractor for the Hobson's Bay Main Sewer for appointment as engineer-in-charge. By February 1894 he was aware that further retrenchments were planned, and began a vigorous campaign among friends of the commissioners. It was no use—in mid-March he knew he was doomed—but he made a desperate counter-attack. He wrote again to Zox, claiming his support for 'the only Jewish engineer in good practice in Victoria'. He wrote formally to the chairman of the Trust, was indignant to find that the letter had not been tabled, and distributed copies to the commissioners. A review committee extended by a month the original proposal for leave on pay until 1 July. He received notification of dismissal on 13 April and left on the 20th. In July he was disconcerted at an interview with Commissioner Thornley, a powerful businessman and politician, who accused him of gross disloyalty to the chief engineer and of overstating his achievements: 'For the first occasion in my life I have been thoroughly abused'. He stoutly denied the criticisms; Thornley would not believe such a young man could be so highly qualified. But he had made himself unpopular with the commissioners and when in July, with construction of the Saltwater bridge in mind, he applied to be appointed as consulting engineer, the Trust rejected him. Problems arose over construction of the bridge: the Trust came to the view that there was dangerous strain on a girder, and added bracing to the central panel. Monash, having confirmed his calculations with Kernot, protested to the chairman that the additions were 'utterly needless, useless, and only serve to add dead weight to the bridge, while atrociously disfiguring the symmetry of the design'. The alleged sag came about because the contractor had not been supervised: as Monash had predicted, the Trust would have been saved much money if he had not been dismissed.

He was so depressed when sacked from the Trust that his election as graduate member of the Engineering Students' Society committee boosted his morale. An offer of a post in Tasmania as a hydraulic engineer came to nothing. He asked an acquaintance whether it was worth applying for a municipal post at St Arnaud and was warned that the job was prearranged. Advised by Miller that the offices of both surveyor and town clerk of Brunswick were becoming vacant, he waged a vigorous campaign, 'sickening work', and lost the surveyorship by one vote to a seventy-three-year-old local candidate and the clerkship to the incumbent assistant. His mobilization of Deakin and A. R. Outtrim, the politician (via his brother, the major), to bring local pressure to bear was unavailing, but he found Deakin, when he ran into him once, 'very affable'.

Monash's response was boldly to open private practice with Joshua T. Noble Anderson, who had tutored him for the water supply engineers exams. They were of similar age, had met at least as early as October 1891, took warmly to each other, and Vic and Ellen Anderson also got on very well. In March 1892 Anderson suggested a partnership when times improved and Lewis released Monash from their understanding. Later that year Monash and Anderson combined the students they were coaching for government exams. In November Monash found Anderson's picnic for his university students 'one of the jolliest amusements I've had for a long time'. So, after nearly three years' friendship, Monash took up Anderson's offer:

> [I] am guided more by necessity than by choice to reopen this proposal. For myself I can say that in the interval I have greatly improved my business connections and reputation. . . . we combine an excellent array of qualifications. Expenses of an establishment are now extremely cheap, and even at the worst, we could at the very least pay expenses.

Anderson quickly agreed and Monash & Anderson opened at 49 Elizabeth Street in June 1894.

Ambition had to be deferred during these stark years. Monash had summed up at the close of 1892:

> Having come to realise that I am no genius, that I have no originality, and that I can only attain a moderate success and that by very hard work, I have worked hard. . . . I have kept up in what I think is a remarkable degree the resolves, methods, and discipline of my earlier life. I am pleased to feel I am living an earnest, useful, kindly and contented life.

Some feelings of uncertainty and inadequacy remained. He was worried that Professor Kernot sometimes seemed cool, and was elated when told by students that Kernot frequently mentioned him. At a brilliant hospital ball he felt 'very small among these great public men—though Vic is in her element'. At Government House, to which militia officers were often invited, he tended to be uneasy, still something of an outsider. He enjoyed smoke-nights, though 'at these affairs I am usually very much out of it', for he could not sing, recite, or tell a story well enough. Occasionally he would fill in as an accompanist, but lived in fear of being called on to contribute an item—yet when younger he had sought the limelight for his piano-playing and card tricks. He carried a notebook containing some recitations (usually Kipling, who was so much the favourite author of engineers) and ribald rhymes, and jotted down the outlines of jokes. He also had a curious fear of being beaten in an election, which remained through his life;

he would join the Engineering Students' Society committee only if he were unopposed. There were signs that he was becoming more strait-laced, as in his occasional disapproving comments on lotteries and plays such as *Formosa*—'vile, unhealthy'—and his opinion of Dr Scott, M.L.A., a chance train companion: 'a drunken foul mouthed roué—very clever and entertaining'.

John delighted in his baby, but the marriage continued uneasily. In April 1893 they had a dull three weeks' holiday at Daylesford which was judged to be climatically suitable for Vic's weak lungs. John and Mat were estranged for several weeks following conflicts between her and Vic; Mat identified his 'pet failing' as posing as the injured party. Vic was asked to Government House for the first time, to a garden party, which John described as 'a stupid wandering gazing and gazed at', and to a ball. John's separate invitations as an officer had irked her; his arrival home drunk one night, after helping to entertain visiting Austrian officers there, was a further aggravation. Despite increasing financial stringency, they continued to keep a servant. Their attitudes hardened late in 1893; Vic was continuing to go out with other men occasionally, though usually in her sister's company. In December she was pregnant again and, because of her frail health, doctors induced a miscarriage. Their relationship was then so bad that John could provide little sympathy. In January Vic proposed a permanent separation. Max Simonson was trying to keep the peace, but advised John to 'treat her firmly and unbendingly' and persuaded him to allow her to go away to Christmas Hills for a few weeks. Soon after her return she left him for four days until Max persuaded her to return. John received an anonymous letter warning him of her behaviour. There were some brief periods of peace during autumn and winter, but John's diary displays their domestic misery: he no doubt exaggerated to some extent, using his diary as a release.

The break-up came in September 1894. After helping Jack Mackey in his electoral campaign, John arrived home after midnight and Vic abused him roundly. 'I caught her hand to prevent her striking me.' Vic later alleged he had her round the neck. She left the house with the baby and began proceedings for a separation. John dismissed the servant, closed up the house and moved in with his father and sisters at Hawthorn. He implored Vic to return: if she did he would lay aside all hostility, if not he would assert his legal rights; she had deserted him and could present no evidence of misbehaviour on his part. He visited his daughter twice, but when Vic had prevented him seeing her for nearly three weeks, he and his father

> went to Mr. Simonson's house, and saw him in his front verandah. We sat with him and my child was brought to me, and I took

her in my arms. After chatting for ten minutes or so, I told Mr. Simonson I was going to take the child away with me. He said he would certainly object to any kidnapping. I replied I had a right to do what I liked with my own child. Meanwhile my father had risen, and had gone out and hailed a cab. Mr. Simonson then said 'I shall have to tell Vic.' He rose and went inside to do so, and while he was gone I went outside with the child and hastened to the cab. . . . my wife . . . ran a few steps after us. . . .

Mat and Lou were to look after Bertha admirably with the help of a nurse. Guarding carefully against any attempt to abduct the child, John arranged for Vic to see her regularly.

He was expecting her to return, but on 24 October he noted:

Vic having held out so long, I am quite overcome with my feelings. My father calls on Max, who won't interfere. I come home to lunch, and anxiously await Vic. When she comes with Sa, I go in with baby, go to Vic and ask her to give me a kiss and come back to me. She says she is very sorry for me, but wants a rest, and has at present no intention of ever coming back. . . . I though almost brokenhearted brace myself to the inevitable.

Advised by Farlow, John discussed his situation freely with his friends, who rallied round. Vic and her friends began to make wild accusations against John, for which there seem to have been little or no justification. In spite of everything, he hoped to win her back: 'I am continuously oppressed with grief, both at the loss of my wife and home, and the dreadful conduct of the wife I have loved and cherished so much'. He even brought in Rabbi Abrahams to intercede. Not all the Moss family were unreservedly on Vic's side. But Dave Moss had arranged to take Vic and Belle to England and to John's utter dismay they sailed on 10 December. He sent a desperate appeal to her to leave the ship at Adelaide or Albany, and return:

The statements which you have made about me to many people, you must know in your heart are utterly false; and I know that, apart from this, seeming friends of yours have helped to poison your mind. . . .

As you grow older you will find that pursuit of pleasure, to the sacrifice of every good emotion, will lead you to an abyss of mortification. . . .

Sum up all our past life together honestly and fairly, and you will see . . . you have been a selfish, jealous, truthless, neglectful . . . wife and mother. . . . you say you never loved me—but I have made a home and name for you, of which you *were* proud, say what you will. . . .

Now, wife, take counsel with yourself, sit down and think, think hard. . . . You cannot now say that I have not stretched out my hand to you. Be a good, sensible woman, and take it, and come back.

He even asked the ship's captain to keep an eye on her moral welfare. The occasion of Karl Roth's marriage induced some reflection:

> An act of marital authority . . . is ten times more effective, if done with a smiling face, and a kind speech. My mistake was to do just the opposite—to talk a lot, try to argue and appeal, and then quietly give way. . . . a husband *must* be master. . . .

A few days after Vic left, on 15 December, John's father died. Worried by his precarious finances, he had fast been deteriorating in general health. Only two days before, John had had him overhauled by Miller. The end was sudden: John arrived home in the afternoon to find him unconscious, rushed for a doctor, but he had died when they returned. He was sixty-three. Officers of the Melbourne Hebrew Congregation performed the last rites; prayers were said in the house for four evenings and John attended synagogue next day. He probably observed the formalities at the wish of Tante Ulrike and cousin Albert. Concerned that his troubles had contributed to his father's death, he was now saddled with the heavy labour of winding up the estate which, despite book-assets of more than £4000, seemed 'hopelessly insolvent': the assets were largely in real estate which was heavily mortgaged. Most of the properties had to be abandoned to creditors but a few, at Jerilderie and elsewhere, were slowly sold over several years. Almost none of the money owed to his father could be gathered. Within a few months John and his sisters lost the family home in Yarra Street, when the mortgagee foreclosed. John had already realized on his last asset, borrowing almost the whole value of his life policy.

He lived a distracted life in the first half of 1895. He often went to the theatre and passed much time at the Naval and Military Club and the Yorick (to which Goldstein and Kernot had nominated him), and at smoke-nights. Several times he got home with the dawn, sometimes after a 'glorious drunk'. His friends were good to him—notably the Cards, Krakowskis (he had a soft spot for Ada and they both probably eventually considered they would have been wise to have married each other), Steele, C. E. Wright and Gerald Wragge. He took up carpentering, chess and sketching again. He sporadically sought female comfort, without making any serious advances. Against all probability, he continued to hope that Vic would return. Despite all their conflicts, he had grown accustomed to her now, remembered the ideal Vic whom he loved, and was 'troubled almost nightly with tragic and affecting dreams in which my wife plays a prominent part'. But on 9 June he noted: 'Resignation is too humble a word. I am almost content'.

Out of the blue, on 13 July, came a letter from Vic announcing her return. 'My first feeling is one of triumph, but I soon realise it is a bitter one, and that I have a terribly difficult position to face.' He was very disturbed: would it really be worth trying again? Moreover, it coincided with the loss of the family home: his sisters would have to live with them. She arrived on the 25th:

> "Well, what has brought you back?" "I am willing to confess that I had more regard for you than I thought." She spoke well, feelingly and statefully, I could not help admiring her. But I doubted her sincerity. I suggested guarantees, but she laughed at that. . . .
>
> 26th. I do most of the talking today, and attempt to lay the position logically and fairly before her. She is not to be moved to admitting herself entirely in the wrong, but again promises to make me amends. However I point out that my constant fear of her again leaving me would greatly hamper my career. She then offers to leave me. "The child is happy, and does not want me. You no longer love me and I am sorry I have again come into your life. I will go out of it again. Good Bye." I let her leave, but was so deeply moved, that the same evening I wrote asking her to see me again.
>
> 27th. I was not fit for work all the morning, doubting if Vic would not see my evident anxiety and stand out against me. But at 2 oclock she came out again, and we soon arrived at an understanding. . . .
>
> 28th. Vic comes . . . and we pass a pleasant afternoon together. Vic seems greatly changed and her warm affectionate manner, if sincere, augurs for future well-being.

That night he wrote in his Commonplace Book:

> It was dreary and dark, and all joy had fled
> And I lost your face in the shadows falling
> And heard no longer your sweet voice calling
> But only the wail of the storm instead
> And I knew you were cruel, and Hope was dead.
>
> But here at the last I find
> I am holding again your hand
> And now you are cruel no more, but kind
> And I scarcely can understand
> But as long as your hand on my hand closes
> I know that you love me sweet
> And so long will our lives be decked with roses
> And the lilies make paths for our feet.
>
> I am kissing you over and over
> I am holding you close to my heart
> As of old, we'll be lover and lover
> And live in a world apart.

Next day he began a new volume of his diary and a new letter-book.

John immediately took Vic to the orderly room at North Melbourne

nie Gabriel, 1888

John Monash, c. 1888

orge Farlow

Will Steele

Vic and John, 1890

Three generations, 1894 or 1895

to see his brother officers: it was best to meet boldly the curiosity and gossip which they would have to endure indefinitely. Within a week they were settled in a fairly substantial house, which they named Bertmont, close to his former family home, on the corner of Coppin and Isabella Groves, Hawthorn, at the stiff rent of £5 a week; Mat, Lou and a maid moved in with them. But to John's great distress their relations were soon as bad as ever. Whatever the terms of their bargain, Vic would not accept his authority, spent money against his wishes, and went off with friends to the races or the theatre without consulting him. After one row at New Year he 'left the house distracted, and spent a terrible night. How is this all to end?' But after their first twelve months together again, periods of relative calm and content became more frequent; the departure of John's sisters to separate lodgings had helped.

Monash & Anderson had set up as civil, mining and mechanical engineers, claiming between them to have been responsible for works worth over £1 million; they also announced themselves as patent agents. Their fees—two guineas a day (three for country work)—were the lowest allowed by the Institution of Civil Engineers (London). They drummed up custom, suggesting to shires that they engage them as consultants rather than employ a shire engineer. They concentrated on South Gippsland where coal and gold mining companies were carrying out construction works. The Coal Creek Pty. Co., the most successful of the mines, employed them as consultants, and through letters to the *Age* they became eloquent propagandists for the new local industry against the importing coal-ring trying to destroy it by cutting prices. Briefly they considered one of them setting up a headquarters in Gippsland. Their most profitable early engagement was in litigation over a lift accident. They arranged to sell Moorooduc clay on commission—which led to acquaintance with John Gibson, the manager of David Mitchell's cement works. They made a feasibility study of the navigability of the Barwon River, lobbied for employment by the Mount Lyell Co., and joined a syndicate hoping to salvage a sunken ship. They took many jobs for expenses in hope of future employment. Mining companies were bad payers: one even paid in shares and then made calls!

Josh Anderson was a charming man, lively and entertaining, in some respects more brilliant and possibly a better mathematician than his partner, but erratic. Monash quickly realized that he was no businessman and took charge of the book-keeping. 'Though Anderson is a good hand at making business, and has a much better first impression general aspect, I am far his superior in all practical details.... he cannot work hard, continuously or accurately.' In December 1894 Anderson was distressed by losing his part-time university lectureship in mechanical engineering. When it was advertised, Monash and Anderson applied jointly: Monash lobbied vigorously, but in the end the post was eliminated. No doubt worried by his partner's domestic troubles, Anderson was talking of 'breaking up and leaving Victoria'; they even reached the point of agreeing that Monash would carry on the business for his sole benefit. Monash was looking to Western Australia, where there were promising railway-construction jobs. However, they struggled on. The firm now advertised itself as architects as well as engineers and found minor commissions from designing shops and factory extensions. An invention by one Galopin concerning the gearing of bicycles caused much exploratory work. The Shire of Cranbourne employed them on a legal case; Monash had to spend a week based on the Tooradin Coffee Palace and ultimately arranged a happy compromise, earning much good will. They failed to capture the Korumburra lighting contract, for which they had been negotiating to raise capital overseas, but Healesville shire (where Anderson owned land) employed them as consultants from mid-1895 and they introduced electric lighting there. But the Healesville connection was to prove an almighty nuisance.

Their first large contract of £1201 from mid-1895 was to design and install an 'aerial tramway' at Landys Dream Gold Mining Co., seven miles out of Walhalla in Gippsland on the Woods Point track. The tramway, for transporting quartz, was to be one mile long; they had no local precedents to guide them and had to make a totally novel design. Serious delays ensued: the company had not cleared the ground properly, the ropes ordered from England were late, so was the ironwork. Their carrier was always difficult to contact, then delivered the parts in almost the worst possible order. The contracted date passed, but fortunately the directors had demanded new work. Monash spent three weeks there in January 1896 camping in a bark hut on the banks of the Aberfeldy, then Anderson had to spend months desperately trying to make the thing work; trials were indefinitely delayed. By late February the directors were restive; in mid-April they delivered an ultimatum. The shareholders were tense. Monash told Anderson: 'I have become an object of huge interest to many, as I walk the streets, feel like a marked man. The fate of the district seems to depend on the Tramway!' Monash was unwell with haemorrhoids and diarrhoea amid this suspense, and their debts were mounting. Their bank obliged with £100 overdraft. Monash and Anderson held shares in Landys and used their inside knowledge to buy and sell as they fluctuated wildly.

Eventually on 12 May the directors rescinded the contract and demanded possession, probably at the very point when the tramway was about to work satisfactorily. Monash & Anderson went to law.

Monash laboured on the documentary evidence and before a judge and jury of four spent three days in the witness box late in August. The jury found against the company, which appealed. In December a compromise was reached: Monash & Anderson gave up £190 of the £320 which the jury had awarded. It was better to compromise, John told Mat, than suffer the 'horrible suspense of waiting till April, the want of money in the interim and the risk of having the verdict reversed'. In the end they probably gained nothing but hard-won experience from the contract.

Another Walhalla contract was more successful. In February 1896 they agreed with the Golden Fleece Co. to move about 28 tons of machinery, mainly a huge boiler, from Daylesford to beyond Walhalla, and to erect a battery. It was working out well until in June they could not afford to pay the carrier who would not continue; an agonizing correspondence followed until he agreed. They employed as foreman C. Christensen who stayed with them for years; Monash worked with him on the installation early in July. They ended up amiably with the carrier and finished the contract early. The inevitable final argument with the directors followed: when Monash & Anderson threatened to take the matter to arbitration the company paid nearly all the sum in dispute.

Anderson infuriated Monash with his inefficiency—yet they remained very good friends. In 1896 especially, when one or other was usually out in the field, they reported fully and frankly to each other. Monash did blow up occasionally, as when Anderson submitted a grossly underestimated tender to Golden Fleece and Monash had the humiliation of having to submit a revised version. They often wrote bluntly to each other but usually had the sense not to put it all on paper: 'We'll talk about this'. Anderson came to understand Monash's self-righteousness and passion for orderliness. Monash had been learning to admit his own mistakes. He was very considerate to Anderson during the tense period when he was working on the tramway. Some of their messages were in Greek, Latin or cipher—as much for fun as secrecy.

They struggled on through 1896. Anderson found useful work advising the Mildura irrigation trust and they reached a more favourable agreement with Healesville shire. Monash had a triumphant confrontation, as consultant to the Strzelecki Collier Co., with a difficult contractor, and they improved a steam tramway they had previously designed for the company. They won a lift-inspection contract. Monash gave evidence to the Railways Standing Committee on behalf of the Fitzroy Railway League, advised Graham and Wadick again with regard to final payments on the Outer Circle line, was engaged by the Crown Solicitor on another Railways case, was employed in a dispute over patents, and examined for the South Australian School of Mines. He nevertheless had to allow his five-guinea subscription to the Institution of Civil Engineers to lapse, was subject to debt collectors' letters, and had to borrow horse-furniture for formal military parades. Monash & Anderson were just managing hand to mouth.

Military prospects at last began to improve, and Monash renewed his flagging enthusiasm. He had been disappointed about promotion and was bored with the unrewarding routine. Some of the other subalterns were restive under his 'bossy manner' and his taking too much into his own hands. He knew his two seniors in the Battery, Outtrim and Miller, were about to retire; an offer from Major W. H. Hall of a captaincy in his battery came to nothing, but he continued to live in hope.

One avenue of self-promotion was through the United Service Institution of Victoria whose council he joined in July 1894. He suggested a conversazione, an exhibition of naval and military equipment with lecturettes on recent innovations in weaponry, drew up a plan and, for fear of seeming to push himself too much, gave it to Hall to propound. The plan was adopted, the conversazione was a triumph and Monash got full credit; the General, Sir Charles Holled Smith, paid formal compliments and Colonel Hoad and other senior officers were generous in praise. He was then snatched for the secretaryship of the Institution, but found the post dull and burdensome; though a lecture by the Governor, Lord Brassey, in June 1896 was a feather in his cap, he was glad to be able to resign in 1897 because of absence from Victoria.

He was at last promoted captain on 18 October 1895; that week he was an aide at the Governor's levée. Monash's friendships—genuinely affectionate—with Outtrim and the state-school headmaster Hall, now lieut-colonel in command of the Metropolitan Brigade, were to serve him well. More than anyone, over a ten-year period Hall acted as Monash's mentor. In the scramble for promotion and seniority, he and Outtrim were conspiring in Monash's interests. Monash used his acquaintanceship with the journalist, Donald Macdonald, to get a paragraph on his promotion into the *Argus*. His immediate application to sit for his major's exams was rejected and a twelve months delay imposed; Outtrim wisely persuaded him not to appeal. Outtrim promised to remain in command until the most favourable moment for the succession, but rejected Monash's suggestion that he take three months leave so that his junior might acquire 'such a vested interest in the battery as it would be hard to shake'. In imminent hope, Monash threw himself into the work. By July 1896 Outtrim had brought it off: he arranged for Monash to be given acting command until he qualified for his majority, and himself joined the Reserve. Monash's appointment in command of the North Melbourne Battery, Garrison Artillery, was gazetted late in September.

Again Monash asked Macdonald to mention his appointment in the *Argus,* but he appeared—disastrously—as Major Monash, and was consequently described as such in a Yorick Club circular. The mockers had a field-day. Monash wrote to Hall:

> some have supposed that this paragraph was inspired by me. I take the most direct way that lies to my hand of stating that there is no truth whatever in such an insinuation, and ask you to be good enough, should occasion arise, to let it be known that I disclaim any responsibility.

Hall replied:

> ... very provoking just at this juncture when I want all my tact to steer the machine. Of course I give you credit for too much sense to believe you inspired it, but that does not prevent comments. . . . You cannot but be aware that as good a man as you are necessarily has detractors and these small minded gadflies annoy one with their buzzing. I suppose there is nothing for you to do but be quiet and go slow for a little.

By late October Monash had the Battery running smoothly but, he wrote to a former officer, 'Poor old Outtrim let things drift terribly, and it will be many good days' work before I can get everything fixed up to my liking'. He revelled in the task: 'My success here is one of my only comforts in the midst of much grave trouble'. Hall persuaded him to wait till December, without protesting, for his major's exams (which, he calculated, made ninety-four written exams in seventeen years). He scored 99 per cent for drill, 98 per cent for Coast Artillery Tactics and 87 per cent for Regimental Duties. He failed his riding exam, however, but was passed overall. His promotion to major was announced on 2 April 1897 and gazetted on the 9th together with confirmation of his command. His hopes had long been deferred, but to have risen so far at the age of thirty-one was still uncommonly good going.

6

Little Accomplished
1897–1906

IN WINTER 1897 Monash came suddenly into demand as an advocate and expert witness in legal-engineering work. Over the next two years he spent three-quarters of his time in other colonies—four times in Queensland, six times in New South Wales, twice in Western Australia. He had spent a week at Portland in May, representing the Austral Otis Engineering Co. against the Portland Freezing Co. He was pleased with his performance, having given the opposition's expert witness such a hot time in the box that 'I thought really he would commit some violence upon me'. However, a young articled clerk who was present, Frederic Eggleston, was 'struck with a certain almost childish egotism about him'. After defeat, Monash learned that it was a put-up job: the arbitrator was in collusion with the Portland Co's expert.

His first major employment was by Baxter & Saddler, contractors for a section of a Queensland railway from Bundaberg to Gladstone, whose final claims against the government were in dispute. In June he was away for a fortnight, travelling with V. J. Saddler through Bundaberg by ballast engine to the contractors' camp where he spent six days mastering details. In September he again made the long train trip—playing euchre and yarning with other first-class passengers, delighting in the Darling Downs. He worked up the case for a week and decided to make twenty claims totalling about £25 000. 'I regard this work as the chance of a lifetime', he wrote to Vic. 'If I win a success, it will be the biggest thing I have ever done, and my name will be made.'

Monash was in poor health. His haemorrhoids were better, but his diaries of the two previous years also frequently refer to being ill, depressed, bilious, and having diarrhoea. This was perhaps the worst period of general health of his life, in some part a product of his many anxieties. He wrote to Vic from Brisbane: 'I have followed your advice and have not touched liquor in any form . . . and I certainly feel better for it. But I have not yet recovered from the feeling of nervous depression and lassitude'. And later: 'I wish I could tell you I am well, but I'm not. I'm all over pains, and feel like lying still on my back for a month'. But in November and December, when he returned to Brisbane for the case, he was much better. He was feeding frugally, largely on pineapples and other fruit. The 'muggy moist heat' was dreadful—on the whole he would rather be roasted than stewed. Three clean collars, two changes of underclothing and two or three showers a day were necessary. He soon became 'quite a bananalander', having gone in for Assam silk suits, porous cellular shirts and a pith helmet.

The case began on 10 November and was to last ten weeks. Monash was paid five guineas a day. He had to work long hours, often to midnight, organizing the dozens of assistants and witnesses and conferring with Saddler. For a start, the Railways Department objected to Monash's appearance since he was 'expert in arbitration'; it had been agreed that the case would be conducted by engineers. Saddler misled the three arbitrators by stating that he employed Monash on an annual salary; they ruled in his favour, whereupon (Sir) Arthur Rutledge, leader of the Queensland Bar, was engaged in opposition. Monash opened the case well when his expert witnesses on the vital cement-testing issue, Professor Warren of Sydney and John Gibson, so exposed the Railways' case that Rutledge did not cross-examine. Monash found Warren a 'jolly nice fellow' and they became good friends. The case went excellently, Monash holding his own with Rutledge. 'Everyone from the highest to the lowest, enemy and friend alike', John exulted to Vic, 'is saying nice things to me. . . . Saddler struts about like a peacock. . . . I really believe he thinks he owns me'. He began to dream of the bonus Saddler would give him and of how he might increase his future fees: 'I feel that very soon I will be able to command a constant income of nearly £2,000 a year'. Although still living hand to mouth, he allowed Vic to buy the Behrends' piano for £55.

He had only a fortnight at home over Christmas and New Year and had little rest, let alone a holiday. But on New Year's Day he made a final entry in his Intimate Diary:

> Five years since last I wrote. A great piece out of a lifetime, yet how short it seems. Five turbulent, struggling not very happy years— except latterly. For at last I seem to have got into smooth waters. I have been successful—very—yet what a long way short of my early ambitions. More than ever has it been born in upon me, that my only chance of success lies in hard work. This, and rigid method in all my affairs, has brought me my success, and this only. I have had many griefs—death and time have torn away great gaps in the past, which I still cherish so fondly. I am happy in my domestic sphere and try to do my duty to my dear wife and darling

daughter, and I feel they love me. My sisters too are cared for—I feel now that my position and future are assured, and that nothing but unexpected calamity can injure me. I fear I am as self-conscious as ever, yet I have grown sober—more contented, and single of purpose. I have fewer friends than ever; success does not foster new friendships. I look forward now to a time of more material comfort, and less feverish striving; inwardly I feel that worldly prosperity is less than nothing, and I yearn for rest and time to think, time to dream again the pictures of my younger years. Today I am more hopeful, more stable-minded, and steadfast in good resolve than ever before.

The case resumed on 13 January. Monash took four days over his final address to the arbitrators and was happy with it: 'Win or lose, I have made my reputation'. He had told Saddler in September that the claims were worth at least £8000, and as the case proceeded he confidently expected twice as much. The award of £7722 was very disappointing; after costs, Baxter & Saddler gained very little, and Monash had no hope of a bonus.

His other major engagement in late 1897 and early 1898 was as adviser and expert witness for pastoralists, farmers and townspeople in the Jerilderie area, combined against David and Samuel McCaughey who were damming much of the water in the Billabong and Colombo creeks for irrigating their properties. So, after twenty years, Monash saw Jerilderie again. He spent a fortnight in the area in July when the cases began before the Land Board at Urana. He was there for most of October also, between Queensland trips, surveying the creeks and dams, travelling by horse and trap, camping out several times, then appearing in court. His employers appealed against the Board's attempted compromise and issued writs against the McCaugheys for damages. Monash had bright prospects of much more work. Just before Christmas he gave evidence in Sydney before the Land Appeal Court, which agreed with him that the McCaugheys must greatly modify their damming.

In March he had to spend four days in the Riverina on the way to Sydney for *Blackwood* v. *McCaughey*, the first of the Supreme Court cases for damages. Monash was advising the barrister Sir Julian Salomons. Proceedings were adjourned and Monash spent ten more days in the Riverina, making water conservation surveys. When the cases resumed late in May he 'had a heavy time running about seeing solicitors, counsel, draughtsmen and departmental plans. . . . I have been the mainspring of the whole business'. J. H. Want, Q.C., had not cross-examined him, but devoted much of his final address to attempting to discredit 'this gentleman from Victoria', an epithet which he used with 'damnable iteration' Monash said. During the lunch-break he protested to Want who replied, 'It's all in the game, come and have a drink'. The jury was not swayed—one of them told Monash it was 'a fool of a speech'—and awarded £2000 damages. After long negotiations in which Monash took part, the McCaugheys settled the remaining cases for £10 000 and £17 000 costs and a guarantee that they would desist from grabbing so much water. Samuel McCaughey sounded Monash out on possible future work for him. Monash believed that damming the Murrumbidgee was the best remedy for the problem, to allow for irrigation but preserving navigability of the rivers, but deplored the disunity and petty jealousies into which the district fell, following the 'seemingly equitable settlement' of 1898. The following year he turned aside a suggestion that he should stand for the New South Wales Legislative Assembly to provide a lead on the question. Between 1903 and 1906 he was to make several more trips to the Riverina and Sydney as adviser to the Lower Murrumbidgee River Locking League.

During his long absences Jack wrote to his 'Dearest' with great affection but undemonstratively, constantly assuring her of his sympathy with her loneliness and that 'it is no fun up here', persuading her of the material benefits which would flow from their separation. She was as mercurial as ever: 'I cannot tell you how much I miss you. I feel as I should or wish I had felt long ago—that you are part of myself and that it would be impossible for me to live without you'. And—'Upon my word I shall forget how to do it'. When he had time, his letters, though dashed off, were sparkling:

> I spent the greater part of yesterday afternoon in the streets of Sydney, which were bubbling over with excitement. . . . I began to realise how far reaching and Australian in its character is our great Cup Race. In a right of way off George St. I saw a remarkable sight. A long string of men and women to the number of several hundreds were pushing their way into the lane, so I took my place and was carried along with the stream. . . . I found myself in a long low room like a warehouse basement. All along one side was a long counter and behind . . . seven young men coatless and collarless, hoarse and perspiring, crying the odds and gathering in coin by the shovelful. . . . I watched the show for half an hour in amazement and pity. Old men, clerks, out at elbows vagrants, women factory girls, bell-toppered men and little boys swept past in an endless stream. . . . About 10 to 4, I went to join the crowd in King St. opposite the Telegraph Office. . . . When the Post Office clock began to chime, a deathly hush fell on the crowd, . . . out flashed the name GAULUS on the large front window. It was instantly repeated by thousands of throats, many hats went up, and there were not a few curses. Slowly the crowd dispersed, but business for the day was done. . . .
> So you see I had my Cup day fun after all.

While still in Brisbane, John heard that Vic was suddenly seriously ill with a high fever. He *could* not go home—he was in the middle of his final address. Anderson assured Monash he could rely on him to send the 'absolute truth' and to tell him he should let the case 'rip' if necessary. She was out of danger fairly quickly.

> It leaked out that you were ill, and from all sides, even from perfect strangers, I have been overwhelmed with sympathetic enquiries. Whenever any telegrams have arrived, the proceedings have been stopped.

It had been a serious illness. She was eventually allowed to convalesce in Sydney; John wrote reassuringly about her improved health to her elder sister whom he still addressed as 'Mrs. Simonson', reflecting earlier hostilities. On return home they took on a second maid-servant. Vic accompanied him to Sydney (with Tante Ulrike) again in May-June.

'With so many responsibilities on my shoulders', he wrote to Behrend, 'I really cannot entertain any other thoughts, but the sordid one of making money'. Monash & Anderson seemed as though they might be turning the corner but John and Josh both still had to watch every penny to avoid their bank-manager's icy attention. According to Monash's income tax return they cleared £298 each in 1897 and £208 in 1898. They treated each other with the utmost consideration over sharing their earnings. Both suffered losses from bushfires in January 1898 (John on his father's Thorpdale property). He wrote to Anderson: 'I don't grudge you the freest hand in operating on the business a/c for private purposes. My turn to need it may come any day'. They occasionally made tiny joint investments from their earnings, and usually had to realize on them quickly. As always, the great problem was getting in earnings due: the Mildura trust eventually had to be threatened with legal action. The fact that Monash was earning more than Anderson inevitably made for tension, but early in 1898 Anderson won new Mildura work and a contract for installing machinery at the Ballarat Woollen Mills. The problem then became how to carry on the firm with both partners so often away from Melbourne. They had taken on a junior, but they had to consider whether another partner was necessary. Their tender for an aerial tramway for the Mount Lyell Co. was unsuccessful and prospects of another in New Zealand came to nothing. Anderson was advising the Victorian Railways on routes for a track from Healesville to Woods Point, and impressing Monash with the possibilities of dirigible balloons. Monash was frequently worried by what he considered Anderson's tendency to 'finesse', to be over-clever and create 'complications where none exist', but he had the grace occasionally to ask Anderson to pardon his 'preaching attitude'. He confessed: 'I am not good at feeling my way. I like to mature or at least *outline* my whole plan before commencing any negotiations'.

Anderson made the contact which ultimately shaped Monash's business and professional career. In September 1897 Anderson met Frank Moorhouse Gummow, a Sydney contractor-engineer whose firm Carter, Gummow held the Australian patent rights for Monier reinforced concrete construction, and negotiated a temporary agreement whereby Monash & Anderson became their Victorian agents. This led directly to their building the Anderson Street (Morell) bridge over the Yarra and becoming contractors for the Fyansford (Barwon River) and other bridges. For the moment, Monash had little to do with these enterprises, but in Sydney in March 1898 he spent some time with Carter, Gummow, viewing Monier works and being thoroughly coached.

Saddler had engaged Monash to prepare and conduct Baxter & Saddler's case against the Western Australian government for claims arising from their contract for the 200-mile Mullawa–Cue section of the railway from Geraldton to the Murchison goldfield. The 3' 6" line had taken three years to build. When Monash eventually left for Perth early in July 1898 he believed he was going only for five weeks: it turned out to be twelve months. On the voyage he played cards and chatted with Saddler and his friends—'all men of immense wealth and their talk made my mouth water'. On arrival he could not start work on the claims for several days because Baxter, following racing wins, was on a spree and then hid himself 'in shame and contrition'. But within a week Monash had gone north to inspect the line. Back in Perth he began steady work on the claims, aided by a staff of nine including a personal secretary, and enjoyed the luxury of dictation.

Baxter & Saddler gave Monash the entrée to Perth society. He was asked to a 'very select and very choice' small dinner at the Weld Club which included the premier Sir John Forrest and his brother the mayor, the Speaker Sir John Lee-Steere, C. Y. O'Connor the engineer, 'old Dick Speight' formerly head of the Victorian Railways, and J. W. Hackett, 'an old Melbourne University man [of] great influence here'. Monash considered he held his own very well. Sir John and Lady Forrest invited him to dinner which was followed by an 'At Home':

> About 50 people turned up. I then understood for the first time the conservatism and real cliqueism of the genuine original Sandgroper. . . . in this country there is only one ruling caste; all the "blarsted t'othersiders" are out of it—in politics—in influence—in Sassiety. The Naicest are all real original Sandgropers. Well, this ruling caste is made up wholly and solely of the *six great families*—hold your breath in awe—and they are the Forrests, Venn's, Lee-

Steere's, Shenton's, Hammersleigh's and Leake's; and they are all intermarried in the most bewildering and interminable confusion. Everybody in Sassiety is a cousin, second cousin, brother-in-law, uncle, aunt or something of the kind to somebody else. . . . Well the great six did the grand in approved style, stood around in stiff groups, while a few artists tried to make music, talked scandal for 2 hours, and after a very nice supper, went quietly home. . . . I left at last more heartily amused than edified. I fancy you and I could manage a politico-social function of this kind a good deal better.

Thus wrote the thirty-three-year-old from the metropolis. He told Vic that

the reason why I got on so well is I suppose because I am a stranger. No man is a hero in his own country. In Melbourne everybody knows all about me—and the extent of my experience and familiarity breeds contempt, whereas here—when I talk—as I can talk now of my extensive travels—people are inclined to place on one the same kind of halo that is put on an English stranger.

But he soon tired of dining with the great.

Monash was keeping a sharp eye out for business. 'My chief trouble is that odious slave driven feeling I have. I sadly want rest from anxiety.' If only they could accumulate some capital, he told Vic again and again, impressing on her the need for self-denial: 'Nothing is truer than that money makes money'. He was excited when Saddler, boasting of how he stood by his friends, offered financial help when needed and dangled prospects of Monash taking charge of a huge oil works he was planning in New South Wales or of the Zeehan–Strahan railway in Tasmania he was angling for. John and Vic began to discuss whether they could bear to move to Tasmania. Seeing so many easy opportunities around him in Perth, he told her she could 'look forward with confidence to a time not very far distant, when you can lord it with the best of them in Melbourne Society'.

Regretting that he had not gone to the West when gold was first discovered, Monash had found his great investment opportunity within two days of arrival in Perth. His friend from the Outer Circle, W. B. Shaw, and a partner owned a promising quarry, suitable for supplying road-metal, but lacked capital to develop it. Monash put in £200 of his own money but could not persuade Anderson to invest more than £100 of their joint funds; nevertheless he now had about a 30 per cent interest and was entirely confident it would yield him £500 a year. Anderson would not be convinced—it was essentially 'pure speculation' and they could not risk more. The gentlemanly but deeply-felt exchange was a minor crisis in their partnership. Monash—and Anderson too—could write strongly and angrily, but not offensively, to each other. Monash essentially was hurt at not being able to convince Anderson of his good judgement. It probably was a *very* good speculation, but Anderson turned out to be right. The manager absconded with the funds.

The preparatory work in Perth dragged on, seemingly interminably; Monash was consoled only by his three or four guineas a day (of which, by his bonus arrangement with Anderson, he took about two-thirds). He avoided society, largely to save money, and joined a lending library. He often spent Sundays with his old flame Ada Krakowski, now Ada Benjamin, and her husband, but did not tell Vic who was on bad terms with Ada. Through her he became active in Perth's musical life and took up the piano again for at least an hour a day, playing occasionally in an amateur orchestra. He looked forward to resuming the duet-playing he and Vic had so neglected. In mid-September he was involved in an extraordinary incident when Saddler, being seen off at Perth station, came to blows with another elderly businessman. 'The fight was viewed by a crowd of Knights and society people—and K.C.M.G.'s, porters, policemen and toffs were all mixed up in a furious turmoil.' Early in October he visited Kalgoorlie on the first of three small private advisory jobs and wrote an account of his trip (which does not survive) which roused the admiration of the Andersons as being worthy of de Rougemont and well worth publication. He then had a hard few days on the northern line, though he did not as he feared have to carry out the check with the government inspector of the depth of the ballast, brought back finally two truck-loads of papers and kit, and knuckled down to work. This was further delayed when his chief associate, Prince, suffered an attack of dysentery; Monash nursed him and they became fast friends.

John had been trying to buoy Vic up with hopes of an early return, but by early November suggested that she and their daughter Bert join him—and hang the cost! The case was obviously going to drag on into the New Year. Saddler's Tasmanian venture was proceeding too quickly for Monash possibly to be engaged. Vic was delighted and she and Bert joined him early in December—and were to stay for six months. Vic launched herself into Perth society—Government House, the Forrests and 'all the elite' received her with open arms. She was in her element at the New Year racing carnival: 'Mrs Monash, in a unique dress of black voile patterned in stripes . . ., wore a picture hat of blue velvet, with wastrel-looking ostrich plumes nodding over the brim'. She developed her friendship with Harry Boan, the draper, and his wife. When John rushed back to Melbourne for three weeks to attend the Easter camp, Vic wrote to him about her success at the mayor's reception: 'I wore my pink and blue, and really dear although I say it as shouldn't I looked awfully well. As I entered there was a buzz and the men simply rushed me'. Someone sent her a diamond ring through the post, anonymously.

The government was in no hurry to bring the case to a conclusion. Monash and Prince had by January lodged the final claim of £150 000, and prepared their brief while trying to convince the government that it would be wiser to settle. Monash was conducting Baxter & Saddler's affairs under power of attorney and was content up to a point with the accumulating fat daily fees. He was troubled that, as in Brisbane, he might be challenged with not being a bona fide full-time employee of Baxter & Saddler and was dissembling about his partnership with Anderson, whom he warned: 'Your story must be that I have been with B & S for the past 2 years'. He had a leisurely time in February, including some days fishing with Prince. Eventually the case was heard in late April and May. The arbitrator was O'Connor, engineer-in-chief of the colony, whose great goldfields water scheme was at a critical stage and whose views on money-grubbing contractors were well known. Walter James, the distinguished barrister and federationist, worked with Monash in opposition to the crown solicitor and Septimus Burt, the leading local barrister-politician. O'Connor proceeded brusquely and awarded some £15 000 on forty-two of the forty-six claims; the remainder were referred to the Supreme Court but were settled out of court, to make a total judgment to Baxter & Saddler of £45 000. It was a satisfactory outcome, but Monash waited in vain for any bonus; he had, however, cleared over £1000 from his year's work. The last month's delay waiting on the settlement, which he largely negotiated, was infuriating. He had seriously considered staying, however, especially when a large contractor urgently sought his advice. He finished on very friendly terms with James, but O'Connor was not pleased with him and Monash wrote him an ingratiating letter asking, from professional interest, for copies of his goldfields water supply plans.

On his return in July 1899 Monash was very glad he had stuck with Anderson. Both knew that if Monash continued to earn three times as much, they would have to part, but Monash was content to postpone the decision, largely out of respect and liking for his partner. He was impressed by Anderson's handling of the three Monier bridges—over the Yarra, at Fyansford and near Creswick—which he was building under the close tuition of Gummow and his men. It had been a triumph to persuade William Davidson and Carlo Catani, the Public Works Department engineers, to allow a Monier experiment: the negotiations had been extraordinarily thorough. With three arches of 95 feet, the Anderson Street bridge was the largest Monier work Gummow had yet attempted. There was intense interest within the profession—and some scepticism over whether the slender arches could possibly bear the weight. All was well: a fortnight after Monash's return a large crowd witnessed the successful test of the bridge by a 15-ton roller and hundreds of tons of dead weight. Though he had had little to do with it Monash always gloried in this first local Monier work, the most elegant of the Yarra bridges. A few people continued to assume that 'Monier' derived from his name.

Monash described Monier concrete construction as

> a combination of ordinary cement mortar with a grid or lattice-work of iron rods. Monier . . . applied the process originally to the manufacture of flower-pots, but it was soon apparent that he had hit on a combination of materials which combined exceptional strength and elasticity with comparative cheapness—so that the process came to be adopted for the construction of fire-proof floors and arches of all descriptions, also pipes, etc.

The tensile strains were taken by the iron, the compressive strains by the concrete. It was a much cheaper process for bridges than iron or steel—about the same cost as timber—and the 'fine plastic substance' (Monash was never to tire of telling architects) 'could be moulded to any form of beauty'. On his return he instructed himself in Monier principles of bridge design, consulting Gummow's technical expert, W. G. Baltzer, and, at Fyansford and Creswick, mastered the building process itself. Pipe manufacture was an even more promising prospect. Monash & Anderson displayed pipes from Gummow's Sydney factory and persistently lobbied the Melbourne & Metropolitan Board of Works, which agreed to trials late in 1899. Gummow and Anderson had been planning to establish a Melbourne pipe factory. Monash was soon in contact with the wealthy contractor and cement manufacturer, David Mitchell, through his manager John Gibson, who was offering land in Burnley next to his works provided his cement was used.

Monash's return coincided with a lull in demand for ordinary engineering work. Baxter & Saddler provided a useful job, supervision of the construction in Melbourne by Dorman Long & Co. of a 100-foot span bridge for the North Mt Lyell Copper Co.'s railway. Monash had a few days' work as arbitrator for the Board of Land and Works in a dispute. The obvious path of advance came to be further contracting for Monier work. Saddler had partly kept his promise by arranging for the Bank of Australasia to lend £500, but he could not be brought to the point of agreeing to provide capital and share profits. Monash had been sure enough of his financial situation to pay in Vic's name £40 on a £140 cottage at Port Melbourne as an investment. But by October 1900 the firm was seriously over-extended. In order to take on a series of eight small bridges at Bendigo and a large one at Bruthen, and later to install engine-beds and a roof at a gold-mine near Maryborough, Monash had to 'inaugurate general retrenchment' in the firm and domestically. Moreover, they had to persuade Gummow and

Richard Taylor of the Fyansford cement works to wait for payment of large sums, and justify themselves to the Bank of Australasia.

Monash and Anderson had underestimated the potential appalling delinquency of impoverished shires and their engineers refusing to pay their debts. Fyansford was their Waterloo. It was a hazardous enterprise from the start. Anderson had designed the handsome four-arched bridge by late 1897, in consultation with Gummow and Taylor. The shires of Corio and Bannockburn, having struggled to borrow money and gain a government subsidy, could not sign the contract until February 1899. The work itself went smoothly: the bridge was ready in November with weeks to spare before the contract date. But the shires, in breach of contract, systematically delayed payments in order to reduce their interest charges. Advised throughout by George Moir of Gillott & Moir, Anderson suspended work more than once, but antagonized shire councillors with his proper, though blunt, demands. The testing of the bridge was postponed in order to delay final payment: Monash & Anderson had to call in the agreed arbitrator to set a date. On 16 February 1900 a huge crowd witnessed the successful progress of an 18-ton roller. Though a replacement was built in the 1970s, the bridge still stands.

The original contract had been for £4507, which had been paid. Forgoing several hundred pounds, Monash and Anderson agreed with the supervising engineer on a final sum of £6142, taking into account the new work authorized by him in writing. After two months the partners were horrified to learn that the shires did not propose to make the final payment, on the seemingly absurd ground that they were not responsible for their engineer's written commitment. Assured of their position, Monash & Anderson issued a writ. But the case was not to be heard for fourteen months and all their capital and savings were tied up. It was a terrible month for Monash: Anderson went down with typhoid, his relations with Vic were again at a low ebb, and his cousin Louis Roth was charged with embezzlement.

The Wheeler's Creek bridge, some seven miles from Creswick, had been designed for Kingston shire in 1898 by Anderson, under Gummow's supervision. Monash began the Monier work in September 1899, the job seemed to turn out well and the test in March 1900 was satisfactory. But by August the bridge was in danger of collapse, not from the Monier work but probably from inferior cement in some of the supports. The firm agreed with the shire to carry most of the repair expenses, as it was preferable 'to err on the side of extravagance and future security'. They could have made little profit in the end.

Their building in 1900 of the Tambo River bridge at Bruthen was marred by another hazard—harassment by government inspectors. It was an apparently straightforward job—a large timber bridge of 440 feet—but there were constant rows between the foreman, Christensen, and the inspectors, usually over the quality of the timber. Monash settled some disputes directly in Melbourne with Catani of the Public Works Department. But when Christensen made errors in measurement the spans had to be adjusted under Catani's supervision and the inspectors demanded that Christensen be replaced. Monash eventually won this battle, and had managed also to demonstrate that no better timber could be obtained within a reasonable distance. But he had to go down to Bruthen at least eight times for several days and endure many heated arguments with Catani and the inspectors, while the profit margin slipped away. But the bridge was sound and remained in use for more than seventy years.

After sustained lobbying, the Bendigo city councillors were persuaded in October 1900 to agree to construction of eight small Monier bridges for about £7000, and work began early the following year. Monash & Anderson shared their large purchases of cement between Mitchell's cement works and Taylor of Fyansford, two of their main creditors. A Bendigo journalist caught Monash during the long day's work of turning an arch. Twenty-two men were working, wheeling up the barrows of cement composition and ramming it into place, Monash rapping out his orders. The composition, he explained

> is 'punded' closely and carefully between the iron network, first with those little hand pounders, and then with heavier sizes, and watered lightly. We keep on working continuously, 'punding' and watering, watering and 'punding', so as to form one solid homogeneous mass.

On 14 May 1901 the arch of the King's Bridge, Bendigo, collapsed under testing. The traction engine fell through and mangled an onlooker. Monash immediately called his workmen together to check that no one was buried; he, like many others, had a close escape. 'Things are pretty bad for us', he wrote to Mat, 'but the only thing to do is to face it, and live it down'. The inquest exonerated the contractors. All expert witnesses agreed the bridge had been designed on thoroughly orthodox lines; but it had been extremely skewed and the concentration of stress on one corner of the abutment, together with the unusual severity of the 25-ton test, had caused the collapse which had nothing to do with the Monier work. Kernot believed that the occurrence brought into question the whole orthodox theory of skewed bridges. Monash & Anderson's design for the bridge had been revised by the city engineer; Monash had done most of the supervision. His and Anderson's problem was to avert criticism of the Monier process; inevitably the newfangled method was widely assumed to be responsible, though the *Building, Engineering and Mining Journal* reassured the profession. They agreed to rebuild at their own cost—possibly

£1000—and Gummow, Mitchell and Gibson, all interested parties, became further involved in backing them.

Next October, when another of the larger Bendigo bridges came up for testing, thirty tons were required—an extreme check. The city council was considering cancelling the contracts. Monash was very anxious, but all went well. The rebuilt King's Bridge was tested satisfactorily in January 1902. The usual violent arguments about lagging payments followed.

Monash & Anderson carried out other minor works in 1900–1, advised Saddler on various questions, and filed many patent applications on behalf of inventors. They lobbied and tendered unsuccessfully for a large dam, a lighthouse and many shire bridges. They were now employing on their various contracts, as regularly as they could, a small staff of foremen (including Jack Anderson, Josh's brother) and artisans. Late in 1899 Monash accepted an invitation to join an inquiry into the operation of the Melbourne & Metropolitan Board of Works. The inquiry sat sporadically throughout 1900 and Monash came on much closer terms with his fellow member and old friend, Jack Mackey. The report broadly cleared the M.M.B.W. of vague charges and made some minor suggestions for reform. In 1901, pursuing his attempts to involve Saddler as a financial backer, Monash plotted with him in lobbying the Melbourne and Footscray councils to secure the contract for a new major bridge over the Saltwater River; Saddler lent the necessary deposit, but Monash & Anderson's tender was narrowly defeated. Monash spent Christmas and New Year 1901–2 in western Tasmania, roughing it at 'Hell's Gates', Macquarie Harbour (he had read Marcus Clarke's *His Natural Life*), advising on an arbitration case heard at Strahan.

The pipe factory project took about two years to organize. Monash and Anderson cultivated as best they could the main potential customers: the Public Works Department remained broadly favourable, the Railways thoroughly prejudiced, and the Board of Works open to conviction. There were difficulties in arranging to preserve secrecy of the process and to deal with possible infringement of patent rights, and in settling terms with the Sydney company. Monash made progress in Sydney in January 1901 when he and Gummow together attended the celebrations of the inauguration of the Commonwealth, and negotiations soon reached harmonious agreement. Monash & Anderson had agreed with David Mitchell to form the Monier Pipe Co. Pty Ltd of Victoria, each holding 40 per cent of the shares with the rest distributed among officers of the company. Gummow agreed to sell his rights in Victoria to the process for £500 and, until paid, a royalty. Mitchell in effect was providing the working capital. His employees, Gibson, E. A. Newbigin and A. Lynch, were to be manager, secretary and foreman at the Burnley factory. Early in 1902 a few sales were made to the Public Works Department and to the Prahran municipality, but the Board of Works and the Railways were not yet committing themselves. Late in the year Monash sent Alex Lynch to Gummow's Sydney factory for a week, with immediate benefit. Monash was giving the factory about half his time and concentrating on mastering the technology. In October he showed Mitchell's daughter, Madame Nellie Melba, over the factory.

The business and professional association with Gummow remained highly conscientious. The patents seemed safe enough. Gummow had warned Monash of the danger of spies seeking employment or breaking in to the factory on Sundays or at daybreak. Monash reassured him of his and Gibson's precautions: casual callers were not admitted, only high officials and engineers known personally were shown round, parties of municipal councillors were allowed only a rapid tour. A weak challenge by a syndicate, backed by an English company, was successfully defended in the Patents Office without going to court.

The Fyansford case had been weighing on their affairs. Through the long delay of more than a year, they had tried to persuade the shires to settle. They were totally confident when they learned that the shires were so alarmed by the strength of their documentation that they proposed to make accusations of fraud and manipulation of measurement of quantities. The case was eventually heard in June 1901 before Mr Justice Sir Hartley Williams, who declared in favour of Monash & Anderson for £1900 and costs, and condemned the accusation of fraud as scandalous. Egged on by combative lawyers, the shires determined to appeal to the Full Court, and proposed to levy a special rate and sell property in order to meet the costs. Monash & Anderson seized the shires' office furniture and other belongings and had them auctioned in an attempt to frighten them into settling. Leo Cussen was conducting Monash & Anderson's case; on the other side, however, were the formidable Edward Mitchell and Isaac Isaacs. The appeal before Judges Holroyd, Hodges and à Beckett was heard in February 1902. Judgment was deferred and, scandalously, was delayed for more than six months, the amount at issue, with costs, now being some £4000.

To general amazement, the eventual judgment granted Monash & Anderson only about one-fifth of their claim; although the judges, in effect, declared justice was on their side, the law was not. Cussen was staggered. He had no doubt that the judges had 'overlooked or forgotten' aspects of the case including one key argument; moreover they had reversed the judgment of the primary judge on a question of fact. A few days later he took the extraordinary course of asking the Full Court to justify its decision; they frankly admitted overlooking certain points. The *Herald* published an editorial headed 'Sharp Dealing', condemning the shires. Cussen favoured appealing to the Privy Council, if only in order to negotiate a more favourable settlement; old David Mitchell was indignant and he and Saddler, as outraged contractors, promised financial aid. Anderson wanted to fight it out to the bitter end. Mat Monash, who was no typist, to save money laboriously began to peck out the proceedings for the Lords of Appeal. Cussen remained militant but the solicitors Farlow & Barker, wanting to make sure of their fees, advised against proceeding. Monash eventually decided to give in: it was ridiculous for impoverished litigants to go to the Privy Council—how could the loser meet the costs? Even if they won, most of the gain would be eaten up by expenses. So finally in April 1903 he negotiated a slightly more favourable settlement than the Full Court verdict. A blazing row followed with George Farlow about the limited concessions his firm made on fees. For the rest of his life Monash avoided the Fyansford bridge.

Monash calculated that the firm had lost almost £3000 over the case. They were now at least £1000 in debt to Mitchell, Gummow, Taylor and others. In May 1902 Anderson, who had a large family to support, had taken up a post in Dunedin, New Zealand, in charge of the sewerage works, but the partnership survived for the moment and he returned to Melbourne briefly that year. Monash told Gummow that they were determined 'to face the position and see it through. . . . We calculated that on the basis of our past business proceeds, and leaving the prospects of the pipe factory out of consideration, we should be able to pay off everybody within two years'. And he told his sister Lou it was a matter of choosing 'between an insolvency which could have . . . destroyed my credit for ever, or of facing the music, and building up my shattered fortunes'.

Monash had been inclined privately in the past to be contemptuous of 'failures' who had not been prepared to work hard enough and apply their intelligence, and to boast of his own success in spite of his background of poverty. With much excuse, he sometimes now—though not very often—complained of the 'cursed bad luck which seems to cling to me'. It was agonizing to have to implore his major creditors to stay their hands. For years he was to be humiliated by his indebtedness, suffering scores of demands for payment and solicitors' letters. He was often months behind with his rent and life assurance payments, and years in arrears with his club subscriptions; he had to let his associateship of the Institution of Civil Engineers lapse and he did not join the Victorian Institute of Engineers until 1904; he did not send a cable to his sister Lou on her wedding day and did not always give Mat a birthday present. Worst of all, on a sad day about 1890, expecting he would be able to sell it, he had taken over from the Roth family a heavily mortgaged house in Armadale. The Victorian Permanent Building Society would not allow him to sell it and year in year out persecuted him for weekly payments and threatened legal action.

Though it was not as bad as during the mid-1890s, Monash's health stood up only moderately well to the pressures of these years. In 1898 he had a troublesome skin complaint and in August 1899 a serious attack of influenza; the doctor visited seven times. During the next four winters he was laid low briefly by influenza or heavy colds. His diary has sporadic entries noting 'decided evidence of brain fag' or 'overwork—far from well' or 'mental over-strain, may be merely liver'. In 1899 he began dieting. He did not have a proper summer holiday after New Year 1897 when with Vic he stayed at St Bernard's Hospice, in 'the glorious amphitheatre of the Great Australian Alps' (and where 'J & V Monash 31/12/96' is carved on a survey cairn). He did not return to Buffalo until Christmas 1904. He was taking no regular exercise: he never rode now, except occasionally on parade, and neither he nor Vic ever owned a bicycle. However his professional and military activities from day to day were enough to keep him in reasonable nick, though barely enough to stay the onset of corpulence. He was allowing his moustache to grow more bushy; his hair was receding.

John doted on his daughter Bertha, seemingly an uncomplicated cheery girl. He wrote to Lou when she was about to become a mother:

> You will soon find out what a different aspect life will assume, when you come to realize your newly assumed responsibilities, and the joys, tempered also by troubles, which are their outcome. A child of one's own links one strangely both to the past, and the future—and one both starts life afresh, and lives one's childhood and youth all over again.

He kept and dated all Bertha's childish letters. He had strong views on starting children young: when Bertha was four he was reading her Bible stories and began to teach her writing; she began piano lessons at five; when she was twelve he asked Mat to suggest twenty English classics for her to read. She was sent to Stratherne, then to the Presbyterian Ladies' College, and he envisaged eventually sending her to a Continental finishing-school. In one of her letters during the war Bertha thanked him for her education, especially in music and for helping her to become so broad-minded. Late in life she remembered above all how much time he devoted to her and his inexhaustible patience. 'He enjoyed nothing more than our walks through the bush and simply sitting quietly and listening to the bird calls and watching the birds hopping close to us.' And her birthday parties, always with new games and entertainments, were unforgettable.

John and Vic's marital relations slowly improved over the years.

The quarrelling continued, but periods of serenity lasted longer. John's brief diaries make sad reading, but he used them as a release; they reflect neither the warm affection Vic displayed in her letters nor their obviously satisfactory sex-life. John tended to complain that Vic did not give him 'whole-hearted sympathy, support and loving care'—she did not *believe* in him enough and plagued him with 'petty annoyances'. She retorted that he tended to treat her as a child, did not trust or confide in her, always wanted 'such a frightful lot of discussion about everything'; obviously, also, she did not know how to display interest in his work. John had long abandoned any attempt to educate her in his image and, when involved in a quarrel, had given up arguing, trying rather to jolly her. He was infuriated by Vic's suspicions of his carrying on with other women, which had little if any basis. He was still gravely worried by the threat to her reputation through her casual behaviour. She also resented having to economize and liked to bet. They seem not to have resumed their duet piano-playing. There was only one further major crisis, when she left him for a week in 1901. Many years later, John told Walter Rosenhain, his brother-in-law: 'After some years of severe suffering, in which my own married life was irksome and almost intolerable—nevertheless, gradually, tho' slowly—a change came, and my domestic affairs reached smooth waters'.

Vic's precarious health and highly nervous condition explain much. She had presumably been tubercular and after her illness of early 1898 had lost at least two stone. John delighted in her putting on weight to about eleven stone for in that generation the amply-proportioned Gaiety Girl was the model of pulchritude. She also suffered from bronchitis and asthma. In 1903 they left the Hawthorn house because of her health and moved to a boarding-house in East Melbourne, The Bungalow, on the corner of Gipps and Powlett Streets, which was surprisingly comfortable. John had to store his workshop equipment and some of his papers. Two years later they moved nearby to Varzin, on the corner of Gipps and George Streets where they became close friends of the Cathie family, their landlords. John now walked to work every day, as he had as a schoolboy, through the Fitzroy Gardens. In 1904 Vic took up shooting with the Commonwealth Ladies' Rifle Club and immediately became very proficient, but she does not seem to have pursued the hobby. As an indication of growing domestic harmony John at last began to call his sister-in-law 'Sa' instead of 'Mrs Simonson'.

Despite the urgent need to economize, John and Vic maintained a heavy programme of balls, concerts and theatre-going. He did not much enjoy any longer the social round: 'When men get rotund in bulk, and just a little balder—they wonder how they used to find pleasure in the mazy dance'. But Vic had to have what diversion they could afford, and it remained essential to be seen at Government House, military and club balls. She delighted in dancing in the first set, occasionally, with the commanding General or with Sir John Madden, the lieutenant-governor and chief justice. And there were the Cup and the Show and occasional conversaziones, fêtes, bazaars and picnics by paddle-steamer down Port Phillip Bay.

They went, about fortnightly, to almost everything the theatre offered: visiting operatic companies, all J. C. Williamson performances, and especially Rickards' Tivoli Co. variety shows. As well as the tickets pasted in his Souvenirs books, John kept a comprehensive list of the shows they saw over twenty-five years. He led the testimonial committee for Robert and Florence Brough when they retired in 1902. And they supported to the full the limited musical fare which Melbourne now provided, mainly through Marshall-Hall's concerts and the Liedertafel. Other notable occasions were the opening of the first Commonwealth Parliament in May 1901 and the associated festivities, and Melba's arrival home in 1902—John and Bertha were among the crowd at Spencer Street station. He saw his first film in August 1897 at Rickards' show: 'a complete cinematograph view of the jubilee procession—the Queen, Princess, English and colonial troops all complete—a startling experience'.

John and Mathilde had had periods of falling-out, but by the time they were around thirty had settled into a loyal and intimate association. Mat had an equally sharp mind, but was clumsy and reserved in her social relationships, frequently 'in dread of doing the wrong thing', and frail in her capacity to make a professional career as a teacher. She was also more instinctively radical than her brother. Her health was never strong. She managed to teach languages full-time for short periods at University High School and elsewhere, but usually confined herself to private coaching. John asked her in 1898 exactly how much she and Lou could 'both live on *comfortably*, without any necessity to earn *anything*. It is my great aim to provide an investment for you which will meet all your needs'. She replied that the weekly £2 John gave made all the difference, more money would probably make her no happier, and she would keep teaching without grumbling but it was difficult to earn more; things would be easier if Lou were to marry (as she herself was unlikely to) and it was not fair for him to be so burdened with his sisters. John replied:

> You see Mat, I am painfully conscious of the fact that—while having every good intention I am often so absorbed in affairs, and carried away by the Sturm and Drang of my fight for position and reputation, that I am likely to be blind to the most obvious smaller obligations unfulfilled.

He managed to increase the allowance to his sisters to £3 a week.

Louise, eight years younger than John, had been brought up by Mat since she was twelve. After schooling at P.L.C. she studied for three years to be a teacher of physical education at Miss Elphinstone Dick's Melbourne Ladies' Gymnasium. She also learned typing and shorthand and helped John in the office occasionally, but like Mat she had difficulty in finding regular employment. Lou was far less shy than Mat; witty and outgoing, she made friends easily. Her problems were solved by her engagement to Walter Rosenhain, a brilliant engineering graduate of the University of Melbourne, also of a Jewish German-speaking family. He and Lou had written by every mail since he had left for Cambridge in 1897, and in March 1901 he wrote to John seeking his consent. John had disliked the Rosenhains: the mother had dressed him down when he was twenty-three for alleged discourtesy to her daughters, and he had thought young Walter 'a little prig' whom he delighted in beating at chess. However, he could not but be impressed by his developing work in metallurgy, and warmly approved the marriage: 'I will regard you with all love and sympathy as a friend and a brother, and more than that I cannot say'. Lou sailed alone, well provided for by John, and married Walter late in 1901. John's subsequent warm letters were often superbly well done, even though he might conclude with 'Oh, so much left unsaid that I wanted to say!!' Lou sent the news of her first pregnancy as a cryptogram which took John 'over an hour to unriddle'. He took much interest in her first daughter, a real niece as distinct from numerous nephews and nieces by marriage.

John had worried about Mat being parted from her sister and hoped to send her off briefly with Lou to England, but could not afford it. Indeed, for economy, Mat went to live with Aunt Ulrike Roth. Her health was bad in 1902 and she had an operation; John reported to Lou that she was subsequently much more vigorous and looked younger. She was immensely proud of the success of her matriculation students. He tried unsuccessfully to persuade Vic and Mat to live together again.

John also had to carry the burden, with what is commonly called Christian resignation, of the widowed and impoverished Tante Ulrike and her daughters Mathilde and Sophie. For the three Roth boys, to say the least, 'turned out badly'. Karl failed in his business as a pharmacist in New South Wales, was in bad health, became a door-to-door hawker and was reduced to begging for support from John and even from his mother. In 1900 Louis was tried for embezzlement and sentenced to eighteen months: John stood bail, arranged and paid for his defence, and provided letters of introduction when he made a fresh start in Western Australia. And in 1903 Herman, whom John had for several years employed as a clerk, was discovered misappropriating funds. Not surprisingly, in view of the further damage to the Roth womenfolk and the treachery to himself, he in effect roughly dismissed Herman from the family. John was his aunt's comfort and stay in her misery; their struggle to make ends meet was pitiable, he told Lou; again and again Ulrike wrote: 'However can I thank you for your goodness to me'. He managed to pay the rates and the mortgage interest, and to take the girls occasionally to balls and dances. Louis was making good as a clerk in the West: he gradually repaid the money he owed John, contributed to his mother's expenses, and was proud to regain his cousin's respect.

Albert Behrend, too, eventually became a burden. Although John had long outgrown him and lost close contact, he had been shocked when in 1897 Albert decided to take his large family back to Europe. Albert failed to find any satisfactory job in Vienna and returned after four years. Now in his mid-fifties he struggled, with some success, to maintain his family. John was bound to help his old mentor.

Membership of several clubs suited Monash's convivial nature and desire to be widely known, was good for business, and handy for lunch. He was fairly regular at the Naval and Military, going on to it often after parades, occasionally playing billiards or snooker badly. He was always glad to be well received at the Old Scotch Collegians' Club. He enjoyed the Yorick Club, which he used a great deal; indeed he was elected auditor in 1896 (although late in the year he was still unfinancial); in 1902 he told the treasurer that, though he did not want to resign, he could not afford membership. The year before he had been one of the leading originators of the University (graduates') Club, moving the founding motion, joining the first committee and active in financial planning and equipping the premises; he gave chessmen and a cyclostyle machine to the club. In 1902 he was elected top of the poll for the committee, but next year lost for the post of vice-president. The University Club became his main social centre. Although he had quite often enjoyed a 'jolly conclusion' to the various annual meetings and smoke-nights he regularly attended in the 1890s, and even occasional evenings 'rambling from club to club', in the years of stringency from 1900 such break-outs were rare.

During his thirties, when he was so hard pressed, Monash tended to drop away from old friends. The holiday hikes had to be abandoned and family responsibilities prevailed. George Farlow, his staunch prop as military deputy and legal adviser whom he saw week in and week out, despite passing strains remained his most intimate associate. Poor Will Steele, even before they were thirty, had withdrawn himself. He had been forbidden by her father to marry the girl to whom he was engaged and, later, when he was again thrown over, approached John with suicidal intent, and seemingly was warmly comforted. Several times he wrote to John in his times of deepest trouble: 'Don't write—shall see you some day'. They hardly saw each other again and, having become a total recluse, Will died in 1912. Joe Miller died in 1902: Monash sadly remembered 'my almost constant companion since my school days'. He was out of touch with Arthur Hyde, a *Herald* journalist. Jim Lewis was in Tasmania. The Card girls were scattered in Europe and America; Arthur Card, a staunch admirer of John, appealed to him for advice in 1904 when in desperate trouble. Monash's friendships were diluted widely among military, business and club associates; his annual guests to military balls were a mixed assortment of family, business patrons and others to whom he owed hospitality, and old and new friends. An outstanding social occasion was the bucks' party for Jack Mackey, attended by the lawyers Arthur Robinson, George Maxwell and P. D. Phillips, and the politicians T. R. Ashworth and J. A. Boyd: 'A most delightful evening, among men of my own time—good speeches—good stories—good fellowship. Alas for the many lost opportunities'. At the time, in 1902, he felt he was falling behind.

He had neither time in these years for serious reading nor cash to buy many books. Nevertheless between 1899 and 1904 he subscribed to sets of the *Encyclopaedia Britannica*, the *Masterpiece Art Portfolio*, a *Library of Famous Literature* and a nine-guinea (by instalments) edition of the *Arabian Nights*. Early in 1901 he took up photography—he never became much good at it. Late in 1902 he told Lou: 'Music I never touch. My camera has been stored unused for months past; and my old hobby for carpentering and pottering about the house and garden has not been indulged'. He rarely drew now.

Monash's German associations had fallen away; he gave up going to the German Club after his marriage. In 1899 he gave his collection of more than four hundred German novels to the Turnverein and as a consequence was elected an honorary life member. His few conscientious letters to German relatives were usually in English. He explained to his cousin Bruno: 'While, in a sense, it was my mother tongue, and while I still can perfectly well read and understand the language, I can no longer speak it with fluency and correct idiom, and least of all write in German, except in the plainest and most infantile terms'.

He continued to abhor any formal religious practice. Vic usually attended synagogue on Yom Kippur: John would not. 'Day of Atonement so I stay in office all day out of sight', he entered in his diary in 1893. In 1897, referring to the approaching Day of Atonement, Vic flippantly wrote: 'Of course you will fast?' 'Did you fast last Monday?', John wrote to Vic the following year. 'I did, between lunch and dinner.' They were seat-holders of the Melbourne Hebrew Congregation, where Vic's family had been members, but from about 1896 he did not pay his dues. Eventually in 1905 the seats were forfeited and his name was removed from the list of members, but in 1907 he paid the arrears and re-joined. He subscribed sometimes to the United Jewish Education Fund and was an inactive member of the Jewish Literary Society formed in 1897. He disliked a certain type of Jew and could comment on parties: 'a crowd of Jews—few of them to my taste' or 'a brood of better class Jews'. There is no evidence that in these years he was discriminated against as a Jew, unless his and Vic's omission for several years from the invitation list to the lord mayor's ball (and their usually successful protests) are regarded as relevant.

Monash had broadly the political views to be expected of an Old Scotch Collegian, university graduate and militia officer. He took the conservative *Argus*, not the radical *Age*, and was conventionally free trade and anti-socialist: in 1895 when at Port Melbourne to give a lecture on artillery he found himself 'among a den of ill bred ungrammatical socialists'. He had little sympathy for the poor: 'Physical deprivations are the least of human sufferings by a long sight'. But he could be a good Samaritan: in 1902 an unadorned diary entry was 'On way to Varsity Club committee I find old woman in gutter and take her home'. He had supported the Patterson government's policies of retrenchment and land settlement and was 'dreadfully' disappointed when it was defeated at the 1894 election. He broadly voted the *Argus* ticket for the election of delegates to the Federal Convention in 1897, placing Duncan Gillies first, Sir Frederick Sargood second and Murray-Smith third, supporting the older generation of conservative migrants and opposing Isaacs, Deakin and other Liberal native sons. But in Sydney six months later he called in at the Convention and 'met Deakin and Isaacs who were glad to see me'. He was no ideological warrior, took little interest in politics except at election times, and worked actively only for friends like Mackey and Boyd. During Mackey's first campaign in 1894 Monash spent a night armed, guarding the committee room. He remained a conservative voter but did not join a political party until 1912 when Robert Harper, the politician, signed him up for the Liberals. He seems never in his adult life to have attached himself to any political or intellectual father-figure or leader.

He attended the farewell in January 1900 to Deakin who was off to England to see the Australian constitution through. When Queen Victoria died, like any loyal citizen of standing, he attended the undenominational service in the Exhibition building, the Grand Sacred Concert at the Melbourne Cricket Ground, George Reid's town hall lecture on the Queen's reign, and the proclamation of Edward VII. He was also involved for some years in the Imperial Federation League which locally was in part a properly loyal response to the nationalism of the Australian Natives' Association. Monash joined its council in

1896 and was briefly acting secretary. He was probably acting the part expected of a militia officer rather than serious about the highly theoretical solution of imperial federation to the problem of the growing colonial sense of nationality. He remained on the league's committee for several years, but it was largely inactive. In his time Monash was fairly liberal in his attitudes to the Chinese. On the one hand he witnessed in 1897 the burning-out of the Chinese quarter of Narrandera:

> It was the most pitiable yet the most excruciatingly funny performance I ever witnessed... Nothing could be done to save the buildings, though we pulled down 2 houses in an effort to make a fire break. I will not soon forget the poor Chows with their goods, josses and womenfolk. There were the most ludicrous scenes.

But he was very interested when he met them on trains and greatly admired their mining skills: 'They can do almost anything with water-power as on the Ovens River'.

The University became a compelling interest. From 1894 Monash began attending meetings of its Senate, then a powerful legislative body, composed of all graduates with higher degrees, which elected most of the council. In 1900 he became very active in the reform movement deriving from bitter divisions over the sacking of Professor Marshall-Hall for allegedly licentious tendencies. It was both a conflict of generations and a matter of support for the professoriat which had backed Marshall-Hall. Monash joined the committees of support for the election to council of Dr J. W. Barrett and Leo Cussen, two young native-born professional men. Intense lobbying went on for months before great victories were won. The University's already stringent financial position suffered drastically from the substantial defalcations by its accountant discovered in 1901. In a desperate situation, a Senate deputation waited on the Premier who coldly replied that it was first the duty of graduates to restore the situation; Monash rebuked himself for having made a 'very bad speech'. He was henceforth active in fundraising. In a comprehensive analysis he made of the University's finances, he was especially concerned to protect 'modern technical training' and the lecturers in science and engineering who were in imminent danger of dismissal even though their salaries were only about £200 a year—'little enough in all conscience'. He put four exclamation marks against the item showing only £1400 for exhibitions and scholarships. He also for once displayed a passionately held radical conviction: 'Shall we raise fees, and make higher education only a rich man's ambition, or shall we practically shut down the schools? Unless we get help, one or other result must inevitably follow'. Governmental lack of support for higher education was a scandal.

In June 1903 Monash was approached to lecture for three months in Hydraulic Engineering, and he became a member of the faculty. Bernhard Smith, who was going on leave, lent him his notes, his cap, gown and hood, and advised him on access to sources. Monash lectured to a class of about eight, gave his version of Smith's notes, and found it hard work. Later that year he was appointed honorary co-examiner in Civil Engineering I and II, and for the next few years worked happily with Higgins, T. W. Fowler and, occasionally, Kernot. He took part in setting papers, recognized that the outside examiner found it easier to rank candidates then determine the pass-level, and took the view that no one should be failed unless both examiners agreed; he was stern with candidates who regurgitated lecture notes without attention to relevance.

He continued to devote much of his Sundays to the relaxing routine of ordering his papers. After necessary private correspondence and payment of bills, he would write up his diary, sort in-letters—neatly folding them, noting on the back the author and date of receipt, tying them with string in chronological bundles—paste up his Souvenirs book, and make up his private accounts. His letters were usually written straight out at speed, almost without correction; he hardly ever made drafts. He press-copied nearly all his letters until about 1900 when he began to dictate most of them in the office for typing. His Souvenirs books include programmes of concerts, smoke-nights and complimentary dinners, his 'trip-lists' for camps and walking tours, theatre programmes and tickets, dance programmes, invitations, personal mementoes and such curiosities as 'a hair from the head of Mrs Knorr taken from the knot after execution'. By the mid-1890s his diary had become scrappy and fell off steadily. From 1899 he used small annual diaries (before this he made notes which were written up later), and kept none at all from 1904 to 1913.

He had no time or inclination to loaf. The 'flight from introspection', which Will Steele had predicted, had probably come about. He was both phenomenally busy and buffeted by circumstances with, he felt, little freedom to choose and act. From the late 1890s, to the great disadvantage of this biography, there is little indication, despite the vast surviving correspondence, of his deeper thinking and motivation. The biographer can only leave open the question of the degree of self-scrutiny which continued, and wonder to what extent from now on his life was a development according to a pattern already set, and how much the public face concealed the private.

The contrast remained between the fluent lecturer, speaking without or with only bare notes on military and other subjects of which he was master, and the nervous dining or smoke-night guest, fearful that he might be called on to say a few words or relate an anecdote. He strongly objected to being called on to speak impromptu at a public function, and had a low opinion of his powers as an after-dinner speaker. He was asked beforehand to move the main toast at Mackey's bucks' night and tried to get out of it: 'This is not much in my line'. He was aware that his manner could be ponderous, that he was deficient in wit and coining of epigrams, and perhaps did not tell a story very well. He was averse to be seen not to excel at anything he undertook; he possibly remembered that in his youth his attempts to be the life of the party had not always been appreciated. The extreme sensitivity to criticism remained. He did not have that memory for yarns which is so handy an asset for the traveller in chance company, as he so often was. He still carried a small wallet containing a tiny joke-reminder booklet, various cuttings of common misquotations or of examples of unusual slang, transcriptions of parodies or of verses such as W. T. Goodge's 'Great Australian Adjective'. He of course also carried photographs of his wife and daughter.

Approaching his fortieth birthday Monash had not a great deal on which to congratulate himself. His marriage was hardly very successful; he locked up within himself the hurt of lack of a son and a large family. He was still in debt. His military career seemed to be petering out. His great ambitions had been put aside. He had written to Albert Behrend in 1900:

> I am beginning to feel severely the strain of constant work, and the responsibility for keeping up two households. . . . One can only retrench down to a certain point if one does not wish to throw aside the position and standing one has to maintain. In other words, in younger days I strove and drove to make a position, and now the position drives me. . . . If I had only had Capital to start with I might have done well but there is fearful competition in contracting work as well as in everything else, and the nett result is a bare comfortable livelihood for those for whom I am responsible, and for myself a steady continuous grind and mental strain week in, week out.

And in 1902 he told Lou: 'The adverse experiences of recent years have made me something of a pessimist. [I] find myself with fast waning energy and enthusiasm, and with very little accomplished'. The recollections, thirty years on, of a journalist ring true:

> The Monash of that day is well recalled, a black-moustached, pale-faced Jew, forlorn, anxious, and dejected of mien, . . . with an old black bowler shoved down hard on the back of his head. [However] to those who were associated with him in his work as an engineer, John Monash appeared as a towering intellect, a giant mind that in a few hours of ferocious concentration, smoking furiously and incessantly the while, would produce a solution to a problem that had baffled his contemporaries for months.

He had that 'faculty of complete absorption in his subject' which promised great things.

1902 and 1903 were slack years for public works and in the building trade. Small Monier bridges at Kyneton, Ballarat, Mansfield and the Upper Coliban were useful but not very rewarding tasks. Monash advised the Dunlop Pneumatic Tyre Co. on alterations to machinery and plant. Patents applications provided a few guineas, but he disliked the work:

> I have come to the conclusion that patents—the best of them—are not worth the paper they are written on to the patentee. I have myself, as agent, put through nearly 100 patents, and in no single instance has the patentee ever realised a sixpence—though some of the inventions were clever, good, useful and valuable.... The whole question of patents is a rotten swindle, and no one knows it better than the patent agent of experience, who in a sense is as great a fraud as the fortune-teller—or any other business that fattens on the foibles of humanity.

Preliminary work for an electric tramway in Essendon was wasted, for the project collapsed. He applied unsuccessfully through Deakin for appointment as a commissioner to investigate possible sites for the national capital.

He came increasingly in demand as a technical adviser or expert in court cases or arbitrations. Sir Isaac Isaacs recalled:

> He came to the Court with a perfect grasp of the points at issue, a perfect understanding of the rights and wrongs of the dispute, a perfect power of expressing with lucidity the opinions he held, and of pointing out whatever fallacies lay in contrary opinions. More than once, he was invited, instead of waiting to answer questions, to state in his own clear and connected way, how the matter stood from his professional standpoint. I believe his view was almost always accepted, for its accuracy and its sincerity.

Phil Jacobs and George Moir, the lawyers, considered him the best witness they ever heard. According to Sir Robert Menzies, Cussen said that 'any solicitor who failed to retain John Monash as an expert on any patent matter was prima facie guilty of negligence'. Monash's best-known case was perhaps *Kannaluik v. City of Hawthorn* of 1903; after going to the Privy Council it became a leading case on the liabilities of municipalities for drainage and the flooding of ratepayers' properties. Monash appeared for Kannaluik with Cussen against Isaacs. Monash's view that expenditure of a mere £150 would have settled the situation weighed with the judge who was caustic about the council's obstructiveness. His judgment was confirmed by the Full Court and sweepingly by the Privy Council to which the Hawthorn Council had foolishly, on Isaacs's advice, taken it. There Monash's notebook, which he had consulted in the witness box and which Isaacs had demanded be produced as an exhibit, was telling evidence. By 1905 Monash was advising or appearing at least once a month in the courts and often negotiating settlements. It was, however, a dangerous professional pursuit. Professor Orme Masson, for one, was worried by expert witnesses being employed to argue in the courts and not to present the whole truth.

One day in December 1902 Isaacs gave Monash a lift into the city, and they improved their slight acquaintanceship. The brilliant but unpopular barrister and former cabinet minister, ten years Monash's senior, was Melbourne's most distinguished Jew. Monash had little reason to feel friendly towards his famous elder after the Fyansford case, which was still unsettled. They clashed again in the City of Hawthorn case and Monash was no doubt amused by its outcome. In January 1904 Isaacs asked him to Mount Macedon to advise on a dispute with a neighbour over their titles and water rights. Four days later Monash was invited again for two nights. He pasted in his Souvenirs book notes of their talk about the law, world politics, the United States and politicians, and reminders of anecdotes Isaacs told him. Their religious convictions were not dissimilar, but they were to diverge over Zionism. Twenty-six years later they were both to be on the short list for the governor-generalship.

Monash was hoping to work himself out of his difficulties by means of another major bridge contract—the Koondrook-Barham link over the Murray, near Kerang on a major stock route. The project was to be managed by the New South Wales Department of Public Works whose able inspector, J. B. A. Reed, had been supervising an almost identical Murray bridge at Cobram. In 1902 Monash & Anderson, backed by Saddler, tendered for a largely timber 270-foot structure with an iron and steel central lift-section, set on a concrete base supported by piles, and won the tender easily. Monash was blithely hoping to clear about 15 per cent. Saddler, temporarily short of funds, had almost entirely to withdraw his support; Monash quickly gained new financial backing from the contractor, A. G. Shaw.

The gamble was on the weather. In autumn 1903 the rains came early, just before the first piles could be finished, and the river remained up for the rest of the year; work was held up for eight months, with large standing charges. Early in 1904 serious technical problems occurred: 'I am battling with a leaking coffer dam 32′ x 9′ in 14′ of water—a beastly job'. Then they struck 'a blow hole right in the centre of our large coffer', and 'heartbreaking' costs of concreting. A diver and an expert on coffer dams had to be employed. Monash had to

Mathilde, 1908

Walter Rosenhain

Lou Rosenhain

With wife and daughter, 1908

apply for six months extension. Then Reed and Christensen fell out and had to be mollified, and employees threatened militant action in response to Christensen's 'black-guarding' of them. Two carpenters got poisoned hands, another went on the spree. The two governments had not completed financial arrangements so their payments were delayed—a 'monstrous shame'. 'Finish, finish!' Monash told Christensen. At last the bridge was opened in October and after more than a dozen Commonwealth and State politicians had orated interminably, Major Monash modestly responded to the toast to the contractors. Once again he had made little from the contract. The one great gain—despite everything, despite his dependence on him—was a warm friendship with Reed.

The need to gain Gummow's approval for every move with regard to reinforced concrete and to consult Baltzer, his expert, was becoming increasingly irksome. Early in 1903 Monash asked them to send him the Continental literature or a list of references; they supplied him willingly. Monash's knowledge of German remained important: he began to correspond with German authorities, subscribed to the monthly *Beton und Eisen*, and built up a collection of technical German literature. Gummow had been carrying out experiments with Professor Warren; Monash determined to follow his example, partly as demonstration to his professional colleagues. Kernot agreed to supervise tests held in December 1904 which Monash reported next May to the Victorian Institute of Engineers: 'Tests of Reinforced Concrete Beams'. He did not claim that they were any more than elementary experiments to 'verify the physical constant presented by foreign writers as a basis for safe practice in the design of beams, or, if necessary, to establish fresh constants for local materials and conditions'. He later reported further tests of June 1906 on 'soundness of practice as regards design of T-beams'. In 1905 Monash was still tactfully seeking technical advice and approval from Gummow and assuring him that he would not break away from proper conservative practices: 'By and bye I trust the need for detailed criticism will disappear, as I come to more fully understand your methods and working principles'. He became so bold as to challenge a formula of the Austrian expert Emperger himself, by writing to *Beton und Eisen*, and was convinced that Emperger's reply was evasive.

The propaganda battle for adoption of the revolutionary reinforced concrete against sceptical professional opinion and vested industrial interests had constantly to be waged. Monash missed no opportunity of lobbying officers of instrumentalities and local government about the advantages of Monier in cost and durability for bridges, culverts, drains, water tanks and dams as against cast or wrought iron, brickwork, stoneware or ordinary concrete. Engineers visiting Sydney were steered to Gummow for demonstration of Monier work in New South

Wales. In June 1904 Monash gave a carefully prepared talk, with many lantern-slides, to the Royal Victorian Institute of Architects.

Monash looked to the Monier Pipe Co. to restore his solvency. By early 1903 the company had won several small contracts for pipes of various sizes from the Board of Works, Department of Public Works and local councils. A larger contract from the Board followed and others could be expected, as the commissioners were determined to resist price-raising by the pottery ring which had supplied the vitrified stoneware previously almost exclusively used. Aware that unreinforced concrete pipes were commonly used in Germany, Monash imported some moulds and presses with the intention of creating a 'valuable adjunct to our concrete-iron pipe manufacture'. But he was beaten to the punch by Taylor of the Fyansford Cement Works, who had recently visited Germany and won a large contract with the Board early in 1904. By the close of 1903 the company had paid for its plant and Gummow's rights to the pipe-making process. Monash anxiously looked forward to rich dividends, but for the moment all profits had to be ploughed back. Too quick a development would not be in his interests; he could not meet any call for capital, and Mitchell could easily have insisted on a reduction of his 40 per cent interest. The formal directors' meetings with Mitchell and Gibson were tense. The first small distribution was made late in 1904. Profits for the two and a half years to June 1905 were £3392. Monash looked forward also to interstate expansion: Gummow was generous in reaching an understanding whereby Monash would have sole patent rights in South Australia and possibly Western Australia, a matter Monash had first raised in July 1903. His explorations in Adelaide that year came to nothing.

Monash's main utilization of reinforced concrete came to be in general building construction, not bridge-building or pipes. Early in 1905 he completed a reinforced concrete flat roof for a ballroom at Raveloe, Domain Road, South Yarra, for the especial use of Mabel Emmerton (Dame Mabel Brookes), and a reinforced concrete porch and portico for Chastleton, Toorak. 'After many disappointments' in mid-1904 he had won an order for a reinforced concrete interior for a seven-storey block of offices and apartments in Bank Place; following a prolonged contest with the city's Building Surveyor's Department during which the fireproof qualities of reinforced concrete were well publicized, it was built in 1905–6. A large store at Kensington for the Australian Mortgage, Land & Finance Co. was built over the same period. Monash consulted Gummow and Baltzer on the details for both.

It had become clear that Monash & Anderson's use of their licence for building general Monier work and the developing operations of the pipe factory required formal clarification. The pending large-construction works demanded quick action, so early in 1905 a new company, The Reinforced Concrete & Monier Pipe Construction Co. Pty Ltd, was formed. Gibson became managing director and Monash superintending engineer, with a commission of about 5 per cent on all works as well as his share of profits; commission still had to be paid to Gummow for constructional work. By agreement the Monash & Anderson partnership was dissolved. Monash considered that Anderson had no remaining rights, a view which depends largely on the nature of their informal understanding. But Monash held the view that Anderson and not he had been primarily responsible for the Fyansford disaster, and he resented having to work off the firm's debts without his partner's help. He gave Anderson a discharge of his liability, calculated at £2372, and from April 1905 Monash & Anderson ceased to exist. It was rough justice, in view of Monash having worked the partnership out of debt, that Anderson was to have no share in the future profits from Monier.

Anderson's departure in 1902 had greatly increased the strain of carrying on the business. John wrote to his sister Lou Rosenhain in November: 'Latterly it is all I can do to keep pace with the really important current work. I find too that I can work neither as fast, nor so long as I used to, and require more regular and longer sleep'. He had had poor luck too with his employees. His cousin Herman's peculations and neglect cost him more than £100 and—far worse—gravely damaged his reputation as a patent attorney, for payments had not been made to register patents; one irate client imposed a stern settlement. The able and loyal foreman Christensen often quarrelled with the supervisors of contracts; moreover Monash had to observe a court order to garnishee his wages for the benefit of his deserted wife and children. Jack Anderson, whom he employed as foreman for smaller jobs, had to be dispensed with when he broke out twice on blistering benders.

Monash had another scare in 1905. His ramshackle financial edifice tottered when the London Bank presented one of his promissory notes and it was dishonoured. The Bank of Australasia was alarmed and insisted on reduction of his overdraft which, backed by Mitchell and Saddler, it had previously been happy to renew. He was now so close to solvency that he managed to ride a blow which a year earlier might have knocked him out. Several minor construction jobs helped to make the year profitable; these works were undertaken by the Reinforced Concrete Co., no longer by him as a private engineer.

The struggle to survive had toughened him. He laid down basic business principles to his cousins badly in need of advice: analyse the flow of business from week to week to detect fluctuations; do not allow customers to run up big accounts; gain confidence of creditors by punctiliously meeting engagements and thus improving one's credit rating; stay fully insured; build up a reserve fund in a separate account and don't touch it. Take nothing for granted in business relations:

> nip in the bud any transactions which have in them the slightest opportunity for "getting at" you. My experience is that the dishonest man never carries his hall mark in view, and that the man who protests most, and is most obviously honest is the most to be feared. The moral I draw is to assume every man a rogue till he is proved honest—a sorry maxim for humanity, but, I believe, a necessary one.

Extortionists had to be abruptly put down: a debt collector was informed that 'to charge a full 10% commission, for a simple preliminary service . . . would make it impossible for us to put any future business in your hands'. Woe betide a business associate, like the Bendigo city engineer, whom he caught in the wrong: this was not the first time he had 'had to suffer insinuations . . . and the irritation caused thereby is very irksome. . . . you should now withdraw the imputation that I promised a thing which I failed to perform',—but a few weeks later he was making peace by offering to show him over the pipe factory.

Contracting was a rough game. Monash was not above carefully instructing his foreman on ways and means of getting the most favourable agreement on measurement of quantities of material—'every *inch* tells', and when the evidence was recorded it should be covered over—but this was a game played by both sides, reasonable (or unreasonable) profits depended on interpretation of the fine print and obscurities of contracts, and on successful bullying of opponents. Professional men like Monash and Anderson were not nearly ruthless enough, or heartless sweaters enough, to be successful contractors. Nonetheless Monash was now well practised in the manipulation of men, both in that assertive browbeating and that friendly blandishment by which most arguments are won. 'Reasonable men can't be expected to see eye to eye on all points so personal feeling need not arise', was one of his standard approaches. His articulateness, ability to maintain arguments and to make the best of poor cases established ascendancy—or that feeling of confused inadequacy which made opponents give way. If not, he would exercise all his power of charm, appeal to friendship—which as often as not was entirely genuine—and add a judicious element of self-pity which may not have been so effective. The pattern of an astounding work-load combined with almost entire self-control was well established.

The Militia Garrison Artillery (Coastal) was organized in two brigades—the Metropolitan, and the Western District based on

Geelong. The Metropolitan Brigade, under the command of Lieut-Colonel Hall, consisted of three batteries—the North Melbourne, Williamstown and Harbor Trust. Including some permanent troops, the coastal artillery in its seven forts comprised just under one thousand men. The demoralizing aspect to the senior officers was the quick turnover of volunteer militiamen; they seemed always to be training novices and battling to improve mediocre standards.

Monash had taken over the North Melbourne Battery in 1896 with great ease. According to Farlow,

> His orders were models of conciseness and at the same time completeness. Nothing appeared to be overlooked.... He never buzzed about the tents of his men to see if they were properly provided for but what he did do was to think out all things and detail officers to work out the details and report to him as to their satisfactory development.
>
> He supported his officers by asking each one as if casually to let him know later on how that particular officer was arranging his part of the scheme. I have often heard such a conference in which Monash would quite approve the officer's scheme and then make what appeared to be a casual suggestion. The officer was probably unaware that the smooth working came about 1/10 from him and 9/10 from the casual suggestion.

Monash sometimes recorded the burden of routine administration:

> I have a board on helmets, an enquiry on an injured man, half yearly stock takings, inspection of quarters, some lengthy reports to prepare for Hall . . ., a new candidate for commission to overhaul and pilot through, selection of NCOs to fill vacancies, recruiting of about 20 new men, a new manning detail to prepare, to draw up rules for all competitions and my practical exam and above all the preparation of all hands for the coming camp.

Recruitment of officers and their performance was a continuing concern. In 1897 one was arrested for forgery: Monash had to suspend him but, perplexed by the case, helped him indirectly; he was acquitted, but a year later his military conduct was so unsatisfactory that he had to be sacked. Another officer suicided. Monash took up Lieutenant Dave Bevan, son of the famous Congregational minister, helped him with his military exams and became a close friend; Bevan was later a regular member of the annual trip to Buffalo. Competition for commissions made for awkward dilemmas. One unsuccessful aspirant was introduced by Lieut-Colonel Tom Price by means of a pushful mother; in the end Monash was summoned to the General to justify himself. In another case political pressure was applied: the Premier himself came to the assistance of a sergeant in Monash's battery whom he had passed over for a commission. A report was required: Monash stressed the tradition of the battery's officers being university graduates almost to a man—this applicant was too old, a bank clerk, not the senior or most efficient sergeant, and had 'none of the smartness, initiative, elegance of manner or personality which I aim at in my officers'.

Relations between the militiamen and the British permanent officers were always uneasy. Colonel J. M. Templeton, the senior militia officer, was a firm proponent of militia prestige. In 1895, during the Commandant's absence, he had marched into the Barracks and insisted on taking command, to the delight of the militia officers. Monash, whom Templeton had to lunch to let him into his confidence 'regarding his campaign against the General', believed his assertion of the militia's equality of status had far-reaching consequences. The British gunners did tend automatically to assume, as Lord Roberts was to say about the British Territorial Artillery, that civilians could never master the mysteries of the gunner's art and would be a danger to the country. Monash frequently chafed at the incompetence of the permanent instructors which led to bad shooting by his men. Worse, he suspected them of intrigue: he warned Miller about the 1895 Easter Camp that they would 'play a little game, and do all they can to show how helpless the militia are'. Later that year the *Argus* reported 'ceaseless picking to pieces' of the Garrison Artillery by the permanent men. Monash protested to Hall in 1897:

> I don't object to any amount of legitimate supervision and criticism of my work, but [Sergeant-Major] Howie's presence on battery parades is becoming more and more suggestive of a superior sort of espionage. If the position becomes much more aggravated, his attendance far from being of any real assistance to me in the instruction of the men, will become an intolerable nuisance.

However, his relations with successive battery sergeant-majors—permanent men who in effect were administrative officers—were close and cordial. At some stage, probably about 1896–97, Monash used, or attempted to use, the press to ventilate his frustration. An undated memorandum in his Papers marked 'Criticism for the press' runs:

> In 1894 Dean-Pitt made a final attempt to work all the forts as one fortress. It was an egregious failure, clumsily planned, without previous instructions, and the few hours during which the work lasted were spent in abusive messages to the various fort commanders, for alleged errors which were due not to incompetency of the Militia, but to neglect to keep the forts and armaments in a proper condition for carrying out such a scheme as fortress fighting. ... None of the present V.A. [Victorian Artillery] officers have the

necessary largeness of intellect, skill of administration, or general scientific knowledge to grapple with the larger and critical questions.

He was probably broadly correct in his judgement.

Monash's absences in Queensland and Western Australia for most of 1897–99 almost ended his military career. His fellow chess-player, wise observer of the oddity of human beings and immediate superior, Lieut-Colonel Hall, saw him through. In 1897 Monash gained permission to leave Victoria from time to time so as not to be technically absent without leave. When first away in Queensland he kept closely in touch with Farlow about battery affairs, but as his absence lengthened he grew concerned. Hall reassured him: 'You know my advice, never to sink private business for the military'. He managed to survive the Queensland episode: 'They are not only very lenient with me, but I have contrived to be on the spot on all important occasions, and as for the rest Farlow looks after things very well'. But during his long absence in Western Australia he was very pessimistic: his last leave application had been granted only after a strong minute from Hall. 'That General is a beast', Monash commented. He wrote to Vic:

> I will have to choose sooner or later, between my military work and my business career. . . . one of the chief attractions which the military has for me is the social opportunities which it has given, and will in the future give you. . . . please be quite frank. [It is] not an easy thing to put away a hobby of 15 years. . . . [I] will simply have to swallow the bitter pill. . . . You can't imagine how it grieves me—but there is simply nothing for it.

It was better to resign than be shoved out. Yet he managed to survive his nine-months absence, rushing back from the West for the 1899 Easter Camp and making such a mighty personal demonstration there that he was convinced he was safe. The only trouble was that he omitted to apply for leave for May and June. The genial Hall reported:

> H.Q. have been disagreeable about the matter in a quiet way. I have to mat you. So if Monday at my office will suit you Why Dill Dill come and be Killed. I do not know what you expect Justice or Mercy!

It was a precarious survival, which owed much to Farlow's loyalty.

His command had been enlarged: in 1898 the Turner government, 'stirred by wars and rumours of wars', increased the defence vote. Monash's battery was enlarged to 186 all ranks and divided into two companies, each with a captain and permanent sergeant-major. 'Won't it be a fine command!' he rejoiced to Vic. The battery's shooting at the 1899 camp was magnificent. 'Both my companies were classed as per British regular service regulations as "First-class shooting Companies".' No. 2 set a record for Australasia, scoring 12 hits out of 16 shots at a target being towed at 12 knots at 2000 yards: 'a cruiser would have had a very poor show against us'. Colonel Bingham said that the performance was rarely beaten in the British regular service. Monash then had to take charge of the funeral of a sergeant: a 400-strong parade marched through the city. 'Oh Lord how tired and weary—footsore and aches all over. To wear a stiff tunic for 5 hours ain't no joke.'

Like the great majority of senior militia officers, Monash did not volunteer for the South African War. Coastal artillerymen were irrelevant, thirty-five-year-olds with family responsibilities were hardly expected to go, it would have crippled his shaky business, and he received no invitation from a senior officer raising a unit. Late in life he said that it was his 'misfortune not to be chosen for service' in South Africa. But he may have seen little virtue in Australian participation. In reply to Bevan seeking advice on whether he should volunteer, he wrote:

> This is certainly not an occasion where patriotism demands the making of any personal sacrifices. It simply amounts to this, that to anyone who aspires to military experience in the field, whose private circumstances permit, and who allows himself to be moved by sentiment, an opportunity is now offered.

For once his non-British background might have markedly affected his attitude. Monash may have revised his earlier attitude to the war as the successive contingents departed and popular and political opinion in Victoria developed to brush aside doubts. He did his duty in organizing proper farewells and welcomes home for the volunteers.

Until about 1905 Monash's business concerns were so pressing that his military activities became very much a sideline. 'I have had to almost entirely neglect military matters', he wrote to Lou in June 1903, 'and have only been able to retain my position of command by the loyal assistance of my subordinate officers, and the goodwill of my seniors'. Farlow, under Hall's benevolent eye, kept efficiency high. But in July 1903, at a time when he could not attend a parade for two months, Monash noted: 'Battery going to the Devil'. Major-General Hutton, in command of the Australian Military Forces from early 1902, was making things hum, in uniting the colonial militias and improving standards of organization, training and equipment. The artillery was reconstructed and from July 1903 Monash's battery became No. 3 Victorian Company, Australian Garrison Artillery. He lectured only rarely now. The routine continued. The annual ordeal of the Commandant's inspection usually ended happily with Monash entertaining his officers at the Naval and Military Club. In 1903, however, his comment after Major-General Gordon's inspection was 'rotten show, rotten speech'. The Easter camps at Queenscliff were usually exciting and enjoyable. He occasionally umpired at field-firing exercises. In 1902 he was appointed to revive the United Service Institution, but the task proved to be too difficult. He attended the frequent welcome and farewell dinners to senior officers and to a visiting Japanese naval squadron in 1903. He conscientiously organized benefit funds for the widows of deceased members of the battery. In 1904 he slashingly refuted the allegation of a ship's captain that he had almost been hit by a shell from practice-firing at Fort Gellibrand and vigorously cross-examined him at the inquiry. In 1905—both because his own authority to deal with the matter was challenged by Barracks bureaucrats and from a sense of outraged justice—he resisted an attempt to dismiss without trial some raw recruits to the battery for an offence against the civil power, for alleged minor fraud. That year at the May camp, astonishingly, every member of the battery was present. In 1906 he arranged a successful reunion dinner for members of the 'University Corps'. He sympathetically supported claims by N.C.O.s, instructors and qualified specialists for increased pay. And the normal military social life continued—brigade and regimental balls where Vic sometimes was senior lady, and the North Melbourne Battery's own dances where John and Vic were hosts to two hundred or more guests and led the opening set of lancers with the senior officer attending and his lady.

In March 1905 Monash qualified for the long-service medal and in March the following year for the Volunteers' Decoration. He had applied for the latter in 1904, twenty years after enlistment, but the brief break in his early service, to his chagrin, delayed the award. Hall's promotion to another post became imminent in 1906; Monash hoped for the succession but the other company commanders, Majors Hanby and Tope, were both senior to him. In August–September he was given leave to prepare for his exams for lieut-colonel and attended classes under the permanent officers Major Julius Bruche, who was to become the closest of friends, and Captain Cox-Taylor. Monash passed the first part with 93 per cent, 90 per cent and 60 per cent—top of five candidates in two subjects and second in the other. Nevertheless Hanby was given command of the Garrison Artillery. Immediately after commanding a three-day camp at Queenscliff of four artillery companies, Monash sat the second part of the exam in January 1907, but had to write indignantly in May and June to protest against results being withheld:

> Having, for very many years, devoted myself loyally and diligently to the service of the military forces, at the sacrifice of very considerable business interests, and having in the interests of the Service, and this Regiment, without demur, suffered, in connection with the reorganisation of the Forces, substantial derogation of status, I feel

entitled to have received greater consideration, and I do not think I would be doing justice to myself to submit without protest to a failure of such consideration calculated to further prejudice my status and seniority, and to put a strain upon my sense of loyalty, which cannot but impair the efficient performance of my duties.

Such letters probably did him more harm than good. Eventually he was notified in October that he had passed. But he seemed to be in a dead end. He was over forty now, his service experience in the Garrison Artillery had been highly specialized, and advancement within it was unlikely. There seems to be no evidence of prejudice holding him back; it was perhaps rather a matter of neglect from above in not providing scope for his talent. He began to refer to himself as a has-been and to indicate that his days as a soldier were numbered.

7

Pillar of Society
1906–1914

AT LAST, from 1906 to 1908, Monash broke through to prosperity, good fortune and some measure of fame. 'For three years past', he wrote to Lou in May 1906, 'I have had as rough a passage as falls to the lot of many. Although it is not the story that is told to the world'.

> By dint of hard work and the assistance of influential friends [I] have placed my business in a condition which is now safe from the possibility of ruin. For 2 years it was touch and go, and any undue pressure of an impatient creditor would have smashed the thing to splinters.

He had paid his debts off at the rate of £1000 a year. A minor Australia-wide boom was developing and the Reinforced Concrete Co. was steadily expanding; in the first two months of 1908 it booked more work than in the whole of any previous year. Monash was 'working harder, and with less relaxation than ever' but affluence was in sight.

> Much to my surprise, I approach the age of 43 with a feeling of immense juvenility, and less feeling than ever of any exhaustion of energy. I am afraid that in some subtle way, our poor mother's early death gave me the idea that one became old at 40. . . . my experience is that the calming down of youthful exuberance brings with it a much stronger, much more real and solid sense of vigorous living, and a calmness of spirit which makes life ever so much more enjoyable. [I] can enjoy the fruits of a first rank position fairly won—doubtless by much hard work, but then work which I have keenly enjoyed.

The long trials he had undergone had strengthened him.

From 1906 the company undertook as many as a dozen different jobs at a time—country bridges, tanks, culverts, siphons, the University dissecting-room, additions to the Government Printing Office, country post offices, suburban banks, a five-storey warehouse off Flinders Street, then several silos, construction of abattoirs and a £26 000 contract for the Preston reservoir. The running start of patent protection enabled domination of reinforced concrete construction for some years yet. Monash's staff expanded to four assistant engineers, three clerks and an outside agent; his assistants—Lindsay, Laing, Upton, Sexton, and P. T. Fairway who stayed with the firm, were all University of Melbourne graduates. He could now dictate nearly all his immense business and private correspondence in the office—though he often apologized for sending a typed letter. From 1905 he abandoned private consulting engineering work and almost all law court work, although he took on odd jobs for those to whom he was under obligations like Gummow and Shaw. As an engineer in private practice, he had won a position at least comparable with any Melbourne rival: the aged T. B. Muntz, H. V. Champion or A. G. M. Michell. In 1906, having paid his arrears, he rejoined the Institution of Civil Engineers (London) as an associate and was immediately promoted to full membership.

The South Australian Reinforced Concrete Co. Ltd. was a great success. Monash had established it in June 1906 with E. H. Bakewell as managing director; they and Mitchell, Gibson and the pastoralist C. H. Angas were the five shareholders, contributing initially £200 each. As consulting engineer Monash earned 2½ per cent gross on all business. In 1907 the company was engaged on a railway bridge at Port Victor, and next year on a wharf at Port Adelaide and commercial buildings.

In a sense Monash owed everything to David Mitchell and his manager, John Gibson. They would have said that they knew their man. Mitchell's linking of his Richmond cement factory with the neighbouring reinforced concrete pipe factory and its later development was the major interest of his old age. When Mitchell died in 1916 Monash, 'deeply grieved', could 'never forget how he befriended me when I needed help so badly'. Monash's relationship with his contemporary John Gibson, the industrial chemist, was the key to his business success. Gibson, a tall, strikingly handsome Scot, had joined Mitchell in 1890; his younger brother Robert eventually became the Commonwealth Bank chairman who dictated financial policy in the depression of the early 1930s. John Gibson wrote formally in 1907: 'It has been a long and trying fight but the honorable manner in which you have discharged the liabilities of your late firm has earned for you the esteem and respect of those who are acquainted with the circumstances of the case'. Early in 1909 Monash wrote to him: 'Please favour me by accepting enclosed cheque of £250, as an attempt to express in a tangible form my sense of the many obligations I am under to you, in the assistance you have so generously given in re-building my shattered fortunes'. Their association was to become much closer still. Similarly, Monash's right-hand man, the company's foreman, Alex Lynch, was devoted to him.

Prejudice against the use of reinforced concrete was gradually breaking down. The contemporary rebuilding after the earthquake of San Francisco, largely in concrete, was a handy advertisement. But the building trade remained hostile: contractors and brickworks faced loss of business and craftsmen a threat to use of their skills. Gradually the trade recognized that reinforced concrete had come to stay, and turned towards educating itself in the techniques and breaking down the Reinforced Concrete Co.'s dominant position. Monash kept up the propaganda battle. In 1907 and 1908 he read papers on the use of reinforced concrete to the Victorian Institute of Engineers, the Royal Victorian Institute of Architects and the Society of Chemical Industry of Victoria. He conducted parties of doubting architects round works in progress. Rosenhain supplied him with details of reinforced concrete works in England for, Monash explained, 'nothing talks so strongly with the profession and State Departments in this country as to be able to quote *English* practice. America is regarded as unreliable and speculative, while anything savouring of being "Made in Germany" is unwelcome as a precedent'.

The two chief battles in the war with the building trade were over the Preston reservoir contract and the Melbourne Public Library's domed reading room. The Board of Works advertised the Preston contract, alternatively for concrete or reinforced concrete, but obviously intended to adopt the latter and thus in effect employ the Reinforced Concrete Co. Individual contractors and the Master Builders' Association complained loud and long: this was no competitive tender but a private arrangement. A strong minority of the Board friendly to the Master Builders bitterly criticized the decision. In May 1908 *Building* came out with a sensational attack: 'A GRAVE DANGER. How the Australian Building Profession is Threatened with a Great Rival'. The Reinforced Concrete Co.

> embraces in its methods the cleverness and ingenuity of the smartest of American combines. . . .
> Here is a private company designing and carrying out buildings and other constructions; . . . usurping the positions of architects and builders; eliminating that element of check that is the sole protection of the client.

And the journal revealed that the company had recently held an extraordinary meeting in order to increase its capital of £300 in 2000 three-shilling shares to £4050 in 27 000 shares, in order to provide better evidence that it could guarantee against failure of large contracts. The row continued at the completion of the contract. E. G. Ritchie, the Board of Works engineer for water supply, was hostile to reinforced concrete and worried about minor defects in the work, some of which had to be repaired. Photographs of cracks were shown round to discredit Monash. The Board eventually took the company to arbitration over full payment. Monash fought it out over seven days of hearing early in 1910; the award was almost entirely in favour of the firm. The Board was very unhappy—some members were shrill—and sought legal advice before paying up.

Monash did not win all his battles against business opponents. The defeat over the Public Library hurt him deeply. The chief librarian, his friend E. La T. Armstrong, persuaded his trustees to build a domed reading room like those of the British Museum and the Library of Congress, and N. G. Peebles of Bates, Peebles & Smart drew preliminary plans. Monash was drawn in to work on structural details with Peebles who became a good friend and joined the annual trip to Buffalo. There was a presumption that the company would do the job: it submitted a tender for the reinforced concrete work in May 1908 and provided evidence to justify the price. A deputation from the Master Builders' Association to the Library trustees requested rewriting of the specification to allow for open tendering. To Monash's fury, without hearing him, the trustees gave way; in May 1909 the company lost the tender to Swanson brothers, and Trussed Concrete Steel Co. of England redesigned what briefly became the largest reinforced concrete dome in the world. (Nine years later Gibson and Fairway had the pleasure of reporting on the structural defects.) Peebles replied to what he described as a pessimistic and somewhat petulant letter from Monash by prescribing a holiday:

> The idea of a man of your vast intellect and attainments, unimpeachable honor and social standing being in any way affected or disturbed by fancied humiliations and the puerile calumnies of a few of the members of the Master Builders' Association is simply preposterous, as is also your anxiety with regard to the future of your business affairs.

Their friendship survived intact. By 1909 the Master Builders and several contractors had mounted a massive attack on the Reinforced Concrete Co. through the journal *Building*. They were demanding normal competition for reinforced concrete work, raising sniping doubts about the safety of the company's work, asserting that Monash's claim to patents was a bluff and challenging him to go to law. He chose not to, no doubt partly because the patents were about to expire. After 1910 reinforced concrete construction, in effect, was open to all.

His imminent enrichment had led Monash to dismiss an opportunity which a few years earlier or later he might have seriously considered. Late in 1907 Mackey, now a member of Sir Thomas Bent's government, asked Monash if he was willing to be considered for appointment as chief commissioner of Victoria Police.

Monash's annual income, almost entirely from the companies, climbed from approximately £2000 in 1907 to about £7000 in 1909. He began to keep carefully tabulated statements of conservatively estimated assets and liabilities, calculated every few weeks. At the end of 1908 he estimated he was worth £3146, two years later £14 097, and at the close of 1913 over £30 000 (now equivalent to more than $1 million). He invested solely, apart from some debentures, in suburban houses of which he bought more than a score. He still had a weakness, however, for a 'spec': £350 invested in 1909 in a syndicate promoted by the Gibsons to produce tar-chlorinated briquetted fuel was wasted. He began to donate occasional guineas to the Austin Hospital, the Salvation Army and Jewish good causes.

Almost the first of John's responses to financial security was to look after Mat. The episode displays him as the pivot of his family, caring for his sisters verging on neuroticism. In May 1906 he wrote to Lou Rosenhain about Mat:

> this dread . . . of a penurious old age, is very much fostered by the poverty-stricken, not to say squalid surroundings in which she lives [with the Roths]. . . . She is slow at making new acquaintances, and of new friends she has none at all. With the departure from these shores of one after another of her youthful companions, . . . a pathetic loneliness has come into her life. . . .
> The result of all this is a regrettable but gradual narrowing of her character, . . . and a withdrawal into herself.

He had determined to send her on a long trip to Europe; Lou enthusiastically agreed to accommodate her in England and in February 1907 Mat set off. In 1906 Walter Rosenhain, at the age of thirty, had become superintendent of the department of metallurgy and metallurgical chemistry at the National Physical Laboratory.

Mat's first responses to Lou and Walter were alarming: 'I have not yet felt my old feelings of love and protection towards her returning. . . . Why did I come!' With awful candour she described Lou's excitability and nervousness, their skittishness, their self-absorption and lack of friends. But she told John she was 'sometimes racked with envy at their happiness in each other and their children'. Lou found Mat 'moody and morbid' but kind and unselfish in looking after the children and freeing her and Walter. Mat made long trips to the Continent and she and Lou began to get on much better and to discuss whether she might stay permanently. John squashed this quickly, with the promise that Mat could return to Europe every two or three years—but she stayed for over eighteen months.

Mat reported that Lou's warped views on her past treatment in the family made her blood run cold. John replied:

> I am really sorry that you are allowing Lou's vagaries to disturb your peace of mind. [If her remarks] amount to nothing more than a recrudescence of the delusion she used to suffer from that she was badly treated by you and me, financially and otherwise, and a failure to recognise how much she owes to you in particular, well, why not let it go at that! Personally, I bear her no grudge. I have the satisfaction of knowing that during all the time I was solely responsible for her material welfare I did the best I could for her. ... I think you would regret very much afterwards, if you allowed those occasional collisions to embitter you even temporarily against them. The best way is to take such matters lightly and airily, because really compared with the other evils of life such ills are but skin deep.... You are now surely philosopher enough to know that so far as emotional troubles are concerned—they are almost wholly of our own making.... If people allow themselves to really suffer from such things as jealousy, wounded pride or ingratitude they have themselves to blame more than those who cause such feelings.

Mat had had enough: 'Walter says that the whole of our family require to learn to bear criticism—well I think I have learnt it pretty well now'. She ached to be among people who weren't candid and critical; Australian heartiness, good comradeship and informality would console her. When she did return home, Lou was very upset.

Mat had also told of Walter's joking references to the commercial application of John's talents; she believed Walter was a little envious of his making money. John was stung into replying:

> Frankly, I have always suspected that undercurrent of jealousy. ... The position simply amounts to this that Gummow in Sydney, and I in Victoria have simply and boldly been the pioneers of a new era in Engineering. We are the precursors of a new development in the Engineering profession, viz: the Civil Engineer of the future will be first and foremost the commercial directing head of Engineering enterprise and industry—the scientific side of him will be merely an adjunct or subordinate function to the main purpose of his being a personal Director of Engineering enterprise. Science has advanced so rapidly and so deeply permeates all industry, that the day of the mere commercial managers, and the mere unscientific building contractors are numbered. The great Engineers of the future will not sit in offices and draw plans for others to work to,—they will post themselves at the head of the actual industrial operations. The result here is very plain, and only follows in the lines worked out by the great engineers of the day in Europe and America, such as Hennebique (Paris), Adolf Wayss (Vienna), Dr Emperger [Vienna], Ransome (U.S.A.), Mouchel (England) etc. etc. Every one of these truly great engineers is the actual controlling head of a *Contracting Company*. What is the result here—why that Gummow and I are unquestionably at the very top of the *profession*, and far from having

lost caste, are looked *up* to as leaders of scientific thought. . . . since you left my standing and influence and power have grown enormously.

It must be said that his claims were broadly true.

During 1907 Monash had soldiered on rather glumly, having been beaten for the command of the Garrison Artillery by his senior, Hanby. Early in December, however, his old schoolfellow Colonel J. W. McCay, already a former Commonwealth minister for defence and now in command of the newly created Australian Intelligence Corps, offered him command of its Victorian section. Monash was excited by the prospect, knowing that his military future must lie in some such new departure; as usual he consulted Colonel Hall. Monash played it hard to McCay. He was, 'with one exception, the senior combatant major in Victoria qualified for promotion'; no fewer than thirty-two lieut-colonels had been junior to him when majors. Eleven days later, after assurances from McCay, he accepted the offer.

McCay saw him through; Monash was promoted lieut-colonel, dating from 7 March 1908. The new rank took some time to gain daily recognition: he had been known so long and so widely as 'Major Monash'. As always he punctiliously did the right things. He had already written to Hanby, asking formal permission to accept his new post, and to his sergeant-major, Hollingworth, to thank him warmly and to attribute to him much of the success of his work. Hollingworth replied:

there are so many things I would like to say. . . . I commenced Soldiering in January 1883 . . . and during the whole of that period I have never had a better Officer and a Gentleman to deal with. Nor have I had to deal with a better Artillery Officer either Permanent or Militia.

Monash thanked Hall: 'the best years of my life have been spent under your guidance and encouragement'. He wrote again to Hanby to make sure that Farlow succeeded him. His North Melbourne officers and men farewelled him at a smoke-night: 'a splendid send off . . . and I have a beautiful memorial photo of my old officers and non-coms'. And when the Garrison Artillery officers gave him a dinner, Monash 'spoke feelingly of his 21 years service with the corps'. After all, it was in the coast artillery that he learned to know and understand Australian volunteer soldiers, how to command them and guard their welfare with fatherly authority.

The prime mover for the formation of the Intelligence Corps had been Colonel W. T. Bridges who was appointed Chief of Intelligence in 1905. He and Lieut-Colonel H. G. Chauvel and Major C. B. B. White who were to be outstandingly brilliant professional soldiers during the 1914–18 war, were 'Hutton men', chafing under the control of Major-General Hoad. Bridges was aiming to create a General Staff and saw the Corps as its precursor. The determination of the 1907 Colonial Conference in London to promote an Imperial General Staff had been the ultimate stimulus. The Corps' main duties were to collect information about the topography and military resources of Australia and its dependencies and of foreign, especially Pacific, countries, and to prepare strategic and tactical maps and plans. The almost entire absence of military mapping was a grave embarrassment. In 1909 after the Australian section of the Imperial General Staff was created, the Corps became intimately linked with the General Staff, with no clear distinction made between intelligence and other staff functions.

One of the Corps' first exercises was to test the efficiency of Australia's warning system against an unexpected invasion or raid. Its first school of instruction, at which McCay and Bridges did most of the lecturing, was held for a week in Melbourne in January 1909; the first annual camp followed in April. The Corps established a monthly intelligence diary, prepared military handbooks, and gathered data on transport and supply problems. Monash was in his element in supervising classifying, indexing and filing in a district military library. Checking the activities of suspect foreigners, in Victoria at least, took little attention. Mapping was the main work. After asking shire engineers to spend part of their leisure-time preparing maps, Monash soon pressed on McCay the hopelessness of part-time militiamen making much impact on the immense task; a small group of permanent force cartographers was consequently established. The Corps ran into some adverse criticism and mockery because of press reports that it was 'the brains of the Army'. McCay's abrasiveness, tendency to argue about orders like the lawyer he was, and his capacity to irritate the Military Board, did not help. But he got on well with Monash and gave him his head.

Even before Lord Kitchener's whirlwind visit in December 1909–February 1910, Australia's ramshackle military forces were showing signs of new vigour. British reforms, following the Boer War blundering, were filtering through. At a meeting of officers in September 1907 the United Service Institution of Victoria was re-formed on Monash's motion; monthly lectures began again and war games were conducted, but by 1909 the U.S.I. had again lapsed into inactivity. In October that year a conference of officers, including Monash, considered Major Bruche's secret defence and mobilization scheme. Monash went on to attend the seventh course of instruction in staff duties held by Colonel Hubert Foster, director of military science at the University of Sydney; he joined another course there in 1911. In 1909 also, he served on the founding committee of the Aerial League of Australia, promoted with defence interests primarily in mind, and secured inside information from Rosenhain on current developments of aviation in England. It is unlikely that any other Australian soldier was writing to Berlin booksellers requesting catalogues and notice of new works on military science, topography, transport and supply, the history of warfare, the making of military maps and textbooks on strategy and tactics.

Australia went 'Kitchener mad' when the veteran arrived. Vic wrote to John: he 'looks just lovely . . . how some woman has not stolen drugged and married him, I don't know'. The Deakin government, broadly supported by the Labor Opposition, astutely calculated that the compulsory training of youths, which had already been passed into law, would after Kitchener's advocacy gain wide public support. Kitchener judged his report nicely. Australia was prepared to respond both to the growing German threat to the security of the Empire and to the new local fear of emergent Japan. He produced a scheme whereby the old militia would be abolished and a new citizen army created, based on the compulsory training in cadet forces of boys who would proceed to brief annual service for seven years. They would be trained by the graduates of a national military college at Duntroon, Federal Capital Territory. The scheme came into operation in 1911.

Monash was temporarily attached to the Victorian commandant's staff to assist preparations for Kitchener's inspection of manoeuvres. The Intelligence Corps worked over the Christmas holidays and produced a map of the Seymour–Avenel area in three weeks. Monash was determined to show it—almost the only proper military map in Australia—to the great man, and he very likely did. He won pleasant publicity from the task.

With Bruche's help, he was easing the Corps into general staff work—suggesting tactical exercises, umpiring, and having his officers attached as brigade staff officers for manoeuvres. He joined three senior permanent officers in planning and reporting on the daily exercises for the Kitchener camp. At the exercise at the 1909 Easter camp, isolated in a tent for four hours, he so ably planned both the attack and defence of Langwarrin by Colonels Hall and R. E. Williams that neither could prevail. He also regularly drafted the section of the State commandant's annual report on camp-training, criticizing the tactical handling of the infantry brigades.

Monash was making some good friends among the permanent officers. The best was Julius Bruche, also born in Melbourne of German (though not Jewish) parents, seven years younger, fellow Scotch Collegian, and a lawyer. In supporting him in 1907 for the chief commissionership of police (as he was to do three more times unsuccessfully), Monash described him as 'the one real live and up to date man among our Victorian permanent officers'. Bruche and Monash were to correspond on a quite unusual, for him, level of intimacy though, despite frequent hints, he never brought about any improvement in Bruche's appalling handwriting. 'Do you remember', Bruche would write, 'the day of the Kitchener Camp when you and I . . . rode out of camp and we talked. . . . I often think of it. . . . The very best of good wishes to you always John Monash and don't you forget it please'. Colonel John Stanley was now Victorian commandant. Monash had previously been ill at ease with him, but they now came to be on close gossipy terms. Colonel J. W. Parnell, a former University colleague who succeeded Stanley and then became commandant of Duntroon in 1914, was another friend.

Over the Cup weekends of 1906–8 Monash took parties of six or eight friends up Mt Buffalo; they usually camped for two nights. George Farlow was always first choice. Others were W. E. L. Wears, of the engineers Wormald & Wears, with whom Monash lunched frequently and who acted as an agent for his company; the architects Bates, Peebles and Wright; John Gibson; and Bevan and other militia officers. Monash issued comical mobilization orders, though his planning was of course meticulous. Hearty badinage prevailed: they went in for amateur theatricals and in 'The Buffalo Buster', their facetious typed journal, Monash was known as 'Thunder Roars' because of his mighty snore. In 1908 they explored the underground creek and caverns, gaining access by rope. It was a 'long time since I got so much fun and real enjoyment out of £4.9.2', Wears once wrote. 'Thanks very largely to your wonderful powers of organization and consummate tact', said Peebles, the trip 'was the most glorious and memorable I have ever experienced'. In summer, John, Vic and Bert holidayed more than once at fashionable Lorne.

But he did not get enough exercise and at the close of 1908 wrote to Eugen Sandow, the London physical culturist, requesting 'a course of exercise or treatment' which would reduce his weight and stimulate digestion. He gave the following particulars:

Occupation: Civil Engineer; chiefly sedentary; about 1/5th of time occupied in travelling, but involving only light exertion and little exercise.
Health: With the exception of a tendency to bilious or dyspeptic headaches (not severe), health is excellent; never had a serious illness; quickly shake off a cold.
Habits: very temperate, but not a total abstainer. Use tea at every meal; smoke rather heavily (pipe). Diet moderate (below the average) and very plain. Have a preference for starchy and fattening foods, because I find that vegetable diets such as fruits, raw and

cooked, give digestive trouble. Cold shower every day, all the year. Take from 5 to 10 minutes stretching and light dumbbell exercises every morning after bath, before breakfast. Fairly supple. Sleep well.

Measurements: Height 5' 10" [in boots].
    Weight 15 st. 5 lbs in clothes, varying very little; have been the same for 3 years past within a few pounds. Neck 16½". Chest empty 40½" expanded 43", waist normal 43" contracted 41".

Sandow's course of exercises arrived but, though he may have followed them, Monash did not return the report requested. He now had to wear spectacles for reading and close work.

In August 1909 Melbourne *Punch* jabbed him unkindly:

The Intelligent Corps . . . was well represented. Its colonel and his adjutant . . . were present. Have you ever seen them? They look like two comic characters out of a pantomime or a music hall. The colonel is inclined to be large. His waist measure cannot be a day under sixty. He is not tall either, and his girth makes him look short. When he wears the candle-extinguisher helmet of the Intelligent Corps he is strongly reminiscent of a large mushroom.

One measure of Monash's hard struggle over the years is that he did not go overseas until he was forty-four. He had longed to travel—for pleasure, to taste the sources of the European culture of which he was part and to visit the great centres of industry. Stabilization of his business and the growth of his income made a trip in 1910 feasible; moreover Bertha would be leaving school and could accompany her parents. He began to plan for March–November 1910, writing to relatives for advice, consulting with Cook's. It would be a 'preliminary canter', in the expectation of further trips every two or three years. He sought reasonable comfort, not luxury—first class by sea, second class by train on the Continent. Eventually he settled the itinerary: twelve weeks on the Continent, eight in Britain and a fortnight in the United States.

Methodical preparations proceeded. He gave Gibson power of attorney and left instructions for Fairway about jobs in hand; Mat was to control collection of his rents. McCay's election to the Senate was pending: Monash left code-words for telegraphing if he were offered permanent or temporary command of the Intelligence Corps, but McCay was not elected for Labor had a sweeping victory. He armed himself with letters of introduction. He itemized every garment in their seventeen pieces of baggage, charted the disposition of luggage keys, and listed everything worn or carried down to pipe-cleaners, toothpicks and handkerchief. While away, he detailed every item of expenditure including tips, stamps, newspapers and cups of coffee, analysed weekly expenditure, made a comparative survey of hotel bills, and eventually listed 468 souvenir items, including a toothpick from

Maxim's, Paris, and pieces of the wall of Edinburgh Castle, with his laundry lists filed as an appendix.

Monash was at first uneasy with lethargic ship-life and his 'indisposition to settle down to anything'. He read a lot, especially George Meredith's novels. He was warming to the company, people were very amiable: 'I am not sorry after all that we chose an Australian ship'. A close friendship was developing with the Meyers—Felix, a gynaecologist, and Mary, a painter; they all drove round Naples together.

After leaving the *Otranto* they set off for three or four days in each of Rome, Florence, Venice and Paris. John Monash was the model tourist, fitting in nearly all the major historic sites and galleries, closely observing transport systems, photographing, and enthusing over almost everything. He was delighted that his French and German stood up well. A fortnight followed in London—in mourning for King Edward VII; they watched the funeral from the Horse Guards Parade, the Victorian agent-general having supplied the tickets. Monash was already uneasy at inadequate news from home of the business. June and July were spent on the Continent, beginning with a few more days in Paris. John took Vic to the Folies Bergère and the Moulin Rouge and went off alone one night with a concierge to several night-spots:

> I must confess, I was horribly bored with it all—it was so palpably 'got up' for the benefit of strangers. No man of the world could possibly be in any way allured or taken in by that kind of show. . . . It was exactly like the stage beauty, who (as the experienced one knows) is all wig, and paint and powder. That is just what midnight Paris is. . . . It is all a hollow sham—for there is *no* real genuine *Paris* night life.

Three days in Brussels followed, then a long swing round Germany into Austria, from Cologne to Berlin, Dresden, Breslau, Vienna and Munich, paying his respects to his father's surviving brothers and sister—none of his mother's were alive—and a dozen or two cousins. At Stettin he visited the graves of his Manasse ancestors. Having left Breslau at 3 a.m., he spent a day in Krotoschin, seeing the houses his grandparents had lived in and bringing back leaves from their graves; he was shown his grandfather's hand-press and founts of type. Four weeks in the Alps followed, mostly round Lucerne, Zermatt and Chamonix; he walked and climbed often, but his chief delight was in the variety of mountain railways. Then followed six weeks in Britain, including a week on the Isle of Wight with the Rosenhains and a week in Scotland, more than a dozen visits to the theatre, and the usual traveller's irritation at a delayed bank draft, before sailing for America. He left Europe, convinced that war with Germany was imminent.

The greatest gain from the trip was the development of affection for 'Walterlou' Rosenhain. Before they left home Lou wrote to John that after nine years apart she was worried he would still treat her as a child. Walter was 'most charming', John told Mat in May, but patronizing; Lou was all he could wish, but for a little hastiness with the children:

> At first they both started to be critical of us—I think they took my (reputed) dignity for pompousness—but I [accepted] their views about every mortal thing—so gradually this air of criticism wore off.

Mona was very clever and understood all his best jokes. Nancy was 'the dearest, sweetest little girl'. They began to hit it off famously: John delighted in their domestic life, found his and Walter's scientific and general attitudes were in harmony, and was enthralled by his laboratory. Months later John told Mat: 'The critical bantering—lightly chaffing—demeanour entirely disappeared, and an excellent, more intimate, affectionate, frank and sympathetic attitude took its place. Lou began to realise that I was a real sort of brother'. When John, Vic and Bert left, Lou wrote emotionally to say how marvellous it all had been: she would always be glad to have John nearby to play with her babies; couldn't she be proud of them, hadn't she redeemed herself for her reputation as a rather irresponsible child? But six weeks later she wrote to complain that they had cut themselves off. John hit back with devastating candour: they had sent eighteen communications before reaching home. It was 'an illustration of what I preached so much to you, that one must learn sooner or later in life that one *must not* write on paper the things one may freely speak aloud'. She and Mat should 'cut it out'. Walter explained that she was pregnant and disturbed; John replied, 'Peccavi'. Walter had written when they left:

> You and I have each found a new and close friend where we *might* only have found an acquaintance whom circumstances had made into a relative! I haven't often come to a close understanding with any man such as that which has sprung up between us.

John replied:

> Your few warm-hearted lines of farewell touched me very deeply. . . . The fact is, I felt our parting a great deal more than an onlooker might suppose. . . . The coming to an end of a happy episode has always been a very tragic experience for me. Perhaps I am rather too emotional for a hardheaded businessman. At any rate, our many happy hours together were a linking up of ties which neither distance nor lapse of time are likely to weaken; and I am sure the consciousness of this will be for both of us a happy mental resting point when other troubles and disappointments of life beset us.

From now on he would confide in Walter as in no one else.

They had the time of their lives in the United States: a few days in New York, partly with Alice and Arthur Card, then via Niagara Falls to Chicago where a stream of distant relatives greeted them, then five emotion-charged days in Minneapolis with Leo and his branch of the family. They journeyed on through Banff and the Rockies to Vancouver, and took ship for home via Honolulu, Suva and Brisbane. John won the chess tournament and Vic the Ladies' Deck Quoits. John summed up the essence of his travel experiences for a colleague:

> The great secret of doing things in comfort and making the most of your time is to plan out beforehand exactly what you want to do, and then stick to your programme. A lot of valuable time is lost in indecision and change of plans. In a party, a leader should be chosen, and his orders obeyed implicitly by the whole party—particularly as regards lagging behind, and straggling.

On his return to Melbourne, Monash found 'everything shrunken and dingy'; Australia seemed 'a little provincial place'. His trip had been 'a liberal education' which had adjusted his 'sense of proportion with a vengeance'.

> America was a most fascinating, stimulating and wonderful experience. New York puts London and Berlin in the shade altogether. The country, the people, the cities, the industry, the organization and achievements . . . are far in advance of anything we have read or understood.

He told Walter:

> I say that a visit to America would astonish and stimulate you to an extent that you have no present idea of. You can discard the accepted impression about America and her people as confidently as you can discard the average Englishman's impression of the Germans. It is not so much the achievements of the people—great as they are—that made such an impression on me; but the altogether new and vigorous, and arresting attitude of mind towards life in all its activities.

Its cities were 'monuments of human achievement'; skyscrapers were not freakish, they were perfectly suited to their environment. (The new cities of reinforced concrete, to a man in his position, were the realization of a vision.) The recently built Pennsylvania station was 'the last word'; in Chicago it was a 'superb sight to see the automobiles by regiments moving in opposite directions along the streets'. There were few trade secrets as businessmen were so imbued with the necessity of progress. 'The brain power behind all the American undertakings' would ensure their dominance. So an acute boy from the bush, well placed to be objective, recognized a world shift in economic power.

To a man who was fascinated by innovations and gadgetry America provided constant joy. One could telephone anywhere in the country from a hotel room. Express lifts, domestic heating by radiators, the toaster on the breakfast table, moving advertising signs, were examples of the revolution produced by electricity. He delighted in the Dewey library cataloguing system; the availability of iced water; the simultaneous attentions of barber, manicurist and shoe-polisher; ready-mixed mustard; American idiom and slang.

His other main theme in press interviews and talks on his trip to the institutes of architects and engineers was modern use of electric power, especially in transport. Apart from the marvels of Swiss railways, the underground systems of London, New York, Paris and Berlin were swift and clean and had 'almost completely banished the effete steam system' and its associated smoke nuisance. His 'scornful comments on our backwardness', especially the need to electrify railways, reflected the deeply felt disappointment of an engineer of a colony which twenty years before had been in the van of technological progress.

Monash had arrived home acutely anxious about his business and private finances. His whole future depended on his property investments, he told Mat; he had to assess urgently how much independent income he could rely on. The company's business had fallen off in his absence; they had lost their monopoly as the patents were expiring, and rival specialist firms and builders were competing successfully; the opposition of the Master Builders to use of reinforced concrete was stronger than ever; and the pipe business was being damaged by Taylor producing more cheaply. John wrote to Walter at New Year:

> The outlook is very unsatisfactory. A monopolistic business breeds jealousies, enemies and competitors; . . . I fear that in order to maintain a steady increase in financial prosperity, I shall be compelled to throw into my business affairs a still greater amount of personal industry and energy than ever. I suppose, at bedrock, this is no serious hardship. I shall continue to enjoy all the excitement in the ardour of the chase and the battle. And I feel particularly energetic. The holiday has done me an immense amount of good, mentally and physically. My work is a great deal more a pleasure to me than formerly, I tire less easily and don't feel so much tendency to worry over petty annoyances as before.

Before he went overseas Monash and Gibson had been planning to buy out the aged and ailing David Mitchell and to take Lynch into a new proprietary company. If indeed they approached Mitchell at all, he must have refused. In November, immediately he returned, Monash and Gibson were conferring, and by the New Year had got as far as drafting a letter to the Bank of Australasia, announcing their purchase and seeking overdraft arrangements. Strangely, on the face of it, on 13 March 1911 Monash formally asked his fellow-directors to discuss his analysis of the situation:

> the prospects of profitable business become daily more meagre, and the effort to secure work is increasingly difficult. . . . I personally view the future with much alarm. . . . the administrative expenses are so heavy that if we have to face a steady shrinkage in volume of business, the present assets will gradually be absorbed. [Possibly the time is] ripe to stop operations and realise the assets while they remain at an unimpaired value.

He had not yet renewed his agreement as engineer to the company and would prefer not to continue unless 'the business could be reorganized on much restricted and more concentrated lines, and on much narrower profit margins'. He also raised the possibility of retiring from the company and competing with it himself. Mitchell and Gibson asked him to submit specific proposals. On 2 April he suggested three options, to any of which he was prepared to agree: first, that he take over the company entirely; second, that he take it over but for the pipe factory (for which he would continue as engineer); third, that they pay him out and leave him free to compete.

These letters were specious: in collusion with Gibson, Monash was trying to frighten Mitchell out. The company was not in trouble, for on 27 March Monash wrote to Rosenhain:

> I was chiefly anxious about the maintenance of a sufficient volume of business, . . . and I was rather afraid of certain competition which was threatening. However, I have had a run of particularly good luck, and one good contract after another has fallen to my net at a satisfactory figure. . . . Of course, this is a time of very great prosperity in Australia, and I am at the period of life of most efficient work and greatest influence, so I feel it is "now or never" with my affairs. If in the next 2 or 3 years I can manage to put by another £10,000 or so, it will mean, not only absolute security for all of us . . ., but also a considerable measure of luxury in the form of ability to travel whenever we feel inclined. . . . I am following the policy of making hay while the sun shines.

The proposals came to nothing; Mitchell would not budge and very likely saw through the bluff. But in December Monash persuaded Mitchell to allow Gibson an equal shareholding; he may have threatened a bust-up if Mitchell did not agree. Monash and Mitchell had held 40 per cent each, Gibson 19 per cent and Newbigin 1 per cent. Now Monash, Mitchell and Gibson were to hold 97 per cent in equal shares, and Lynch and Fairway were each given 1 per cent. The episode is curious: Monash and Gibson may have been worried about what provision Mitchell had made for his interest in his will, but their tactics seem clumsy. Gibson's relations with Mitchell are one of several unknown factors.

1911 was a very profitable year indeed. In July John wrote to Lou:

> The position is now so satisfactory that hardly anything but some altogether unforeseen disaster affecting the community and business as a whole, can have much influence upon my position of independence.... Strangely enough, I find it difficult to realize yet. As long as I can remember, the lives of our parents, as my own, have been more or less of a struggle to barely carry on in very modest comfort; and the feeling that one has reached the point of being quite independent, financially, of the success or failure of one's business undertakings, is one that it takes a long time to get reconciled to.
>
> Naturally, this state of affairs is reacting very beneficially upon my health, plenty of leisure for physical exercise, and sleep; no overwork, no brainfag; no serious worries; with the result that I feel extremely well, and full of energy.
>
> Our easier circumstances enable us to have a very good time indeed; and there is nothing that is worth while doing and seeing that we do not participate in. Of course, this is life for Vic, and she too is enjoying excellent health, and has improved greatly in appearance since her travels. With increased good looks and weight, and the better dressing which she can now afford, she is really as much admired as she is admirable.

The formal relationship with Gummow and nearly all patent protection were now ended.

The company's works included extensions to the Town Hall and the Melbourne Hospital, the State Savings Bank head office in Elizabeth Street and the Centre Way Arcade; bridges over the Maribyrnong River and at Flemington and Janevale; extension and widening of the Glenferrie Road bridge and a stormwater drain in Hawthorn, local government works at Prahran; a government cool store, and a bank at Launceston; pipes for the Trans-continental railway. The building of Collins House in 1911 and a subsequent extension brought Monash into close touch with the Baillieus, Robinsons and other captains of Melbourne finance. Early in 1912 he moved his office from 49 Elizabeth Street into the 'palatial modern office building' with 'a suite of nine rooms'. McCay was just across the passage—they were 'Jack' and 'Jim' to each other. That year, also, Monash helped George Higgins to build a reinforced concrete house at Beaumaris, probably the first in Victoria. He also cheerfully met unexpected growth in demand for pipes by the Board of Works and local authorities. In mid-1913 there was a slump in business but it had picked up by the close of the year. The South Australian company, which had also established a pipe factory, was doing well. Monash was sometimes defeated, however: he was angry that the Railways could get away with building a new Port Melbourne pier with timber.

It was Gibson's turn to go overseas and for most of 1912 Monash had to handle the managerial as well as the engineering side of the business. It meant immense work for him, he told Mat; the commercial side was not much to his taste. He managed to settle a wage claim at the pipe factory by judicious compromise. In 1913 the Metropolitan Gas Company employed him to give evidence before Mr Justice Higgins in the Arbitration Court that nine shillings a day was too high for coke-workers, whose tasks he considered to be much less arduous than those of most labourers. He hardly ever now appeared in the courts and he had abandoned patent work. He told Walter he had 'a rooted objection to the policy of spreading myself too thin over too many matters, and have constantly to resist the temptations which are daily offered'. But he gave evidence at the bar of the Legislative Council on proposed public works, and advised Rear-Admiral Creswell on concrete oil-storage tanks in Sydney. He was interested enough in competing in the designing of Canberra to write for particulars. After Walter Burley Griffin had won, he commented: 'I hope that the Government will embark upon the scheme of laying out a Capital worthy of the nation to be built as the nation develops; but there are many narrow minded people in the country who scoff at the scheme and attempt to ridicule it'.

A well-to-do man like Monash, now in the inner swim of the city's business, was continually being sought to join syndicates and offered enticing investments. He was by no means immune from a flutter. He joined the board of a company manufacturing automatic postage-stamp machines (in the hope that the Post Office would buy them), sponsored an anti-shock spring for car doors, invested in Tasmanian greenstone mining, was on the lookout for 'novelties' to import, and in 1914 began serious discussion with C. P. Monash of Chicago on introducing to Australia vacuum heating of buildings. His most adventurous enterprise was to become chairman of directors of Luna Park Ltd; £30 000 was spent on construction, including the all-important scenic railway, before the opening in December 1912. Its promoter had been the American, J. D. Williams, of cinema fame; but within a few weeks Monash was threatening resignation unless business was conducted on proper lines, and was instructing the secretary on proper arrangement of an agenda. Moreover, shareholders were hot on Williams's trail; Monash seems to have taken over with another American, Herman Phillips, and held off a counter-attack. He and Vic and

Bert made a 'weekly pilgrimage' to view his new toy. Late in 1913 good dividends began to be paid. He also joined the board of Wiltshires who, among other things, made Worcester sauce.

Monash had full biographical treatment in *Punch's* 'People We Know' column on 9 March 1911. The author singled out some of the qualities clear to others when Monash later became famous, but was slightly malicious, especially in the emphasis given to 'racial' origins. He had 'the Teutonic habit of study, of logical thought, of ordered method', 'the phlegmatic German capacity for work', was 'system personified'. He had the Jewish knowledge of men, an 'uncanny insight into character'; and his 'superb quickness at figures and accurate mental calculations, which astound those who deal with him', resulted from his Jewish heritage. He was 'a hero of concrete'; few engineers in the world surpassed him 'in daring, in ability, in skill', but he was curiously unrecognized as an engineer in Victoria. He was possibly the finest citizen officer in the Commonwealth: 'There is no doubt that if the day comes when Australia has to take down the rifle in real earnest, it is upon men such as Monash that she will have to depend'. But he was 'neither romantic in appearance or in style', was 'stout and ruddy, with the typical Hebrew mouth and the typical Hebrew eye'. Monash privately agreed that the article was 'anything but a satisfactory advertisement'.

Vic had long been looking forward to having a motor car. In July 1911 John ordered from E. Schultze, motor manufacturer (body builder), a four-cylinder, 15-20 horsepower Berliet, seating eight (two in the tonneau), for £575. It was to have eighteen coats of paint in vertical black and dark green stripes, dark green upholstery, brass lamps and the monogram JM in gilt on the tonneau door. The car was delivered late in September and a chauffeur engaged. Vic delighted in it, especially when going to the races: 'I do hope I have not overdone it but it is such a temptation', she told John. He attempted to learn to drive but, having little talent, gave up—everything he did had to be done well—but Bertha soon won her licence. He became a pillar of the Automobile Club and the Good Roads Association.

Although they were comfortable in their East Melbourne lodgings with the Cathies, and Vic was cautious about taking up housekeeping again and possibly worsening her health by moving, they had decided to seek a house of their own; John considered that 'our inability to entertain, if continued, would be a serious bar to our social advancement'. In May 1912 he advertised in the *Age* and *Argus* to rent or lease a modern house, preferably in Toorak. But when they were offered the late F. W. Prell's property in St Georges Road, Toorak, they bought it for £4750. It was 100 feet by 380, just under an acre, the very pick of the suburbs at absolutely the highest point in Toorak, John wrote exultantly to Mat, exaggerating as so often. The house was 'not much to look at externally being designed by an architect who had scanty aesthetic ideas, so that it has a rather square, cold and inartistic appearance from the front', but internally it was perfectly planned with four 18-foot by 24-foot rooms, a handy basement, and gas and electric lighting and heating. The surrounds were in poor order: the front fence was an eyesore, there was no drive, the garden was a wilderness, while the back was overrun with thistles and weeds and sheds would have to be pulled down. But it was 'capable of being turned into a really sumptuous home'.

Monash called in his friend Ernest Wright to redecorate and bought much new furniture, including a brown-leather-topped walnut office table with a double lock for the top centre drawer. When, however, they unpacked their stored furniture and other belongings, they found nearly all the crockery and picture-glass were broken, and John's framed diplomas, some books and some letters had been consumed by rats or damaged beyond repair. Their plan of decoration proceeded: they hoped to 'avoid the mistake of overcrowding either walls or floors'. They moved in, with a cook and a maid, within six weeks of purchase and Bert gave a successful dance a fortnight later. They retained the house's name, Iona.

The front garden was reconstructed and planted, including two hundred standard roses, by the end of the year: much concrete went into a drive, gateways and Monier slabs here and there. The back was still a chaos of mud, gravel and brickbats, but was being reshaped as a vegetable garden, a tennis court (asphalt on a concrete base) and a glasshouse; the incinerator was concrete. Monash got a workshop into order and began to 'potter about the place in the way that I like to and was used to in the old days'. They began to keep chooks. He installed a clothes hoist and allowed a photograph of it to be used in an advertising brochure. When he again began to keep a diary—or rather appointment book—from August 1913, its contents were largely gardening notes. He now began systematically to build up his library: the works of Dickens, Lytton, de Maupassant, Meredith and of major poets; dictionaries, reference works, law books; Bernard O'Dowd's *The Bush*, Emerson, G. B. Shaw and many others. They had bought at the auction of Prell's effects 'a quantity of very choice statuary and ornaments for less than one quarter of their value including a beautiful Carrara marble statue of Ruth, which on its pedestal, stands 8 feet high'. With these purchases went several fashionable European paintings which included Ralli's *Snake Charmers*, and also works by Strutt and Scheltema. In 1913–14 he added Australian works by E. Phillips Fox, Norman Lindsay, Dora Meeson, Jessie Traill, Hilder and Heysen.

Monash's marriage was never happier than in these years, but Vic still suffered 'a good deal from nervous troubles' as well as asthma. Each year from 1906 she had a holiday on her own in Sydney or Adelaide. All things considered, John must have been satisfied to read, after twenty-three years of marriage:

> I have come to the conclusion that there is no man alive, or at least that I have met, that can compare with you in any way, but of course this is only as it should be isn't it. . . . You want to go away from your hubby to realise how much you think of him.

They went to the theatre as often as ever: John had arranged with J. C. Williamson's for permanent first-night dress circle seats and they also subscribed to Gregan McMahon's repertory company. In 1911 they revelled in Melba's Grand Opera season, attending every first night. Good concerts were few, but John once wrote to the under-appreciated Czech pianist, Edward Goll, to thank him for the 'exquisite pleasure [of] your magnificent and artistic performance'. They bought a new piano, a rosewood Ronisch Baby Grand, and a home cinematograph and joined a film library. Motoring retained its novelty. John had not been to Buffalo for some years but at Christmas 1912 had a pleasant five-day tour to Marysville, Yea, Woodend and Ballarat, and in February 1914—his first real holiday since the overseas trip—they spent a fortnight in Tasmania, motoring from Burnie through Launceston to Hobart via the east coast.

Family obligations had become less onerous, once he was able to ease the financial worries of his sister and the Roth womenfolk. Mat was still teaching part time and occasionally had the joy of producing a first-class student; John sent her off on another overseas trip in 1912, but she and Lou did not get on well. Tante Ulrike's health was worrying; he gave the ailing Soph Roth the pleasure of a trip to Ceylon; the vagrant Karl from time to time caused alarm by appearing in Melbourne. Albert Behrend was struggling on: one son became an electrical engineer, another a dentist, and a third a Labor Party activist who tried to borrow the Monash car for electioneering purposes. John was very close to the children of Vic's sister Sa and Max Simonson. He gave Vera a diamond ring, was a good uncle to Karl who entered his father's business, and he helped Eric in his engineering course, advising him that 'steady conscientious work . . . a good and wide education is the very best asset, better than wealth and influence'. Early in 1914 John carried out the melancholy duty of arranging the affairs of Max who was deranged and going blind, while Sa had a heart condition. After his overseas trip, he had a formidable load of continuing correspondence with German and American relatives. One of his most hopeless tasks had been the request from Bruno, his very bright engineer cousin, son of Uncle Max who had been naturalized while in Australia, to help him escape German or Austrian military training and gain British nationality.

Monash's club life was based on the University (president 1909–12 in succession to Sir John Madden, the founding president) and the Naval and Military (vice-president from 1908), but he was active in several others. From 1906 he was a vice-president of the Old Scotch Collegians Club. He sometimes moved the toast to the school at annual reunions of old boys and represented the club at gatherings of kindred bodies, conscientiously insisting on the right to precedence against the historically ill-based claims of Melbourne Grammar. But when the Geelong Grammarians at their gathering called first on an Old Melburnian, he told his secretary: 'If they had the bad manners to commit a breach of precedence, it would not have mended matters for me to have shown myself ill-mannered also'. In 1911, at the Scotch diamond jubilee dinner in the Town Hall, he moved a toast and was one of the six hundred dinner-shirted gentlemen who, to the air of *The Cock of the North*, marched in fours up Bourke Street to the Exhibition Building where they joined boys of the school. About 1907–9 he was a member of the Sloperian Society, a dining club. After being invited to walk by Felix Meyer, he was elected to the Wallaby Club in 1913. He belonged briefly to the Stock Exchange Club, probably as a convenient place to lunch, and was elected to the Victoria Racing (Flemington), the Victoria Amateur Turf (Caulfield), the Melbourne Cricket and the Gisborne Country clubs. He also joined the Royal Society of Victoria, the Royal Geographical Society of Australasia and the Microscopical Society—with promises to be active some day. His various clubs called on him to lecture (with slides) on his travels, as he did, with good houses, to the Prahran Literary Society, College Church, Parkville, and others. The British Medical Association made him chief guest at an annual dinner. The demands for formal speeches, movements of and replies to toasts, presidential introductions and votes of thanks, came thick and fast.

Monash was in top form in 1912. He told his sisters that his business was booming and his prestige was mounting steadily: 'All is right as right can be'. 'I enjoy every minute of it. . . I find that things which used to worry me greatly . . . now pass me by untouched.' Although he was carrying Gibson's work, his energy seemed boundless: he now became president of the Victorian Institute of Engineers and joined the University council. 'I returned home', he wrote to Walter,

> with all sorts of resolutions about slacking off, and keeping myself from entangling outside interests, but it was all no good; and whether my motives have been the altruistic ones of helping along the multifarious interests which have succeeded in imposing themselves upon

a, c. 1914

e library

Monash in 1912

me, or merely flattered vanity at being sought out to do these things, the result is that I am just as heavily involved as ever in lots of things which I had better have left alone. . . . I can occasionally do a little good here and there, and that is a satisfaction.

Lou remarked in reply that she had often heard him say that 'the more one has to do the more one can fit in'. His health was excellent: he had had a severe attack of lumbago following his trip to Scotland, he was following a 'diet for obesity' (which included abolition of bread and sugar, limited fluid intake and increased consumption of fish), but he showed 'no signs of nervous wearing down'. He now regularly ordered a gallon of Dewars whisky from the University Club.

Assured status tended to accentuate Monash's peremptory, punctilious style. Any correspondent who did not acknowledge a letter or promptly answer a query was sent a speedy reminder. Woe betide any bureaucrat who was blatantly inefficient. The deputy postmaster-general was sternly informed of the inconveniences caused by delays and corruptions in telegrams. On the other hand he was unusually courteous in praising good service: on return from his overseas trip he wrote to Thomas Cook's Melbourne office to express his entire satisfaction with the courtesy and efficiency with which he had been treated by Cook's everywhere. He would point out that he had been under-charged as well as demand justification of apparent over-charging. He was not infallible himself: he sometimes left things behind in hotel rooms.

One of Monash's keenest ambitions was to take part in governing the University. He had continued to examine in Engineering and occasionally lectured on hydraulics or reinforced concrete. In 1907 he had agreed to write the engineering chapter of a history celebrating the University's first fifty years but the project came to nothing. When Kernot died, the University consulted the Victorian Institute of Engineers on the proper qualifications for a successor and Monash gave his opinions; when he was consulted on the short-listed applicants he supported the successful candidate, Henry Payne. In 1911 the University decided to promote a graduates' association: 260 attended a dinner at the Grand Hotel. At a subsequent executive meeting Monash was elected chairman and moved the resolution which became clause 1 of the objects of the association. He had managed to override a minority of the University Club which feared for its independent existence, by arguing for the necessity to cater for the broader intellectual needs of graduates (including female graduates) which the club could not meet; the objects of the association were literary and scientific rather than social. After the annual dinner in April 1912, over which Monash presided and moved the toast to the 'Alma Mater', he was happy to hand over the chairmanship to J. G. Latham. One new ally

Monash had made was Dr Georgina Sweet, lecturer in zoology, for whom he wrote a reference in support of her unsuccessful application for a chair in Western Australia.

The engineers had no representative on the University council; as one of the smaller professions they found it difficult to carry the vote of the body of graduates. In October 1908 Monash made soundings on whether councillors would welcome an engineer and whether he would be personally acceptable; he would be 'most disinclined to embark upon anything like a contest or a scramble for a vacancy'. When an opportunity came in 1910 he could not stand as he was about to go overseas. By 1912, knowing that he had strong backing from his profession, he was ready to move. He passed up an opportunity in February when the engineers decided not to contest a vacancy against the medical profession, provided the medicos supported them next time. Next month Leo Cussen, on Monash's request, ascertained that Mr Justice Sir Thomas à Beckett did not intend to stand again. Within a week the campaign was won, though not without difficulty. J. A. Smith, retiring president of the Institute of Engineers, Higgins, Payne and the architect Anketell Henderson were Monash's chief supporters. But he had to persuade Professor Masson not to run Professor Harrison Moore against him on behalf of the professoriat; he probably pledged his support to Moore next time. He was then opposed as an engineering candidate by A. H. Merrin, who was supported by a group of young graduates. When it came to the point Monash had a two to one majority at a stormy meeting of about twenty engineering graduates—'Merrin and his party were very furious'. The medicos stood by their written pledge and Monash was elected unopposed. He regarded it as 'perhaps the highest honorary position in the gift of our community outside of politics'. He wrote to George Higgins:

> I am already greatly indebted to you for many previous kindnesses. It was you who introduced me into my Profession, and guided my first faltering steps. You also nominated me for the Institution of Civil Engineers London, and more recently for the Victorian Institute of Engineers. So that you have been throughout a 'Professional Sponsor' to me, for which I tender my sincere thanks.

He exulted to Mat, after a graduation ceremony, at 'taking a *senior* place [on the platform] to the great professorial dons—those revered deities of our youth'.

He was soon a member of the building and finance committees, and of the large 1913 committee reviewing the general state of the University. He was enthusiastically active in the Senate, in effect as a representative of the council in the upper house helping to force legislation through. He lobbied Mackey to try to improve government funding. He sensibly insisted on resigning in 1912 both from the chairmanship of the graduates and from the presidency of the University Club but, as he told Mat, they had 'really served their turn'. He gave up examining, but was happy to relieve Higgins by lecturing on reinforced concrete—six lectures in 1912, continued in 1913 and 1914. Sir Walter Bassett recalled him as the best lecturer he had, especially when railing against the 'economic madness' of using imported steel for construction rather than reinforced concrete. In 1913, on the occasion of Albert Mansbridge's visit from England, Monash warmly supported the objectives of the Workers' Educational Association. With the other University reformers—his friends, Barrett, Cussen and Fink—he had great satisfaction in redressing the wrong inflicted on Marshall-Hall in 1900. When Professor Peterson died in 1914, Melbourne's musical public campaigned to have Marshall-Hall reappointed. A sub-committee of council, which included Monash, divided evenly between appointing him immediately or advertising in the normal manner. After a hard-fought debate on council, the battle was won by ten votes to seven.

On the nomination of A. G. M. Michell, Monash had joined the council of the Victorian Institute of Engineers in 1906 and became a vice-president in 1908. In 1907 he was active in rounding up contributions to a purse of sovereigns for his 'old friend' H. C. Mais, the senior engineer who was eighty and hard up; five years later he took the lead again in another whip-round. When Kernot died in 1909, his University colleagues proposed to commemorate him with a tablet. Monash felt strongly that there should be a worthier memorial and became secretary of an appeal committee based on the Institute: 'I strongly favour a public statue. The late Professor Kernot exercised a far-reaching beneficial influence upon our community.... We have done but little in the past to honour our great dead'. In the end it was agreed to found a memorial medal for distinguished achievement in Australian engineering.

The presidency of the Institute was attractive to Monash as a means of reforming his profession. As vice-president, he was regarded as president elect and was willing to succeed in 1911, but did not force the issue as J. A. Smith wanted to continue. He spent much time at council meetings and on sub-committees such as those on building regulations and the Federal capital site. Next year Monash seemingly tried to avoid the presidency because of Gibson's absence, but he eventually submitted. Monash supported, through the V.I.E., the foundation of one Australia-wide body, which came about in 1919 with the foundation of the Institution of Engineers, Australia. Specialist local institutes of mining, municipal, electrical and chemical engineers and a graduates' association complicated the situation. Eventually he and

Smith forced through in 1914 incorporation of the Institute and a change of name to 'Australian', which was intended to encourage federation of the profession.

He had been storing up much which he wanted to say. He wrote an anonymous editorial for the *Varsity Engineer* on the need for graduates to be men of character:

> there are few callings which in their higher levels make so many and so heavy demands upon the purely temperamental qualifications of the individual, calling for the constant and long-sustained exercise of quite special phases of character. The engineer must above all things be a man of the world, ... meaning a man of broad education and outlook, free from petty bias and prejudice, full of sober common sense, of human sympathy and understanding, in nothing an extremist, and in nothing a faddist. He must understand men, because he has to organise, direct and lead men to the attainment of the best fruition of his own labours. The arts by which a man can inspire in his subordinates enthusiasm, loyal service and obedience are simple. They rest upon the force of example, and no engineer can really succeed who has not himself the loyal, disciplined and optimistic temperament. These qualities again are founded upon earnestness, habits of industry and strength of character.

Those who succeeded and deserved to succeed were those who had the courage of their opinions, were not afraid to take responsibility, and who said what they meant. This must have been close to an idealized self-portrait.

In his 1913 presidential address to the Institute, he pleaded for more 'mutual sympathy and support' among engineers, ' a more energetic striving after higher ideals, higher standards of educational and technical efficiency, and a fuller realization of responsibility to the community'. Two major features of the profession in Australia made for inefficiency: most engineers were in public employ, and there was 'no well-defined general standard of training and competence'. Employment in governmental and municipal service sapped initiative and encouraged conservative and stereotyped approaches. 'Engineers' could be university graduates, be entirely unqualified, or have one of several certificates of widely varying merit: 'in effect there is no standard at all'. The 'average status and competency' of the profession was lower than in older countries, largely because of lack of standards of admission. The profession was divided into numerous bickering societies and riddled with cliques. Contributions by Australian engineers to scientific knowledge were negligible. It was a passively insular profession, out of touch with overseas thought and practice and suffering from acute conservatism. Melbourne's trams and trains were antiquated, its harbour facilities crude and primitive, Victoria's main country roads a disgrace, the practice of forestry was backward, provincial centres were unsewered, water power remained wholly undeveloped. It was due to lack of enterprise, not lack of capital. Senior State engineers should travel abroad to regain touch and then disseminate the latest knowledge.

He had proved himself a worthy pupil of Kernot. But he was embarrassed when the *Age*—not his favourite newspaper—took up his 'diatribe' in one of its slamming editorials and claimed him as an ally on the side of 'the people'. 'If the indictment be half as true as it is explicit we are driven to the conclusion that Australia is served in engineering matters by one of the most incompetent and lack-lustre groups of soi-disant scientists to be found in the whole civilised world.' Perhaps the greatest confirmation of the trend of his remarks was the lack of controversy they aroused. One warm letter he received was from Gummow:

> Strive on, it is good to see someone take on the work, and I must add that I know of no one better able to fight the cause than yourself, but I am pessimistic enough to feel that you will only sow the seed and that it will be for future generations to reap the benefit.

Monash's presidential address in 1914 was on the state of reinforced concrete construction and its implications for the profession; he emphasized the superiority of German and Austrian practices over American, English backwardness, and the inadequacies of American and English technical literature.

Monash was closely involved in the split in the Boy Scout movement in 1911 when for once his conciliatory powers were ineffective. The Imperial Boy Scouts were formed in Victoria in 1908–9 with a loose structure; his friend Wears was chairman of the central executive committee and in February 1910 Monash joined the committee of control. That year, while he was away, a split developed between many scoutmasters and the executive, Wears fell out with the Chief Scout Master, E. G. Lister, and a movement for a revised constitution developed through the Scoutmasters' Association. At the committee of control in February 1911 Monash was as vehement as the rest in demanding disciplinary action against the dissidents. Yet there are hints that in some aspects he sympathized with them, despite his friendship with Wears and the strongly Establishment and military composition of the controlling body. He agreed, allegedly as a neutral, to chair a committee of constitutional revision to clear up what he privately described as 'disruption and petty squabbling owing to a loose and ill-organized form of administration'. Preparation and adoption of a new constitution seemed to proceed harmoniously and Monash became vice-president under the new order; but dissent continued, perhaps partly because Wears was appointed chief commissioner, and late in the year Lister and others were expelled and formed a rival body. At this stage Monash was as hostile as anyone else to the intrigue and disruption of the dissidents. He continued to attend meetings regularly, was prominent in receiving Sir Robert Baden-Powell when he paid a visit in May 1912, and took the salute at the Australasian rally in January 1914. Although he well knew that the movement had no avowed military purpose, he was equally aware of the benefits of scouting as a preliminary to military service.

In 1911 and 1912 the Intelligence Corps concentrated on mapping; little was done to gather intelligence information. Kilmore was the site for the major camp at Easter 1911 and a thorough inch-to-the-mile map of the area was prepared. 'My corps has had to do the whole of the topographical work, and the organising of road and rail transport and so on, and a gang of 15 high spirited young men take a lot of driving and guiding towards a harmonious and efficient result.' Later in the year maps of 2000 square miles near Melbourne were almost completed. In the next two years Monash organized staff tours for his officers—imaginary battles between Eastland and Westland in which they reconnoitred and gathered information. Because of his seniority, he now had a growing burden of administration as a member of the District Defence Officers Promotion Board (for which he had to conduct exams) and as chairman of the District Inventions Board. A colleague on the latter, C. H. Foott, recalled:

> No one could fail to be impressed by his grasp of detail, his infinite patience in examining any idea put before him, and his kindness towards inventors, even when (as was often the case) their ideas were valueless or chimerical. He would often go to some trouble to explain . . . just exactly why the invention failed to be of any use.

He had to take the lead for a time in the Aerial League of Australia and found a recent book, *The Aeroplane in War*, 'very startling and suggestive'. Late in 1912, as Victorian representative, he attended a senior conference on the problems of compulsory military training.

He was studying military history and the principles of warfare much more intensely. E. W. Perry, the military historian, has said of him that

> If conversation turned on famous campaigns he would take out a pencil and paper and show how Napoleon had handled his forces at Austerlitz, Ulm or Marengo; how Wellington had constructed in Portugal the lines at Torres Vedras in the Peninsular War; . . . or how Moltke had worked out the plans for the military operations of 1870–71. The details of the major campaigns in modern history

were engraved upon his mind, and he could describe them in conversation with the utmost vividness and clarity.

Few if any of his peers were more widely read. G. F. R. Henderson's *Stonewall Jackson and the American Civil War* had become his favourite text—he used it to set problems for his officers—and in 1911 he was showing round a new photographic history of the Civil War. He now had time free from business cares, and the added interest excited by his American trip led him to enter and win the first Gold Medal essay competition, sponsored by the Army, on 'The Lessons of the Wilderness Campaign, 1864'. The essay was published in the *Commonwealth Military Journal* for April 1912. By any test it is an illuminating original article, expounded with utter clarity in a moderate scholarly manner but drawing firm conclusions. Apart from works on the Civil War, his bibliography of eleven items included Henderson's *The Science of War*, Tovey and Maguire's *Principles of Strategy* and Hubert Foster's new work, *Organization*.

The Wilderness campaign in northern Virginia, fought out by the great generals Grant and Lee, was one of the turning-points of the war. Monash argued that 'the character and training of the troops engaged, and of their leaders, . . . the topographical features of the theatre of war, and the circumstances which influenced its strategical and tactical development' bore 'a close analogy to Australian conditions'. Substantially, these were citizen armies, 'bred in an atmosphere of personal liberty and independence, well qualified physically. . . and well skilled in bushcraft and horsemanship; . . . an accurate prototype of any fighting force which could be placed in the field in Australia'. The terrain and the density and distribution of population and its resources were similar to those of inhabited Australia (he was mistaken about the similarity of terrain). Lee's brilliant instant fortifications, by timber breastworks, carried out by troops expert in use of pick and shovel and axe and saw, suggested that 'the nature of the field works described and prescribed by our service manuals may not necessarily be the best for Australian conditions'. The poor tactical employment of cavalry should be an object lesson to the Light Horse. There were many general lessons to be drawn: the most successful commanders were graduates of West Point, with high professional education and previous experience of war; although the United States was a popular democracy subject to 'public clamour', Grant partly owed his success to the absence of political interference; he carried out 'the fundamental principle of strategy . . . to seek out and destroy the armed power of his antagonist' and to wear him down rather than try to capture his capital; his greatest weaknesses were looseness in the chain of command and inadequate use of artillery; all depended on the personal qualities of the leaders and the morale of their troops. Perhaps the most interesting lesson was that 'the subordinate should not be hampered by too precise or detailed instructions, but is to be encouraged to act according to local circumstances'. Finally, he recognized that chance and accident—wounding or illness of senior commanders, weather conditions, bushfire—vitally affected the issue. John Monash had the makings of a good historian.

In mid-1912 the affairs of the Intelligence Corps became critical. McCay had fallen out beyond reconciliation with his superior officers. He threw his hand in and, seemingly not taking Monash into his confidence but leaving him to act in his stead, went overseas. John wrote to Mat on 11 September:

> His back was scarcely turned when Head Quarters decided to abolish his position altogether and thereby deprive me of the opportunity of rounding off the matters which he had left unfinished. I made a great protest over this . . . the whole thing has involved a lot of worry.

He may have come close to talking himself out of a command, for the plan to decentralize the Corps by placing it under the control of the general staff of the six military districts and abolishing its headquarters proceeded. Early in November, he told McCay, he saw Brudenell White but could not pin him down and tried to draw him by saying:

> "It seems to me, Major, that, under the proposed organization, you are not going to have any suitable place or duty for a Senior Lt. Col. like myself," and the man had the hardihood to look me straight in the face and say, quite coolly, "No, I do not suppose we will."

Monash concluded that he had no future in Intelligence: 'I shall either have to face the prospect of going out of active duty, or of looking for some soft place to fall on'. Some permanent officers were encouraging him to apply for command of a brigade, but he had no Infantry experience. He was 'a good deal disgusted' at the 'shabby treatment' he had received, and was not surprised that they had almost broken McCay's heart. McCay replied briefly—from Florence, in French, on an open postcard!

> I very much regret all your trouble with Headquarters, but it doesn't surprise me. I hope you can bring yourself to be charitable. I shall do all I possibly can to help you when I return. . . . It is useless to try to serve one's country when Headquarters always opposes everything one does.

Acting on a broad hint from White, on 18 November Monash applied for an infantry brigade, and received the usual cold acknowledgement. White also sent him for comment the draft order on reorganization of the Intelligence Corps. Monash replied temperately and constructively, though he began by restating his general objections; however, the matter was decided. He admitted the plan was 'logical and workable'. He had long contended that the Corps should form the Intelligence section of the General Staff, but warned against it becoming too much of a 'Watertight Compartment'. He pleaded for higher status for the Corps as a means of attracting the best officers, and for a return to the function of collecting intelligence information on resources of the Commonwealth and of foreign countries, and made suggestions about the organization of companies of guides. 'I have now exhausted my time and your patience, so I let it go at that', he concluded. His acting command of the Corps was terminated on 5 December, but he remained in charge of the Victorian section until mid-1913, a military period he found 'very dull'.

After the war Monash concluded that what reputation the Corps had won rested on 'the training of our officers in staff work, which qualified them to act as Brigade Majors, Staff Captains etc.'. Perhaps he recognized that reorganization had been inevitable: the work was too important to be left to militiamen. Stanley, as Victorian commandant, had reported in 1912 that Monash's 'energy and capacity' had 'brought his officers to an astonishing standard of training'. There may have been some truth in one journalist's assertion that the Intelligence Corps had been really successful only in the Victorian district. And Monash himself was no longer a narrow specialist but something like an all-round soldier, with particular knowledge of staff work, transport, supply, engineering, and intelligence.

He was appointed to command the 13th Infantry Brigade from 1 July 1913. Bruche, asserting that Monash was a genius, and Stanley outvoted a reluctant staff officer. Monash was delighted: the 13th was a blue-ribbon brigade taking in the southern suburbs and not the less reliable north, 'the pick of all the commands'. It 'will I suppose be my last military office'. He would have to deal with an inherited undercurrent of conflict between brigade and regimental commanders, some of whom were not on speaking terms with each other: 'They shall have to shake hands and make friends, or I shall want to know the reason why'. He had them to dinner at Iona to confer. In August the Intelligence Corps gave him a farewell dinner; McCay proposed the toast. In his spare time, Monash had been translating *Kavalleristische Monatshefte*, the German cavalry journal, for the General Staff.

Monash fought for his rights, and for those of his fellow citizen-soldiers, with regard to promotion; he was sure that attack was the best means of defence. A recommendation for promotion to colonel, to go with his new appointment, had been rejected by the Military Board which deferred a decision until his work had been observed.

Monash immediately protested convincingly; he was not superior in rank to his battalion commanders. It was intolerable to be so long on probation, he told Bruche: 'It is still quite possible that I may have to take extreme measures to enforce what is due to me'. In September he encouraged an Adelaide colleague to press his rights: 'My impression is that they usually go where they are pushed. I hope this is not talking treason'. Monash was indeed promoted colonel early in September, back-dated to 1 July. Bruche had been worried by Monash's letter and told him that promotion was normally deferred until after attending the first camp in the new post and that it was not worth worrying about:

> Remember you may be a "hell of a fellah" but you have never yet *commanded* a Battalion or any body of troops *in the field*. So it is a compliment selecting you. . . . Don't jump at my terse way of expressing things. . . .

Monash replied:

> Sorry you don't agree with me about that question of rank. Just as emphatically as you put it, I consider *you* are wrong, and that the views you put don't do credit to your known logical faculty and clearness of vision. . . . As to my "fighting and getting licked"—that would be rather a new experience for me, and I don't think its going to happen *this* time either! Now what in the world do you mean by this: "Besides, do you think its a right thing to start and get pressure from inside, and no doubt outside to make your case? I thought you were above this". . . . It's certainly pretty straight, and rather offensive. . . . The only "pressure" I recognise, or in my wildest imaginings ever contemplated applying in this or any other case, is the pressure of reason, logic and common sense.

Bruche was distressed:

> I write and talk straight but to be offensive is not my desire to you above all others. Surely you ought to know this. Our relationship in the past has been too close and on my part too happy for me to do or say anything which might be offensive to you.

And two days later he wrote again to say that he was delighted to realize he was mistaken, but that Monash should look again at his original letter to understand why he Bruche had been misled. Monash replied again:

> You have made out a very good case for having been led to believe that I had entertained thoughts of sinister action. I can quite see that my words can fairly be thought to mean what you did think they meant. But I thought that you, knowing me, would be ready to believe, that the measures I contemplated would be within the

bounds of propriety. The fact is, that letter was dictated in the rush of a busy day. . . . That other expression in mine . . . "rather offensive" was plainly from its context used in a spirit of banter. . . . Well, . . . I have had my way, or is it better to say 'the authorities have graciously seen fit to accede to my application.' I think they have made rather a foolish muddle of it, don't you? The bedrock truth is that time had to be gained to promote certain other people first, and that talk about postponing Brigadiers' promotions till after a period of probation was a mild official bluff.

The fact is that Monash sometimes resorted to bluster and bombast when thwarted, and that it was rare for someone like Bruche to call his bluff.

Late that year Monash led a revolt by the citizen-brigadiers. The culmination of 'a good many pin pricks' from Headquarters was a circular laying down peremptory dress regulations; Monash had probably provoked the issue by improperly wearing full dress at a public function. All the Victorian citizen-brigadiers protested at discrimination; their colleagues in New South Wales were equally irritated; and Monash set out to rouse South Australia, warning that it must not be known in official quarters that he was in communication. They won their campaign. That same month Monash urged the senior brigade commander to remonstrate about a junior permanent staff officer implying in the press that the senior citizen-commanders were in a 'condition of close tutelage'.

Monash's militia command when he took over was 'a composite Brigade of all arms', 'not really an Infantry job', but by the end of the year it contained five infantry battalions, as well as two batteries, a survey company, an Army Service Corps unit and an ambulance. His characteristic style had firmed. In October 1913 he lectured to his company commanders on their duties and responsibilities. They were soldiers in order to train for efficiency in war, not for personal or social kudos. They had to make the 13th Brigade a complete machine, depending on mutual support, co-operation and sympathy, and on unity of thought and method. Discipline must not be mere obedience based on fear of punishment, but instinctive conformity to the will of a superior officer. Officers would develop strength of character by cultivating self-control, self-confidence, courage of their opinions, quickness and firmness in decision-making, and sane and not extreme views. Further requisite qualities were zeal, good temper, common sense, punctuality, tidiness, self-sacrifice, dignity towards subordinates, methodical habits, and coolness under stress. They must study textbooks and manuals and military history, and practise writing précis. They had to learn to take responsibility in the absence of orders, and think constantly on how they might act in difficult situations. They must care for their men's welfare, always give a square deal firmly and fairly, be severe rather than lenient when punishment was unavoidable. They must be patient with men of varying intelligence, allow time for orders to percolate, and (doubly underlined) explain to all what was going on. (How unusual was that advice?) They must learn from Generals Lee and Jackson how to face difficulties courageously; they must bear all cheerfully. He published his advice as a pamphlet, *100 Hints for Company Commanders*. A scribbled note he made in January 1914 on 'The Development of a Soldierly Spirit' was on the same lines. Another note, '3 principles of Arrangements for Battle', shows him thinking in a general's terms:

> 1. When battle imminent, always be ready to fight quickly on *suitable* front; this helps you to decide on disposition for approach.
> 2. Envelopment is more effective than frontal attack; this helps you to select your main objective.
> 3. Keep control as long as possible, i.e. don't throw in all at once; this helps you to concentrate on decisive point.

He had learned, long ago, to 'administer a rocket' in terms appropriate to the man. For example, after beginning a letter, 'I am writing quite unofficially, as I feel that the sins which I am about to lay at your door have been committed unwittingly', he made his charges mercilessly but concluded, 'Trusting you will not think, under the circumstances, that this is putting the matter too harshly'.

Monash prepared for the first large-scale eight-day manoeuvres of the 13th Brigade in February 1914 with that thoroughness and careful attention to detail which occasionally was to lead to envious criticism that he was 'showing off'. On 16 October he wrote to his brigade major:

> I am sending you herewith the first draft of my proposed syllabus of training for your frank and exhaustive criticism. While the draft will probably disclose deficiencies, it would also benefit by judicious compression.

In December he held a tactical exercise in the chosen area, Lilydale. By now it was known that the manoeuvres would be the first reviewed in Australia by General Sir Ian Hamilton, Inspector-General of the British Overseas Forces. Monash confessed to 'Walterlou' that he was a little anxious.

Early February was very hot, with bushfires close to Lilydale; dust and flies were to plague the 2500 troops. Monash himself wrote the orders for the battalion commanders— 'the first and only time in my experience' a brigadier did so according to Lieutenant (later Air Marshal Sir Richard) Williams. He lectured to all officers and sergeants: 'Let all ranks know what is going on. Therefore note, and explain. Inculcate lessons to be taught'. The day before Hamilton's inspection he held a full-dress rehearsal of the mock battle. On the day, Hamilton, the governor-general and the headquarters senior officers watched the exercise. At lunch-time Hamilton called a conference and, after Monash had addressed his officers, himself made some remarks. Hamilton was startled by Monash's talk:

> I was prepared for intelligent criticisms but I thought they would be so wrapped up in the cotton wool of politeness that no one would be very much impressed. On the contrary, he stated his opinions in the most direct, blunt, telling way.

Hamilton reported that in Monash there were the makings of a commander. He stayed for the rest of the day and watched the troops march in to camp in the dust and heat. Several of the Imperial officers were reported to have had tears in their eyes and lumps in their throats at the earnestness and enthusiasm of the conscripted citizen-soldiers, the first they had ever seen in an English-speaking country.

It was a personal triumph, heightened by the mess the 17th Brigade made of its parade next day. The governor-general sent his congratulations. White told Monash he had seen many a regular brigade do its work less well. And for the next fifteen years Hamilton, the gallant Gallipoli commander, almost invariably when he met Monash or wrote to him, would hark back to that conference under the gum-tree: 'Vanity, I suppose, because of the good shot I made then in saying you were a man of outstanding force of character'. 'Nice to think', wrote an old artillery friend, 'that a gunner can show them all the way to do things'.

The press had given Monash extensive publicity. But for some weeks the *Age* attacked him for overworking his troops to exhaustion and questioned the quality of citizen-brigadiers. Seemingly the editor was not aware that armies have to be trained to march long distances and then be ready to fight; he passed for publication the opinion that 'it is too high a price to pay for efficiency if only one man is overtrained'. Monash's position was unassailable. In October he had taken medical advice on the maximum daily distance proper for nineteen- to twenty-year-old youths to march in hot weather, 'leading up to it'. Hamilton had told him to carry on with his plans; the great majority of the troops had been well rested; hardly any were seriously distressed. Monash 'went in among the Companies as they arrived . . . and over and over again they met me cheerily with the remark "Give us a half hour's rest and we will do it all over again"'. 'I shall adhere to my policy of training for war and not for picnics', he told Bruche. However, his request for an official denial seemingly was refused, and some doubts remained in higher quarters about the medical justification.

Monash was involved in 1914 in an ugly reflection in Melbourne of the Irish Home Rule crisis. The president of the Celtic Club, Major McInerney, C.M.G., a Boer War veteran, made some trenchant remarks late in March about the views of Field Marshal Earl Roberts on the Irish question and on his military capacity—technically a gross breach of military etiquette. The committee of the Naval and Military Club, under Colonel James Burston's presidency, decided to recommend McInerney's expulsion from the club to a special meeting of members. He defended himself there, but the club solemnly expelled him, on the motion of the vice-presidents, Colonels F. G. Hughes and Monash. McInerney made a public statement. In reply, Monash wrote to the *Argus* and *Age*, supported by Hughes, to state that McInerney was expelled only after numerous appeals to withdraw his charges, on the grounds of his cowardly breach of etiquette and not because of his political views, and that many of the minority opposed to his expulsion wanted only to prevent him posing as a political martyr. He later told Mat that he had hounded him out 'as a disloyalist, from a club of honest loyal officers'. The Irish Catholics pursued the issue: on 27 May in the House of Representatives, a Melbourne Labor member was informed, in reply to his question, that the three colonels had not volunteered to serve in the Boer War. At a smoke-social in McInerney's honour on 3 July, four Federal Labor members supported the injured warrior. Dr William Maloney derided the three unwilling colonels: 'Are we going to allow these lickspittle little puppies to interfere with our freedom?' McInerney considered that 'centuries of persecution would have seared tolerance into the heart of a Jew'. Thus, quite damagingly, Monash was identified as a supposed enemy of the Irish Catholic–Labor Opposition core.

The great event of 1914 was to be the meeting in Australia of the British Association for the Advancement of Science, which had previously conferred in Canada and South Africa but never in Australia. Monash threw himself into the preparatory work as a member of the Victorian executive committee and of the Scientific Business sub-committee, and prepared a survey for the *Handbook to Victoria* on 'Public Works in Victoria'; it was a careful article, but he freely vented his opinions on the outstanding question of canalizing the Murray River, the scandal of differing railway gauges, depletion of timber resources, poor roads and public distrust of academic training. His particular problem was how to make sure the Rosenhains would attend. He managed tactfully to persuade Walter and Lou to be his guests in Melbourne; Walter still had to ask John to lend him £200 to cover the family's fares.

Now that he could afford to run his business at an easy pace, Monash was uncertain about how to spend the rest of his life. 'I am a little too old', he told Walter, 'to take up with any prospect of a success that would make it worthwhile, anything in the nature of artistic, musical or scientific studies on a really worthy scale'.

> The days and weeks pass more and more rapidly the older one gets, and one seems to become year by year only more and more a piece of flotsam swept hither and thither by the waves of affairs and the tide of crowded incident. . . .
> I have got myself into a rather passive, unenergetic frame of mind so far as money-making activity is concerned. I have worked so hard for so many years, that I feel a yearning for more quiet and peace. . . .
> In outside activities I am afraid I have rather overdone it, and intend to withdraw gradually from some of the public positions. Of these the Military and the University will be the last to go.

He was determined to travel again, probably via Japan, to spend more time in the United States, then to Europe to devote himself to 'the study of European Art, literature and a study of the people'. Early in 1914 he was firmly planning to go in March 1915, partly in order to attend a World Engineering Congress.

His ambitions were tempered down. He was at the head of his profession, had risen almost as high in the citizen army as was possible, was well-to-do, tiring of being a president and vice-president—was a pillar of the Melbourne Establishment. He could look forward to a C.B. when he retired as a brigade commander, and a knighthood if he became chancellor of the University. He was a very genial man now; the fear of unpopularity had long gone. He had indeed an unusually wide range of friends and acquaintances. He was on very good terms, for example, with E. J. Stock, the rising man of the National Mutual Life Association, E. L. Piesse, the Hobart lawyer and Intelligence officer, and Robert Garran, his next-door neighbour and head of the Attorney-General's Department. Another *Punch* profile, though written in September 1914 when any severe criticism was unlikely, rings true:

> He inspires respect, and he also inspires affection. A rigid disciplinarian, there is nothing of the martinet about him. The gods have blessed him with a keen sense of humour, and at the same time with an honest kindliness. He is always ready to sympathise, always ready to stiffen the weak-kneed, and help along the stumblers. This city is full of men who are proud to regard themselves as friends of John Monash.

He continued an affectionate correspondence with the off-beat Card family, including Arthur, 'The English Psychic Entertainer and Exposer of Fables', who asserted: 'If one person in all the world deserves to get on "Thou art the man" as I know of your early struggles and how good you always were to your people'. Like most middle-aged men, however, few intimates remained among his friends: Steele had died and Lewis and Hyde had drifted away, but Gibson, Bruche and Rosenhain had taken their places.

He was at peace with himself, recognized enough now, with a fair measure of fame. He could relax and be more altruistic: 'There is no satisfaction, in the end, in a life wholly spent in the pursuit of selfish ends', he remarked to Vic. But where was he now to go at the age of forty-nine? His career showed signs of a dying fall.

On the other hand, he had superbly developed qualities for any large job which might crop up: absolute self-confidence, entire skill in the manipulation of men to his forceful will, a magnificently developed administrative competence, and an intellect which had never yet been subjected to adequate challenge.

8

Gallipoli
1914–1915

PROBABLY the first shot fired by a British Empire serviceman in World War I was from one of those guns at Port Phillip Heads which Monash knew so well: shortly after midday on 5 August 1914 the German steamer *Pfalz* was stopped by a shot across her bows while trying to escape. Europe's militaristic nationalism was finally out of control. The British, French and Russian governments believed that the only way they could avoid war was by allowing the Kaiser's Germany to become the dominant world power. Whether Germany deliberately went to war as an aggressor, or believed she was waging a preventive war in the face of intolerable provocation, or fell into it semi-accidentally and was obliged by the requirements of the Schlieffen plan to appear to be the brutal aggressor, Winston Churchill expressed the gist of the matter: 'Germany clanked obstinately, recklessly, awkwardly towards the crater and dragged us all in with her'. Australia, as part of the British Empire, was automatically at war.

The country was in the midst of a Federal election campaign which Labor, led by Andrew Fisher, was easily to win. All the political leaders pledged support for the Empire's cause and the retiring Cook government immediately committed itself to raising twenty thousand soldiers and placed the Royal Australian Navy at the British Admiralty's disposal. The populace reacted with exultation rather than apprehension, for none could imagine the appalling, prolonged blood-letting in store: the war would be short and sharp and probably over by Christmas. Support was nearly unanimous. The extensive defence programme of the previous few years had been adopted in fear both of Japanese aggression towards Australia and of the German threat to the Empire. The reality now of the latter brought an overwhelming response of sentiment from a people which was still mainly first and second generation Australian, imbued with the ideology of British imperialism, and deeply conscious of the familial blood-tie. Later generations find it difficult to understand why their great-grandparents and grandparents rallied so willingly to a war which seemingly was none of their business; historians have not succeeded in explaining the elements of the situation. There was no choice in 1914. It was a simple matter, for that generation, of defending British civilization against the barbarians. The underlying realistic appraisal was that, if Australia did not take part, it would almost inevitably be taken over if Germany won the war. But the tiny socialist and pacifist minorities of 1914, whose voices then were not heard, were to rally by 1917 a large minority of the people to support a peace settlement—as a consequence of British stupidity in handling the Irish rebellion, the tragic division of the Australian people by the attempts to impose conscription, deterioration of living standards and the never-ending casualty lists.

Monash's attitude was entirely conventional. The purpose of the war, he told his cousin Karl Roth, was 'to help the Empire to crush a peril which may mean the end of Australia as a free country'; it was essentially a defensive war. To an American cousin, who had told him his sympathies were naturally with Germany, he replied:

> It may cause you and your people surprise that I should myself take up arms in this quarrel, but then, you must not fail to remember that I am Australian born, as is my wife and daughter, that my whole interests and sympathies are British, . . . and that every man who can, and is able to do so, must do his best for his country.

Monash for several days in that first week of August had to work hard perfecting plans in case of call-up of the militia, before it became clear that the outgoing Cook ministry was keeping its head. His other concern was the meeting of the British Association; about four hundred British scientists and a sprinkling of foreign guests were making the long voyage to assemble in most of the Australian capitals in turn. Monash was a member of several planning committees, but could take little part in their deliberations. His more immediate concern was that the Rosenhain family was coming to stay. He was rather harassed in those first few days, with 'the ends of dozens of strings' in his hands.

The call that soon came was unexpected. On 9 August McCay rang to say that he had been chosen to command a brigade of the Australian Imperial Force; would Monash take over from him as chief Censor? After brief reflection Monash agreed, provided he was regarded as a stopgap and could have a week to put his affairs in order—he assumed duty on the 17th. The British War Office had laid down strict rules for security procedures in a war emergency; Bridges had planned the local machinery. Monash found he was faced with a 'most worrying, anxious and strenuous job'. All wireless traffic, the communications of German trading houses and letters sent to enemy countries had to be controlled, and attempts to supply information to Germany of troop or shipping movements intercepted. At the end of his first week he promulgated principles of press censorship: unconfirmed, unofficial or unauthorized reports of victories or defeats, especially if alarmist or sensational, would have to be suppressed, as would anything seditious or likely to give offence to allies, notably Japan; also adverse criticism of naval and military administration or anything likely to foster public alarm. From the start the press complained, especially about lack of uniformity of treatment in different States. John had immediately told Mat to warn everyone in the family not to write to German or Austrian addresses. It was a dirty job and he was glad, after four weeks, to hand it over to Colonel Hall. When, many years later, he was invited to attend a reunion of censors, Monash replied that censorship was 'a grievous and deplorable necessity of war' which was best buried in oblivion.

The eager volunteer soldiers had been organized into three brigades to form the 1st Division, A.I.F., under Bridges's command and were to sail to the Middle East late in October. Colonel Monash was appointed to command the 4th Infantry Brigade, A.I.F., on 15 September. He later attributed this early selection to command to Hamilton's favourable report on him and to McCay's influence. A dinner given by the Old Scotch Collegians on 1 September to McCay and others who had immediately volunteered probably precipitated his thinking. After the first appointments early in August, no more were expected but, because of the remarkable success of recruiting, formation of a fourth brigade was announced; it was to be recruited Australia-wide. Eager aspirants to the command rushed to apply. Monash did not do so until 10 September:

> I have not volunteered for active service, because of the consequences of such a step to the business and public interests which I represent. I am virtual head of four large industrial companies, operating in Victoria and South Australia; also member of the University Council, and many of its committees, also Chairman and member of a number of scientific bodies. These large interests would be so much affected by my withdrawal, that I do not feel justified in gratifying my personal impulse to volunteer for service; or to urge my claims for selection in competition with other men equally suitable. At the same time my services are at the unreserved disposal of the Government, and if . . . the Authorities consider me qualified for so great a responsibility and that it is in the best interests of the community that I should take up this task, I am entirely ready to do so, without any qualification.

Despite the strange tone of the application, he knew that he had to serve. He had perhaps been waiting to be asked. His German origins may have made him uncertain, but it is unlikely, after his contemporary McCay's appointment, that he thought he might be regarded as too old. Colonel J. G. Legge, the chief of the general staff, had probably at the last minute urged him to apply. Legge gave the minister for defence, George Pearce, the choice of Monash and Colonel G. R. Campbell, a fifty-six-year-old New South Welshman, with the comment that both were capable men with similar qualifications, but that as a rule he would prefer the younger man.

Congratulations flooded in. One battalion commander in the first contingent wished he could join him: 'Your brigade will be second to none *I know*'. Another told him: 'I don't think you realise the great effect your leadership [of 13th Brigade] has had upon us all . . . I want to thank you before we go'. Walter Rosenhain chaffed him that he would end the war as 'Major-General Sir John'.

Monash was told that his brigade had to be ready to leave in seven weeks—an almost impossible task in that the 13th Battalion was New South Welsh, the 14th Victorian, and the 15th and 16th from the other States. His first appointments were of a brigade major and staff captain—Lieut-Colonel J. P. McGlinn, a militiaman from New South Wales, and Captain C. H. Jess, a permanent officer; he soon had them to dinner at Iona to begin planning. The complicated processes of selecting battalion officers proceeded slowly while Monash chafed at the delay. Legge would release few of the small number of permanent officers, but Monash managed to acquire permanent men as regimental sergeant-majors, and most of the second class going through the Royal Military College, Duntroon, as junior officers. Bruche, in Queensland, was very helpful, but he was not allowed to join the brigade—he had once told Monash he was the only militia brigadier he would ever willingly serve under. Monash told him that

> I started this job very much overwhelmed with the sense of responsibility, but, now that I have got well into the work and done a lot of thinking ahead, and have moreover had repeated opportunities of observing how not to do things, I am rapidly gaining not merely confidence, but a considerable measure of enthusiasm.

At this stage, in October, Monash was subjected to a whispering campaign about his origins: it was alleged that he could not speak English properly, that he had been born and educated in Germany as had his children, and that the 'c' had only recently been dropped from the name. Letters attacking him were sent to Pearce and even to Lord Kitchener, and a petition, protesting at his appointment, was got up. Monash was not the only one: as he himself noted, Bruche and Sellheim suffered particularly, also Rosenthal, Jess and 'crowds of junior officers of the A.I.F. . . . whose names are a sure and certain index of foreign descent'. The Military Board had judged purely by British citizenship and ignored enemy parentage, but the public pressure was such that by late 1915 it ceased to commission officers of foreign origin. Intelligence reports were called for in some cases: on 2 December Pearce saw a scrappy Defence Department report on Monash's background (which included three errors). He recalled proudly in his autobiography that 'If I had listened to gossip and slander, as I was urged to do, Monash would never have gone to the War'. Late in October the *Argus* published more than fifty letters in a wild controversy on 'the alien danger'; Monash must in the vulgar view have been seen as the prime example. Conspicuous among the minority calling for fair play and tolerance was Gerald Robinson, one of the Collins House brothers and Monash's fellow Luna Park director. Monash clipped for his cuttings book a letter asserting that children of German-born naturalized Australians would, if taken prisoner, be treated as deserters as having been subject to German military service. Pearce was even accused of sheltering Monash because their wives were related! The hysterical prejudice was not totally unfounded: while the great majority of the Australian-born of German origins were entirely loyal, a few of them and some of the older generation of migrants were markedly pro-German. Monash had some immediate worries about his family: the Behrends were subject to embarrassing investigation and Tante Ulrike, who spoke to her children in German, was at risk. At one of his send-offs he replied obliquely to the vicious gossipers: 'It puzzled him completely to think that people could doubt, or even openly question, . . . that a native-born Australian, such as himself, could fail to do his utmost in such a crisis'. The University vice-chancellor, J. H. MacFarland, wrote to him next day: 'When I heard of the thing first I thought of a counter-demonstration but it would only have given the critics an importance to which they are not entitled. . . . God has given you a good nervous system. I hope it will wear well'. Monash had not been in the least disturbed. He tended to attribute the personal campaign against him to 'the McInerney clique'.

The period of training for the brigade before departure was extended by several weeks and Monash was glad to be able to slip away for a last quick trip to Buffalo. The Rosenhains had stayed on for several weeks, but he had seen much less of them than he had hoped. After he had made quick visits to New South Wales and South Australia to inspect troops, the brigade assembled in Victoria late in November, Monash moving into Broadmeadows camp with it. Following a brisk campaign for improvement of the water supply and latrine conditions, he began to impose his methods on commanding officers and to lecture to their juniors. He reissued *100 Hints for Company Commanders*.

There was time for tactical exercises on the outskirts of the northern suburbs. On 17 December, with Monash riding at the head, the brigade marched through Melbourne, twenty-two miles all told from Broadmeadows and back; he himself calculated the yardages, stages and timing. The governor-general, Sir Ronald Munro Ferguson, was 'much impressed by the condition, discipline and marching of the men'. The brigade was predominantly made up of countrymen, often of splendid physique. Collins House—the first three Victorian brigade-commanders were all tenants—gave Monash a great send-off, cheering him long and loud and presenting him with 'a military travelling kit-bag and camper's dining outfit'. Gibson and the Luna Park directors and the Wallabies dined him and warmly wished him well. And he called on Annie Gabriel, who had recently moved to Melbourne, to say goodbye.

On 22 December the brigade sailed to rendezvous with the New Zealanders at King George Sound, Western Australia. Eleven trainloads cheered and sang their way to Port Melbourne—especially 'Australia Will be There', which was adopted as an official brigade march-tune, and 'We're here because We're here'. Despite the secrecy a crowd of some four thousand saw off the *Ulysses*, flagship of the second contingent, with the traditional streamers and 'Auld Lang Syne'. As commander of the convoy, Monash had a torrid time during the three-day pause at Albany. The hurried embarkation arrangements had been partly botched: many men and many of the stores were on the wrong ships, and orders and other papers had been dumped on the flagship only half an hour before sailing, for distribution at Albany. Communication between the seventeen ships largely broke down there: a half-gale was blowing, the Navy frequently overrode his orders, tugmasters went on strike and refused to work after dark, some senior officers were disobedient. He could not confer with unit commanders about training on the voyage. Fearful of a black mark being recorded against him, he wrote privately to Legge and Lieut-Colonel Dodds at Victoria Barracks to explain his difficulties, and facetiously described to Vic some of the continuous requests for decisions at Albany and the answers he would have liked to have given.

It was a relief to get away on the long voyage—to Egypt, as everyone now knew. For a couple of days Monash had a 'nervous obsession of falling overboard', which he attributed to a slight gastric upset. After the sinking of the *Emden* the convoy of twenty ships was safe and escorted only by one submarine.

> The fleet at sea is a truly magnificent and impressive sight. . . . Standing on the bridge of the flagship . . . I can see the whole fleet spread out in regular formation and responsive to every signal as to course, speed, distance and interval. I feel it is something to have

lived for, to have been entrusted by one's country with so magnificent a responsibility.

Daily he had to send signals 'directing, advising, scolding, bullying and criticising'. A few deaths from pneumonia following measles led him to contemplate the folly of not bringing nurses. Inoculations were proceeding well: he proudly claimed that he seemed to be 'impervious to pain which makes other people squirm'. C. P. Smith, the *Argus* correspondent, was preparing numerous despatches. Of Monash, who had already charmed him, he wrote: 'His powerful personality and impregnable sense of justice were . . . revealed to all ranks . . . at Broadmeadows, and there is not a man on board who would not follow him to the ends of the earth with perfect confidence'. In the Indian Ocean Monash began a 'systematic perusal of text books' and lectured on reconnaissance to assembled officers. He had to sack the officer in command on one ship who had fallen out with the captain.

Colombo was 'full of hard work and trouble'. First the formalities had to be observed: the local commandant visited the flagship, Monash then lunched with the governor and returned the commandant's call, then the governor returned Monash's call and was shown over *Ulysses*. On the second morning the water police relaxed their vigilance and a shoal of boats soon surrounded the fleet. Men from two ships swarmed down anchor-chains and ropes or dived off the decks, and boarded the native craft. Monash sent three officers and fifty men in a fast launch who rounded most of them up, but about two hundred got away, many to the bars of the Galle Face and Grand Oriental hotels. Eventually the European garrison had to be called out to control the roaring drunks. All but about twenty were captured by next morning when the convoy sailed. The commandant submitted an exaggerated report and two months later Monash had to defend himself at length. Like so many Australians voyaging to Europe, he was impressed with the Ceylonese—historically, Australians' favourite Asians.

Each night, now, Monash and Captain Brewis, the naval commander, discussed the next day's disposition of the convoy in the light of naval intelligence; they could not be entirely sure that no armed merchantman was in the region. Shipboard life was extraordinary: at any one time an observer might take in classes in machine-gunning, signalling and languages, a court-martial, cricket and chess matches, wireless telegraphists operating, band practice, and officers and men 'in all sorts of dress and undress . . . sitting, sprawling and lying about, yarning, reading, and sleeping'. 'You can hardly realize', Monash wrote home,

what a rooting up of everything in which I have any interest, this business has been. . . . I suppose the only thing to do is to set one's teeth, and go straight ahead. . . . I can only form the guess that for the time being the Australian troops will be left to garrison Egypt, and may quite possibly be left there till the end of the war, that is of course unless the war goes on over next spring and summer.

And he was worrying about how Vic was managing domestic finances and assuring her that 'if all goes well, and the war is over', she should improve the library at Iona by putting a walnut grille into the window-bay and installing a walnut mantelpiece instead of the old-fashioned marble.

After the Colombo experience, Monash anchored the convoy four miles out of Aden. At Suez they were inundated with wild rumours; as a precaution he built up cover on the ship's bridge against snipers. They were arriving just when the Turks were about to make a futile assault on the Canal. 29 January was a day of 'sustained excitement', a 'revelation of Empire'. It took from 9 a.m. to 5 p.m. to steam the forty-five miles to Ismailia between infantry entrenched on both sides cheering all the way—Gurkhas, New Zealanders, Lancashire Territorials, Sikhs, Bengal Lancers. The band saluted a French warship with *La Marseillaise*: 'The ships company yelled and danced with delight. Round after round of cheers (Heep, Heep, Hooray) followed us on our way'. Then came Sepoys, more Gurkhas and New Zealanders, an Egyptian Camel Corps, King's Own Scottish Borderers, and many more. 4th Brigade disembarked at Alexandria and settled into camp five miles out of Cairo near Heliopolis, fifteen miles from the 1st Division at Mena.

4th Brigade, Chauvel's 1st Light Horse Brigade and the New Zealand Infantry Brigade and Mounted Rifles, were to make up the New Zealand and Australian Division under Major-General Sir Alexander Godley.* With the 1st Australian Division they formed the Australian and New Zealand Army Corps under Lieut-General Sir William Birdwood.† Both the senior generals were courteous in welcoming Monash and reviewed the brigade at church parade on the first Sunday. He found Birdwood

> a small, thin man, nothing striking or soldierly about him, speaks with a stammer and has a rather nervy, unquiet manner, but there is no mistaking his perfectly wonderful grasp of the whole business

---

* A battalion at full strength was about 1000 men. There were four battalions to an infantry brigade which was 4055 strong plus ancillary units. A division, consisting of three brigades and ancillary units, amounted to nearly 18 000 men. A corps could vary widely in size, from two to six or seven divisions. An army similarly might include two or several corps.

† Monash, Birdwood, Chauvel (and Ludendorff) were all born in 1865 (Ludendorff in Posen Province, Prussia).

of soldiering. . . . I have been around with him for hours and heard him talking to privates, buglers, drivers, gunners, colonels, signallers and generals and every time he has left the man with a better knowledge of his business than he had before. He appeals to me most thoroughly.

Birdwood told the governor-general that Monash struck him as being

an exceptionally able man on paper, observant—and with knowledge but I am doubtful about his being able to apply this knowledge in the field, partly perhaps because he does not seem to possess enough physical activity on horse back. Lord Kitchener recently sent me a certain amount of nasty correspondence about him from Australia with reference to his alleged German proclivities, but I told him [Kitchener] I am not prepared to take any action in the matter which I understand was fully enquired into in Australia.

But Birdwood had taken the precaution of consulting the medico Charles Ryan from Melbourne about Monash.*

The 6' 6" Godley was a British Army regular who had been commanding the New Zealand Military Forces. Monash described him as 'elegant, graceful, genial and expansive. He also shows great ability, but is mentally a long way behind Birdwood. His strength lies largely in his magnetic and stimulating personality than in high technical ability'. He could deal it out hot and strong at his 'pow-wows', but was willing to admit his mistakes. Godley considered Monash to be 'a very energetic and capable commander, and believe that he will do well in the field. He is always very ready to act upon all suggestions and orders . . . an excellent officer'. Monash found Birdwood's staff officers to be 'charming amiable people, the very essence of considerate good breeding, and modest, simple, earnest and sincere'. Godley's staff, all New Zealanders, were going out of their way to help him.

Monash liked to be liked and usually thought well of people on brief acquaintance; he was to modify his opinions soon enough. He had seen McCay several times and found him 'jumpy':

I am afraid the First Division are not at all a happy family; there are a good many mutterings about overwork, and unsympathetic administration. I have heard Battalion Commanders . . . talk as I hope and believe my Commanders would never dream of doing. . . . I think we have been most fortunate (I mean Chauvel and I) to get into Godley's Division.

---

*   He probably passed the letters on to Bridges, for when Major J. G. Gellibrand recommended sending home members of the A.I.F. of foreign origin, Bridges showed him a bundle of letters and said, 'Then charge Monash as an alien Jew with suspicion and his wife with open disloyalty. Would you recommend his discharge?' 'Yes', replied Gellibrand, 'if his men distrust him he should go'.

For a time Monash attempted to assert independence from Bridges as senior officer of the A.I.F., on the ground that 4th Brigade was an 'Australian Formation' raised by the Military Board, as distinct from 1st Division, A.I.F., which had been raised at the request of the War Office. Legge and Dodds had told him not to accept Bridges's authority while the brigade was in training, and his orders as officer-in-charge of the convoy placed him under the control of the senior Imperial officer at his destination. But it was impossible to maintain for long that 4th Brigade was not part of the A.I.F. Oddly, however, for three years until late in 1917, Monash was to remain more or less apart from the main Australian force.

After 4th Brigade's first exercise, Godley commented: 'All I need say is that they fell into their place, and did what they were ordered to do, with a punctuality, precision, steadiness, and thoroughness, which makes further comment unnecessary'. Next day, 12 February, Monash noted: 'A very heavy field day on foot in which everything works out splendidly and whole Brigade receives great praise at pow-wow'. On the 15th Godley sent for him to say that he and Birdwood considered 'my Brigade is best Aust. brigade in Egypt, and that we are to go straight on to advanced training'. From now on Godley's division trained as a division, which 1st Division never did. There was some resentment at the praises heaped on the 4th Brigade, but Monash was proud that the eight weeks' lag had been caught up. Henceforth the training was intense, with much night-work. Monash stood up well to sleeping when he could and was pleased with his riding prowess: 'in saddle from 7.50 to 6.15 p.m. and do a deal of hard riding successfully, and without stress. Most satisfactory and stimulating day'. His staff was shaping well: McGlinn, though a little slow, was entirely reliable and they were becoming intimate friends; Jess was satisfactory; and his A.D.C., Lieutenant (later Major-General) Locke from Duntroon, was 'a charming gentlemanly lad'. Monash himself wrote *Operation Standing Orders* for the brigade. Three or four days each week were spent in the field; after twenty miles' march, the men came in to play football. The division had 'fought' the East Lancashires, and his brigade had 'fought' and licked the N.Z. Brigade, mainly by means of a flank attack. He inspected and addressed the four battalions separately. They would need to cultivate patience, endurance and self-sacrifice; there were a few 'slackers' and 'wasters' who could best be disciplined, not from above but by public opinion in their battalions; they were shortly going on active service and he called on them 'with confidence to do your level best for the sake of your manhood, for the sake of Australia and for the sake of the British Empire'. In late March he remarked that 'our War Training is finished, and we are now all standing by for orders to move'.

Monash initially thought no better of the 'land of sand, sin, sorrow and syphilis' than any other Australian; all were eager to be off to France. 'Everything is dirty, squalid, smelly and repugnant to any refined sense', he wrote after a week. The wind, dust and cold were highly unpleasant. A day at Memphis was disappointing:

> my principal impression was of a yelling screaming crowd of dirty, smelly Arabs, donkey boys, Bedouins, Dragomans, donkeys, camels and mules, whirling along in a pandemonium of confusion, noise, shouting and muddled arrangements.

He was amazed to receive 'a deputation headed by the Grand Rabbi of Cairo, in resplendent robes of many hues'. Conversing in French, Monash agreed to muster Jewish officers for the Purim service and was implored to lead the Australian troops in reconquering Jerusalem—he promised to use his 'great influence with King George and Earl Kitchener to that end'. He began to visit the museums and one night even witnessed some 'fancy dancing'. His usual companions were McGlinn and Smith of the *Argus*—he had barely met the Sydney journalist, the lanky carrot-haired Charles Bean, the official war correspondent and eventually the great war historian, who showed little interest in 4th Brigade. Smith became one of Monash's greatest devotees and professed to 'love him as a father'. On St Patrick's Day 'McGlinn and all the other Paddys in the Brigade' took him to a Greek Catholic service at Heliopolis (so the influence of 'the McInerney clique' was not far-reaching). Late in March, with a party of a dozen, he had a two-day trip to Luxor—'by far the most wonderful and impressive sight I have seen anywhere'. 'Some day I hope you will see it all with me', he told Vic.

Like any soldier, Monash lived for letters from home, which he read again and again. The first batch included the news that Vic and Bertha, on holiday at Clifton Springs, were at the same table as the Commonwealth attorney-general, W. M. Hughes, and his wife. 'What a pity he is so hard of hearing', Vic wrote, but Mr Hughes was 'a dear', and had presented Bert with a copy of his *Case for Labor*! Vic was forming a branch of the Purple Cross Service for wounded horses and was working hard for Belgian Flag Day. Bertha worked throughout the war as a nursing aide. John wrote when he could, in considerable detail, reassuring them about his health. He did not mention the influenza-cold he had immediately on arrival which made him 'feverish' and 'seedy' for ten days, and was proud of feeling 'robust' and 'thoroughly good'. He was, however, worried by the absence of news of the business from Gibson. He anxiously awaited a locket he had asked for, which would both serve as an identity disc and include miniature photographs of Vic and Bert. When it arrived, he was highly excited:

> In the middle of a busy Cairo street, surrounded by newspaper vendors, chocolate merchants, bootblacks and people who were assuring me that they had "vair gude ohrangees" I tore the parcel open, and feasted my eyes upon the long looked for locket.

He wrote very freely to Vic, revealing much current information. At first he sent his letters through Hall, but soon abandoned this practice. When Bert chaffed him about breaking the regulations, he replied that he intended to keep relating 'what everybody knows', but never to pass on confidential information. Sometimes he went much too far; on 22 March he adopted the transparent subterfuge of referring to the recent arrival of Mr Hamilton, 'the same gentleman who came to see me at Lilydale', who was launching a business at a place across the water. And he sent official documents for safe keeping. No doubt he was a very good judge of what would still be relevant several weeks later, and he knew that Egypt swarmed with spies from whom little could be concealed. But he was open to the criticism that he would not keep the rules by which his juniors had strictly to abide. It was a common failing among generals: Birdwood, for one, in his letters told his wife almost everything.

When the third A.I.F. contingent arrived early in March, Monash was alarmed by the lurid rumours they brought of the second contingent's misbehaviour, and sat down to write to Senator Pearce:

> our Australian relatives and friends have been asked to believe that at every port of call . . . the soldiers committed to my charge landed in considerable numbers and indulged in drunken and immoral orgies. . . . the exact contrary has been the case.

He admitted the Colombo trouble, but no soldier had landed at any other port of call, and since arrival in Egypt,

> no one could wish to command a finer and more earnest, more worthy and well behaved body of men. . . . I am addressing myself to you, Senator, as our official and political representative, with the earnest request that for the sake of our Parents, our wives and our children, you will not allow our good name to be tarnished in Australia.

When Pearce showed the governor-general this letter, the response was that while 'exceedingly interesting', it was in places 'somewhat emotional'. Munro Ferguson probably reacted similarly to an effusive letter Monash wrote him about 4th Brigade's quality. Monash had had in mind the alarming incidence of venereal disease among the first contingent. By the time 4th Brigade arrived, stern measures had been taken and few of them fell victim.

Early in April Monash had the 'very disagreeable' job of acting on a court of inquiry into the 'battle of the Wazzir'. On Good Friday a few drunken Australians and New Zealanders began to break up a notorious house in the brothel area of Cairo, in protest at rising prices, the incidence of V.D., adulterated grog and robberies. About two thousand troops gathered and several houses were fired. The town picket, the fire brigade and the military mounted police were in turn repulsed, before order was restored. The hastily assembled court examined some fifty witnesses and inspected the area. Monash had never seen such a 'sickening revolting and disgusting spectacle'; swarms of 'revolting black women' screamed 'filthy abuse' at them. 'Phew! I'm glad it's all over.' The court made heavy weather, against a conspiracy of silence, of making its inconclusive report.

At last they were to move. Wild rumours blossomed, especially after General Sir Ian Hamilton's arrival. They busied themselves with 'final overhaul of kits, seeing that every man had all he needed and nothing more, serving out the Emergency Ration, examining the . . . rifles, sharpening the last of the bayonets and swords, trying the revolvers, loading forage and stores'. On 11 April the brigade broke camp and took train for Alexandria: 'The men are in the highest spirits and I am sure we shall do well'. They sailed on the 13th and, on opening the sealed orders, Monash could reveal that they were sailing for Port Mudros, Lemnos, to prepare to invade Turkey on the Gallipoli Peninsula.

They crossed the blue Aegean in calm sunny weather, past Karpathos in the west and Rhodes to the east, then caught a glimpse of mighty Mount Olympus 'tipped with sparkling gold as the sunlight bathed its snowclad peaks'. Did Monash recall that famous battleground on the plains of Troy, only a few miles to starboard? Mudros was crowded with the great armada. For almost the only time during the war Monash's letters were censored. He was given charge of a trial disembarkation of most of the division; for days the men practised climbing down rope-ladders with heavy loads. No one knew yet when the attack was to be made. In long periods of inactivity he made pencil sketches of shipping in the harbour. On the 21st he was unable to attend a conference because of rough weather, but that night wrote his first operation order, 'without a tremor and with as little excitement as if it were merely all pretence like our peace manoeuvres'. On the 23rd, to his great delight, a mail arrived—and, in case of his death, he wrote farewell letters to Vic and Bert. Early on the 24th he was summoned to a divisional conference five miles out: it was a 1½-hour 'rough and perilous journey in the little cutter. . ., and I was wet through with spray'. He wrote again to Vic anticipating 'great events which will stir the whole world, and will go down in history . . . to the eternal glory of Australia. . . . It is astonishing how light hearted everybody is, whistling, singing and cracking jokes, and indulging in all sorts of horseplay and fun'. So the innocents went to their slaughter. A young lieutenant, to be killed next day, recorded in his diary: 'Australia tomorrow founds a tradition. God grant it may be a great one'.

The Gallipoli venture, the 'promising sideshow' to break the stagnation of trench warfare on the Western Front, made good strategic sense. If Turkey could be knocked out, the Middle East would be liberated and the threat to Egypt removed, pressure on Russia in the Caucasus would be relieved and exchange of military material and grain made easy, and Italy and even Bulgaria would be attracted to join the Allied cause. It was planned first as a naval operation: after forcing the Dardanelles, the Navy could enforce the surrender of Constantinople (Istanbul). The failure of the attempt to force the Straits on 18 March meant falling back on a military invasion to help the Navy through. The commander-in-chief, Hamilton, hurriedly prepared an assault by English and French troops at Cape Helles on the tip of the peninsula together with a landing by the Australians and New Zealanders near Cape Gaba Tepe, a dozen miles north of Cape Helles on the Aegean side. Hamilton saw the Anzac landing as 'a strong feint, which may develop into the real thing'. With much administrative bungling, preparations proceeded with the full knowledge of the Turks; their army was presumed to be no serious match for British troops, even on such easily defensible ground. So this beautiful borderland of Europe and Asia, historically the most important strategic waterway in the world and the source of innumerable legends and classical associations, once again was to be the stage for mankind in agony.

4th Brigade was to be in reserve to the 1st Division and the N.Z. Brigade and was intended to land late on the 25th. On the 24th, warships and transports slipped away from Lemnos in twos and threes. 4th Brigade headquarters and the 14th Battalion joined the long line at 9.30 a.m. on the 25th in mild sunny weather. About noon, still out of sight of land, they heard the first rumble of naval guns. 'My only feelings', wrote Monash, as he closed his last letter for three weeks, 'are those of the keenest expectation, the thought of the world stirring drama in which we are taking part overshadowing every other feeling'. In his diary he later wrote:

> At 2 p.m. we passed the entrance to the Dardanelles, and witnessed the furious bombardment of Achi Baba, and the enemy's shelling the beach at Cape Helles. About 4 p.m. we came opposite Gaba Tepe and ANZAC Cove, and commenced to hear musketry and saw Enemy Shrapnel on the ridges. At 7 p.m. first boat load of wounded came alongside, and then followed a dreadful night, over 700 wounded being taken aboard. About 11 p.m. an excited Commander

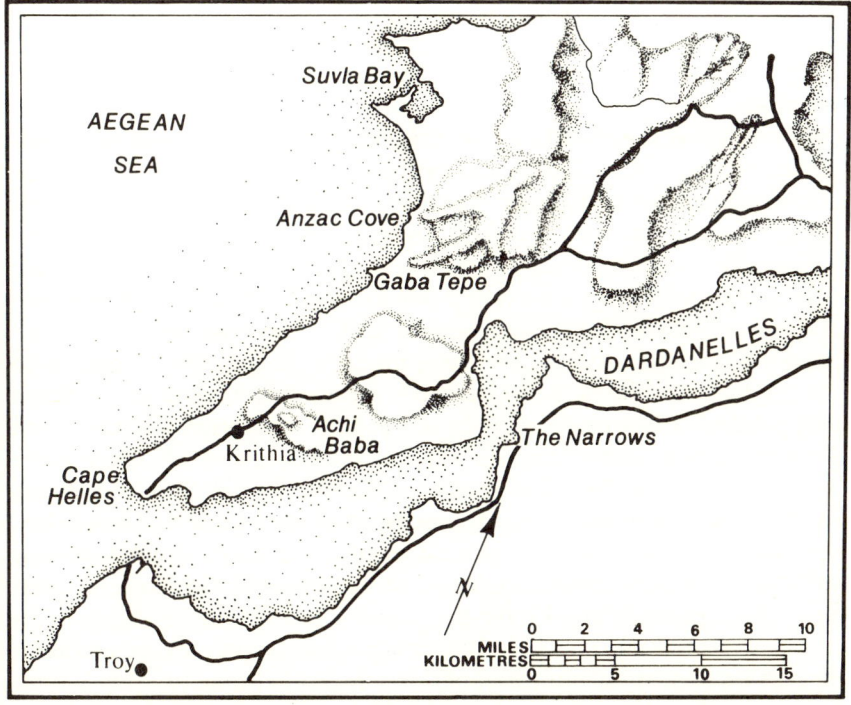

Gallipoli

of a destroyer came alongside and yelled orders to lower all boats, ready for the shore in case the "Admiral decided to reembark the whole force."

4th Brigade's landing had been delayed by the confusion on shore. The 16th Battalion went ashore about 6 p.m.; the 15th, badly split up, between 5 and next morning; the 13th before midnight; Brigade headquarters and the 14th not till the following morning.

The plan had been to land on the open beach one to two miles north of Gaba Tepe and, after securing the hills on the left flank, to push east through low country across the peninsula to sever Turkish communications. The landing was mistakenly made a mile further to the north, mostly on what came to be known as Anzac Cove, a narrow beach about 1000 yards long. While disembarking in congested confusion, the units of Bridges's 1st Division were inextricably mixed up, and most of the troops were faced with precipitous cliffs to assault. The detailed events of that day when the Australians, imbued with their instructions to press on, and out of control of their commanders, are largely unknown. Anything might have happened—total success or total failure—following the fierce encounters in the mallee-type scrub and the wildflowers. Isolated groups penetrated further than ever was to be held again, but late in the day the outnumbered enemy under the inspired leadership of Mustapha Kemal forced them back. By nightfall the Anzac position was critical: Bridges and Godley recommended to Birdwood that the troops be evacuated. At midnight Hamilton decided to deny the plea: 'You have got through the difficult business, now you have only to dig, dig, dig, until you are safe'. So the position was inspirationally secured.

Monash and the 14th Battalion landed about 10.30 a.m. on the 26th under heavy shrapnel, and were sent to a bivouac on the beach. The previous evening Godley had ordered most of the 16th Battalion to occupy Pope's Hill (named after their commander), and some of the 15th were near Courtney's Post by sunset; after midnight, half the 15th filled the gap between 2nd and 3rd Brigades on the 400 Plateau; early in the morning the 13th was sent to reinforce Quinn's Post and Pope's and to clear Russell's Top. During the afternoon of the 26th Godley sent Monash to confer with MacLagan of 3rd Brigade about how best 'to collect the scattered fragments of my Brigade, which had been distributed piecemeal all over the line. I went up the valley under a hail of shrapnel, and in a chorus of whistling and crackling bullets'. He was hit by a spent shrapnel pellet, which of course he souvenired. After a night back at the Beach, at 9.15 a.m. on the 27th he took the 14th into Shrapnel Gully, 'under fairly heavy fire' according to Locke's war diary. Three-quarters of an hour later, he was summoned back to Plugge's Plateau to confer with Birdwood and Godley. The previous day it had been settled that Godley's division would take the left and Bridges's the right. The party stood viewing the second ridge until the shrapnel got too hot and they moved to an old Turkish trench. Birdwood decided that the New Zealanders would take the left quarter (Walker's Ridge and Russell's Top), Monash the left centre (as far as Courtney's Post), and MacLaurin and McCay (under Bridges) the right centre and right. Monash returned to the waiting 14th Battalion, detached two companies for MacLaurin's sector and, under severe sniping, pushed on with the remainder who climbed up to reinforce Quinn's and Courtney's. From now, the whole upper valley was to bear Monash's name. Brigade headquarters was established under Courtney's, a rough dug-out was built, and telephone contact made with the 14th and 16th Battalions. The brigade medical officer continued to marvel, over the years, at how men of Monash's and McGlinn's build—Tweedledum and Tweedledee they were sometimes called—managed to scramble up (though the way in to Shrapnel Gully from Anzac Cove was easy).

Unknown to the higher commanders, Kemal's major counter-

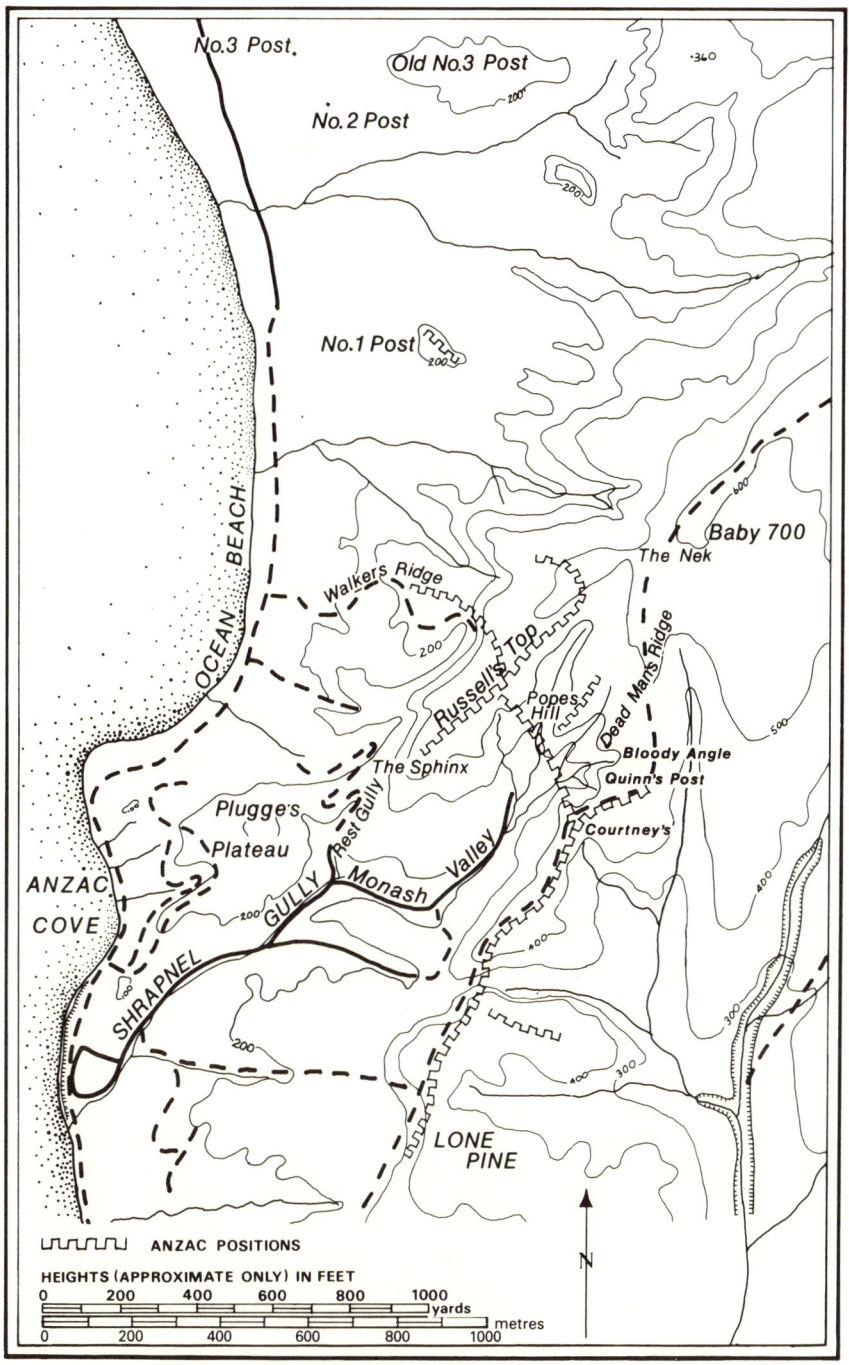

The Anzac Perimeter

offensive had already begun. Monash was again sent for early in the afternoon to join Birdwood and Bridges at MacLaurin's headquarters to work out the boundaries of their sectors and their fire-plans. Soon after Monash left the conference, MacLaurin and his brigade major were killed by snipers. Monash took over his sector officially at 4 p.m. The Turkish counter-attack, right round the perimeter, though it continued sporadically for most of the night, failed everywhere, partly because of murderous shelling by the Royal Navy. Late in the afternoon 4th Brigade beat off determined attacks on Pope's, Quinn's and Courtney's, repeatedly using the bayonet to clear the immediate front.

Monash's sector at the head of the triangular valley was the most difficult. From the higher ground of The Nek and Baby 700 the Turks controlled the field of fire, they occupied Dead Man's Ridge and Bloody Angle at the head of Monash Valley, and some snipers were within the Anzac lines; movement up the valley by day was perilous, even after sandbag barricades were built. In the history of warfare few positions have been as bizarre as Quinn's Post. Here and at Pope's the crest could not be occupied during the day for it was swept by fire from the flanks and left rear; the Turks were able continually to congregate just over the summit. For the moment it was a matter just of hanging on, digging and digging. After the Turkish failure on the 27th, next day they charged Quinn's again and again, but the following two days were relatively quiet. Monash was constantly conferring with Captain Skelsey, the engineer who was developing the defences of Quinn's. Monash's diary for the 28th reads: 'All energies devoted to gathering up scattered details of the Brigade and getting them arranged in groups'. On the 29th he managed to reinforce Pope's, form a reserve and start probing in the gap on his left, and reported that his men were well dug in. But on the 30th, one and a half of his four battalions were still elsewhere. That day, however, he had a conference of commanding officers; his notebook contains an orderly agenda of sixteen items—arrangements for regular alternation in the front line, placement of machine-guns, sapping, links between the posts, bivouac areas, keeping the roads clear, sanitation, casualty returns, etc. Some weeks later he told his wife:

> It needed a lot of nerve to keep cool enough . . . to reinforce at the critical points, to hold the proper reserves of men at the proper times and in the proper places, to organise the ammunition supply, and the food and water supply, and to keep everybody cheerful and hopeful, and to make exhausted men do just that little bit more that turned the scale.

On the 30th, observing from below, he sent in two companies of the 13th Battalion to counter-attack at the right of Courtney's, when the

British Marines gave way. Quinn's was again attacked several times; the troops appealed desperately for bombs and periscopes whose manufacture on the beach was being contrived. Somehow the 14th and 15th Battalions hung on, but with heavy casualties.

To make the position safe Baby 700 would have to be captured. Knowing something was in the wind, Monash reported to Godley on the 30th that his brigade was not yet fully gathered and incapable yet of co-ordinated action; in particular, the 16th Battalion at Pope's was utterly exhausted. But Birdwood issued orders for a general advance on 1 May at 5 p.m. That morning, Colonel H. B. Walker, commanding 1st Brigade, objected to the plan and conferred with Bridges and Monash, who supported him. Birdwood decided to modify the plan, confining the attack to Godley's division, which was to move at nightfall on the 2nd after a preliminary bombardment. Monash noted: 'I have difficulty in dissuading Godley from undertaking a partial advance by N.Z. Div.'

The night offensive was a disaster. At 7 p.m. a heavy bombardment by naval and land guns opened on the Turkish positions and was followed by sustained machine-gun and rifle-fire until 7.25. The 16th Battalion which had had two days 'rest' and the 13th which had had none climbed to the crest singing 'Australia Will be There' and 'Tipperary' and cheering as they went over the top—they could be heard down at the beach. Their objective was the ridge to the right of Baby 700. Although met by heavy fire and suffering terrible casualties, the 16th and part of the 14th established themselves and dug in as an extension of Quinn's to the left, as did the 13th in front of Pope's. But the attack had gone off half-cocked: the Otago Battalion, which was to attack Baby 700 at the same time as the 16th, had not arrived, and the 13th's left flank was open and under orders not to advance without the Otagos. Godley and the Otagos' commanding officer had allowed far too little time to march from Walker's Ridge via the beach into Monash Valley. Divisional headquarters must have known an hour before zero that they could not arrive on time. Yet the action proceeded. When, nearly two hours late, the Otagos made their advance, they met withering fire and could not get far over the crest. A company of the 15th Battalion, which Monash put in between the 13th and the Otagos, reached the Turkish trenches on Baby 700 but had to retire. About midnight the front gained was semi-circular, in the centre an advance of some 600 yards. Godley had already made the desperate throw of sending part of the Canterburys over The Nek, which had not been intended until Baby 700 was taken; they inevitably failed, retreated into Monash Valley, and thence advanced to the Otagos' left. Their position was terribly exposed and at daylight the entire left crumbled.

Meanwhile, about 2 a.m. Monash was given two supporting

battalions of British Marines and the impossible task of connecting the line of trenches across his whole front. The Marines were slow to make their dispositions and eventually were caught by machine-guns in the dawn, Jess attempting to place and rally them. The top of the valley was jammed with wounded and reinforcements and ammunition carriers crowding up. At about 5 o'clock artillery, unasked by Monash, shelled the ridge, destroyed some 80 yards of the 16th's trenches, and demoralized some of the 16th and the Marines into withdrawal. The 13th and the core of the 16th hung on desperately. Now Brigadier-General Trotman of the Marines formally asked Godley whether, as senior officer, he should not take over command of the sector. Godley concurred, because of the seniority principle and because Trotman was the fresher man—the battle was lost anyway. 'Monash and myself given a day's spell', Jess wrote in his diary. Monash bore no grudge against Trotman whom he judged to be 'amiable and helpful' though he thought his men were useless.

The 16th dribbled back during the morning; the 13th in their well dug-in positions remained out in front, but as they could not be supplied or supported, withdrew next night. Monash did not rest much that day. He wrote urgently to Godley about this first slaughter of his brigade: it was at less than half-strength—the 16th had overnight been reduced from about 637 to 300 men, and the 15th was down to 350. 'It is imperative that this Brigade should be withdrawn for reorganization and the appointment of new staffs and leaders.' There was no chance of that.

It was a demoralizing initiation into battle. Monash could comfort himself that he had had no part in preparing the battle plan, had been scrupulously careful in his area of responsibility, his men had no chance after the Otagos failed to arrive, and the chaos in the hours before dawn was not of his making and beyond control. He could learn much from the hurried nature of the operation, with its lack of attention to obvious detail. The semi-destruction of his brigade rocked his confidence in his superior officers and confirmed his inclination to speak out: he could hardly do worse than they had. On the other hand he knew that all were exhausted, and rational leadership was hardly to be expected.

Bean, the official war correspondent, talked to him on the 3rd. Major Blamey had already told him that Monash's reports had given Birdwood and Godley the impression that he was shaken in the crisis. Monash talked excitedly to Bean of a 'disaster. . . . They've tried to put the work of an Army Corps on me'. Bean eventually wrote in the *Official History* that 'the disastrous attack by his brigade . . . had left [Monash] unstrung, as well it might'; and elsewhere he concluded that 'he was in no way responsible'. The great Murray, V.C., of the 16th

Battalion looked back on it as 'the worst stunt I was ever in' except Bullecourt, 'a blunder . . . a sad and terrible business'.

Birdwood came round on the 4th and ordered vigorous digging. Work continued on connecting the posts and carving out saps and T-heads towards the enemy; the word went round that trenches had to be wide enough for Paddy McGlinn and deep enough for Godley. At Quinn's especially, which for several weeks now was to be the centre of the fighting, a warren of tunnels and trenchworks was constructed. Monash established a routine of the 15th and 16th Battalions alternating there each 48 hours, while the 13th held Pope's and the 14th Courtney's. On the 6th and 7th he welcomed five hundred sorely needed brigade reinforcements.

Following Hamilton's order to undertake minor operations in order to 'compel the enemy to maintain a large force in your front' while Helles remained the chief battleground, Godley insisted on actions which would disclose the Turks' strength and the nature of their defences; Monash and all his battalion commanders were opposed. On the night of the 8th, five non-commissioned officers of the 13th were sent out from Pope's to ascertain the enemy position on Dead Man's Ridge; one was killed and three badly wounded. Next night Lieut-Colonel Cannan's 15th Battalion made a reconnaissance in force from Quinn's. All went well at first and advanced Turkish trenches were captured. But when the Turks counter-attacked in strength, the 15th could not reply to bombing attacks and, with the dawn, were exposed to heavy crossfire and had to be withdrawn. There were more than two hundred casualties. Turkish casualties were heavier and useful information had been gained about enemy dispositions, but a disgusted Monash wrote in his diary:

> Godley visits us. Professes to be very pleased at result of last night's operations and now declares he knew all along the Turks were still present in large numbers. He yields to my request for a little pause to recoup and reorganize.

Birdwood was up again that day and asked some of the 15th whether they were in the charge the previous night. They told him they had been reserves: 'Our Brigadier Monash was standing by and he chipped in "Most of those who were in the charge last night didn't come back Sir"'.

Help was at hand in the form of the 1st Light Horse Brigade who were to be used as infantry in relief of the Marines. Colonel H. G. Chauvel, Monash's senior, took over the left-centre sector on 12 May. Monash showed Chauvel round Quinn's and Pope's and they discussed schemes of manning. Chauvel described Monash's headquarters dug out, as 'a somewhat dissolute-looking rabbit warren', 'within practically a stone's throw' of the front line. Next day the Light Horse replaced 4th Brigade there but, after the raw newcomers had been subjected to severe pressure from bombing attacks, Birdwood and Godley decided that the 15th Battalion would have to return. One squadron was left, in order to make another futile raid ordered by Godley: forty-six of the sixty who went over became casualties. Monash noted: 'Godley orders 3 sq 2d Regt to its doom'. On the 17th his diary reads:

> Chauvel rather annoys me by undue interference with internal administrative matters, but I can easily hold my own, if I take the trouble. He is always grateful for my help, when he gets into a tangle. [He] is very fidgetty, and frequently calls to consult me during the night.

Birdwood later was critical of Chauvel's pessimism and considered relieving him, though he had displayed great bravery and coolness; very likely, in contrast, Monash was displaying the determined cheerfulness which came to be one of his characteristics. On the 20th, after the Turks made a massive assault, Chauvel wrote home that the infantry were 'simply magnificent':

> I am living cheek by jowl with Monash here and find he is really a very fine soldier. He has been of very great assistance to me the last few days, and very willing indeed considering I have ousted him out of the command of the sector. . . . I was astounded by the coolness and grit displayed by our men, my own and Monash's.

The two men formed a lasting bond of brotherhood: 'I shall never forget those early days at Anzac . . . when we got along so well together', Chauvel told Monash after the war.

On 7 May Monash had got away for the first time to the beach for a swim and to 'dine' with Godley. By the 12th he was writing letters: almost the first was to ask Vic to tell Theodore Fink how his son had died. Gradually be began to tell the story, though he never wrote very revealingly about himself:

> Those first three weeks were pretty tough and solid. We had nothing but what we stood up in for the first 5 days, then gradually came water, and food, and boxes to sit on, and boxes to burn to boil our camp kettles, then blankets and waterproof sheets, then sandbags to build dug outs and cabins, then tools and timber to make roofs . . . and by and by came my kitbag with a change of underclothes, and so for the past week or two we have been quite comfortable and respectable.

He described the noise: the 'gentle purring hum' of a bullet passing close by and the sharp sudden whipcrack of one well overhead; the 'low rumble or growl' of their own rifle-fire; the kettledrum rattle of machine-guns; shells 'like a gust of wind on a wintry day . . . ending in a loud bang'; the ear-splitting discharge of the artillery and the reverberating echoes.

> We have been amusing ourselves by trying to discover the longest period of absolute quiet. We have been fighting now continuously for 22 days, all day and all night and most of us think that absolutely the longest period during which there was absolutely no sound of gun or rifle fire . . . was 10 seconds. One man says he was able on one occasion to count 14, but none believe him.

He described the scene behind the line:

> We have got our battle procedure now thoroughly well organized. . . . There are orderlies carrying messages, staff officers with orders, lines of ammunition carriers, water carriers, bomb carriers, stretcher bearers, burial parties, first aid men, reserves, supports, signallers, telephonists, engineers, digging parties, sandbag parties, periscope hands, pioneers, quartermaster's parties, and reinforcing troops running about all over the place, apparently in confusion, but yet everything works as smoothly as on a peace parade, altho' the air is thick with clamour, and bullets and bursting shells, and bombs, and flares.

The men

> are as docile and patient and obedient and manageable as children, yet they are full of the finest spirit of self-devotion. For the most perilous enterprises, whenever volunteers are called for, every man in sight offers instantly, altho' often it means certain death. . . . They are always cheerful, cracking jokes, always laughing and joking and singing and as I move among them and ask "Well lads, how are you getting on", the invariable answer is "First rate Sir" or "Ryebuck", or "We're ready for another go". There have been scenes of awful slaughter, with heaps of dead and wounded and ghastly wounds and long lines of stretcher bearers with their gory burdens, but men march cheerily past and take up positions for attack & defence. . . . I am convinced that there are no troops in the world to equal the Australians in cool daring, courage and endurance. . . . our boys, capably led, can give the British regulars points and a beating at *any* part of the game, whether it be in digging a trench, or in a bayonet assault, or in steadiness under fire, or in boiling the billy or in ambulance work, or in cheerfully suffering fatigue and privations, or in marching, or personal bravery. Our wounded are most amazing: they sing, they cheer, they smoke their cigarettes, even when so badly hit as to have to be carried on a stretcher.

Under heavy shelling, they would derisively cheer the Turks. But

Monash was too shocked and too weary, though he might have been capable of it, to make an adequate literary response to some of the most heroic events in the history of warfare. No Australian who fought at Gallipoli managed convincingly to describe what it was like. Nor did Monash really understand the Australian ethos or begin yet to apprehend the apotheosis of the Australian common man which was occurring.

He had plenty of humour to retail, sometimes with an anti-officer twist: the colonel with a sprained ankle who ran flat out for cover from an approaching shell; the man buried by an 8" shell who when dug out cursed 'those damn snipers'; the orderly officer who, berating a cook for his slovenliness, asked what company he belonged to and was told, 'Yours Sir'. He tried to keep the 'horrible side' out of his letters home, but in writing to Professor Masson mentioned 'the woeful waste of life, energy and time . . . nothing to be done but to see it through'.

Brigade commanders were at risk on Gallipoli as rarely occurs in battle. McCay and all his brigade staff were wounded. A dozen of Monash's headquarters personnel became casualties, some of them killed or wounded close beside him by sniping or shrapnel. He collected spent bullets which fell close; shrapnel burst where he had been only a moment before. During the first week when he heard a call to the telephone, the man holding it fell dead, another who took it was hit, and having unthinkingly seized it himself he was dragged away. 'There was no courage in what I did. I was merely so intent on my objective . . . that the danger . . . did not occur to me.' Reminiscing after the war, he recalled that most men, if at work, lost much of the consciousness of danger; it was a curious psychological fact, moreover, that they felt that other men were more likely to fall than themselves. 'And a man as temperamentally phlegmatic as I am, and as occupied as I was then, had small space for consciousness of the fact that he was under fire and in personal danger.'

From the start, he had resolved not to worry; but he always insisted on 'all my people exercising reasonable caution in not remaining stationary in spots which are obviously dangerous, and in doing their observations and reconnaissances from covered places'. The track along the valley was still perilous; everyone had to double through the exposed spots. Bridges had been shot there on the 15th on his way to visit Chauvel and Monash, just short of their headquarters, and died three days later. Bridges's death and MacLaurin's too had been avoidable: 'such unnecessary exposure not only does no possible good, but seriously impairs morale'. The argument is a traditional one about the propriety of a commander inspiring his men by personal bravery and thereby risking grave damage to the cause—Plutarch's rule that a good general should die of old age; Bridges and Birdwood were conspicuous examples of the other side of the argument. Monash, though he very sensibly did not visit the trenches as often as younger and more agile commanders, did his job. He often had to show his seniors the front line, but he and McGlinn could not squeeze through some of the tunnels. He wrote home casually about the 'everlasting tramping about, mile upon mile, up and down these steep hills—my Wallaby walks have proved an excellent training'. He was proud to be doing his duty and not 'skulking at home'. He was insensitive about the 'sheer nerves and funk' of two senior officers who had broken down, and was amused when one of his superiors avoided 'going to the foremost point'. It is absurd to suspect that he did not show adequate bravery on Gallipoli—and only worth mentioning because of occasional slanderous gossip. He must have conformed to the local code of behaviour of usually ignoring shelling. If he had not so behaved he could not have survived the contempt of his men.

The Anzac position was by now secure enough, as the Turks found when they launched a general offensive at 3 a.m. on 19 May, preceded by a heavy artillery bombardment. About 4 o'clock Courtney's was rushed, but was cleared within the hour by Albert Jacka and his Bendigo mates of the 14th Battalion. About 4.20 the brigade machine-gunners cut down the attack on the 15th in Quinn's. With the dawn the defenders picked the Turks off in hundreds. Still they came again and again until nearly midday: their dead lay thickest opposite Courtney's. From that day, much of the Australian bitterness faded, in tribute to the enemy's bravery. 'Everybody exhausted with want of sleep and heavy mental strain', Monash recorded. The Turks never again made a general assault on Anzac.

The thousands of stinking corpses, and some wounded, in No Man's Land now presented a problem. The contest could not continue, it seemed, for health reasons, unless an interval were called. Turkish initiatives were made on the 1st Brigade front. Opposite 4th Brigade a cry of 'Docteur, Docteur' was heard and a flag was raised. Monash sent out two doctors with a Red Cross flag, and 'instantly from all over the place sprang up Turks out of their trenches waving white flags, white rags, and red crescent pennants'. A young Turkish officer was conducted to Monash who explained how an approach might be made at a higher level. Birdwood had already planned to pass a message arranging for a meeting to discuss an armistice, which was eventually fixed for the 24th.* In case it was all a Turkish plot, they were heavily

---

* It rained on the night of the 22nd–23rd and some wag composed a parody of 'Little Grey Home in the West', which Monash jotted down:

> We've a little wet home in a Trench
> Where the rain storms constantly drench
> There's a dead Turk close by
> With his heels toward the sky
> And he gives off a beautiful stench. . . .

bombarded with 18-pounders overnight. During the armistice, while burials proceeded, Monash recorded,

> we noticed a Turk about 100 yards away trying to repair a loophole. ... We signed to a Turkish officer, pointing to it, and he at once understood and ran over to the man and gave him a sound belting with a stick. He then returned to us and, still in sign language, with a polite salute, expressed his regrets ... and then very politely intimated that he would esteem it a favour if we refrained from using our field glasses.

Both sides were of course breaking the rules. Birdwood, Godley and Monash were reconnoitring in front of Pope's, Quinn's and Courtney's. That day Monash explained to Birdwood his plan for taking Baby 700, with which Birdwood agreed, but nothing came of it. A few weeks later Monash still held that they were 'well able to push forward'.

On the 21st Monash had welcomed an order to man Hamilton's personal bodyguard: 'Nothing could more eloquently tell of the esteem in which the Fourth Brigade is held'. Better still, Hamilton ordered Godley to send Monash, one of the first to be so honoured in the Expedition, to rest for a couple of days on the *Arcadia*. Sixteen years later, Hamilton remembered: 'He did splendidly at the Dardanelles, but was a little old for front-line work. I believe I saved his life by pulling him out and making him take a ... rest'. On arrival at Imbros, Monash refused to climb the ladder, telling the ship's officer he had 'come for a rest, not to do gymnastics'. He had 'a plain dinner' with Hamilton who was 'most gracious and charming and considerate' and recalled Lilydale and the Naval and Military Club. Monash told him a story, at which Hamilton 'laughed consumedly', about a brawny Australian taking a Turkish prisoner to the beach, who so persisted in telling him about his wife and children that 'he got on my nerves so I shot the [bugger]'. A King's Messenger present said he would make a point of telling the story to His Majesty. (So war brutalizes civilized men.) Everyone treated Monash kindly and considerately. 'I have been able to get a complete night's rest, with all my clothes off, and a proper bath and clean up.' He returned on the 28th, calling at Helles on the way, and learned, to his delight, that he and about twenty others in the brigade had been mentioned in despatches. On the 30th Hamilton visited Anzac and viewed Quinn's from 4th Brigade headquarters.

The day after Monash returned the Turks had broken in to Quinn's. The Queensland miners of the 15th Battalion had long known that the post was being undermined, and had been counter-tunnelling. On the 25th Chauvel and Monash ordered the firing of a counter-mine and another two days later. But at 3.20 a.m. on the 29th massive explosions blew up part of the post, which was rushed by Turkish troops. The 13th was in occupation, with the 15th in close reserve. Cannan, the usual commander, was away resting; Burnage, commanding officer of the 13th, was soon wounded; Pope of the 16th took his place. Chauvel had rushed up the slope, leaving Monash to organize below. All was well, and by 8 a.m. the position was restored after some two hundred casualties. 'The men behaved like heroes', wrote Monash, 'their battle discipline is perfect, they never flinch, and never hesitate'. The last cornered Turks were taken prisoner and given cigarettes and biscuits, even though stretcher-bearers were carrying out wounded and dead all around them: 'Gallantry can surely touch no higher pinnacle'. 'One old fellow went on his knees, and made a long speech to me in Turkish with many salaams and gestures of homage.' Burnage, the 'gamest old man' of the 13th, was cheered down the valley and out of the war.

At last, 4th Brigade was relieved from Quinn's and Courtney's on 1 June; they had remained there because they knew the ground so well and it was risky to hand over to anyone else. Monash believed, with good reason, that no other brigade had had 'so *continuously* hard a time', had done better or suffered more—most of the original brigade were casualties. They went down to bivouac behind Walker's Ridge, below The Sphinx, 'out of the eternal rain of shrapnel', and the men delighted in bathing, shaving and cleaning up. Next day, in Rest Gully, Godley addressed them, rising to the occasion to recognize their heroism, and announced eleven decorations. Monash thanked him, 'then called for three cheers for His Majesty the King which were lustily given from three thousand throats in true Australian style—the echoes rolling from valley to valley and far out to the sea'. Next morning Birdwood and Monash spent two hours chatting to the troops.

Monash was conscious of the danger of the brigade being neglected in publicity because it belonged to the mixed division and was angry with Bean for his neglect in his early despatches of their exploits in the first few days.* He told him off at the first opportunity, and on the day of Godley's parade jotted down a not entirely accurate summary of the brigade's actions on the first three days. He ordered a clerk to take down Godley's speech in shorthand, wrote an introduction and conclusion, and sent it to C. P. Smith, who placed it in the *Argus* and other newspapers. 'It is due to this fine Brigade that the fullest publicity should be given to its historic doings', he told Vic. Moreover,

> One ought not to hide one's light under a bushel, nor fail to have an eye to the future, and any little discreet publicity may weigh

* Bean had seen nothing of 4th Brigade in the first week and did not visit Quinn's until 24 May. On 2 June he noted in his diary that the 4th was 'a fine brigade, rather easier and freer with their officers and not so neat or rigid as our [*sic*] division'.

heavily in the scale when later on it becomes a question for those in authority to decide on recommendations for the War Honours list.

He recommended promoting the term, 'the Fighting Fourth'. Convinced of the hostility both of permanent soldiers and of the official correspondent, he was adopting a dangerous policy of self-promotion. However, he had not planned for his letters to be published in the press at home, though many of them were written for showing round to family and friends. Vic and Bert had taken the initiative: he did not regret it, in so far as the letters were an 'appreciation of the fine work of the Australian soldiers', but he did not want to suffer the charge of 'atrocious self-advertisement' made against McCay when his wife placed some of his letters in the press. When the Censor eventually decided that no names would appear, Vic and Bert did not think it worthwhile to persevere with publication.

In reserve, for some time 4th Brigade expected imminent recall to the front line. Early in June Monash was busy dealing with reinforcements and the returning wounded, and appointing new officers to the battalions which had been so knocked about. The men did not have it easy, for they had to carry food, water and ammunition to the front line, unload at the beach (often under fire), dig trenches, terrace, make roads, and suffer occasional casualties from shelling. Water was the key to the campaign: the Turks always had plenty, the Anzacs never more than the barest ration. But life was distinctly easier with weekly church parades (which Monash of course attended as the main communal occasion), improvised concerts and time at the beach; there was even a rum issue on the centenary of Waterloo. With the warmer weather, Monash relaxed dress restrictions (he claimed to have been the first): everyone wore cut-down khaki overalls as 'shorts', even Godley and the brigadiers; in shorts and boots only, the men burned themselves as dark as any Turk. In July the 14th and 16th Battalions were given a few days spell at Imbros.

The choice by the Australian government of Legge to succeed Bridges in command of 1st Division outraged Monash, Chauvel and McCay, whom Birdwood tried to soothe. Legge was their junior, had not served in the campaign and was personally unpopular. Moreover, Birdwood should have made a recommendation to Pearce who had indeed concentrated on finding a suitable commander for the A.I.F. rather than a successor to the division. But Legge had only a month on Gallipoli before Birdwood sent him to command the 2nd Division in Egypt. The government then transferred administrative command of the A.I.F. to Birdwood. On 21 July Monash learned by cable from home that he had been promoted temporary brigadier-general, as had six other colonels. The government had at last given way and removed the senior officers' grievance that they held rank junior to British and New Zealand officers with comparable responsibilities. Monash was now addressed as 'General' and an eventual knighthood was clearly in view.

About this time wild rumours circulated in Cairo, London and Melbourne that Monash had been shot as a German spy and traitor. Burnage, for one, was told this on the hospital ship to Egypt. Returned men in Australia claimed to have been present at his execution. Rosenhain reported from London 'no end of lying reports about all over the place'. Vic was made seriously ill when told by one officer in good faith that things had been made too hot for John, he had been forced to resign and was on his way home; then by another that he was in hospital with a nervous breakdown. Vic cabled for reassurance; Bert told her father that it had seemed impossible to her: 'You are positively the strongest man both mentally and physically, I know'. Frequent rumours of spies on Gallipoli and arrests of suspects, combined with the hysteria at home and mankind's infinite gullibility, are probably sufficient explanation. Monash advised his 'dear old muddleheaded worriers' to keep their heads. But, he told Mat, 'If there are people who are making it any harder for [Vic] or any of you I should like to know all about them and what they do and say, so that I may remember it when I get home'. Some of them in fact were vicious gossips within the Jewish community. He believed that his 'old enemies' were 'stirring up trouble in Egypt', and wrote to a trusted officer there asking him to send *'fullest possible particulars'* of rumours and allegations. The reply gave no specific details:

> It may surprise you to know that you have been shot in several places on the peninsula and here in Egypt. Directly one asks for the authority for the story . . . the recounter becomes alarmed and forgets from whom he heard it or says "oh everybody is saying it".

Monash does not seem to have found evidence enough with which to confront his enemies. Early in 1916 he wrote indignantly to the Behrend family, who were calling themselves Monash-Behrend, demanding that they stop: 'openly and deliberately bruiting about the fact of my connection with a family of German name and origin' might do 'incalculable harm to my interests. . . . I have many enemies, who are only too glad to seize upon anything that may injure me'. (A terrible row followed between Minnie and Mat.) Monash's eagerness to gain promotion, honours and decorations may be explained partly by the need to have his loyalty acknowledged; when he heard of his first mention in despatches, he remarked that it should 'shut up some of my enemies for good'. It was to be convenient to have his old friend and subordinate in the Intelligence Corps, George Steward, the governor-general's secretary, in charge of the Counter Espionage Bureau.

Monash spent much time visiting and receiving colleagues. Early in June the New Zealander Brigadier-General Russell walked him over 1, 2 and 3 Outposts, to the north towards Suvla Bay—'hot and arduous work' which slightly lamed him. He visited the other New Zealand brigadier, F. E. Johnston, and Legge, White, Lieut-Colonel 'Pompey' Elliott and others at their stations. He showed C. P. Smith round Quinn's and Courtney's. Godley frequently dropped in to exhort and confer, but he saw little of Birdwood. In mid-June he spent a day visiting Cape Helles on a trawler with other senior officers, under fire on the way and bombardment when there—'an exceptionally thrilling and never to be forgotten experience'. On return he found that he had escaped, by his absence, being called on to take command of a section of the line. He ate sparingly, had his drinking water boiled and was taking plenty of exercise. He still had his teeth and they stood up well to the biscuits. In the hot weather, when the atmosphere at the beach was almost like Manly or Sorrento, he went several times to bathe. He had never known such flies: 'They fight you for your food, and make for the eyes, nostrils, ears and mouth'.

Monash was woken on 27 June, his fiftieth birthday, by the row of a Turkish attack on Walker's Ridge. At 6 o'clock his battalion commanders and their seconds gathered to shake his hand, the 14th Battalion (Victorian) sent collective greetings, and 'all day long, officers from near and far, came to wish me happy returns'. Lady Godley had baked a cake for him in Alexandria, Legge had brought a box of cigars, the Army Service Corps found some rare matches, and the cook provided a 'specially sumptuous' four-course dinner. Such attention was very welcome to a man who took commemorative occasions unusually seriously. The day was marred by a funeral, but he finished it by sharing with his staff a bottle of champagne someone had given him. John Monash inspired far more affection from his officers than did his divisional commander and most of his fellow brigadiers.

In June and July, when he was largely out of things, Monash had time on his hands. Delays in mail were distressing: he read and re-read letters from home and replied in great detail. Vic, who was calling herself 'Victory' again now and was active in the Friendly Union of Soldiers' Wives, wrote as a good wife should: 'Life is very empty for me and I miss you dreadfully'. She was cultivating all the people who might be of use like the Pearces. All Melbourne had congratulated her on his promotion and Rabbi Danglow had based a sermon on him. Mat, who in her first letters had remarked that they had never 'sentimentalized' to each other and that she could not write intimately, did in fact do so very affectionately, as well as informatively and wisely.

Several of his old girl friends, who still called him Jack, did not let him down—the Card sisters and Ada Benjamin especially. Billie Card wrote from England:

> I guess that you are just the same good old Duke of York that you were when you marched four or five girls up the Bogong or the Geebung mountain to see the largest gumtrees in Victoria. Don't you dare think how many years ago that is, just get on with your bombthrowing.

Lewis, Wears, Frank Tate of the Education Department, Meyer, Taylor (his old business rival) and many others wrote warmly to rejoice in the glory of 4th Brigade, to tell him of Marshall-Hall's untimely death, or to chip him about a new soft hat in Melbourne called 'The Monash'. Reading-matter was short and eagerly exchanged; 'Walterlou' were sending *Punch*, the *Sphere* and the *Weekly Times*. Monash sent home a report on painless childbirth which 'appealed to me as of vast interest and importance'. When he heard of the death of Rupert Brooke, whom he had met in Egypt, he was reminded of the German poet, Körner, and asked Vic to buy Brooke's published works. He played much chess and spent many hours trying to solve problems; 'Do you play chess?' he often asked. He applied his mathematical talent to trying to make a foolproof system for roulette. He made algebraic calculations, drew a maze, listed non-English words of English form like 'nate' and 'nope', and made a tabular, classified history of the officers of his brigade. Tobacco was a solace. And, when winter approached, he appealed to Lou to provide, for a fatty diet, his 'old friend' Schmaltz—pig's kidney fat with apples and onions.

Senior army officers tended to be demanding in their requirements of their batmen. Monash was seemingly an exception:

> You ask about Dawson. He is my thoroughly devoted slave, who would mother me if I would let him, but he is absolutely the clumsiest, unhandiest man I have ever met. He spoils every job he touches, is hard of hearing—never remembers anything, is untidy—although perfectly honest he is a habitual fibber, or rather bluffer—in short he is almost everything a good batman ought not to be—yet I have not the heart to send him about his business.

No man is a hero to his valet, but Dawson's views on his boss are not recorded. They remained together for the duration.

During that long hot summer, the Anzacs lost all their romantic illusions. They had expected a war lasting a few months or perhaps a year, after which they would return to the adulation of cheering crowds, with fabulous tales to relate. Now they knew the score. There was no end to the war in sight, no hope of home leave, only the prospect of battle after battle from which there was no escape except death or a serious wound. They lived amid the stench of corpses and in their own filth; their agony was traced on every face and was palliated only by their tenderness to each other. Though the horror was hardly so intense for senior officers, Monash's reactions reflected those of his men. He still wrote of the possibility, his duty done, of gaining an honourable discharge after twelve months. But he knew he was in for it, that it would be 'a case of hanging on till the job was done'. If he was conscious of the possibility of a great destiny in store, he by no means welcomed it. Nearly always cheerful in his letters home, he occasionally dropped his guard as when he referred to 'this weary squalid iron time', and to yearning for his 'home and family and roses and creepers'. He professed to be utterly confident about the progress of the war—it was his constant policy, he did not allow himself not to be. Late in July, when all were waiting tensely on a massive Turkish attack on the bridgehead and standing-to every night, he was sure that all was safe and that after their defeat the Turks would sue for peace. Moreover,

> We have dropped the Churchill way of rushing in before we are ready, and hardly knowing what we are going to do next, in favour of the Kitchener way of making careful and complete preparations on lines which just can't go wrong.

There was no future for the British and French assault at Cape Helles. As early as May Birdwood had begun planning to break out from Anzac and attack the main range to the north. Hamilton took up the scheme enthusiastically and, on Kitchener's insistence, the British government agreed to large reinforcements. A massive landing by British troops would be made at Suvla Bay and 25 000 more be sent to Anzac. The operation would begin with feint attacks at Helles and then at Lone Pine; that night the foothills to the north would be cleared, mainly by the N.Z. Mounted Rifles, and a several-pronged attack on the ridge be made by the N.Z. Brigade, the Gurkhas and 4th Brigade, which would be on the extreme left and eventually link up with the Suvla Bay force. The commanding heights would be won by daybreak; an attack from the Anzac bridgehead would then be made on Baby 700, after which it would be easy to make a final thrust across the peninsula and enclose the Turkish forces.

On a hint from Godley, Monash had begun thinking on 20 June about a northern left hook. On 12 July he reconnoitred the country from 2 and 3 Outposts with his staff officers, Eastwood and Locke; the spare diary entry gives no indication of how bold a foray it was. Next day, with three battalion commanders, he joined a destroyer 'cruising up and down coast . . . making a reconnaissance of spurs' under desultory fire. Divisional and brigade conferences followed on the 19th and 21st. On the 26th he showed Lieut-General Sir Frederick Stopford, who was to command at Suvla, the Anzac position. At the end of the month the brigade was jubilant over the announcement of Jacka's V.C.—the A.I.F.'s first.

Five days before the intended attack, Major-General H. V. Cox, an acerbic Indian Army veteran, was brought in to take command, under Godley, of the left assaulting column. On 2 August Monash was suddenly summoned to go on another destroyer trip with Godley, Cox, and the other brigadiers; they embarked just following heavy shelling of the pier, and after lengthy inspection of the country to the north had a full-dress conference. Next evening Cox called to confer. On the 4th Monash worked on the plan and visited Cox to settle details. He recommended Pope rather than Cannan as his successor, if he were hit. Next day he attended in turn conferences held by Birdwood, Godley and Cox, then had a session with his battalion commanders. That night Monash told Bean the plans. Bean had

> strolled round to Reserve Gully, where he and his troops were perched in dugouts, as in pigeon holes round the great amphitheatre of sandy cliffs.... As a clear logical exposition of a scheme of operations, it surpassed any that I had ever listened to.... it was a masterpiece of lucid explanation.

On the 6th, *the* day, when the great battle of Sari Bair began, Godley and Cox addressed the officers and N.C.O.s of 4th Brigade. According to one who was present, they 'hummed and hawed', then Godley said, 'What do you think, Brigadier?', whereupon all sat rapt for half an hour during Monash's exposition. He repeated Birdwood's instruction that they must press on and not hesitate; they must keep cool and calm; messages must clearly show time, place and sender; when they reached Hill 971 they must dig in and expect a counter-attack as they had at Quinn's, Pope's and Courtney's. 4th Brigade had been given star billing and 'had to fight and fight, good, hard and plenty'. He had been interrupted by shelling—several men were hit. 'It meant some effort to keep one's voice steady and an uninterrupted thread to one's remarks', he recalled.

The details of the plan were Cox's. Assuming there would be slight resistance, 4th Brigade and the Gurkhas were to move at night into unreconnoitred country with totally inadequate maps and no air photographs. They were to proceed up the Aghyl Dere, which spread into five branches issuing from 'a wild tangle of at least thirty scrub-covered gullies and ravines'. Their route was twice as long as the New Zealanders' attacking Chunuk Bair, and far more difficult to follow. Monash had drawn up a provisional time-table for the four-mile march which, assuming there were no checks, would reach the turn into the

Aghyl Dere at 11.15 and the forming-up position on the Abdel Rahman ridge for the attack on Hill 971 at about 1.40 a.m.

Mayhem began at Lone Pine at 5.30 p.m. 4th Brigade moved off along the beach road at 9.25, with Monash in the middle of the line by divisional order.

> It was like walking out, on a stormy winter night, from a warm cosy home, into a terrible hail, thunder and lightning storm. We had not gone half a mile when the black tangle of hills between the beach road and the main mountain range became alive with flashes of musketry, and the bursting of shrapnel and star shell, and the yells of the enemy and the cheers of our men as they swept in to drive the enemy from molesting the flanks of our march.

They got away smartly; indeed, the later detachments had to jog in their heavy equipment in order to catch up. But the covering forces clearing the foothills were taking longer than expected and the brigade was ordered by division to stop between 2 and 3 Outposts. They had already suffered casualties from shelling, now there were more from stray bullets. At least half an hour was lost and then after brief progress the line shuffled to a halt again. Major Overton, the chief guide, had adopted the advice of a local Greek guide to take a short cut straight ahead to Taylor's Gap instead of going on round to the opening of the Aghyl Dere. It was a disastrous decision, against orders, which was to delay both 4th Brigade and the Indian Brigade following behind. The 13th Battalion, in the lead, began to encounter fairly strong fire, the pass narrowed and was so thick with scrub that it had to be hacked and bashed aside. The harassing Turks were cleared away, but the path was choked and at least two hours more were lost. It was a very dark night, with no more than ten yards visibility.

Monash had already sent McGlinn forward to hurry things up, but he had suffered an accident. Now, with Cox's permission, Monash himself forced his way to the head—and it was as well for his military future that he did.

> I found Overton, Eastwood and Tilney conferring and arguing, and apparently unable to decide what to do. I vividly remember saying "What d— nonsense! Get a move on, quick."

'By dint of yelling and swearing' he directed the 13th, followed by the 14th, from Taylor's Gap across the Aghyl Dere and into Australia Valley, himself supervising the sorting of the men into platoons; then hurried back to direct the 15th and 16th up the Aghyl Dere to the right. He moved on with the 15th about 500 yards and established his headquarters, then showed the last company of the 16th the way. It was now after 3 a.m. Overton told Monash to 'march two fingers S. of moon', and departed to guide the Gurkhas. Having been punched

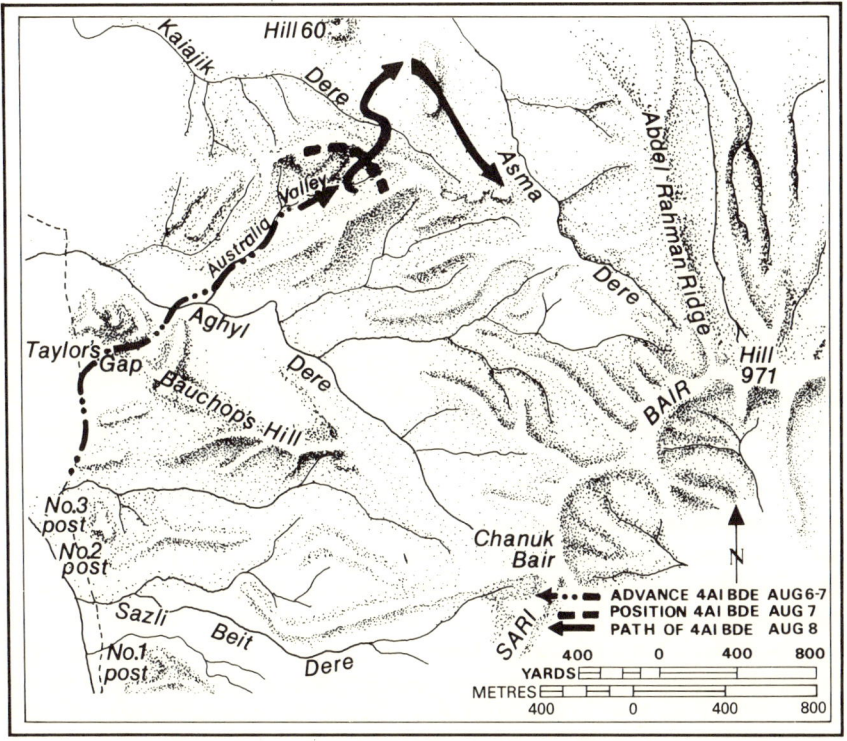

The August Offensive

into position, between 3.30 and 4.30 the 15th and 16th made fine progress for a mile or more under 'pretty heavy firing', but both battalions had to fight their way with the bayonet—the 15th had 112 casualties that night. But they inflicted heavy casualties—Monash claimed fully five hundred Turkish dead and wounded and six hundred prisoners—and overran a Turkish camp with much equipment; Monash eventually acquired a folding bed and a copper bathtub. He also captured two Turks himself: 'I heard a slight movement near me, and soon spotted them. They crawled out quite tamely when challenged, and holding up their hands, gave themselves up'. The 13th and 14th Battalions on the left reached what they believed were their proper positions to cover the assault by the 15th and 16th on the ridge, and began to dig in. The 15th and 16th had reached a rise perhaps 1000 yards from the main ridge which was the objective. Pope reported by telephone that he believed his right flank was actually on one of its spurs. But many of the men were sick, they had had no marching practice for months, were weary from the digging and carrying of the last few days in preparation for the reinforcements, and had been dropping down to sleep whenever there was a lull.

This was the turning point of the battle. The Turks had been surprised and most of their scanty forces defending the ridge from the thrusts from the coast had been dealt with. The Indians on 4th Brigade's right had made fair progress after their delay. The New Zealanders further right had done best; theirs was the great opportunity, and they could not quite take it. The attack on Baby 700 at The Nek by the 3rd Light Horse Brigade—outrageously—proceeded: they were butchered. The landings at Suvla Bay had been successful, but the incompetent generals and raw troops were incapable of advancing. It was still a close-run thing: the Gurkhas and New Zealanders that day very nearly captured the heights. During these vital hours 4th Brigade stopped still. On going forward to consult, Monash recognized that Pope was probably mistaken about his position and that there was still rough country to cross before tackling the Abdel Rahman ridge on the way to 971. Pope and Cannan insisted that their men were exhausted—and if those two brilliant, gallant commanders said so, then that was the case. Monash persuaded the slightly wounded Cox soon after sunrise that they could not advance and must dig in. This decision to rest and re-form was indubitably correct; the 15th and 16th Battalions were still scattered late in the afternoon. However, the order came from Godley that they must attack—at about 11 a.m., with reinforcements; Cox sent instructions to the artillery about 8 o'clock. But Godley called off all further action that day. About 9 Monash conferred with his battalion commanders and arranged to form a continuous line with the Indians on the right, and for digging and consolidating, water and ammunition supply, evacuation of wounded and burial parties.

There is much that will never be known about that morning; the precise order of events cannot be stated with certainty. Major C. J. L. Allanson, commanding the 6th Gurkhas, who two days later was briefly to reach the top of the ridge, was ordered by Cox to support 4th Brigade, probably for the assault at 11. Allanson provides the most damning evidence against Monash in all his military career:

> I discovered him hopelessly tied up . . . in the low hills, a lot of shooting seemed to be going on, and there were some wounded lying about, but what I mostly saw were men hopelessly exhausted lying about everywhere, all movement and attempt to advance seemed to have ceased. . . .
> What upset me most was that Monash himself seemed to have temporarily lost his head, he was running about saying 'I thought I could command men, I thought I could command men'; those were his exact words. . . .
> I went up and told him that my battalion had been placed in reserve at his disposal, but he said to me "what a hopeless mess has been made of this, you are no use to me at all".

I said nothing more, but got back to my battalion as soon as I could, wrote a message to General Cox to say that Monash had come up against a dead-end, did not require my battalion. . . .
It was obviously useless to lie in cover in the low hills, when every minute counted. . . . I was in reality anxious to get away from Monash as quickly as I could, as I felt thoroughly upset by what I had seen.

Allanson's account is not what it seems: it was written long after the event, possibly twenty years later, and may have been malicious. It contradicts his own evidence in 1917 to the Dardanelles Commission in which he said that he found 4th Brigade

> engaged with a large body of Turks, and there was an apparent precipice in front. I saw no hope of ever getting to the top of the hill if I supported them. . . . I think they got into an impossible country. I think my battalion had tremendous luck in striking good country.

It may be that, if credence is to be given to his later account, he did not know that when he met Monash, probably about 7 a.m., the decision to dig in had already been taken: it was no longer a matter of every minute counting. If, as he asserts, Monash had 'temporarily lost his head', it is remarkable that no hint of supporting evidence has survived for, if true, it probably would have quickly become notorious. Nevertheless, it is possible that Allanson caught Monash briefly out of control. In his *Gallipoli* (1965) Robert Rhodes James set out to debunk Monash's performance, basing the most serious assault which has been made on his reputation on the Allanson account. Rhodes James's attack, however, was tendentious and ill informed.*

On that very hot day, before they could rest, the brigade had to dig in. This had to be abandoned on the right, as enemy snipers and field-guns came into action. On the left, groups strolled over to a farm to fill their water-bottles, crossing a rise—it was Hill 60, scene of bloody battles two to three weeks later. Monash unsuccessfully tried to persuade the Wiltshires on his left to occupy the position. Godley planned a general advance next morning. Monash's diary reads: 'At 6 p.m. get orders to attack at 3 a.m. tomorrow. Reconnaissance 6 to 7.30. Issue orders to C.O.s at Conference at 8.30. Sleep 10 to 2 a.m.' He had advised against 4th Brigade taking part, in view of its condition. Godley instructed Monash to have his men on the crest so that as soon as the bombardment stopped they could assault 'with loud cheering'. They had had precious little rest that day and were to have little that cold night.

Neither Godley, nor Cox, nor Monash, nor anyone else knew where 4th Brigade was. Another valley and spur had to be crossed before

---

* See Appendix II.

reaching the Asma Dere and the Abdel Rahman ridge, 'the most forbidding ridge on the peninsula'. The country ahead was so precipitous and overgrown that they could not have reached the objective in less than several hours. Captain H. V. Howe, who covered the ground in 1919, concluded that 'only complete idiots could have expected it to be carried by infantry assault'.

At about 4.15 a.m., at dawn, the 15th Battalion, with the 14th and 16th behind, was caught by heavy machine-gun fire, 'an inferno', then by shelling and counter-attack by infantry in much greater strength, and the movement became hopelessly confused. Some of the troops were too exhausted either to fight or run. On a high knoll above his headquarters Monash was out of touch, as his telephone lines had been cut by shellfire. In the *Official History* Bean implies that he should have been with the assaulting column; his view would be generally supported unless there was a special reason, such as an order by Cox. When the lines were repaired and Pope reported on the hopeless situation, Cox and Monash ordered a withdrawal, at some time between 5 and 7.30 a.m. The Brigade's machine-gun sections—'possibly the finest unit in the A.I.F.'—covered the retreat, mowing down counter-attacks. Many wounded were evacuated with great bravery; the retreat was over by 8.30. There had been about 750 casualties that morning, more than half of them in the 15th Battalion which had almost been cut off, about 1000 since the night march began. According to the Official Medical History, 'The medical arrangements were deplorable'. It seems that Monash and his staff were largely to blame.

For the rest of the campaign, 4th Brigade as such was no longer a fighting force. Monash still believed they had crossed the Asma Dere. Only on the 19th, when Cox raised doubts and Monash sent out 'numerous reconnaissances', did he realize the facts. 'Much worried about previous error, for which Eastwood and Locke are to blame', he confided to his diary.

4th Brigade was left out of the general attack on the 9th, but when the Turks counter-attacked, the 13th Battalion, supported by the 15th, repulsed them; the 16th had to relieve a British battalion which had had heavy casualties. The massive Turkish effort continued next day and, at heavy cost, succeeded in forcing back the British front, and no more. On 4th Brigade's line, the 13th and 16th held on early in the morning. Monash warned that he would need reinforcements and machine-guns to repel a stronger attack. Cox called two hundred men of the 15th and a hundred of the 14th to plug dangerous sections of the line. 'Everybody exhausted and rattled', noted Monash, 'but self and Eastwood doing all possible to calm people down'. All Cox's force was confused, with units jumbled up and grave problems of supply of water and ammunition. Monash's men were sleeping out without covering, and bronchitis was becoming common. Yet the brigade dug in well and had few casualties, in contrast to the English battalions nearby which lost heavily. Each side had slugged the other to a standstill.

8 August when, as Monash put it, 4th Brigade 'was so badly (and needlessly) cut up', was one of his and the A.I.F.'s blackest days. The British Official Historian makes a rare criticism when he suggests that Birdwood was mistaken to attack 971 at all; that concentration on Chunuk Bair would have been better; and that the task given to 4th Brigade would have tried peacetime troops in perfect health as a daylight manoeuvre. Bean concluded in the *Official History* that the country was the most difficult Australian infantry had to face during that war: 'the attainment of Hill 971 . . . was never within the range of human possibility' when largely undefended on the 7th, let alone on the 8th. Birdwood had considered the best chance was to attack where least expected: the country into which he ordered 4th Brigade was, he knew,

> covered with deep ravines and precipices everywhere over which we must attack at night, so it will be a very high trial. Lots of men will lose themselves, but will have to keep pressing on and will I hope find themselves again in the morning, and with real determination they will I hope succeed.

He saw the battle as 'a great gamble'. (The Australian government was instinctively right in its determination to force on the promotion of senior Australian officers in order to protect the A.I.F.) And yet Birdwood's offensive came so near to success. If only, as so often in the Gallipoli story, *if only*. . . . The assault from Suvla Bay should have succeeded; had it done so, 4th Brigade might have taken 971 in spite of everything; but the Suvla attack was one of the greatest disasters in British military history.

Monash and 4th Brigade remained immensely proud of what they had done. Godley reported to Pearce:

> The 4th Aust. Infantry Brigade made a most wonderful night march through this really desperately difficult scrub-covered country, and at the end of it attacked the ridge with the greatest possible gallantry; that they were not successful was due alone to the extraordinary difficulties of the country, and the fact that they were so enormously outnumbered. . . . General Monash handled his brigade excellently.

Birdwood in his autobiography referred to the brigade's 'magnificent night march through appallingly difficult country'. Cox, writing to his wife on 11 August, enthused about 4th Brigade's performance and wished he had more Australians. In his semi-public letters home

Monash cracked hardy, professing himself not only to be 'more than satisfied with the work of the Brigade', but also on having had 'no actual defeats in any of my operations'; he even claimed Sari Bair as 'our most successful work of all'. Keith Murdoch, the journalist, considered 4th Brigade's advance was 'one of the most glorious efforts on the Dardanelles. There is a disposition to blame Monash for not pushing further in, but I have been over the country, . . . and I cannot see how even as much as he did could have been expected'. Major T. W. Glasgow was another who concluded at the time that 4th Brigade had done splendidly.

To the degree that 4th Brigade did fail, it was mainly because most of the men were desperately sick. Neither the senior medical officers nor Monash had realized how serious the situation was; the men's stoicism and his own hardiness had misled him. During the summer, the Official Medical Historian relates, the troops had been 'swept by a wave of intestinal disease, predominantly fly-borne; of which the nature and cause were only gradually recognized'. Medical officers had concentrated mainly on trying to ensure purity of water. The effects of inadequate diet, primitive sanitary arrangements, and infection spread by flies in dixies and mess tins became catastrophic. Monash had asked his medical officers late in July whether the brigade was fit for severe operations. Three out of four replied that it was not. They agreed that the men's health was declining; that they were suffering from gastric derangements, bronchial infections, rapid pulses, loss of weight and heart dilation; and that the causes were irregular rest and meals, unvaried diet, hot weather, flies and dust. Nevertheless Monash concluded that the powerful stimulus of the prospect of an offensive would improve their condition. The medical men on the spot, just too late, were recognizing the full gravity of the situation. G.H.Q. was unaware: on 1 August the senior medical officer noted 'a good deal of diarrhoea amongst the Australians, possibly due to sea bathing'. In the 15th Battalion history (1936) Monash was sternly criticized for his inadequate appreciation of the health of the men—a rare example, in the genre, of criticism of high authority.

In August it came to be recognized that much of the disease was paratyphoid, and by then, as one medical officer remarked, 'You might as well have spat on a bushfire'. Later that month, according to the newly-arrived medical officer of the 15th Battalion,

> The condition of the men . . . was awful. Thin, haggard, as weak as kittens, and covered with suppurating sores. Practically every man had dysentery. . . . if we had been in France every man would have been sent to hospital.

This unit had already suffered heavier casualties than any other

Australian battalion. Approaching winter would put an end to the epidemic; meanwhile all the original Anzac brigades were almost in total collapse.

How could a man who had with such pride created a first-rate fighting force carry on, seemingly without utter distress, when it was cut to pieces, when so many comrades were killed, maimed or demoralized? In so far as he revealed himself, Monash was unperturbed:

> The great essential is to entirely suppress all personal considerations, and to take no notice whatever of one's losses. There is the definite tactical objective, and that is all important—to capture a hill, or seize a road ...—and whether it costs 100 or 500 men to do it, the great point is to *do* it, and having done it, to reorganize ready for the next move. If one stops to count the cost or worry over the loss of friends, or the grief and sorrow of the people at home, one simply could not carry on for an hour. The moment a man becomes a casualty, ... he must be ruled out completely, as if he never existed—get him away, get him out of sight, forget all about him—pick your man to take his place, and go right ahead with the work in hand. There is absolutely no other way. ... it is the *whole* secret of successful leadership in war.

About the same time he wrote:

> Letters from Australia continue to express grave misgivings about my nervous stability. They appear to think that a nervous breakdown is inevitable. But that is entirely a matter of temperament. ... as time goes on I get steadily more and more indifferent to all the influences which are calculated to unnerve and upset one's mental equilibrium. It is merely a question of adaptability to a new environment, and the familiarity which breeds contempt.

Both these extracts from letters were written reflectively, away from the battle, on leave in October. This formidable man had schooled himself not to admit natural emotions and to adopt the necessary outlook of a senior military commander. He did at least reflect that war tended to 'bring out the non-spiritual and purely brutal characteristics' of men.

The gravely weakened 4th Brigade had to campaign for another month yet before being relieved. Hamilton's next throw, having belatedly sacked his generals there, was to advance from Suvla. The left of Godley's mixed force had linked up with the Suvla force and on 21 August was to attack Hill 60. On the 17th Monash had a weary day in the sun, showing Cox, Godley and Birdwood in turn over his lines: they remarked on the excellent trenchwork. Conference followed conference: five hundred of 4th Brigade were to form the right flank under the command of Cox and Russell. All the relatively fit men of the 13th and 14th Battalions would have to make a dash in mid-afternoon across more than 200 yards of open ground, weighed down with 50 pounds each. They would be protected by a barrage.

The artillery planning was botched. While the New Zealanders made some progress on the left, nearly half the first two charging lines of 4th Brigade were cut down; the rest had to shelter and dig in that night. Next morning the newly-arrived 18th Battalion of 2nd Division was sent out to charge and lost half its strength, but an insecure line was established. The 4th Brigade men were taken out that night, having suffered more than two hundred casualties. The attack from Suvla was a total failure.

In future years Monash used this battle as an illustration of the grave danger of altering orders at the last minute, as had happened with the artillery arrangements: 'everybody got rattled, . . . it was altogether a mis-timed, mis-calculated, and mis-directed operation. The result was considerable loss of life and little gain'. He was not impervious and displayed his bitterness when he used the word 'survivors' in a message to Godley urging relief of his men out front. Godley took exception and an undignified, though polite, correspondence followed about the meaning of the word, the exact number of casualties and the desirability of not exaggerating them. That day also, Monash urgently asked for relief of his brigade which was now at 30 per cent strength: the 17th Battalion, 2nd Division, came in to the line with 4th Brigade veterans left among them.

Birdwood gained permission to assault Hill 60 again on the 27th. 250 of the remnants of 4th Brigade were called on to attack again under Russell. Cox, against the advice of Russell and Monash who wanted to attack at night, decided on a daytime assault, relying on artillery. Again the bombardment was almost useless and the Australian attack was blotted out within a few yards. After the next two days, Hill 60 was half-captured. 'For connoisseurs of military futility, valour, incompetence and determination, the attacks on Hill 60 are in a class of their own', Rhodes James has remarked. 4th Brigade was now down to under a thousand effective men. 'The whole was a rotten, badly organized show', Monash wrote in his diary, '—and those who planned it are responsible for a heavy loss to this Brigade'. Lieut-Colonel Adams of the 14th was broken and had to be relieved. The redoubtable Pope at last cracked; Monash asked for him to be rested for, as his 'mainstay', it 'would be better for him to recoup now, while I myself am in good going order'. Monash had a row with Cox who was almost at the end of his tether. Cox had deplored 4th Brigade's failure: 'I do not understand how they can bear to see the N.Z. troops on their left carry two lines of trenches, and not do the same themselves'. Monash replied that every officer taking part had been killed or wounded: 'I do not see what more can be expected of the men'. Cox followed with a rebuke about the incomplete state of a linking trench he had ordered to be constructed. Eventually Monash protested to Godley about Cox's 'bullying'.

At last 4th Brigade was pulled out at the end of August to occupy a peaceful stretch of line on Bauchop's Hill. The incumbent English troops were highly inhospitable and Monash had to sleep out for two nights. His daily calculation of brigade strength continued sickeningly. However insensitive he may earlier have been, from mid-August he was totally concerned to get the brigade out and was referring to its 'absolutely rotten condition'. The arrival early in September of canteen stores, which varied diet, was long overdue.

The arrogant Australian contempt for British troops had its origins on Gallipoli where the British Army was far from its best. Surprise and dismay were mixed in with the new-found pride. Writing to both Vic and Walter, Monash reflected what every other Australian was saying. The cause of the August failure was insufficient troops and inadequate munitions, but especially

> the poor quality of the British troops. Over and over again they have allowed themselves to be driven out of positions which have been hardly won by Austr. and N.Z. troops. . . . altho' some are better than others, they can't soldier for sour apples. They have no grit, no stamina or endurance, poor physique, no gumption, and they muddle along and allow themselves to be shot down because they don't even know how to take cover. . . . Over and over again I have had to mix up a few platoons of Australians among them to keep them steady and teach them how to dig trenches, how to prepare their bivouacs, how to cook their food, how to take cover, how to fight, and how to stand their ground. They have a willing enough spirit, and plenty of dull stupid courage, but they simply don't know enough to come in out of the wet. Much of the fault lies in the leadership. . . .

He had briefly had two New Army battalions under his command. In late September he summed up the campaign:

> we give the Turks ample notice of our intention to land a military force. We almost tell them in detail the date and place. . . . Then we land a force which is adequate *only* to secure a bare landing and hold it *defensively*. . . . And the latest English papers talk of the whole undertaking as a strategical blunder, and say that the whole future effort should be concentrated on Flanders, which means that the sacrifice of nearly 15000 magnificent Dominion troops has been useless and to no purpose!! . . . during the first 48 hours after the landing at Suvla while there was an *open road* to the Dardanelles, and no opposition worth talking about, a whole Army Corps sat

down on the beach while its leaders were quarrelling about questions of seniority and precedence; and it was just this delay of 48 hours which enabled the Turks to bring up their last Strategic Reserve from Bulair and render futile the whole purpose of that landing which was to protect the left flank of the Anzac advance; and the failure to do this, held up our further offensive. Cheerful! isn't it.

But to be fair, 'The real army disappeared at Mons. The thing we have now is a very poor imitation'.

The remnants of 4th Brigade—including only about three hundred, less than one-tenth, of those who left Melbourne with Monash—were sent in mid-September for rest on Lemnos. Monash had at last fallen victim to dysentery a week before they left; then he was further crippled by his old enemy, lumbago. He recovered enough to enjoy 'some *beer*' and a hot bath on board ship, had a relapse, but was confined to his tent only for a couple of days. He began riding and taking long walks in fine autumn weather; he rode with Lieutenant Locke ten miles out one Sunday for a hot sulphur bath, and loafed in a lush orchard, nibbling grapes, figs, pomegranates and quinces. He was inspired to write a nostalgic letter about the garden at Iona, requesting a detailed progress report and suggesting planting a walnut tree; later he sent holly acorns from Gallipoli for planting.

Monash enjoyed being a general and a very senior Australian officer, but it was a nuisance to have to become camp commandant for nine days. He struggled for adequate tentage, to hurry up the distribution of mail, and to get hold of the canteen stores due. Mudros and chaos were synonymous in popular parlance. He was landed with one 'prize fool' and another 'superlative idiot' of an English officer to work with. He was appalled by the 'inefficiency and muddle and red tape':

> There are ever so many gentlemen earning their war medals on board luxurious transports, decked all over with gorget patches and arm bands and lace, acting as deputy-assistant-acting-inspector-general of something-or-other.

He overheard a couple of them sneering at those Australians' ignorance of real soldiering:

> those are the blighters . . . for whom Australia has been spilling her good red blood. . . . And it's about time too that somebody asked about the treatment of Australian soldiers in Tommy hospitals. . . . the sooner they hang somebody for gross mismanagement, the better.

Despite lavish fresh food and a daily issue of stout or beer, the 4th Brigade men were slow to recover health. And few reinforcements were arriving—Monash began to worry about whether the brigade could be built up to anything like its former standard. But the men were at last settled in reasonable comfort. At a camp concert Monash made a speech of welcome and he and the New Zealander, Brigadier-General Hughes, 'ragged each other' for general entertainment. At smaller concerts Monash gave short talks on various subjects: 'his elocutionary powers seemed to cast a spell over the men', according to the 15th Battalion's history.

Three weeks leave in Egypt followed. On the restful voyage Monash yarned with 'a very interesting R.C. chaplain'. Apart from five days in Cairo, he stayed in Alexandria at the Savoy Palace Hotel, sleeping in most mornings. He had to confer about reinforcements, hunt up convalescents, inspect his brigade transport, and visit the sick and wounded in hospital. Though Alexandria was 'a hive of idlers and shirkers', he found none belonging to 4th Brigade. With Locke and others, he sampled the night-life: music halls, variety shows, the Folies Bergère, the Casino, cinemas, and a boxing tournament which he unexpectedly enjoyed, but the Moulin Rouge was 'a sick show'. He dodged the Jewish community 'for fear of their wanting to rope me in for religious ceremonies', and was chagrined that when he looked up Rose (Blashki) Slutzkin he 'had to go through Sabbath ceremonial'. He spent two days with his favourite nephew, Eric Simonson, and went for walks of five or six miles. He saw his horse Tom and, as a souvenir, sent home one of his shoes, requesting that it be mounted on a plush base 'in memory of a very fine faithful animal, who has served me well', and who could not be taken home. Finally, he attended the Sultan's departure from his Summer Palace for Cairo: 'When I was presented to him he remarked: "Ah Australien! Je vous faire mes compliments, mon cher général." A pretty compliment was it not, to be congratulated on being an Australian!!'

In Cairo Monash heard that he had been appointed a Companion of the Order of the Bath—and 'went straight around and got my new ribbon—a bright magenta'. The C.B. ranked higher than the C.M.G., C.V.O. and C.S.I. Walker had been awarded it too, and Jim McCay— Monash was very glad about this: 'the poor man has had more than his fair share of worry and sorrow and disappointments'. But, amazingly, all four of Monash's battalion commanders had also got the C.B. 4th Brigade's honours and decorations were 'far and away above anything achieved by any of the other Australian or N.Z. Brigades'. Monash was a little piqued, however, that Russell was knighted; it only showed that New Zealand looked after its officers better. He wrote to McCay, urging him to stir up the authorities. He was pleased that *Burke's* and *Debrett's* quickly asked for his particulars. But he recognized that 'the matter of awards is all a gamble and a fluke. Most men get either much more or much less than they really deserve'.

In November Monash ran into trouble on the seniority question. After promotion to brigadier-general, he believed he was now the senior A.I.F. officer after Legge, because of the back-dating to September 1914 which seemed to have lifted him over Chauvel and others who had been his seniors as colonels. But when Brigadier-Generals Chauvel and W. Holmes were given temporary command of the 1st and 2nd Divisions in place of the incapacitated Walker and Legge, he was 'much perturbed', and formally objected to Godley. He drafted a polite letter of explanation to Chauvel, which he eventually decided not to send, in which he said: 'One has to consider that the war will go on for a long time, . . . and I have my aspirations, and like every other man, a desire to have my activities employed in the widest possible sphere'. Godley replied that the appointment of brigadier-generals was always temporary and local and that the announcement in the Commonwealth *Gazette* had erroneously proclaimed substantive promotion (it was subsequently amended). Monash then asked for a formal ruling and wrote to Pearce, stating his case, and to McCay, who was in a similar situation. Monash did have a case for claiming seniority: there were other tangles and inconsistencies. But Birdwood rebuked him: 'The Army Corps Commander deprecates the assertion by officers of their claims to appointments which are filled by selection. The seniority and claims of all eligible officers are fully considered before a decision is made'. Monash continued to believe he had been improperly overlooked.

He was held up, waiting for a ship in Alexandria, and returned to Gallipoli on 8 November, three days after his brigade. They returned to the mile of trenches on Bauchop's Hill, a quiet but interesting sector with the Turks on the other side of the valley, 300 to 600 yards away. On the 13th Monash was summoned to meet Birdwood at Anzac Cove. After the long walk in, mainly through trenches, he and all the other senior officers waited on the beach for the visitation from Field Marshal The Earl Kitchener of Khartoum. Birdwood went to the end of the jetty to greet the tiny picquet-boat and conducted the great man off to meet the assembled generals, while cheering troops crowded round. Birdwood took him up to Russell's Top to examine the battle-ground. Kitchener said little, and didn't stay long.

The brigade, built up with reinforcements, had to be taught and nursed back to something like its former proficiency. All four battalions were now commanded by majors who had left home as captains. Monash applied some firm rebukes, after inspection of the line, on the state of weapons and discipline. The main task was to dig in deeply for the winter and as a precaution against possible use against them of German high explosive shells. Monash applied his engineering skills to tunnelling and constructing galleries, chambers, vents and drains. No serious military projects were in view but the brigade undertook some aggressive patrolling in order to dominate the wide no-man's-land. They regarded stalking the enemy's patrols and bagging two or three prisoners or potting a few snipers, as good clean fun, with relatively little danger. Listening patrols would go out to note 'the time, direction, objective, number and movements' of enemy patrols. Next night, fighting patrols would waylay and bomb them, and collect rifles, ammunition, equipment and occasional wounded prisoners. Late in November Monash was laid up for two days (through the snowstorm) with a slight attack of jaundice, which had been widespread. On 6 December Birdwood and Godley inspected his front and were complimentary about the thoroughness of the defences.

Several weeks earlier, vital decisions had been taken. Hamilton had been dismissed in mid-October. The visiting Melbourne journalist, Keith Murdoch, had helped to precipitate the decision with a wildly exaggerated condemnation of the conduct of the campaign, which glorified the Australians and reviled the British; yet, as convenient to the anti-Gallipoli faction within the British government, it was published as a state paper. Although many disillusioned Australians agreed with Murdoch, Monash and almost every other senior officer despised his report. General Sir Charles Monro was appointed in succession and, when he reported in favour of evacuation, Kitchener made his visit and reluctantly agreed on 22 November, placing Birdwood in command of the operation. As a consequence, Godley succeeded to the Corps command and Russell took charge of his division on the 26th. The British cabinet confirmed the decision to evacuate on 7 December.

Monash was sure there was nothing to the rumours. When he was told on the 12th, the 'stupendous and paralysing' news came 'like a thunderbolt'.

> It is of course, an absolutely critical scheme, which may come off quite successfully, or may end in a frightful disaster. But orders are orders. I need not say I feel very unhappy. . . . I am almost frightened to contemplate the howl of rage and disappointment there will be when the men find out what is afoot, and how they have been fooled. And I am wondering what Australia will think at the desertion of her 6000 dead, and her 20,000 other casualties.

For himself he wanted to be 'the last man of the Brigade ashore, and to see everybody safely off'.

He decided to keep a diary-letter—realizing how dramatic the episode would be and the historical value of a day-to-day account— although no one might ever see it. On 13 December the 15th Battalion 'disappeared into the night, at 2 hours' notice'. Already the plan was an open secret, though Monash could not formally instruct his commanding officers till the 16th. 'Every man knew, and felt it more keenly than he had felt anything in his life', the 13th Battalion historian eventually wrote. It was 'curious and interesting to watch the machine unwind itself as methodically and systematically as it was originally wound up', Monash remarked. The postal organization was disbanded, supplies of fresh food ended, the military police withdrawn and defaulters returned to their units; the mule-trains stopped and supplies again had to be carried by hand; most of the hospitals packed up and departed; collective cooking was abandoned.

The date of the final embarkation depended on the weather and the moon, but eventually the nights of the 18th and 19th were chosen: fifteen thousand had left over the previous nine days; twenty thousand remained.

> We had our final Divisional Conference,—and took mutual farewells of each other!! General Birdwood . . . went along my whole line, and shook hands with all the officers and expressed the hope that many of them would come through alive.

On the 18th 'Corporal Palmer, my best typewriting clerk, was hit in the leg, while I was talking to him outside the Brigade office, by a stray bullet'. Many of the men visited the graves of their mates. McGlinn got away with eight hundred troops that night, taking with him the remaining records—they were already planning to write the history of the brigade together. At midnight Monash wrote:

> Everything is normal, just the usual sniping, and occasional bombs and bursts of machine gun fire. If we get thro' tonight, I feel sure that all will be well. My bed tonight will be a heap of old sand bags.
> As to the 'die-hards', a list has been drawn up of the names of each of the last 170 officers and men, shewing for each man, the *exact* time that he has to leave the front trenches, and exactly what he has to do—whether to carry a machine gun, or its tripod, or its belts,—or to throw a bomb, or to start an automatic rifle. . . . Every one of these 170 officers and men has been given a card, containing all these particulars.

In preparation for the last night the Turks had been made accustomed to periods of silence—'the Silent Stunt'.

The weather for the last day was perfect—calm, foggy and drizzly. The hours passed agonizingly slowly—Monash later told Dr J. W. Springthorpe that the strain of those last two nights had been the worst he had experienced. At 8 p.m., after the first of his last three parties had left, Monash exulted:

> If the Turks only knew!! . . . The next hour or two will be decisive . . . we shall have succeeded in withdrawing the great bulk of the

Leaving Port Melbourne:

flanked by wife and daughter...

and with McGlinn

4th Brigade headquarters in May 1915 and on 7 August

Army Corps without any loss—a wonderful piece of organization, beyond any doubt. If it succeeds, it will be due to splendid preparation on the part of the leaders, and splendid and intelligent obedience on the part of the men.

About 9 his last patrol came in to report nothing abnormal, and he left for the beach with the second-last party of 425 men, leaving 170 of 4th Brigade of the 2000 Anzacs who were to stay in the line for several hours yet; there were many dryly emotional 'Cheeriohs' and good-luck handshakes. But Monash forgot his leather portfolio containing his diary-letter and the orders for the evacuation, which had been ordered to be destroyed and which he was keeping as a souvenir; he had to send a man to hurry back and collect it.

By midnight, after a crowded barge journey, Monash was on a small transport:

Officers and men, of both Army and Navy, from upwards of 50 different units—who had not seen or heard of each other since the days of the war training in Egypt, or since leaving our home lands, foregathered. The strain being over, the reaction came in wild and hilarious greetings, mutual felicitations and hearty handshakes all round. . . . Gradually the ship's company, worn out with want of sleep, and the tremendous strain of the closing hours, fell asleep.

But he later imaginatively continued his diary-letter to cover the last party remaining on shore:

at 1.55 my last man left his foremost position—leaving only the automatic devices working. All other Brigades and Divisions were similarly timed according to their distance from the embarking piers, of which we had four. Down dozens of little gullies leading back from the front lines, came little groups of 6 to a dozen men, the last (in every case an officer) closing the gully with a previously prepared frame of barbed wire, or lighting a fuse which an hour later would fire a mine which would wreck a sap or a tunnel by which the enemy could follow—all these little columns of men kept joining up, like so many rivulets which flow into the main stream, and so at last they coalesced into four continuous lines. . . . There was no check, no halting, no haste or running—just a steady, silent tramp in single file. . . . without check each line marched (like so many ghostly figures in the dim light) in single file onto its allotted jetty, the sound of marching feet having been deadened by laying a floor of sand bags; and so onto motor barges. . . . there was a short pause to make sure that no one had been left on shore . . . then the landing and loading staff, chiefly naval officers, stepped aboard—'Let go all over'. 'Right away' was the last order, and slowly we moved out. Just before the barge at Anzac pier cast off, the last Engineer officer on shore joined the terminals of an electric battery and thereby fired three enormous guncotton mines which, with a terrific explosion, blew up 'Russell's Top'. . . . a couple of hundred Turks must have gone up into the air, but nothing could be seen except a volcano of dust. Instantly a most terrific tornado of rifle and machine gun fire burst forth along the whole length of Sari Bair shewing that the Turks, far from suspecting our real manoeuvre, had been actually expecting an attack, of which they took the firing of the mine to be the first signal. Thus, dramatically, with the bullets . . . whistling harmlessly overhead, we drew off in the light of the full moon, mercifully screened by a thin mist—and so ended the story of the Anzacs on Gallipoli. We had succeeded in withdrawing 45,000 men, mules, guns, stores, provisions and transport to the value of several million pounds, without a single casualty, and without allowing the enemy to entertain the slightest suspicion. It was a most brilliant conception, brilliantly organized, and brilliantly executed—and will, I am sure, rank as the greatest joke in the whole range of military history.

It is good that someone so described the event. It was so incredible that many in Australia believed that the Turks must have let them go. It was a magnificent piece of organization by Brudenell White, Birdwood's chief of staff, but it could not have so succeeded at Anzac and Suvla but for the unusually beneficent weather conditions.

About midday and 4.30 p.m. the two batches of the Brigade 'diehards' marched through a mile-long cheering lane into camp on Lemnos:

First came the band, blowing as they had never blown before, followed by a neatly dressed and very portly brigade major [McGlinn], and then a company of dirty ragamuffins who held themselves up like guardsmen.

Monash made triumphant speeches.

He sent home his diary-letter of some four thousand words and Mat typed copies which were 'positively fought for'. Catherine Deakin read it to 'Alfred and Pattie and Ivy'; many said it was as good as Scott's Antarctic diary. Vic sent it to Hall, seeking permission to publish, but leave was not granted, even though the *Argus* brought pressure to bear. Dr Springthorpe had already published in the *Age* his brilliant account of the evacuation, which owed much to an interview with Monash—though Monash had hoped to 'scoop' him. He assumed that the Censors, Springthorpe and the *Age* were conspiring to prevent publication of his account and that if only Smith of the *Argus* had known of it earlier he would have beaten the censorship.* But the Censors, Monash's old associates Hall and G. G. McColl, may have been protecting him from his own reckless folly. It was an immensely exciting document, but in Army terms it was illegal—which Monash knew, he later

---

* Excerpts were eventually published in several journals late in 1916.

referred to 'smuggling' it home—and the Censors may also have been aware that it was not altogether what it seemed. For, carried away by literary hyperbole and possibly deeply regretting that he was *not* one of the very last off Gallipoli, Monash had implied that he was. Under orders he had left for the beach nearly five hours before the last. It was a clumsy deception, as so many people knew the facts; Bean became aware of it and held it against him. Though Monash intended it to be published anonymously, the authorship would inevitably have become widely known.

Three weeks later Cape Helles was evacuated. So ended that dreadful campaign, lamentably prepared and blunderingly carried out. As Churchill said, it was 'impossible to assemble the long chain of fatal missed chances... without experiencing a sense of awe'. Monash never wavered in his view that it had been good strategy—a 'magnificent conception' but 'miserably ineffective in execution'. Nevertheless it was not a total failure: it was a constant threat to the enemy on his weak flank, it temporarily kept Bulgaria out of the war, saved a major battle for Egypt, and so weakened the Turks that for the rest of the war they could easily be contained. And the Anzac landing, Monash was certain a year later, would be seen as 'one of the most famous events in history—putting into shade such events as the "charge of the Light Brigade" at Balaclava'.

Received opinion has it that Monash's performance on Gallipoli was mediocre. It derives largely from Bean and to an uncertain extent from contemporary prejudice against Monash because of his origins; the initial impression also lingered that at Sari Bair 4th Brigade had let down 1st Division and the Light Horse, which had made such sacrifices at Lone Pine and The Nek. In the second Gallipoli volume of the *Official History*, published in 1924, Bean noted Monash's limitations as a fighting commander when compared with men like Walker, McCay or Chauvel, and made his well-known remark: 'Monash was a leader of whom it was already said that he would command a division better than a brigade and a corps better than a division'. He also concluded that Monash had undoubtedly shown 'defects in leadership'.

Bean and Monash never got on easy terms with each other. They had hardly met before 3 May when Bean caught Monash at a time of great stress. A few weeks later they clashed over Bean's lack of attention to the exploits of 4th Brigade. Bean knew little of his background and what he knew he did not much like. He was in a position to pick up the malicious tittle-tattle about Monash, whoever was spreading it. In his diaries he struggled to be honest about him, admitting that he was obviously very able and had extraordinary powers of exposition, and noting the constant praise: 'Like every one who worked under Monash [Skelsey] has the highest opinion of him'. Late in August he expressed the view that 4th Brigade was not as good as the 1st or 3rd, its 'want of success [that month] can't be accidental every time' and was perhaps partly a consequence of the units being 'left to themselves more than in any other Brigade'. It is doubtful whether Bean realized how little Monash had to do with the actions late that month. He picked on him as an example of a man too old for his job—no brigadier should be over forty-five—and remarked that choosing him for the action of 6–7 August, which required extreme energy in leadership, foredoomed it to failure. 'Sleepy old John Monash—cautious if ever a man was—is one of the worst sort of men for such a move; but he's probably brilliant compared with [many British brigadiers]'. In the *Official History* Bean ultimately made great amends: in volume 4, published in 1936, he listed the 'holding of the head of Monash Valley by 4th Brigade' as one of the four greatest achievements of the A.I.F.; the others were the landing, Lone Pine and 6th Brigade at Bullecourt. And in volume 2 he had absolved Monash and 4th Brigade for the Sari Bair failure. He later remarked that 4th Brigade was every bit as good as 1st Brigade and that although Monash did not have the special qualities needed for such an enterprise as Sari Bair his leadership had been 'strikingly efficient'. The military historian H. V. Howe, formerly on Gallipoli with the 11th Battalion, 1st Division, and a friend of Bean, went so far as to state that 4th Brigade 'was universally regarded among Australian troops as the best brigade on Anzac' and that 'from the beginning Monash was regarded throughout the Australian Forces as an exceptionally competent Brigadier'.

No one of senior rank did very well at Gallipoli (except possibly Walker). In general, brigadiers were given hair-raising tasks. Monash did far better than most of his peers. No other Australian senior officer outdid him in hardiness: several officers of similar rank could not stand more than two or three weeks of the campaign; no other brigade commander (leaving out Monash's two days on the *Arcadia*) lasted the first eight weeks, let alone remained on the peninsula from the first landings to mid-September. Chauvel, White and several others were in hospital for several weeks; Monash's resistance to disease was such that he had only two brief periods of lying-up. He may possibly, naturally, once or twice have been rattled, but his nerve stood up remarkably well; MacLagan, for one, had to be spelled more than once. Brudenell White later concluded that Monash was lacking in the requisite physique, youth and physical vigour, but his 'indomitable will carried him through'.

His superiors' opinions of him were mixed and fluctuated from time to time. Against all of them charges of incompetence could be laid much more easily than against Monash. Hamilton, remembering their Lilydale meeting, commented that his conduct had been fully up to the sample he showed then. Late in November Birdwood remarked:

Monash has, I think, certainly done well. He looks after his Brigade thoroughly well—knows all details concerning it, and is an excellent organizer. At the same time, I cannot look upon him as a leader in war.

Though 4th Brigade had done 'excellent work', Monash was not resolute enough and Chauvel and Holmes had better claims. Late in 1915, writing to Pearce, Godley named Monash as one of several excellent brigadiers and continued to speak highly of him in 1916. But he told General Hutton that Monash was only 'quite good'—'he was not quite as active as a Brigadier should be in these days'. In 1918 Paddy McGlinn ran into Godley: 'my word how did he speak of the old Brigade and your work. He said the Brigade never gave him the slightest anxiety—it was so well run'. McGlinn was entirely confident about their achievements: 'We, or our administration, were never found wanting nor were they [Birdwood and Godley] given an uneasy moment'.

Monash had the respect of his peers like Russell and White. Chauvel congratulated him on his C.B.: 'I don't think there is any Brigadier either from Australia or New Zealand who has earned it more'. But in 1918 he told his wife that the infantry much preferred Walker to Monash as a leader. Brigadier-General G. J. Johnston, the artillery man, was 'very proud to be a member of the same order which claims you, old friend'. Major (Major-General) A. C. Temperley, serving with the New Zealanders, later wrote: 'I knew General Monash intimately [on Gallipoli]. He was excellent company, and took with both hands all that life had to give him'. But, as always, the most significant opinions are those of immediate subordinates, all of whom greatly respected and liked him. McGlinn remained the most faithful admirer of all: Monash was 'one of nature's noblemen', and 'one of the whitest men God ever put breath into'. To a man, the battalion commanders supported him. Pope and Burnage became close friends; the young Cannan, whose judgement as leader of the troubled 15th Battalion, is worth much, and Adams and Dare of the 14th, revered him: 'From the day we started training with you as our Brigadier', wrote Adams, 'everyone recognized your surpassing qualifications for the anticipated ordeal in front of us'. These were not obsequious or dissimulating men.

But what of his reputation with the rank and file? Some favourable reports and near-absence of known criticism indicate strong negative approval at least; for what it is worth, Walter and Lou Rosenhain reported that the 4th Brigade wounded in England all spoke of him 'with admiration and affection'. There may have been more: whereas Godley and McCay had already acquired unenviable reputations for willingness to make rash and injurious sorties, Monash had a reputation for proper care. Captain J. F. McGlinn, the brigade signals officer, considered that

he saved some of our battalions from being more severely cut up at various times by showing the seniors they had no idea of the front line ground. Maps are all very well but the man on the ground knows best; at any rate the general proved it to them more than once.

There remains Bean's statement in the *Official History*: 'It was averred against Monash in those days that he was seldom seen in the front line, the complaints from Quinn's Post . . . being sometimes bitter'. As we have seen, the implied charge is probably put far too strongly. Assuming there was something to it, the men in Quinn's did not know that there was a large school of military opinion which held that he had no business to be there, except occasionally, and many military historians would agree with Warren Perry that Bean's remark was 'characteristic of an attitude to war which is instinctive and romantic rather than rational and scientific'. Yet Bean probably reflected prevailing opinion at the time.

Major criticisms of Monash's performance seem to be difficult to justify. He did not plan but had to carry out the 2–3 May offensive, which was quickly beyond repair. On 6–7 August he was not responsible for the broad plan or for its more important details or for the delay in the advance, and he adequately resolved that delay; his recommendation not to press on in the morning can hardly be criticized in view of the condition of the men and the firm advice of his subordinates. The disastrous decision to attack on the 8th, made at short notice and in general ignorance of the position on the map, was not his. His hurried reconnaissance was inadequate but could hardly have been otherwise. Sari Bair was the old story, to infantry, of drawing arrows on small-scale maps. At Hill 60 he was subordinate and powerless. Neither Bean nor anyone else ever made specific suggestions of how a 'fighting commander' with 'the touch of a Stonewall Jackson, and the recklessness of a J. E. B. Stuart' might have behaved on 3 May or 7–8 August. Just what was possible on 3 May? In the light of the evidence it is futile to assert that on 7 August a great commander would have got his men moving, however sick. Perhaps brigade headquarters should have been further forward on 8 August, but what precisely could a dynamic fighting brigadier have done beyond going to a glorious idiotic death?

At least two of his main critics at the time—Birdwood and Bean—were mildly antagonistic towards Jews, while others still suspected him for his German background. It will never be possible to judge satisfactorily how reasoned were the criticisms of Monash's performance and how much was simple prejudice. But it seems clear that Monash did rather better on Gallipoli than has generally been believed.

9

Egypt and Salisbury Plain 1916

AFTER THE WAR a journalist asked Monash to recall his most memorable wartime Christmas. 1915 on Lemnos was the obvious answer: winter sunshine, green fields around, a wonderful Christmas mail and, above all, relaxation and freedom to move about. Not surprisingly, there was general confusion in receiving the evacuees from Gallipoli and despatching them to Egypt. Eventually 4th Brigade got away, Monash in command of a North Atlantic liner and worried about submarines. They made a rough camp near Ismailia on New Year's Day.

The weary task of training the reconstituted brigade began again. Monash lectured to officers, many of them new, about their duties to the Empire, Australia and the dead, and on map-reading and night navigation. He was already preaching that 'staffs exist to help units and not to make difficulties for them'. He argued for decorations for those he had recommended and who had been refused. He fought the everlasting war for adequate tentage. He planned exercises and applied discipline to improve appearance and bearing.

> It is the same rush and bustle and hustle as in a big industrial business. . . . I am working now with blunted tools, and instead of a newly raised, experienced and competent body of regimental officers, I have only the remnants—mostly war weary. . . . Mere administrative work is enormous, and there are a thousand and one things to do and think of simultaneously. There are questions of personnel, getting in reinforcements, allotting same to units, gathering in convalescents, digging out shirkers, evaluating the qualifications of new officers, promotions, transfers, appointments, punishments, courts martial, boards of enquiry on injuries, on accidents, on lost stores, questions of supply of food and forage, their quantity and quality, tent accommodation, sanitation, water supply, conservancy, horses, their numbers, health and distribution, vehicles, repairs to, painting and equipment for them, clothing and equipment of the men, regi-

> mental equipment, signalling stores, machine gun equipment, ammunition and its distribution, interior economy, finance, pay allowances, leave on business and private affairs, military police control of the Ismailia district, training, programmes for training, supervision of training, lectures to officers and N.C.O.'s—dozens of interviews every hour of the day on these and hundreds of other matters—besides having to dance attendance on visiting senior officers, and having to give time to and be polite to dozens of Australian, British and Indian colleagues who drop in for a chat and to fight our battles over again.

General Sir Archibald Murray, the new commander-in-chief, Middle East, inspected the brigade—'in rags, and a lot of lame ducks'—but they did well. Pretty Ismailia town and its French Club, where Monash could dine and get a bath, were a comfort. Meanwhile 'rumours that we go to France are followed by equally persistent rumours that we are not to go to France!!'

That January Monash's guard slipped revealingly when he wrote to his very old friend Billie Card. He was

> refitting and recruiting and training and knocking discipline and a semblance of fighting capacity into a few thousand more Australians ... so that in a month or two they may, with all due circumstance, get blown into little pieces, or get holes drilled into themselves, for the honor of Australia and for the good of posterity. I am a pretty patient individual, but this beastly war is getting to be rather a bore, and not nearly so much fun as building bridges, or touring around the world, or tending roses in my garden.

They would no doubt soon be moving to 'some fresh scene of slaughter and bloodshed'. This from a man who normally would *never* show 'weakness' to his womenfolk and friends.

He was under severe stress. On 19 January Gibson had cabled to tell him Vic was seriously ill and to seek consent for a major operation. For a week he heard no more, then came a succession of cables after the operation until on 1 February—'beside myself with relief and joy'—he could write to 'Walterlou' to tell them that all danger was past. Only in mid-February did he learn that it was cancer of the uterus. The mails were very slow, and the relevant rush of letters did not arrive till the end of the month. Vic, who had a horror of cancer, had not been told. She had written him a brave letter before the operation, revealing that for months she had spent much of her time in bed. The surgeon, Rothwell Adam, wrote candidly: the condition had been very serious, but the prognosis was reasonably good. Monash had already consulted Birdwood and Godley about the possibility of getting home; they had convinced him that the War Office would not allow it and that it was 'not possible without a sacrifice of honour'. Nevertheless he asked Adam for urgent advice if Vic's health deteriorated; he would seek release from his military duties if the emergency was 'real and urgent and great'.

Vic recovered remarkably well. John sent a tenderly affectionate cable in April for their silver wedding anniversary. She told him, 'You were the only man I ever loved'. Bertha, uncharacteristically, wrote that 'sometimes I could just cry and cry, for wanting you back so badly'. John had to frame carefully his letters to his wife, daughter, sister and sisters-in-law, in the light of what he knew they knew, and of what they knew he knew, of the seriousness of Vic's condition. Without undue self-pity, he ruminated on the traditional predicament of the soldier far from home.

Family links pursued Monash on Gallipoli and in Egypt. His nephew Aubrey Moss was doing well as a sergeant in various jobs. Sa Simonson wrote often, affectionately and bravely, in her own great troubles, and asked John to look after her sons Eric and Paul. Monash appointed Eric as his aide in January and was delighted with his personality, manliness and the quality of his staff work. Paul was claimed as a brother and became a sergeant in the 14th Battalion. Most remarkably, John's cousin Karl Roth, having understated his age, turned up in the infantry on Gallipoli. John told the 'frightfully filthy object' that if he spruced himself up he would recommend him as a corporal pharmacist in the brigade ambulance. It was a failure—the brave attempt at self-redemption collapsed. Back in Egypt Karl fell victim again to alcohol, was hospitalized and repatriated, and died in July. From afar Monash helped Gershon Bennett, Bert's great friend whom she was eventually to marry, a dentist who had been studying in the United States, to get a commission in England. And on Gallipoli he kept an eye on the able mining engineer, Corporal Gordon Gabriel, Annie's son, and helped him win promotion.

News of the business at home was worrying. Before he had left, Monash and Gibson had formed the Concrete Constructions Co., to consolidate their pipe-manufacturing interests, bringing in Richard Taylor. It did reasonably well, but in 1915 the Reinforced Concrete Co. made a loss and the South Australian company was also in trouble. From mistaken kindness, Gibson rarely wrote, and was eventually roundly rebuked: 'I have faced disaster and defeat before, cheerfully; but it is hard to have to face uncertainty and doubt'. Monash was relieved to hear there was no calamity and reassured Vic that she must not stint herself. 1916 was a better year, but Monash arranged, without Gibson's knowledge, for the engineer P. T. Fairway to keep him regularly informed. Other news from home was reassuring. Theodore Fink told Vic that 'Springthorpe told me a lot about "Jack Monash" which it would do you good to hear'. The founder of the Australian navy,

Rear Admiral Sir William Creswell, wrote: 'I can assure you we look up to all you Anzacs as super men and the more that you have all taken your big work with such modesty. I can understand your being almost heart broken by the Suvla business'. Sir John Madden had referred to him as a hero, and C. P. Smith had named him 'the finest soldier I saw'.

In February and March 1916 the A.I.F. underwent radical reorganization, doubling its divisions, brigades and battalions to accommodate the mass of recruits. There was talk of an Australasian Army; for the moment two Anzac corps were developed, with Birdwood and Godley as commanders. Amid much heartburning the veterans of the 1st Division and the 4th Brigade were divided up to form daughter units; on 13 February Monash wrote his orders for selection of officers and men from the 13th, 14th, 15th and 16th Battalions for transfer to the new 45th, 46th, 47th and 48th Battalions in 12th Brigade. 4th Brigade took affectionate farewell of the N.Z. Brigade, their mates in the former N.Z. and Australian Division. Monash dined at their headquarters, attended a Maori camp-fire (a haka was performed in his honour), a concert at which he made a parting speech, then 4th Brigade's final concert in tribute to the Kiwis. He had mixed feelings about losing Russell as his divisional chief; he was 'a splendid chap . . . a close friend . . . urbanity itself', but he doubted his capacity. 'Our proceedings as Divisional Manoeuvres here would make you scream!', he told McCay. 'Those years we spent at War Course, Staff exercises etc. were so much labour wasted.' 4th Brigade was to go to the new 4th Division in Godley's corps.

> Godley always gave me a square deal . . ., yet I am bound to say that he was cordially hated by all New Zealanders, and is now hated by all the Army Corps Staff. The truth is that he belongs to the Army Clique, which holds all Militia officers in contempt as *'mere Amateurs'*. Yet he has done my Brigade very well, and for that I am grateful to him. [He] has a violent temper. . . . He is also very pernickety. He is also very selfish. While in a formal way, he is very dignified, a fine speaker and a strong administrator, he has not that urbanity and tact which makes a man really liked by his Staff and Commanders.

Cox, Monash's superior in the battle of Sari Bair, was to command 4th Division.

As soon as he heard this news, Monash wrote to McCay, who was now briefly inspector-general at home.

> Surely Australia won't stand this! I have a very live interest in the matter, because I am the only Australian Brigadier who has served continuously throughout the campaign, without a single day's

absence from duty; and have secured three 'mentions', and have been recommended for special distinction in connection with the closing phases at Gallipoli. . . . there will be at least two, if not three, commands of Australian Divisions vacant very shortly, and it is surely not an unreasonable aspiration, that in the light of my training and services, I should be selected for one of them.

Other senior officers, some of whom had gone in for 'some pretty warm cabling', also thought it a 'scandal that Australia should acquiesce' in War Office appointments to Australian commands of British and Indian officers 'at a loose end for a job'. Monash suspected that both Birdwood and Godley were prejudiced against promotion of Australians, especially citizen-soldiers. But he did not suspect Brigadier-General Brudenell White, Birdwood's chief of staff, whom he described in April as 'far and away the ablest soldier Australia has ever turned out . . . a charming good fellow'. He took it for granted that permanent soldiers like Legge, Chauvel and MacLagan would be preferred to Holmes and himself.

Monash was not well informed. Since mid-1915 the Australian government had been pressing strongly for appointment of Australians to senior commands. Neither Birdwood, nor Hamilton before him, was prejudiced on this matter, but the fact was there were few possible claimants. Early in 1916 Birdwood exclusively appointed A.I.F. men to brigade commands. Walker and Legge had to have command of 1st and 2nd Divisions, and, on Pearce's insistence, he accepted McCay for the 5th. Pearce was disappointed that so few Australians stood out, and asked Birdwood to give every consideration to Chauvel, Monash, Holmes and White. Birdwood appointed the 'slow but very loyal' Chauvel to the A.N.Z. Mounted Division. White was too valuable as a staff officer, Holmes too inexperienced and, on Monash, he replied:

> I regard [him] as a man of very considerable ability and with good administrative powers. [But] he has not shown that resolution which is really essential, [and there is] among a considerable number of the force a great feeling against him on account of what they consider his German extraction.

Legge had told Birdwood that, because of his German connections, it would be 'very inadvisable' to promote Monash.

He knuckled down. He *should* be promoted, he felt, in justice, and pretended to his family that he did not care:

> I am not at all sure that I should like the command [4th Division], except for the kudos. The worry and responsibility I now have are more than enough, already. At any rate, I have firmly resolved not to intrigue or canvas for promotion in any way, if Australia chooses to let her forces be exploited to find jobs for unemployed senior

British officers, that is not my affair. . . . I am not going to stir a finger to intrigue for promotion.

At the same time he told Vic: 'Do all you can to cultivate Hughes. He is one of the Wallabies, and I like him very much. It may help me for you to be chummy with Mrs Prime Minister'. And it would be as well to get what snippets of publicity she could about the 4th Brigade and him into the press.

In mid-February the brigade moved to Tel-el-Kebir, seventy miles from Cairo and thirty miles west of the Canal. For a few days early in March, in Cox's absence, Monash acted in command of some forty thousand of the A.I.F. in the area. Training proceeded vigorously. More than two-thirds of the officers in the brigade had been promoted from the ranks of their own battalions; the Official Historian notes that 4th Brigade had a higher proportion of state school products among its officers than the New South Wales brigades which tended to recruit subalterns on social grounds from the Light Horse. In the 3rd Division, later, most of the warrant officers and sergeants gained commissions in their own battalions. Monash's was still the only Australia-wide brigade; he deliberately used interstate rivalry—'the most powerful weapon in my hands'—in promoting competition for efficiency among the battalions, whose territorial basis he would not allow to be infringed. Pope and Cannan had returned to take command of their battalions, but to his great sorrow he lost McGlinn to 5th Division, and replaced him with Major J. M. A. Durrant.

From mid-March 1st and 2nd Divisions began to leave for France, and the 4th and 5th took their places in the local defences. Most of the two latter divisions had to make a forty-four-mile, three-day march to Serapeum, carrying full packs and ammunition. Monash and Durrant made careful preparations, which were not adequate. Heavy sand, heat, thirst, dust, flies, chafing new boots and cotton trousers, and the effects of recent inoculations, produced great distress. On the second day, though the main body marched in with bands playing, the New Zealanders went out to aid more than one hundred who had fallen out. On the third day the brigade 'dissolved into trailing groups'. E. J. Rule of the 14th Battalion wrote in *Jacka's Mob*: 'Within two miles of our destination General Monash rode up and tactlessly told some of the stragglers that their sisters could do as well. It was the only time I've heard men curse him'. Monash rebuked some of the 15th for diving into the Canal before the end of the march; he galloped away when they began to count him out. The 13th were ashamed that 'the heads' would sanction such a march and allow them to be humiliated in front of the Kiwis. But 4th Brigade did better than most. McCay, who had just taken over 5th Division, never lived down the collapse of 14th Brigade, though he sacked its commander.

Two months now followed east of the Canal, on the fringe of the Sinai Wilderness—'at the end of the world', Monash described it. There were rumours of a Turkish attack. The heat became fierce, and training was confined to early morning and evening; the flies were even worse than at Anzac. He vividly described the khamseen which hit them in mid-April—the gale of sand and pebbles, the pitch-dark lasting twenty hours:

> It was impossible to move about, or eat, or cook, or sleep. There was nothing to do but huddle together in the most secure of the tents, and swear, and wonder if it was ever going to stop. But stop it did at last . . . it left us gasping, choking, eyeballs inflamed, chests raw with coughing, with severe headaches, and symptoms of catarrh in nose and throat and generally down and out.

He rode in to Serapeum through the tail-end of it, on the way for a few days in Cairo—he would never forget that ride. Having already a respiratory infection, he took more than three weeks to throw it off. In Cairo he set about reforming the mails:

> Didn't I just wade in hot and strong, criticising the whole system, brushing aside their tales of difficulties, and making them sit up all around. "If it's not *your* fault, but that of the Australian Department, are you going to sit still like a lot of mummies? . . . Have you written? Have you cabled? Well then get busy and cable—do it *now*".

There was time to spare in the desert. Monash was translating, and trying to write stories—the diary entries are tantalizingly brief. The *Saturday Evening Post* was the 'sheet anchor of myself and staff' and he was interested in Hilaire Belloc's journal *Land and Water*. He delighted in a copy he received of C. J. Dennis's *Songs of a Sentimental Bloke* and showed it round widely; the brigade chaplains preached sermons on it. The first commemoration of Anzac Day was memorable:

> I turned out the whole Brigade . . . at 6.45 in the morning. Every man who had served on Gallipoli wore a blue ribbon on the right breast, and every man, who, in addition, had taken part in the historic landing on April 25/15 wore a red ribbon also. . . . Alas, how few of us are left who were entitled to wear both! We then had a short but very dignified Service. . . . We spent the morning in cricket matches and other amusement, and in the afternoon, the whole Division went down to the Canal to swim and take part in a great Aquatic Carnival . . . one teeming mass of naked humanity—at times there were over 15,000 men in the water. . . . Of course we had many comic items on the programme, including a skit on the memorable landing.

The Prince of Wales and Godley attended and 'in the evening we had mess dinners everywhere, and finished up with band concerts, and wished each other the opportunity of enjoying many happy returns of this famous Day—*Our Day*'. Monash had twice to entertain Prince Edward, who was attached to Murray's staff.

> Birdwood brought him on a visit to Tel-el-Kebir, with a small retinue of noble lords, who were youngsters just like the Prince himself—and he rode around seeing the troops at work and shaking hands with the various C.O.'s. He was not very talkative—but he made quite a long speech to me—to the envy of a number of others. What he said to me was: "M-m-m-m-m-". The fact was the youngster was completely bewildered, and most evidently ill at ease.

Monash was happy with the progress of the brigade and, when Godley inspected it, considered it the finest performance he had seen for 'turnout, steadiness, set up and precision of drill'. At a meeting of divisional officers, Cox spoke, then called on Monash who was satisfied that he had made a 'great impression'. He attended a demonstration of the Stokes mortar; the only record of an untoward happening is a label in his collection of records in the Australian War Memorial: 'Fragment of Stokes Mortar Bomb, which wounded me at Serapeum, on 8th May, 1916'. For more than a week in mid-May Cox was away ill and Monash took charge of the division, finding it 'anything but a picnic' with much rushing round and hard riding. Later in the month he conducted night manoeuvres. He used W. H. Fitchett's *Deeds that won the Empire* as a means of interesting the men in British military traditions.

Monash was getting on splendidly with Cox even though he was 'one of those crochetty, peppery, livery old Indian officers, whom the climate has dried and shrivelled up into a bag of nerves'. Cox had good reason to be grateful for he had carpeted Lieut-Colonel Tilney of the 13th Battalion on very shaky grounds, and Tilney was determined to take the matter higher. Monash's tact smoothed things down, but he told McCay and McGlinn that the incident was an example of the evil of 'putting Australian troops under a Divisional Staff who wholly misunderstand the Australian attitude and temperament'. Cox became quite intimate with him 'in very unreserved and extremely flattering terms', and recommended him to Birdwood for a divisional command. Godley also was now convinced of Monash's worth, supported him to Birdwood, and wrote to Pearce on 31 May:

> I wonder who you will appoint to command the 3rd Division. Monash has come on a great deal lately, and, having commanded his Brigade in the field for eighteen months, is I think, deserving of a trial, and I believe would do it well if he had really good, well-trained staff officers to help him.

Birdwood recommended Monash early in June.

They were all utterly weary with Egypt. 'I shall be more than content if I can see my wife and daughter once again before my time comes', Monash told an American cousin. Confirmation at last came of the move to France. He addressed each of his battalions: 'The average Australian by his nature feels a healthy amount of contempt [for Egyptians]. But in France we shall be the guests of a great, a brave and gallant nation, a people in every way as good as ourselves', so their behaviour had to be 'dignified, courteous, and gentlemanly'. On the 29th when Murray inspected the division, Cox was very pleased with 4th Brigade: the march past was *'extremely* good considering heavy ground and flying sand. . . . It is very satisfying when men *try* like that'.

The brigade sailed uneventfully to Marseilles in the first week of June and learned at sea of the naval battle of Jutland and Kitchener's death. Monash was as busy as ever as G.O.C. troops. Starting their long train journey up the Rhone valley, as though through a perpetual garden, the brigade eventually reached the Armentières section near the Belgian border. Monash and Durrant spent two days in Paris sightseeing, before moving on through Calais to Bailleul; a week later brigade headquarters moved to Erquinghem and a comfortable farmhouse. Monash was soon dining with Birdwood, White, Legge and Russell. First impressions of the front were misleading:

> the people here don't know what war is. It is true they get an intensive bombardment now and then, and that is pretty bad for anyone who gets in its way—but in between times you'd hardly know there was a war on at all.

And even after a month of it he held that 'war in France is simply child's play to what it was in Gallipoli'.

Immediately they arrived, however, 4th Brigade was tagged for a substantial night raid, one of many diversions from the massive British offensive on the Somme on 1 July. On 18 June the brigade was temporarily attached to the 2nd Division, and part of the 13th and 14th Battalions joined 5th Brigade to be tutored by them in the line. Monash worked closely with Brigadier-General Holmes: 'He is a real good fellow, and is giving me a lot of help', he told McGlinn. Monash nominated the 14th Battalion to provide the raiding team which was under the immediate control of Lieut-Colonel G. H. F. Jackson, a British specialist in raids with the 2nd Division; 4th Brigade took over the line at the end of the month. Monash had reconnoitred on 19 June and with Jackson worked out the detailed plans for 'Monash's Muddle', as the Artillery jocularly termed it. The raid on the night of 2 July was by no means successful. After the preliminary bombardment, the eighty-nine officers and men, armed mainly with revolvers and coshes, were held up by wire which had not been cleared by the mortars, and only about twenty-five of them reached the German trenches—three-quarters of the party became casualties, more than they inflicted. Monash had been perturbed at losing contact with the leader, through failure of signal-rockets. 'Only their thorough training saved the raiders from complete disaster', the Official Historian summed up; no prisoners were won. Monash made the best of it to senior officers and misleadingly bragged to Walter Rosenhain: 'Our scouts and wounded threw themselves on the enemy wire to form a bridge for the rest of the party to walk on!!' Next night the enemy replied in kind and the 14th suffered severely in holding them off. It was no easy time: the Brigade had had three hundred casualties in four weeks in holding its two-mile front, and Monash was very short of sleep.

3rd Division was beginning to arrive in England from Australia, still without a commander. On 24 June Monash heard from Jackson that his appointment was unofficially approved. On the 26th Birdwood called in to notify him; Godley and Cox followed with their congratulations, and McCay wrote to reassure him:

> You know without my telling you how jolly glad I am; and I congratulate you most sincerely. I fear you'll find discipline indifferent . . . but you'll be able to remedy that. Good luck to you.

But nothing happened for nearly a fortnight and Monash grew edgy, fearing some last-minute political veto or that the new division might be broken up for reinforcements. A letter from Birdwood implying no immediate action 'much disturbed' him. He wrote inquiringly to Cox and was rebuked for his pains by Birdwood, from whom on 9 July he heard full details: the new divisional staff was already under orders. His departure was complicated by the move of 4th Division to the Somme. But eventually he handed over the brigade to C. H. Brand and on the 14th, after a little speech of farewell to his C.O.s, set off for England. There, four days later, he wrote reflectively to Vic:

> Coming now to look back upon it, I recognize the disadvantages I had to labour under to get to where I now stand. . . . there is the question of religion, and the question of parentage, and it is rather gratifying, in spite of these very solid handicaps, and without any intrigue whatever on my part to have got the honor and status of my present rank. I am wondering what my enemies out home will be saying.

And he later added:

> While I know that [Birdwood] has been very helpful to my interests, yet I also know that I should have had no chance of commanding an Australian Division in the Field had it not been

for the Australian Government and Defence Department (Hughes, Pearce, Foster etc.) insisting on an Australian being appointed, and pressing my claims on Birdwood.

Paddy McGlinn exulted: his promotion was 'such an effective slap in the face to those miserable curs' who had tried to injure him. In Melbourne, Hanby and other elderly gunners met at the Naval and Military to drink his health. Sergeant-Major Garcia, D.C.M., of 4th Brigade sent some doggerel entitled 'Farewell to our C.O.'. A lieutenant also wrote to tell him that everyone in the brigade regretted his departure:

> altho' I know you have not sought popularity, there isn't a man amongst us who does not love and respect you. I personally ... will never forget you at Monash Gully during those strenuous days of Pope's Hill and Quinn's Post.... you were so fatherly and considerate and altogether different to the terrible personage that a N.C.O. pictures his G.O.C. to be.

Monash had 'bucked up' many of them when things were very grim.

He stayed ten days with the Rosenhains in Surrey before moving to Salisbury Plain. Calls at the War Office and A.I.F. Headquarters in Horseferry Road provided little enlightenment on immediate duties, but after sending Simonson off to reconnoitre, he went down to Salisbury for a day and met his staff officers. He arranged with Burberry's for new uniforms, inspected Walter's laboratory, went several times to the theatre, visited Westminster Abbey, and took Vic's friend Lizzie Bentwitch to tea. He also had a severe case of uncle-worship on his hands. Since their visit to Melbourne, his three Rosenhain nieces had been enraptured by him; the eldest kissed his photograph every night and wrote to her Dear Uncle Jack regularly. He delighted now in cuddling them and taking them for walks. It was eighteen months since he had had more than a glimpse of family life. He could even play the piano, but he was not altogether pleased when Walter exposed the flaw in his roulette system. He was surprised by the rigour of life in wartime London, especially the blackout precautions against Zeppelin raids, but exaggerated the situation in writing to Vic and Bert to dissuade them from attempting to join him—for the submarine threat was already ominous and by the time they might arrive he would be in France and would rarely be able to see them.

On 25 July he moved to his headquarters at Larkhill, nine miles north of Salisbury and one north of Stonehenge. Birdwood, not quite confident of Monash, had, with White's assistance, done him proud with regard to staff. His general staff officers were Lieut-Colonel Jackson, with whom he had already worked in France, already becoming a famous trainer of soldiers; Major G. G. E. Wylly, V.C., an Australian-born Indian Army officer; and a Duntroon man, Major George Wootten. His senior administrative officer, Lieut-Colonel H. Mynors Farmar, D.S.O., from an ancient British military family, like the others had served gallantly on Gallipoli. Monash liked the look of his staff:

> a very mixed but a very fine lot; some are younger sons of peers while others are promoted from the ranks; one is a Baronet; one a Professor [H. A. Woodruff of the University of Melbourne], and another an ex-storekeeper—but there are no longer any social distinctions in England, and it is only a man's intrinsic worth that counts.

His brigadiers, with whom he immediately began to confer, included W. R. McNicoll, A. Jobson, and H. W. Grimwade in charge of artillery. He was worried (he uncharacteristically admitted in a letter home) over whether he could impose his authority on them, but they gave him no trouble in that regard. Monash immediately began riding round with Jackson, inspecting the units—the 33rd to 44th Battalions of the 9th, 10th and 11th Brigades, and associated troops. The men, he soon told Birdwood who had asked him to write regularly, were 'equal in every way, in physique and in bearing, to the earlier Divisions', they were out for business and there would be no trouble with discipline:

> Most of them are men of standing—a great many master tradesmen, owner farmers, miners, professional men, and several members of parliament. . . . It is a great honour to command 20,000 such men. And the officers seem also very good. I am beginning to feel that it is going to be a pleasant and agreeable job, and not a difficult one to create a very fine fighting Division out of these men.

They were largely countrymen: 9th Brigade was from northern New South Wales, the 10th from rural Victoria, the 11th from the other States. They had a hard and independent look about them; crime was almost negligible even though 11th Brigade had been 'grossly mismanaged'. His first unpleasant task was to dismiss its brigadier: it had been a political appointment—the man was a prominent State politician—and he was incapable and drinking heavily. They had at least two painful interviews, and Monash had to battle with the bureaucrats at Horseferry Road before he could replace him with Cannan. He also had to sack one battalion commander, but refused a brigadier's request to remove another. During these weeks he grieved at the downfall of Pope, recently a brigadier in 5th Division, whom McCay had had sent back to Australia because he was allegedly drunk—though it was rather a matter of exhaustion after prolonged action. Monash believed his old friend had been unjust, and when Pope confided in him comforted him as best he could.

Monash had comfortable quarters, living with Farmar and his family, a mile and a half from divisional headquarters, sharing expenses. Farmar had immediately arranged for him to be made an honorary member of the Cavendish Club in London, then suggested he accommodate him. The Farmars were 'very tony people', John told Vic, who 'know all the nobility and the gentry, but are . . . very bright company'. The first time he met the small Farmar children, he noted in his diary: 'Susan, Hugh and baby play with me uproariously'. Sixty-five years later Susan and Hugh remembered him clearly as an anything but frightening man who romped with them, did not mind their noise when working, and encouraged Farmar's groom to take them riding. Mrs Farmar wrote to Vic of the pleasure it was to have him as a guest: 'He would cheer up any house by his sunny ways and delightful conversation'. Monash kept in touch with the Farmars for the rest of his life.

Monash's substantive promotion to major-general went through in mid-August. He enjoyed but was amused by the trappings:

> Of course, a Major-General commanding a fighting Division is a quite tremendous person, and it is a little hard to live up to it. I must not travel by rail, except in a reserved compartment, and there are lots of other things I mustn't do; and wherever one goes people stare and follow one about. . . . I have now donned my red armlets, and this attracts even more attention than the gold peaked cap and gorgets, and ribbons.

He had appointed a new senior A.D.C., Lieutenant Colman, son of a Jewish bookmaker originally named Kohlmann. 'He's certainly not ornamental', John told Vic, 'and talks with a strong nasal hebraic accent, but he's an absolutely ideal man for the job of Camp Commandant . . . and he's also extremely popular'. But he was disappointed in his performance and in November aided his return to Australia on medical grounds.

Monash's relations with Birdwood and Brudenell White, as controllers of the A.I.F., were close and cordial. He had a problem about the authority of Brigadier-General Sir Newton Moore, a former premier of Western Australia who was commanding the A.I.F. depots and training camps in England. They had an immediate altercation, whereupon Birdwood made it clear that Moore had no authority whatsoever over the 3rd Division. Birdwood looked to Monash, as senior officer in England, to keep an eye on things there. Monash had long known Moore from his days in Perth and managed the confrontation with aplomb, for he looked on him as 'a very charming good fellow'; moreover Julius Bruche had recently arrived to act as Moore's second-in-command.

Birdwood and White also supported him totally over a much graver matter—the attempt to break up 3rd Division in order to reinforce the other divisions after their terrible casualties at Pozières and Fromelles. The initial decision by the Army Council to withdraw a large draft, taken over Birdwood's head and communicated to Monash on 16 August, was part of the murky plot to win Australian consent for conscription, which Britain and New Zealand had recently introduced; it would seem to the Australian voter that there were insufficient men to maintain six divisions. The Australian government was informed that the only way to keep 3rd Division in existence would be to send about seventy thousand more recruits over the next four months. Monash stormed and raged over the loss of his men; it was stupid—there were twenty-five thousand other Australians available in the training camps—it was a 'cruel shame', no useful end was served: 'Men are now being torn asunder who enlisted together, represent the same districts and home interests, and hoped to work and fight side by side'. But by 9 September 2800 men had been marched out. Monash asked Bruche to send the best possible replacements. Expecting imminent further withdrawals, he continued the struggle. But no more was heard of the matter: among other things, Birdwood had persuaded Haig to intervene.

The referendum in Australia on conscription was to be on 28 October. In hope of the troops showing the way, they were to vote on the 16th. At the last moment, because of well-judged fear about their intentions, Prime Minister W. M. Hughes, the diminutive superpatriot of demonic energy, asked Birdwood to appeal for a 'Yes' vote. Birdwood had tried to 'avoid doing the politician' but felt he could not refuse, so sent telegrams ordering postponement of the poll until his message to the troops could be distributed. In France the poll, which had begun in some areas, was cancelled and delayed. But the telegram was not received by Monash on Salisbury Plain till about midday, when 80 per cent of the division had already voted. He wired Birdwood to say the poll was almost completed, but was told that voting must stop. He disobeyed: in consultation with the returning officer, he decided to complete the poll, and did not issue Birdwood's message when it arrived late in the day. In a letter to the returning officer he mentioned his 'serious quandary' and misgivings: he could imagine the outcry of 'antis' at home and the probable damage to Birdwood's reputation; 3rd Division, to whom Birdwood was only a name, would have been angry if the poll had been cancelled. The returning officer entirely supported him: *no one* could order delay, it was simply unlawful. Nothing more was heard of the matter. The 3rd Division poll stood.

Like almost every officer, Monash of course broadly supported Hughes and strongly favoured conscription. Their pride in being volunteers came second to the need for recruits. But his reaction to a letter of January 1917 from the journalist Agnes Murphy, a former dancing partner at Government House, is interesting. She made a strong anti-conscription case: the censorship had deluded the public about the gravity of the military situation and was unfairly used for political purposes; Birdwood's interference in a political issue was scandalous; the government's incessant attacks on the Industrial Workers of the World awaiting trial were an outrage on justice; thousands had voted against conscription 'to mark their indignation at the brutal treatment of the Irish rebels'; Hughes's tactics had killed the voluntary spirit, especially his 'persistent statement that all who voted against Conscription wanted Germany to win'. Monash was probably sincere when he replied: 'I fully agree with many of the sentiments you have expressed . . ., although it would be inconvenient for me to be quoted'. He later told General Sir Henry Wilson that 'it was the way Hughes had handled the conscription question which had made Australia vote against it'. Monash may have been one of the few capable of recognizing the disastrous divisive effect of the conscription campaigns. He doubtless shuddered when he heard that Minnie Behrend, an active anti-conscriptionist, had embarrassed Vic in the company of 'nice' friends by calling out to her from a procession. Incidentally, he wrongly believed—Birdwood had told him so—that the A.I.F. had voted heavily in favour of conscription.

Impressive though they looked, the men of 3rd Division had to be trained virtually from scratch:

> No single Brigade had met till they reached England. Even some Battalions had never been together, all in one place. Officers didn't know their men, and vice versa. The men had no rifles or bayonets, and had never seen a Mills bomb, or dug a trench, or seen a Vickers or Lewis machine gun, or a Stokes Mortar, or handled their transport. The gunners had never seen an 18 [pounder] or a Howitzer. All they had learned to do was to stand up straight in rows and behave themselves. All the bayonet fighting they had been taught in Australia had to be unlearnt.

Almost his first action was to send off hundreds of specialists for training at schools. Yet he told White that the fourteen weeks training period laid down was unnecessarily long, and almost a scandal with regard to the need in France.

That fourteen weeks was roughly taken up with four of company, four of battalion, three of brigade, and two of divisional training. Monash spent long mornings in the saddle and afternoons at his desk. An area was given over to digging 2000 yards of opposing trenches, which were wired; billets were established a mile behind. Under the tuition of a staff experienced in trench warfare, each brigade had to occupy the line, remaining there for several days before being relieved by another. Battalions practised raiding and making a major attack with artillery and air support. Patrols were sent into no-man's-land, attacks in gas masks were made, and sniping instruction given. Every battalion had to practise billeting: marching twelve to fifteen miles to Nether Wallop and other villages, finding quarters with the help of the village constable, muddling through somehow. The 37th Battalion historian remarks that this was all very well, but that in some ways they were ill prepared; for example, they had had no practice in following barrages. The outstanding occasion was the 'crater stunt' early in November when two thousand troops took part in the blowing up of a mine, rushing and fortifying the crater. The word had got around:

> early this morning there arrived a special train bringing upwards of 120 generals and senior staff officers. . . . It was the biggest audience the Third Division has yet had, and it is to be noted that they came, not to supervise and criticise, but to *learn*. . . . I had to get up on to the top of the mound created by the explosion and give a long address to the whole crowd, explaining the means and principles employed, the reasons for all the arrangements, and the points brought out as a guide to future operations of this nature in the actual war zone. I think it will be a long time before I shall face so distinguished and critical an audience again. . . . The whole thing was entirely our own idea, worked out by myself and staff.

Monash told Rosenhain that many of the senior officers found it difficult to believe that he was not a professional soldier, and that no one patronized him because he was not. A little later he entered in his diary: 'The Signalling Exercise with the Divisional Commanders all present was a veritable triumph for me—my criticisms causing a sensation to Staff College officers present'.

Monash insisted on 3rd Division wearing the brim of their slouch-hats turned down, and not looped as had become the rule in the other divisions. The parallel with the 9th Division's T-shaped colour-patch in World War II is close. The matter is sometimes cited as an example of Monash's allegedly crude psychological approach, here as an attempt to instil a sense of the division's distinctiveness. In the *Official History* Bean remarks that the 3rd Division's 'most cherished desire was to be just one of the five, and, if General Monash had known how his order as to hat-brims burned in the men's hearts, the brim would possibly have been looped up that same hour'. Here, as quite often, Bean adopted a black and white simplification to Monash's detriment. We may be sure that Monash was well informed on the state of opinion; and there is evidence that opinion was divided on what was not an important issue. When 3rd Division eventually came under Birdwood's command fifteen months later, he ordered Monash to comply with the general rule, but admitted that when first consulted he had allowed him to do what he liked. In his good-humoured submissive reply, Monash asserted that his policy had been based on practical reasons rather than any desire to make 3rd Division distinctive. In the Citizen Forces, he argued, many units, including his own and Grimwade's brigades, had worn their hats down. It had been the invariable practice in Cox's 4th Division in Egypt. In the bush the felt hat was worn 'with the flap level all round and with the whole hat slightly tilted to one side, having one deep dent in the top of the crown'. He further argued climatic, practical and aesthetic reasons, and remarked in conclusion that a large proportion of the other divisions, on and off duty, continued to wear the flaps down. He was on the side of history, for in World War II his campaign was justified by practice.

Late in October Monash gave three talks to his brigadiers and battalion commanders, speaking freely from limited notes (with a shorthand writer in attendance). Firstly he advised them to study again Field Service Regulations, covering the whole range of an officer's duties; every line was of absorbing interest. Discipline could be enforced only by unrelenting supervision—'unremitting pressure and vigilance'. He stressed the importance of sticking to the battle plan. Officers should query the meaning of orders if in any doubt; it was far better to 'take your snub' than to make a mistake, though he would take care that officers were not snubbed for asking questions. However, he went on,

> There is an unfortunate tendency among a minority of Australians to criticise one another, and their superiors, and senior officers as well as junior officers are the offenders. It is a bad business and quite prejudicial to military discipline. Loyalty to your superiors is a fine thing, and Commanders should always try to earn it. But unfortunately they do not always have it. It is mighty easy being loyal to a man who is your superior when you agree with him, and he does what you expect him to do, and you are pleased to be with him. But the loyalty we want is loyalty to the man when you think he is unnecessarily severe, critical or wrong, when he is adopting a course of action which you feel and know to be incorrect. It is when he *knows* he will get your obedience in letter and spirit even though you don't agree with him and his commands, that counts. That is the only kind of loyalty that is worth a damn, or counts at all. I do not suggest that you will do behind your seniors' backs things you were told not to do. Or fail to do things you were instructed to. But there is a tendency to criticise. Wipe it out Gentlemen: Do not permit it with subordinates. Not even with your senior officers. ... It creates a bad spirit which leads to inefficiency and failure in battle.

Officers *must* be cheerful and never grouse: it had not always been so on Gallipoli. Any officer tolerating a man feeling sorry for himself was in effect a traitor. They had to instil into their men the will to kill: this was war, they had to make them feel that the Germans were vermin to be exterminated. The Gallipoli armistice had been alarming: there could be no fraternization with the enemy. Officers must steel themselves to bear heavy casualties:

> Over and over again I have seen [officers] paralysed because they have lost men whom they have relied upon. They are overwhelmed with the loss and death and bloodshed. You must get yourself into a callous state of mind. A commander who worries is not worth a damn. . . . Make up your minds you are not going to worry. It will do after the war. . . . Hypnotise yourself into a state of complete indifference as to losses. . . . you have got to carry on.

And a final point from Gallipoli experience—in prolonged battle conditions, men needed sleep much more than food.

According to Farmar, Monash was very concerned with formal discipline, largely as a consequence of slackness on Gallipoli, and enforced strict saluting. He told his men that war was like a game with rules. The saluting rule was soundly based: it was visible evidence of loyalty to the Crown and recognized the relative degrees of responsibility under the King. Remarkably, Farmar relates, on Salisbury Plain voluntary parties from 3rd Division patrolled the camp to remind recalcitrant soldiers of the need to salute until it was no longer necessary. The division was sometimes called 'The Guards'.

Through all this period the terrible battle of the Somme had been bleeding the A.I.F. At Pozières and Mouquet Farm, 4th Brigade had fought its way forward superbly. Brand wrote to recall that, when handing over, Monash had told him how good a brigade it was. 'My opinion is the same as yours—second to none.' Durrant, too, told Monash that he could be prouder of them than ever. 'No-one glories more than I', Monash replied to Brand. But what was Monash's thinking on this shattering demonstration of the failure of the mass, frontal advance to break the stalemate of trench warfare? And, in view of the massive British casualties, what were his views on the policy of attrition? He was at least trying to keep up with the flood of technical literature on infantry tactics.

Monash was plagued with inspections. His immediate superior, Lieut-General Sir Henry Sclater of Southern Command, was pleasant to work with and a helpful mentor. On 6 August the Chief of the Imperial General Staff, General Sir William Robertson, called in, but stayed only an hour after Monash had presented his staff and commanders; he and Robertson dined with the Sclaters at Government House, Salisbury. Major-General Sir Francis Howard, Inspector of Infantry, spent two days with the division and was highly complimentary. Field Marshal Lord French, Commander-in-Chief Home Forces, looking 'old and worn and lifeless', followed, and also gave warm approval; the Sclaters again had Monash to dinner with the exalted party. 'We are being inspected to death, and it does disturb the training so', Monash complained to Rosenhain. Having heard she was in the neighbourhood, he had Lady Birdwood to tea with Lady Moore and showed them round the camp. Birdwood himself visited in mid-October and concluded that the 3rd Division was 'going on capitally'.

French had promised Monash—whose suggestion was it?—'to ask the King to come down and have a look at the Division before the weather got too cold'. It was quickly arranged for 27 September. Monash thoroughly rehearsed the division. He described the outcome to Vic:

> Apart from being by far the biggest and most splendid, it was much the most successful Review I have ever been present at. . . . the parade was a grand total of 27,000. . . . we marched past in close column of platoons (i.e. 100 men every 10 paces) and even with this crowding, the march took nearly 2 hours. . . . What you will doubtless most wish to hear about is what the King did and said. I suppose it does not happen to very many people to have the unique privilege and pleasure of spending 2½ hours continuously . . . with the King of so mighty an Empire, and talking with him the whole time on a footing of perfect freedom and equality. . . .
>
> As the King rode up to the Flagstaff, the great Royal Standard . . . was "broken" out, and fluttered out into the breeze precisely as I gave the 'Royal Salute' and 27000 bayonets flashed together into the 'Present Arms' and the 16 massed bands played 6 bars of the Anthem. It was a moment of glorious sunshine, in an otherwise dull day, an impressive and magnificent spectacle. The King remained with his hand at the Salute, while I gave "The Parade will slope and order arms and Stand-at-Ease". Then I trotted out towards him, and he trotted up towards me, extending his hand as he came near, with a cheery winning smile: "How do you do, General" he said in a deep, clear vibrating voice; "I am so *very* glad to be able to come down to see you all. It is the first time I have been able to see Australian troops in England. Shall we go up to the right of the line? . . . You used to command the Fourth Brigade didn't you? They've done awfully well. I hear you were on Gallipoli all the time; that *was* splendid." . . .
>
> In short, he was chatty, and breezy and merry all the time, and hardly waited for me to answer him before he went on. . . . As we rode at a walking pace down the whole line (nearly 2 miles long it was) I told him where each Battalion or Battery was raised, and he was always ready with an appropriate comment. He asked me what part of Australia I had come from, and said he'd been in Melbourne twice, and that it was a fine city. Had he met me there?

... When we came to the end of the Third Division ... he stopped and looked back and said "Well, General, I heartily congratulate you. It's a very fine Division. I don't know that I've ever seen a finer one. The men look just splendid and so soldierly and steady." I continued to ride with him to the extreme end of the line, when he said "I should like to see them march past now. Shall I go to the Flagstaff?" ... I and my staff went full gallop across the front of the parade.... We posted ourselves at the head of the Column; Eric leading, next Jackson and Farmar, then myself, and 50 yards behind me Grimwade and staff leading the Artillery.... I gave the signal to advance, and then commenced a march which continued without a break for nearly 2 hours. As I wheeled around, after passing the Saluting Point, and reined up alongside the King, he turned to me with a broad smile and said "And yet those silly Germans say we've no ear for music. Listen to those beautiful bands, and how their instruments shine!" ... he did not once take his eyes off the troops, and asked hundreds of questions and criticized dozens of small details, such as the quality of the Artillery horses, the relative utility of leather or web equipment, the rifles, the clothing, the hats, the platoon commanders and their training and so on and on. He talked nearly all the time, jumping from subject to subject—every now and then breaking off, to mutter "splendid"—"splendid". He told me he had reviewed already 1½ million men since the war began, adding with especial emphasis "Isn't it *perfectly wonderful*. No man could have done it but Lord K." He made one remark commencing "If we win this war ..." and I smiled and said "*If* we win?" and he threw back his head and laughed a full laugh and said "Oh yes! we'll *win* right enough, nobody need make any mistake about *that*"— and then "Those stupid Germans! They started out to smash the British Empire!—smash it to pieces!—and look—just *look*"—with a sweep of his arm up and down the marching column "see what they've *really* done; they've *made* an Empire of us." ... And so the show went on, the King talking all the time, ... of our recent successes and of the splendid efforts of the British colonies. "Think of it—600 000 men—marvellous—marvellous", and of our being now able to beat the best German troops, man to man, "And make no mistake, they *are* good troops and hard to beat." Again, as the long column came to an end, he turned to me with shining eyes and said "Perfectly splendid; magnificent." I then presented to him my Brigadiers and Battery and Battalion Commanders—on foot—and then we rode down together to the Burford station—about a mile away—I riding on the right of the King. ... And then came the climax of it all. For I had had the troops drawn up, closely packed together 100 deep, on the sloping field adjoining the road, and, as the King rode by, each Unit broke into deafening cheer upon cheer—raising hats aloft on bayonets. It was a stirring sight, and our horses—though terrified—behaved splendidly. The King rode with his head bowed, looking grave and solemn, and when he had passed the last of the troops, he turned to me and said "It makes a lump come in my throat, to think of all these splendid fellows coming all those many thousands of miles; and what they have come for." And he said not another word till we reached the station and he dismounted. . . . Then he shook hands all round, and with me last of all, saying "I'll send you a message for the men tonight when I get home. Now, good bye, General, thank you very much; and don't forget to come and see me. Good bye to you all" as he stepped upon the Royal train, which slowly moved away.

As soon as he left, the rain came down in sheets and all got thoroughly soaked on their way back to camp. In fact many of the troops had been extremely disgruntled at having to turn out yet again, even for the King.

The boy from Richmond might have been forgiven for chortling more than he did. *How* the coup must have been envied. The Rosenhains had come down to share in the triumph. Springthorpe was on hand to write it up for the *Age*. Three weeks later Monash attended Buckingham Palace to be invested with the C.B. by His Majesty 'in his usual chatty and informal way'.

Early in October Monash had four days' leave in London. He stayed at the Cavendish Club, went four times to the theatre, lunched at the Cheshire Cheese, tried on uniforms (and ordered a chamois vest and underpants to keep out the winter cold), and spent an afternoon in Richmond Park with the Rosenhains. Walter gave him two pieces of a Zeppelin recently shot down, which he sent home as priceless souvenirs. Four weeks later his assistant provost marshal, Major Sir Henry Dering, a baronet, invited him for the weekend to Surrenden, his estate in Kent, which his family had held for a thousand years. The house-party spent Saturday shooting pheasant and partridge—'a very fine sport', Monash concluded, 'however cruel'. Next day he was shown over the mansion and viewed furniture and paintings by van Dyke, Holbein, Gainsborough and others. It was the first time he had been entertained in a stately home.

Lack of equipment was holding up the division's movement to France. On 22 September he wrote urging action to Birdwood, who informed Haig who replied that he wanted 3rd Division as soon as possible, whereupon equipment flooded in. It was simply a matter of priority; Monash was immensely impressed by the scale of British war production which he was convinced made ultimate victory certain. By mid-November most of the division was ready. Monash reported that Southern Command believed it 'the best trained Division that has left since the old Army disappeared'. However, the improvised artillery had to wait: Grimwade was doing very well, but his senior officers had been inadequate and the batteries had to be brought to a higher pitch of training. The division made its last march on 13 November—it was strung out for fifteen miles and took five hours to pass. Monash reported to Sclater on the many serious faults and issued the severest of rebukes to the 43rd Battalion, the worst-performed.

The division began its move to Southampton in eighty-seven trains over six days from 21 November, and thence to Le Havre and Rouen: 'You should just have heard the men cheering as train after train went out today'. Monash issued a message to all troops. He managed a little more time in London, crossed to France on the 24th and began to take over from the British division in the line.

10

3rd Division in Action 1917

So, AT THE START of the coldest winter in thirty years, 3rd Division moved into the Armentières sector, known as 'The Nursery', on the Belgian border where it was to remain without a major action for six months. It was part of Plumer's Second British Army, and of Godley's II Anzac Corps together with the N.Z. and a British division. The other Australian divisions were fifty miles away to the south on the Somme—just as well, perhaps, for there was astonishing irrational feeling against the 3rd. 'What in hell are they doing, eating their heads off?' had been the cry; they were nicknamed 'The Neutrals' or the 'Deep Thinkers' and, when they did eventually meet up, were taunted with the inquiry, 'Declared war at last, have you?' Godley was delighted with the division, he told Pearce: it was

> in every way an excellent one... and as regards smartness, discipline and general appearance and turn-out, is the best of your Divisions I have yet seen. General Monash is proving himself to be as capable and excellent a Divisional Commander as he was a Brigadier.

Birdwood came and spent a full day, chatting to hundreds of the men; he too was very pleased, telling Munro Ferguson that 'Monash has so far proved a tremendous success and is quite a Napoleon in his language'. Then on 22 December came the commander-in-chief himself, Field Marshal Sir Douglas Haig; the King had perhaps suggested that he should look at 3rd Division. Monash turned out his reserve brigade and detachments from all other units in pouring rain. The slippery march-past was rather absurd, and many of the troops believed it should have been called off. But the reserved Haig, riding beside Monash whom he had never previously met, put his arm round his shoulders and 'with much feeling and warmth' said: 'You have a very fine Division. I wish you all sorts of good luck, old man'. Haig recorded: 'The men looked splendid and marched past in excellent style. M.Gen. Monash seems a clever Australian of Jewish type. I believe an Auctioneer in civil life'. (Haig was confusing him with Currie, the Canadian commander.)

He was in good nick, he constantly reassured the family. 'Everybody I meet always tells me how well I look, "as hard as nails", and that's just how I feel—young and vigorous, and full of punch, and not a bit tired.' He had reduced his pre-war weight by at least three stone to 12½ stone and his waistline from 45 to 37½ inches (31 contracted). Gallipoli had begun the process and in England he had been rigidly dieting: no sugar or potatoes and little fat and starch, only a slice of buttered toast and coffee for breakfast, a light lunch, and a good dinner but only enough to satisfy hunger, alcohol in strict moderation. Almost every day he walked or rode several miles with Eric, and later Paul, Simonson, and did dumb-bell and stretching and bending exercises in the morning. He slept well. He admitted to more wrinkles and lines on his face, but denied he was greyer or noticeably balder, and was proud of his trimness. He still occasionally had a touch of lumbago, and dosed himself with aspirin. In his later militia days his corpulence had made it difficult to take him altogether seriously as a soldier. His appearance now added considerably to his authority—an extraordinary feat of will-power had been necessary.

He was comfortably housed in a chateau at Steenwerck, four miles behind the lines, with electric light and hot water. The Plouvier family still occupied part of their house, together with Monash, Jackson, Farmar, Simonson and their servants; offices in huts were scattered about the grounds. Monash was soon on the best of terms with Madame Plouvier. After two months he was ordered to move his headquarters to Croix du Bac, a smaller village, with spartan quarters. There he was amused by his landlady's small twin daughters' imitation of him demanding his cap and stick from his batman.

Monash had control of an area stretching back some twenty miles from his five-mile front. It included the large town of Armentières, desolate and shattered with only a few thousand civilians remaining, but useful still as a base; he established battle headquarters there in a basement. Bailleul was a smaller town, with an officers' club as a social centre. Fighting was a small part of his duties. The front and a mile behind was a sea of mud; no transport could move within 3000 yards of the line. Wherever he went he returned splashed in mud from head to foot, and he suffered from chilblains. The front line was merely ditches in the slime and could be lightly held, but for hundreds of yards back a complex system of supporting trenches provided security. The chief effort went into draining, building repair-works after bombardment, and food and ammunition supply through the railhead at Steenwerck. Whale oil and turpentine were not enough to meet the danger of trench feet; Monash issued a card of instructions on the subject. The most important divisional enterprise was the daily collection of wet, and supply of dry, socks and gumboots. Daily, two thousand men washed at the divisional baths—'great beer vats'—where they received a change of underwear. Hot food and drink—porridge, stew, Oxo, coffee—was carried forward in dixies packed in straw-lined boxes. Out of the line, the Y.M.C.A. man, Frank Beaurepaire, the champion swimmer, was amusement manager and sports secretary, running a cinema and a theatrical company. Monash made a point of attending regularly: 'Many of the songs and jokes are topical—very personal and very funny—. . . directed against Godley and me and the Brigadiers—. . . the men simply roar with delight'. His most difficult and time-consuming task was to administer Armentières and district, even with the help of a French Military Mission and twenty-seven interpreters.

Although the country was so flat and boggy and there was no chance of any serious attack by either side, high policy was to keep up pressure. So patrols were constantly sent out—often to find the enemy line deserted—and frequent night raids planned; Godley had immediately ordered Monash to bring in prisoners for identification. During December and early January he made the rounds of brigade and battalion headquarters. The sector could hardly be described as quiet: artillery and mortar bombardment was kept up steadily. The Germans got in first in mid-December with raids on the 38th and 39th Battalions which were satisfactorily repulsed. The 33rd Battalion replied on Christmas Eve and Christmas night, and found no one at home; but the 37th identified their opposing regiment. On 9 January the 39th's raiders killed a few Germans; on the 10th the 44th entered the German line without finding any enemy; on the 13th the 40th withdrew when faced with unbroken wire; on the 28th a party of more than two hundred of 10th Brigade penetrated to the third German trench, had some sharp fighting and secured a prisoner, but overall probably only broke even; on the 31st an 11th Brigade raid was stopped by heavy machine-gun fire. The Germans had replied on 3 January, and on the 22nd when 9th Brigade was kept very busy—four Australian prisoners were taken and forty-seven casualties suffered and next day Monash taxed Brigadier-General Jobson with 'errors and delays'; another German raid followed on the 29th. In two months the division suffered six hundred casualties; Monash reported to Godley that their aggressive attitude had made the enemy nervous and jumpy and had produced heavy retaliatory shelling. On 26 January the divisional front was widened to seven miles. Five more minor battalion raids followed in February (and three German replies), building up to the 'Big Raid' ordered by Corps for 27 February, 'the most important ever undertaken by Australians' according to the *Official History*.

The 824 raiders from 10th Brigade had been carefully rehearsed.

Monash wrote the preliminary orders himself and commanded from Armentières. He introduced a novelty whereby the bombardment, three hours before zero, mixed smoke and gas shell, gas being abandoned towards the end; some Germans were tricked into wearing masks. The steel-vested raiders trotted across no-man's-land on a half-mile front, behind the barrage which then formed a box round the raided area. The German line was occupied for more than half an hour; one company was badly hung up on wire but the other three penetrated to the second and third lines. Seventeen prisoners and some useful equipment were brought in and at least one hundred and perhaps two hundred of the enemy were killed; the cost to Australia was about thirty dead and one hundred wounded. Haig sent a congratulatory telegram. Monash proudly reported to Walter that 'every man in the Division now thoroughly believes that with adequate artillery support we can enter the Bosche lines at any time and in any place and stay there'.

Monash remained happy with his brigade. They were magnificent, a different type to the Gallipoli men, older, more intelligent and responsible, though less imbued with the 'spirit of mere adventure'. Their formal discipline was splendid, the incidence of crime, drunkenness and gambling extraordinarily low. 'It is wonderful how well we have got through the rigorous winter under most distressing conditions.' The low crime rate was a matter of special pride, and it continued to be by far the best of all the divisions. From his arrival in France Monash had been harried by the army provost marshal who, bound by preconceived notions about wild Australians, was convinced that crime was being concealed. Godley backed up Monash well. His men weren't saints, Monash told him,

> but I can assure you that since the early days of my arrival in England, when things were admittedly a bit willing in the villages around Larkhill Camp, such a thing as an organised disturbance or interference with police ... or anything worse than the rare case of an individual drunken man, was absolutely unheard of. My policy was to extend great indulgences to the troops and to punish most severely the slightest trespass upon the privileges accorded.

He took strong exception to the provost marshal's attitude. Dering and his police had successfully prevented crime; he was proud of them as a fine body of men. Dering, however, came to a bad end in June when he stupidly told the local civilian authorities of pending military operations, and his provost seniors pounced. Monash had warned him he must get on good terms with them, he had not done so, and his position was indefensible. However, he parted with Dering on very friendly terms.

3rd Division Headquarters staff, November 1916: Jackson is on Monash's right, Farmar on his left

General Sir Hubert Plumer, drawn by John Monash

The case of Quartermaster-Sergeant A. T. Ozanne, the forty-year-old Labor member for Corio, did Monash considerable damage at home. Late in 1916 Ozanne had gained an extension of leave from A.I.F. Headquarters for treatment for a medical condition which was serious enough to bring about his discharge a few weeks later. He thus missed embarkation for France with 3rd Division. After advice from his subordinates, who may have misled him for Ozanne was a notorious 'stirrer', Monash took the view that he was a 'coldfooter' who never intended to go to the front; he expected him to be sent to France under arrest to stand trial for absence without leave. Ozanne now became the victim of a sordid political plot. The election of April 1917 was pending and Corio was a swinging seat. Prime Minister Hughes broke the understanding that members of parliament serving in the Forces would not be opposed and ordered his agent, the journalist Keith Murdoch, to supply material detrimental to Ozanne. On demand, Monash officially reported his view that Ozanne was virtually a deserter. Without Monash's consent or knowledge, Hughes published his report as a cable under Monash's signature. Ozanne narrowly lost his seat and the cable destroyed him as a public man. Dr William Maloney, Labor member for Melbourne, was outraged and denounced his old acquaintance Monash at public meetings as the 'cowardly German general', and the Victorian Labor Party abused him. Later, however, Maloney was convinced that he had done Monash an injustice and made great efforts to profess his respect and friendship. The weight of surviving evidence is against Monash in terms of political prejudice and fair play. It is difficult to understand why he did not recognize that his original view was at least open to grave doubt. But he was not a willing participant in the political plot.

Monash was not satisfied with his senior officers as a whole. The brigadiers were broadly satisfactory. Cannan was surpassing all expectations. McNicoll was 'a bit dour and acidy' and often difficult to manage, but was doing well. Grimwade, whom he had at first doubted, turned out to be a great success, converting the improvised divisional artillery into the best in the A.I.F., Monash asserted. Jobson took some handling: he

> lacks military experience and broad acquaintance with fundamental principles, but he makes up for this by an active mind and great industry. He is still far from being as efficient as I would desire, but he is learning every day, is easy to manage and influence, and is gaining strength and experience.

Jobson was deeply grateful for Monash's congratulations after Messines early in June: that 'you, who know just what my limitations are, should think so highly of what I have tried to do. . . .' But when at a conference he showed himself to be unnerved Monash tried to silence him, then wrote to him humanely, asking for his resignation. They, too, parted the best of friends. Brigadier-General Charles Rosenthal, a Sydney architect, replaced Jobson, and Monash gave him the great gift of Wootten as brigade major. 'I had the privilege of a long confidential talk' with Monash, Rosenthal later recalled, and 'mutual confidence' was established. Monash continued to delight in 'how *all* my Commanders and staffs work to do their very utmost to help me in all things'. He retained the total respect and affection of all his brigadiers.

The casualty rate of battalion commanders, however, was heavy. To Monash's dismay, one whom he had sacked on Salisbury Plain as quarrelsome, obstinate and egocentric, turned up in charge of the divisional training group. He wrote urgently to McCay, requesting his removal. Others dismissed were 'weak and unreliable', 'could not stand the strain', or 'did not take his job seriously'. After Messines, two more were to get the boot as inadequate. Senior majors, promoted in their places, did well. Monash developed his gift for stern decision with the minimum of offensiveness. 'As you know', he told Cannan, 'I always say quite frankly what I mean . . . without any desire to be disagreeable to anybody'. An officer had to be shown an adverse report: Monash usually convinced his victim that his good qualities did not outweigh lack of personality, force of character or adequate military knowledge. He persuaded the strict McNicoll to relax the rules of marching at ease and to intersperse some lecturing with monotonous hours of close-order drill. He very firmly ordered a C.O. to discipline an officer who was swearing filthily at private soldiers. Sergeant-majors were not to be martinets or bullies. Of course, he did not always succeed. One notable rebel was Major Story of the 37th Battalion, who in July protested to Godley against a rebuke by Monash and who in September 1918 was to be the centre of major trouble.

Part of Monash's continuing good fortune was to belong to Plumer's Second Army during 1917, and not Gough's Fifth Army as the other Australian divisions did until late in the year. Plumer's high reputation remains almost unchallenged, and his chief of staff, Major-General 'Tim' Harington, likewise is generally accepted as having been gifted and successful. Their scientific approach, and their doctrine that staffs existed essentially to *help* units and that explanation down the line was essential, suited Monash and the A.I.F. very well. Plumer visited Monash regularly, at least once a month. Neither of them left any account of their meetings, but Monash certainly held his senior in high respect. According to Farmar, Monash's personal relationships with Plumer and Harington were close.

In February changes had been made in three of the A.I.F. divisional commands. Legge, who according to Monash was 'lazy and pedantic and quarrelsome' and disliked by Birdwood and Godley, was relieved from 2nd Division and went home; Brigadier-General N. M. Smyth, V.C., of the British Army replaced him. McCay, who had been unwell, was transferred to command A.I.F. depots in England. Monash at first believed McCay was going home and remarked to Vic, 'I wish I were in his shoes!' When he visited him a few months later he reported:

> He declares he has become an old man and will be able to see no more active service. . . . in spite of the adverse repute in which he seems to be universally held, my old liking for him strongly revived during the few hours I saw him. He showed all his old clearness of grasp and power, and was as nice and amiable and friendly as it was possible for any one to be.

He was replaced at 5th Division by Talbot Hobbs, an architect and artilleryman whom Monash had known since his days in Perth. 'We both thought we knew a great deal about soldiering in those days!', Monash recalled to him in a warm letter of congratulation. In deference to the Australian government's pressure for appointment of Australians to high command, Birdwood also arranged for the replacement of Cox at 4th Division by Holmes. Walker remained with 1st Division. Thus, of the six commanders (including Chauvel) of A.I.F. divisions, four were Australians of whom three were citizen-soldiers; and Monash was now the senior A.I.F. commander on the Western Front. His personal and professional relationship with Brudenell White was close. White had written in January: 'A respect for you which began in 1902 has gone on steadily increasing!! I would like, and would greatly value a further long association the even tenor of which I hope will not easily be disturbed'. Monash rejoiced in Chauvel's success in Palestine and looked forward to his promotion: 'Imagine an Australian rising to the rank of a Corps Commander!' Monash and Holmes had always got on well, but they had a serious breach late in June. H.R.H. the Duke of Connaught was inspecting troops of the 3rd and 4th divisions: Holmes protested bitterly to Monash that he had 'abruptly interposed' himself and 'without my permission or consent, presented two of my officers', the famous V.C.s, Murray and Jacka of 4th Brigade, to the Duke. Monash replied temperately, explaining that Godley had motioned to him to come forward and that he had hesitated and gestured towards Holmes, but Godley had beckoned again; Godley had made the presentation, he had not said a word. Holmes rejected the explanation and said he was taking the matter higher. The trivial truth hardly matters: perhaps Holmes misunderstood what happened or was sensitive to Monash's alleged 'pushiness', perhaps Monash was so carried away by meeting his 4th Brigaders as to be forgetful of etiquette. Holmes was killed a few days later by a shell. He was replaced at 4th Division by MacLagan, whom Monash considered had 'developed a pessimistic and obstructive temperament'. Of the six divisional commanders, Monash and Chauvel were now the only native-born Australians.

Monash had been upset that he had not received a mention in despatches for his services in 1916; the omission might be held against him. White explained that orders were that mentions could only be made of those serving on the Western Front in September 1916, and all the A.I.F. knew that his promotion was equivalent recognition. Godley was unsympathetic when Monash asked him to mention his name to Pearce:

> You can't have it both ways and be training and raising a new division in England and at the same time be mentioned for fighting in France. The standard of mention in despatches is very high now I believe, for general officers and one has practically no chance of being mentioned unless one has been in an offensive and not merely holding trenches.

Amends were made in Haig's April 1917 despatches released in June—alas! Monash's name was by clerical error omitted and, when corrected, his rank was wrongly given as temporary. But eventually his fifth mention was formalized.

In March Godley gave Monash a fortnight's leave. He had no desire to go to cold London, 'a city of the deepest gloom' he now considered it, and made for Menton on the Riviera, spending four days in Paris on the way. Watching Parisian life, he found himself coming more and more to admire French *égalité*, camaraderie, humour, and especially their 'marvellous *politeness* to each other and to strangers'. 'They rush to help you. . . . everybody talks to everybody else. Obvious strangers argue the news of the day together.' He was amused by the ritual, the 'immense business', of ordering a meal, and by French officers always wearing all their decorations and medals. The rail trip along the Mediterranean, the scenery and the sun excited him, but his main purpose was to rest. He strolled along the gravelly beach watching the fishermen, took the tram to Monte Carlo, roamed round the hills, enjoying the ancient villages and the views of the Alps and the sea. The highlight of his holiday was *The Barber of Seville*; he exuberantly described to Vic the excellent performance and the Monte Carlo opera house.

It was a time for reverie and reflection. Inspired by Vic sending him her photograph, he had recently written the only love-letter, properly so described, of his four years' absence: 'It is perfectly wonderful how you keep so young, and you must be the envy of all who know you.

In short, if I were not in love with you already, I am certain I should fall in love with you again'. He reacted strongly, however, against her suggestion to let Iona: 'You can hardly imagine the yearning I feel to get back to my home, and have a few months peace and rest. The idea of strangers having the run of my books and papers and souvenirs etc is most repugnant to me'. Vic had somehow got the idea that he might after the war want to take a British military appointment:

> I hate the business of war and soldiering with a loathing that I cannot describe—the awful horror of it, the waste, the destruction and the inefficiency. Many a time I could have wished that wounds or sickness, or a breakdown of health would have enabled me to retire honorably from the field of action. . . . My only consolation has been the sense of faithfully doing my duty to my country, who have placed a grave responsibility on me, and to my Division who trust and follow me, and I owe something to the 20,000 men whose lives and honor are placed in my hands to do with as I will. But my duty once done, and honorably discharged, I shall with a sigh of relief turn my back once and for all on the possibility of ever again having to go through such an awful time. Of course, if Australia wants my services in some administrative capacity in connection with her future army, worthy of my rank and record, and permitting me the freedom of an independent citizen—well that is another matter; but not unless it becomes necessary for our bread and butter, and all other means had failed would I dream of becoming a paid servant of the State in any capacity whatever. I have fought all my life for personal independence, and shall not give up what I have won except as a last resort, and only if your absolute livelihood depended upon it.

He considered Iona

> an ideal home in which to spend our declining years in great personal ease and comfort. . . . I wonder can you realize the deep yearning I feel for a few months *peace* and quiet life, within the portals of my own home? To be rejoined to it and to you and Bert is my constant daily longing, and the extinction of that hope would make my present life of turmoil and strife and horror almost unbearable.
>
> Then, also, consider the public position I have won in and for Australia. On this side of the world I would be a mere nonentity, and I would hardly count at all. But in my home country, I shall hereafter be able to wield all the power and influence that you or I could desire—socially, financially or in any other way, in any sphere we may desire.

Their assets, together with a few directorships, ensured a future income of some £3000 a year—luxury for the rest of their lives.

He had some reason to be perturbed about what was happening

at home. Neither Gibson nor Fairway had written for six months about the state of their business, and Vic had fallen out with Gibson. She had been misled by the clerk, McNaught, whose salary Gibson had reduced and who was soon to leave for another job; either maliciously or from misapprehension he had persuaded Vic that Monash's interests were being undermined. John had to reassure her of Gibson's absolute integrity and of the entire security of their holding in a limited liability company, and to implore her to make peace: 'He is at heart the very best fellow I have ever met, and it is a cruel injustice to him to even suggest that he has not your, and my, interest at heart'. He made it clear to Gibson that it was impossible to return home to relieve him of the burden of the business: it could not happen unless he was rendered useless by sickness or wounds or was a proven failure.

> [War] is not a business in which one can take any pride or pleasure, or even pretend to. Its horror, its ghastly inefficiency, its unspeakable cruelty and misery has always appalled me, but there is nothing to do but to set one's teeth and stick it out as long as one can.

He implored Gibson to continue to accept his necessary duty.

Monash remained happy with his division which was working like 'a well oiled machine'. Plumer visited to present decorations. Monash lectured to officers on forms of attack, and was told by Godley that it was 'the best lecture that he had ever heard'. The sick-rate of the division was the lowest in Second Army, less than half the average. On his return from leave, Monash found that the policy of regular raiding had changed to emphasis on defence works, for fear of a major German attack. The boot was now on the other foot: from late March the Germans raided almost weekly, while 3rd Division confined itself to occasional offensive patrolling. Although the Germans took a few prisoners, casualties were light; according to the *Official History* the division was 'singularly successful' in keeping them out.

The desk work was never-ending. Monash was punctilious in replying to the steady flow of letters from home from parents, wives and fiancées—imploring him, perhaps, to look after 'our boy, our only son', or, more commonly, asking him how their loved one had died—and would strive to make cold comfort meaningful:

> I need not say, my dear madam, that I entertain for you the sincerest sympathy, that you should have suffered such a cruel blow, but trust that it will console you to know that your husband played the part of a brave man, and that he fell nobly doing his duty in the defence of his country.

Regularly he had to rebuff efforts to bring influence to bear on behalf of a relative or friend—usually a request to award a commission. His standard answer was that the soldier would be judged purely on his performance, but that he would keep an eye on him.

The Allies had begun 1917 with ambitious plans for offensives on a wide front around Arras by the British, then by the French in the south, then by the British in Flanders. The Kaiser's spurious 'peace offer' had been scornfully rejected. Few, on either side, desired the compromise peace settlement which was so obviously needed. The Germans resumed unrestricted submarine warfare, which soon seriously threatened Britain's resources but brought the United States into the war from April. Before the Allies could attack, however, the Germans late in February and in March had made their remarkable tactical withdrawal to the Hindenburg line—on the Somme and to the north but not in Flanders—laying waste the country between. In April and May the British assault on the Arras front proceeded: the Australians suffered heavily at First and Second Bullecourt, increasing distrust of British management and especially of General Gough. In April Nivelle's offensive foundered. The British assault in Flanders was to go ahead: the plan aimed to wear down the enemy and ultimately to break through or at least free the ports of Ostend and Zeebrugge. Before the main assault could begin, the Messines–Wytschaete ridge, from which the Germans looked down on the British south of Ypres, would have to be cleared.

As early as January Monash had noticed the 'stupendous' preparations for supply of ammunition, food and equipment. On 7 March Godley disclosed to him the plan for the attack on Messines Ridge; the divisional commanders discussed it on the 23rd when Monash was pleased that he was better posted than the others although he had been away on leave. On the 26th, 3rd Division's line was extended to eight miles including Ploegsteert Wood; they side-stepped to the left and for weeks continued to adjust their line. Divisional headquarters were moved back to Steenwerck, where Monash strolled round the well-kept garden of the chateau before breakfast and, to keep himself sane, hung photos of his garden at Iona round his bedroom. He was very active in controlling dispositions, travelling hundreds of miles a week by car and on horseback. He was working long hours on his battle plan which he named 'Magnum Opus'; on 15 April he released it to his brigadiers, asking for comments and encouraging discussion of detail with battalion commanders. He then proceeded to write detailed objectives and procedures for each battalion, 'particularising in some cases the employment of platoons and even of sections'. 'Wonderful detail but not his job', Harington later commented. According to the *Official History*, 'there was concentrated upon the plans an amount of thought and care far beyond that ever devoted to any other scheme of operations produced by a staff of the A.I.F.'.

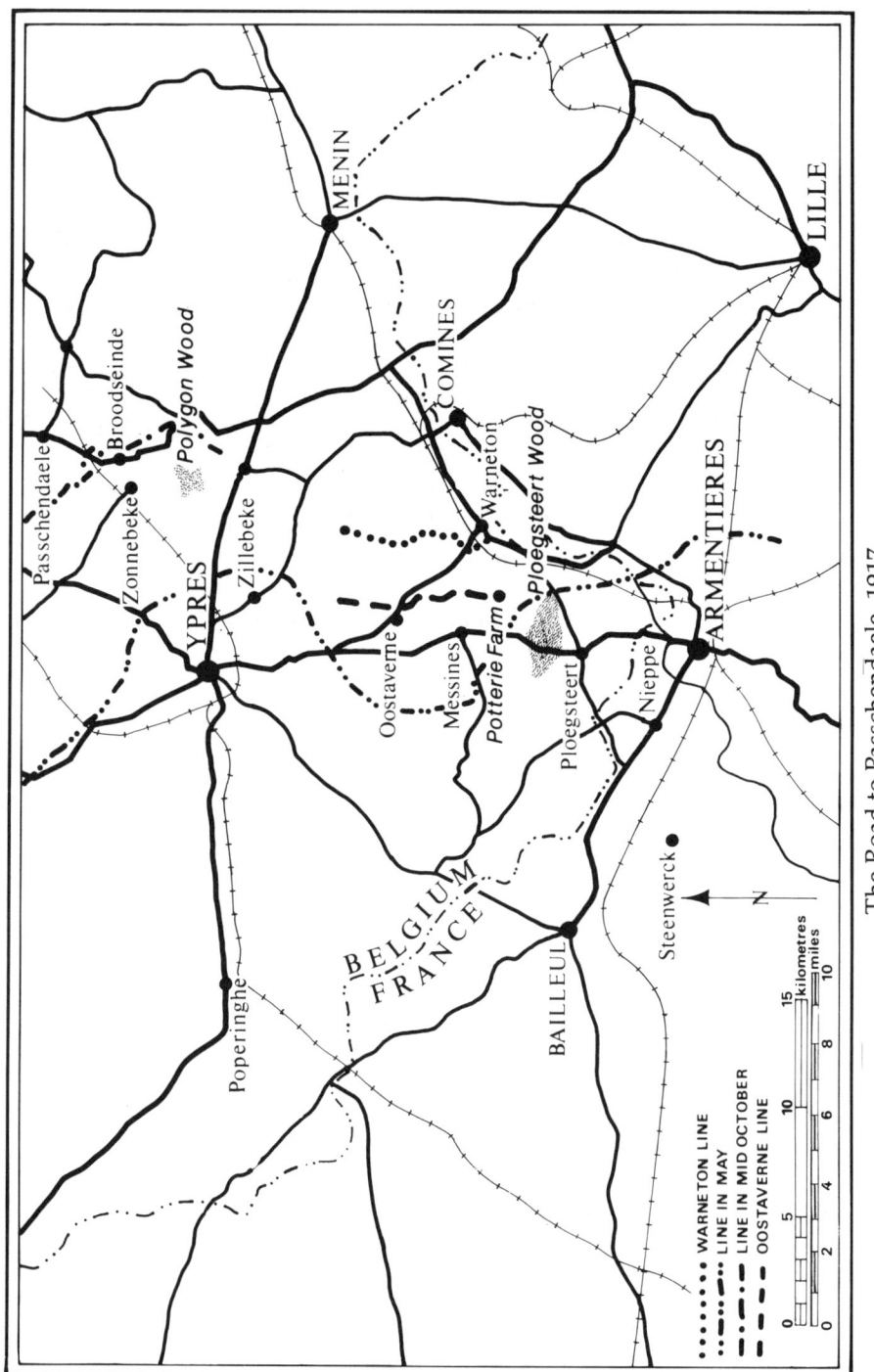

The Road to Passchendaele, 1917

By May 27th, on which day the 3rd Division's operation order was issued, its schemes had already been elaborated in thirty-six successive circulars, of which one, the instructions for the machine-guns, comprised seven parts. The attack had been practised by each brigade in the training area, and the objectives and arrangements explained to companies and platoons by reference to two large models of the battlefield which had been constructed beside roads a few miles behind the front, showing in miniature the trenches, entanglements, streams, roads, and ruins.

Monash had gone south to watch the early stages of the Vimy Ridge battle and later visited the Canadians after their remarkable assault, meeting Major-General Currie, establishing pleasant relationships and learning from what they had to tell.

'Magnum Opus' depended on detailed application:

> For weeks past, we have been making roads, building railways, and tramways, forming ammunition-dumps, making gun emplacements and camouflaging them, preparing brigade and battalion battle head-quarters and laying a complex system of underground cables, fixing the positions of machine-guns, working out barrage time-tables for machine guns, field-guns, heavy guns and howitzers. For this operation I shall have added to my own artillery five army brigades of field artillery. The heavy and siege artillery will not be under my command. Then there is a mass of field engineering work to be done, in large dugouts, approach-avenues, assembly and jumping-off trenches; most voluminous orders to be got out, controlling the action of the whole of my 20,000 men and animals—feeding organization, transport organization, ammunition supply, cutting the enemy's wire ... the preliminary destructive bombardment of his field works, the completion and blowing up of mines, and finally the preparation of the 12,000 infantry, for the actual work of 'going over the top.'

He issued notes for themes for company commanders to use to sharpen their men's fighting spirit. He wrote at length to Godley with suggestions to counter the one thing which might ruin the attack—enemy knowledge of zero hour and their bombardment of the troops forming up. He constantly studied aerial photographs. Conference followed conference: on 15 May Plumer visited to go minutely through his plans. Haig arrived on the 24th and later noted that Monash was

> a clear headed determined Commander. Every detail had been thought of. His Brigadiers were equally thorough. I was much struck with their whole arrangements. Every suggestion I made was most carefully noted for consideration.

Godley called his divisional commanders together, Monash his brigade and battalion commanders, to cross-question them. He explained to

Jackson that he did not doubt the clarity of their joint orders, but wanted to be quite sure that, going into their first battle, his units knew precisely what was expected and that the orders were being properly passed down the chain of command. With three days to go, he reminded his brigadiers that determination was the key to success and that, if in difficulties, they must not assume reserve troops would be forthcoming. He had done all he could. They would either have a brilliant success or a hammering, he told Vic. 'The attack always had everything against it, the defence always everything in its favour. . . . I have every confidence in the men, and I know they have in me.' He could not sleep the night before the battle 'on account of excitement, mosquitos and noise'—and anxiety.

The plan was for three corps to pinch off the German bulge in the line south of Ypres and capture the ridge and its further slope in one day:

> The northern corps would strike south-eastwards on both sides of the Ypres-Comines canal; the central corps due eastwards through and past Wytschaete; the southern corps east and north-east from Hill 63 and Ploegsteert through Messines. The southern army corps was II Anzac.

3rd Division was on the right flank, with the New Zealanders under Russell to its immediate left; Monash rejoiced that he had the 'star turn'. 4th Division, A.I.F., was brought in to act as corps reserve. As a preliminary, over eleven days three and a half million shells, including gas, were pumped on to the Germans, who replied systematically but were greatly outnumbered in guns. Twenty-three deep mines were ready for firing at zero hour. For ten days before the battle 3rd Division raided almost nightly in strength, but brought back few prisoners and suffered substantial casualties. On the day, over their mile-long front, 9th Brigade on the right would not have to penetrate as far as the 10th on the left. 9th Brigade would be protected by smoke in the creeping barrage, and saps had already been prepared for quick construction of safe communication trenches. At the last minute Monash issued an account of the savage treatment of Australian prisoners after Bullecourt, in order to enrage his men; the effect was uncertain.

The Germans of course knew a major assault was pending, but not when. Zero hour was kept secret until six hours before. When on the night of 6 June the eight attack-battalions of 3rd Division began their three-mile approach through Ploegsteert Wood, they ran into heavy gas-shelling and, despite their respirators, at least five hundred men were overcome. (Their gas training had been good: the British Army gas expert had held them up as an example.) Nevertheless the battalions reached the start line, within 200 yards of the enemy, largely intact and on time. The Germans were surprised in the end: Monash's fear of overwhelming shelling of the assembling troops was not realized. At 3.10 a.m. the big guns opened fire and the mines went up—four of them in front of 9th Brigade. Over they went into the dust and smoke. It was difficult to keep order and direction in the dark around the vast craters, but the troops soon sorted themselves out.

Monash described to Rosenhain what had already been done: every enemy trench, wire entanglement, strong-point, farm, dugout, machine-gun, mortar emplacement, gun-pit, signal station, buried cable, tramway and dump that could be identified from aerial photographs had been noted; and for every one detailed plans had been made for bombardment and capture. The time-table for all grades of artillery, machine-guns and mortars was 'co-ordinated so as to agree to a second'. The initial attack was 'child's play compared with the nightmare of the approach march'. The Germans were cowed by the days of bombardment and demoralized by the mine explosions, and their guns had largely been knocked out. No troops could have stood up against the overwhelming onslaught. Only the 33rd Battalion, under Lieut-Colonel Morshead, had to crush serious resistance. The first stage was over within the hour; a planned pause followed while the New Zealanders occupied Messines. At 5 a.m., in daylight, the second phase began; although there was more serious resistance, 9th and 10th Brigades reached their final objectives on time, in less than half an hour. They now had to fortify, in expectation of a counter-attack. Monash described how he proceeded

> to rapidly consolidate the ground and organise it defensively by placing out wire entanglements, readjusting artillery action, placing Vickers and Lewis guns and trench mortars and reorganising units in depth, so as to get rid of the heavy congestion of men in the forward lines and thereby reduce casualties due to enemy shell fire. . . . by nightfall I felt my position was absolutely secure on my new lines.

The victory had essentially been won, but late in the day the 37th Battalion ran into trouble supporting the New Zealanders' drive to the Oostaverne line. Next day the situation of the 44th Battalion was for some time obscure and the 10th Brigade suffered severely from shelling. During the next two days the thrust to Potterie Farm continued and the Germans withdrew nearly a mile to the Warneton line. The division was relieved on the 12th.

So Plumer's masterpiece, 'the most perfect attack with limited objective of the whole war', came off brilliantly, with only a fraction of the expected casualties. It was the first major battle victory for the A.I.F. which was greatly heartened by this evidence of British capacity. Monash, too, was impressed with the higher command:

> I am the greatest possible believer in the theory of the limited objective. So long as we hold and retain the initiative, we can in this way inflict the maximum of loss when and where we like. It restores to the offensive the advantages which are natural to the defensive in an unlimited objective.

But he began to ponder over the need to go in far enough to capture the enemy's guns and prevent retaliation.

3rd Division was in high favour. Haig visited on 9 June and in his diary described Monash as 'a most practical and capable commander, and has done well'. Madame Plouvier photographed them shaking hands. Plumer also had called in to thank him. Godley was cock-a-hoop and gave high praise for the execution of the difficult swinging round on the right flank, and then clearing the enemy out. The *Official History* concluded that though the careful digging of communication trenches was wasted labour, the 3rd Division's 'spirited yet controlled advance in precise accordance with plan, in spite of the powerful effort of the German artillery to crush this flank during the approach march and afterwards, was altogether admirable'. II Anzac Corps had suffered more than half the casualties of the three corps engaged. 3rd Division had four thousand, almost as many as the New Zealanders. Although the casualty rate was nearly as high as at Passchendaele later, less than 15 per cent were deaths and a large minority were gas casualties who soon rejoined their units. Most of the casualties, Monash told Birdwood, occurred from shelling during the period of consolidation, despite his thinning out of forward troops. 'The operations', he went on, 'disclosed a few weaknesses here and there, which will have to be remedied, but . . . there were astonishingly few disappointments'. One was the C.O. of the 37th Battalion, who was mercilessly grilled and sacked. Doubts remain about the justice of this. Another disappointment to Monash was Bean's reporting of the battle: 'the apotheosis of banality. Not only is the language silly tosh, but his facts are, for the most part, quite wrong'.

When relieved, Monash moved to Bailleul but was kept busy: he was constantly conferring about the lessons of the battle and addressing units or groups of officers. When the town of Nieppe came under shellfire, he set 3rd Division to evacuating old people, invalids and children, and to fighting fires, to the extreme gratitude of the mayor. He paid a courtesy visit to a Tank battalion and had a ride in one of the 'very wonderful, and very terrible machines'. Then after ten days the division was sent back into the line east of Messines to bury the dead. Plumer had a long yarn with him.

He had eleven 'delicious' days leave in London from 30 June, staying at Prince's Hotel, Piccadilly, 'the smartest place in town'. The Simonsons took him for his birthday to Oscar Asche's *Chu Chin Chow* and he saw *Aida* and some plays. He was distressed by his sister Lou's behaviour: 'Will you let me say', he wrote, 'that I think that happiness comes only from within. You must try—you must really—to cultivate a placid temperament, and put yourself under a strong discipline so as not to allow outside happenings to worry, irritate and arouse you'. Overall, he found leave 'a distraction, but no rest' because of official business, including a day inspecting his training battalions, and press interviews. Immediately he returned, in the absence of Godley and Russell, he acted as corps commander for six days; he had to move corps headquarters because of heavy shelling.

Late in July, 3rd Division took part in a feint against Lille by Plumer's Second Army. While the French were racked by mutinies and the Russians were clearly out of the war, the British had to carry the burden. The British government at last authorized Haig's step-by-step assault in Flanders, of which Messines had been an essential preliminary, as possibly leading to vital penetration if German morale were to break. Massive bombardment on the Ypres front began on 15 July, and the great assault leading ultimately to Passchendaele was launched on the 31st. Preparing to attack the Warneton line, 11th Brigade had been constructing a new trench system, during an eighteen-day stint under constant damaging shelling. The Germans held the Windmill Ridge in strength. Cannan's plan to clear his front was elaborated on by Monash and adopted as part of Plumer's feint. Plumer ordered an end to aggressive actions until the main attack—which was just as well, for Monash was extremely worried about Jobson's handling of some skirmishes by 9th Brigade which had failed. Intensive conferences at high and low levels followed. Monash saw Haig, and Plumer at least twice. On 31 July, before dawn, the 11th Brigade attacked and won the Windmill and all its objectives, and repelled counter-attacks, but at the cost of 550 casualties. Whether the assault was of diversionary value is obscure. Plumer and his staff were critical of some aspects of the operation. As usual Monash held a prolonged review, and wrote a long memorandum on methods of attack and repelling counter-attack—at one 'long and heavy conference on tactical questions' with his C.O.s he spoke for three hours. He again stressed how much quicker air observation was than any other means of learning the position of troops in attack. Warneton had been an unsatisfactory episode in a subsidiary role, and on 9 August he was happy to hand over the sector to MacLagan and 4th Division.*

3rd Division had a six weeks thorough rest back near Boulogne,

---

* During Warneton a private, who had absorbed the order that it was urgent to identify and interrogate prisoners, turned up at divisional headquarters. 'Does Mr. Monash live here? I wants to see him. . . . You Mr. Monash? You want some Fritzies. Well I've brought you two.' Monash gave him a lift back to the front in his car.

recruiting, refitting and retraining; ominously, Haig and Plumer were getting them back to battle strength as quickly as possible. Divisional headquarters were at the Chateau Hervarre near Bléquin. Monash toured the units regularly, attended the divisional sports, horse shows and cricket matches, and entertained his battalion commanders to dinner, usually two at a time. I Anzac Corps was now in the area and he exchanged visits with Birdwood, White, Hobbs, Walker, Smyth and others. He went to points of vantage to watch the bombardment, then the opening of the second phase of the Ypres battle—which was 'magnificent and terrifying, putting into the shade the most terrible lightning and thunderstorm ever witnessed. The whole country simply trembled'. His divisional headquarters was bombed from the air, and he souvenired several fragments. He presided at a demonstration of new smoke-bombs. He combined business with pleasure on visits to his divisional base depot and machine-gun and camouflage schools, resting overnight at Dieppe and at Paris-Plage, meeting French ladies and English nurses. By chance Monash and his French liaison officer, the Baron de Gail, attended a charity fête in the form of a military horse show, an extraordinary international assemblage. As senior officer he was conducted to sit between two beautiful women—the Duchess of Westminster, in charge of a hospital, and the show president, the Marquise d'Armaille, who chuckled when he asked her not to speak 'comme mitrailleuse'. Back at his headquarters he entertained Matron Kellett and Melbourne nurses of the 25th Australian General Hospital. That month he was suffering from lumbago. Gershon Bennett scraped his teeth. Keith Murdoch, the plotter, called in for a long talk.

Early in September, training 'in most beautiful rolling country', in pleasant autumn sunshine, was intensified. By the middle of the month he was thinking hard about preliminary plans for attacking Broodseinde. On the 22nd Haig reviewed the division—'a brilliant success. The chief stayed for an hour ... chatting to me and my senior commanders', and he had Monash to dinner that night. The division began its five-day march towards the front on the 25th.

The rainfall in August—five times as much as in 1915 or 1916—had largely wrecked Haig's plans for Third Ypres. The second stage, postponed to 16 August, had been only partly successful and subsequent heavy fighting probably wore down British morale as much as the German. Haig turned the main attack over to Plumer and Second Army, and a series of step-by-step set-pieces was planned from 20 September. I Anzac Corps was prominent at Menin Road and Polygon Wood. The third and most important step on 4 October was to be at Broodseinde, the section of the ridge east of Ypres which was the main enemy stronghold, headquarters and observation point. The date depended on the speed with which II Anzac Corps could organize. This was no long-prepared Messines, nor was 3rd Division familiar with the ground. Harington eventually described as 'beyond all praise' the manner in which the division made and carried through its plans at short notice. One great joy was that at last the two Anzac Corps were to fight side by side. 'We passed the 3rd Division (11th Brigade) on the road ... yesterday', wrote Bean, 'and I must say they looked magnificent. I'll swear they knew they were passing through the 1st Division'. The greetings were now totally cordial. The New Zealanders to the north were to capture the Gravenstafel spur; the 3rd, 2nd and 1st Divisions to the south had the main ridge as their objective; the 3rd would have the longest advance of about 2000 yards. On both flanks the Anzacs were supported by some of the finest British divisions. All were buoyed up by the hope that this might be the decisive battle leading to a breakthrough.

On 1 October Monash moved to headquarters at the Menin Gate in Ypres. Waiting for his staff, gear and papers to arrive, he spent an hour in dashing off a graphic letter to Vic, describing the town and the mêlée of traffic he had passed through. In the old walled town, 'a stark pitiable ruin' which had been shelled daily for two years, tunnelled dugouts, cabins and galleries had been established, like underground mine-workings. It was 'cold and dank and overrun by rats and mice, and altogether smelly and disagreeable'. Accommodation was so limited that he had unwillingly to leave his administrative staff in the rear, which ultimately delayed evacuation of the wounded. Preparation was intense: 'Very busy harassing day. Finally see Brigadiers', was the diary entry for the 3rd. He instructed them carefully that if the enemy attempted to disorganize the offensive by attacking first, the men must stand fast and not go to meet them; the barrage would take care of them and those who survived could easily be shot down. He and Jackson had had effectively less than three days to plan the battle in detail.

The men spent most of the 3rd sheltering in shell-holes. When they moved on that night it was drizzling, with occasional squalls. 10th and 11th Brigades had to cross the swampy Zonnebeke valley: several of the duckboard tracks were destroyed by shelling and many of the men had to wade through the bog. About 5.30 a.m. a heavy barrage fell: the Germans were indeed attacking. When at 6 the British barrage crashed down and the Anzacs went over the top they ran into advancing Germans—the two zero hours were almost identical. The 37th and 43rd Battalions suppressed scattered resistance, particularly from 'pillboxes', and pressed into the next valley, bounded by the Gravenstafel ridge. Here, at the first objective, they paused and dug in, according to plan, while the 38th and 42nd went through and, hindered by shelling, reached the next objective about 7.15. Already many prisoners had been taken, 'in swarms beyond all previous experience of the A.I.F.'. The 41st and 44th Battalions ran into wire in swampy ground, fell behind the barrage and were briefly checked. The 39th and 40th similarly were held up, fell behind and struck intense fire. This final stage saw the stiffest fighting. The 41st quickly reached its objective. But the 40th suffered heavy losses in suppressing strong-points; nevertheless they reached their final objective by 9.15. 3rd Division dug in, protected for another two and a half hours by the precise barrage: the *Official History* remarks on 'perhaps the most complete and accurately-sited front and support lines ever made by Australians in battle'. The 41st held off two minor counter-attacks; some of them went forward to get a better view and Monash, fearing they would be caught in the barrage, sharply ordered Cannan to get them back.

Broodseinde was a triumphant victory, the greatest A.I.F. success yet, and there was immense elation. Monash, necessarily lagging hours behind, had had almost nothing to do. The jubilant corps commanders considered immediate exploitation; when Monash was consulted he agreed that an advance to a better future start line was possible, and briefed McNicoll. However, Plumer rejected the proposal. But this third hammer-blow within a fortnight, one of the greatest victories of the war, raised hopes of a stunning culmination of the Flanders campaign—if only the weather held. 3rd Division's casualties had been 1810, 27 per cent of its fighting force engaged, the lowest proportion in its four major engagements in 1917. On the 6th they handed over to a British division, but knew it was to be only a short spell 'to get the men bathed, dry underclothes and fresh equipment of ammunition; repair of Lewis guns, etc. etc.'. Monash wrote exultantly to Rosenhain:

> All the enemy's manifestations ... strongly point to very serious demoralisation. In fact, he is staggering, and we are all praying for the weather to keep up; so that we can keep on hitting him. ... everything depends upon the rapidity with which we can bring up the guns. I have my whole Pioneer Battalion and all my Engineers working night and day. ...
>
> Both Plumer and ... Harington have told me that they do not consider that any other two Divisions on the Western Front ... could have marched into the Battle Line and, at three days notice, carried out so big a task so completely and with such perfect synchronisation and small losses.
>
> We are, naturally, very much elated and not a little excited. ... Unless the weather balks me I shall capture P—— village on 12th.

But the weather had broken—and saved the Germans from disaster. It rained from the 4th and became torrential on the 8th. Knowing what was involved, yet unable to accept failure of his grand plan and believing he was sustained by 'the great Unseen Power', Haig resolved to proceed with the assault on Passchendaele. Plumer and Harington, triumphant, allowed their doubts to be allayed; Birdwood hoped for postponement but did not protest; Godley, of course, was all for it. Haig's great modern champion, John Terraine, justifies the decision, essentially on the grounds that the Germans were very close to breaking-point and that the assault had reached an exposed point which could not be defended, if it stopped over the winter. The Germans may have been near breaking, but not near enough. The British bombardment, by destroying the drainage system, had created impassable bogs. The height of absurdity was that the cavalry were being held ready: they probably could not have got through even if the Germans had laid down their arms.

The preliminary attack on the 9th, in which 2nd Division was heavily engaged, could make only small gains. On the 12th, 3rd Division, with the New Zealanders on its left and 4th Division supporting its right flank, was expected by Corps to advance 3000 yards on Passchendaele ridge to beyond the village. There were to be three stages, taking six hours. They would have to start at a pace which had not even been attempted in the attacks of dry September.

9th and 10th Brigades spent the night of the 10th–11th in the open, east of Ypres; their tents had not arrived. The preliminary bombardment was thin; despite superhuman effort, many of the guns could not get through the mud into position or find a stable platform, and ammunition supply was lagging. On the 11th, despite the heavy rain, Plumer with the support of his corps commanders let the assault proceed. Monash had been pleading to Plumer and Godley for twenty-four hours delay. At 6 p.m. the men began their approach march under persistent shelling and arrived at the tapes in heavy rain by 3 a.m. They 'pulled their waterproof sheets over their heads ... and slept', and further shelling brought more casualties. The British barrage broke out thinly at 5.25; few enemy machine-guns were eliminated; moreover, when the infantry went over they had no hope in the mud of keeping up with the barrage, and their Lewis guns were soon choked. The 38th Battalion was flamboyantly carrying a flag to fly from Passchendaele church. Both brigades had been disorganized by the shelling and the battalions became thoroughly mixed up. 9th Brigade on the right reached its first objective very late, after heavy losses; then, under phenomenally heavy fire, took part of its second objective. 10th Brigade on the left did worse; darting from one shell-hole to another and in places floundering in mud up to waist-deep under machine-gun fire, they too had heavy casualties—some even drowned—but reached their first objective. Both brigades did much bayonet-work and captured hundreds of prisoners. Parties of the 10th pressed on to Crest Farm and even to Passchendaele church, but the advance as a whole was held up by enfilading fire from the left where the New Zealanders, attempting an utterly impossible task, were hopelessly bogged in the swamp and wire. For what it was worth, the rain had stopped.

In the Ypres ramparts, Monash had no news that the battle was going seriously wrong until nearly 10 o'clock and no clear picture until after midday. Two of his observation planes had early been brought down; 'runners' could not get back to battalion or brigade headquarters. He altered his dispositions, and arranged for artillery support and use of his reserve battalions. But it was all futile: the advanced troops were suffering so heavily that their commanders had already decided to withdraw. 3rd Division retreated by mid-afternoon to within 100 yards of its starting point; the action had been almost an exact repetition of that on the 9th. 3rd Division's casualties were 3200, 62 per cent of those engaged, almost as many as the New Zealanders'.

In his official reports Monash properly stressed the effects of the condition of the ground and advised that Passchendaele could be won only if the defences were deluged with artillery fire. The time for preparation for battle allowed had been totally inadequate: communications, reconnaissance, taping approach routes, laying of duckboards, bridging, platforming of guns and ammunition supply had not been properly carried out. In writing unusually objectively to Rosenhain, he concluded that the plan was fully justified and would have succeeded in normal weather conditions with 'first-class fighting divisions' such as the New Zealanders and 3rd Division. He asserted that they probably would have brought it off with forty-eight hours preparation, and in normal weather might have succeeded in the twenty-four they were allowed. But the rain intervened and the attack on the 9th had failed:

> Even in the face of this the Higher Command insisted on going on, and insisted, further, that the uncompleted objectives of this fourth phase should be added to the objectives of our fifth phase; so that it amounted to this that Russell and I were asked to make a total advance of 1¾ miles.

The weather had grown steadily worse. The ultimate decision to proceed he condemned as hare-brained. The A.I.F. was being put into the hottest fighting and sacrificed where the British Army had failed, and was not being properly protected by the Australian government. Monash did not face the implications of not attempting to go on. He may have allowed his opinions to be fairly widely known; a rumour spread that he had lost his command because of plain speaking.

On the 14th McNicoll came to breakfast 'looking haggard', and Monash walked to N.Z. headquarters to commune with Russell. The funeral of Major Adams, C.O. of the 3rd Division Pioneers, took place on the 16th: Monash brushed up every verse of the 'poem' Chaplain Cuttriss had composed for the grave-side service. 3rd Division was now briefly part of the command of Lieut-General Currie of the Canadians who, with firm adequate preparation, stage by stage, were heroically to take Passchendaele four weeks later and secure a tenable front on the ridge—for what little use it was. Meanwhile 3rd Division pushed posts forward half-way to the first objective of the 12th, while those in the rear were 'shelled to hell' and had mustard gas poured on them night after night: this was the worst experience of gas the A.I.F. suffered. G.H.Q. then 'actually insisted' that 3rd Division be bussed, and not march, forty miles to the rear for rest. Bitterly, the remnants of the battalions returned to their old billets to be succoured by their good French friends. Monash had a good rest for three weeks, in which he enjoyed walks in the country and building up his collection of shoulder-straps taken from prisoners, and, of course, conferred with his brigadiers about the 'lessons of recent offensives'.

3rd Division longed for the day when it could join the Australian Corps. Monash had had to serve two masters: he had kept in close touch with White about A.I.F. policies and procedures and resented the time spent on making irrelevant British Army returns. He once asked White for a direct order from Birdwood that he was bound by the A.I.F. organization for fighting and training, not by Corps or Army: it was very important, they would be fighting together one day. The Australian government had long been anxious to bring the divisions together. In mid-1916 Haig had refused Hughes's request to permit formation of an 'Australian army' (for an 'army' had by then grown in size to eight or ten divisions) or to bring the divisions together in Birdwood's corps. Birdwood was ambitious to command an Australian army brought up to strength by New Zealand and British divisions, or a 'Dominion Army' including the Canadians.

During 1917 feeling in the A.I.F. and from the government end had intensified: the divisions must be brought together and entirely officered by Australians. Direction of the campaign to these ends was undertaken by Murdoch the journalist, a protégé of Hughes, his intermediary to Lloyd George, and his adviser with regard to mobilizing A.I.F. support for the National government and conscription. In mid-July Fisher, the High Commissioner in London, and Murdoch cabled Hughes, strongly urging renewed pressure on the British government. The A.I.F., they argued, greatly prized its national identity and had suffered in battle at Fromelles and Bullecourt from failure by British divisions on its flanks. 3rd Division remained under Godley who was 'notoriously anti-Australian' and prevented 'enforcement of Australian democratic policy by Monash'. Murdoch and Bean wrote to Lloyd George to explain that Australian nationalism was 'the one great motive working in our people'; and that G.H.Q., which regarded Australian divisions as interchangeable with British divisions, rejected this view as a sort of treachery to the Empire. Hughes acted immediately, cabling the British government on 30 July. He eventually had a deprecatory reply from the Army Council, whereupon he referred the issue to the Imperial War Cabinet; as a consequence, in October Haig was asked to consider the matter. Murdoch had already been in direct negotiation with Haig and Birdwood.

Murdoch was fishing in deep waters. He was also trying to persuade Hughes that Birdwood should be replaced by an Australian and was asserting that the senior A.I.F. officers agreed that White should 'have the Corps'. The Canadians had a commanding officer in the field and a G.O.C. in London. McCay was angling for the equivalent position of G.O.C. and looking to Murdoch to support him.

Monash knew little of these plots. He was of course well aware of the possibility of further promotion. Early in August he wrote home that with the gathering of the forces before Third Ypres he was seeing a good deal of Birdwood and White.

> I am almost convinced that there is some change afoot. Possibly it may mean a transfer of my Division to 1st Anzac. B. told me the C.in-C had a very high opinion of my Division and of me personally, and had gone out of his way to express himself in terms of praise of my work. B added it was rare for the Chief to do this. White entirely confirmed these statements. . . . There have been vague rumours for some time, in well-informed circles, of a contemplated regrouping of the Australian forces. It has even been suggested that B. may get an Army Command—in which case, there will be a Corps Command vacant. As I am senior Australian officer in France, the gossips have naturally coupled my name with these rumours.

On 22 September he dined privately with Haig. Such hospitality by Haig to a mere divisional general was rare indeed—he must have been assessing him—and rumours began to circulate. John reported to Vic:

> I dined with him and Lt. General Kidgell [Kiggell], Chief of General Staff, and Maj. Gen. Butler, Deputy Chief of General Staff. There were only the four of us present. After each course was served, the mess steward went out of the room, and the doors were locked from inside, until the chief gave a sign for the next course. So you may imagine that some very important and confidential matters were discussed—about which I need say no more than that there is no question that we are very rapidly wearing down the German military power, and it is now only a question of time and weather. Nothing could have been more charming than the affability and camaraderie of these three great soldiers.

Seemingly the meeting confirmed Haig's favourable opinion. He had told Paul Simonson, 'Your uncle is a great man'. Despite his royal favour and aristocratic connections, Haig was not entirely a snob: he was a Scot, educated at Oxford, with some liberal inclinations, and much less inclined than the standard army product to look down on a colonial Jewish engineer and citizen-soldier. But the large unknown question is what Monash really thought of Haig after Passchendaele.

About this time Bean interviewed Haig and had the impertinence to promote the cause of White against Monash. He noted in his diary:

> Monash for an Australian Commander in Chief we cannot have. He is not the man. The purity and absence of jealousy or political intrigue in Birdwood's administration, is worth anything. There is no "eye-wash"—bluff and humbug and insincerity—in it, and there is in Monash's. White would do, but not Monash. Besides we do not want Australia represented by men mainly because of their ability, natural and inborn in Jews, to push themselves. Monash and Rosenthal have both the quality, though Monash does not use it shamelessly. Rosenthal does.

Bean's assumption that Rosenthal was a Jew was mistaken.

Haig let it be known that he and the War Office objected to an Australian corps of five divisions as unwieldy, and that he had been considering creation of a second Australian corps and giving Monash the command; White should have a divisional command before being considered for a corps. Birdwood's position was obscure: on the one hand he might remain in command of the existing corps, on the other Haig was suggesting he might be confined to administrative duties, presumably as G.O.C., A.I.F. Murdoch and others were confused and not sure what to suspect. Was Monash in command of a second corps to keep 3rd Division, and were the divisions not to be united? Were Birdwood's army enemies determined to prevent him commanding a united Australian corps? Would the removal of Godley from command of II Anzac Corps and his replacement by Monash or Russell be an adequate solution? Murdoch was inclined to swing back to support of Birdwood as the united Australian commander, though he pleaded to Hughes that White was preferable. When Haig conferred with Birdwood and White on 29 October, a happy solution was reached. The Australian divisions had been so bled during Third Ypres that the reinforcement problem was acute—another corps was now out of the question. Haig was happy to accept their suggestion that 3rd Division join the existing corps and that 4th Division be temporarily withdrawn and regarded as a depot division. It was an astute and popular solution; moreover Haig accepted entire Australianization of A.I.F. commanders. On 15 November 3rd Division officially transferred.

Partly by chance 4th Division soon rejoined the corps which after all was allowed to have five divisions.

Monash might genuinely have persuaded himself that his division was, as he asserted, 'universally regarded as the best of the 5'. He did not know that in July Birdwood had confessed that, although he was appalled at the prospect of breaking up any of the divisions, if it had to be done, 'in ordinary fairness I presume it would have to be the 3rd', as it had been in the field for a much shorter period than the others. Nor did Monash know that Murdoch was belittling his reputation to Hughes:

> Birdwood will try to arrange that the Third Division will be the first to go, and there is much to be said for this. It was the last into France, and has least prestige. Moreover, Monash has organised it in a way that does not make for free and spirited fighting. G.H.Q. has a great idea of Monash, and Haig said to me that he intended that Monash should get an army corps. We all hope it will not be the Australian army corps, because the handling of the old Fourth Brigade and the Third Division does not justify great confidence in Monash's ideas of strategy. On the other hand, he is certainly a better divisional commander than the Englishmen Smyth and MacLagan.

Perhaps it was just as well that Vic and Bert got on so well with Billy and Mary Hughes and that 'Bob' (Sir Robert) Garran, Hughes's close adviser, was Monash's next-door neighbour in St Georges Road.

Monash's popularity was growing. The Messines and Broodseinde victories greatly enhanced his reputation: Passchendaele could not have. At home his former officers—Pope, Dare, Locke, Woodruff and others—were constantly praising him; in Melbourne especially, in contrast to McCay who was generally unfairly reviled, he was becoming a hero. In August 1917, in a despatch in the Melbourne *Herald*, Murdoch had reported that 3rd Division swore by him, by no means the case with all divisional commanders. The 37th Battalion probably did not, after Messines. At any time a large proportion of the troops were hostile to the 'heads', who were anyway difficult to distinguish. One grievance was Monash's policy of not normally issuing rum: he provided soup, Oxo and coffee to exhausted and cold men coming out of the line, but his experience with the 4th Brigade led him to believe, on purely medical grounds, that rum did more harm than good. It was standard A.I.F. practice to issue rum after, not before, action. But a sense that he knew his job, was a careful general, and outstanding in providing welfare services was growing. His practice, copied from Cox, of sending a card of congratulations to anyone decorated or who had done very well, was appreciated. Several of his men advised a lady running an entertainment and rest centre for Australians in Paris to write to 'old Monash' for help—'he's dinkum'—and help enthusiastically he did. He was spontaneously applauded at a 3rd Division Pioneers' concert: 'Those fellows knew what they were doing and only voiced in unison what they all feel individually', one officer told him. Chaplain Cuttriss referred in his book, *'Over the Top' with the Third Australian Division*, for which Monash wrote an introduction, to the 'rousing and prolonged cheering which greets him when presiding over or addressing an assembly of his men' on informal occasions. Exaggerated, no doubt. But not all the junior officers who wrote warm letters of congratulation when he was eventually knighted were crawling to him.

He was disregarding the Censor as much as ever. When senior officers were seriously warned, he would be discreet for a few weeks, then would break out again. More and more he confided in Walter Rosenhain: sometimes he would write triumphantly and misleadingly, sometimes quite objectively, but not often very revealingly. He was also sending Walter official documents for transmission to Melbourne. In June 1918 he reached the height of folly when he sent his initial plan for the battle of Hamel before the event—when Walter was under surveillance because of his German origins!

Monash lost his two senior staff officers, Farmar and Jackson, in September and January as a consequence of the deliberate Australianization. He approved of the policy but had regrets in these cases. Both Farmar and Jackson, whom Birdwood had placed with Monash to strengthen and guide him, ended up his devotees and intimates. Farmar had told an Australian friend after Messines:

> General Monash as a leader is a genius, and the thought he has given to every detail inspires every man in the Division with confidence. The men are trained to the minute. I never knew a finer lot, they are magnificent. I am proud to live with them.

He was heartbroken to leave, he wrote in his reminiscences. Monash had a brain of the highest quality but was 'of most humble mind'; he was a master of teamwork; there was no waste anywhere.

> He brought all concerned into his confidence from the first beginning of an enterprise. . . . He wanted to employ only the exact number of personnel necessary, and that every man should have his own share in a job and know that he was responsible for it. He used great care to ensure that as far as it possibly could be arranged all should share in turn rough times and smooth.

Farmar was fascinated by Australian troops. They tended to look on officers as 'General Managers and Intelligence Service'; the rank and file thought out how to win; 'great stress was laid on having level teams and no weak links'. 'They tested everyone. General Monash was passed for his thoroughness and care for every detail which mattered without any fuss and frills.' *

Jackson moved on to command a brigade in 29th Division, and between the wars was a distinguished instructor at staff college and theorist of warfare. He wrote to his 'reasoning friend' Monash, to tell him that his new job was 'like coming back many many years'. He was in a 'very good division but I wish you were commanding it. The lack of attention to detail is very apparent'. His general did not know his job and was a dangerous madman. Jackson was afraid he himself had become too democratic in outlook. 'Please burn when read.'

In 1935 Jackson estimated Monash's qualities for the military historian, Liddell Hart. Monash was of course a man of outstanding ability, very methodical, who as an engineer trained to accuracy gave attention to detail to a degree which few British generals could rival. He did a great deal of the work himself, yet trusted his staff and was 'a delightful man to work with'. He was in marked degree ready to discuss, and a big enough man to change his mind. He would call Jackson in and say, 'Now listen to this'. If Jackson gave good reasons for disagreeing, he would sometimes say, 'Yes, I have thought of all those, but I think it is worth trying'; but sometimes he would say, 'Oh! I had not thought of that. No we won't do it'. He was far-seeing, had great powers of analysis and constructive thought. He had an 'amazing aptitude' for seeing through other men's eyes; no divisional commander in France knew his front line better, because of his detailed discussions with officers and his study of air photos. Jackson remembered some of Monash's pet sayings. If he received unworkable instructions he would describe them as 'a policy of perfection impossible of attainment'; of ambiguous orders he would remark, 'Same old thing, using words to disguise their meaning'. Jackson criticized him for being inclined to write up Australians and himself rather too much (presumably in *Australian Victories in France*).But, in all, he was 'a remarkable character'.

---

* Farmar recalled an inspection by Haig. A portly Jewish officer was tossed by his horse during the preparations. Haig had been preoccupied and the inspection was an anticlimax. The mess that night was rather depressed. As was customary, Monash read out the weather report which began: 'A heavy dew fell this morning'. 'The tension broke. The General shouted with laughter, so also the victim . . . and the two nephews. . . . We all did.'

11

Something to have lived for
1918

FROM 4 November 1917 the 3rd Division spent six weeks in the quiet Ploegsteert sector, which they had captured five months before, and Monash returned to Steenwerck chateau. For a fortnight the division and II Anzac Corps ceremonially farewelled each other. Monash was happy to leave Godley although 'towards the end he was very nice . . ., and gave me a splendid farewell banquet'. As senior general, he immediately took over acting command of I Anzac Corps, while Birdwood went on leave. But when Birdwood returned, adjustment to control by a different corps staff had awkward moments. It was not just that hat brims went up. Corps had various minor points of criticism, largely concerning the divisional artillery. White was tactful: 'Of all this you and I will talk again and I daresay that we will find our views are not much at variance', he wrote. Jackson and White quickly settled most of the points at issue. A more serious brush came on Christmas Day when Birdwood and White criticized some of the rear defensive works. An altercation followed and Monash spent the afternoon writing a justification. Two days later he and White had 'a heart to heart and satisfactory talk'. In all, however, it was a quiet period and Monash found time for some pencil sketching.

Having received no honour for two years, Monash expected a knighthood but knew it was a lottery. Australian generals were due for preferment—the Canadians were doing far better—and since Bridges only Chauvel, two medicos and an administrator had scored. Birdwood and Dodds were determined to secure proper recognition for the senior generals. When Birdwood rang Monash on New Year's Day, he was surprised and grateful to be told it was not a mere knighthood, but Knight Commander of the Bath. He saw the hands of Haig and Plumer rewarding him for Messines. Hobbs and Walker also had K.C.B.s, while McCay had a K.C.M.G. Mat Monash 'did a little war-dance' to celebrate John outstripping McCay at last; Monash telegraphed him 'most cordial congratulations from his oldest friend', but Birdwood told him that McCay was very jealous and added: 'He's got more than he has earned'. A happy celebratory mess dinner followed, and hundreds of congratulatory messages poured in.

John immediately sent 'heartiest congratulations' to Lady Monash, and told her he believed only Lady Munro Ferguson and Lady Madden would have precedence over her in Australia. Her correct title was 'Victoria Lady Monash', not 'Lady Victoria Monash' or 'Lady John Monash'. Vic was overwhelmed: 'My darling. Best love wonderful man. What a genius you are. Jewish community gone mad, off their heads. K.C.B.!!!' 'I don't think that I have anything left to wish for as a title and to dine at Government House were both my greatest ambitions.' It was a pity she had not had a better education, 'but it is too late now to regret all that, and all I can do is my best'. She asked John what he really felt about it, and received a revealing reply:

> I think I can say quite truthfully that my pleasure at the event has been far more on your behalf than on my own. We started from small beginnings—but it has been from the first my ambition to provide for you the utmost that life can give. The two essentials for that were money and position and the one without the other would have been very little use. . . . That is why, while working hard for so many years to get the most out of my profession in the way of monetary results, I devoted so much of my labours, also, to non-productive effort—both in military and in University spheres. . . .
>
> . . . we have now accomplished both ends to a moderately successful degree. While we are not wealthy, yet our means are such that dignified comfort, at the least, is assured to you. Of course, as you so often said, and as I know well, one cannot ever have too much money. But it is a good thing to have a financially secure position . . . altho' there is much, both in the way of self-indulgence, and in the way of help to others, that one would also like to do. . . .
>
> As to the future, who can say? If I am spared to return, and if my health and energy hold out there is scarcely any possibility which I need now deny myself. Of course, it would not be right for me to sink into oblivion and make no further effort in the service of Australia. In what direction this may come it is quite impossible to foresee. The University is pretty sure to claim my services in a still higher capacity—if I were willing—possibly soon as Vice-Chancellor, and later on perhaps as Chancellor. That they will desire to confer on me a high honorary degree is quite probable. . . . The Government is bound to offer me some very high post in the military sphere. I shall be senior Australian Commander in the field (except Chauvel) and if the war ends in a way that makes it necessary for Australia to maintain her ability to defend herself, they simply cannot, on my record, afford to pass me by. Of course, I do not say that I should accept anything in the shape of a permanent post:

I am too keen on preserving my independence ... and I have also my present business affairs to liquidate, even if I decided to retire altogether from the active practice of my profession. There will be so many openings offering, and so many public and semi public positions which in the past I aspired to, that the difficulty will be to know what to choose and what to leave alone. There is still another possibility. Don't be amused—I merely write of it, because I am in a frank humour—and that is a Governorship. The day when State Governors will be chosen from Australian citizens is rapidly approaching. When that day arrives, the field of choice will be very limited.... It is therefore a quite legitimate ambition for a man in my position; and nothing like so difficult a job as that of commanding a Division in the field. Birdwood has been quite openly mentioned as Governor-General....

Now, please don't laugh, but regard with equanimity the prospect of your, one day, becoming an Excellency!!

John asked Vic to have confidence in his judgement for the future; he had not always had it in the past. He continued:

It is strictly true to say that, so far, the possession of a knighthood has made not the slightest difference to me.... I have been to everybody—either "General", or "Sir",—for the position and authority of a Divisional Commander are in themselves greater than anything the mere possession of a title can give. Of course I value the knighthood very highly indeed;—as a mark of achievement; but I don't think it will really make a ha'pworth of difference to my personality, or my temperament or my outlook on life. In other words, I don't feel a bit that I now have something I have got to live up to. I did have that feeling when I first got a Division—but now that I know that I am commanding one of the Crack Divisions of the British Army, I have acquired a feeling of complete confidence and mental poise....

Now, this is a monstrously egotistical letter, but I suppose—like the male peacock before the pea-hen—one may be permitted to do a little strutting before one's own wife, once in a while....

The Messines mudflats which the Australian Corps occupied for the winter were in general quiet, but were nevertheless an area of 'miniature warfare' with the emphasis on aggressive patrolling. No-man's-land was wide, the front line was waterlogged, both sides probed to locate enemy posts and make identification of opposing units. In raids on the night of 30 November–1 December the 39th and 40th Battalions captured prisoners and inflicted many more casualties than they suffered. Minor raids followed on 7 and 8 December. The policy changed from the 14th and Haig ordered urgent defence preparations in depth for a German spring offensive. The Russian collapse had enabled transfer of a million German troops to the Western Front;

they would obviously make a supreme effort for victory before the Americans could arrive in strength. Meanwhile the Allies had not agreed on unity of command, the French were semi-paralysed by the effects of the 1917 mutinies, and the British were wracked by distrust between Lloyd George and Haig.

When 3rd Division was relieved on 16 December it was called back unexpectedly on Haig's direct order for ten days to man the old Armentières area, because of the unreliability of the Portuguese. The division was then rested for nearly a month but from 29 January to 8 March reoccupied the line at Ploegsteert. Opposite Warneton again, Monash continued large-scale raids, sometimes in such strength that German regimental historians believed them to be attempts to seize the Warneton defences. On 10 February some two hundred of the 37th and 38th Battalions took thirty-three prisoners and inflicted heavy casualties, suffering fairly lightly themselves. The London press made much of the success. On the night of 3–4 March, 235 raiders from 9th Brigade took eleven prisoners, almost without loss. There were several other minor skirmishes, sometimes in retaliation to German raids. Monash gave pep talks to the raiding parties, dwelling on the evil of German brutality as exemplified by the torpedoing of the *Lusitania*, the shooting of Nurse Cavell and the sufferings of the Belgians. He told Vic that he

> definitely established the important fact that, whether the Boche intends to launch a great offensive in the West, or not, he certainly has *no* intention of doing so on the front of the Australian Corps. All the prisoners, many of whom I interrogated myself, were quite clear, and in agreement on that point.

He sent to Corps a draft plan for capturing Warneton, using two brigades in a night attack.

It was an unusually busy time. Monash lectured to intelligence and machine-gun schools, and wrote a pamphlet on machine-gun tactics, which he discussed with White, emphasizing the use of the weapon in attack. He was experimenting with the uses of smoke, especially in order to blind enemy machine-gunners. He appointed a new commander of his machine-gun battalion and guided him closely, stressing the need for tact in managing men and for constant attention to their welfare. On 26 February he held another of his regular full-scale conferences of senior divisional officers, and spoke for more than two hours. He demanded entire uniformity of thought, policy and attitude throughout the division, analysed the general military situation, detailed the possible kinds of surprise German attacks, and asserted that the coming enemy offensive would provide the great opportunity for final victory. He covered a huge range of subject-matter, down to cleanliness of cooks. It was all straight to the point, without any showing off—so unlike his mouthing of conventional exhortations in his addresses to troops on parade. About this time Major Geoffrey Drake-Brockman attended a conference of divisional engineers. He described Monash as 'a man of medium build, with large nose, dark skin and eyes that penetrated, who looked more like a professor than a soldier; and sartorially, in his old and ruckled top-boots, he might have been a lieutenant in charge of transport'. The brigadiers gave their views, then the field company engineers—a new experience for Drake-Brockman. Then Monash made an analytic assessment and laid down policy. He could understand the 'configuration of the terrain, from the study of maps, better than any of us from our physical contact with our particular zones'.

John explained to Vic why he was now rarely sending handwritten letters:

> A Division is such a big affair, and takes a lot of looking after;— always some loose screws somewhere that want tightening up, and some stiff bearings that want oiling, and the furnaces need constant stoking, or else the fire will go out. The trouble is that I never have a moment's privacy. . . . often and often I am referred to even at meals or when in bed.

He was exaggerating: he quite often attended the Corps boxing contests or concert party performances. But listing some miscellaneous events illustrates the demands on his attention. Jackson left in mid-January and was replaced by Jess, who had been Monash's staff officer on Gallipoli; Monash noted with amusement that he also, as well as Major G. F. C. Wieck, his G.S.O.(2), was of German descent. He had to protect Grimwade from Brigadier-General Coxen, who had recently taken command of the Corps artillery and was interfering with the divisional artillery. Four American commanders visited him in turn, and he also had to entertain a party of Japanese officers. Lieut-Colonel P. P. Abbott, a Member of the House of Representatives, at Birdwood's suggestion stayed with him for three weeks in order to find out how a good division was run; they argued the toss on all sorts of subjects. Abbott had been met with a 'breezy greeting' and soon concluded that 'Monash is one of the "biggest" and brainiest men I have ever met—a big grasp of his job with his ever watchful eye on everything'. General Plumer thought so highly of 3rd Division that he wanted to take it with him to Italy: Haig quickly scotched that notion. Monash's curiosity was never sated: in mid-February he sent off for a full description and synopsis of lessons of the Pelman system of memory training. He subscribed to the *Times* and his favourite casual reading remained *Punch* and *La Vie Parisienne*; he had recently been reading O. Henry's short stories, and was enjoying the complicated jigsaw puzzles Walter Rosenhain was making for him. He relied on supply from home of his favourite pipe tobacco—Capstan, full strength, brown label—and of Kiwi boot polish.

Early in March 3rd Division went out of the line to rest. Monash was due for a month's leave but, in consultation with Birdwood, decided to take only three weeks. He set off with Paul Simonson, who had replaced Eric as his aide, for three days sightseeing in Paris, using his 25 hp Vauxhall limousine for he had found that 'other Divisional Commanders were not so squeamish as I had hitherto been about using Government Cars and petrol for pleasure'. He moved on to Menton, and spent the first day 'just lolling about in the sunshine, on the sea beach—not even reading', before settling down to write letters home. His first reading was Bernard Shaw's book on Wagner's *Ring* cycle—'in the true Shavian style of brazen revolutionary cynicism, but is very clever and ingenious'. He enjoyed a new opera at Monte Carlo, *Manole* by Gunobourg, and spent a happy day with Rosenthal walking vigorously round the hills.

After eleven days he was urgently recalled. The great German offensive had begun, and they were streaming over the old Somme battle-ground. It took him thirty-two hours to reach his divisional headquarters on 25 March at 7 p.m.; he had wired for his car to meet him in Paris. 3rd Division back near Boulogne had been one of the divisions kept in reserve in expectation of an emergency. They were bitterly disappointed, never having fought on the Somme, when on 22 March they were sent towards Ypres, but on the 24th they were ordered south to Doullens to X British Corps, as G.H.Q. Reserve. Overnight on the 25th–26th the division moved by train, while Monash snatched some sleep. He spent the early morning searching by car for X Corps Headquarters; at Frévent he was ordered to help occupy a line between Arras and Albert. Doullens, where a G.H.Q. conference was in progress, was in 'indescribable confusion'. 'An exhausted and hungry soldiery was pouring into the town from the east and south-east, with excited tales that the German cavalry was on their heels.' But within half an hour of arrival Monash met the first of the trains bringing Rosenthal and a battalion of 9th Brigade which he ordered into a defensive position. He motored then to Mondicourt where McNicoll's first train soon arrived and elements of 10th Brigade were similarly deployed. McNicoll forcibly gathered hundreds of retreating British troops and put them into line. Monash set up a headquarters at Couturelle in a chateau 'whose owner hospitably provided a much needed meal', then made contact at about 4 p.m. with MacLagan of 4th Division and arranged a continuous line. He issued orders to his three brigades and returned to Couturelle about 8 p.m.

There, orders soon came that 3rd Division was to come under VII British Corps, on the right flank of Third Army, twenty miles further south on the Somme. Monash was to report immediately at Corbie. Fortunately, a message arrived just before he left to say that the Corps headquarters had been forced out of Corbie back to Montigny. He took two car-loads of his staff and two despatch-riders; it was moonlight but they moved painfully slowly through the swarms of troops and vehicles. They arrived about midnight:

> I found them sitting very disconsolately in a dark building, practically wringing their hands, as all the Divisions of the Corps had been biffed badly that day. The only men in the crowd who seemed to have their wits about them were the Corps Commander, Lieut-General Congreve and . . . Hore Ruthven [later Lord Gowrie]. Both these men are V.Cs. They were seated at a little table with their maps spread in front of them examining them by the light of a flickering candle. As I stepped into the room, General Congreve said 'Thank Heavens—the Australians at last'.*

He was 'brief and to the point':

> At four o'clock today my corps was holding a line from Albert to Bray, when the line gave way. The enemy is now pushing westwards and if not stopped to-morrow will certainly secure all the heights overlooking Amiens. What you must try and do is to get your division deployed across his path. The valleys of the Ancre and the Somme offer good points for your flanks to rest upon. You must, of course, get as far east as you can, but I know of a good line of old trenches, which I believe are still in good condition, running from Méricourt l'Abbé towards Sailly-le-Sec. Occupy them, if you can't get further east.

MacLagan then arrived and got orders to move his division in on the 3rd's left with the 35th British Division between. Monash recalled that

> It was already 1 a.m. of 27 March, and I had left my division twenty miles away. Everything depended now on quick decision and faultless executive action. It was fortunate that a telephone line to G.H.Q. had been found in good working order, and that the services of three large motor-bus convoys could be arranged for to proceed at once to the Doullens area, in order to transport my infantry during the night. . . . I worked with my staff till nearly break of day, considering and settling all detailed arrangements.

Amiens, ten miles to the west, lay almost open. Following a misunder-

---

* In his six accounts of the incident, it is only in this letter to Vic that Monash reports Congreve saying this. No doubt he said something like it. 'Thank Heavens—the Australians at last' is a family joke among Monash's grandchildren, when meeting each other.

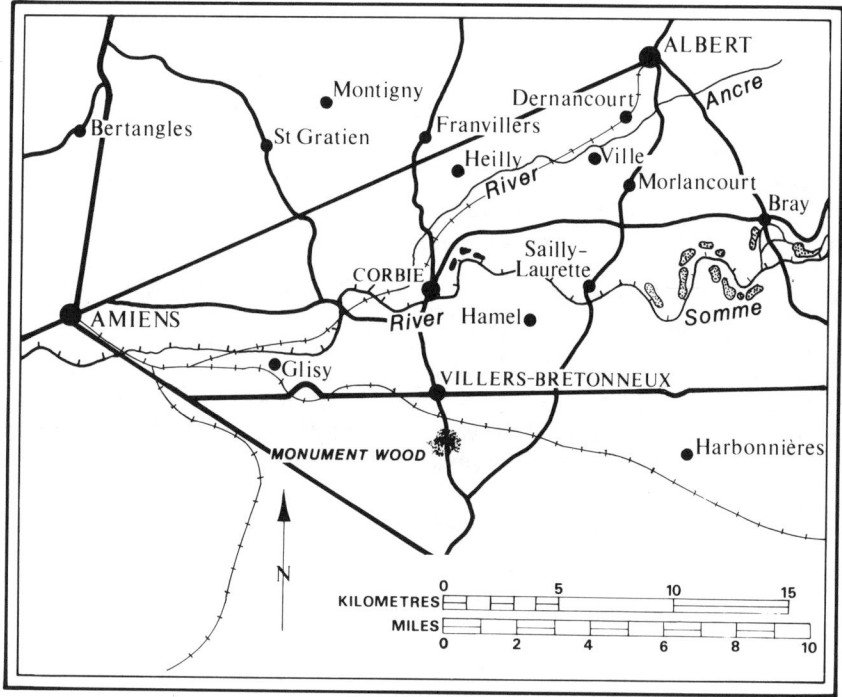

March–June 1918

standing between Congreve and a divisional commander, a ten-mile gap in the line was covered only by a small scratch force, mainly cavalry. Monash managed a little sleep. Shortly after daybreak he and a staff officer and Paul Simonson moved to Franvillers, high up, from where they could see the German cavalry and advance guard near Morlancourt forcing back scattered troops of British cavalry. 'It was really a question of an hour one way or the other whether we could intercept him or not. You can imagine the state of my mind.' He was 'momentarily expecting to be mopped up by Bosch armoured cars' which he could see. Soon after 8 o'clock, however, two battalions of Cannan's 11th Brigade arrived in sixty London buses and were quickly deployed through Heilly. By 10 the first two battalions of McNicoll's 10th drove in, and a little later the first of Rosenthal's 9th. In spite of two near-sleepless nights the 3rd Division infantry marched out eagerly 'on that crisp, clear spring morning, with heads erect and the swing and precision of a Royal review parade', delighting in their great task—on the Somme at last, where their mates had so suffered, and looking forward to open, real warfare. Some of Bean's finest writing in the *Official History* is his depiction of the glorious Australian self-conceit in the face of the defeatism of so many British stragglers; the welcome of the distressed local population to 'Nos Australiens' ('Fini retreat Madame,—beaucoup Australiens ici', is one of the great national statements); the delight of the officers, reading Monash's orders by torchlight, in the ' "old man's" masterly touch'; the contacts between the advancing battalions and the gallant remnants of the British rearguard. By mid-afternoon, six battalions of the 10th and 11th Brigades, five thousand troops, were in line and sending out patrols, and had induced great caution in the enemy. There was only one real brush that day. From about 6 p.m. the divisional artillery began to arrive. Having established his front, Monash had to worry about his right flank on the Somme; on the other side of the river, in the Fifth Army area, the situation was obscure. In fact the Germans were breaking through three miles south of the river. Haig switched the remaining British cavalry across the river to feel for Fifth Army's flank, thus removing the screen in front of 3rd Division. Congreve and Monash anxiously conferred by telephone; at 7 p.m. Congreve consulted again and ordered transfer of 9th Brigade to the right along the river—which was carried out during the night.

The day before, Foch had taken supreme command of the Allied armies. The thinly covered gap south of the Somme between Third and Fifth British armies which the Germans were beginning to exploit was to be covered by the French reserve.

At 10 in the morning of the 28th Monash reported to Birdwood that his position was 'quite secure against all but an attack on a grand scale':

> My troops are in the highest spirits; my ammunition supply, about which I was very anxious, is now on a fairly satisfactory basis; food and water are all right; one ambulance has arrived, and the others are in sight. By tonight I hope to have all departments thoroughly well organised. The men are, of course, very sleepy . . . but every hour that we are left unmolested is improving their condition.

The main strain that morning came on 4th Division to the north who beat off a strong attack at Dernancourt. On the extreme left of 3rd Division the 38th Battalion also helped the 35th Division repulse a firm German move. Monash was anxious to push forward and had been out to see Cannan and McNicoll to discuss the chances of stealing the ground ahead by daylight patrolling, but he was anxious about his right flank. Here, however, the 61st and 1st Cavalry Divisions counter-attacked at 11, aided by the 3rd Division artillery across the river. Then Congreve instructed Monash, at Foch's desire, to attack on his front. At noon Monash ordered an advance in two 1000-yard stages, at 4 and 7 p.m., towards Morlancourt.

The hurried attack was half successful and the Official Historian was later unimpressed:

With what strength each brigade should attack, and how its troops should be disposed, appears to have been left by Monash to the discretion of the brigadiers; but, possibly through lack of time, or difficulty of communications, or even through general inexperience in the sudden operations of open warfare, that prudent and normal procedure was not accompanied by close consultation between the brigadiers to whom it was committed or by such action from above as would ensure that the detailed plans of the two subordinates dovetailed.

No substantial artillery support was possible. Not expecting strong resistance, McNicoll sent the 40th Battalion on a frontal advance over level ground; by some blunder, the 41st Battalion did not support them on their right. The 40th came under heavy fire and by 5.30 its advance stopped half way to the first objective. The 42nd and 43rd Battalions proceeded rather to conduct offensive patrols, but most of their movements were late. By dusk the troops were digging in. An attempt on the far right to take the village of Sailly-Laurette failed. An advance of half to three-quarters of a mile had been made, with three hundred casualties all told. 'The A.I.F. was still inexperienced in open warfare', Bean summed up; the ground could probably have been won with little loss by patrol approaches and by night attacks. No doubt; but Congreve and Monash had settled on an immediate attack.

The front was advanced slightly on the 29th with artillery support. On the 30th at noon, while Monash was at 11th Brigade, the Germans suffered severely, despite the artillery they brought to bear, when they made a mass frontal counter-attack and were shot down in hundreds without the second and third Australian lines being involved; the 3rd Divisional and British artillery, sometimes firing over open sights, did great damage. The British front north of the Somme was now secure. 35th Division was withdrawn and 3rd Division extended to the left to link with the 4th.

South of the river, the battle had been fluctuating. In a desperate moment on the 29th, Rosenthal's 9th Brigade was taken away from Monash. Discomfited and importunate, he argued successfully for its replacement, as guardians of his river flank holding the bridges, by 15th Brigade, the first of the 5th Division to arrive from Flanders. So began his close relationship with Brigadier-General 'Pompey' Elliott. Monash was alternating bursts of planning work at Franvillers with tours of brigade headquarters. Franvillers was exposed and, after shelling on the 30th, Congreve ordered him to withdraw divisional headquarters to St Gratien where he found 'a very fine old Louis XI Chateau belonging to the Comte de Thielloye, who made us very comfortable'. On 1 April Monash arrived at 11th Brigade ten minutes after shelling had killed three brigade officers. A letter from Major-General Mullens, commanding the 1st Cavalry Division, thanked him for his courtesy and support, especially by artillery: 'It was a pleasure and an honour to be fighting alongside troops who displayed such magnificent *morale'*. Monash claimed to Birdwood that 'the advent of Australian troops ... has had an instant and extraordinary effect in steadying the whole line and in giving confidence to a lot of people who had become very "windy"'. White wrote to say that he was reading his messages to Birdwood with intense interest and pride. Meanwhile the troops out of the line were enjoying the picnic atmosphere, the green fields and crops, and the chicken and pork, champagne, *vin rouge* and milk for the taking in the evacuated villages. But Monash methodically organized collection of goods worth nearly £100 000—94 tons of wool alone, wheat, oats, bran, livestock, wine and furniture—for transfer to the French authorities. It was a highly unusual transaction in this or any other war.

3rd Division had done its job well in the last days of March. The overnight move and the forming of a front could hardly have been more speedily or efficiently carried out. And though it was only partly successful, the advance on the 28th had very few parallels. Writing to Jackson next day, Monash claimed to have made a

> real and tangible impression upon a very critical situation as I found it three days ago. It is a splendid illustration of the old doctrine which you and I have so often preached, that any sort of a plan was better than no plan at all, and all that was wanted in this immediate neighbourhood ... was some clear definite plan communicated promptly.

There was to be hard fighting yet, especially south of the Somme. On 4 April when the detached 9th Brigade so magnificently defended Villers-Bretonneux and 4th Division saved Dernancourt, the Germans captured Hamel and Monash's right flank was exposed when a new British division was 'biffed out'. 'These Tommy Divisions', Monash wrote home, 'are the absolute limit, ... bad troops, bad staffs, bad commanders'. Elliott's 15th Brigade crossed the river and Monash received a British brigade, and later Glasgow's 13th Brigade, then the 7th Brigade, in exchange. 5th Division was put in south of the river on the 5th when Monash had minor attacks and heavy shelling on his front. Haig did not issue his 'Backs to the wall' order until the 11th when the dangerous assault on the Lys in the far north had begun. But later in the month it was evident that the great German spring offensive had been held, and some realists were now convinced that effectively the war was won, for the Americans were coming—though remarkably slowly.

At the time Monash and nearly all the Australians exaggerated their impact on the battle for Amiens, not surprisingly because the German assault did almost peter out in front of them and they had seen so much evidence of a beaten British army in shocking disarray. Monash referred to Fifth Army's collapse as 'almost a debacle ... quite avoidable'; there had been 'a gross lack of leadership and efficiency'. The A.I.F. was indeed given pride of place in shoring up the dangerous gap on the Somme; at several places it blunted German attacks and counter-attacked brilliantly and its presence immensely rallied the British on their flanks. But hardly anywhere was the A.I.F. actually first to stop the offensive, neither Fifth nor Third Army had entirely broken: however weakly, the line was being held, and the Australians were used as strategic reserves by commanders who had not lost control. By the end of March the Germans were almost exhausted, and when they rallied to make their last throw at Villers-Bretonneux late in April, again it was the A.I.F. who repulsed them. With regard to 3rd Division in late March, just as they arrived the Germans were switching their main assault to south of the Somme. Monash and the main body of his division had to deal only with limited challenges, were in the eye of the storm.

Nevertheless Monash and the A.I.F. as a whole could not but be proud of themselves and seek recognition. They had nowhere yielded an inch; they were bitter about the loss up north of Messines, Armentières and Ploegsteert Wood—1st Division had had to be sent back there to save the day. Arrogantly, after what they had seen, they circulated derisive stories about the British Army (though making exceptions) and joked about British criticism of their lack of discipline. Monash liked such stories and sent them home, but instructed battalion commanders to try and stamp them out. They had had little publicity from the events of late March, for the Germans had been slow to identify their presence which hence was censored from the news. After Anzac Day at Villers-Bretonneux, however, Philip Gibbs and other correspondents impressed the British public with their stories of Australian valour.

Monash's new Fourth Army commander, General Rawlinson, who called in at least twice in April, was satisfied with Monash and Hobbs as 'good commanders'. The Australian Corps had now gathered again except for 1st Division, with headquarters at Bertangles chateau near Amiens, and formed the right flank of the Fourth Army, linking with the French south of the Somme. Monash frequently visited or received the other divisional commanders and was often out conferring with his brigadiers. Most days he walked several miles to keep in trim. On 11 April he issued a message to all ranks—Stick to your hard digging, hard wiring, and instant readiness—and on the 13th sent another to the brigadiers urging them to concentrate on keeping spirits up, for this was the critical stage of the war. The 12th was a very bad day—Owen Lewis, one of Jim's boys, was shot down in flames, and Lieut-Colonel J. A. Milne of the 36th was killed by shellfire: 'It is hard, sometimes, to keep up one's spirits, but it has got to be done, for, if the Divisional General were to start to despair, and wring his hands, the Division would go to pieces in just ten minutes'. On the 18th the 33rd Battalion was badly gassed. The 24th, when Villers-Bretonneux fell, was an 'anxious and tiring day' because of gas-shelling and cutting of communications. Its recapture the following night by the 5th Division Monash always held to be the real turning-point of the war, quoting Hindenburg's admission that it finally destroyed German hopes of a decisive victory. On the 21st he was convinced, making his contribution to the everlasting argument, that Australian Lewis-gunners had brought down von Richthofen—he was soon on the spot. On the 29th he gave a glass of wine to and chatted with a German airman who had been shot down.

3rd Division remained between the Ancre and the Somme until early May. They and the rest of the Corps had an immense advantage in morale over German troops who were dispirited and weary. Throughout April Australian harassment by shell-fire, gassing, mortar bombardment, air attacks and sniping intensified. It was necessary to gain ground to allow more room for defence and continually to capture prisoners and identify their regiments in order to gain information about German intentions. So began the great period of 'peaceful penetration', mainly by night patrols, in which 3rd Division was most prominent of all; over a period of forty-five days it captured three hundred prisoners on three nights in five, making forty-one separate identifications. Cannan's 11th Brigade was particularly active, battalions competing with each other, and companies within battalions.

At the close of April and early in May developed what Monash termed four 'minor battles' at Morlancourt, during which the line was advanced by about a mile. First, 10th Brigade advanced near Ville, almost without loss, by dint of sustained aggressive patrolling. Then the combative Rosenthal gained Monash's permission for 9th Brigade to move in force right of Morlancourt on 4 May; again several hundred yards were quietly stolen. Next, 9th Brigade attacked on a 1500-yard front with artillery barrage on 5–6 May. They were largely successful, but the right flank especially was precariously lodged. Next night another limited objective was won. But operations went badly wrong on the 7th–8th when a company of the 34th Battalion, pressing on too far and losing itself, had to surrender. Some of the muddle had been caused by indecision: Monash and Hobbs had disagreed about moving forward a battalion of 5th Division on the right; White had supported

Hobbs, but Birdwood ruled in favour of Monash. Then Monash, on Hobbs's request, had to postpone zero hour, but orders within 9th Brigade were still fatally late. In his diary Monash referred to confusion and worry. He and White analysed the causes of the 'fiasco'. The operations of 4–9 May had been entirely successful until the night of the 7th, at the cost of some three hundred casualties. 2nd Division now relieved the 3rd and over the next ten days made brilliant advances.

Jess looked back on these 'wonderful days' when the depressing reports in the newspapers of other parts of the front were always relieved by the sentence: 'North of the Somme our advances were again successful and resulted in many prisoners'. Monash was deploring Birdwood's lack of aggression and refusal to attack south of the Somme. Much of 3rd Division's ground was in full observation of the enemy over the river and subject to shelling from well-concealed artillery positions there. In fact White had been ordered to draw up a plan for an attack on Hamel, but believed it would cut up a division for no great gain and convinced Rawlinson and Birdwood of its foolishness.

Monash's resting headquarters were at Allonville. He now could give several sittings to the official portraitist, John Longstaff. On overnight notice, Haig yet again inspected the division on 17 May and Monash turned on a brave show of ten thousand men. Haig entered in his diary: 'The Australian is a different individual now to when he first came, both in discipline and smartness. Altogether it was a most inspiring sight'. The division's rest was brief: on the 22nd it took over south of the Somme from 4th Division, with headquarters at Glisy near Villers-Bretonneux. They were on the extreme southern flank of the British Army and immediate liaison had to be made with the neighbouring French—'right good fellows', Monash and his troops found them. Shelling of his headquarters village was unpleasant and Monash had tunnelled dugouts constructed, 'far underground in rather wet, stuffy and smelly surroundings'. Bean was impressed, when he visited, by the 'terrace verandah for offices' and the 'wonderful set of dug outs'. On 25–26 May the enemy launched an appalling gas bombardment and 11th Brigade alone suffered hundreds of casualties. But before the end of May Monash was being warmly farewelled by the division and had issued a parting message, for he had been translated to a higher task.

In January, Matron Kellett, Lieut-Colonel E. A. Drake-Brockman and others had written to Monash to tell him of the strong rumour that he was to be promoted corps commander. Monash was genuinely surprised and replied that the rumour was not well founded. He was seeing much of Birdwood at the time and believed himself to be on terms of 'most intimate confidence'. Birdwood had told him that

> McCay had coolly asked B. to resign the Corps Command and give it to McCay. Upon his refusing, McCay then asked B. to give him command of the Third Division, and send me to England to command the Depots. B. said "I told him I didn't want the Third Division ruined like he had ruined the Fifth".

Then on 26 March Jackson wrote to congratulate him: 'How are you going to make up yr Cabinet . . .? . . . Wish the authorities would let me go back to you we would have the devil of a good show'. Again, Monash did not believe it.

On 12 May Birdwood told Monash that he had recommended him to the Australian government for the Corps command. Birdwood had been ordered to take over Fifth Army. He would have preferred to remain where he was, but submitted when told that he would block the way of an eligible Australian, was half-promised that the Corps would be part of his army, and that he would be allowed to retain administrative command of the A.I.F.

'Birdie' had justified Kitchener's trust in him as the right man to command the Australians because he 'went among men as a man'. Few other British officers could have so understood Australian attitudes to discipline, or have been so absolutely fair in his dealings with them. He was a great leader of men, full of fighting spirit, of fine instinctive judgement, who believed in his luck. He was bold in dealing with his superior officers and served the A.I.F. well in remaining so independent of G.H.Q. Yet he was only a mediocre battle commander, never drew up plans for operations himself, and was unreliable in his frontline observations; on the other hand his trust in his juniors earned him great devotion. At Bullecourt and elsewhere he had stood up against the madness of his army commander, but had eventually given way too readily. These are the considered judgements of Brudenell White, his loyal prop and stay. In retrospect Monash himself, mainly remembering Gallipoli, described Birdwood as 'a master of the art of inspiring men to persevere, to show fortitude under privations and suffering'. But there were also many senior officers like Gellibrand and Elliott who considered that Birdwood's protection of Australian interests had been inadequate.

Birdwood had warned Pearce in March that McCay, the senior officer, was ambitious to succeed him: that would be a disaster, in view of McCay's abrasiveness and unpopularity. If he, Birdwood, were to be promoted, he would recommend Monash for the Corps, while if possible he himself would remain G.O.C., A.I.F. Now, in May, he cabled the government and scrupulously wrote at length to support his recommendation. Any one of White, Monash and Hobbs might succeed him but, able though he was, Hobbs could not compare with the other two. He had the utmost admiration and the deepest affection for White. But it was impossible to overlook Monash, his senior:

> He has commanded first a brigade and then a division in this force without I think a day's intermission since our training days in Egypt in Jan. 1915, to the present time. Of his ability, there can be no possible doubt, nor of his keenness and knowledge. Also, he has had almost unvarying success in all the operations undertaken by his division, which has I know the greatest confidence in him. I am aware, of course, of the feeling there was against him in Australia, ... owing to, I understand, his German origin, but this has, I think, been entirely lived down, as far as the A.I.F. is concerned, by his good work. ... I do not think we could in justice overlook in any way his undoubted claims and equally undoubted ability to fill the appointment.

Birdwood had Haig's approval for Monash; and, being human, he was aware of the benefit of retaining White as his chief of staff. (Could he have put up any sort of show without him?) Monash, White and Hobbs had all encouraged him to continue as G.O.C.; indeed, Hobbs had threatened to resign if McCay were appointed.

The modest White, though he would dearly have liked to take over the Corps, considered his chief was right. When Birdwood put the question squarely to him, he recalled twenty years later, he replied that 'as Monash was my senior and an abler man I could not see on what grounds he could be passed over without injustice. ... I felt strongly at the time that Birdwood chose rightly and events and time have strengthened that opinion'. Moreover, he knew how important it would be to retain his guardianship of the interests of the A.I.F. through his mouthpiece, Birdwood.

The government, in the absence of Hughes who was journeying to England, approved Birdwood's recommendation on 18 May; Birdwood immediately telephoned Monash.

The new appointments were promulgated on the 23rd. So on 1 June Monash became one of twenty corps commanders, commander of the largest corps, and a lieut-general under Haig and the five army commanders. It was 'the finest Corps Command in the British Army', he told Vic, of 166 000 men; he had under him five major-generals and twenty-five brigadier-generals.

> To be the first native born Australian Corps Commander is something to have lived for, and will not be forgotten in Australian history; and the appointment will give me a unique and unimpeachable

standing both in England and in Australia. . . . With best love Your Jack.

And having regard

> to certain disabilities of ancestry and religion, it is I think, a ground for pardonable pride to have achieved such a status. . . . Suffice it to say that I feel the greatest possible confidence in my ability to make a success of the tasks now imposed upon me.

He was amused by Walter's joking, 'We'll see you as C. in C. yet'.

The changes were accepted with satisfaction by most of the senior A.I.F. officers, although with regret at the loss of White to Fifth Army. Monash was reassured: his appointment seemed to be popular. Hobbs and Rosenthal rejoiced: Gellibrand, Glasgow and MacLagan were rather more uncertain. McCay wrote warmly, though he remarked that he would have been a rival if his health had not put him out of the running, and told McGlinn that the appointment had gone to the most capable man in the A.I.F. 'Pompey' Elliott told his wife he 'was never so delighted with anything in my life'. Cannan claimed to 'voice the opinion of the whole A.I.F. in saying the appointment is the most popular one ever notified in A.I.F. orders'. McGlinn, however, warned that there was 'a crowd in London' at A.I.F. Headquarters 'yelping' because of Monash's alleged preferment to Jews. We may surmise that the rank and file of the A.I.F. were very pleased that an Australian had been chosen; that at least it was not McCay; that there was little against Monash; and that White was even less well known to them. Reports from Australia were very encouraging. The federal parliamentarians were delighted. Monash's former officers at home—Pope, Jobson, Durrant and Locke (who according to Vic simply worshipped him), and Brigadier-General George Johnston ('Jack old friend')—allowed no doubt about the state of public opinion. Vic's reports that Legge and other senior officers were lost in admiration and that the secretary of the Returned Soldiers' League had told her not a man opposed the appointment are less reliable. Felix Meyer reported a feeling of deep satisfaction in Melbourne, but another correspondent noted that some regular officers were anything but pleased that a 'mere militia man' had reached the top. Theodore Fink told Murdoch that most Australians were greatly satisfied, but 'he has his enemies'. Sir Ronald Munro Ferguson was perhaps not so pleased: he never admitted Monash to his select circle of intimate correspondents.

Some of White's associates, however, were dismayed. They included some 'disaffected brigadiers' whom Monash referred to in discussion with his divisional commanders. On 16 May, when Birdwood had called him aside, Bean had been shocked at the 'very great blow' that White was leaving the Corps. Next day he 'blurted out' the news to Will Dyson, an official war artist, and Hubert Wilkins, the great photographer.

> There was immediately a great consternation.... We had been talking of the relative merits of White who does not advertise, and Monash who does. . . . Dyson's tendencies are all towards White's attitude—"Do your work well—if the world wants you it will see that it has you". . . . Dyson thinks it a weakness, but he takes it better than the advertising strength which insists on thinking or insinuating itself into the front rank. He says: "Yes—Monash *will* get there—he must get there all the time on account of the qualities of his race; the Jew will *always* get there. I'm not sure that because of that very quality Monash is not more likely to help win this war than White, but the manner of winning it makes the victory in the long run scarcely worth the winning."

Bean and Dyson, at least, agreed now that if White would not act for himself, it was up to his friends to work for him. They agreed that Birdwood must go, that Monash should become G.O.C., and White should command the Corps. Bean sent a telegram to Pearce advising him not to allow White—'universally considered greatest Australian soldier'—to be lost to the Corps.

On the 18th Bean and Dyson left for London to conspire with the brash and forceful Keith Murdoch who soon began ruthlessly to manipulate men and news. He cabled Hughes in the United States, asserting that A.I.F. opinion overwhelmingly opposed Birdwood's retention of administrative command and Monash's appointment over White:

> Some officers . . . claim that in operations strategy and understanding of Australians [White] is much superior to Monash whose genius is for organization and administration and not akin to the true AIF genius of front line daring and dash.

Hughes cabled, too late, to Pearce urging postponement of the decision. Murdoch sent a cable to the Sydney *Sun*, which was blocked by the Censor, claiming there was a 'strong unanimous view' that Birdwood should not be G.O.C. and that Monash was likely to become the 'supreme administrator' in London while White took the Corps. He persuaded W. S. Robinson of Broken Hill Smelters to cable his associates to lobby the government on these lines. The Australian censorship held up release of the news of Monash's appointment for almost a month, in case the decision was reversed.

However, Murdoch miscalculated in trying to bully Birdwood into abandoning his administrative control. Fully alerted, Birdwood wrote to his political patrons and to the governor-general. Murdoch, he claimed, aimed to be the 'Australian Northcliffe' and his underhand methods had inspired much annoyance and resentment. Colonel Dodds, Birdwood's deputy adjutant general, also wrote to Pearce to assure him that Murdoch was totally misrepresenting A.I.F. opinion, and rebuked Bean to his face as an 'irresponsible pressman'. Bean told Dodds that Monash had worked for commandership of the Corps 'by all sorts of clever well hidden subterranean channels' (and nearly forty years later shakily wrote in the margin of his diary, 'I do not now believe this to be true'.)

Murdoch also wrote to Monash to offer his 'hearty congratulations and felicitations'. Monash answered politely, but for once was caught slightly off balance; realizing he had been perfunctory, he replied more fully the next day. While resenting the arrant impertinence of the journalist, he well knew how dangerous he was. 'I profoundly distrust this man', he told Vic. After consultation with Birdwood, he wrote to Hughes on 2 June, urging him to suspend judgement and to visit him and the troops as soon as possible in order to discuss the matter. He also emphatically advised that 'upon *every* ground, and in the best interests of the A.I.F., ... the present organization should be left undisturbed'. He did not admit Murdoch's claim to be 'spokesman of the A.I.F.' and would prove to Hughes that his assertions were 'absolutely incorrect'.

The issues were by now confused: the campaign to replace Birdwood with Monash was much more prominent than the plot to replace Monash with White. Murdoch had a case in that, although he was ignorant of military considerations, the Australian government was determined both to Australianize the A.I.F. command and to gain a louder voice in the conduct of the war: a G.O.C. in London might serve the purpose—moreover it was becoming urgently necessary to begin to plan repatriation. On the face of it Birdwood, even with White at hand, could not run the A.I.F. as a sideline to his Army; moreover he had little capacity for handling broader semi-political issues. But the senior A.I.F. officers opposed removing the senior post from the army in the field. They recognized that Birdwood's and White's administration had worked well and had kept the A.I.F., as Monash said, largely 'free from intrigue or cabal'. Nor could they see how there could be a clear division of authority between a G.O.C. in London and the corps commander.

In the *Official History* Bean summed up his and others' criticisms of Monash as potential corps commander:

> though a lucid thinker, a wonderful organiser, and accustomed to take endless pains, he had not the physical audacity that Australian troops were thought to require in their leaders, and it was for his ability in administration rather than for tactical skill that he was then reputed. Moreover, a few of those who knew both men doubted

whether Monash's judgment would be as resistant as White's to the promptings of personal ambition or whether he was as well equipped to overbear a wrongly insistent superior or the strain of a great disaster. They knew that Monash had an almost Napoleonic skill in transmitting the appearance of his capacity, and there was some belief—quite erroneous, as appeared later—that he had sought his appointment by every means in his power.

Bean at the time went much further in writing to White:

> You know and I know and Gen. Birdwood knows and everyone knows, that our men are not so safe under Gen. Monash as under you. You know that no one will safeguard them against a reckless waste—or useless waste—of life in impracticable or unnecessary stunts, or will get so much effect out of them in a good stunt—as you can or would.

No evidence survives of any senior officer agreeing that Monash might sacrifice lives to his ambition. There were also long-standing enemies, whom we cannot identify, at the Barracks in Melbourne, decrying him. (McGlinn referred to them as 'the Melbourne swine'. 'What a hell of a smack in the face your success must be to them my dear old chap.')

On 6 June Murdoch made his explicit bribe to Monash: 'You as a full General with supreme authority . . . would be the solution of many of our country's difficulties'. He wrote flatteringly to him of his genius, pointed out the alternative to a G.O.C. of a cabinet minister stationed in London with a military staff, and reminded him by the way that his cables went to 250 newspapers. 'It is a poor compliment', Monash noted, 'both for him to imagine that to dangle before me a prospect of promotion would induce me to change my declared views, and for him to disclose that he thinks I would be a suitable appointee to serve his ulterior ends'. He wrote a friendly reply, avoiding argument. Later, however, he began to draft another letter to Murdoch, to explain why he wanted to prove himself as Corps commander: 'You and your friends believe my abilities are mainly administrative, you probably think that a non-professional soldier is unlikely to be a good commander, that in the past I have been a figurehead controlled by professional staff officers'—but it was too undignified to continue. He did not deign to join the rush to London of McCay and other urgers when Hughes arrived on 15 June.

Bean now tackled Monash, who told him it was unreasonable to try to prevent him leading the Corps when Haig had full confidence in him and had told him he would have given him a corps command anywhere if the Australian position had not been vacant. Bean persuaded himself that he had half-converted Monash to his views.

> Monash is a man of very ordinary ideals—lower than ordinary I should say. He cannot inspire this force with a high chivalrous patri-

otic spirit—with his people in charge it would be full of the desire to look and show well—that is the highest. There is no question where the interest of the Australian nation lies. It lies in making White one of its great men and makers.

Birdwood had written to Murdoch: 'I dare say you will beat me, but, I warn you, I shall make a hard fight before I die'. On the 24th Monash conferred again with Birdwood, who brought him up to date. Birdwood had had a cool reception when he saw Hughes. Fisher, the High Commissioner, was enraged and spoke contemptuously of Monash; Birdwood told him he didn't know what he was talking about. Murdoch had paid a deferential visit and when he asked whether Monash really was fit to be corps commander, Birdwood had told him, 'Of course. . . . He can do it much more ably than I'. White would not accept the Corps, if offered: it 'would suggest he had been intriguing with Murdoch'. Monash did not fail to recognize that he stood to win both ways. But he told Vic that he could not give up the Corps command without loss of prestige until he had made a success of it; and furthermore it would be disloyal to Birdwood. 'It is a great nuisance to have to fight a pogrom of this nature in the midst of all one's other anxieties.' This is a very rare instance in his life of Monash acknowledging that he was subject to anti-Semitism.

Meanwhile the thirty-one-year-old Murdoch dined and wined the great: Lord Milner, Secretary of State for War, General Sir Henry Wilson (now Chief of the Imperial General Staff) and others, in order to meet Hughes; then Lloyd George himself at the Ritz—Lieut-Commander J. G. Latham was a guest and made notes about the plot on the back of his menu. Bean wrote a memorandum for Hughes, setting out their case. Murdoch and Bean vigorously argued with senior A.I.F. officers. Birdwood told Hughes that he was 'absolutely confident' in Monash, whom Plumer and Rawlinson both greatly admired, and he confided to the governor-general that Monash had said he would ask to be sent home if he lost the Corps. Monash and Hobbs wrote vehemently to Pearce. Hobbs described Monash as 'a commander of very great ability and exceptional energy and experience, who enjoys absolutely the complete confidence and respect of the A.I.F. as a fighting leader'. The letters ultimately were important in persuading the government at home to attempt to restrain Hughes. Rawlinson agreed with Birdwood that Murdoch was 'a mischievous and persistent villain'. Bean wrote emotionally and at great length to his hero, White, and received a totally dismissive though friendly reply. Monash reassured McGlinn: he had powerful trumps to play if necessary. He had indeed—the commander-in-chief and three army commanders! He had also come to realize that, as word got around, the A.I.F. was rallying behind him.

But the sabotage continued. Hughes and the deputy prime minister Joseph Cook eventually arrived at Corps headquarters on 1 July and with Birdwood and Monash visited the troops out of the line. Hughes did not know that three days later the battle of Hamel was to take place; Monash remarked to Birdwood that the time could hardly be more inconvenient. Presumably Bean felt some shame later in the week. Monash found Hughes and Cook almost impossible to collar; when he did, Hughes wanted to postpone the issue, whereupon Monash said:

> I am bound to tell you, quite frankly, that any arrangement which would involve my removal from the command of this Corps would be, in the highest degree, distasteful to me, and that I would regard any such removal as a degradation and a humiliation.

Hughes gave the politician's answer: he 'laid his hand on my shoulder and, breaking in upon me, said, "You may thoroughly rely upon your wishes in this matter receiving the greatest possible weight" '.

Three of the divisional generals had also managed to convey their opinions to Hughes, who was shaken and told Murdoch he had met no one who agreed with him. That night at Corps headquarters, Bishop G. M. Long spent hours trying in vain to persuade Bean and Murdoch of the error of their ways. Bean had disturbed White by telling him Monash was certain to accept the bribe of promotion. On the 29th White wrote to Monash to say that if he acquiesced, 'the basis is knocked from under my resistance'. On the 2nd Monash sent a quick P.S. to Birdwood to reassure White and next day, just before Hamel, found time to write. White's letter had been cryptic, there was something behind it; he, Monash, had not budged, he would not voluntarily forgo the command, and had told Hughes and Cook so. White replied on the 6th, agreeing he had been cryptic and that Monash had divined correctly; and furthermore,

> in case there is any suspicion lurking in your mind, may I say once and for all and very definitely that if the conspirators in this matter do happen to be General White's friends, they are not acting at the suggestion or with the approval of General White.

The Monash–White relationship remained impeccable.

After Hamel Birdwood wrote exultantly to Monash: the battle had entirely justified his promotion. Monash had a frank talk with Murdoch about the 6th. Bean reported it as follows:

> there is no doubt of the old man's strength. . . . When he had won 'battle honours' he would be well content to take up the other position. . . . I still urged Murdoch to advise Hughes not to give time.

A week later White roundly rebuked Murdoch for impropriety, ignorance and dangerous meddling. The impervious journalist brushed him off as subservient to England and politically unaware. There is a hint that about this time Gellibrand, Glasgow and MacLagan conferred and, while not certain about Monash but reassured by the success of Hamel, decided that he had to be supported. Bean again wrote desperately to White. He saw it as probably his 'major job in life' to ensure that the two senior appointments went the right way: 'This seems to me one of those big turnings where the nation goes either right or wrong'.

> I am inclined to agree with you that Monash is a very big man. I think he might lift us through [repatriation] not only without trouble but with actual benefit. His work with the third division is most visible still in the low—the very low—percentage of their crime. That is precisely the form that his genius takes. I do think that that position is made for a man of his particular capacity, and that Australia is the loser if he is permanently devoted to a position for which he is not so conspicuously suited.

Murdoch again wrote reassuringly to Monash and received another polite answer which perhaps indicates that Monash was getting a little enjoyment from 'managing' him. But Monash knew very well that his position with Hughes was delicate, although they had not had things out. Murdoch had made it clear to him that Hughes wanted a G.O.C. to take over 'much of a semi-political, semi-national, economic and financial character', that a supremely important immediate post-war job was in store for him. Monash was letting it be known that this was a politician's task and not a soldier's; Hughes, doubting whether any politician could gain sufficient support from home in view of the divided nation, was 'getting steadily angrier' with Monash; but Monash was determined to have his chance in the field before accepting the job. Briefly on leave in London late in July, Monash failed to meet Hughes, partly because he was urgently called back to France. He told Birdwood that all seemed safe. However, Murdoch was not beaten and, by persistent nagging, forced Hughes towards a decision. He told Bean that Hughes was vacillating:

> White does not impress him as Monash does and he has a tremendous and very inflated idea of the Hamel battle. I doubt very much if he will give White the corps, and I am not pressing this upon him. That will follow ultimately, if White stops fooling about—he is every day proving himself less sound in his judgment than he should be. Monash will sooner or later want the GOC-ship.

Hughes cabled cabinet to recommend that Birdwood should go, but that he was so impressed by Monash that he should have the choice of G.O.C. or the Corps; a resident minister in London would be necessary—it would have to be Pearce.

The 8 August offensive effectively closed the issue for several months. However, on 12 August Hughes offered Birdwood the post of full-time G.O.C., assuming he would not be willing to resign from Fifth Army. To his surprise Birdwood accepted—but in the urgent military situation it was agreed to continue the status quo until 30 November. At the last moment, Chauvel complicated the situation from the Middle East by making a claim to be G.O.C. A rash despatch by Murdoch to the Melbourne *Herald* caused a flutter: the governor-general was shocked and Mat Monash correctly judged that it was 'deliberately done to insinuate a doubt as to your ability'.

Almost forty years later Bean regretfully referred to 'our high-intentioned but ill-judged intervention. That it resulted in no harm whatever was probably due to the magnanimity of both White and Monash'. There might easily have been much harm: the Australian higher commanders were distracted during some of the most vital days of the war. It is perhaps the outstanding case of sheer irresponsibility by pressmen in Australian history.

12

Feeding the Troops on Victory 1918

BIRDWOOD and White settled the changes in divisional command over Monash's head. Birdwood did ask Monash whether he would like to have McCay; Monash refused—it would be 'disagreeable' to command his old senior and friend. He suggested McNicoll and, it may be, Elliott, but the decisions had effectively been made. Monash was content that Glasgow (a Queensland grazier whose wife was of German parentage) and Rosenthal were to replace Walker and Smyth, the last senior British commanders in the A.I.F., at 1st and 2nd Divisions. He was less happy about the promotion to command of 3rd Division of White's friend Gellibrand, a Tasmanian orchardist and former professional soldier, whom Bean regarded as 'a great leader but a sensitive and often difficult subordinate'. In July Monash recommended Brand to Birdwood as first emergency for divisional command, and Grimwade for trial with an infantry brigade. By this time eighteen of the twenty divisional generals and infantry brigadiers were citizen-soldiers.

Gellibrand was soon at loggerheads with McNicoll whom he found argumentative and inefficient; McNicoll objected to Gellibrand's expression and manner, and requested a transfer or permission to resign. Monash smoothed them down as best he could, but in August Gellibrand complained that he had to administer a separate system for 10th Brigade. Monash told Birdwood that basically it was a personal difference and largely due to Gellibrand's manner. Despite the disharmony, Monash did not separate them until October.

He did not have much say, either, about his corps staff. The brilliant Brigadier-General Blamey was the obvious and entirely acceptable choice as White's successor. (He was a 'work and burst' man—would slave for long hours, then drive off for a night in Amiens.) Monash's administrative head was a Britisher, Brigadier-General R. A. Carruthers, an old friend of Birdwood whom Monash considered to be a charming loafer but backed up superbly by Lieut-Colonel

G. C. Somerville. Monash wanted Bruche to replace Carruthers, but Birdwood forbade it because comment on their German origins might be revived—'stupid in the extreme', John told Walter. The only other senior British officer remaining was Brigadier-General L. D. Fraser, in command of heavy artillery. The other brigadiers whom Monash inherited were the permanent officers W. A. Coxen, the artillery man, and the cultivated engineer C. H. Foott, son of the poet Mary Hannay Foott and a man who had worked in ferro-concrete. Major R. G. Casey had a subordinate part in composing the battle orders. As personal staff Monash retained Aubrey Moss and Paul Simonson. Not knowing that they were his nephews, Bean noted that Monash's 'personal staff was Jewish, and men honoured him for this loyalty'. One junior officer recalls Simonson as 'a first-class A.D.C.' whereas Moss was 'that bastard'; both moustachioed, they were widely known as 'Mo' and 'Arf a Mo'.

Headquarters at Bertangles, a few miles north-west of Amiens, was in an elegant chateau. Monash inherited from Birdwood a Rolls-Royce, flying the Australian flag. Everyone at Corps was watching him, when he moved in, with intense interest. His diary entry, after Birdwood and White left on 31 May, was 'I commence organizing'. Interviews in the next two days with senior staff officers were followed by visits to neighbouring corps, to his divisions and to artillery headquarters. His army commander, Rawlinson, and his chief of staff, Montgomery (later Field Marshal Sir Archibald Montgomery-Massingberd) called in. Junior staff were highly uneasy. Birdwood used to wander through, waving to or stopping for a chat with anyone of lowly rank, touching them on the arm or shoulder. Monash was a new broom, expecting salutes from junior officers down—within a few days, the other ranks were gravely perturbed. He did not fraternize, was abrupt on the telephone, and yelled at his A.D.C.s. He found Corps headquarters to be too cosy.

He took over a wonderful fighting machine, rivalled only by the Canadians, New Zealanders and a very few British divisions. It was the only volunteer army, experienced, proud, war-weary and intensely homesick but not dispirited, united now with hardly a remaining trace of State parochialism or inter-divisional jealousy. They were 'incorrigibly civilian' still, and their morale was such that they saw the funny side of war as few soldiers ever have anywhere. The Corps was virtually at full strength, though few reinforcements were coming through now; another series of battles like Third Ypres would finish it. Early in 1918 the British Army had been reorganized on the basis of three instead of four battalions to the brigade. The A.I.F. had to begin to follow suit, and shortly before Monash took over the Corps three of the sixty battalions were disbanded. For months he passively resisted any further break-ups, preferring four battalions in a brigade to three stronger ones. Fifty thousand non-Australian troops were attached to the Corps, mainly British heavy artillery, British labour battalions and an American engineer unit.

Monash had his first conference with his four divisional commanders (1st Division still being absent) on 6 June. Hobbs made a little demonstration, drawing attention to the fact that for the first time in the history of the A.I.F. all the commanders and their senior staff officers present were Australian. (MacLagan was an honorary Australian, having been instructing at Duntroon before the war.) The agenda was wide-ranging, the most urgent matter being discussion of possible defence against concentrated trench-mortar bombardment, with which the Germans recently had been all too effective. Monash put on the agenda: 'Safeguarding troops against casualties' and 'Cumulative small gas losses'. He began by announcing that he planned regular, possibly fortnightly, interchanges of views. In the following weeks he systematically went the rounds, concentrating on the divisional and brigade commanders he knew less well, and regularly had them and battalion commanders to dine at Bertangles. On 11 June he had a narrow escape when visiting 12th Brigade: as he got out of his car, a shell burst on the other side of it, spattering it with splinters.

June was a relatively quiet month for the Australians. Although the great German offensive of March–April on the Somme and the Lys in Flanders had been held, they were still bringing into battle divisions from the Russian front. Throughout May the Allied armies waited tensely: the blow eventually fell on the French, far to the south-east on the Soissons–Rheims front on the Aisne where the Germans reached within fifty miles of Paris, and again on 9 June at Noyon. Meanwhile Foch was itching to make counter-strokes. Monash was engrossed in the secret information now made available to him from G.H.Q.

Rawlinson's orders to Monash were emphasizing precautions against a probable German attack; a drive between the British, whose right flank the Australians were guarding, and the French must have tempted them. Of the four Australian divisions, one was to the north and two to the south of the Somme, and the other in reserve. On 10 June, in operations to the north of the river approved before Monash took over the Corps, the 2nd Division grabbed more of the Morlancourt ridge and took 330 prisoners. Impudent raiding south of the river continued, especially after Foch's request, amplified by Monash to his divisional commanders on 10 June, for minor offensives.

'Taking it all in all', Monash wrote to his sister Lou, 'I am having, from the point of view of work, anxiety and responsibility, a much harder time than ever I had before, although of course the work is intensely interesting, and the power and authority which I now wield, are ... most satisfactory to me'. He was about to launch the battle of Hamel (strictly Le Hamel), which was to win him instant fame. It was by no means all his own work—major battle plans never are—but it was largely his battle.

From early June Monash, MacLagan and Gellibrand had been discussing the possibility of attacking to straighten out the German bulge—for which there were many good tactical reasons, especially future artillery requirements. They drew up a plan for a six-battalion attack on Hamel, but on the 13th, biding his time, Monash recommended deferment. He was keen to satisfy the aggressive temper of the A.I.F. and to give it the satisfaction of proving the British Army still had some kick left in it. 'It was high time', he later wrote, 'that some commander on our side of No Man's Land should begin to "think offensively", and cease to look over their shoulders in order to estimate how far it still was to the coast'. The precipitating factor was the arrival at Fourth Army of a battalion of a new type of tank. By the 18th Monash and Rawlinson both were seized with the possibility that these tanks would make the Hamel operation possible by greatly reducing infantry losses; with Blamey and Montgomery, they sat down to thrash it out. Next day Monash was making preliminary notes and on the 21st formally submitted to Rawlinson his proposal for a four-brigade dawn operation, using all the Corps artillery and tanks and aircraft, and asked MacLagan to work on a detailed plan. After another conference on the 22nd, Rawlinson sought Haig's permission, stressing, as had Monash, the need to assess whether the proposition was attractive enough to justify casualties which would weaken the precious Australian Corps. Permission was granted on the 26th.*

Monash had conferred with Brigadier-General Courage of the 5th Tank Brigade on the 19th, and his original plan in effect adopted the tactics recommended by Tank Corps Headquarters: it would be essentially a tank operation, with infantry helping to take strong-points, mopping up and consolidating. The infantry was to be remarkably thin—only eight battalions for a 6000-yard front. Monash added important details. Gunfire would disguise the noise of the approaching tanks; a daily gas and smoke-shell barrage would be introduced so that, on the day of attack when gas was omitted, the enemy would still be hampered by wearing gas-masks; and smoke would conceal the actual point of attack. But Monash's own senior officers forced

* Rawlinson himself and his biographer F. Maurice exaggerated the army commander's contribution both to the original decision and the plan adopted. One eventual ludicrous consequence was that Sir John Smyth, V.C., in his *Leadership in Battle* managed to write four pages on the battle of Hamel without mentioning Monash. But Monash also exaggerated his own claims when writing to Bruche on 10 October 1919: 'It is undeniable and unchallengeable that the whole conception of the battle of Hamel, ... rested upon my own unaided efforts. ...'

revision. Blamey and Coxen were unwilling to rely so much on the tanks: full-scale artillery support would make success certain. They were strongly backed by MacLagan and 4th Division which had suffered so much from the failure of the tanks at Bullecourt in 1917. Monash had to withdraw diplomatically and he and Courage accepted a basic change of plan. In the end the novelty of Hamel was that each tank was assigned to and controlled by an infantry commander, and they followed close on the creeping barrage, despite all fears that their height would expose them to short-falling shells. Meanwhile, the battalions were bussed daily to play with the tanks: they were taken for joy-rides, climbed in and out and all over them, even drove them. They were shown how the tanks could mow down wire, leap trenches and suppress strong-points—'pirouetting round and round, would blot them out, much as a man's heel would crush a scorpion', as Monash put it. The diggers were converted and took the tanks to their hearts, each company adopting one. The Tank Corps had put its future in Monash's hands.

Another modification came at Rawlinson's instigation. American divisions had recently arrived in the area and were being attached for experience, by companies and platoons, to Fourth Army units. Rawlinson asked Monash whether he would like Americans to join the battle: Monash 'asked for about 2000 men organised in eight companies'. Happily they were able to set 4 July as the day of attack. Blamey held a conference on the 27th, and Monash another, with an agenda of 118 items, on the 28th. Two days later he held his last major conference, for about twenty-five officers, with an agenda of 133 items, lasting nearly four and a half hours. On 1 July Haig spent an hour examining the battle plan. Monash found him 'affability, courtesy and consideration personified'. Next day Hughes made his visit and Birdwood too went through the plan which he deemed 'practically perfect'. Rawlinson had been having private doubts: on the 27th he noted that the Australian Corps was 'not functioning very well' and that he was 'not altogether happy about the operation'. Over the next three days he became more satisfied that they were coming to understand the tanks. On 1 July he noted: 'Too much talk is going on—old Monash talks too much but is very good at all the preliminaries'.

The day before the battle there was a crisis. First, half the Americans were withdrawn, to their great distress. There was time to make adjustments without great difficulty. But at 4 p.m. Monash learned that General Pershing had forbidden the use of *any* Americans: he had not known of their involvement and considered them insufficiently trained. Monash resolved on bold resistance: fixed plans must not be changed. He managed to meet Rawlinson with MacLagan at 5 o'clock. According to his own account

> It was a meeting full of tense situations—and of grave import. . . . the whole of the infantry destined for the assault at dawn next morning, including those very Americans, was already well on its way to its battle stations; the artillery was in the act of dissolving its defensive organization with a view to moving forward into its battle emplacements as soon as dusk should fall; I well knew that even if orders could still with certainty reach the battalions concerned, the withdrawal of those Americans would result in untold confusion and in dangerous gaps in our lines of battle. . . .
> . . . disguised in the best diplomatic language that I was able to command, my representations amounted to this: firstly, that it was already too late to carry out the order; secondly, that the battle would have to go on either with the Americans participating, or not at all; thirdly, that unless I were expressly ordered to abandon the battle, I intended to go on as originally planned; and lastly, that unless I received such a cancellation order before 6.30 p.m. it would be in any case too late to stop the battle.

He told Rawlinson that the commander-in-chief could not have realized that his order to withdraw the Americans would mean abandonment of the battle, and that it was open to the army commander to disobey in the light of the situation as known to him. According to Bean, Monash told him that Rawlinson said: 'Do you want me to run the risk of being sent back to England? Do you mean it is worth that?' And that he had replied, 'Yes, I do. It is more important to keep the confidence of the Americans and Australians in each other than to preserve even an Army Commander'. Rawlinson was in an awkward position. He might have called Monash's bluff, if it was a bluff, and ordered him to carry on without the Americans. He did not, probably being convinced of the danger of last-minute confusion—and he could not risk putting the Australians in unnecessary danger, or offending them. He agreed that if Haig did not countermand his order by 7 o'clock, the battle would proceed on his own authority. He did manage to make contact with Haig who, just before 7, ordered him to carry on, with the Americans. 'And so—the crisis passed as suddenly as it had appeared', Monash later wrote. He had warned the artillery to stand by for a possible order to restore their defensive organization. Outwardly unperturbed, he had met the Australian war correspondents at 6 o'clock to expound his plans for the morrow, before the news of Haig's decision came through at 7.30. He went to bed early.

It had been a major test for the new corps commander. He had made up his mind quickly and coolly, and had persuaded Rawlinson, by force of argument and personality, to risk supporting him. If Rawlinson had insisted that they both had to obey orders, he probably could not have held his ground: disobedience at such high level might have had extreme unpredictable consequences. It was perhaps as well that he was to be so successful on the morrow. Otherwise, Haig and Rawlinson might have been disposed to ponder on the pressure he had brought to bear on them.

Before 3 o'clock next morning the infantry were lying out on the grass and in the crops on the start line. R.A.F. night-bombers were at work along the front and at 3.02 the pre-dawn harassment by the artillery began as usual; under cover of the noise the tanks began their run to the start line. The only thing which could have saved the Germans now was an artillery bombardment, in knowledge of the attack—but it was a complete surprise. At 3.10 'the main barrage crashed down', and 'the infantry at once rose and, lighting their cigarettes and with rifles slung', the tanks close behind them, walked towards the barrage which every four minutes would creep forward; fortunately it was foggy. '. . . not even Messines passed off so smoothly, so exactly to time-table, or was so free of any kind of hitch', wrote Monash. 'It was all over in ninety-three minutes. It was the perfection of team work.' J. F. C. Fuller of the Tank Corps agreed: 'In rapidity, brevity, and completeness of success, no battle of the war can compare with Hamel'; it was 'the perfect battle'. In 1972 Major-General H. Essame wrote: 'A war-winning combination had been found: a corps commander of genius, the Australian infantry, the Tank Corps, the Royal Artillery and the RAF'.

That was the general's eye view. It was likewise for some of the battalions. 'It wasn't a battle at all', wrote one participant,'—just a Sunday morning stroll through the park. No rifle fire, no machine gun fire, no shell fire, no casualties, nothing at all'. It was by no means so easy for some of the other battalions who met stern resistance. But they took 1600 prisoners and inflicted at least as many casualties and gained much booty, at a cost of 1400 casualties. The tanks came back laden with cheering wounded. None of the tanks was lost and only three were temporarily disabled. The bombardment and diversionary raids far along the line prevented the Germans realizing where the main attack was coming from. It had been the first unqualified success of the tanks; they had proved even more useful in consolidation than in the attack itself, and four carrier-tanks had followed up with ammunition and supplies which 1200 men would have been needed to carry—an outstanding lesson. Moreover, for the first time ammunition was experimentally dropped by parachute to the Vickers gunners. The German gunners had been confused whenever their infantry sent up flares by contradictory ones put up by the Australians. The American collaboration had been a triumph.

The lessons of Hamel—'the first modern battle'—were many: notably the example of co-operation between tanks, infantry and aircraft, and the discovery of low German morale. The prime question raised with all ranks—stated with feeling in the front line—was: 'Why not in such operations go on through to the German guns to prevent their retirement and immediate retaliatory bombardment?' British staff officers and war correspondents began streaming into Corps headquarters to find out how it had been done. 'All England is talking about it and me', Monash soon wrote home—and France too. G.H.Q. paid the great compliment, which gave Monash immense pleasure, of publishing for guidance of commanders his battle orders with a commentary. The Supreme War Council, sitting at Versailles on 4 July, rejoiced in the victory and the statesmen sent congratulations. Prime Minister Georges Clemenceau visited 4th Division—Rawlinson and Monash were there—and spoke in English to a large gathering of the men, of how the Australians had astonished the continent of Europe by their valour and of the special place they had in the hearts of his countrymen. And when they gave tremendous cheers for the old tiger in response, he remarked, as he turned to leave, *'Des jolis enfants'*.

Monash had formal engagements to carry out with the French. The prefect of Amiens, although the city was still evacuated and under bombardment, decided to celebrate the national day and the relief of his city with a lunch in the partly destroyed *hôtel de ville*. Monash made his first speech in French. A few days later he had unwillingly to entertain for two days the members of the French mission which was about to visit Australia; as it turned out, he enjoyed it. The head of the mission was Albert Métin, scholar, cabinet minister and soldier, author of *Le Socialisme sans Doctrines*, the product of an earlier visit to Australia. Monash was much impressed with him and the veteran General Pau. Sadly, Métin was to die on the voyage out.

On the day of Hamel, Monash had ordered MacLagan and Hobbs to take advantage of evident opportunities for advances by vigorous patrolling. The enemy was reeling, with defences unusually unprepared. But the Corps had a ten-mile front; Monash implored Rawlinson either to narrow it or get 1st Division back from Flanders. He was warned also by Brand that, after Hamel, 4th Brigade and all the 4th Division were stale and needed a long rest. This may partly have induced him to issue a message to the Australian people on the 13th pleading for reinforcements to come quickly, for famous divisions were decaying and battalions being broken up. Meanwhile he visited brigade after brigade, explaining that relatively the A.I.F. was not overworked. The men appreciated the straight talking, according to one brigade diary.

Immediately after Hamel, all along the Corps front, the troops had a high old time, peacefully penetrating and nibbling, advancing the line by hundreds of yards and capturing prisoners and machine-guns. Monash was considering a variety of tempting prospects. He rejected for the moment a proposal by Hobbs to tackle the Morlancourt heights. The more important need was to iron out the bulge south-east of Villers-Bretonneux on the far right, and on 7 July he submitted a plan for a major attack on Monument Wood, which dominated the town. In the next few days 2nd Division penetrated about a quarter of the distance he had in mind. Haig had sanctioned a full-dress attack with tanks, which was considered by Rawlinson at a conference on the 11th. But Rosenthal's men, by nightly encroachment, soon occupied almost all the thousand yards advance planned as a battle. On the 15th, Rawlinson, Montgomery, Monash and Rosenthal planned an attack on the 'Mound', whose capture would provide a highly satisfactory front. The formal assault with artillery support was successfully carried out from the 16th to the 18th.

In his book *Australian Victories in France in 1918* Monash made an exaggerated assessment of the longer-term effects of Hamel. It was

> the first offensive operation on any substantial scale that had been fought by any of the Allies since the previous autumn. Its effect was electric, and it stimulated many men to the realization that the enemy was, after all, not invulnerable, in spite of the formidable increase in his resources which he had brought from Russia. It marked the termination, once and for all, of the purely defensive attitude of the British front. It incited in many quarters an examination of the possibilities of offensive action on similar lines by similar means—a changed attitude of mind, which bore a rich harvest only a very few weeks later.

In fact Foch and Haig, though hardly in command of events, were imbued with aggression. Before Hamel, in June, Mangin had counter-attacked successfully, as had the First British Army near Ypres. The great French attack of 18 July owed nothing to Hamel. However, Haig had long had in mind a major offensive and ordered its preparation within a fortnight of Hamel, which may have encouraged him to the point of action. Monash's greatest claim to military fame may lie in the model example he gave at Hamel of the concerted use of infantry, artillery, tanks and aircraft and its subsequent application by the British Army.

The degree to which Monash specifically inspired the great offensive of 8 August is a vexed question. It has often been asserted that he did: it became a commonplace of patriotic journalism and a Returned Soldiers' League article of faith, sometimes with the assertion that the A.I.F. thus 'won the war'. Many of the senior A.I.F. officers believed that he did, especially Blamey who in later years put the claim very strongly: the victory at Hamel 'decided Sir John Monash to stage the great battle of August 8, at Villers-Bretonneux'. Blamey was certain that Monash had persuaded Haig and Rawlinson to adopt his plan.

> Men like Monash, by sheer logic ... are so able to impress others who lack initiative, individuality, and decision, that they actually persuade them to do what otherwise their lack of energy and enterprise would never venture.

Similarly in 1920 F. M. Cutlack, the war correspondent, was convinced that 'If "Yes" or "No" to the plan lay with Rawlinson ... the plan and the organization of the attack were indubitably Monash's'.

Monash himself was never quite sure. On 2 August 1918 he told his wife that 'towards the end of the third week in July [sic], I propounded certain proposals to Sir Douglas Haig'. On 11 August he told Murdoch that he *believed* he was responsible for the battle, that after Hamel he had told Rawlinson he could go in five miles or more, with support on the right flank—and that when Rawlinson had mentioned the Canadians he had leapt at the suggestion. Reporting the conversation in his diary, Bean wrote: 'So it was John Monash's battle, and he has certainly made a great name for himself in it'. In 1954 Bean made a marginal note: 'Monash thought it might be so. I found later that this offensive was Foch's and Haig's'. On 16 August 1918 Bean noted a conversation with Blamey who rather thought that the idea was his:

> anyway it arose over afternoon tea cups. It was becoming clear, after Hamel, that the Germans opposite our front were so deteriorated as to offer a prospect of breaking through. Blamey and Monash each spoke to the Army staff and managed to persuade Rawlinson after a time.

In *Australian Victories* Monash did not pitch his claim very high, or indeed directly. He had

> expressed the readiness of the Australian Corps to undertake and maintain a long sustained offensive, provided that arrangements could be made to shorten my frontage from a three to a two division battle front, and to increase my resources from the present four, to five, or even six divisions. It was further essential that in any advances attempted by us, other corps must co-operate on both flanks.

In August 1919 he wrote to Blamey asking him to help find a vital letter he had mislaid—his proposals to Rawlinson for the great offensive, written some time between 4 and 17 July, which he remembered Blamey had helped him lick into shape. It was still worrying him in 1928 when he wrote to the Australian War Memorial asking for a search of the records: he had never verified his memory that he had made a verbal or written case to Rawlinson or Montgomery—he and the Corps had never received proper credit.

In a letter to Bruche on 10 October 1919 he claimed to have been 'the prime mover in the events from July 1st to 21st', but undeserving of 'the whole credit'. His part was 'analogous to that of an inventor who conceives a new scientific idea and who talks it over with his colleagues or friends, who all make suggestions which are discussed, some being adopted and others rejected, so that ultimately the new idea takes a definite form and substance'. Between 4 and 20 July he had seen Rawlinson or Montgomery almost every day, and urged on them the desirability of a large-scale offensive. Eventually Montgomery had said, 'Well, General, let us have some specific proposals'. Monash replied: 'Reduce my front, return 1st Division and use the Canadians'. The attack had to be deep enough to capture the enemy's artillery line. Montgomery promised to talk it over with Rawlinson. They returned a couple of days later to go further into the proposal, after which Rawlinson referred it to Haig. At Rawlinson's first conference on the 21st, Monash, Currie and Butler of III Corps 'elaborated the outlines of the plan'.

Monash was never in a position to grasp the context fully. Haig and Foch had been discussing possible offensives since April. In mid-May Foch asked Haig to study the possibility of a major Anglo-French attack south of the Somme. On the 23rd Haig elaborated to Rawlinson a plan for joint use of the Australians and Canadians involving a deep leap-frogging attack. Birdwood and White drew up a secret detailed commentary for Rawlinson. The plan was dropped after the major German assault of 27 May. It seems that Monash remained in ignorance of this proposal for the rest of his life. After Hamel, writes Bean, 'Rawlinson resuscitated the plan, or rather the British part in it, which he greatly expanded'. On 17 July Rawlinson submitted formal proposals to Haig which were approved on the 19th; on the 21st Monash and Currie were put to work. The decision to proceed was effectively taken by Foch on the 24th. The repulse of the last German attack at Soissons and the French counter on 18 July was the ultimate turning-point: the German offensive was over, they could not now win the war. Foch and Haig had been considering several alternative possibilities for a major British attack. Bean, who in the *Official History* handles the matter admirably, reasonably claims that the decisive factor which led Haig to decide on the Amiens front was the 'peaceful penetration' of the Australians there from April on. He concludes:

> It is in his efforts to impress on Rawlinson the chance created by the activity of the "Diggers" that Monash's claim to a share in origination of the scheme really lies. . . . How far Monash contributed to bring about that realisation can probably never be assessed.

And elsewhere he remarked: 'the great stroke was made at the place where he [Monash] asked for it to be made, and . . . it was delivered in accordance with the methods that he had urged and had applied at Hamel'.

Essentially Haig, Rawlinson and Monash were thinking along the same lines. Rawlinson probably encouraged Monash to believe he had had more to do with it than was the case, as a means of involving the A.I.F. more deeply in the offensive and making it more difficult for Hughes to attempt to withdraw it from battle. There is little to add to Bean's appraisal except to remark that Monash's cryptic diary records five meetings—there may have been more—with Rawlinson and/or Montgomery between 6 and 15 July. Monash believed also that Rawlinson did not seriously take up the project until the 20th, and he recalled his 'very great difficulty in persuading' him to advocate it to Haig. It seems certain that Rawlinson had not been confiding in Monash.

At his conference on the 21st Rawlinson assigned frontages to the Australian and Canadian corps and gave them a free hand on tactics. Monash, with Fuller of the Tanks, successfully argued for an extended objective, to make sure of capturing the enemy's guns. This was probably his most important contribution. Next day Monash and Blamey made their outline plans, broadly following Hamel, and prepared a memorandum on details which was sent to Army on the 27th. Knowing there must be delay, Monash snatched a few days leave in London, making arrangements for speedy recall: 'a Destroyer would stand by at Dover to rush me across if necessary, as I was not quite prepared for the alternative proposition of flying across'. (Few were in those days, and it would quite likely have been no quicker.) He deliberately arranged publicity for his leave in order to allay German suspicions about pending employment of the Australians; Haig, similarly, golfed at Le Touquet for several days. Monash's leave was the usual mixture of official business, press interviews, seeing the Rosenhains, and the theatre, with time for sitting to portraitists and photographers. He had five days, returning urgently on the 29th, but by train, ferry and car as usual.

Monash and Blamey got to work. Blamey recalled that Monash

> spent the whole of the next morning with me in going into details of the alternative plans for the attack which the Corps general staff had prepared. [He] selected the plan he preferred, went minutely into the mass of detail of supplies, movement, auxiliary forces etc. required. He shut himself up in his room for the afternoon.

His comprehensive proposals on 1 August at Rawlinson's Army conference set the pace for the other corps. The day before, Monash had met his divisional commanders, demanded their plans and asked for questions. Haig visited during the meeting: Monash told him he was delighted to be recalled from leave and that he had 'all the threads of the operations' in his hands; Haig instructed him that he must be prepared to use cavalry and rather unnecessarily told the major-generals that he had absolute trust in their corps commander. Monash recalled that he was given an entirely free hand to work out the deployment of the Field and Heavy Artillery, the Tanks and Armoured Cars, and the Cavalry Brigade, 'the dispositions of the Infantry, the methods of attack and the tactics to be employed'. He issued a memorandum to the divisions, clarifying obscurities, on 1 August and at a final conference with their commanders on the 4th settled queries. Rawlinson was finding 'Currie and Monash very pleasant and easy to deal with. No friction or argument of any sort'. Haig called in again on the 5th and Birdwood on the 7th.

Rawlinson planned an attack by three corps—the Australians and Canadians south of the Somme, divided by the railway line, and Butler's III Corps north of the river—with full tank, air and cavalry support. He laid down three stages and objectives for the five- to eight-mile advance on the day; the first under a creeping barrage, the second supported by mobile artillery and tanks, and the third a period of exploitation. The Canadians had a more difficult task than the Australians, and III Corps was known to be in for stiff fighting. The Australians had had a more arduous time than the Canadians in recent months; perhaps, if given the easier task they might be expected to break through further, or perhaps it was largely a chance consequence of occupying the ground they did. Foch and Haig were not satisfied with Rawlinson's plan and Haig urged him to think in terms of a vital breakthrough. In line with his orders Monash told his commanders on 1 August that there was 'no intention of carrying the exploitation of the success' beyond the third objective. On the 5th he explained to the war correspondents that it was a matter either of going for the railway at Chaulnes or the guns. The latter was the objective and Allied guns would then attempt to neutralize the railway. In fact it had been decided, after Haig had pressed Rawlinson, that the Canadians, not the Australians, would lead any further exploitation.

The Corps front was 7000 yards, just on four miles, two miles for each attacking division, a thin concentration compared to Messines or Third Ypres. The day's objective was 9000 yards distant, more than five miles—3000 yards in the first phase with creeping barrage. The artillery line was 'the simplest ever drawn'—dead straight—though it meant that on the right the infantry would start half a mile behind the front. The curtain of shellfire, including much smoke, would be lifted forty times and conclude after 143 minutes. After a pause of 100 minutes the second phase of open warfare would begin. As at

Hamel, the tanks, one to a company, would initially accompany the infantry but would take the lead in the open warfare phase; some of them would transport machine-gunners. Leap-frogging of small formations was not new but Monash used it on a scale rarely if ever before attempted: two divisions side by side would make a double leap-frog, in a highly ingenious scheme to minimize approach distances. The troops were to be drawn up in the reverse order to that in which they would enter battle. The brigades of 2nd and 3rd Divisions which were to carry out the first phase were to come through from behind the brigades of the 4th and 5th allocated for the second and third phases, which would in turn move through. (1st Division, which arrived from Flanders only just before the battle, was in reserve.) Monash recognized that his plan was risky, 'enormously increasing the labour of preparation and the mass of detailed precautions'. It was 'unique in this war or in any other war', he told Bruche. The aim was to aid deep penetration by reducing the stress and fatigue imposed on troops to the irreducible minimum.

Surprise was everything and 'never was a secret better kept'. The main problem was how to bring in the Canadians without the enemy suspecting their presence. Extraordinary measures were taken to delay informing subordinate commanders of what was in store until the last possible day. But by about 4 or 5 August, such was the movement that it was obvious what was afoot. A few Australians were captured in a raid and nearly three hundred English troops were rounded up in a German counter-attack at Morlancourt—remarkably, the enemy learned nothing from them. Visual observation from the Australian front line was discouraged; instead, aerial photographs and local area-maps were distributed in huge numbers. 'It was inspiriting to me to see', wrote Monash, '... numerous small groups of men gathered around their sergeant or corporal, eagerly discussing these maps and the photographs'. A new system of calibration of guns enabled doing away with 'registration' fire: thus the enemy had no warning of the vast number of guns concentrated. Monash delighted in a 'modest little stratagem' whereby his batteries 'methodically engaged' deserted enemy gun positions, knowing very well the detailed positioning of their artillery. As at Hamel, every morning before dawn the noisy bombers promenaded in preparation for the night when the tanks would approach the front. The enemy seemed still to suspect nothing, though the extent of his gas-shelling was worrying; if it became a deluge, it was to be smothered by full artillery attack on gun positions. Monash's main fear was of a withdrawal by the enemy to a prepared position, which would wreck the plan of battle.*

* No attempt has been made to cover the full extent of the battle plan. To appreciate its magnitude, complexity and ingenuity the reader needs to consult chs 5-6 of Monash's *Australian Victories*.

Monash knew there was likely to be trouble on his left flank, north of the Somme, where already there was desperate fighting. Under pressure from Monash, Rawlinson had told Lieut-General Butler of III British Corps that he had to keep attacking until he captured Chipilly Spur. Monash warned MacLagan on the 6th to prepare a defensive flank in case Chipilly remained in enemy hands. On the morning of the 7th he issued his prophetic message to the A.I.F.:

> TO THE SOLDIERS OF THE AUSTRALIAN ARMY CORPS.
> For the first time in the history of this Corps, all five Australian divisions will tomorrow engage in the largest and most important battle operation ever undertaken by the Corps.
> They will be supported by an exceptionally powerful artillery, and by tanks and aeroplanes on a scale never previously attempted. The full resources of our sister Dominion, the Canadian Corps, will also operate on our right, while two British divisions will guard our left flank....
> Because of the completeness of our plans and dispositions, of the magnitude of the operations, of the number of troops employed, and of the depth to which we intend to overrun the enemy's positions, this battle will be one of the most memorable of the whole war; and there can be no doubt that, by capturing our objectives, we shall inflict blows upon the enemy which will make him stagger, and will bring the end appreciably nearer.
> I entertain no sort of doubt that every Australian soldier will worthily rise to so great an occasion, and that every man, imbued with the spirit of victory, will, in spite of every difficulty that may confront him, be animated by no other resolve than grim determination to see through to a clean finish, whatever his task may be.
> The work to be done to-morrow will perhaps make heavy demands upon the endurance and staying powers of many of you; but I am confident that ... every man will carry on to the utmost of his powers until his goal is won; for the sake of AUSTRALIA, the Empire and our cause.
> I earnestly wish every soldier of the Corps the best of good fortune, and a glorious and decisive victory, the story of which will re-echo throughout the world, and will live for ever in the history of our home land.

The message was well received. As Bean said, 'the men felt that, whatever might be in front, all was right behind them'. It was a rare occurrence in that war.

We must allow Monash himself to describe the opening of the battle of Amiens:

> A strange and ominous quiet pervaded the scene: it was only when the explosion of a stray enemy shell would cause hundreds of heads to peer out from trenches, gun-pits, and underground shelters, that

one became aware that the whole country was really packed thick with a teeming population carefully hidden away....

Zero hour was fixed for twenty minutes past four. ... In black darkness, 100,000 infantry, deployed over twelve miles of front, are standing grimly, silently, expectantly, in readiness to advance, or are already crawling stealthily forward to get within eighty yards of the line on which the barrage will fall; all feel to make sure that their bayonets are tightly locked, or to set their steel helmets firmly on their heads; company and platoon commanders, their whistles ready to hand, are nervously glancing at their luminous watches, waiting for minute after minute to go by—and giving a last look over their commands—ensuring that their runners are by their sides, their observers alert, and that the officers detailed to control direction have their compasses set and ready. Carrying-parties shoulder their burdens, and adjust the straps; Pioneers grasp their picks and shovels; Engineers take up their stores of explosives and primers and fuses; machine- and Lewis-gunners whisper for the last time to the carriers of their magazine and belt boxes to be sure and follow up. The Stokes-mortar carrier slings his heavy load, and his loading numbers fumble to see that their haversacks of cartridges are handy. Overhead drone the aeroplanes, and from the rear, in swelling chorus, the buzzing and clamour of the tanks grows every moment louder and louder. Scores of telegraph operators sit by their instruments with their message forms and registers ready to hand, bracing themselves for the rush of signal traffic which will set in a few moments later; dozens of staff officers spread their maps in readiness, to record with coloured pencils the stream of expected information. In hundreds of pits, the guns are already run up, loaded and laid on their opening lines of fire; the sergeant is checking the range for the last time; the layer stands silently with the lanyard in his hand. The section officer, watch on wrist, counts the last seconds: "A minute to go"—"Thirty seconds"—"Ten seconds"—"Fire."

And suddenly, with a mighty roar, more than a thousand guns begin the symphony. A great illumination lights up the eastern horizon; and instantly the whole complex organization, extending far back to areas almost beyond earshot of the guns, begins to move forward; every man, every unit, every vehicle and every tank on their appointed tasks and to their designated goals, sweeping onward relentlessly and irresistibly....

The artillery barrage dominates the battle, and the landscape. The field is speedily covered with a cloak of dust, and smoke and spume....

Monash had asked Major Walter Berry to call him before 4 a.m. They paced up and down the gravel drive at Bertangles, Monash from time to time looking at his watch. At 4.15 they stood on the steps, counting off the last minutes until the 'tremendous thump' of the

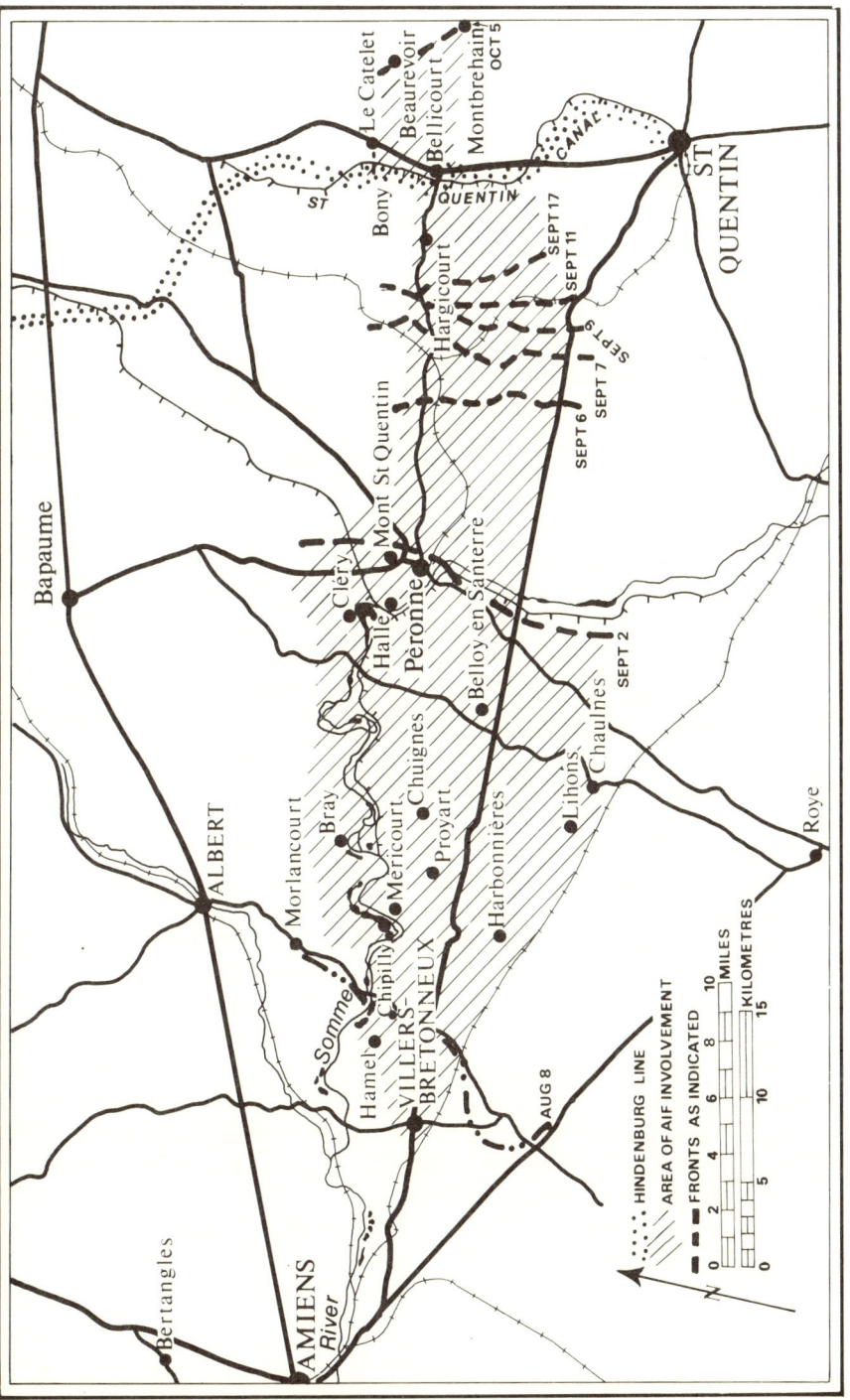

The July–October 1918 Offensive

barrage came. Berry said, ' "Sir, this is a most wonderful day for you." He turned to me and, putting his hand on my shoulder, he said "No, Berry," he said, "it is a very wonderful day for Australia, and history will bear this out".' He slowly climbed the steps and went to his office. There was Blamey, with his feet up, smiling and peacefully smoking a cigar. 'He said "Sir, I have nothing to do, so we can wait while they count thousands of prisoners".' Surprise was virtually complete. A fairly thick fog caused some jumbling of troops, erratic advances and temporary lagging. Otherwise the first phase went entirely to plan. 'The advance was the most bloodless ever made by Australian infantry in a great battle', wrote Bean. At about 8, when the sun broke through, an extraordinary panorama was revealed: groups of infantry and tanks waiting to resume the advance, mobile artillery dashing up to take their positions, pioneers and engineers at work clearing and repairing roads, droves of prisoners bemusedly stumbling back. At 8.20 the second phase began and, although here and there stiff fighting was necessary, the tanks demoralized the enemy and the armoured cars and cavalry began to probe. The leap-frogging went entirely smoothly: to Rawlinson it was a remarkable demonstration of 'the discipline and high organising capacity of the Australian Corps'. The messages coming through to Monash by telephone, telegraph and the pigeon-loft were all favourable; the most useful were those conveyed by the relays of aeroplanes which dropped them close to Bertangles, to be picked up by cyclists and delivered often within ten minutes of writing. Monash himself drafted progress reports and telegraphed to Rawlinson: for example, 'Australian flag hoisted over Harbonnières at midday'. 'The Huns never knew what hit them. [It was] not so much a defeat as a stampede', was a typical comment on the day. However, as feared, there was trouble north of the Somme where the green boys and middle-aged men of III Corps were making little progress in the Chipilly bend. German artillery shooting across the river knocked many tanks out and some astounding artillery duels followed. As planned, MacLagan formed his defensive flank. But it was quite safe to proceed with the third phase, which was completed by 1.30 p.m. Monash had had few important decisions to take: he was soon able to order abandonment of defensive works on the line reached in the first phase. They had taken at least eight thousand prisoners, seized a huge number of guns and, according to Ludendorff, 'documentary material of inestimable value' following capture of a corps and a divisional headquarters. Australian casualties that day were only about two thousand. Rawlinson noted: 'The Canadians have done splendidly and the Aussies even better—I am full of admiration for these two corps'.

The almost perfect co-ordination that day deeply impressed the

A.I.F. And, as Bean wrote in the *Official History*, 'the main responsibility for the organization as they saw it they attributed, with justice, to General Monash'. Bruche saw him in the evening and congratulated him, 'but he as usual in his quiet way smiled and said "Yes, it's been a wonderful day, Julius, it's been wonderful," and so on, but not at all in a conceited sort of way'.

Hindenburg described 8 August as 'our first great disaster from which there could be no recovery'. Ludendorff called it 'the black day of the German army'. It was the most sweeping advance in a day that the Allies had enjoyed on the Western Front; everyone was congratulating everyone else. But despite Haig's intentions it was not immediately exploited. There was virtually nothing ahead of the Australians after about 11 a.m., but the battle had been planned by Army as a set-piece: the objectives gained were to be fortified. At the time Bean was angry with Monash and in the *Official History* judged that the opportunity for unopposed advance could have been snatched if brigades and battalions had been allowed discretion to exploit. Monash was, of course, under Rawlinson's orders and, as we have seen, the tentative decision had been made to exploit on the Canadian front. Monash had probably not been prepared to urge further immediate exploitation on Rawlinson, as he was so aware of the threat on his left flank. And like everyone else he had not expected the extent and ease of the success. A few weeks later he privately confessed that he had 'had no idea how far-reaching and decisive' the operations beginning that day would be. By noon he had warned his divisional commanders that advance the following day would probably be on the southern flank. After Rawlinson told him that the attack would be south-east towards Lihons and Roye and that the Australians would form a defensive flank for the Canadians, he worked on a plan which he forwarded to the divisions that evening, but he was disappointed: he had hoped to be allowed to drive on due east into the great bend of the Somme in open-warfare formation, push the enemy back six or seven miles and force him to make his line on the devastated battle-ground of 1915 and 1916.

The successful attack on Lihons from the 9th to the 11th required heavy fighting, for the Germans had reorganized very efficiently. Monash had planned for an advance in three stages with strong tank and artillery support. Glasgow's recently arrived 1st Division was to make the main attack along the railway next to the Canadians, but they had not arrived when the Canadians were preparing to move at 11 a.m. Elliott's 15th Brigade, nearest to the Canadians, filled the breach and, though it had a rough time, completed the first stage before 1st Division arrived about 2 p.m. On their left 2nd Division—also late—was relieving the 5th; between them 1st and 2nd Divisions broadly completed the second stage against patchy resistance but at considerable cost. Moreover most of the tanks had been knocked out; the Tank Corps' contribution had almost ended for the time being. The attacks had been poorly co-ordinated. Since the Canadians were setting the start-time, Monash had been forced to delegate responsibility for liaison between the Australian divisions and with the Canadians to his divisional commanders. The eventual arrangements were hurried and faulty.

On learning that Currie would attack again at 8 a.m. on the 10th, Monash ordered 1st Division to begin on the third stage at the same hour; there was no tank support but there would be a barrage. They were moving now into the old battlefield. Again co-ordination was faulty: the Canadian warning that they had to delay went astray. There was solid fighting in the next twenty-four hours and heavy casualties were suffered, but despite German counter-attacks Lihons was taken. Bean in the *Official History* sums up the Lihons operation as 'a classic example of how not to follow a great attack'. Fourth Army primarily, and the Australian and Canadian corps commanders and staffs, were all to blame for hasty planning and inadequate communications—all were unprepared for the novel requirements of open warfare. The transition in planning from a battle with the limited objective of freeing Amiens and its railway to a far-reaching advance had never properly been made.

Monash had been concentrating on his left flank. In order to remove the threat from Chipilly, he had persuaded Rawlinson on the 9th to allow him to operate on the north bank, so that he found himself where he 'had so strongly desired to be from the first, namely, astride of the Somme Valley'. He moved 13th Brigade across, but the Chipilly spur had already been captured by an English regiment led by a small patrol from the 1st Battalion, A.I.F. MacLagan was able to withdraw his defensive flank. At 11.30 a.m. on the 10th Monash conferred with Gellibrand, MacLagan, McNicoll and other brigadiers and laid down a bold plan: 'The German is in a condition of great confusion, and we have only to hit him without warning and roll him up'. Monash had an eye to the terrain—the Somme here flowed in a series of tortuous U-shaped bends; drawing cordons across two bends would surround the enemy. 13th Brigade would attack north of the river that night, and 10th Brigade south, both assisted by tanks whose noise might panic the enemy; this was only the second attempt anywhere to use tanks by night. Monash instructed the brigadiers directly. North of the river the plan worked excellently: the enemy did panic, though most of his troops escaped. Brigadier-General S. C. E. Herring of 13th Brigade left an account of his conference with Monash who had already—movements were so urgent—settled the times for Herring's conference with his commanding officers and for the action. He asked Herring how he proposed to attack, broadly agreed with the proposals and went on to discuss how the tanks and artillery might best be used. 'The best of luck, Herring', he concluded. It was very different south of the river near Proyart. Gellibrand and McNicoll believed the plan to be feasible, but many battalion and tank officers were gravely concerned. The attack was entirely repulsed. The enemy was prepared, made an aerial bombing attack, severely damaged the tanks with artillery and anti-tank guns, and covered the vital crossroads with guns and heavy machine-guns. The 37th Battalion, sometimes unfortunate in its dealings with Monash, suffered over one hundred casualties. In 1936 the battalion historian condemned the unnamed general responsible as a fool. It was a temporary setback, for the enemy was doubly outflanked. In the next two days he was harried beyond Méricourt and Proyart and the objectives set for the Corps on the 9th were all gained.

Two astonishing days of pride followed. On the morning of the 11th, John wrote to Vic:

> Quite early I had a call from Mr. Winston Churchill, Minister of Munitions, and at 11 o'clock . . . a call from Field Marshal Sir Douglas Haig, who came formally to thank me for the work done. He brought with him the Chief of the General Staff, Sir Henry Lawrence, and . . . I received a further call from General Sir Julian Byng, the Commander of the British 3rd Army. The Chief thereupon seized the opportunity to have a conference with General Byng on certain contemplated operations and would not hear of my withdrawing, so that I was present during the whole conference and was frequently asked for my opinion.
>
> I had, earlier in the morning, arranged to meet my own five Divisional Commanders at Villers Bretonneux . . . at 2.30 p.m. and I mentioned the fact to the Commander-in-Chief. He said at once that he would very much like to come up, so as to be able to meet [them] personally. . . .
>
> About noon, Sir Henry Rawlinson . . . rang me up to say that there had been important developments and that Marshal Foch was coming up this afternoon to give fresh orders about the tactical policy of the next few days. . . . I told him at once about the arrangements . . . and he at once said that . . . he would arrange for his own Army Conference to be at Villers Bretonneux also at 3 o'clock. . . .
>
> In due course, I . . . selected a place on the western outskirts of the town, suitable for the Conference, under a bunch of trees. All around was a scene of the greatest activity. On one side of the main road was a large wired-in prisoners cage, in which there were over 3000 Boche prisoners, who had been captured during the last twenty-four hours. . . . An immense stream of traffic was pouring up the road towards the Front. . . . the first railway train which had

succeeded in getting through Amiens since the battle was actually steaming through the cutting at 2.30.

At the appointed hour, my five Divisional Commanders [arrived]. We had scarcely assembled and sat down with our General Staffs, when another car drove up, bringing General Sir Henry Wilson. ... Shortly after came the Commander-in-Chief. ... The Field Marshal made a little speech to us and was very complimentary to me, saying that, as always, my plan was perfectly worked out and deserving of the greatest credit, etc.

In the middle of it all, arrived Sir Henry Rawlinson for *his* Conference. ... There followed, in quick succession, Lieut.-General Sir Arthur Currie, commanding the Canadian Corps, Lieut.-General Kavanagh, commanding the Cavalry Corps, Lieut.-General Sir A. J. Godley, temporarily commanding the III Corps, Major-General Elles, commanding the Tank Corps, and Major-General Charlton, commanding the 5th Brigade Royal Air Force. ...

The Commander-in-Chief particularly insisted that our Conference was not to be delayed in any way and so we all squatted down on the grass, while great maps were spread out and Rawlinson commenced to expound the situation and ask for our opinions.

We had scarcely started when still three more motorcars arrived, out of which hopped Monsieur Clemenceau, . . . Marshal Foch, and the French Minister for Finance. This completed the gathering, met literally, *by pure chance* on the actual battlefield and on a site which will live forever in Australian history. ...

Of course there was no thought of serious work or discussion for some twenty minutes, while everybody was being presented to everybody else, and I was personally, naturally—with General Currie—the leading figure in the show, for everybody was highly complimentary and marvelled at the completeness of our success.

There was rather too much mutual congratulation that week. According to Blamey, when Haig met the Australian generals he 'uttered a few words of thanks and said, "You do not know what the Australians and Canadians have done for the British Empire in these days." He opened his mouth to continue, and halted. The tears rolled down his cheeks. A dramatic pause, and we all quickly filed out'. Monash presumably considered such weakness should not be mentioned.

Next day the King invested him with his knighthood. Birdwood had arranged it. With a bare twenty-four hours' notice Monash gathered a guard of honour of six hundred men to line the long Bertangles drive. 'An imposing and varied collection of war trophies' was dragged in from the battlefield to the chateau's quadrangle. The King inspected the guard and the troops, had a few words with each of the divisional commanders, then proceeded to invest Monash. He examined the battle trophies and departed; the whole ceremony had taken only half an hour. Monash had carefully arranged for photographers and film cameramen to record the occasion for posterity.

The ceremony had not gone entirely smoothly. After the King had tapped Monash on one shoulder he had hurriedly to wag his sword to the other when Monash mistakenly began to rise—and some of the onlookers laughed. Then, when the King was leaving in his car, Monash after farewelling him called on the troops down the drive to give 'Three cheers for his Majesty'—to which there was little response. 'Come on!'— Monash tried again—but the cheers were as ragged as before. Drivers and other troops had been worked hard in hauling the German guns to Bertangles and could see little point to the occasion. Bean angered Moss and Simonson by telling them that it was a lot of nonsense. When Monash later showed Murdoch a photograph, he said 'Bean kindly arranged for it to be taken—I did not know anything about it of course'. Bean commented: 'The old poser! Well—there are many like him and he is a most capable man'.

The intention was to launch another major attack on the 15th or 16th on the Roye-Chaulnes line; the Canadians and French would lead, with the Australians making a flank. Monash planned his dispositions accordingly, but the battle was called off. Both the French and the Canadians feared the consequences: as Monash said, 'the possibility of further cheap exploitation of the success of 8 August had come to an end'. The Canadians were transferred to their home ground near Arras and the French moved in on the Australian right. Currie made his bluff farewell:

> It is a pleasure for me to say, Monash, that there are no troops who have given us as loyal and effective support as the Australians, and I am sure I speak for all Canadians when I say that we would like to finish the war fighting side by side with you.

The A.I.F. had a week's breathing-space, which it occupied with peaceful penetration, forcing outposts back closer to the real line of resistance. On the 13th, Corps headquarters advanced to Glisy and Monash visited all his divisional generals; on the 15th he held a conference with them. He was carrying through some basic reorganization. The Australian front, having expanded to the north of the river and at an angle along the railway to the south, had grown to 16 000 yards—far too great for adequate resting of troops. Monash asked Rawlinson either to shorten his front or to expand his resources and was given a British division as a reserve. He was already in charge, north of the river, of an American regiment and set up there a Liaison Force based on 13th Brigade. He gave the command to Brigadier-General Wisdom and had to withstand an indignant protest from Brand. Thus the Corps had expanded virtually to seven divisions, and indeed a little later briefly to eight, almost the size of an army.

During this week Monash shuffled his divisions carefully. It was natural for some units to believe they had been worked harder than others; the 4th Division, especially, considered it had recently done more than its share and Monash knew that in his old 4th Brigade there was mutinous talk.

The decisions which had to be given regarding the times and alterations of these divisional reliefs became from now on really a basic importance, and affected the main framework of the whole of my future plans. It was no longer merely a question of earmarking certain divisions for a specified single operation; but of planning, many days ahead, the rotation in which the divisions were to be employed in a continuous series of operations. . . .
 . . . Each division had to be kept employed until the last ounce of effort consistent with speedy recovery, had been yielded, and each division had to rest a sufficient time to enable it fully to recover its spirit and tone, and yet had to be ready by the time it was wanted.

It was one of Monash's particular points of pride that, until the very end, the complicated divisional reliefs were 'carried out with precision, freedom from iritating hitches, and a minimum of stress on the troops', and that buses were usually found to meet them when they were near exhaustion.

On 19 August Rawlinson told Monash the plans for the next phase: on the 21st, Third Army would strike at last, north of Albert (General Byng and Haig on the 11th had discussed with Monash the methods he had used on the 8th); on the 22nd, III Corps next to them would push forward north of the Somme assisted by the 3rd Division; and on the 23rd there would be a general offensive on a front of 33 miles covering most of the Third and Fourth Army fronts. The Australian front south of the Somme would be shortened to 7000 yards.

Third Army did very well on the 21st. On the 22nd Gellibrand used the 9th Brigade in support of III Corps, aiming ultimately to take Bray. All went fairly well that morning and Albert was taken, but in the afternoon the Germans counter-attacked successfully north of 3rd Division. Monash ordered abandonment of any attack on Bray that day or the next. But the battle of Chuignes on the 23rd, which aimed to push the enemy back to the Somme where it bent south, was brilliantly successful. Two brigades of Glasgow's 1st Division were to attack along the river in a three-phase operation, while a brigade of the 32nd British Division was to capture the village of Herleville, with full artillery, tank and air support. Monash's battle conference on the 21st was prolonged, for both the 1st and 32nd Divisions were unfamiliar with his special methods, were strangers to each other and, some of them, to Corps staff, and the tactics of Hamel and 8 August 'had to be re-opened and elucidated'. The barrage fell at 4.45 a.m. and 'one of the hardest blows ever struck by Australian troops' was thrown. By dusk the objective was won and nearly all the ground intended for exploitation, over most difficult country against stern resistance, at a cost to 1st Division of about one thousand casualties; it had taken at least two thousand prisoners. Monash had been worried about the difficulty of the third phase, especially when there was some delay, but—'I had the satisfaction that night of contemplating a victory far greater than I had calculated upon'. 3rd Division was enabled to take Bray that night. Monash took huge delight in the capture of an immense naval gun which had been bombarding Amiens—the 'largest single trophy' won during the war, he claimed. He began to wonder—the prisoners he saw were so dispirited—whether the next few weeks might not prove to be decisive.

Monash saw his task now as being to drive the enemy back over the Somme near Péronne. 3rd Division pressed on steadily north of the river and the engineers and pioneers restoring the bridges and crossings followed close behind—which was to be of critical importance a week later. Twice, orders transmitted by Monash from Army to 3rd Division to hold back and let III Corps take the lead were too late; vital advances had already been made. Monash now withdrew 1st and 4th Divisions; at the very end of their stint they suffered badly from gas-shelling. They were intended to have a good rest and indeed had three weeks, but Monash had them in mind for a major future task which he said he felt intuitively rather than by any reasoning. On the 25th and 26th he conferred with Rosenthal of the 2nd and Hobbs of the 5th who were taking over, and with Gellibrand, and planned an attack on the 27th with full artillery support. But Haig and Rawlinson ordered him to confine himself to aggressive patrols; First and Third Armies were attacking on the 26th. Monash could understand their view: Fourth Army had done its job, it had drawn the German reserves, it had hardly any tanks left, there was no great strategic urgency to force evacuation of the Somme bend. But it is also likely that Haig and Rawlinson wanted to minimize Australian casualties, both for fear of Billy Hughes and to keep the Corps as strong as possible for a future major action.

Monash was displeased: he considered they were underestimating the Australian 'reserve of striking power', with the enemy on the run. So he began a private war, falling back on his orders to keep in touch with the enemy and using them to justify continual pressure and infiltration while avoiding dangerous assaults. There followed from the 27th to the 29th 'a merry and exciting three days of pursuit': the enemy was harried all the way, leaving behind huge quantities of stores. The 3rd Division north, and the 2nd, 5th and 32nd British south of the river drove on towards the big bend across the desolate maze of the 1916 battlefield. Hundreds of prisoners were captured daily. Monash was proud of two innovations in gunnery in which Hobbs and

Rosenthal, former gunners, entirely concurred against the textbooks. One-fifth of shells were smoke, thus blinding the resolute German machine-gunners, and guns were detached to come under infantry control in order to engage machine-guns directly. The main difficulty was to repair the roads enough for the heavy artillery to be brought up. Indeed the rate of advance depended, especially for supply, on road repair as much as enemy resistance. At any one time, only three brigades were employed—one-sixth of Monash's infantry strength.

It was a matter of time. Monash saw a great opportunity if he could cross the river quickly enough. They reached it on the 29th. On the 28th and 29th he was conferring with the divisional commanders, and very likely the bold Rosenthal spurred him on. All his previous major operations had been set-pieces such as Messines and Broodseinde, when there had been little he could do during the action: the temptation was now irresistible to prove himself in a fluid battle, with a great prize to be won, in a purely Australian operation. But he had to gain Rawlinson's permission: on the 30th they and Montgomery and Blamey conferred at length. According to Monash, the final outcome was Rawlinson saying 'And so you think you're going to take Mont St Quentin with three battalions! What presumption! However, I don't think I ought to stop you! So, go ahead and try!—and I wish you luck!'

'The strategic object in view', wrote Monash, 'was to make the line of the Somme useless to the enemy as a defensive line, and thereby render probable his immediate further enforced retreat to the Hindenburg Line'. The objective was the ridge to the east of the river, and first the dominating hill of Mont St Quentin with its slopes almost bare of cover; a mile to the south lay Péronne, a famous fortress. A prerequisite was further advance by 3rd Division north of the river and round the bend past Cléry. They were driven hard, day after day, especially 10th Brigade on the 29th and 30th. The main problem was how the 2nd and 5th Divisions were to cross the Somme canal and the marshes beyond. In his original plan of the 28th Monash envisaged direct crossings about Brie and Halle and a frontal attack on Mont St Quentin. Next day, accepting that there was little chance that any of the bridges would survive, he decided to send both the divisions to cross near the bend behind the 3rd Division front and to attack Mont St Quentin and Péronne from the north through Cléry, a plan which had been 'vaguely forming' in his mind ever since he had been given control north of the river. 32nd Division, as a conjuring trick, would draw as much attention to itself as possible, by demonstrating noisily along the river opposite Péronne. One junior officer at Corps believes to this day that Monash never knew how near-run a matter it was of getting the ammunition up through the limping French railway system and truck convoys. It might have been a disaster: the ammunition arrived only with a couple of hours to spare.

On the night of the 30th the complicated switch of ground began. Before dawn next morning 5th Brigade of 2nd Division, weary and weakened, without tanks but with massive artillery support and a rum issue for once, faced a daunting task. Amazingly, somehow, they did it, an absurdly small force of a few hundred men against far greater strength in a heavily fortified position. Then and since it has been constantly asked: How was it done? The speed of their rushes (and their yelling), 'according to textbook principles, each section alternately giving its neighbour covering fire', astounded and swamped the outposts; those behind broke and ran; the bombardment had been highly effective. Use of the rifle-grenade, constantly practised, in conjunction with Lewis guns had much to do with it. The battalion commanders, writes Bean, 'could hardly believe their eyes as the prisoners flooded through'. By 8 a.m. Monash had telephoned to Rawlinson that a footing high up on Mont St Quentin had been won.*

They were not yet on top of Mont St Quentin. 5th Brigade was two miles out on its own and had to beat off several counter-attacks. Monash hurried in 6th Brigade in support and the 7th behind them, and called next on 14th Brigade of 5th Division to come in on the right and attack Péronne, pushing them all round as quickly as possible. But it took ten hours, until dusk, for 14th Brigade to march the seven miles round across the river; Monash considered Hobbs and Brigadier-General Stewart should have driven them much harder. Hobbs that afternoon, backed by his brigadiers, anxiously drew attention to the stress on his troops: 'I was compelled to harden my heart', Monash later wrote, 'and to insist that it was imperative to recognize a great opportunity and to seize it unflinchingly'. Meanwhile 3rd Division pushed ahead to safeguard 5th Brigade's left; Monash had told Gellibrand that 'casualties no longer matter'. He could not continue to exercise close control; the battle now was largely to be run by the brigadiers and battalion commanders whose conferences that night lasted far into the small hours. Presumably, however, their plan of attack for the morning was referred to Monash and approved. There was murderous fighting next day, but the mount was entirely taken.

---

* According to one version, the conversation went:
  'By the way, we are on the top of Mont St Quentin.'
  'I don't believe it.'
  'Come and see.'
  'You have altered the whole course of the war.'
Another version has it that Rawlinson said, 'You spoiled a damn good battle'.
  Both are likely to have been blown-up versions of what Monash told pressmen; according to the Official Historian, Montgomery was the first to tell Rawlinson.

So was most of Péronne, but it was lost again; Monash and Blamey were upset, believing the Germans should have been chased right through the town. It was entirely taken next morning. By the 3rd it was all over, and the Germans were retreating to the Hindenburg line, fourteen miles back.

It had been an exceedingly risky enterprise, Monash knew.

> In the absence of properly co-ordinated action, there was every chance of confusion, and cross purposes. . . . But the only alternative was to do nothing and attempt nothing. That would have been the worst of bad generalship.

It was brought off, Monash concluded, 'firstly and chiefly' because of the 'wonderful gallantry of the men who participated', and because of the rapidity and 'sheer daring' of the plan. Haig was staggered: he had intended a quite different approach to turning the German line on the Somme. Monash had forced his hand and altered his intention of allowing Fourth Army a quiet time. Rawlinson sometimes referred to it as the finest feat of the war. Writing to Generals Allenby, Cavan and others, he claimed that

> By this bold and successful action . . . the heart was knocked out of the Boche. [It was] not only a tactical victory deserving the highest praise, but it was strategically of first importance, for it broke the Somme line of defence and showed that the enemy had failed to defend successfully . . . a position which was very strong by nature, had been improved by every means which modern engineering skill could devise, and was defended by troops second to none in the German Army.

Bean concluded in the *Official History*: 'Within Australian experience of the Western Front it was the only important fight in which quick, free manoeuvre played a decisive part. It furnishes a complete answer to the comment that Monash was merely a composer of set pieces'. A. J. Smithers remarks:

> If one is tempted to criticize Monash by reason of the things that might have happened, he would be perfectly entitled to reply: "But they did not happen, and I knew that they would not happen. The Australian Corps at this point of the war was an instrument so perfect that it could be trusted to carry out the task I gave it without undue risk. And that is what it did." It demands great hardihood on the part of any man, more than half a century later, to assert that he knows better. . . . If he had no other claim to consideration, Mont St Quentin assures John Monash of a place amongst the great captains.

Monash himself privately considered the capture of Mont St Quentin to have been 'reminiscent of some of the surprise tactics of Stonewall

Jackson, which depended on accurate calculations of time and space and punctual execution of orders by all concerned'. The casualties had been slightly over three thousand.*

The chase went on, far along the front now, with the Australians in the van. For Monash the problems of getting the railhead up, restoring bridges and crossings, and road repair were paramount. The weary 2nd and 5th Divisions, and after a few days 3rd Division again relieving the 2nd, pressed hard on the enemy's heels and denied opportunities to devastate the country and salvage supplies. For the first time in the war the Corps Cavalry went into action, cyclists leading the chase. By 7 and 8 September the infantry reached the outer defences of the Hindenburg line, and halted. On the 10th and 11th the 1st and 4th Divisions took over again; after probing they established that the Germans proposed to stand on the main British line of 1917–18 and they proceeded to snatch several tactical strong-points. Meanwhile Fourth Army was reorganized by adding IX Corps on the Australian right, Godley's III Corps remaining on the left. Monash now commanded only the five Australian divisions on a shortened front. Corps headquarters had moved on 31 August to the derelict Méricourt chateau and on 11 September to Belloy-en-Santerre, just short of the Somme, to an uncomfortable former German hutted camp. Monash was frequently out at divisional headquarters and surveyed the lie of the land from vantage points, but neither he nor Blamey considered it necessary to make any close reconnaissance themselves. The prestige of the Australian Corps was now such that they could get from G.H.Q. all the resources they wanted, whereas earlier it had been a matter of 'scrapping and fighting' for everything.

Because of tactical developments the Hindenburg defence system was no longer the impregnable fortress it had been in 1917. Nevertheless the four and a half miles deep-trench system, the warren of underground shelters almost impervious to artillery, and the maze of wiring, based on the barrier of the St Quentin canal, were highly formidable. But the Germans were being hammered now on almost every front and their reserves were committed. The Hindenburg line could not possibly be overrun in one attempt, so Fourth Army proposed a formal assault in two stages. After a preliminary conference on 10 September, on the 13th Rawlinson and his corps commanders, at Monash's headquarters, 'quite informally, over a cup of afternoon tea', planned the preliminary battle. Montgomery—on 'Archie' and 'John' terms with Monash—always fondly remembered 'the Australian teas'. That evening, with Glasgow and MacLagan, Monash defined the start line.

---

* Barrie Pitt, the only military historian I have found who criticizes the operation, as unjustified, bases his argument on a gross mistake about the number of casualties.

With Third Army on the left and First French Army on the right, the front would be seventeen miles, of which the Australians would be responsible for four. Fewer than seven thousand Australians would attack, expecting to drive in more than three miles in three stages, the first two under creeping barrage. Only eight tanks were available. Worried by this and fearful of casualties, Monash adopted the 'amusing' expedient of having dummies constructed and left in full view in order to frighten the enemy; more effectively, he doubled the normal machine-gun resources to provide a horrifically dense barrage. The artillery line was again perfectly straight. At the final Corps conference on the 16th 'we all began to understand each other so well that most of what I had to say could almost be taken for granted'. Zero hour for the battle of Hargicourt was set for 5.20 a.m. on the 18th. It poured with rain, but the men got their hot breakfast and rum.

The first two stages went like clockwork. In addition to the artillery, '256 Vickers guns opened up with a single roar. . . and kept up a steady lift three hundred yards ahead of the infantry'. The old British front line was captured by 10 o'clock against a demoralized enemy. The real Hindenburg outpost line remained a mile ahead. Monash had been cautious about this third exploitation phase; it was not to be considered a definite objective, the wire had not been cut, fresh troops might be waiting for them, an honest attempt was to be made but no desperate measures taken. 1st and 4th Divisions won further glory. By nightfall the 1st had got there, while the 4th, all but exhausted, was 500 yards short. Monash and MacLagan consulted, the artillery was brought up, and at 11 p.m. the last conclusive assault to a commanding position over the canal and the Hindenburg line proper was carried through. Monash had hardly 'dared to hope' that it could be done, and with only 1260 casualties and 4300 prisoners and 76 guns captured (apart from enemy killed and wounded)—'about a record for a major operation', Rawlinson enthused. German officers admitted that their men would no longer face the Australians. And it was a greater victory than had been expected, for the captured posts were in fact the chief defensive position of the Hindenburg line. The British on either side had done well, but had to fight hard for several days more to catch up. When, the previous day, Monash had told what was in store, Bean had judged it an 'extensive ambitious plan for troops as worn as these . . . and I think that he can scarcely hope that the exploitation phase will succeed'. He was entirely surprised:

> If this attack had gone against them, we should all, I expect, be ready to blame the General for putting on the Corps a task which was too heavy for it. As it was, he was clearly right in his estimate—that the Germans in front of us were so broken that . . . Infantry would not stand and face our men.

It was one of the very best days the Corps had ever had, he concluded. Indeed, Hargicourt was a triumph which almost rivalled Mont St Quentin. The 1st and 4th Divisions, unknowingly, now marched out of the war, their job superbly done.

During late August and September Monash successfully campaigned for better publicity for the A.I.F. in the British press. He had switched the emphasis of his messages to the troops to an appeal to the prestige of the A.I.F. rather than to patriotism, and circulated news sheets of press extracts. The A.I.F., however, was hardly mentioned in reports of the great successes of *British* (ambiguous word) troops on 8 August: G.H.Q. was concerned to combat enemy propaganda that Lloyd George was 'climbing to victory over the corpses of Canadians and Australians and putting them in wherever the fighting has been hottest' (as Monash put the problem). The A.I.F. reaction was angry. Bean and Murdoch strongly held that Australia could not afford to forgo the credit, that 'how far we put the civilised world under an obligation to us' must be driven home, that Australia's reputation in the United States might someday be a matter of life and death. Hughes, too, was angry, and concerned that Australia should have as strong as possible a voice at the peace settlement. Monash was primarily concerned about the effect on morale of the troops, and protested to Wilson and Rawlinson. He told them plainly that Australians were 'by nature and intellect, sportsmen and that they would refuse to go on playing any game in which their scores were not put up on the scoring board'. He was not a sporting man and his idiom was slightly astray; Bean, a great public school man, thought the statement itself was rather unsportsmanlike. But the increased publicity in September was remarkable, after three press parties had been conducted round the Australian front. Sir Arthur Conan Doyle was one visitor who fell to the Monash charm:

> The men were great ... but greatest of all perhaps was their Commander, ... a rare compelling personality, whose dark flashing eyes and swarthy face might have seemed more in keeping with some Asiatic conqueror than with the prosaic associations of the British Army.

The journalist Arthur O'Connor described Monash as in appearance

> somewhat rugged. His broad shoulders and deep chest are surmounted by a big head, thickly covered with tawny-grey hair, brown eyes, alert yet kindly, moderately heavy moustache, and strong mouth. ... He speaks quietly, deliberately, unhesitatingly. ... a *strong man* ... intellectual, original, democratic ... ruthless.

Throughout September Monash had several serious problems, apart from military operations. Hughes, since his arrival in June, had been shaken by Lloyd George's lack of confidence in the British high command and believed that the British government, desperately worried by shortage of manpower, was withholding troops from the field until 1919 when the Americans could be expected to sweep all before them. He consequently was highly aware of the danger of the A.I.F. being overworked and of the need to conserve it, and demanded power of veto over its future use. If Haig knew of this, he ignored it, for the first Hughes knew of the 8 August offensive was in War Cabinet that day. He held his hand for some weeks during the glorious offensive but, some time in September, instructed Monash that the Corps must be withdrawn from all action by early October. According to Bean, Monash

> demurred that the needs of the campaign might render it impossible to withdraw the Corps when the weather broke.... The Prime Minister's reply was that the Corps must be out of the line by the date mentioned and that General Monash's position would depend upon this. There is evidence that Mr. Hughes at this time, although sure of the Australian Government's approval of his aims was not always certain whether it would support the methods, and even feared that Monash by cabling to Australia might have him overruled.

The alleged encounter may have occurred between 13 and 16 September when Hughes was visiting the Corps. Yet all the indications are that Monash and Rawlinson had already agreed that after Hargicourt the Corps could stand only one more battle, at the end of September. Certainly, Murdoch was acting as Hughes's runner: in later years Monash recalled he 'was chasing me round promising hell if I didn't give leave and rest'.

Hughes sprang a most embarrassing coup by ordering the immediate return to Australia on two months leave of six thousand of the original Anzacs. He did not consult A.I.F. Headquarters for fear the generals would upset his plan. Birdwood was ordered by G.H.Q. on 12 September to send off eight hundred men immediately. The trouble was that they were nearly all from 1st and 4th Divisions which were about to go into action. Monash protested: he was upset not merely because of the damage to the relevant battalions but because selection had to be hurried, the men could not get at their belongings, and no proper farewells could be made. He protested to Hughes, but he had to comply. In the end only 450 of the 800 were drawn from the two divisions about to go into action. Monash's considered reaction was, in order to protect the Corps, to inform Fourth Army that the 1st and 4th Divisions had been weakened and would probably have to be relieved immediately after fighting at Hargicourt on the 18th, and that rather than recall two other divisions from rest, it was desirable to gain the services of

Monash, May 1918

Presenting a decoration

ertangles chateau, 11 August 1918

The 'dubbing'

Monash at Menton, March 1917 or March 1918

Senior officers, Corps staff, late 1918: Blamey is behind Monash

two American divisions. Hughes's other intention, which he rashly began to announce to the troops, was that they should winter in the south of France or in Italy.

On 21 September, as an extreme case of stress, occurred the saddest incident in the history of the First A.I.F. Following Hargicourt, III Corps was attempting to advance its front to level with the Australian line. After two unsuccessful days Butler asked Monash to assist by taking over 500 yards of the front. Monash consented. 1st Brigade was just coming out of the line but, knowing the ground, they had to be called on. 119 men of the 1st Battalion refused to move: they considered it unfair, they had too often had to do the job when the Tommies failed— they had lost many of their officers and did not realize the task was relatively minor. The rest of the battalion carried the action—their last of the war—through successfully. Mutiny, even a 'fatigue mutiny' such as this, was technically punishable by death. All but one of the 119 were convicted, instead, of desertion, sentenced to up to ten years imprisonment on Dartmoor, and kept under close arrest. But Monash did not confirm the sentences and eventually Hobbs, when Corps commander, pardoned the men.*

Late in August the War Office moved to enforce on the A.I.F. the ruling that battalions must be reduced to three to a brigade. Monash fought hard against the order, chiefly by procrastinating. He did not consider reduced numbers was a serious problem: 'I welcome any pretext to take the fewest possible number of men into action. So long as they have 30 Lewis guns [per battalion] it doesn't matter very much'. He knew how bitterly the men of battalions to be disbanded would react, feared the effects on morale, and argued optimistically that, as in previous years, the battalions would recuperate over the winter. He asked to be given discretion to disband particular battalions only as special cases. He and Birdwood agreed that none of the battalions of the original four brigades would be touched, a compromise which may largely have satisfied him. A few days later the instruction came to send the original Anzacs on leave, which greatly weakened Monash's case, then on 19 September a peremptory order to disband eight battalions forthwith. He and the divisional commanders decided which battalions would be broken up.

---

* After the Armistice, probably at the conference of senior officers late in November, Monash and Hobbs suggested to Glasgow that he remit the sentences. An orthodox disciplinarian, Glasgow refused to do so and Monash gave way. Glasgow told Bean that he considered Monash showed 'moral cowardice' in not enforcing his opinion. The incident is suggestive in showing how some admirable but strait-laced generals like Glasgow found Monash difficult to understand when he was taking a broad view of situations. Monash and Hobbs probably had good reasons for not acting themselves at that moment. Glasgow similarly believed Monash did not act straightforwardly enough over disbandment of the battalions.

Seven of the eight battalions went on strike after their officers had obeyed orders. Lieut-Colonel Story of the 37th had to be sacked when, in his bitterness, he lost his head. All the battalions stated their willingness to fight, elected their own officers who kept strict discipline, and ignored appeals by their generals, brigadiers and colonels. Monash met delegates from the 37th, and told them 'I have done a thing unprecedented in military annals in holding an informal conference such as this, but I realise that the A.I.F. is different from any other army in the world'. But he quietly made it clear that while there would be no arrests, dispersal would inevitably proceed and the battalion would die with a stigma attached to it. But the rebel battalions stood firm, the pending major operations were threatened, and the generals, fearing a sympathetic strike by other battalions, had to give way. After a conference on the 25th between Birdwood, Monash and the divisional commanders, Rawlinson and Haig were asked to allow another fortnight, and agreed.

It had been an act of folly by the high command to attempt such disruption while operations were in train, which Monash had to resist. It placed him in a very difficult situation, but he was not displeased by the outcome. For in the end, the battalions were disbanded only after the A.I.F.'s fighting was over. Monash may even, as he claimed to Murdoch a few months later, have been playing a double game— attempting to enforce the disbandments while hoping and expecting that they could not be carried out. But he could not have welcomed such indiscipline and was not in control of events.

At the close of the fighting early in October the disbandments had to be carried out. Monash told the divisional commanders: 'The last thing that any of us desire is that there should be any public scandal, such as would arise from the wholesale arrests of men for disobedience of orders: nor can we afford to have orders, deliberately given, openly defied'. They would proceed indirectly and gradually: the battalions would receive no convalescents or reinforcements; officers and N.C.O.s would be individually transferred, the men would be given a chance to form companies in other battalions. He would proceed 'with as little fuss and strong talk as possible, so that there should be no wounded feelings and no bitterness'. By mid-October only one battalion, the 42nd, still held out. Monash remarked to Blamey: 'I was taking a chance, but it seems to have come off quite well'. After the Armistice he stalled and argued again when Birdwood ordered disbandment of four more battalions.

By September the pressure was telling on him. 'At times, when I feel very tired, I am tempted to hope that it will be the last serious work I shall have to do in my life', he wrote to Springthorpe. On 7 September he unsuccessfully asked Rawlinson for three or four days off in Paris. Blamey, who watched Monash more closely than anyone, recalled that he suffered severely from the strain, and became quite thin with the skin hanging loosely on his face. His characteristic attitude was deep thought: 'With his head carried slightly forward, he would ride in his car for long periods in silence', concentrating. His weight was down to 11 stone 5½ pounds on 26 July. There was no time for his regular walks now, though he was using the dumb-bells in the mornings. But he could relax like a cat, it was said. He still pencil-sketched occasionally: several drawings survive including a comic sketch of Plumer and another of a tin-hatted soldier (copied from the current issue of *Punch*) which he drew during the battle of Hamel. His confidence prevailed during battle; he would not show anxiety. He wrote to Felix Meyer in April:

> I often have to carry on my heavy correspondence, official and personal, in the short interlude between stirring events. It is astonishing how one learns to do a number of things simultaneously, for I have frequently had to keep going with dictated correspondence in the very midst of directing a battle. This isn't, in the least, 'swank', but only the bare truth, and I find that to do so is the very best way of relieving the tension, of filling in the intervals between moments of stress, and of keeping one's mind elastic and one's thinking machinery cool.

The last task was to break the Hindenburg line. It came close to being a disaster. But the strain Monash had been under, the constant distraction of visitors and the worries of the disbandment crisis did not necessarily affect the soundness of his planning. Rawlinson wanted the Australian Corps to take the lead and they had been discussing ways and means. The difficulty was that Monash had only three divisions available. When, at his prompting, Rawlinson offered two American divisions Monash was delighted for they were fresh, at full strength, much larger than British divisions and with many more machine-gunners. Foch and Haig arranged for four successive massive blows along the front, starting on 26 September. Fourth Army's would be the last and most important, on the 29th.

Monash produced his written plan for Rawlinson on the very day of Hargicourt; they had discussed it twenty-four hours before. Next day at an Army conference it was adopted with modifications; in the evening Monash conferred with his divisional commanders. On the 20th he began discussions with Major-General G. W. Read, the American corps commander, and Courage of the Tanks, and daily conferences followed. Monash's basic plan was for the Americans to attack and cross the 6000-yard-long St Quentin Canal tunnel, in effect a bridge; the Australians would exploit, then the British corps on left and right would follow and deploy to north and south. Tanks and a crushing barrage would be employed. He would not attempt to cross the canal itself, as it was too dangerous. Attacking the tunnel involved the Australian Corps side-stepping to the north. Rawlinson enlarged the plan to allow for a direct attack on the canal to the right by IX Corps. It required great tact on both sides for the American corps of nearly fifty thousand men to place itself entirely under Australian control and for Read to retire to the position of an 'interested spectator'. To coach the Americans in Australian practices, Monash established a mission of two hundred officers and non-commissioned officers from the resting divisions, led by MacLagan. It took nearly a week to sidestep the Australian front, placing the American 27th and 30th Divisions in line opposite Bellicourt and Le Catelet.

Rawlinson and Monash were perhaps over-optimistic in their belief in the shattered state of German morale and the probable effects on their front of smashing blows elsewhere. According to Gellibrand, at the conference on the 19th Monash said the operation would be 'more a matter of engineering and organization than of fighting'; Gellibrand asserted that, throughout, Corps considered the enemy defence to be 'little more than a M.G. [machine-gun] bluff'. And the plan had to be modified by an unforeseen check: Rawlinson and Monash had assumed that III Corps would be able to make good the ground it had failed to take on the 18th, but despite repeated assaults it failed, stopping 1000 yards behind the proposed start line for the 29th. Monash wanted to accept the situation and pull back the planned start line, but Rawlinson insisted on the Americans attempting to take the ground on the 27th. At his corps conference on the 23rd Monash expounded their task to the Americans, but was met with such a rain of questions that he spent three hours 'with blackboard and chalk, maps and diagrams . . . in an endeavour to explain methods and reasons, mistakes and remedies, dangers and precautions, procedures and expedients'. He dwelt at length on the fundamental importance of 'mopping up', and in retrospect doubted the efficacy of his message. His conference on the 26th of American and Australian commanders and their staffs, the last he was to hold and a 'heavy strain', was tense and expectant. Haig called in to give encouragement by detailing the other offensives. Gellibrand noted that for once there were no precautionary instructions for any failure.

The preliminary American attack on the 27th seemed at first to go well but by noon there were conflicting reports and by evening the situation was clearly serious. But it was not until the following morning that Monash realized quite how alarming it was. The main problem was that both active and wounded Americans were lying out in front; the Americans next day could not have the support of the barrage on the ground immediately ahead. Monash asked Rawlinson whether a day's delay might be possible and was told it was out of the question in view of other armies' operations, but more tanks were allocated. When Haig visited, according to his diary, he 'found Monash in what he called "a state of despair", Americans not heard of, not mopped up. Told him not a serious matter, he should attack tomorrow morning in force as arranged'. We cannot judge Monash's condition of mind: he may have been in something like a 'state of despair', or the uncharacteristic admission may have been one of his verbal exaggerations, made unguardedly, to possibly the one man to whom he might confess a rare weakness. Be that as it may, he had been compelled to 'gamble on a chance', on the success of the preliminary operation. 'It was contrary to the policy which governed all my previous battle plans, in which *nothing* had been left to chance. . . . It was the only occasion in the campaign on which I was compelled to accept preliminary arrangements which were not such as would absolutely guarantee success.'

For the assault on the 29th Monash commanded some two hundred thousand troops, more than he had ever had in his charge. His thousand guns bombarded for three days before, beginning with the new mustard gas and following with high explosive, including shells with instantaneous fuses which were highly effective in cutting wire. The two assaulting American divisions were to be followed by 3rd and 5th Divisions to exploit. At 5.55 a.m. the monstrous barrage broke out and the Americans went off into the mist and smoke; the Australians marched up behind, light-heartedly, though having to wear gas-masks much of the time. But the Americans on the left were soon in grave trouble from counter-attacking Germans and 3rd Division was quickly involved among them. The Americans on the right had done much better and 5th Division joined them a mile ahead of the 3rd. And, by one of the great feats of British arms during the war, further to the right the canal had already been stormed and crossed by the 46th Division. But on the left most of the tanks had been knocked out and the Americans had gone into the blue. At Corps headquarters the situation remained obscure for much of the day. Eventually Monash and Blamey were led to believe by air-reports that the Americans were on their objective and that relatively few enemy pockets could be holding up 3rd Division, and insisted that they push on. A few hundred yards were gained with great difficulty, and late in the day they were obliquely astride the Bellicourt tunnel, their right well across, their left far back. 5th Division had taken the southern end of the tunnel and the two divisions had made effective tactical contact.

Monash had told the war correspondents that he doubted whether the inexperienced Americans would succeed. When he saw them again on the 30th the first thing he said, according to Bean, was 'Well, you see what I expected might happen has happened. . . . The Americans sold me a pup. . . . They're simply unspeakable'. Blamey had got hold of an American divisional commander and sworn at him like a bullock-driver. Bean concluded in the *Official History* that 'the most brilliant battle plan that Monash ever drew . . . broke down largely through his underestimation of the human element. For the first time since August 8th his attack did not go "according to plan" and the American divisions paid dearly for their first experience'. He and Gellibrand believed that the task given the 27th American Division was far beyond it and perhaps any other division. Yet, what options did Monash have after the failure two days before?

Late in the afternoon of the 29th, Rawlinson, Montgomery, MacLagan and Monash conferred, and scrapped the original plan. The reserve brigades of both A.I.F. divisions would next day attack northwards along the main Hindenburg trench system and capture Bony and the northern end of the tunnel. A telephone conversation, with Gellibrand at 7.22 p.m., has survived, taken down in shorthand:

> Monash: There have been great successes down south and up north [and it] is likely to reduce the amount of opposition. It has been decided to withdraw Americans and push up the 13th Corps and our front will be shortened to a very narrow front of 4000 yards. I have got to put the responsibility on you and the 5th Division of working together to square up the rest of the tunnel up to Le Catelet to get the 13th Corps through there. The really important thing is if you can get on to the knob everything must fall and if 5th Division can get along the railway ridge to the Le Catelet line. . . . Put as many tanks as you can get to go up the Hindenburg line in a body. I will get Hobbs to do the same on the railway spur.
>
> Gellibrand: My real trouble is artillery action in view of possibility of Americans being in this line.
>
> Monash: Exactly so. The question is whether you cannot do without artillery action. We cannot tell where the Americans are; there ought to be no harm in bombarding Bony itself. However you have the artillery in your hands. Work it out. I will not withdraw the Americans so long as they are doing any good but when we can do without them we will. The knob is the key to the whole situation. In view of the success in other parts things will be better tomorrow than today.

The situation on the 30th was ugly and the issue remained in doubt amid desperate and stubborn fighting. It was 'a day of intense effort', Monash wrote, 'slow and methodical hand to hand fighting, in a perfect tangle of trenches . . . but by nightfall the line of the 3rd Division had advanced fully 1000 yards'. Monash and Gellibrand had serious disagreements. Monash objected to the absence of a divisional reserve and demanded its reconstitution. Gellibrand considered the 'peremptory' order caused 'unnecessary fatigue and trouble'. Moreover, he later wrote, 'time and again I was right in my reports and inferences and disbelieved'. At 5.15 by phone, Monash was tetchy: he reprimanded Gellibrand for not reporting loss of tanks, deplored his attacking on such a narrow front, and was surprised that the situation had not been cleaned up. He said Gellibrand was being bluffed and that he was strong enough to force the issue; Gellibrand admitted to his diary that his problem was to 'ginger up' his brigades. Monash ordered a set-piece frontal attack under barrage next day; Gellibrand protested that a flank attack was preferable; Monash later rang back to agree. Gellibrand noted that when Monash called in next day he apologized.

But all went well that day. The Germans were outflanked by IX British Corps on the Australian right and abandoned any hope of holding the tunnel. Bony fell and 3rd and 5th Divisions cleared right up to the Beaurevoir line, the last of the defences. Monash visited his divisional commanders and issued messages of congratulation; his old 3rd Division, in particular, had covered itself in glory.

3rd and 5th Divisions were relieved, as had been arranged with Rawlinson a fortnight before, and the 2nd, after its month's rest, was brought in for the final effort. On 3 October, after suffering severe gas attacks during the night, 5th and 7th Brigades with only 2500 rifles in the line made a frontal attack with barrage before dawn on a wide 6000-yard front. By midday, after stiff fighting they had taken the Beaurevoir line. A captured German officer said: 'You Australians are all bluff. You attack with practically no men and are on top of us before we know where we are'. In the afternoon 2nd Division moved on towards Beaurevoir spur but in their weakened condition were held up; Rosenthal settled for a secure foothold on the heights. It had been 'an astonishing performance . . .', Monash wrote, 'fighting under open and exposed conditions'. Next day the Hindenburg line was finally broken.

2nd Division was to be relieved by the Americans, but they needed another day to come into the line. Monash submitted to one more demand:

> General Rawlinson desired me to retain control of the battle front for one day longer, and . . . to advance our line still farther to the east. I selected as a suitable objective the village of Montbrehain, which stood on a plateau that dominated any further advances.

Most of 6th Brigade were fresh and they and the divisional Pioneers brilliantly carried out a particularly nasty operation, with tank support, suffering some 430 casualties—a severe loss for such a limited gain. The infantry of the First A.I.F. had fought their last battle.

Between 8 August and 5 October A.I.F. casualties were about twenty-four thousand, of whom just over five thousand died. John Terraine writes:

> In that war of 'bloodbaths', of 'murderous offensives', ... this figure of 5,000 dead in sixty days of incessant attack seems all wrong, misplaced, incongruous. Yet there it stands, a reminder for ever that even on the bloodiest fields good training, high morale and sound leadership can procure victory at a price that does not make a mockery of the word.

Over the same period, though the A.I.F. was often the spearhead, British and French casualties were relatively far higher. Monash maintained that

> It was the least costly period, for Australia, of all the fighting that her soldiers underwent. Had it been otherwise, the effort could not have been maintained for so long, nor could the spirit of the troops have been sustained. It was the low cost of victory after victory which spurred them on to still greater efforts.

The assertion is not strictly true: it depends on the periods taken for comparison, but in terms of what was achieved in relation to casualties it is clearly justifiable. Bean was unjust with regard to Monash's period as corps commander, when he remarked in the *Official History*: 'the losses of his brigade, division and corps were, if anything, higher than the average in the A.I.F.'. The casualties during seven weeks on the Somme in 1916 and during Third Ypres in 1917 were higher than in the August–October 1918 offensive; and the proportion of killed was markedly lower while Monash was corps commander. Moreover Bean's statement does not allow for the fact that, in his time as corps commander, Monash was constantly called on to attack.*

Monash wrote in *Australian Victories*:

> It may be that hereafter I may be charged with responsibility for so relentlessly and for so long committing the troops of the corps to a substantial aggressive policy. Such criticisms have already been whispered in some quarters. But I am sure they will not be shared by one of the men whom it was my privilege to command. They know that an offensive policy was the cheapest policy. . . .

There had been great stress, especially about the end of August. Mont

---

* It is hardly reasonable to hold a brigadier on Gallipoli closely responsible for losses. Monash's losses as divisional commander were unremarkable. Casualties on Gallipoli were 27 000+, in seven weeks on the Somme in 1916 28 000+, at Third Ypres 36 500+ (33 000 for Sept.-Oct.); and from 8 Aug. to 5 Oct. 1918 24 000+. Casualties in the five months Monash was corps commander were under 35 000. Bean's figures can only be made to add up if Birdwood's two years of command (including two long inactive winter periods) are compared proportionately with Monash's five months.

St Quentin and Péronne and immediately after had been the worst period, when some battalions were driven to exhaustion and beyond. Some of the 59th Battalion had mutinied at Péronne when, having at last been relieved and having settled to sleep, they were called out again, and there were other incidents. Some of the men, trapped and desperate, went through particular hell. One of them wrote, soon after the war: 'Drunk with success, the Australian leaders continued to hurl their decimated battalions into the thick of the bloody conflict. . . . in order that a group of mad militants might appease their inhuman appetite for blood and glory'. But nearly all the troops, in full pride, drove themselves on. They knew they were being used as shock-troops—*all* of them, the whole Australian Corps—and required guarantees that they would not be so continually used that they would be largely wiped out.* According to the 13th Battalion historian, 'We always knew that [Monash] would do everything to save the lives of men'. War correspondents are sensitive to 'the everlasting contradiction which any soldier . . . knows, between the fatalistic courage of most fighting men and the pushful vanity of their leaders'. The ever-watchful Bean, though he was in agony over the losses throughout and suspicious of Monash's motives, eventually exonerated him, except for the last day at Montbrehain.

In this decisive fighting, for such it was, he was right to work his troops to the extreme limit of their endurance, which normally is beyond the limit to which men themselves think they can endure. At such times victory often goes to the troops that hold out longest, withstanding strain, toil or exhaustion in perhaps unbelievable degree and for an unbelievable time; and the value of different armies depends largely upon how far they are ready to do this.

Another war correspondent, H. S. Gullett, remarked in 1923:

Some critics have declared that in the last grand advance Monash overworked and overdrove the Australians. But I have never heard the fighting man say so. They were pushed on with heavy wastage to the verge of prostration; but it was victory all the way. The result was the justification.

The critics to whom he refers seem not often to have committed themselves to print. Monash did not suffer after the war the terrible charges of butchery levelled at Haig, Currie and many others. He was under Hughes's orders to withdraw all troops by early October, but he had

---

* In proportion to population Australia put in the field only 61 per cent of the contribution Britain made, much less than New Zealand and much more than Canada. But of those who did take the field Australia had a far higher proportion of casualties than any other part of the Empire.

independently decided that they could last no longer. He made a point of not mentioning Hughes's instruction in the reasons he gave in *Australian Victories* for withdrawal of the Corps.

Monash had not foreseen the sudden end of the war. In September in a morale-boosting statement for home consumption he predicted that with favourable weather the enemy would be pushed out of France, though probably not from Belgium, by Christmas. Early in October he was assuring Pearce that, after rest over winter, the A.I.F. would have fifty battalions ready for the spring 1919 campaign. A few days later Germany sued for peace.

Monash immediately began to proclaim his mistaken interpretation that the breaking of the Hindenburg line was the cause of the peace offer. In fact Hindenburg and Ludendorff had previously been seeking an immediate armistice. Monash was soon writing to Pearce:

> the performance of my five Divisions and Corps troops has not been surpassed in the whole annals of War. . . . We ourselves are under no delusion in entertaining the belief that . . . the work of the Corps was the dominating factor, first, in converting the enemy from an offensive to a defensive attitude; next, in compelling him to seek a refuge in the Hindenburg Line from which he could attempt to reorganise his resources; and, thirdly, in forcing him out of the Hindenburg Line and into a situation which is compelling him to sue for peace. I am quite aware that other troops of the Imperial Forces helped materially in all this, but I am able to assert without contradiction that the performance of the Australian Corps . . . far transcends the performances of any similar body of troops on the Western Front.

And he soon tabulated the Australian achievement: from 27 March, 29 144 prisoners and 338 guns captured, 116 towns and villages relieved, 394 square miles taken, 39 enemy divisions engaged. They had captured between 20 and 25 per cent of the prisoners, guns and territory taken by the British Army, in ratio more than twice as much as the rest. As Terraine has remarked, the Australian Corps had been 'to all intents and purposes, the spearhead' during a series of victories unsurpassed in the annals of the British Army.

The Australian infantry fighting was all over. On 2 October Rawlinson told Monash to go on leave; he arranged to go on the 5th. 'Take your leave with delight at all you have done', wrote Birdwood. Monash was exhausted: a bald diary note of 21 December—'Final disappearance of tremors'—is suggestive. He asked Dodds in London to keep people away for a few days and to provide him with a car. He largely avoided business for ten days, feeling 'dull and dispirited, and not very well'; the plays he saw 'rather bored' him. He had to see Hughes, and on request wrote for him a pithy account of the Corps' achievements.

General Wilson sent for him to confer about future use of the Corps. He spent time with Springthorpe briefing him for the articles he was preparing on the A.I.F.'s victories to be published in the Melbourne *Age* in January 1919; and he gave several press interviews. He had one demanding public engagement when he and the Foreign Secretary, Arthur Balfour, were principal guests of the Dominions Luncheon Club at the Savoy. His own account seems not to have been very wide of the mark:

> As [Balfour] had spoken for nearly an hour, in a very solemn and weighty tone, during which the audience sat in perfect silence, I adopted a breezy, whirlwind style, which woke them up and my speech was punctuated with rounds and rounds of cheers and laughter.

It was a punchy call to finish off the war and a review of the success of the Australian Corps. Balfour congratulated him, saying he wished he could speak as well; Garran thought it was magnificent. Monash was a celebrity now and began to savour heady success. Lord Swaythling, brother of Montagu, the Secretary of State for India, had him to lunch with famous English Jews. He lunched and dined with Surgeon-General Sir Charles Ryan, Sir Douglas Mawson, Captain Muirhead Collins, and his old superior, Major-General John Stanley, now elderly and 'pompous and stodgy'. And he took to lunch his very first girl-friend, Clara Stockfeld, the 'chit of a girl' who remembered throughout her life a conversation on Elsternwick station: 'I have blessed you for it often'.

In mid-October Rawlinson asked Blamey what he considered would be a fair delay for further actions by the A.I.F.: Blamey replied, two months. On the 20th, however, Rawlinson rang to say that the Corps would have to be used about the 27th. Hobbs and Blamey visited him, asking for reconsideration, and Rawlinson promised a further week. Hobbs and Blamey immediately wrote to Monash: 1st and 4th Divisions were not fit, MacLagan was very disturbed, the men would consider faith had been broken after Hughes's assurances. Monash wrote to Hughes in alarm: their participation could not be indispensable, would he intervene? They met and went to see Wilson separately. Wilson referred the matter to Cabinet. Monash had told him that he was instructed by Hughes not to allow his divisions to fight any more. He was wriggling and trying desperately to moderate the conflict between his prime minister and G.H.Q. He told Rawlinson he had had a heated interview with Hughes and had told him he took his orders from G.H.Q. and not from a politician. Wilson was indignant: Hughes's promises to the A.I.F. were damnable. Slanted casualty statistics were rushed out to prove that it was 'manifestly unfair' not to put the A.I.F. in again. Monash arrived back in France late on the 27th and he and Birdwood made representations to G.H.Q. Haig was insistent, but promised that the 1st and 4th Divisions would go into action only in an urgent situation. Monash wrote to Dodds asking him to assure Hughes that he had done everything possible. In fact Hughes had given way. Monash summoned his divisional commanders to confer on 1 November with Rawlinson. Actually, Monash was glad to be moving in again in the conviction that the rested battalions would want to be in at the death. Blessedly, events outstripped him: Corps headquarters approached the battle-zone only on 11 November.

Monash spent that day driving 120 miles through rejoicing villages to Le Cateau. He had been brooding on the future, filling in time at his headquarters at Eu, writing a long letter home at last, showing Springthorpe round the battle-grounds (suffering many punctures on the way), visiting Dieppe, taking walks again, attending a conference of his commanders with General Maxse, the inspector-general of training. He was instructed that the Prince of Wales would join him for a month as an aide. He reminded Rawlinson that his proficiency in German might be useful in the next few weeks. It was a period of running down. If there was great emotion or elation, he did not display it in his letters or brief diary.

The previous occupant of the quarters at Le Cateau had been Crown Prince Rupert of Bavaria; in 1914 Field Marshal French had fought the battle of Mons from it. The chateau was spacious but badly knocked about and cold and cheerless. Monash settled down to plan the march by the Corps through Belgium into Germany where he assumed he would be required to administer a district. There were army and corps conferences on the 12th and 14th. Monash wanted the Corps to be part of the occupation forces—the triumph would not be complete otherwise. As it turned out Foch decided that the proposed occupation force would have to be greatly reduced: Fourth Army was to stop at the frontier for the moment, and no Australian infantry units entered Germany. Four divisions of the Corps congregated near Charleroi.

On 13 November Monash was summoned to see Hughes in London on the 18th. It was generally expected that Birdwood would retire, or be forced out, as G.O.C., A.I.F. In the previous months Monash had been uncertain about what he would do if the government offered him the appointment. It would mean promotion and increased status and power, but he would lose the kudos of a fighting commander. However if he did accept it he would probably be able to impose almost any conditions he desired. When he went on leave early in October he was hoping to press Hughes to make a decision, and discussed the matter with Birdwood and White on the way. He had conferred with

Hughes twice, but the prime minister wanted to defer his decision until the military situation clarified.

At the Armistice Monash was no clearer about his future. He knew that Hughes was angry with Birdwood for wanting still to cling to the A.I.F. command, and he assumed whoever was G.O.C. would control demobilization and repatriation. But he did not fully realize what doubts Hughes, under Murdoch's influence, had about him. 'Birdwood is the man I would rather live with', Hughes said:

> Monash is a far more capable man—he has the ability, but he is out for himself all the time, like a Jew, showy. . . . Do you think he has the kindliness or the humanity . . . to deal with men at a time like this? . . . Is he human enough to run repatriation?

Murdoch was trying to persuade him that White should have the job. When summoned again to see Hughes, Monash immediately loyally informed Birdwood who told him that he expected to remain G.O.C. and that he intended White to control demobilization. Indeed, White had already ordered senior officers to start work and was developing a scheme of organization which he had long been pondering; he established a Demobilization and Repatriation branch on 16 November.

Hughes, however, eventually decided he wanted Monash, and surprised him by offering him the post of Director-General of Repatriation and Demobilization and not command of the A.I.F., which Birdwood retained. The department would be under political, not A.I.F., control. Monash was pleased: it would be difficult and satisfying work, far preferable to 'sitting down on the Rhine for several months with nothing particular to do' in winter and famine conditions.

White was keen to take part and content to serve under Monash, but Monash either froze him out or convinced him that his proper job was to go home to run the Army. On the 21st some sort of scene occurred between them. According to Bean, when Dodds asked White what was happening, he said 'Bloody Hell!'—and White was not a swearer. Dodds tackled Monash who replied that he had suggested to White that he go home. Had he been ruthless, or merely tactless? If the latter, he certainly would quickly have tried to restore good relations. Two days later they were lunching together in France with Birdwood. How cordial a gathering was it?—it is likely that from now on Birdwood deeply resented his own down-grading. Bean claimed White was 'deeply hurt', but if he bore any resentment to Monash, it did not last. Monash told Hobbs on the 23rd that White was in no way disappointed.

Monash summoned a conference of senior officers at which he announced his new post: Hobbs would be his successor and the Corps would not be going into Germany after all. He addressed the gathering at length on his plans for repatriation. Corps staff gave him a warm farewell dinner; after a day clearing up and handing over to Hobbs, he made a rushed trip to Waterloo and Brussels with Paul Simonson; and then after saying goodbye to the staff officers individually, returned to London.

On 20 November he wrote for Vic and Bert to come and join him, but to wait until the English spring by which time the journey might be reasonably safe and comfortable. On almost the same day Vic was writing: 'Your name is a household word in Melbourne. You are loved by everyone officer soldier and civilian. You are such a wonderful man'.

13

The Best Man in France?

AT THE CLOSE of the war, Monash in reputation stood far above any other Australian general, in the eyes both of the A.I.F. and the Australian public. In future years he was to enjoy rather more than his fair share of the glory. He had the first attribute of a great general—good luck—in that he took command of a magnificent instrument just when the tide was about to turn conclusively in the Allies' favour, and he was never compelled to fight with the odds against him. But the task could hardly have been better done. Hamel and Mont St Quentin were brilliant achievements and several other engagements were more than notable. He had bad days and made mistakes no doubt, as on 10 August and in the last days of September, but a champion boxer has to suffer blows in the process of outpointing or knocking out his opponent; they were merely temporary checks. Blamey once remarked that, as corps commander, Monash made only one important mistake, which he did not specify. The corps command was the critical leap to fame; without it, Monash would have remained a sound and successful divisional commander of limited repute. Either of the very able White and Hobbs, if preferred to Monash, would have done very well, but they were simply not comparable in intellect, articulateness or personal magnetism, though White was in administrative capacity. They could not have won the fame Monash did. Outstandingly successful though the divisional commanders were, it is similarly difficult to imagine any of Rosenthal, Glasgow, Gellibrand or MacLagan, as corps commander, rivalling Monash's achievement. Chauvel was the other outstanding general of the war, but although his record as a light horseman in the desert was superb he was an unlikely corps commander on the Western Front.

Monash won undying respect from nearly all the senior A.I.F. commanders. Elated by their great team achievement, the men at Corps headquarters swore by him. Blamey stressed his flexibility of mind.

Coxen remembered 'his capabilities of visualising and marshalling requirements to the minutest detail, in the proper order of sequence', as though dealing with 'an abstruse mathematical problem'. Foott recalled his patience, kindness and even-temperedness. Writing privately when Monash died, he remarked: 'John Monash was a fine man, a fine soldier, and I am proud that I was able to satisfy him as an Engineer, for that was his own profession'. Among the divisional commanders, Glasgow, although he had some reservations, described Monash as 'a cultured gentleman, . . . a great soldier, and a masterly organiser and administrator'; his care for the men was outstanding and he had an 'almost uncanny capacity for appreciating a difficult situation, and being able to make provision for it'. Hobbs, on taking over the Corps command, revealingly wrote to Monash to remark 'how very good and kind you have been to me and how very helpful in times of difficulty or stress'. He later described Monash as 'a great judge of men and character, calm and deliberate, resolute and determined'. Rosenthal was the staunchest of loyal friends. Among the brigadiers, McNicoll and Grimwade worshipped Monash; Elliott, so critical of his peers, entirely approved of him; Cannan considered him the greatest man he knew; Jess recalled especially his days with 3rd Division which 'had a staff in which there was not the slightest element of discord, due entirely to your fairmindedness'. Many battalion commanders similarly revered him: 'You, Sir', wrote Morshead, 'have always held and will always hold our deepest respect and highest esteem'. So did his staff officers in the 4th Brigade, who shared many dark days—Locke and Durrant, who became generals. Albert Jacka, V.C., who had little time for the top brass, always spoke highly of him.

Among the British generals, Haig admired Monash throughout; in his diaries, Terraine notes, he approved of him more than anyone else perhaps. Hamilton, in retrospect, judged Monash and Russell outstanding among the Anzacs, Monash 'as a thinker, an administrator, and an outspoken firm character'; Congreve considered him the best divisional commander he had struck; and Plumer, Harington and Fuller all held him in very high regard. Rawlinson's attitude is uncertain: while he worked well with Monash, he disliked him as a Jew. When Colonel Repington, the *Times* military correspondent, tardily met Monash in 1919, he was highly impressed by 'a very alert, wideawake, shrewd man'.

From mid-1918 many talked of Monash as 'the best man in France', including members of the British government, notably Walter Long. Towards the close of the war and after, many Australian soldiers asserted that Monash would have been a far better commander-in-chief than 'Butcher' Haig. (Successful though Haig was in 1918, few then or since have been able to forgive the casualties on the Somme and at Passchendaele.) In October 1918 it was rumoured in the A.I.F. that Monash was about to be appointed. In 1920 *Smith's Weekly* referred to the common belief that 'If the war had lasted one year more Monash would have been British Commander-in-Chief'. In 1923 Sir William Beach Thomas, the war correspondent, named him as the best soldier on the Western Front. Among many Australian ex-servicemen it became an article of faith that the war would have ended much sooner if Monash had held the high command.

Monash's ultimate reputation eventually owed most to the steady advocacy of Sir Basil Liddell Hart, widely recognized as the outstanding military commentator and historian of his generation (but for Fuller, perhaps). Despite the spate of war reminiscences, little serious military history was written in the inter-war period, apart from the slowly appearing official versions. In his obituary of Monash, Liddell Hart paid a remarkable tribute:

> He had probably the greatest capacity for command in modern war among all who held command. . . . If that war had lasted another year he would almost certainly have risen from commander of the Australian corps to command of an army; he might even have risen to be Commander-in-Chief. If capacity had been the determining factor he would have done so. . . .
>
> He was in some ways an utter contrast to the traditional idea of a great military commander. He, more than anyone, fulfilled the idea which gradually developed in the war—that the scale and nature of operations required a 'big business' type of commander, a great constructive and organising brain. His views were as large as his capacity. Perhaps the strongest testimony to his capacity is the distance he went in spite of a tremendous compound handicap of prejudice. . . .
>
> His grip of situations silenced all doubters and compelled the admiration of even the most critical professional soldiers.

Liddell Hart had not made any deep investigation and his conclusions were reached largely from discussions with senior British officers. His antipathy to Haig and his bitter clashes with the military establishment perhaps inclined him to extol Monash as the new type of military leader.

Liddell Hart was one of Lloyd George's advisers when he was writing his memoirs. In volume 4, which appeared in 1934, Lloyd George remarked that 'the only soldier . . . who possessed necessary qualifications' for commander-in-chief 'was a Dominion General'. The reference was generally assumed to be to Monash, though some Canadians thought it was to Currie. In volume 6 (1936), however, he was specific.

Unfortunately the British Army did not bring into prominence any commander who, taking him all round, was more conspicuously fitted for the post [than Haig]. No doubt Monash would, if the opportunity had been given him, have risen to the height of it. But the greatness of his abilities was not brought to the attention of the Cabinet in any of the Dispatches. Professional soldiers could hardly be expected to advertise the fact that the greatest strategist in the Army was a civilian when the War began, and that they were being surpassed by a man who had not received any of their advantages in training and teaching. . . .

Monash was, according to the testimony of those who knew well his genius for war and what he accomplished by it, the most resourceful General in the whole of the British Army.

The trouble is that Lloyd George was using Monash's reputation as a weapon with which to bludgeon Haig and other senior officers; his judgement is worth little. Certainly, in 1918 he had desperately been looking for a replacement for Haig and there was no obvious successor. The Dominion prime ministers, Borden of Canada being especially critical of the high command and like Lloyd George and Hughes suspicious of the British military caste, were eager for a change. Monash only began to be known to the government in July and August. He could not possibly have been seriously considered for commander-in-chief: he was still a junior corps commander, and not even Hughes would have been bold enough to put his name forward. And by this time Haig, with Foch, was winning the war.

Some conjecture is allowable. If the war had continued into 1919, Monash must have been offered an army. He was already virtually an army commander and it would have been easy to add one or two British divisions, and possibly the New Zealanders, to the large Australian corps. Monash had shown in August 1918 that he could handle seven or eight divisions; Liddell Hart used to cite him as an example to contradict the 'fetish' that 'a commander cannot effectively control more than three or four sub-units'. But the jump to the lonely eminence of commander-in-chief would have been far higher. It is an open question whether Monash could have handled higher strategy well; his capacities are not in doubt as much as his limited apprentice training. And it is very unlikely that professional soldiers could have submitted to the indignity of being led by a Jewish colonial militiaman, who had never seen active service in his youth. The war did not last long enough for him to come to full stature—or to fail at the highest tests. And, to restore a sense of proportion, we should note that in each of John Buchan's *History of the Great War*, Cyril Falls's *The First World War* and Fuller's *The Decisive Battles of the Western World* Monash was granted only one passing mention.

Over the years the myth took wild forms. Major-General Sir Kingsley Norris wrote in 1970: Monash 'was considered in 1918 for the appointment of Generalissimo of the Allied Forces in France, a command which fell to Foch'. The son of one of Monash's senior British officers in the 3rd Division recalls his father maintaining that Monash would have been supreme commander but for French and Italian prejudice against a Jew. The author of a letter to the *Australian* in 1979 asserted that Lloyd George did not replace Haig with Monash only because the King threatened to abdicate! On the serious level, Liddell Hart's judgement prevails. The historian A. J. P. Taylor described Monash in 1963 as 'the only general of creative originality produced by the First World War'. Anthony Eden (Viscount Avon) in his reminiscences (1976) recalled Monash as 'the ablest soldier of the war'. And in his *History of Warfare* (1968) Montgomery of Alamein wrote:

> I would name Sir John Monash as the best general on the western front in Europe; he possessed real creative originality, and the war might well have been over sooner, and certainly with fewer casualties, had Haig been relieved of his command and Monash appointed to command the British Armies in his place.

(Both Taylor and Montgomery were in close touch with Liddell Hart.) Almost alone among the senior generals of World War I, Monash's reputation has never declined. Major-General H. Essame in *The Battle for Europe 1918* (1972) wrote possibly the most extreme eulogy of all: he understood his men as profoundly as did Napoleon, Rommel and Montgomery; Monash and Blamey 'unquestionably outshone all their British counterparts in ability and battle expertise'. In 1980 Terraine broadly confirmed Monash's stature, although not allowing any legitimate comparison with Haig, in a chapter of his *The Smoke and the Fire*. The American John Toland in his *No Man's Land* (1980) agrees.

The English press and a few politicians used to make much of the success of the 'amateur' Dominion generals when compared to the professionals of the British Army. They were not amateurs. Their militia training was in quality often as good as that received by British professionals. After three years of war they were professional enough. Monash always held, saturated as he was in the history of the American Civil War and the writings of G. F. R. Henderson, that the civilian soldier had an advantage over the professional. In 1910 he remarked privately on the 'confinement of scope' characteristic of professional army training. In 1923 he complimented George Wootten on 'abandoning professional soldiering: I have never regarded it as an adequate career for an ambitious man'. He always stressed the greater importance in the exercise of high command of preparation for war—training, administration and maintenance—over actual combat; and he always deplored the narrow specialization of British permanent officers. In contrast to the wide training of engineers, architects or 'captains of industry',

> In the regular Army one knows all about one or two Applied Arts very thoroughly—horsemastership, or gunnery, or musketry, or chemical warfare, or military law, or military engineering, and very little about anything else. It was indeed characteristic of the Senior Army Officer of the best type that he could talk well and informatively of his particular arm of the service, and of polo, or fox hunting, and of the traditions of the Army, but that he was dilettante, if not entirely uninterested, in every other subject of science, art or philosophy.

During the war, he argued, civilians with scientific and technical experience were far better equipped than regular officers to handle innovations such as aircraft, tanks, automatic machine-guns, grenades, new forms of high explosive, poison gas, smoke and camouflage. Another important argument for the civilian's advantages which he did not use was that the permanent soldier was not accustomed to a life of high pressure. Haig, for example, when commanding at Aldershot just before the war, from early morning supervised training on horseback, spent from 11 till lunch in his office, played golf or tennis in the afternoon, and finished the day's work with a couple of hours professional reading. Though in the event Haig for long stood up to pressure as few men could, the contrast with the amount of work, concentration and crises to which Monash was accustomed is striking. The 'captain of industry' had developed the qualities of coolness in emergency and capacity to handle volume of work under strain. He was at least as likely as the professional to have what Lord Wavell laid down as the essential quality of a general: robustness—'the ability to stand the shocks of war . . . a high margin over the normal breaking strain'.

Monash held to his view that warfare was essentially a problem in engineering, or that conduct of war was basically a 'plain business proposition' like directing a large industrial undertaking, being a general manager. His assertions were strengthened by a vivid extended metaphor:

> A perfected modern battle plan is like nothing so much as a score for an orchestral composition, where the various arms and units are the instruments, and the tasks they perform are their respective musical phrases. Every individual unit must make its entry precisely at the proper moment, and play its phrase in the general harmony. The whole programme is controlled by an exact time-table, to which every infantryman, every heavy or light gun, every mortar and machine-gun, every tank and aeroplane must respond with punctu-

ality; otherwise there will be discords which will impair the success of the operation, and increase the cost of it.

However, this view emphasizes mobilization of resources rather than battle. Training as an engineer (and his civilian experience in studying maps, making field-sketches, especially his knowledge of mathematics with regard to gunnery) was of course useful, but it is difficult to accept its overriding importance. 'Engineering is a mode of looking at things, a way of doing things', it has been remarked with reference to Monash. 'The engineer is the man with the genius first to recognise the real conditions of the technical problem before him, and then by skilful effort to discover its adequate solution.' But the same may be claimed of other disciplines. Alignment of resources by a large-scale engineer-contractor was what Monash had in mind, but it tends to assume that all battles are set-pieces and to neglect tactical battle-planning and the response of the enemy. Successful conduct of battle is mainly but by no means only the engineer's or businessman's allocation of resources.

At Corps headquarters Monash had no time or concentration to spare to cultivate the affection of junior officers and other ranks. Most captains and lieutenants at Corps found him a remote being; one, a staff brigadier in World War II, even compared him to MacArthur in his aloofness. He behaved very differently with his senior officers and those juniors who, from the nature of their duties, had to see him frequently. At this level he demonstrated his great gift for extracting the best efforts they could give and for winning their personal liking as well as respect. According to Blamey, 'The most affectionate and cordial relationship existed between Monash and his staff'. He had 'a warm and sunny personality'. 'With the Corps staff he was never happier than when joking and chatting in the mess. . . . Probably no commander was surrounded by less formality.' Durrant recalled that 'a good story at the mess table never failed to bring forth much merriment from him'; he especially liked Jewish stories.

Monash and Blamey made a great team, remarkable if only because they had barely been acquainted. They remained devoted admirers of each other. Conjectures about Blamey's contribution to Monash's successes cannot be satisfactorily settled. Normally, during operations, Monash would confer with Blamey (or with Coxen, Fraser, Foott or others), then retire to settle the outlines of a plan. His surviving pencillings indicate that he frequently drafted in detail; which of them worked out details depended on immediate circumstances, although it was Blamey who finally produced the orders. Monash in his *Australian Victories* gave Blamey more extensive and effusive praise than anyone else, and after the war took every opportunity to commend him. Thanking him in 1920 for his remarks, Blamey wrote:

I cannot express the ease with which my work was carried on with the Corps, chiefly owing to your own completely human outlook and generous support. I have never served a commander who made my task easier. I think the unity of aim and entire absence of friction on Corps Headquarters will make it always one of the happiest epochs of my life.

F. M. Cutlack, who had been Intelligence Officer with 3rd Division and in 1918 became an official war correspondent, wrote in December 1919:

> Officers of his headquarters staff who set out to work as long a day as the G.O.C. found themselves committed to the most continuous hard work they had ever done in their lives. . . . In his office he was always more like a newspaper editor, or the chief of a large engineering construction staff, or the director of a great corporation than an army leader. He saw everybody; he forgot nothing. He left nothing to chance which industry and foresight could make certain. He made no plans until he had exhausted the ideas of all staff and subordinate commanding officers; then he would suggest a scheme which embraced the good points of all. . . . Sir John has about him an unfailing magnetism.

In 1926 Monash addressed the Beefsteak Club on 'Leadership in War' and laid down the desirable qualities of a commander:

The capacity to form judgments, rapidly and soundly, is, I believe, more temperamental than intellectual. I grant that a well-stored mind, a well-exercised mentality, and a fund of varied experiences in the affairs of life are a necessary stock-in-trade. But these would avail a man little in war if he had not the right temperament for that environment.

A successful leader must be unemotional to the extent of being callous to the external influences which evoke joy or sorrow, elation or despondency; he must be indifferent to praise or blame; he must have the capacity to persevere calmly and dispassionately with the business in hand, undisturbed either by the menace of imminent calamity, or by the exultation of success. He must be patient to a degree. He must have determination and steadfastness of purpose of a very high order. He must have an exalted confidence in himself and in the correctness of his judgment, amounting to an intellectual arrogance. His capacity to appreciate the working of the minds of others must be automatic and swift. His personality must be of a kind which inspires confidence in others, and which dominates their instinct to exercise independent judgment.

He should be, in short, temperamentally a paragon of excellence, which, I fear, none of us, in spite of earnest aspiration, ever completely reached. . . .

Perhaps the highest and most critical of all the tasks of a leader are the creation and maintenance of the morale of his men. . . . It is the responsibility of that leader to infuse, by his example, by his methods, and by his self-expression, that spirit of just and humane exercise of his absolute powers, that devotion to the cause, that will to victory, . . . and that application of his utmost intellectual and physical powers, which together make up morale. . . .

On becoming Corps commander, he told Springthorpe, his first task was 'to acquire a moral ascendancy' over his senior commanders and staffs, and

> to secure complete domination over their thoughts, action and policy. The first consideration was the creation of complete unity of thought, and complete unity both of administrative and tactical policy. This could not be ensured without . . . inculcating high ideals, high aims, and a high standard of conduct. In particular, it was necessary to create and foster among all officers, and particularly among junior officers, a sense of responsibility to themselves, their commanders, their comrades, their men, their country and their cause.
> These results were achieved by close personal contact with hundreds of officers, by the holding of conferences, and by lectures and addresses, and by a constant process of critical supervision.

The quality Monash perhaps stressed most was capacity for quick and clear decision; nothing was worse than indefiniteness.

His creed of optimism and his offensive spirit were in harmony with his corps. 'A passive defence involved just as great an average daily wastage of fighting strength as active offensive operations, if well planned and executed.' 'The lethargy engendered by weary months of trench warfare' could easily become chronic. Thus he encouraged constant raiding or peaceful penetration. An 'energetic offensive policy', 'feeding the troops on victory', was the short way to end the slaughter and misery. The troops 'themselves recognized this. They learned to believe, because of success heaped upon success, that they were invincible. They were right, and I believe that I was right in shaping a course which would give them the opportunity of proving it'.

In 1924 an interviewer commented, probably paraphrasing Monash, that 'in so many cases those in command of our troops failed for one of two reasons. Either they were unable to stand the horrors of the situation, or they became so hardened that the men were only pawns in the game'. Monash came well out of the terrible test of victories versus casualties, of having to throw his men again and again into the 'blood tub', not without appalling strain on himself. He almost satisfied Bean on this matter. He did satisfy Hughes: Monash 'was the only general with whom I came in close contact who seemed to me to give due weight to the cost of victory'. If only he had withstood Rawlinson and saved those men of the 6th Brigade at Montbrehain on that last morning. Perhaps he would have, if he had not been at the end of his tether.

Monash had a deep-rooted attachment to 'fixity of plan':

> once a plan had been crystallized and promulgated, no alterations (except perhaps of a trivial and quite minor character) were permissible. In previous years, failures and sometimes disasters had flowed from a disposition to tamper with a plan of action in the hope of bettering it. As a Brigadier [on Gallipoli] I had suffered more than a few times from receiving eleventh hour orders to alter, fundamentally, the task . . . for which I had completed my preparations; and I had had bitter experience of the consequent stress upon my whole Brigade. . . .
>
> I carried this principle to the extreme of insisting that, if an operation could not, for any reason, proceed on the lines originally planned, it was better to cancel the operation altogether and begin *de novo* on a different plan.

Hamel was the chief occasion when he put his convictions to the test. Another of his basic tenets was 'never to entrust a critical operation' to tired troops—obvious enough but not by any means generally applied and sometimes impossible to apply. But the immense organizational difficulties in bringing about regular relief and short spells in the line were largely overcome; he considered the 'recuperative effect' of a week out of the line was 'almost unbelievable'.

Monash's procedure in making a battle plan was broadly as follows. Eventually, he and he alone would have to formulate the general conception and construct the framework. But he would constantly be discussing with Blamey and individually with divisional commanders, and occasionally in conference with them, the possibilities of future action. When he was ordered to prepare an operation, he would confer with Blamey, prepare a plan himself, refer it to the divisional commanders—discussing it by phone or face-to-face or in conference with them all, as time permitted—eventually demanding from them their detailed plans. The final battle conference would be an inspiring exposition of the plan and a resolution of difficulties, rather than a discussion. 'These battle conferences', Monash wrote,

> proved a powerful instrument for the moulding of a uniformity of tactical thought and method throughout the command. They brought together men who met face to face but seldom, and they permitted of an exhaustive and educative interchange of views. They led to a development of team-work of a very high order of efficiency.
>
> The work of preparing for, and the actual conduct of these conferences was always a very arduous business; but they more than repaid

me for the effort they entailed. They served two paramount purposes. They enabled me to apply the requisite driving force to all subordinates collectively, instead of individually, and thereby created a responsive spirit which was competitive. In addition, each commander or service had the advantage not only of receiving instructions regarding his own action, but also of hearing in full detail the instructions conveyed to his colleagues. . . . he had an opportunity of considering the effect of their action on his own.

These conferences were not an Australian innovation but, though unknown in Birdwood's time, became characteristic of the A.I.F. and general practice in World War II. Most other corps relied exclusively on written orders. 'With us, the written orders were promulgated just the same, but the conference was regarded as their consummation.' Bruche recalled that officers at conferences would say:

> "That can't be done, you can't do it that way." And he'd say "General, I think it can, you know," in his smiling way. He was always so imperturbable and never ruffled, never showed any personal animosity.

When Bruche came to him with a grave difficulty, he would say: 'Julius, they all yield to treatment'.

In the great set-pieces like Messines, Broodseinde, Hamel and 8 August, Monash forbade any variation from the plan, however promising the opportunity, if only because the artillery would always know where the infantry was. Terraine has argued: 'Opportunism defeated itself by silencing its own artillery; Monash's rigid method, by ensuring the co-operation required for the success of each stage, made possible a flexible approach to the directness and timing of the next bound'. Too often, allowing troops to exploit a local victory permitted Ludendorff's tactic of 'counterattack at the moment that our attack has spent itself' to prevail. Monash knew very well that during a battle a higher commander, unless things went seriously wrong, could do little more than exhort and trust the man on the spot, whether it was a set-piece battle or an improvisation like Mont St Quentin. Monash had to try to verify in set-pieces that the plan was being adhered to; in fluid operations he had to trust the initiative of his major-generals, brigadiers and lieut-colonels. Except for the conflicts with Gellibrand on 30 September, there is no evidence of his control being too close or of resentment from his juniors. Elliott, for one, lavishly praised the freedom he was given: 'Birdwood and White constantly were at fault many times in fettering or attempting to fetter the initiative of Front line leaders. When Monash came the change was instant and what a relief it was'. Rosenthal agreed. Cutlack reported that 'his subordinate commanders always bore willing tribute to his loyalty to the man on the spot, and the free rein he always gave to tried individual judgment and initiative'. Foott concluded that 'those whom Monash trusted, he trusted fully. He never interfered with his subordinates. A mistake made in good faith never brought censure from him, beyond a quiet explanation of what might have been done'.

At Hamel and on 8 August Monash made a minor contribution to the development of tank tactics, but cannot be claimed to have made much impact on subsequent tank use. He had absorbed the lessons of the battle of Cambrai in November 1917 which indicated the potential of tanks in breaking the stalemate of trench warfare. The use at Hamel of relatively few troops and as many tanks as possible, and the use of tanks as carriers of ammunition and other supplies, was straight tank doctrine. Monash contributed something there in his insistence on tanks advancing as close as possible to the barrage and on their giving particular attention to searching out enemy machine-guns. Possibly against his will, he had adopted his advisers' view that there had to be full artillery preparation, and he had placed the tanks under infantry control. 8 August was similar in the limited independence allowed to the tanks. This was no forerunner to the wide-ranging Panzer-type attacks by armoured divisions in World War II. Yet one historian of the Tanks has claimed that 'in relation to the machines at his disposal, Monash's tank-infantry tactics have rarely been equalled, and probably never surpassed. . . . to read his orders for [Hamel] is to discover once more the strange little thrill which comes from lifting up the edge of the curtain of war and looking at the future'. Smithers' conclusions are understandable:

> One can easily see Monash as a commander of the Eighth Army in the Second War. The name of no other First War general of whom this could be said comes immediately to the mind. . . . He was, above all things, the first twentieth-century general, a man with petrol in his veins and a computer in his head. . . .

His main innovative thinking was, perhaps, in his open-minded and adventurous use of all available arms to assist the infantry:

> I had formed the theory that the true role of the infantry was not to expend itself upon heroic physical effort, nor to wither away under merciless machine-gun fire, nor to impale itself on hostile bayonets, nor to tear itself to pieces in hostile entanglements . . . but, on the contrary to advance under the maximum possible protection of the maximum possible array of mechanical resources, in the form of guns, machine-guns, tanks, mortars and aeroplanes; to advance with as little impediment as possible; to be relieved as far as possible of the obligation to *fight* their way forward; to march, resolutely, regardless of the din and tumult of battle, to the appointed goal;

and there to hold and defend the territory gained; and to gather in the form of prisoners, guns and stores, the fruits of victory.

Thus he took as many tanks as he could get, developed the Canadian use of the machine-gun barrage, and recalled that

> Australian troops were the first to use, just before Messines, poison gas bombs propelled by Stokes mortars; and ... the first to use the Mark V tank, aircraft as ammunition carriers, and the artillery projectiles laden with a recently invented and very deadly form of so-called "mustard" gas.

It was the combination of tactical innovations into a standard battle drill by 8 August which was so effective. Among them were: detailed explanation of orders at platoon level, no change in battle orders once issued, a perfectly straight barrage line, gas shell changing to smoke, leap-frogging, individual tanks under control of company commanders, tanks carrying Vickers guns and crews and supplies to far objectives, parachuting of ammunition, and use of coloured smoke to indicate positions reached to aerial observers.

However, Monash's success perhaps did not depend on innovation so much as soundness of principle. As Terraine puts it, he was 'a brilliant, meticulous organiser' applying the 'same cool, rational, methodical approach' which he once used in building bridges. Monash argued strongly that in set-piece battles success was only a matter of good planning and applying superior force:

> It is only necessary ... to concentrate upon a given front such a density of artillery barrage fire, tank and air-attack, as to make it reasonably certain that it would overwhelm any possible defensive measures....
>
> In a well-planned battle of this nature, ... given a resolute infantry and that the enemy's guns are kept successfully silenced by our own counter-battery artillery, nothing happens, nothing can happen, except the regular progress of the advance according to the plan arranged. The whole battle sweeps relentlessly and methodically across the ground until it reaches the line laid down as the final objective.

All going well, the story of the battle was 'a mere paraphrase of the battle orders prescribing all that was to take place'. Fluid battles such as the later phase of 8 August and Mont St Quentin were very different.

Monash owed or acknowledged inspiration for his success to few: he was essentially a self-made soldier. Hubert Foster, under whom he had sat at the University of Sydney, was one to whom he paid deference. He learned a little from his pre-war associations with McCay and his juniors White and Bruche. He had small reason to believe that his seniors on Gallipoli improved his education. In 1917 he was fortunate to be led by Plumer and Harington, and probably gained much. He worked harmoniously with Rawlinson and Montgomery in 1918 but seems to have owed little to them. Brudenell White watched him, with fascination, developing in capacity and stature. Monash and Haig got on very well. Monash was no doubt deferential: he was loyal to his superiors and almost never criticized them, though Bean once caught him commenting on Haig's obscurities. Privately, he regarded Haig's views on discipline as 'peculiar'. And after the war he recalled:

> Haig was, technically speaking, quite out of his depth in regard to the minutiae of the immense resources which were placed in his hands to wield. I was, at first, quite dismayed to find that he obviously did not know the composition in detail of his own formations, as, for example, when he criticized me for the dispositions made, just prior to the battle of Messines, of the Heavy and Super-Heavy Artillery with which, of course, I . . . had nothing whatever to do; just as, on a later occasion, in 1918, he appeared to blunder badly, and be out of touch with the details of the situation, when he came to discuss with me how best to exploit the great victory of August 8th, before Amiens. But I learned to appreciate that it was not indispensable for a Commander, placed as he was, to have a detailed knowledge of such matters, and that it was his personality and his influence upon his environment that counted so heavily. He was once kind enough to say to me that it always cheered him up to come and have a talk with me. I can say with unreserved candour that the reverse was far more true. It was . . . a source of immeasurable relief and consolation to find him calm, resolute, hopeful and buoyant, in the face of apparently irretrievable chaos and disaster.

The two determined optimists buoyed each other up. Monash could and did stand up to his superiors on important issues, and not just at Hamel. Blamey vouched for his 'great moral strength and tenacity of purpose' and judged that the fact that he was usually right in his conflicts with the higher command led to their placing 'great reliance on his judgment'.

Monash made no attempt to emulate Birdwood's hob-nobbing with the troops. He knew he could not do it well: although he was a genial man with his peers and could unselfconsciously meet rank-and-file individuals on a basis of equality, he was not a backslapper. There was a trace of awkward shyness in his nature and an impatience with insincere play-acting. He also knew that Birdwood's stereotyped *bonhomie* had worn thin. But essentially he regarded it as a waste of time spent away from the real job. After the war he told a friend that Birdwood

> was always "buzzing about", looking people up, perambulating all

over the place, hardly ever at his headquarters, and not *really* exercising any command at all.... I spent as much as possible of my whole time at my Headquarters... considering reports, planning, organizing, and directing, with the result that the Corps at once began to do things and finished by doing great things.

Time away from the office was best spent inspecting technical units of the Corps rather than troops in the line. Monash knew that personal popularity was not essential: 'A force which finds itself well-equipped, well-fed and well-quartered, and which is able to achieve victories in battle without serious losses, will speedily elevate its leaders in its regard and esteem even if it has but rare personal contact with them'. The prevalent 'inspirational' school of opinion continued to disagree with him; Wavell, for example, believed the more time a general spent with his troops the better. Montgomery was not the only World War II commander who paraded himself to develop his mystique. Men of the old school like Gellibrand and Brand continued to sneer at the distance Monash kept from the front line. So did some of the troops who despised the brass hats in their chateaux. Others detested their arrival because they 'drew the crabs'. During battle, it came to be generally accepted during World War I that commanding generals should avoid becoming involved in the confusion of one corner of the action, and seclude themselves in order to exercise what control they could. In the conditions of warfare on the Western Front personal reconnoitring was rarely of any use to a divisional commander, let alone a corps commander. White and Blamey, as staff officers whose job it really was if relevant, reconnoitred little.

In Bean's opinion Monash adhered to prudence as a principle: 'There was never any sign that he lacked physical courage; rather he was determined to avoid all except inevitable risks'. But the fact was that in ordinary daily circumstances going up towards the line involved little additional danger. Shelling was more regular immediately behind the line, but it ranged constantly several miles behind. Monash was exposed to it whenever he made the routine rounds of divisions and brigades. In mid-1916 he wrote:

> it is quite futile to try and dodge shell fire [except that] certain places are more vulnerable than others.... ordinarily one is following an occupation which is not much more dangerous than that of any civilian dangerous calling such as motor driving, cordite making, bridge building etc.

It may be that after Gallipoli and several subsequent narrow escapes, he had become a little 'dodgy'; it would not be surprising, but there is only one piece of supporting evidence. Jackson, who was a fire-eater, mentioned by the way in his eulogy of Monash to Liddell Hart: 'I never got him nearer than the third line and he did not seem to enjoy even that. . . . he had the moral courage to get rid of an officer who did not like bullets while he himself I really believe hated them just as much. He was, as you know a Jew, and I have only met one Jew who was physically brave'. Apart from Jackson's prejudice and his inability to understand Monash's attitude, it is odd that he referred to bullets—which were almost irrelevant compared with shelling. He misled Liddell Hart who inferred too much when he replied that Monash 'had quite enough good points to allow candid admission of his lack of physical courage—a somewhat overrated quality in comparison with moral courage'. The contrast between physical and moral courage was a commonplace in military discussion: high physical bravery was frequent, high moral courage rare.

Monash did give an impression of aloofness and masterfulness. One boy who met him on Gallipoli was struck by 'something undefinable and intangible' about him, allied to greatness. Another young officer felt he 'was in the presence of the "great architect of the universe himself" '. Impressionable youths are often awed in the presence of men wielding great power, but a British war correspondent in 1918 wrote: 'You can interview any of the great British Generals, including Field Marshal Haig, and not feel any great trepidation; but immediately you come before General Monash you know you are in the presence of a great man'. And yet Monash was renowned for his private informality and lack of swank, as distinct from his public display.

Early in 1918 Lieutenant Harold Lilya was sent for by his divisional commander. In some trepidation, he recounts, he reported to Monash and slung his smartest salute. 'He said in the friendliest way possible Lilya sit down and be comfortable—would you like a cigarette?' He quietly explained that he wanted Lilya, a famous bomb-thrower, to command a demonstration team to show 'what a platoon in attack can do if held up'. 'I am sure no Senior Officer anywhere . . . could be as modest and calm and exhibit so much charm as General Monash . . . charm I have never known in any one else', Lilya concluded sixty years later. 'Sit down and light your pipe', Monash used to say to Lieut-Colonel Harold Cohen. But he would usually conclude: 'Do you understand what I want?' 'Yes, Sir.' 'What is it?' Many letters from junior officers thanked him for his kindness and unfailing courtesy; Frank Beaurepaire of the Y.M.C.A., for example, wrote of his 'fairness and approachableness'. While commanding 3rd Division Monash seems to have acquired no nickname; at Corps 'Old Monash' was used fairly widely, even by Rawlinson and Bean, in the sense of him being a wise old head. He came to be regarded, as the *Bulletin* put it in 1924, as 'the absolute antithesis of the unapproachable, self-conscious brass-hat'.

Though he came to be trusted, he may have seemed remote and dull to the men in the line. There are many examples of his humanity, which may have percolated down. Early in the war, a recruit sitting smoking had not saluted him. 'I am nothing but a mere brigadier-general, my boy', Monash told him, 'but one of these days some second-lieutenant is going to come along here and reprimand you severely for your lack of observation'. Docking at Alexandria in October 1915 he fell into conversation with a private next to him on the rail about horses being landed. On leave at the theatre, he invited an A.I.F. sergeant and a private sitting next to him to have a drink during the interval, thus scandalizing English officers. The gunner who, as an outstanding advocate, defended many prisoners, had the utmost regard for Monash's fairness at courts-martial. One would like to know what he said when awarding decorations for valour—something simple but striking no doubt, for he had a sense of theatrical occasion.

Major-General Durrant in 1941 attributed the success of the First A.I.F. largely to 'the detailed explanation of the plan, and description of the objectives, given to all ranks by their officers before zero hour'. The practice had been developing through the war and was carried out far more consistently than in any other army. It followed from the nature of the Australian soldier, whom Monash described as follows:

> The democratic institutions under which he was reared, the advanced system of education by which he was trained—teaching him to think for himself and to apply what he had been taught to practical ends—the instinct for sport and adventure which is his national heritage, his pride in his young country, and the opportunity which came to him of creating a great national tradition, were all factors which made him what he was. . . .
> In him there was a curious blend of a capacity for independent judgment with a readiness to submit to self-effacement in a common cause. He had a personal dignity all his own. He had the political sense highly developed, and was always a keen critic of the way in which his battalion or battery was 'run', and of the policies which guided his destinies from day to day.
> His intellectual gifts and his 'handiness' made him an apt pupil. It was always a delight to see the avidity with which he mastered the technique of the weapons which were placed in his hands. . . .
> He was always mentally alert to adopt new ideas and often to invent them. His adaptability spared him much hardship. He knew how to make himself comfortable. To light a fire and cook his food was a natural instinct. A sheet of corrugated iron, a batten or two, and a few strands of wire were enough to enable him to fabricate a home in which he could live at ease.
> Psychologically he was easy to lead but difficult to drive. His

imagination was readily fired. War was to him a game, and he played for his side with enthusiasm. His bravery was founded upon his sense of duty to his unit, comradeship to his fellows, emulation to uphold his traditions, and a combative spirit to avenge his hardships and sufferings upon the enemy.

Monash once remarked, *contra* Bean, that 'while you could distinguish between the social scales you could not tell whether a man was bred in the city or bush, nor could you discriminate between one State and another'.

The A.I.F.'s greatest strength, perhaps, was its training of officers to look after the men. In January 1918 Monash wrote to Springthorpe:

Try as one will, it proves quite impossible to organize an Army on the basis of an industrial undertaking, or on the basis of any ordinary organization of civilization. There is the personal factor; there are the rough and ready means to ends; there is the wide disparity in the competence and point of view of individuals. It is a trite saying, and one which I am always preaching, that the inevitable consequence of any lack of perfection in our administration and in our organizing methods, the inevitable result, is to bring discomfort and suffering to the men in the ranks. ... it is *they* who get it 'in the neck' every time, whenever some regimental or staff officer makes any sort of blunder or commits any sort of neglect.

.... Our whole and continuous efforts are directed day and night to an attempt to eliminate, as far as possible, the evil consequences of inexperience, want of knowledge, want of tact, and want of the qualities of leadership on the part of hundreds of individual officers. ... One can only lay down broad principles, and then watch carefully. ...

... the leading principle in the exercise of command in this Division is care for the welfare of the men and you will please note that I have put this principle, not so much on the grounds of humanity as upon the grounds of expediency; ... it is our business to bring [them] to the place and moment of battle well fed, well clothed, well rested, in a contented frame of mind, and with [their] offensive spirit at top water mark. We do this because we want to win the battle, and not purely out of love for our fellow-men.

He constantly preached Plumer's and Harington's saying that 'the staff officer is the servant of the troops'. He could be ruthless in sacking officers and sending them home, and made enemies thereby, though some critics believed him not to be ruthless enough.

'Very much and stupid comment has been made upon the discipline of the Australian soldier', wrote Monash in reaction to the everlasting parrot-cry of British officers who were ignorant of the A.I.F. in battle. He attacked 'the barrack room discipline of the regular army, which destroyed individuality and made a man a machine'. 'We release the individual's intelligence and initiative. There is no evidence that soldiers marshalled under an autocracy can boast of any superiority to a citizen army. There is abundant evidence to the contrary.' Monash had been a moderately strict disciplinarian in 4th Brigade and 3rd Division. He probably relaxed his view for he eventually concluded that discipline

> does not mean lip service, nor obsequious homage to superiors, nor servile observance of forms and customs, nor a suppression of individuality. . . .
> In the Australian Forces no strong insistence was ever made upon the mere outward forms of discipline. The soldier was taught that personal cleanliness was necessary to ensure his health and well-being, that a soldierly bearing meant a moral and physical uplift which would help him to rise superior to his squalid environment, that punctuality meant economy of effort, that unquestioning obedience was the only road to successful collective action. He acquired these military qualities because his intelligence taught him that the reasons given him were true ones.
> In short, the Australian Army is a proof that individualism is the best and not the worst foundation upon which to build up collective discipline.

But Monash took the traditional view that 'It is more expedient that the authority of a commander in his treatment of his subordinates should be upheld under all circumstances than that occasional wrongs and petty tyrannies should go unredressed'. This more than any other factor—that injustice so frequently was seen to prevail, as in any other army—qualified the loyalty of innumerable members of the A.I.F.

With regard to relations between officers and men, Monash wrote:

> From almost the earliest days of the war violence was done to a deep-rooted tradition of the British Army, which discouraged any promotion from the ranks, and stringently forbade, in cases where it was given, promotion in the same unit. . . . The Australian Imperial Force changed all that.

In Egypt early in 1916 he had had his way in a fierce encounter with Cox over commissioning a sergeant in his own battalion.

> There was thus no officer caste, no social distinction in the whole force. In not a few instances, men of humble origin and belonging to the artisan class rose, during the war, from privates to the command of battalions. The efficiency of the force suffered in no way in consequence. On the contrary, the whole Australian Army became automatically graded into leaders and followers according to the individual merits of every man, and there grew a wonderful understanding between them.
> [Officers had] to dress like the men, to live among them in the

trenches, to share their hardships and privations.... No officer dared to look after his own comfort until every man ... had been fed and quartered.

'If the Australians hate anything, it is the superior airs which put a gap between them and their leaders.... artificial distinctions irk them badly.' Mutual confidence was everything. Nevertheless Monash exaggerated the absence of social distinctions; a high proportion of those promoted to officer were private-school products.

Monash prided himself on his psychological understanding of his men. He told Felix Meyer that

It is because we do not consider psychology enough that we are taking so long to win the War. Personally I have always found it to pay well closely to consider the psychology not only of the enemy, but also of my own troops, ... to study the methods of keeping up the morale and the fighting spirit of our own soldiers. Indeed, it is psychology all along the line.

One had to judge, depending on the circumstances, he later said, on what grounds to base an appeal to the troops—patriotism, the instinct of self-preservation, desire for revenge, etc. Psychology, in that age, was a novel concept. Bean, Gellibrand and Murdoch deplored Monash's alleged psychological failures—the hat style of 3rd Division, the 'scores on the board', his handling of the disbandment mutinies. Murdoch referred to 'his somewhat shallow interpretations of the deeper feelings and instincts of his men'. Their criticisms are trivial in the face of Monash's psychological achievement in maintaining morale. His message to the troops on the eve of 8 August thrilled many of them (though some were as cynical as ever) and his eventual organization of publicity satisfied them. All the senior A.I.F. commanders were limited by gulfs of class, education and experience in understanding their rank and file. It is doubtful whether any of them except Elliott had better understanding than Monash. His quickly written analysis of the qualities of the digger in *Australian Victories* stands comparison with Bean's long-considered treatment in the *Official History*.

An example of his good sense in the face of orthodox British Army practice was his successful protest, when still a divisional commander, against an attempt by Carruthers to impose ruthless police action against looting of civilian property. There were very few potential criminals, Monash argued, the great body were 'decently behaved men'. When he had been commanded to issue a strongly worded order about horse-thieving, he had merely directed, quite effectively, that officers would be held personally responsible for any stray horses within the lines not accounted for.

You call upon all officers to make lists of civilian property in their possession, stating whence they obtained it.... In plain language you call upon every officer to prove that he is not a thief.... I should not envy the task of the military police in making a house to house inspection of all billets.... the true remedy for the whole evil, if it exists,... is prevention, and not cure.... you cannot ask a whole Army Corps to turn out its pockets for inspection, merely because there may be a score of thieves discovered in the process.

The troops, quite rightly, would 'indignantly resent anything in the way of a general imputation'.

In common with probably all the Australian generals, Monash favoured occasional imposition and carrying-out of the death penalty for desertion. Alone among the Allied forces, the death penalty was never inflicted in the A.I.F. for an army crime. It was provided for in the Defence Act only for mutiny, desertion to the enemy or treachery, not for desertion to the rear. The Australian people and the A.I.F. itself would not tolerate applying the death penalty for desertion from a volunteer army, and the government knew it. In 1917, especially, the Australian rate of desertion and proportion imprisoned, though less than 1 per cent, was far higher than in the British and other Dominion armies. Haig and the War Office were fearful of the effects of the bad example to British troops; the senior Australian officers worried about the contagion spreading among the younger inexperienced men, and recommended one or two salutary executions—preferably of deserters who were known criminals—and announcement that terms of imprisonment would have to be served in full even after the war ended. While acting corps commander in July 1917, Monash had to deal with several serious cases and recommended to Birdwood a further request to the Australian government; Glasgow and Holmes approached Birdwood similarly. But the government, despite repeated appeals, stood firm.

The senior A.I.F. commanders only gradually came to realize the effects of 'shell-shock' and to recognize men at the end of their tether as distinct from simple cases of 'cowardly desertion'. In the earlier years of the war unqualified black and white notions of bravery and cowardice prevailed. Medical opinion was still primitive, but the number of proven brave men who were breaking down forced reconsideration. A memorandum from Birdwood to divisional commanders in December 1917, requiring that 'the medical aspect of the case should be carefully gone into before the man is charged with desertion', was a turning-point. Monash had dealt considerately with several lieut-colonels and majors who could no longer stand the strain, and in May 1918 directed commanding officers to withdraw men with long service suffering from 'nerves'. Hobbs believed that many desertions by men who were 'more to be pitied than blamed' would not have occurred if there had been a better spirit of comradeship in their company or platoon, and that some officers had not been looking after their men well enough. Monash told Blamey he was 'much struck by this Division's handling of this question; and shall talk to the others about it'. In the later stages of the war men convicted of desertion or absence without leave had their sentence suspended if they were willing to return to their units. Many whose nerve was breaking were transferred to support units.

Almost the last thing Monash had done before he went on leave, near-exhausted, after the fighting was over, was to draft some notes for Springthorpe to use in newspaper articles. 'I do frankly', he wrote, 'put forward to *you* the claim that the success of the Corps, as a fighting machine, has been, in its totality, very largely due to my own efforts'. He was perhaps remembering Henderson's dictum that 'no army has ever achieved great things unless it has been well commanded'. He was justly proud of his achievement and fearful that he would not receive proper recognition, but he never said anything like it again. He knew very well what a superb force he had commanded and was again and again to say, 'With such an army a general can work miracles'. His book of 1919, *Australian Victories*, was dedicated to 'The Australian soldier, who by his military virtues, and by his deeds in battle, has earned for himself a place in history which none can challenge'. He could not have maintained his unchallenged leadership of the returned soldiers if he had been suspected of arrogance or patronizing of the rank and file. He was indeed deeply moved by the fellowship of the A.I.F. in which he was humbly proud to participate. It was a code which, in the face of the blinding simplicity of life and death, returned to something like primitive Christianity. Their strong sense of nationality was reinforced by their distaste, which Monash and Bean shared, for the class divisions between officers and men in the British Army and the gross physical differentiation between those from the hereditary class and the stunted subservient products of industrial areas—the success of England in breeding one class at the expense of the rest. Like many senior officers—White is another—Monash came to appreciate the common man as he never previously had. With widened tolerance, he largely abandoned his surviving assumptions that life was jungle-war, and became much more inclined to devote himself, after the war, to serving the people.

Although it was his road to fame (which considerably helped him to endure it) Monash in no way enjoyed the war. 'Every day was filled with loathing, horror, and distress. . . . Yet it had to be. . . .' We must believe him. It had to be: there was no consolation for him in the belief of many of the clergy that it was God's mysterious providence, that through sacrifice and suffering men would be lifted to higher endeavour, or that the war would transform society for the better. He shared the common distress of personal friends and comrades killed or maimed. The burden of letters from distressed parents and wives remained heavy. A Queensland widow who had lost two sons implored him to withdraw her third boy from the line. Another mother wrote: 'Dear General anything you may at any time be able to do for my boy please remember he is all I have may God bless and protect you all'. It was strictly not his business, but Birdwood's, and he wrote recommending inquiry into extreme cases, which Birdwood sometimes acted on.

In minor ways Monash liked to show that he, too, was 'incorrigibly civilian' (as Bean described the A.I.F. ranker) and not a mere cog in the military machine. Blamey affectionately recalled that he was 'neither careful nor careless in his personal appearance' and, as 'a semi-humorous protest against the efforts of his personal staff to have him meticulously correct', 'invariably wore his spurs upside down'. He had a touch of cussedness—according to the viewpoint of the reader, a deplorable inclination to make special laws for himself or a praiseworthy determination not to bow to the system.

If Monash was fortunate in his general treatment by military historians over the years, he was a little unlucky in that the official Australian historian was C. E. W. Bean. Though he eventually came to respect Monash greatly, Bean disliked and did not understand him. Bean was a man of the highest ideals and decency. His *Official History* is probably the most interesting, democratic, honest and fair-minded of those produced by any country. He was a romantic public-school man, brought up on the adventure literature of British imperialism, whose ideal Australian soldier was of pastoral background, a horseman and sportsman, and a dashing battle commander; this was the 'true Australian type'. One of the weaknesses of his *History* is that it is to some extent a factional product: he idealized Brudenell White and other friends like Gellibrand, to the relative neglect of other fine soldiers. From mid-1915, when on Gallipoli they had got off on the wrong foot, he and Monash had bristled at each other, but they rarely met again until 1918. Bean knew little of Monash, who was the new type of engineer-commander who did not meet his ideal. Bean had some conventional prejudices about Jewish characteristics, he disliked Monash's showmanship and his flagrant disregard of the censorship, suspected that he worked deviously behind the scenes for promotion and was subservient to Haig, and believed he had put his finger on basic flaws in Monash's character in that he tended to conceal the truth, was sly and shifty—'not quite straight' enough. In particular, he was sure that Monash was so ambitious for glory that the lives of the Corps were not safely to be entrusted to him. Thus he was misguided enough to plot with Murdoch to replace Monash with his hero White.

Monash considered Bean was inadequate as war correspondent in promoting A.I.F. interests or in sufficiently encouraging the folks at home. Indeed Bean was prematurely too much the historian and unfitted by nature to be a propagandist and public relations man. About September 1918 they were at loggerheads. In his diaries throughout the war, and especially in 1918, Bean displayed extraordinary prejudice against Monash, again and again leaping to damning conclusions. He suspected him of sometimes rewriting his battle orders after the event to fit them to what had actually happened. He never understood that what he regarded as Monash's frequent failure to grasp the details of what had happened in an action, and his tendency to believe the most attractive story, was Monash presenting an official version for public consumption.

Bean largely altered his opinion of Monash after observing his conduct of the Corps in 1918 and, on recognizing how untypical his view of him was among soldiers, he retracted many of his harsh judgements. When Monash died—and before—he paid glowing tributes:

> as a leader for the Australians he gave the Diggers at that time precisely what they wanted—an organiser who would never let them down by the failure of supplies or material. The Digger, trained almost to perfection, required someone behind whom he could trust to see that all such arrangements were perfect. ... And for that purpose the whole British Army ... would probably have picked one man above all others ... John Monash.

He was Australia's 'greatest military leader'—'neither a hero nor a mighty strategical genius [but] probably the ablest and most successful British corps commander in France'. Yet Bean's final considered judgement in volume 6 of the *Official History*, published in 1942, is an uneasy mixture of the highest praise and repetition of some of his old prejudices. He compared Monash with Napoleon at length. 'Monash was eager for military glory; but of none of his battles can it be said that he embarked upon it for that reason.' 'He was naturally humane.' His intellect was 'stored with knowledge sufficient for the greatest of rulers'. But nearly all his minor criticisms were shallow misapprehensions, easily open to rebuttal or qualification.

Bean relied considerably on Brudenell White's opinions in his eventual judgement of Monash. Though he made a magnificent funerary tribute, in his later years White had many private reservations about Monash; he believed he had been over-praised and was irritated by the 'moonshine' talk that he might have become British commander-in-chief. He once said that McCay was 'greater even than Monash', his military knowledge was deeper, and he would have shown himself abler if the war had been one of movement. But Monash 'had unquestionably the greater personality despite an unimpressive presence'.

Cutlack's foreword to the 1935 selection of Monash's war letters is next to Bean's the most important comment by a contemporary. Cutlack had been much closer and had worked with him and knew very well how his working subordinates regarded him. Monash 'was never afraid of responsibility, or of asserting himself in emergency; ... he was never more clear-headed and resolute than when he had set himself to taking charge of a situation'. His supreme accomplishment was his lucidity deriving from 'his great power of mental concentration and analysis'.

> He never left any point veiled in ambiguity, and he could not tolerate ambiguity or carelessness in others. Understanding meant to him complete understanding, the grasping of the full detail of an event or a position and of its proper background. Never, so far as truth was humanly attainable, did he ever half know anything. He would consult with any man within his reach, high or low, in order to perfect his own understanding; and in the utmost good faith, slurring nothing, exaggerating nothing, he aimed at conveying as full an understanding to those with whom he worked.
>
> Any mere pretence of knowledge or capacity was anathema to him. No shrewder judge of men and things has ever lived.

At the same time he had 'that simplicity and unfailing common sense which are the essential possession of all great minds'. His capacity to manage men was legendary and his range of knowledge extraordinary.* In contrast to Bean the hardened journalist Cutlack also worshipped the man:

> His other outstanding and most lovable trait was his humanity. These letters reveal again, what every man who worked under him learned so well—his genial kindliness, his wide-ranging and ready sympathy, his abiding love of life. Few men were rash enough to visit John Monash in anger; none, surely, could ever have left him angry.

He referred to looking into his 'kindly, serious old eyes' and to his gentle, clear voice, and concluded: Monash's good fortune 'left the simple and generous nature of the man, though flattered by success, yet essentially unspoilt'.

---

* Cutlack recalled the arrival at divisional headquarters of an officer of the Medical Corps, 'a man of high attainment in his profession. ... Several of us afterwards received him in the mess and asked him how he got on with "the old man". The new D.A.D.M.S. replied with great feeling: "Get on! I don't know. I've just had the stiffest ten minutes' *viva voce* in my own profession that I've ever gone through. Damn it, I began to wonder whether I knew anything at all about medicine" '.

Bean's friend Gellibrand was another dissident private voice. He had been critical of Monash on Gallipoli, had disagreed with the plans for 8 August 1918, and had had an altercation with him on 30 September. He seemed to arrive on good terms with Monash in the 1920s. But twenty-five years after the war he annotated his copy of Monash's *Australian Victories* with a series of, for the most part, petty and trivial comments and added some general remarks which were highly critical. He was, however, deliberately making the case against Monash, for he concluded: 'For my part it mattered not that the leopard had spots—that was natural. I could admire and follow him with comfort and pleasure despite the fact that I was well aware of his failings'. On another occasion he told Bean that he admired 'a lot of Monash—at a distance'. Some of his criticisms were sweeping: Monash 'was an egoist-optimist and blind to what others could see at a glance'; he never *led*, he *directed* or ordered; he 'accepted all reports as gospel'; he 'suffered from a sense of great mental superiority over all of us'; he was a bad chooser of men and favoured his weaker commanders; he didn't mix. One virtue was the emphasis in his planning on 'the largest factor of safety'. He 'beat all in one thing: his ability to bargain with success on the lines: "I'll take over another mile of front but of course I must have another 3 batteries" etc etc.' Though possibly not meant as such, this is high praise. Gellibrand found it 'difficult to place him above Chauvel or White, and his true level would be nearer McCay, Bridges, Holmes, Walker'.

> Monash and Australia should have rested content with claiming that he was "primus inter pares". . . . There were too many concerned in claiming Monash as *the Leader*—Jews—Victorians—Masons[!]—Engineers and the masses who just follow a lead.

Gellibrand possibly felt some resentment at the fact that he and other fine generals had been allowed so little fame.

On the other hand, the most nationalist and popular of all Australian commanders, 'Pompey' Elliott, made a great case for Monash (in the Melbourne *Age*, 28 May 1921, a remarkable document). Elliott was obsessed with the terrible Australian casualties, which he attributed to rotten British generalship, at The Nek, German Officers' Trench, Fleurbaix, Warlancourt, First Bullecourt and Passchendaele. He detested Birdwood and his minion White for their alleged subservience to the high command, and their lack of protest at British contemptuous criticisms of Australians' supposed lack of discipline and bad behaviour. He believed Monash had been the only British general to see the futility of Passchendaele and to protest against it; he had made the vital planning for 8 August by insisting on going in deep enough to capture the enemy guns to prevent their retaliation; and he had at last achieved proper Australian recognition by insisting on the scores being placed on the board. This reference for Monash, written by one of the A.I.F.'s greatest aggressive commanders who also most considered his men's protection, is strong evidence in support of Monash's stature. His most fervent supporters among the generals included nearly all the great fighting commanders.

'The more one studies the lives of great leaders', writes the historian Stephen Roskill, 'the more one realises that not only is there vast diversity in their characters and methods, but nearly all of them at times exhibited frailties which one would expect to have reacted against their position and authority'. Monash, throughout the war, was driven by the surviving insecurity of the outsider to seek constant recognition of his achievements; the mix of his vanity and modesty is bewildering. His showmanship to superior officers, visiting politicians and war correspondents irritated many who lacked his capacity to show themselves to the best advantage; Birdwood, though he recognized that the goods were there, resented his always so skilfully displaying them on the counter. Monash could always put on a better ceremonial display than anyone else, however hard they tried, just as he was so careful to present himself to the photographer at the best angle at the right moment. He was far more skilled at winning publicity for his division or corps and himself. He was at his worst in his stiff-necked boastfulness in reporting from time to time to the governor-general and minister for defence; he could not strike the right note of semi-formality. Cutlack notes the 'sense of egotism' in his letters—true also of *Australian Victories*—although the egotism is mixed with intense pride in the achievements of the A.I.F.: it was 'a frailty not peculiar to General Monash alone'. Monash was neither better nor worse in the congratulatory or commiserating correspondence between generals, which so often reeked with insincerity, though it was usually a clumsy attempt to 'do the right thing' and keep on good terms. In mid-1918 he began to pester Birdwood to have his promotion to lieut-general made substantive; but he was not in the least unusual among army men in his craving for honours and promotion. Bean's colleague, A. W. Bazley, summed him up astutely (elaborating on a remark by White): 'He was keenly ambitious, but if, being human, he was not without the vanity of most successful men, he had the restraint and intelligence to keep that quality under control; it never trapped him into mistakes in the field'. Much more alarming than Monash's eye for publicity was his habit of exaggerating his and his men's achievements to the extent of serious distortion of the truth. It was not just a matter of putting the best face on things for the sake of morale, but rather an obsessive trait which came out much more when he set pen to paper or dictated than in conversation. The most serious example had been his diary-letter of the Gallipoli evacuation which, as Bean noted, might have destroyed his career if it had been published in full.

In 1976 Norman Dixon published *The Psychology of Military Incompetence* in which he posited a close link between military incompetence and the authoritarian personality, which might be defined as the opposite of the individualistic, tolerant, democratic, unprejudiced and egalitarian. He makes only passing reference to Monash but notes the absence in him of authoritarian traits and that he had not been subject to 'the mind-blunting, routinized career' of a professional soldier. Some of the characteristic personality traits of great generals which Dixon lists, are worth trying out on Monash. He was resolute, quick in decision, radiated self-confidence, was morally courageous, forceful, equable in temper and not anxious, blended boldness and caution, inspired obedience, was compassionate, humane, versatile, fatherly to the young, open to new technology, tolerant of the odd or different and willing to break the rules. He was not afraid of personal conflict, was not introverted, rigid, obstinate, ethnocentric, anti-intellectual, blindly obedient, driven by fear of failure or particularly careful about dress. But he does not fit the pattern in so far as he very much needed approval and was status-hungry.*

Despite all his tense sensitivity, Monash won through to full recognition. A colonial Jewish militiaman of German origin was an unlikely candidate for high promotion but Haig, the 'able inarticulate' Scot with many intellectual friends, and Plumer could recognize quality. And he convinced Birdwood and White and the Australian government on his merits. In Britain and Australia, in the climate of mild Edwardian anti-Semitism, the notion of a Jew being a soldier was a bit of a joke. He had suffered the resentment of permanent British and Australian officers at home and during the war at his upstart claims to military education and his so evident general educational superiority. He had overcome opposition with patience and self-control, without intriguing or wire-pulling—and may be forgiven his exultation. From within the A.I.F., it may be added, there was minimal objection to his preferment despite all grounds of national origin, religion and amateur status.

---

* Like Kitchener, perhaps, as his biographer Philip Magnus describes him, Monash had 'two basic attributes—an unparalleled thoroughness and an unparalleled drive'. Like Admiral 'Jacky' Fisher he had enormous self-confidence, was a progressive technocrat, articulate, incisive, eager for responsibility, unperturbed by enemies and did not shrink from publicity (the phrases are Dixon's). Or like Montgomery his great attributes, as Dixon describes Montgomery's, were capacity for 'sheer hard work, a refusal to conform to the dead hand of military tradition, and the possession of [an] open, clear and sensitive' mind, also 'the knack of creating oases of serenity around himself'. And perhaps too those 'really rather pathetic and naive pieces of conceit [betraying] an underlying need to prove himself to others and thereby to himself'.

No one who associated with him, Bazley concluded, 'could fail to see in him a leader of heroic proportions'. And as a former junior officer at Corps, Sir Hugh Brain, said, his 'tradition of orderly thinking and planning for all contingencies' had immense influence on the generals of the Second A.I.F.

14

The Blare and Blaze of Fame 1918–1920

FROM the beginning of December 1918 Monash set to work on the great task of repatriation. He was not yet rushed with social engagements, though he had quite enough to satisfy him. At the Australian and New Zealand Luncheon Club, Hamilton, Churchill, Hughes and Birdwood all referred to him in their speeches; each time there was 'vociferous applause'—it was 'very gratifying'. During the finals of the British Empire Boxing Tournament at the Albert Hall, Prince Albert summoned him to the royal box and they chatted for half an hour. At the state banquet at Buckingham Palace for President and Mrs Wilson, he sat between the press proprietor Lord Burnham and Rudyard Kipling, who swapped autographs and told him anecdotes about himself. The company stood while the King and Wilson made their speeches. Monash had five minutes with them and ten with the Queen after dinner, and he conversed with Lloyd George, Asquith, French, Balfour and Austen Chamberlain. It was 'a thrilling function of unsurpassed splendour and brilliancy'. He sat at Haig's right hand when the Secretary of State for War, Lord Milner, dined the army chiefs. The 'blare and blaze of fame' was enveloping him. When he was twenty he had believed that any fame he might achieve would prove to be hollow and make him no happier. How often now did he use his ironic inner eye?

Honours aggregated. In October 1918 the French had awarded him a Croix de Guerre avec Palme; the Belgians made him a Grand Officer of the Order of the Crown and gave him their Croix de Guerre. 'Having started at last to do you some sort of justice in the matter of decorations', remarked Carruthers, 'I see that they are making up for lost time'. The Americans (though Monash had to prompt them) awarded the Distinguished Service Medal. At the New Year he was appointed Knight Grand Cross of the Order of St Michael and St George (G.C.M.G.). So far as he knew, in Australia only the governor-general and Sir Joseph Cook had attained this grade, but he received few congratulations; seemingly few people understood how rare an honour it was. He took great interest in the designing of his coat of arms: it included the Southern Cross, a bridge symbolizing engineering, a sword enclosed in a laurel wreath, the Lion of Judah and the compasses of King Solomon; the Latin motto meant 'For War and the Arts'. He ordered a supply of crested notepaper and consulted Sir Edward Wallington at Buckingham Palace about problems of precedence. It was all very pleasant, but had its drawbacks; he implored Ernest Wears never to treat him with 'solemn formality' as many of his friends were doing.

Before he left the Corps Monash had to make his own recommendations for honours. He arranged for a K.C.M.G. for Hobbs and a K.C.B. for Rosenthal and for MacLagan's substantive promotion to major-general. He considered Gellibrand and Glasgow might wait for their Ks, but they got them, nevertheless, as did White through Birdwood. Blamey missed out on any award through a clerical error, and was so enraged that he threatened to leave the Army; Monash hurriedly prompted Rawlinson to provide a C.B. Blamey remarked that he knew honours were 'somewhat meretricious' but their 'worldly value' mattered. Monash fought on through 1919 to try to gain recognition for his particular friends and protégés such as McNicoll, McGlinn and Morshead, and the Simonsons and Moss, but Birdwood could not or would not oblige him.

Repatriation was to be carried out with remarkable speed and humanity by the soldiers under Monash's leadership, rather than by the politicians. It was among the very finest of the A.I.F.'s and Monash's achievements.

Monash built on the preparatory thinking by White and Dodds over a long period. Three days after Hughes had commissioned him, he reported back with his broad plan, then left for France to confer with divisional and brigade commanders at Le Cateau. His chief message was that 'fighting morale' must now be replaced by a 'reconstruction morale', 'a vision of the needs of Australia in the future days of peace'. In London a week later, Private Tom Ryan, a member of the Victorian parliament, saw Monash, Foott and Durrant, and reported to Pearce:

> I thought I knew something of the repatriation problem. . . . these three soldiers . . . have conceived a most perfect, and the most common-sense practical, and just skeleton for this work of repatriation. . . . If the rest of the big military officers have the vision, the foresight, and the indomitable perseverance of these three men, then I can understand why we won the war. . . . On the vocational, educational and industrial outlook, [Monash] is indeed a General, unless one could call him, a Field Marshal.

Monash collared Ryan to work with him and promoted him major.

Monash conferred often with Hughes in December. It seems that Hughes was not unwilling to make demobilization a slow process, for fear of large-scale returned-soldier unemployment. Monash had guardedly reflected this view in his conference at Le Cateau. Nearly everybody concerned was outraged at any suggestion of anything but the most determined policy to get the men home as quickly as possible. Breaking with Hughes, Murdoch began cabling vehemently to the Melbourne *Herald*, to the great embarrassment of W. A. Watt, the acting prime minister. Hughes was delaying vital decisions and on the 20th had an explosive meeting with Monash whom he dressed down for proceeding too fast. Monash eventually noted: 'Mr Hughes not really responsible for any valuable inspirations but, per contra, interfered'. But Hughes capitulated on the main question. Murdoch's despatch to the *Herald*, dated 21 December, was headed, 'Government Surrenders. Speed to be Governing Factor in Problems of Demobilisation. Monash the Driving Force'.

> Twelve days ago General Monash walked into bare, dusty rooms in Westminster. Now he has a staff. A week ago General Monash was settling elementary principles. Now he has a policy.
> The old building hums with life. You breathe the atmosphere of the General's 50 dug-outs. Carpetless floors, plain deal tables, hard work. Graphs are on the walls, not telling of casualties and battle strengths now, or of locations of units, but of movements home. . . .
> The hand was the hand of Monash, the brain that of Hughes. Such was the scheme. But Monash's brain finds a way of directing its own hand. British army commanders found that out when he was a corps commander. . . . If politicians get in the way of this brain now there will be a crash, and Monash will go home.
> . . . never can there be questions about Monash's brain. It is there, a living, searching, strong intelligence, breeding ideas, and judging them shrewdly. His motto is Action, and his energy already pulsates through the demobilisation scheme.

Murdoch continued to support Monash: 'Details of Masterly Scheme Given' headed his next despatch. And he quoted him in an interview:

> I seek to give Australia a 'spiritual momentum'. I mean the influence of brave men, returned to their native country in good condition, equipped for a great future. . . . If we can concert . . . the means and machinery to enable our men to equip themselves for their future industrial life . . . then we are going to render a service to our nation which cannot be measured.

On the 27th Monash promulgated to the A.I.F. a letter from Hughes which laid it down that everything had to be 'subordinated to the task of promptly returning our men to their own country'. They were to be treated as generously as possible, as citizens rather than soldiers; in particular, the ships home must not be overcrowded.

From January on, Monash had things very much his own way, for Hughes and Cook were preoccupied at Versailles. Hughes had originally decided to set up a Demobilisation Board of mixed military and civilian members, chaired by a minister, with Monash as director-general. But events moved too quickly for the board ever to meet usefully. The government at home decided to send Pearce, but he did not arrive till late March when he ran through Monash's plans and procedures and was well satisfied. When the civilian appointment to the board, the capable businessman W. G. McBeath, arrived in May, there was little for him to do.

In December and January Monash and his staff worked prodigiously. Foott was his deputy: Coxen and Durrant held senior posts; and, after failing to get Bruche promoted to the main administrative post at Corps, Monash put him in charge of non-military employment. He relied on McCay to control movements in and out of camps and depots in England. He consulted White often on strategy and tactics. He was to look back on them as 'tumultuous and difficult days' when he was infuriated by the lack of sympathy and 'appalling inefficiency' of British officials. And some of his officers, 'used to the somewhat cumbrous military methods', had to be instructed on how to run things on business lines. Essentially repatriation too was 'a mere hard ordinary business proposition'.

Monash's letters to Chauvel, Hobbs and others are models of sensitive administrative leadership. The recipient could only have replied warmly and enthusiastically. Monash was enjoying being a semi-civilian and not using Army forms of authority. He wrote to Chauvel a week after starting work to say he had to get going without properly considering the problems of the troops in the Middle East; he knew much he was proposing to do would be inapplicable or unsuitable to them. He would modify his plans as Chauvel desired. Chauvel must feel free to suspend orders, refer them back, put up his own proposals; please would he keep in touch fully and frankly. In his many letters to 'My dear Hobbs' or other generals (which he usually concluded 'with kindest regards, yours very sincerely') he wrote without a trace of rank-authority or self-dramatization in explaining his difficulties, trying to sort out authority between Birdwood, Hobbs and himself, suggesting ways and means of arranging the withering away of the Corps, devolving to Hobbs and his staff everything that they considered best to claim, and stressing always his desire for fullest and frankest consultation.

Almost the only serious unsettledness among the troops was in the

3rd Division Artillery which early in January went 'on strike'. Hobbs, Gellibrand and Grimwade handled them with the utmost leniency, and were inclined to blame the officers for over-strict discipline. Monash regretted that these troops had broken out before his paternal policy could become generally known. Marcel Aurousseau, a divisional education officer, has remarked that Monash's series of *Instructions*, 'were examples of such clear, precise and compact English that I recognised them as the expressions of a master mind. . . . The man's ability for organisation was superb'. Monash had drafted by mid-January *Demobilisation of the A.I.F.: Things which Australian Soldiers ought to know*, and had arranged for lecturers at Le Havre base to inform all troops on their way to England of what was being done for them. He was entirely tolerant of the eight hundred men who had enlisted in 1915 or earlier who were absent without leave in England. On 23 January he issued lengthy advice—absolute common sense—to commanders of troop-ships: 'Be strict from the very start about everything that really matters, and indulgent about everything else. Don't fuss the men, and don't irritate them with unnecessary restrictions'. He instructed his own headquarters staff to give visiting troops anything they asked for within reason: 'They were to be treated with the greatest consideration, as men who had done their work were entitled to be'. He knew it was entirely to be expected that many of the troops found it difficult to comprehend that the generals who had so driven them and mucked them around could be devotedly working in their interests.

He had about 160 000 men to repatriate. Birdwood, soon after the Armistice, had been sending convalescent troops home and had extended the home-leave scheme for 1915 men. Monash sent off his batman, Dawson, and asked the Repatriation Department to see he got the fullest benefits to which he was entitled. From the end of November five thousand men moved weekly from France to England. The vexed question of the order of priority for returning home was finally settled on 19 December when Hughes accepted Monash's strong recommendation that the criteria should be, in order of importance, length of service, family responsibilities, and assured employment: men might, in exceptional cases such as 'pivotal business importance' or interrupted university courses, be moved to the head of the queue. 'Family ships' for wives, children and fiancées were to be interspersed at regular intervals. Monash's main contribution was the ingenious arrangement of the troops into quotas of one thousand—a normal train-load and ship-load—and their organization into self-contained units while waiting to leave. By mid-January the details of the scheme were settled.

Though he had little to do with it day by day, Monash had immense pleasure in presiding over the A.I.F. Education Scheme. Compared to the Canadians, the A.I.F. had been slow to prepare for the transition to peace, but by May 1918 Monash was chairing the conference of senior officers which got the scheme going under the direction of Bishop Long. Planning of the enterprise and appointment and schooling of education officers were by the Armistice advanced enough to be just in time for effective action. Monash persuaded Hughes not to set up national workshops in England to train men for industries which Australia needed to develop (such as shipbuilding, aero engines, telephone equipment, potteries, glass and chemicals), but to be content with their original intention to arrange for employment of interested troops by private enterprise; the politicians were assuming that repatriation would take far longer than Monash expected. In the face of Hughes's contempt for formal education, he brought him together with Long and worked out a plan for Non-military employment (or Non-military enjoyment, as the troops commonly referred to it). Monash hoped at least twenty thousand would take part—probably twice that number did. Nearly thirteen thousand completed formal training courses in British educational institutions, apart from those who attended corps and divisional schools in France and Belgium and those who were employed by industry. Nearly all were engaged in agricultural, mechanical and commercial training, but many hundreds sat and passed matriculation, civil service and accountancy qualifications. The scheme boosted morale in the trying period of adjustment and immeasurably benefited the nation by its cultivation of innovatory skills.

Shipping was the great problem: there was intense competition with the other Dominions, India and most parts of the Empire. Hughes's bullying presence had ensured a good start, with sixteen ships to Australia in December. The rest was sheer forcefulness against the Ministry of Shipping. Justifying himself, Monash told Murdoch in April:

> It has been a tough and bitter battle between me and the Shipping Controller, and he has adopted every sort and kind of subterfuge, and every species of bluff to try to make it appear that he has been ready and willing to meet our requirements. . . . They have made a great pretence of being able to produce ships faster than I have been able to produce troops, but they have utterly failed, and the whole of my forecasts have been more than fully realised. I have now got the Shipping Controller absolutely beaten, have created such a pool of troops in England, and have secured such a rapid rate of delivery from France of the small remnant of troops remaining

there, that by no possibility can the Shipping Controller now catch up to me. . . . I am not giving him any rest, and scarcely a day passes that I do not deliver an attack upon him from a new angle.

Pearce was a powerful reinforcement, using his authority to browbeat British cabinet ministers.

Administrative bungles from on high contributed to Monash's problems. He had been assuming that two divisions would have to join the army of occupation in Germany and was not told that the decision had been abandoned. On learning this, late in January, he revised his plans, then was shocked to learn that the 3rd Division was after all tagged for occupation duties. A fierce campaign had to be waged to free it, so that its prepared quotas could immediately embark. The Defence Department was a regular nuisance: until Pearce arrived it could claim to exercise authority. When in January the department cabled its strong support for repatriation by battalions and other units, Monash sent a crushing reply. They protested that not enough senior officers were being sent home and that there had been some mutinous behaviour on the troop-ships which left in December, and wondered why the men were not sailing from France. Monash in late February tardily wrote them a lengthy résumé of his problems.

Of course all did not go smoothly. Early in March he had to stave off the intention of the British general controlling troop-train movements in Belgium and France to reduce the number carried in a single train; he sent a polite letter explaining how this would wreck his quota system, and concluded his appeal to reason with the terrible threat of calling in his prime minister. He was aware of the dangers of men of strong political views seeking to exploit the process of repatriation for party political ends among the troops; in his information service he employed men with widely varying though non-extremist opinions. One sergeant, who allegedly set out to sabotage the system, was smartly sent back to his unit, branded as a 'dangerous agitator' to be treated as 'a carrier of an infectious disease'. Watt, the acting prime minister, warned Monash to watch out for representatives of the Industrial Workers of the World stirring up trouble, especially on the troop-ships. Monash thought it best to withdraw and apologize when, after he had impliedly rebuked Cook, the deputy prime minister, for bringing political pressure to bear in a particular case, Cook angrily denied that he was seeking a special favour. He replied brusquely to a young Federal politician who had served in the British Army, one S. M. Bruce, who had written vaguely to ask what was happening about repatriation. He inevitably aroused hostility from his replies to the many letters of special pleading he received. He was big enough to write personally and apologize for mistakes, as he did to one gunner who had been hustled off home without his English wife and children.

By late March the rate of repatriation was very pleasing. By late May, as the shipping situation eased, it had accelerated fast. Within a month all the troops would be out of France and Belgium. Well over half the A.I.F. had embarked for home, and the bulk of the remainder would leave by July. Monash was preening himself on his extraordinary success, which would bring him great credit. By late July only thirty thousand were left, and most of them were administrative staff or choosing to delay. Monash and his staff got into mufti for normal daily wear. There was some tension and conflict now as he moved to break up the administrative staff; he had to bully Pearce into supporting him ruthlessly. In fact the problems of settling up finances and disposal of stores and equipment provided some of the most difficult work of all. But Pearce left in September, leaving Monash to wind up. There was one bad botch at the very end. Accommodation provided on the *Waimana*, a ship for warrant-officers and sergeants and their families, was totally inadequate and there was a 'jack-up'. Monash listened to the men, granted their case, provided for their maintenance until another ship could be found, and ordered a court of inquiry. At least one wife long remembered his addresses to the men and the women and his kindness 'to all of us "Pommy brides" '.

The repatriation operation had been a triumph. At a time of relaxation of social bonds and military authority when riots in other armies were frequent, the A.I.F. had dispersed remarkably peaceably with discipline as good as ever, reflecting considerate leadership—though there were many strays whom it is doubtful if the administration ever accounted for! The steady progress home of the troop-ships had been blessedly uneventful. As a last task, Monash ordered preparation of a history of demobilization, to which he wrote an introduction. Hughes initially had given him eighteen months in which to do the job; he had almost done it in eight and virtually completed it in eleven.

As the months went by Monash became increasingly bitter toward the government, especially to Hughes. They had clashed over demobilization policy but seem to have had no total breach, although stories to that effect circulated in later years. In 1924 C. Brunsden Fletcher of the *Sydney Morning Herald* gave a hearsay account of one clash (possibly on 20 December 1918): 'It is the picture of two strong men facing one another, and the soldier laying down the law to the politician'. Monash had concluded that Hughes did not like being overshadowed by him in London, and remarked that he had 'behaved in a most discourteous and shabby manner towards me, and I find it quite difficult to be even polite to him'. Monash worked harmoniously with Pearce but was angered by his later claim, for electoral purposes, of the credit for successful demobilization. He continued to regard Joe Cook as one who gave him full credit for what he had done. But the government entirely neglected to honour him and the other senior officers. The British government lavished honours and money-grants on its military and naval leaders: Haig was given £100 000 and an earldom, Rawlinson £30 000 and a barony, Birdwood £10 000 and a baronetcy. The American and Canadian governments promoted Pershing and Currie and provided them with posts of honour. All Monash's wartime honours and decorations were imperial and foreign. The Australian government made no gesture. It would not promote him to general, or offer him any military or other national job, or even consult him informally about his future. They were so ungenerous and tactless partly, perhaps, because they feared a military caste rising to power on the basis of its wartime success.

For the five months before Vic and Bertha arrived Monash led a rather restless life based on his service-flat, usually lunching and dining out at the Naval and Military and other clubs and at hotels and restaurants. He had captured the Corps Rolls-Royce and driver from the protesting Hobbs (and had hopes of 'souveniring' it back to Melbourne), but did not overdo its use, walking vigorously round London and sometimes taking buses and the tube. He was a social lion. Lord Burnham dined him at the Marlborough Club, where Monash found (Viscount) James Bryce, the historian and statesman, 'one of the most amazing personalities I have ever met'; they met several times again. Lord Northcliffe, General Gough, the Earl and Countess of Selborne, all lunched him. Lady Northcote, widow of a governor-general, rather adopted him and sent him pheasants. His old Melbourne engineering friend Lee Murray had him as guest of honour and speaker at the Eccentrics Club, of which he was made honorary life member; the Savage Club similarly honoured him: these were two thoroughly enjoyable evenings. The Smeatonian Society of Engineers likewise was proud to entertain him. He often met members of the royal family, the aristocracy and leading politicians at formal gatherings. He addressed the Overseas Club, the Dynamicables (on 'Engineering in War'), the Lyceum Club, the Ladies' Victory Festival and an A.N.A. Corroboree. He went often to the theatre, was made an honorary member at Lord's and given entry to the royal enclosure at Ascot. He gave portrait sittings to Longstaff, James Quinn, Isaac Cohen, Dora Ohlfsen and Solomon J. Solomon. He was not reading much or seriously: he did read C. J. Dennis's *Digger Smith* (and re-read *The Sentimental Bloke*), Stephen Leacock, Somerset Maugham's *The Moon and Sixpence* and de Morgan's *Joseph Vance*, and he pottered with jigsaws. It was a time for reflection on stirring events and for self-assessment. We may detect in him a new serenity.

On 29 April he joined Vic and Bertha, who had been given free passages by the Australian government, at Plymouth, sailed with them to Tilbury, settled them in to an apartment in Queen Anne's Mansions, and announced their arrival in the *Times*. Bertha wrote home that he looked 'marvellously fit' and the change in his figure was 'positively absurd', but his face was now heavily lined and he was greying and balding. Plenty of festivity remained for Vic, who revelled in it. The Hamiltons, Rawlinsons and Godleys entertained them. They dined with Mrs Hughes and went on to *Chu Chin Chow*. They attended balls, the Ascot races and the jubilee dinner of the Royal Colonial Institute. John attracted much attention when they visited the Royal Academy private viewing where Longstaff was exhibiting his portrait. On 29 May he was invested with his G.C.M.G. at the palace; they attended a royal garden party; then lunched privately with the King and Queen, Princess Mary and Prince Albert. In June and July, John received honorary degrees at Oxford and Cambridge. He and Bert made a four-day tour of the battlefields, visiting the graves of friends and taking photographs for their relatives. He attended a series of formal farewell occasions to Hughes, White, McCay and Chauvel—he was to be the last of the senior generals to go home. His speechifying continued, notably at the American Independence Day dinner, when he recalled Hamel as the first fighting together by American and British troops, and called for closer Australian relations with 'Big Brother'. He listed comprehensively the famous people he met socially that year. Domestically, he cordially approved of Bertha's engagement to Gershon Bennett from whom she had been parted for more than five years. 'I have never hankered for Bert, either after rank or after wealth', he told Mat.

Monash was hailed by the Jewish community in England as the great Jewish general—'our modern Judas Maccabaeus', the *Jewish Chronicle* called him. The daily press also tended to make as much of him as a Jew as an Australian. The comparison with Napoleon's great marshal, Masséna, was often made—irrelevantly, for Masséna was not a Jew. 'But my! isn't it odd the way they emphasize the Jewish business', his sister Mat remarked; they must be forgetting the Old Testament to assume that Jews were unlikely to be soldierly. 'If you have done nothing else I hope that you will have helped to remove some of the prejudices against Jewish folks.'

Monash was forced to consider his position. In the years before the war he had retained his anti-religious views; he had rejoined the Melbourne congregation, perhaps on Vic's insistence, when he could afford it, but had not attended synagogue. In response to appeals, he had subscribed to the *Jewish Herald* and given a donation to the Kadimah library, and had occasionally taken the chair at meetings of the Jewish Students and Graduates' Society. During the war his Jewishness had been little problem, though it affected his popularity in high places. Once on Gallipoli he had taken strong formal exception to an asinine remark in a divisional intelligence bulletin about 'Jewish influence all over the world . . . working against us'. From 1916 to 1918 he often attended Christian and occasionally Jewish church parades—it was his duty, and it was convenient for addressing the men—and he respected the chaplains Freedman and Danglow. He took care to provide for orthodox Jewish soldiers' dietary needs as far as was possible. He noted late in 1916 that four of his divisional staff were Jewish, but two of them were his aides; no accusation of preferment of Jews can possibly be made. But no Jew in a position of high responsibility could ever forget he was a Jew. After the war Monash told a young intellectual, Morris Ashkanasy, that in times of crisis he told himself: 'Remember you are a Jew and that if you muck it up our people will be blamed for it'. The tension was always there, as is shown by a comment of Vic's late in 1918: 'Most people I hear are so sorry that we are Jews, and that both you and I had moneylenders for Fathers, etc. The beasts, I jolly soon had that corrected'.

The great Anglo-Jewish families rushed him. He dined and lunched with Herbert Samuel, Sir Adolph Tuck, Waley Cohen, several of the Rothschilds and the Montefiores, Sir Philip Magnus, Lord Swaythling, the Earl of Reading, Sir Frederick Nathan, Sir Herbert Jessel, and their families; he was taken on once to a Liberal synagogue. He spoke at Danglow's farewell at the Chief Rabbi's home; addressed four hundred of the Jewish Lads' Brigade in the East End, shook every one by the hand, and was made a vice-president; took the chair at a lecture at the Jewish Historical Society; addressed the Jewish soldiers' branch of the Y.M.C.A. and a meeting in aid of an orphanage; and joined the council of the League of British Jews. He spoke at the founding meetings of the movement for an English Jewish War Memorial which was to be devoted to promotion of religious education, and was appointed a council-member; he later gave £250 to the Memorial, and most of his substantial later donations in Australia were to Jewish causes.

Press reports had it that, if Balfour's pledge of a national home for the Jews was to be carried out, Monash would be appointed governor-general or military governor of Palestine. His old 4th Brigade officer, E. L. Margolin, wrote from there to say that though he did not know whether Monash supported Zionism, the Zionists were very interested in him. Israel Zangwill described him as 'designed by Providence to be the first Governor of Palestine'. Late in 1918 Monash had been told that the Palestine Jews were hoping he would become commander-in-chief of the Jewish Army, a suggestion he met with three exclamation marks. In May 1919 he told Mat that the rumours were all 'moonshine', and that he so much wanted to get home he would not consider any appointment for a moment. When the rumours persisted, he let it be known that he was not interested.

Monash's chief formal recognition was at a dinner given him by the Maccabean Society, at which he reinforced himself with Birdwood and White. In his speech of acknowledgement, he made a significant statement:

> In Australia, the land of my birth, perhaps in a higher degree than in any other country in the world, there is and has been throughout at any rate all my life, never a vestige of discrimination against any one class or creed in the community. In the equality of opportunity which the democracy to which I belong offers to every man and woman regardless of social or religious considerations must be found the explanation of the fact that I am able to acknowledge, and gratefully acknowledge, that never at any time since my first schooldays, and throughout my whole academic and professional work, have I been confronted with any difficulty or obstacle or disfavour arising either directly or indirectly from any question of race or religion.

'In Australia we have no Jewish question', he told the *Jewish Chronicle*. He was well aware of the damage both Germany and Russia had done themselves before and during the war by the extent of anti-Semitism, and of his own extraordinary position as a Jew leading the army of one of the world's most democratic peoples.

He involved himself in Jewish politics, however, when he signed a letter to the *Morning Post*, in company with other prominent Jews, dissociating themselves from the Bolshevik sympathies of the left-wing Jewish press; Bolshevism was 'false to the tenets and teaching of Judaism'. His co-signatories were prominent in the League of British Jews which was hostile to the formation of a Jewish state. In later years when Monash was sympathetic to Zionism and was queried about his membership of the league, he frankly admitted he had made a mistake.

His social contacts with so many of England's most cultivated and distinguished Jews revived in him his quiescent communal feeling. In November 1919 the London *Jewish Guardian* published what purported to be an interview with him; he renounced it, claiming that he had no more than a 'cursory conversation' with the journalist. His alleged opinions were striking. The Jewish community in Australia was in danger of losing its identity. Mixed marriages had become increasingly frequent. Most Australian Jews and nearly all the orthodox Jews were of eastern European origin. The older, wealthier Jews of British origin, while proudly Jewish, rarely attended synagogue and, because they themselves were so integrated into Australian society, had little sympathy for the 'foreign' orthodox Jews. Australian Jews did not get 'the best class of Rabbi' and synagogue office-bearers were too often pawnbrokers or bookmakers. Their leadership could not remotely compare with that in the United States or England. He himself would attend synagogue more regularly if his emotions and intellect could be engaged. In England it was an honour to associate with and exchange ideas with ministers and lay leaders: not so in Australia.

> I am now ready to co-operate in any scheme which has for its aim the uplifting of communal self-respect and prestige amongst the Jews of Australia, and I am looking forward to the time when you will send us out more men of earnest and sincere convictions, workers and idealists ... who will help us in coping with the present evil of drift with which we are threatened.

The Melbourne *Jewish Herald* reprinted the article and gloomily accepted it as broadly true. Monash had very likely stated these views in less exaggerated form; perhaps he had been rash and unguarded, not expecting publication. But he had possibly come to recognize that the community could survive only with strong religious leadership and also, perhaps, by the unifying influence of Zionism.

Monash and the Australian Corps made three triumphal marches through London. The War Office had opposed a farewell march on Anzac Day because of the forthcoming parade of overseas troops on 3 May, but was overcome. Monash was in command and Birdwood was relegated to the saluting base at Australia House with the Prince of Wales, Haig, Hughes and Chauvel. Monash rode at the head, with Hobbs close up alongside, and had issued a message:

> It is only four miles and will last an hour and a quarter. It is not too much to ask every man to grip himself. Remember you represent the great and immortal Australian Army Corps. Every man should try and look as he ought to feel, proud of his division and the Australian Army.

The five thousand marching from Hyde Park down The Mall to The Strand and the City obeyed and did not fraternize. Round Australia House the cheering and coo-eeing was deafening. The Australian airmen stole the show—looping, and rolling and banking round the spires and chimney-pots. The press applauded these 'magnificently casual', 'easy-going brothers of ours': 'the people of London yesterday gave them a welcome in which affection was as strong as admiration': the new world had redressed the balance of the old. Monash was 'absolutely devoid of military "swank".' The Australians put efficiency before gold braid. Their officers were 'more "professional" than most professional soldiers, and consequently less theatrical and self-conscious'.

Smaller groups of the Corps marched with the overseas troops on 3 May, when Monash rode behind Chauvel, and in the great Victory

Parade of July, when Monash again led the Australian contingent. These, especially the Anzac Day march, were occasions for Monash to give many press interviews, outlining the record of the A.I.F. When a brief history of the A.I.F.'s fighting achievements was not accepted by London newspapers, he supervised its production as a pamphlet, *The Battle of Amiens and After*. He wrote most of another pamphlet, *The Australians' Fine Record*, a popularized version of his final report to Fourth Army. When the *Manchester Guardian* included a superb leading article on the A.I.F., he wrote appreciatively only to correct one assertion—that Australians called themselves the storm troops of the British Army. That was the enemy's description. Again, he wrote to the *Times* to agree with a correspondent that a report of his remarks on the battle of Hamel had been condensed and slightly distorted: 'The last thing I would have wished to do was to disparage the fine initiative of the Tank Corps'. But when a foolish English brigadier wrote in conventional dismissive terms about Australian indiscipline, he replied sharply:

> With the single exception of a few roods of shell-torn hell on the FLERS-GEUEDECOURT sector in the winter of 1916-17, the five Australian Divisions have never lost a yard of ground taken by them. Briefly, this idea of "indiscipline" among the Australians is, and always was, a ridiculous fiction.

His major public speech to the Overseas Club in March was forthright, but tactful. He made a proud statement of the Australian military achievement and explained the prowess of the A.I.F. in terms of its unique volunteer basis: it was the 'flower of the nation'. Uncharacteristically, he decried the Americans: Australians had an instinct for war 'unlike other nations which came in later and took a great deal longer in preparation, and did not perhaps achieve quite the same success'. He concluded with a graceful tribute to the British troops: 'It had been a glorious pride to fight alongside the crack regiments of the British Army'. When Monash got home he told a pressman: 'I've been the greatest "skiter" in the Empire on the qualities of the Australian soldiers. London is just about sick of me on that subject'. This was hardly true—or not so until his book appeared: he had not been crudely boastful. He had often paid tribute to the Guards, the Cavalry, the Tanks and the 29th and 51st Divisions. Perhaps he might have recognized more often that, after the slaughter of the original army and many of the Kitchener army, no comparison could fairly be made between volunteer Australians and conscript British troops, and that Britain had had to scrape the barrel as Australia never did—but to attempt to say even that was perhaps beyond the resources of any man's tactfulness.

From the very end of the war Monash had hoped to be able to write his account of the victories in 1918. So far as he could judge, the Australian press reports had been quite inadequate. There would be money in it, too. It was widely reported early in 1919 that he was writing a book. He was indeed lunching with Douglas Sladen, the littérateur and student acquaintance at the University of Melbourne, for advice on presentation and how to approach publishers. But he was simply too busy until mid-year. Then an offer by Murdoch, representing the Melbourne *Herald* and Sydney *Sun*, of serial rights, and his suggestion that publication on the eve of Birdwood's arrival in Australia would serve to demonstrate their true relative importance, impelled him to action. From 8 August (by chance or design) for about a month, he wrote *The Australian Victories in France in 1918*, in 115 000 words which he hardly amended, using all his leisure-time—most nights from seven to midnight and some afternoons, but not for thirty consecutive nights as he later claimed privately. It was one of the more astonishing of his achievements. But it was an intense trial: 'Find the effort very exacting. Get writer's cramp and feel very seedy', he noted in his diary on 17 August. He employed a literary agent who arranged a favourable contract with Hutchinson's. Lord Burnham and the *Sunday Times* paid heavily for serial rights, but the *Herald* withdrew its offer and eventually only the *Sydney Mail* serialized it in Australia. Monash won a large advance of £1100 from his publisher and in the end cleared about £2000 (at least $50 000 in current terms). He saw proofs only of the early chapters before leaving England, and Rosenhain saw the rest through.

Monash stated he was writing an 'individual memoir'. It is that, and a proud history too, but it is also to a considerable extent an objective account. There are errors of detail, some of them serious, but surprisingly few given the speed of production. It is, of course, by no means entirely frank: Monash was at various times less in control of events than is implied; the more important occasions when things went wrong are treated fairly honestly, the less important crises are overlooked. It is not overtly personally boastful, though in the nature of the enterprise it was impossible not to some extent to seem so. He eulogized the men and their officers. He was warm in praise of the Tank Corps and the senior British officers of the A.I.F., and largely refrained from invidious comparisons between the A.I.F. and the British Army. It was simply and effectively written. It was propaganda, for the A.I.F. and for himself, but it was not far from the truth. It was the first of the many generals' apologies, and much less misleading than most. Bean fairly summed it up: 'Though Monash's book contains exaggerations and inaccuracies, it does not overstate the fighting value of the A.I.F., nor does it really rate the force higher than did many leaders and writers, British, Allied and enemy'. Bean asserted that its chief importance lay in convincing many Australians, who still tended to decry Australian achievement and assumed that the reports of A.I.F. prowess were exaggerated, that it really had done a remarkable job.

Publication did not give Monash much satisfaction. The extracts in the *Sunday Times* brought an absurd controversy over what happened on the Chipilly Spur on 8–9 August 1918, and some American indignation. When the book was published in London in February 1920, reviews were mixed: some were highly favourable, and others expressed irritation at Australian boasting. Few were substantial—the same applied in April on the book's Australian release. Some readers compared the work with Caesar's 'vivid and simply told chronicles of his doings in Gaul'. The book flopped in England, selling fewer than 1000 copies; the rest of the edition of nearly 5000 eventually sold out in Australia, mainly in Melbourne, at the high price of 27s 6d. Monash was indignant at what he believed to be Hutchinson's breach of promise to bring out a cheap edition. War books everywhere were a drug on the market. In 1923, however, Lothian brought out a cheap edition in 7000 copies. All attempts to persuade Education Departments to prescribe or buy in bulk failed and, after selling through R.S.L. branches and remaindering, the book went out of print in 1930. Monash had been saddened by the experience. Angus & Robertson reprinted in 1936.

Monash and Birdwood had fallen out. Birdwood had never liked Monash but he had been just in his dealings with him and had recognized his supreme ability. They had co-operated in rebuffing the press conspiracy and Monash had been proper and loyal in defining their new relationships in May and November 1918. But Birdwood had been effectively reduced to a minor role; he was human enough to be resentful, was threatened by the rival claim to leadership of the A.I.F., and perhaps feared that his ambition to be governor-general was in jeopardy. Monash, in his all-important role, was irritated by Birdwood's forceful exercise of his remaining power and influence. Legge had warned him that Birdwood was no friend.

In mid-1919 Monash was convinced that Birdwood had schemed to prevent him leading all three of the A.I.F.'s triumphal marches. He was outraged when Birdwood moved in to hand over to the city of Amiens the massive 15-inch gun captured by the Corps, which for so long had bombarded the city; Monash had previously arranged with the prefect that he would present it. He suspected that, in collusion with the government, Birdwood would visit Australia before his return and steal his thunder, and feared that, disastrously, Birdwood would be chief adviser on the future of the Australian Army.

He was exaggerating the conflicts. Yet Birdwood had it in for him. He told the governor-general that while Monash was extremely able and he had 'never failed to get on with him for five minutes yet', he had 'the faults of his race' and his 'ways and methods' put him on edge. Munro Ferguson shared a distaste for Monash's 'offensive' tone and was not surprised that he was 'not altogether a success': 'he cannot laud his offensives in the field apparently except at the expense of all other Divisions'. Birdwood wrote to a later governor-general, Lord Stonehaven: Monash 'thinks he won the war and tells everyone so! He might be very useful but a terrible self advertiser'. Birdwood and Monash kept up a façade of friendship and wrote hypocritically to each other. Monash had to make a speech of praise at a complimentary dinner to Birdwood in mid-July. On 8 July, at a conference, Birdwood seemingly deeply offended him by saying he had always been 'too optimistic' with regard to repatriation. Pearce struggled to maintain peace. *Australian Victories in France* was certainly written in part as a 'counterblast' to expected pro-Birdwood demonstrations at home.

Throughout 1919 Monash was considering his future without being able to reach a firm view. As he was economically secure, there was no great urgency. The first substantial offer was in April from the government of Victoria which, through Sir James Barrett, sounded him out over the chief commissionership of the State Railways. He cabled in reply: 'Entertain strong disinclination surrender individual freedom by accepting any government office except perhaps federal appointment national character'. He commented privately to a journalist: 'No! It's tempting, but I won't accept it. . . . There's nothing further to be done with railways. They're at their last ditch'. He told Barrett by letters that he might consider such a post, if created, as commander-in-chief of the Australian Army or a similar national appointment. Writing in May to Acting Prime Minister Watt, he dropped a very broad hint. As the months passed and the Commonwealth made no offer and his resentment grew at their failure to grant him any recognition, he increasingly inclined to return to business, though not necessarily to reinforced concrete. The Australian managership of Dorman Long & Co. was one possibility.

Several people had suggested that he stand for the Senate. He was both attracted and repelled: he saw himself as a future minister for defence, but he detested the political game and had no desire to serve under Hughes—he would have preferred to stand as an independent, above party. He did not like facing elections, he would only stand if there was a clear popular demand and he did not have to canvass support. The Melbourne *Herald* reported broadly on these lines on 11 July under the heading, 'Monash May Become M.P.'. He allowed Barrett and Springthorpe to make soundings for him. Springthorpe approached Sir George Fairbairn, head of the National Party in Victoria, who liked the idea—but nothing was heard from him.

Springthorpe later wrote to Hughes—and got no reply. The Victorian Nationalists ran 'Pompey' Elliott for the Senate successfully, and Monash chalked up another grudge against Hughes. But, if his intentions were serious, he had made very little effort. Hughes & Co. of course feared him as a politician.

John Monash had landed himself into a dilemma between wife and mistress. The officers and men of the Dominion armies, married or not, with no home leave in prospect, commonly sooner or later sought sexual accommodation. There are indications in Monash's notebooks that he had occasionally made assignations in Egypt and in Paris. From late 1917 he and Vic's old friend Lizzie Bentwitch had been lovers. She was the daughter of a Melbourne tobacconist who left her fairly well off; she had departed for London soon after 1900 and welcomed Vic and John there in 1910. Monash seems to have taken no advantage of his lionizing by attractive women on innumerable social occasions in the immediate post-war celebratory period of 'making whoopee', but he dined out and visited the theatre with Liz so often in late 1918 and early 1919 that there must have been gossip. She seems to have hoped to win him permanently: Monash's diary entries in mid-January and early April read, 'final refusal of extremes' and 'a serious scene re future'. After almost four and a half years he seems to have met Vic on most affectionate terms. She revelled in her social prominence as her letters, when they were occasionally parted, enthusiastically show. But they reverted to the rows and reconciliations of earlier years. John was seeing Liz only in company with Vic, but the deception was oppressing him. The final parting with Liz upset him—'very sad at going away', he noted—and on the morning of sailing there was 'distressful telephoning'.

Pearce had arranged that Birdwood and Monash would sail on the same ship, but that Birdwood would stay in Perth while Monash was hailed in Melbourne. No doubt he would have to take a prominent part in eventually welcoming Birdwood: 'Frankly I would sooner keep out of it', he told McCay. There were many farewells to be made. The *Times* wrote a gracious sub-leader on Birdwood and Monash: 'Australia has reason to be very proud of both'. In his numerous interviews Monash gave profuse thanks for the co-operation of officials over repatriation and for the private hospitality to Australian troops in England who, largely as a result, would 'carry on the Imperial idea which was in the process of expiring'. Farmar wrote in farewell:

> I wish you God speed and continued health and good Fortune. ... Will you let me say that you inspired those of us who served under you with so great a respect and affection that it was hard to leave your staff and hard now to say Good Bye.

They sailed on the *Ormonde* on 15 November.

Monash found the voyage home unutterably boring. There was much rough weather and he had teeth and gum trouble. 'There were few people on board', he told Rosenhain, 'of whom I have not already seen more in the last four years than I want to'. Birdwood was one of them. He played some chess, solved Walter's jigsaws, worked through a mathematical puzzle-book and practised some elementary trigonometry, and did not read much. He was perturbed by his marital situation. After one of several tiffs with Vic, he noted: 'feeling very lonely'; and two days later, 'miserable and dispirited'. Then, in the Indian Ocean, Vic's low state of health led them to consult the ship's doctors, with inconclusive results.

On 19 December they arrived at Fremantle and he and Birdwood had to face what he noted was a more than twelve hours 'hysterical programme'. 'Birdy' stole the show from the start, waving his digger hat from the deck, but it was the local hero, Murray, V.C., who was chaired through Fremantle. Both of them, and not Monash, had headlines in the *West Australian*'s report. At the civic reception at Fremantle Town Hall, at the returned soldiers' gathering, and at dinner at the Perth Club, Birdwood spoke first and, if the newspapers were correct, was greeted with cheers, while Monash had only applause. On the way into Perth Monash set the foundation stone of the Jewish war memorial in King's Park. He was not neglected—the newspapers interviewed him and he concentrated on the success of repatriation; he was prominently referred to as 'The Brains of the A.I.F.'. But in Perth he was not a hero as Birdwood and Murray were. Adelaide was not so exhausting. They were ashore only for five hours, to be welcomed by the premier and cabinet, the lord mayor and the acting governor. He knew now that his triumphant homecoming would not be spoiled by arriving on Christmas Day.

Boxing Day was gloriously sunny. A large crowd welcomed the *Ormonde* at Port Melbourne. Brigadier-General Brand conducted the Monashes to a tender which left for St Kilda where many thousands were waiting. Prime Minister Hughes was not among them. The returned men along the pier were retailing anecdotes of 'the tireless director in the background'; veterans of the North Melbourne Battery had turned out in force. As Monash landed, a wonderful welcoming cry went up. The military and official bigwigs were so numerous that old friends had little chance of getting close. 'With the genial smile which his friends well remember', Monash pumped hands cordially. He had to listen and reply to an address by the mayor of St Kilda before pressing on through the dense crowd. Suddenly he was hoisted up and, enjoying his awkward perch, was chaired (the only time in his life) up the pier and across the lawns, to lusty cheers from those lining the Esplanade. He proceeded by car up beflagged Fitzroy Street to the South Melbourne boundary point, where he was greeted with 'several rounds of full-throated cheers' and another mayor presented his address. Monash and the crowd laughed when the band struck up: 'How are you going to keep them/Down on the farm,/Now that they've seen Paree?' After a call on the governor-general the short procession moved on speedily, surprising the holiday crowds outside Flinders Street station. They gave belated cheers but returned soldier strong-points in Swanston Street were ready. The cars went on to Menzies Hotel where Vic, looking gaunt, retired to bed. Monash got straight into 'civvies'. 'He is still very much of a civilian and a democrat in his views', the *Age* reported, 'and the military caste will never be able to claim [him] as one of its own'.

He went out to Iona, visited Tante Ulrike and his cousins, and also called on old Mrs Lewis, his sometime mother-substitute. Mat later told him 'Lewis' are still dazed with excitement and delight—they think it the noblest act you've done'. She was warning him against false friends, and telling him he must see loyal supporters like Catherine Deakin as soon as possible.

There were hundreds of letters and telegrams. Professor Ernest Scott, the historian, was sorry he had not been able, in the crowd at St Kilda, to get close enough to say a word of welcome:

> Very many of us have watched your brilliant career abroad with the most intense interest, and also with a sense of gratitude. You can hardly realise yourself how big you have seemed to your fellow countrymen. And a thing which would have pleased you most I am sure, . . . was the way which those who have known you longest were not surprised—though they were delighted—at everything you have done. Your old friend Maurice Kernot always jeered at anybody who expressed surprise . . . because he said he could not imagine you *not* doing difficult things supremely well.

Ernest Wears wrote to 'Dear Old Jack':

> I nearly busted when I heard your voice and got your hand. . . . Needless to say I do want to have a little quiet chat with you; but I can see that such is a hopeless ambition pro tem. You've got to be roasted and toasted, and the lord knows what before you are off the chain. . . . But what about a little trip to the Buffalo? It would do you both good. You could then tell me how good it was to look over the Ovens Valley away to Kossy.

J. G. Latham sent 'a hearty welcome home to you—who are, in the most real sense, the leader of Australia'. C. P. Smith took as much pride in Monash's success as if he were his son: it was a 'great thing to have come back . . . from a test that has broken and smeared the careers of so many others'. Barrett asked for 'an hour or so' to discuss necessary matters. Foott was glad their department had successfully repatriated him. The Melbourne newspapers published eulogies. The *Age*'s heading was 'Australia's Greatest General', the *Herald*'s 'A Soldier of the People'—he was amongst the six ablest soldiers in the world.

He was beginning to suffer the full penalties of fame. The next few days saw a confusion of visitors—pests, bores, those just wanting to shake his hand, and those with whom he would dearly have liked to relax and yarn—and telephone calls. It was all a mockery: the problem was to find good medical advice for Vic in the holiday period. She was examined by three specialists and, though she accompanied John to the theatre on New Year's Eve, continued to weaken. A fortnight after their return they moved into Iona; she remained bedridden. Meanwhile John, sometimes accompanied by Bertha, attended the many occasions in his honour—the civic reception at the Town Hall on 12 January (when he was cheered for several minutes, emotional greetings being called from all sides) and those arranged by clubs, societies and the Jewish community. They became progressively more embarrassing; he cancelled some and refused the governor-general's invitation to afternoon tea and a chat. He had to endure the civic reception to Birdwood on the 20th and the dinner for him at Government House. However, he gave active support to the movement in protest at the removal of the original Melbourne cemetery from the Victoria Market site; when he was about seventeen Monash had noticed John Batman's grave there and had been struck by his achievement as founder of Melbourne. He presided at a protest meeting and led a deputation to the lord mayor. They were 'obliterating monuments to the heroes of the past. No piece of ground in Australia was more sacred than this section, and it would be a national crime to wipe it out by uprooting memorial stones and scattering the graves'. It was to no avail.

Vic's condition worsened. John wrote to Walter that he was living in 'a delirium of constant worry and anxiety'. About 12 February the doctors warned him that there was little hope. She rallied remarkably, however. He received a sickening anonymous letter from an old soldier, warning him against a general who had 'said all over Melb. a year ago that your wife and her sister are whores and that you are a beastly dog of a Jew'. Vic died on 27 February of the recurring cancer which had only tardily been diagnosed with certainty. Some of the many hundred letters of condolence testified that, in her own right, she had earned wide respect and affection, especially in giving comfort to bereaved soldiers' wives and mothers. Ellen Anderson and Josh, Monash's former partner, sent remarkable emotional tributes.

Weary and disoriented, Monash struggled to sort out his private

Keith Murdoch and W. M. Hughes, 1918

Hughes and Monash

James Quinn at work, 1919

Monash and Bertha at a war cemetery in France, 1919

Monash, Birdwood and Murray, V.C., Perth, December 1919

John and Vic at St Kilda, Boxing Day 1919

Monash and Lizette Bentwitch at the Melbourne Cup

affairs. He had intended to accept the official invitations of the New South Wales and South Australian governments and make visits in March and April, but he had not the heart. He made only one triumphal excursion, in July to Ballarat where he endured a twenty-four-hour programme of receptions, openings, praise and speechmaking. His bereavement brought little check to the huge correspondence making demands on him—to become patron, president or vice-president; to speak, to write, to be guest of honour; to open fêtes, carnivals and art exhibitions; to send his autograph or to sign a photograph or a flag in support of a good cause. He had to refuse most requests politely. One category he could not refuse was the unveiling of war memorials and honour boards; for many years he carried out this duty knowing that each occasion would be a grim ordeal at which he would have to attempt to give comfort and justification to the nearest and dearest of the slain. The press pestered him for opinions on any and every subject. Within a week of Vic's death he set the foundation stone of the Scotch College Memorial Hall; and he joined the building fund executive for the school's new site at Hawthorn. He gave public support to the Peace Loan. He signed letters to wealthy men seeking funds for the Y.M.C.A. appeal, for he had greatly admired their work for servicemen at the Front. He spoke at the founding meetings of the British Empire League in Victoria, and of the local branch of the League of Nations Union which he urged Chauvel and White to join: 'I think we soldiers know enough of the horrors of war to wish to give every possible support to a movement which may help to minimise the risk of war'. Late in the year he presented the prizes at the speech nights of Scotch and Geelong Colleges and, at the request of Frank Tate, the director of education, at Melbourne High School. He became vice-president again of the Boy Scouts Association.

He joined the Prahran branch of the R.S.L. and spoke at the laying of the foundation stone of Anzac House in Collins Street. He lectured on behalf of the Australian War Memorial; became president of the movement for the City of Melbourne to adopt and succour the town of Villers-Bretonneux; and supported the Australian Children's Society which aided the many hundreds of unmarried British mothers of the children of the A.I.F. He accepted the honorary colonelcy of the Melbourne University Rifles.

Until in August 1920 he agreed to join the State Electricity Commission, Monash had remained quite uncertain about his future. In October 1919, when his hopes either of the offer of a major national task or of a political career had been dashed, he had rashly assured Gibson: 'I have not swerved in the smallest degree from my promise to you to return to our full former activities together and to continue same so long as they afford a reasonable livelihood'. He knew that their business had largely lost its monopolistic character, that it had suffered from restricted building development and industrial conflicts during the war, that Humes had far outstripped them technologically in pipe manufacture, and that their South Australian company had not paid any dividend for several years. Moreover Fairway and Lynch were discontented under Gibson's management. On his return, however, he reassured himself that the Reinforced Concrete and Concrete Constructions companies still seemed to assure a 'satisfactory livelihood', and he resumed his supervisory engineering.

But he was not content. Discussions had made it clear that he was unlikely to have a military future: he was too senior and would not be welcome to the permanent officers, the scale of the proposed Army was inadequate, the inspector-general was paid only £1500 a year. An inclination not 'to spend the rest of my days in mere money making' led him still to look out for a big national job. He jumped at the chance when Watt, the Commonwealth treasurer, early in March offered him the director-generalship of the Institute of Science and Industry at £4000 a year. It would be some six months before legislation could be passed; meanwhile he would be asked to head a royal commission on taxation. In effect Watt was proposing to reward the war hero indirectly: no Commonwealth public servant was paid more than £2000 a year.

The understanding immediately went wrong. He was not appointed to the commission on taxation. Watt left for London on a financial mission, quarrelled with Hughes and resigned from the ministry. Massy Greene, in whose hands Watt had left the matter, soon told Monash that the government could not honour Watt's promise as Parliament was most unlikely to allow a salary of more than £2500. Monash had been consulting throughout with McBeath, who was powerful in Nationalist circles, and on his advice approached Pearce late in April. They agreed to attempt to combine the Science post with executive charge, or at least paid membership, of the Council of Defence at a salary something like Watt's original offer. Monash liked the idea very much. At this point Greene fell ill for several weeks and the matter dragged on through June and July. Monash felt 'sorely humbugged'. Meanwhile, on the request of the prime minister and both sides, he arbitrated a wage dispute between shipowners and marine engineers. His award confirmed the shipowners' offer but granted overtime and other concessions.

He continued his pre-war directorships of Luna Park and Wiltshires. He became chairman of directors of the National Portland Cement Co. and of the associated Maria Island Land and Development Co., hoping to develop a new source of cement. Moreover, he told Walter:

Every day that passes I become more and more entangled in attractive fresh business undertakings, invitations to go on Boards of Directors, duties which involve very little work or time, and which carry an emolument of from £100 to £300 per year, are pouring in. . . . Some of these it is almost impossible to resist. . . . I am beginning to entertain very serious doubts whether it would really be wise of me to cut myself entirely adrift from the environment of my whole past.

He was attracted by Arthur Rickard, the Sydney financier, to become chairman of Melbourne Hotels Ltd, which took over the Grand (Windsor) Hotel, and joined the local board of the Atlas Assurance Co. He was careful not to allow his name to be used as a sleeping director, as unfair to investors. And he refused to act as a patents expert, even on behalf of W. L. Baillieu, and set an impossible fee of a thousand guineas for conducting an arbitration case.

In June-July he had a windfall. Humes made an offer for the Concrete Constructions Co. which could not be rejected: Monash cleared about £10 000. The Hume Pipe Co. (Aust) Ltd was formed, with W. R. Hume, T. S. Nettlefold, L. J. (later Lord) Clifford, A. J. McLachlan and Monash as directors. Gibson would carry on Concrete Constructions in order to give an appearance of competition. The transaction was completed in mid-1921.

Monash had become disgusted with the delay of the Science and Industry proposal; nobody in the government was telling him what was going on and it seemed unlikely that the salary offered would meet his view of what was fitting. He now was assuming he would continue constructing buildings and bridges with the Reinforced Concrete Co. and was putting in most of the day in his Collins House office. Although competition was keen, business was buoyant. He even considered buying out Gibson or at least acquiring a majority interest.

Out of the blue, on 28 June, McBeath sounded him out about the general managership of the State Electricity Commission, founded the year before. The three part-time commissioners, George Swinburne, Professor T. R. Lyle and Robert Gibson, had just advised Harry Lawson, the premier, that a full-time executive officer was essential.* On 29 July the commissioners formed a deputation to Monash. Swinburne followed with a persuasive letter:

There is nothing I have ever been connected with which opens up such possibilities of good in the community and where one's work could be made of immense constructive value. . . . the Institute is attractive if you could only get full play and be properly backed

* W. S. Robinson was a forgetful old man when he recalled in his memoirs, *If I Remember Rightly*, that in 1919 in London, disturbed about Monash's future, he had cabled his brother Arthur, a member of the Victorian government, and that in reply came the offer of the S.E.C. job. Writing intimately to Rosenhain throughout 1920, Monash had not mentioned the S.E.C. All the same it would be surprising if Arthur Robinson, who saw much of Monash early in 1920, had not seen the possibility.

up by the political heads. I do not think you ever would, as the money required is too much for them to appreciate.... Morwell with proper organisational thought and skill will during the next five years be a monument to the men who tackle it and affords an outlet for organising ability, engineering skill in several Departments, town planning, legal practice etc. that no other scheme in Australia presents. To me it is an intellectual treat. I hope to hear that you will throw in your lot with us. It will be a *substantial pleasure* to be actively associated with you.

Monash saw Lawson and, having been assured that legislation was in train to extend the commission's powers and to establish it as an independent statutory corporation, and being offered £3000 a year for an initial period of five years with a promise of an increase to £5000 'as soon as the undertakings proved successful', accepted the offer. So, despite all his protestations he became a government servant again, though a highly independent one. He was excited by the potential of the task. Only *Smith's Weekly*, which had been crusading for his employment on 'our Western Front' as a national director against drought or, alternatively, as the man who might unify and transform the nation's railways, deplored the fact that Australia could find no better use for him than to give him charge of a State instrumentality.

Monash arranged with Gibson to withdraw from the Reinforced Concrete Co. and the South Australian company. Negotiations were not entirely smooth but Gibson agreed to buy Monash's shares for about £6000 and to pay over five years. Fairway succeeded Monash as supervising engineer. After these operations Monash was worth about £60 000. Lawson had probably told him that he must give up his directorships. McBeath had already tactfully advised him that, for the sake of his prestige, he would do well to withdraw from some of his engagements. He immediately resigned from Melbourne Hotels and, later, from Wiltshires, but retained his other directorships.

His resentment at lack of recognition by the Commonwealth government festered. He had been too preoccupied to take much notice of Birdwood's triumphant tour. Currie, writing from Canada, remarked that he could not understand Birdwood's accompanying him home: 'No doubt there is in Australia, as in Canada, a class of citizen who is determined that too much honour shall not come to those prominent in the expeditionary forces, if that person happens to be an Australian or a Canadian'. Though Birdwood was widely popular with them, many returned soldiers were upset by the apparent neglect of Monash. The *Nation*, the organ of the Returned Soldiers' National Party, remarked that he was an infinitely greater man than Birdwood, was 'perhaps the greatest citizen soldier the world has seen', but had been 'made to appear the lesser man'. *Smith's* summed it up: 'So he came back to Australia, which tooted its trumpets round Birdwood, and forgot its own soldier'. Monash complained to Pearce that his recommendations for honours for the Repatriation and Demobilisation staff had been entirely ignored. He was not alone in resenting lack of recognition; White once remarked that while Haig and Jellicoe got peerages and money-grants, 'all we got was a parchment of thanks and permission to retain our swords'. The goverment resisted considerable public pressure. The Melbourne *Herald* was urging Parliament to give Monash special thanks, at least by bringing him to the Bar of the House; a document was circulating in Sydney calling for grants of £10 000 to Monash and Chauvel and £5000 each to White and the divisional commanders. In Parliament supporters were pressing for recognition in tangible form and the raising of a monument to his work, or were attacking the 'military clique' advising Pearce and the 'studied insult' to Monash in the governor-general's speech opening Parliament, in which Birdwood's visit was welcomed and Monash's return ignored. He did resent being ignored, he told Rosenhain, but there had been too much 'disagreeable public comment'. 'Save me from my friends.' The government confined itself to a ceremony of formal thanks to seventy representatives of the Navy and Army at Parliament House in May. Rear-Admiral Grant, Chauvel and Monash spoke in reply. He was finally demobilized on 13 June. In September he wrote bitterly to Watt, reviewing the failure of his negotiations with, and his mean treatment by, the Commonwealth government.

It was all very well: given Australian egalitarian traditions, even a non-Labor government was unwilling to single out individuals for special recognition—it was too invidious a task. Nevertheless, if the will had been there, some simple gestures might easily have been made. The most obvious was promotion of Monash and Chauvel to full general. Hughes's enmity to Monash stood in the way: it was mutual—'I dislike the man intensely', Monash confided.

The visit of the Prince of Wales from May to August was an emotional national occasion which provided a famous incident in Monash folklore. To general outrage in Melbourne, he was reported to have witnessed the Prince's arrival from among the crowd on Swanston Street. The *Bulletin* concluded that 'military officialdom has done its best to snub Australia's citizen-soldier'. Monash privately commented that the *Bulletin* had rather over-stated the matter.

> I am very indisposed to have it appear that I am on the 'grouse' in such a matter. Of course, in a sense, I occupy no official position, being merely 'an officer on the reserve'. If those in official authority have the bad taste to ignore me on important public occasions, I can only leave the matter for the judgement of the public.

The governor-general, government and Barracks rushed to make amends for the oversight, clerical error or insult—whatever it was. Actually Monash, though the senior knight, in the official order of precedence ranked behind judges, Speakers, party leaders and executive councillors—no exception had been made for him. At the private levée the Prince gave him a special smile and an additional handshake. Monash attended official lunches, garden parties and theatre parties, and journeyed to the site of Canberra among two hundred official guests to see the Prince set a foundation stone. The *Bulletin* was in its best ancient form reporting the ghastly protocol of the formal opening set at the Government House ball:

> A plush rope was flung around a sacred circle for the lancers, and the mob pressed to the ringside like a stadium crowd. Lady Helen piloted the Prince through. The G-G blundered in a jovial way. Billy Hughes looked agonised until Edward made him laugh. Monash was the only man who remembered all the moves; but he is a tactician. There was a general air of relief when the old measure was over and the real dancing began.

The next snub, whether by accident or design, was in military terms outrageous: Monash and his senior officers were not mentioned in a military order summing up the process of demobilization. Rosenthal and Bruche wrote to him to protest and sympathize. Monash told Bruche:

> I could hardly imagine that my name was intentionally omitted, but it is significant that I have received no recognition whatever for my demobilization work, not a word and not a line, either from the Minister of Defence, or the Prime Minister, or the Government. But I feel it would be undignified to make any protest. My friends can do that for me if they like.

When the government and military authorities made no gesture on the anniversaries of 4 July and 8 August, Monash was again hurt.

The pattern was now set. The government's lack of generosity or ordinary courtesy to Monash became a lasting grievance of the R.S.L., and was frequently noted in *Smith's Weekly* and the *Bulletin*. Morshead would write: 'The jealous and petty treatment meted out to you, Sir John, is often bitterly commented on in Sydney, and by civilians as well as soldiers. . . . You have the whole-hearted support and admiration of the entire A.I.F.' against the politicians and the Defence Department. In the Senate in July 1922 Brigadier-General Drake-Brockman, later chief judge of the Arbitration Court, remarked that he intensely resented the official attitude to Monash; presumably it was fear that he might reach for political power. That 'wonderful man', who had probably saved the world from another year of war, was given the same gratuity as his batman; it was absurd.

Monash immediately rejoined the University council, but for many months could attend few meetings. In March 1920 he and Birdwood received honorary doctorates of law. He joined enthusiastically in current fund-raising on the Engineering sub-committee and donated £500 himself. He lectured in support of the campaign to raise funds for a women's college and set the foundation stone for an extension to Queen's College. On Professor Payne's suggestion, he submitted *Australian Victories in France* for a doctorate of engineering which was conferred late in the year—the first awarded in Australia. Monash admitted privately that it was much more *honoris causa* than based on a real contribution to science, but leaders of the profession like Sir Henry Barraclough insisted that the University had 'proved itself to possess a clear and very uncommon perception of what it is that constitutes the higher planes of engineering thought and effort'. To Monash's delight most of the engineering societies had recently federated in the Institution of Engineers, Australia, whose State committee he joined.

His advice was not always accepted in matters of state. In mid-year the old enemies Gellibrand and McNicoll, together with Bruche, were rivals for the chief commissionership of the Victoria Police. Monash told Lawson of his support for Bruche ahead of McNicoll and that appointment of Gellibrand would be a mistake, mainly because he was a poor administrator. But Gellibrand was chosen. They 'could not have chosen a more unsuitable man', Monash told Bruche. He intervened in two cases of Australian residents of German birth who, under the government's vindictive policy, were to be deported. One was the Jewish Dr Max Herz, an unconventional orthopaedic surgeon of Sydney, whom Dr Earle Page and the British Medical Association were persecuting. Monash's intervention with Garran at the vital moment may have tipped the balance in the decision to release Herz from internment and allow him to stay. The other case was even more extraordinary. Dr Eugen Hirschfeld was a prominent Queensland physician and legislative councillor who had been thirty years in Australia, but had been German consul at the outbreak of war. Monash had first met him in 1897. His wife was the daughter of V. J. Saddler, Monash's old employer. Although he again intervened with Garran, Hirschfeld was deported. In 1923 Monash wrote to S. M. Bruce, the prime minister, unsuccessfully pleading the case which he compared with Dreyfus's. It was 'a reflection upon the honour of Australia', he asserted. 'I have tried to do the State some service, but have never before asked for any kind of favor.' Three years later Latham, as attorney-general, reviewed the case and readmission was allowed. The Queensland branch of the R.S.L. protested vehemently and, on Mrs Hirschfeld's request, Monash wrote:

> You must be perfectly well aware that I would be the last man

in the world to sanction any action which would permit of treachery or anything of that nature being countenanced in this country, but the days of war hysteria are now over, and one should bring to bear on such a question, a spirit of fair play and charity. . . . it would be assuredly a wicked thing, of which the Australian nation ought to be well ashamed, if a decree of banishment were to be persisted in.

The Queensland R.S.L. was largely cowed. Shortly before Hirschfeld returned, one of his sons was elected Rhodes Scholar for Queensland.

Monash had hundreds of friends in Melbourne, but no one now with whom he was intimate; Rosenhain, Bruche and McGlinn (who regarded him as his dearest friend) were removed in distance, as were close military associates like Hobbs and Rosenthal. Fame brought its penalties, as in the case of his old friend Ernest Wright who wrote to say he had a dread of being thought a toady and considered it best not to see him again:

> I have always been loyal to you in thought and word—even in the dark days before your great fame had got about—when fools said bitter things of you. . . . I want you to know that one who knew you intimately in your early manhood always thought and still thinks of you with respect and admiration. . . . So Goodbye and all good fortune.

Monash replied decently, submissively:

> I have grown old enough to know that it is impossible fully to understand the outlook and view-point of others, and that it behoves us to treat with respect opinions which we do not ourselves hold. . . . All the same, have you considered what your attitude would mean, if shared by *all* the friends of one's youth?

He respected Wright's motives and had kindly thoughts of him, but was rather hurt.

Monash was as soon as possible appointed vice-president of the Naval and Military Club and in 1921 became its 'permanent' president. Presumably he had mixed feelings about the premises in Alfred Place which the club had taken over from the German Club, the scene of much of his social life in the late 1880s, after it was closed down in 1914. He rejoined the Yorick Club. He had to visit the Victorian Club to deny the report that he had said that bookmakers, though doubtless worthy people, were not those with whom one would choose to associate; he was elected an honorary life-member.

There remains the matter, rooted in folk-memory, of his alleged blackballing by the Melbourne Club or, alternatively, his rejection of an invitation to join on the ground that previously it had barred Jews. He was never formally proposed for membership or invited to join.

This does not rule out the possibility that friends wishing to propose him, having ascertained that rejection was likely, did not allow his name to go forward. Monash preserved a newspaper cutting which referred to his declining membership of an unnamed prominent club in Melbourne, and he underlined his reported statement that he 'could not give the club the opportunity to make distinctions in his case'. Another variant of the story is that the Melbourne Club gave a dinner in his honour and he did not turn up—but he did attend and spoke at the club's dinner in honour of him and Birdwood and Chauvel. He accepted private invitations to dine at the club several times in later years, which indicates absence of any strong view on his part. When taxed late in the 1920s on the alleged blackballing, he replied: 'My boy, you surely don't think I'd be such a b f as to give them the opportunity'. The most likely inference is that he had politely rejected the suggestion of friends wanting to propose him, but not on grounds of principle for in fact the club had several Jewish members. Nevertheless an element of doubt remains. It might even have been another club which rejected him. It is not in the least surprising that such a report should have circulated, even if there was no basis of fact.

Through winter 1920 Monash gradually restored order to his affairs. He had been severely disturbed during the first few months back home when he was so overwhelmed with correspondence that he had not been able to keep his filing and accounts up to date and readily lay his hand on documents. He now also had his accumulated war records to organize. He began to use a private letter-book again for family correspondence: 'This is the first attempt at press copying for 5½ years. It is written to test the efficiency of the ink, the press, the pen, the book, the oil sheets and the method. May 15/20'. For most of his private and some of his S.E.C. correspondence, he began using a dictaphone at home, taking the recordings to his secretary in the morning. As he had said many a time he would, he spent happy hours in his garden. Bertha and Gershon Bennett did not marry for more than twelve months after her mother died, probably because Gershon felt he should first establish himself securely in dental practice. Father and daughter agreed to share Iona; Gershon, who continued to address his father-in-law as 'Sir', was presumably not unhappy with the arrangement. Extensive renovations and redecoration followed. In December they toured the Western District, the Grampians and the Mount Gambier area in the family Buick (which had Monash's crest on two doors).

Many women would have liked to marry Sir John Monash. Among others, an actress, a sculptor and a recent Jewish university graduate made advances. But there does not seem to have been any doubt what he wanted. Lizzie Bentwitch arrived on the *Naldera* late in September 1920 and he installed her in the Grand Hotel. (Lizzie had seemingly been deceiving him about her age; he checked her birth certificate and established that she was forty-six.) The Rosenhains were very upset: Lou told John that she was an unscrupulous liar and Walter warned that 'a designing woman may be more difficult to deal with than—shall I say, a Hindenburg system?' John told him to rest easy, there would be no 'undesirable outcome'. But more important, Bertha detested Lizzie, of whom she had seen much in her mother's company in London. There was a crisis betwen father and daughter late in 1920, the nature of which can only be surmised. In December when the *Bulletin* mentioned the probable forthcoming marriage of 'a front-rank war-knight, a widower', Monash wrote to the management to protest and deny—it had distressed his family. If the obvious question is why John Monash did not marry Lizzie Bentwitch, the simple answer is that he preferred to live with Bertha (and her children) with whom he could not contemplate a breach.

Late in 1920 Monash was in poor health. Though he was again passed as a first-class life by the A.M.P. Society, Barrett had advised him to have a long holiday with complete rest: 'If I am any judge of men you have had enough for the present'. At Christmas, though he was fearing a breakdown, he still took only a ten-day holiday. Early in 1921 he lapsed into 'a chronic state of lassitude and abdominal discomfort, not to say pain, disordered digestion and lumbago and rheumatic pains'. In March he consulted Dr Sidney Sewell who described his condition as a 'natural aftermath of a violent change in mode of life', and brought about instant improvement 'by a course of medicine, comprising chiefly intestinal antiseptics, by a carefully rearranged diet, and by a graduated course of physical culture'. Monash attended classes at the Bjelke-Petersen School of Physical Culture for several months. Though he soon felt himself to be thoroughly fit again, he found it convenient to plead 'doctor's orders' as an excuse for refusing many of the never-ending requests for his time.

15

The State Electricity Commission 1920–1931

MANY PEOPLE at the time were surprised, and many have been since, that Monash was satisfied to devote the later years of his career to the State Electricity Commission of Victoria. His was in fact a task of great public importance, difficulty and attractiveness to an engineer. Worldwide, this was the great age of electrification: had not Lenin, for example, defined Communism as 'Soviet power plus electrification'? Victoria had a major power shortage and the small electricity industry was in a mess. The State had only enough black coal of its own to supply its railways, and industrial and domestic power depended on the unreliable and costly supply of black coal from New South Wales. The main political task for the State government was to bring into use the huge deposits of brown coal in the La Trobe Valley, make abundant cheap power available, and remove a crippling handicap to development of local industry.

They needed a strong man for the job. Monash's popularity and, though he was not an electrical or mining engineer, his professional and administrative capacities made him an almost ideal choice. In carrying out a controversial scheme he would be a buffer between vested interests and the government. The aim was, in Monash's words, 'to revolutionise the industrial development' of the State and to free it from its 'industrial vassalage' to New South Wales. Within a week of joining the Commission he reassured Rosenhain, in case he thought it too little a job, that it might be the most important in Australia.

The broad extent of the brown coal deposits had been recognized for fifty years, but although private companies had worked them on a small scale they were unprofitable. They were for the first time seriously considered for generation of electricity when in 1908 the State government brought out from England C. H. Merz, who was familiar with German developments in brown coal, to report on railway electrification. The Victorian Railways embarked on suburban electrification, fuelled by its Newport power-station based on black coal. In

1916–17 during the damaging New South Wales strike, the Mines Department worked brown coal at North Yallourn as an emergency measure. The State government then set up an Advisory Committee into the Utilisation of Brown Coal, including several future senior officers of the S.E.C., which quickly produced an urgent optimistic report recommending establishment of an electricity commission and a generating plant near Morwell. It was the foundation document of the S.E.C. After delay because of political instability, the Harry Lawson government, which was to hold office for five years, legislated late in 1918 to establish the Commission. On 4 March 1919 Professor T. R. Lyle was appointed as chairman and the engineer-politician George Swinburne as a member; Robert Gibson soon joined them. The Commission's first task was to advise on the use of Gippsland brown coal as against possible hydro-electricity schemes; the government regarded it as an open question.

Monash, in London, was now brought into action in a 'cloak-and-dagger' enterprise. The geologist Professor Edgeworth David had returned to Australia, excited about what he had seen of brown coal developments in Germany, and H. R. Harper, about to take up duty as the Commission's chief engineer, suggested asking Monash to mount an intelligence operation. Monash sent in an A.I.F. squad under Major E. N. Mulligan, a mining engineer, to Cologne to assault the Fortuna mine and other installations. By bluff, bullying and bribery, Mulligan gathered substantial information, including a working model of a briquetting machine, which he passed to Monash who wrote a report. In November 1919 the Commissioners recommended strongly in favour of exploiting Morwell brown coal and appended to their report much of the data gathered about the Fortuna workings. By voting considerable funds Parliament committed itself primarily to brown coal development.

The Fortuna foray was a passing incident so far as Monash was concerned. His joining the S.E.C. a year later seems to have been unpremeditated on his part and was influenced partly by his close associations with Lyle at the University, Swinburne as a professional colleague and friend, and Gibson as his partner's brother. Hyman Herman, the 'father of brown coal' and the leading technical man, was also Jewish and an old Scotch Collegian; and Monash was on 'Jack' and 'Arthur' terms with Robinson, the responsible minister, with whom he also shared the school link.

Immediately he was appointed, Monash asked Professor Payne for guidance on basic texts in electrical engineering, F. W. Clements of the Melbourne Electric Supply Co. advised on reading in the economics of electricity supply, and the Commission's background documents had to be mastered. Before taking up his post he ran down to Morwell for a couple of days to spy out the ground. On 1 October he moved into the temporary offices in the Tramways Buildings, Bourke Street, and by November had won Cabinet approval for an eight-storey concrete building in William Street. Naturally the Reinforced Concrete Co. was commissioned by the builders to supervise the concrete work. Monash could not have been expected to tolerate anything but concrete and the company was still leader in the field, but an aggrieved builder wrote to the papers and a question was asked in Parliament. In May 1922 the new offices were occupied.

Monash liked the look of the intricate combination of administrative, financial and engineering questions. He recognized that the task was going to extend him fully—it was 'a big and strenuous job', entirely to his taste. He found that while the Commissioners had been 'groping for basic principles and policies', little practical progress had been made. He had to recruit a staff and virtually create an administrative machine. He was thrown into battle immediately, forced to fight largely unprepared on ground not of his choosing: authority had to be strongly asserted from the start. He had immediately to subdue another 'new boy', H. W. Clapp of the Railways who had just been appointed at the staggering salary of £5000 a year—which could not have pleased Monash on £3000. The Railways had a generating station of 64 000 kilowatts, far beyond its needs for the moment, and was selling its surplus power. The Commission could not tolerate a competing state enterprise and after negotiations with Clapp and Robinson it was agreed that the Commission would eventually become the sole generating and distributing authority.

Before the close of the year Monash had a political triumph. Amending legislation had to be passed to make him chairman of Commissioners (for seven years) and not merely general manager, as he had been appointed; remarkably, he was named, as chairman, in the Act and so could be removed only by Parliament. Moreover, a loan appropriation of £1.43 million and construction of Yallourn township and the head-office building were authorized, and the Commission was given extensive powers over municipal operation and sale of electricity. Thus the Victorian Parliament confirmed its establishment of another example of 'state socialism', a statutory corporation with basic autonomy, qualified by the power of the purse and ultimate parliamentary approval.

On 14 December Monash had addressed Parliament during the dinner adjournment, convincingly explaining that it was not a matter of brown coal electricity *or* hydro-electricity but of both, with the latter necessarily taking only a minor and subsequent part; he promised an era of cheap power and cheap briquette fuel. The following day's debate demonstrated how much conviction he had carried. Nevertheless members of the new Country Party, which tended strongly to support hydro-electricity, remained unconvinced. There was a small sensation when a Nationalist member read out a letter from A. G. M. Michell, the distinguished engineer who was a consultant both to the Commission and the Victorian Hydro-Electric Co., which claimed that Monash had misled members about the comparative costs of Morwell and the company's elaborate Kiewa scheme. Monash accepted the challenge and encouraged Lawson immediately to appoint a select committee. Next day, before the committee, Monash demolished Michell. According to F. W. Eggleston, a member of the committee and a future minister in charge,

> Monash was a brainy Hercules, Michell a blinking, timid scholar, with a practical genius but no presence. . . . Monash . . . stood over the weak-voiced scientist . . . like a colossus. The duel lasted not more than half an hour and Michell was left without a case.

It was 'the most magnificent exposition of the forensic art' Eggleston had ever witnessed. Monash had caught Michell out in several errors, but was running great risks in making assumptions about the costs of brown coal development which to say the least were uncertain. That night the committee reported in favour of Monash and the legislation was passed. From 10 January 1921 Monash was formally appointed as chairman of the State Electricity Commission. But he referred in a letter to the 'rupturing' of some 'life-long friendships', presumably including Michell's. The Kiewa interests continued to fight it out and provincial and rural members remained difficult to convince that the S.E.C. was a State enterprise and not just a Melbourne one. In April a special conference of the Victorian Farmers' Union and country municipalities resolved unanimously that the government should either proceed with both the Morwell and Kiewa schemes or allow private enterprise to proceed with Kiewa and withdraw all restrictions on competition. Monash had played it hard, referring to 'senseless hydraulic works in uninhabited and inaccessible mountain ranges'. Lawson made no basic concession to the rural lobby.

The Commission's major tasks were to develop open-cut mining of brown coal, build the installations which would transmit power State-wide, manufacture briquettes for industrial and domestic fuel, and take over existing electricity-makers and establish a system of power distribution and sale—apart from building Yallourn town and a hundred and one other duties. Its main crisis was to be the devastating discovery that the moisture content of the brown coal was so high that the whole enterprise was jeopardized.

The development of open-cut mining, removing the overburden and opening up the coal to fire the power-station boilers and the briquette-manufacturing plant, aimed at production initially of one million tons a year and eventually ten million. Monash came to recognize that the approach had been hasty, on too small a scale, with indequate mechanization. He had been surprised to find that the Fortuna report had been pigeon-holed. The consulting engineer for coal supply was Lindesay Clark, a Melbourne graduate, an old friend and an able one with extensive Tasmanian mining experience, but, Monash said,

> imbued with a profound hatred for the Germans and a dislike for everything German. This, I am afraid, biassed his judgment, and he brushed to one side as unworthy of consideration all suggestions that our coal supply development should follow German lines, both as to lay-out, developmental programme, and type of plant to be employed. I found the Commission deeply committed to Clark's general ideas, and it would have involved great delay and expense to go back on our track.

Eventually Monash enforced new methods based on German technology.

Early in 1921 the major constructional works were in train: the Yallourn powerhouse with 50 000 kilowatt generating capacity—orders for its six turbo-generators were placed overseas; the Newport powerhouse with 15 000 kilowatt capacity; the La Trobe River weir; the transmission towers for the 110-mile line from Yallourn to Yarraville. Monash was a frequent visitor in the early days of the primitive construction camp, prowling around on his own. He stayed with many of the other Commission men at Mrs Connolon's hotel at Morwell, with no special quarters, dining at table with the others, carrying on friendly banter with the landlady. He 'had a lovely sense of humour in a quiet kind of way', according to one of his 'bright young men'. When there was a conflict of opinion over where to site the temporary powerhouse for the construction works, Monash told the departmental heads to come back after lunch with a decision. When they still differed, he pulled down the map and said: 'That's where the temporary powerhouse will be'. In its three-year existence that temporary plant saw many useful experiments in the qualities of brown coal.

The fact was that the Commission knew very little about brown coal technology. Much depended on the gifted Herman who was sent off to Germany early in 1921. His reports convinced the Commissioners that the briquetting plant could only be built in Germany and that skilled Germans would have to install it. It was a decision fraught with danger, such was the continuing vehement hostility towards everything German. The ordering of the plant from the Zeitz Co. of Halle passed with little notice, but in January 1922 Federal Cabinet, under trade union and R.S.L. pressure, flatly refused to allow the temporary entry of the technicians. Monash held the decision up to ridicule: errors in assembling or in operation would be not merely dangerous but would be extremely costly and jeopardize the whole enterprise, there were no textbooks and they were entirely dependent on German advice. He assumed that the root of the matter was Hughes's hostility to him. Early in March the government backed down and in August the chief constructing engineer and five foremen from the Zeitz Co. arrived to supervise installation.

Late in 1921 to early 1922 the whole enterprise was realized to be in crisis. It had been assumed that the moisture content of the brown coal was no more than 45 to 48 per cent and the orders for construction in England of the boilers for the main powerhouse had been placed in that belief. Successive shaft-sinkings and samplings that year aroused increasing concern as the tests continued to show 65 to 68 per cent water content. Previous testing by the Mines Department had been inadequate: it turned out that the old and new cuts at North Yallourn and Yallourn were different seams. As someone subsequently remarked, it was now a matter of 'burning water with some brown coal in it rather than brown coal with some water in it'. It was not just a matter of delay and expensive cancellation of boiler orders and construction of new: future costs might be overwhelming. Eggleston concluded that inadequate testing was the 'one blot' on the 'remarkable scheme' and that 99 per cent 'of the worry and trouble which occurred later was due directly to it'. He also observed that, in the circumstances, private enterprise could never have gone ahead. There was nothing to be done but to push on and solve the problem. Monash made his own experiment, taking a lump of coal home and weighing it daily. The Germans could help little with the problem as they rarely had to deal with such high moisture content. The engineering profession gradually became aware of the crisis but the press was very slow to pick it up, even though at the 1922 select committee of Parliament Eggleston was well informed; Monash told Herman that he had obviously got his information from officials of the Mines Department who somehow would have to be shut up. It was not until late 1923 that Robinson, after long parrying, had to make a frank statement to Parliament. Monash brushed aside the problem in public and would not admit its seriousness even when writing to Rosenhain in private.

They were running great risks which required steady nerves: if the experiments to adapt failed, the delay and cost would be incalculable and their secrecy indefensible. However, by means of 'modification by experiment, trial and tribulation', the way out was found under the leadership of C. T. Briggs, the mechanical engineer. The boilers were redesigned and modified and an efficient means found of drying on the way to the furnace. The problems were largely solved by early 1924 and completely so two years later when for the first time the S.E.C. confessed its troubles in a formal report.

Very soon after joining the S.E.C. Monash concluded that it had to acquire a monopoly of generation and distribution, though it might take ten to fifteen years to undertake all services. Dozens of municipal and private electricity suppliers would have to be absorbed and their widely varying systems standardized and modernized. As early as January 1921 he was referring to the interests which were 'doomed ultimately to perish' having begun to fight bitterly for their existence. It came to be a matter of rough and tough politics; Monash showed himself to be a master practitioner in the genre when the showdown came in 1922. While public opinion was broadly behind him, and while he could always eventually convince the timid and vacillating Lawson and subsequent premiers of his wisdom, nevertheless a powerful opposition to the S.E.C. developed, based on rural interests, many local government bodies and private power companies. The battle-ground came largely to be the Commission's bold claim to control retailing, not just wholesaling of power. In June and July Monash spent much time with Cabinet, convincing them of necessities, before complex amending legislation was introduced. He also took some of the sting out of Country Party opposition by providing for early power for the south-west, north-east and east of the State. The Commission as yet had no electricity to sell, but the Melbourne Electricity Supply Co. had capacity to spare in its Geelong generating plant, so Monash offered to build a transmission line from Geelong to Warrnambool; the local municipalities agreed, and local costs in the south-west of generating power were removed. He also announced the Commission's first hydro and irrigation scheme, Sugarloaf–Rubicon, and early construction of a transmission line running east from Yallourn.

Monash argued to Robinson that the provincial electrical undertakings were grossly inefficient; their service, construction and maintenance were shoddy; their charges were high, and nearly all ran at a loss. Exclusion of the generating authority from retail distribution was practised hardly anywhere in the world. The economic arguments of scale and efficiency were overpowering. The main problem to be overcome was strong public opinion in favour of local autonomy. The government's answer was half satisfactory, a politically cautious solution: the Commission could undertake retail distribution when local councils requested it. In the long run nearly every shire and municipality came round. The other demand of the rural interests was that there should be a flat State-wide price to the consumer in order to encourage decentralization, despite the costs of taking power to remote areas. Somehow Monash managed to convince the government that, for some years at least, tariffs had to be tied to costs and that a flat rate would endanger the whole enterprise.

The Melbourne City Council led the opposition. It had been running an efficient electricity scheme in a compact heavily populated area, using its large profits to keep down the rates and did not welcome the prospect of having to abide by S.E.C. retail prices. The immediate occasion of conflict was the S.E.C. takeover, on the request of the Essendon council whose area was being neglected, of the North Melbourne Electric Tramways and Lighting Co. The M.C.C. took the lead in forming an Electrical Defence Committee which launched scurrilous propaganda against the S.E.C., flooding the State with leaflets. Journalists were employed to dig up what dirt they could about Monash. Accusations by the M.C.C. of breach of faith by Monash were the immediate cause in September of the government establishing a select committee whose investigations widened into a general examination of the Commission's activities. Monash welcomed the opportunity of meeting his opponents face to face, justifying the amending legislation, and especially denouncing the wastefulness of municipal control.

The select committee, which met for weeks, entirely backed the Commission. It was an astonishing display by Monash of forceful argument, often in a bitter atmosphere. The combative Melbourne town clerk, T. G. Ellery, and the lord mayor, J. W. Swanson, were made to appear stupid and selfish. Monash did not win through without strain: the proceedings were fatuous, he told Robinson; he would do his best but wouldn't be held responsible if things went wrong. They carefully arranged for Monash to have the last annihilating say. He described the outcome to Rosenhain:

> Towards the middle of December the Committee delivered its reports, which were overwhelmingly in favor of my views, with the result that Parliament, in a very few hours, passed no less than five new Acts of Parliament, greatly extending the powers of the Commission, placing large sums of money at its disposal, and, what was best of all, definitely enacting that the finances of the Commission should be entirely separated from those of the rest of the State. . . .
>
> . . . it was a serious matter for me, because, had I failed to carry Parliament and the press with me, it would have been a serious injury to my personal prestige. As matters have turned out, it is again proved that a bold policy is always a sound policy. Now that I have had my fight and overthrown my enemies, it is hardly probable that there will be any recrudescence of this trouble in the future.

The issue of retail distribution was still, however, not conclusively won. In 1924 the takeover of the largest surviving distributor, the Melbourne Electric Supply Co., was a hard-fought battle and the

Commission had to pay a high price. Legislation was necessary, and most of the Legislative Council still supported the local right to retail power; Monash addressed the Council, whose unofficial leader was his friend, H. I. Cohen. The bill was passed only with an enabling provision for Parliament to establish another commission to distribute electricity in Melbourne; Monash had cunningly offered it as a sop, knowing nothing was likely to come of it. Clements, the company's general manager who was soon to become a Commissioner, congratulated him on his success, the product of so much thought and hard work. Monash failed, however, to persuade the Electricity Supply Co. of Victoria, which catered for Ballarat and Bendigo, to sell out. The local municipalities would not bring pressure to bear and the company even refused to use S.E.C. current; for several years the S.E.C. was to be excluded from the two provincial cities.

Yallourn was the first major Australian example, reflecting the English town-planning movement, of a model garden town. Raymond Unwin's *Town Planning in Practice* was a major guide for A. R. La Gerche, the architect, and W. E. Gower, the town planner, who mainly created Yallourn. Monash backed them up warmly. On 24 January 1921 he jotted down 'Some Notes on a policy for the construction and governance of the proposed town', identifying the basic questions which had to be settled before design and construction could proceed far. He agreed that, although private ownership of houses was a desirable ideal, it was not practicable for the time being—it would have to be a publicly-owned town, the Commission would have to be the landlord and subsidize public facilities heavily. Welfare activities would need to be controlled by a body largely elected by residents, with Commission representation; co-operative stores should be encouraged. Monash was firm in demanding that the architect have ultimate control of 'artistic and aesthetic treatment': 'It is the architect, and none other, who can decide how sculptural or horticultural effects are to be employed to emphasize or suppress, to heighten or restrain, in short to create the harmonious whole which he aims at'. He later took pride in the fact that, among his 'many other obsessions', Yallourn was 'a model industrial town, built, organised and administered on what we believe to be the most advanced scientific principles'. He kept a close eye on the school and demanded retention of a good teacher about to be transferred. On the advice of the police, the original policy of prohibition had to be abandoned in 1923, because of the flourishing sly-grog trade, and communal hotels established. He insisted on early founding of a plant nursery, vehemently condemned any unnecessary felling of trees or undergrowth, and eventually delighted in the 'blaze of colour' from public and private trees and gardens and, by about 1930, how little remained to offend the eye.

Monash conducted public relations himself. Journalists admired him for his patience and courtesy and for not visiting on them the sins of their employers. In the early 1920s he regularly spoke to local gatherings and meetings of societies, which were often crammed to the doors, explaining 'the greatest engineering undertaking in the Southern Hemisphere'—preaching that Victoria was under-industrialized and that abundant power would raise the standard of living, increase domestic comfort and provide employment. He made the rounds of the country municipalities and addressed municipal conferences, arguing, pleading, to persuade them of the benefits of coming under the S.E.C. He provided government ministers with notes for their speeches. He composed himself or brushed up his officers' propaganda for the press and technical journals, and wrote patiently to politicians and journalists, explaining how erroneous the criticisms of opposing interests were and how best to support the S.E.C.'s case. He took particular care to keep on the right side of Keith Murdoch, the editor of the *Herald*. His conducted tours of VIPs over Yallourn became famous. Politicians, the press, Rotary, the Chambers of Commerce and Manufactures, visiting dignitaries such as the Imperial Press Conference or the Empire Parliamentary Association, would join the special train from Flinders Street and hear his preparatory lecture on the way down; then follow his guided tour while he lucidly explained and patiently answered the obvious questions. Often he would be in gumboots or old riding breeches and puttees, tweed cap on head, puffing his pipe; opening the furnaces to display the immense heat, he sometimes hammed it up by pretending to push in a known critic. White and Blamey went once and beamed affectionately on him. Few were unimpressed by his masterly exposition.

In 1924 Yallourn came into action. Vast quantities of brown coal were now exposed in the open cut for ready use; 'Mount Monash', made from the overburden, was looming large on the landscape. On 15 June the first generator began work and next day Yallourn was 'turned on'. Power flowed down the main transmission line to Melbourne, through the seven suburban sub-stations, and augmented the supply generated from Newport using black coal. There was no opening ceremony, though Monash proudly announced that he had kept his promise that Melbourne would have power from Yallourn in mid-1924. A few days before, however, he had demonstrated a trial switch-on to visiting Australian railway commissioners. After his dramatic presentation, the operator pulled the wrong switch and there was a loud bang from the boiler-room, whereupon, Monash, looking at his watch, said: 'Gentlemen, we are now long overdue at the briquetting works'; later he sent an apology to the operator for putting him under too much pressure. Robinson, who had just concluded his ministerial career, wrote proudly and warmly: 'Best of luck to you. You have needed all your courage and resource but have vanquished all open to argument'. In November briquettes—'crushed, screened, dried, cooled and pressed . . . hard, shiny, almost black blocks of uniform sizes'—came into production. In 1920 Monash had promised them in 1923; delay in delivery of plant had held up supply. They were cheaper than firewood, and were immediately so popular—and long remained a great propaganda asset—that demand could not be met for several years. Fuel merchants were disgruntled; after some early profiteering their prices were strictly controlled.

From late 1923, however, public criticism of the S.E.C. had been growing. The press had been enthusiastic supporters, but from about September the *Age* became critical, needling and mocking Monash in editorials and special articles, with a judicious mix of anonymous letters of dubious origin. It made much of Monash warning that domestic power could not be as cheap as the public seemed to assume ('Sir John Monash is obviously in a twitter'). In fact, the Commission was beginning to suffer from its own propaganda: the simple public was becoming rather disillusioned by the long delay and growing expenditure. Then the *Age* moved to alarmist criticisms of rising capital expenditure, and ultimately to attacks on Monash's 'megalomania' and 'needless bombast': 'Future generations may be found making complaint against the men and women of this generation that they were severely culpable in breeding enormous white elephants whose services were quite disproportionate to their cost of maintenance'. There is some mystery about the motivation of the *Age's* policy which was controlled largely by Geoffrey Syme. Unquestionably, the criticism was ignorant. Its persistent vicious attacks on state instrumentalities such as the Railways, the Melbourne & Metropolitan Board of Works and the S.E.C. seem to have been due to traditional grudges and idiosyncrasy rather than any particular ideological position or rational approach; perhaps, in line with its high protectionist policy, it took special exception to the S.E.C.'s importation of foreign machinery. Privately, Monash reacted bitterly: it was 'no exaggeration to say that the success of any public undertaking, or the men who control it, may be measured by the amount of abuse, vilification, misrepresentation and criticism which this journal devotes to it'. The *Bendigo Advertiser*, influenced by R. H. S. Abbott, a Legislative Councillor and a frequent foolish critic, was another savage opponent. However, the *Argus* and the *Herald* remained staunch. In December 1924, also, C. Brunsden Fletcher, editor of the *Sydney Morning Herald*, was surprised by the number of cynics and doubters in Melbourne, of whom Monash had good reason to be scornful. New South Wales must somehow attract him over the border:

Just his stamp of mind is our greatest need at the present moment, when urgent public enterprises call so loudly for strong men with the requisite ability and experience, and the like straightforwardness and force of character.... Whereas Victoria was once at our mercy for her main industries, she is now on the highway to independence. Soon she will be competing with us with manufactures born of brown coal and at prices with which we cannot compete.

Nevertheless, public and political confidence in the S.E.C. was badly shaken by 1925. The *Age*, many Country Party members, some municipalities and surviving private electrical interests made a formidable opposition; some Labor members, objecting partly to import of foreign equipment, were also restive. The heavy expenditure beyond the original estimates, partly a result of unanticipated demand, came to be the chief grievance. Unfortunately, in its first full year of operation the Commission made a greater loss than expected because, owing to shortage of loan money, the goverment had cut back on capital expenditure, thus delaying extensions of power supply which would have been profitable. The *Journal of Chemical Engineering and Mining Review* came out with a trenchant attack. Monash wrote to the Rosenhains:

My big job... is not a bed of roses. While the works and schemes are developing quite to my own satisfaction, and to the undoubted overwhelmingly great benefit to the community, there is little thanks for it either from press, or public men, or the people. We have a nasty way in this country of levelling criticism and abuse, and doubt upon all leaders and higher workers, a habit led and engendered by a press which thrives only upon sensation and criticism.... Added to this, I have had four different Ministers in the last two years, and hence no satisfactory continuity of political endorsement of my various projects. All the same I take the matter philosophically, knowing full well that I have builded a great monument—the successful exploitation of our vast lignite resources—the electrification of the greater part of the entire State—and the raising of the standard of comfort of the people.... *I* know that the project is fundamentally financially sound, and will be fully reproductive when fully developed.

But the government's confidence was dwindling—John Allan now led a Country Party–Nationalist coalition.

Monash was also encountering difficulties on the Commission itself. Throughout, he had the total backing of Sir Robert Gibson, who was emerging as the most powerful man of the day in national affairs and was about to become chairman of the Commonwealth Bank Board, and of Sir Thomas Lyle who, though elderly and past his best, was no cipher. It may broadly be true that Monash fashioned the Commission in his own image and put his own stamp on it, but his colleagues nevertheless were very able men. The other Commissioner, Swinburne, was increasingly worrying about Monash's methods and style. He had been concerned about the deal with the Melbourne Electric Supply Co., considering that far too much was paid to purchase its assets. In February 1924 Monash told his daughter of 'a very nasty squabble in the Commission, owing to Mr Swinburne having broken away and taken action which might end disastrously'. After he had concurred with the terms of settlement with the company, Swinburne had withdrawn his signature; the other Commissioners all agreed that they had made a very good bargain, that Swinburne was misunderstanding the facts, and that they should try to save his face. Later in 1924 Swinburne was perturbed by Monash agreeing to chair the royal commission on the police strike, and threatened resignation; he considered the S.E.C. was far too important for its chairman to be so distracted.

From November Monash also had a difficult political chief—Frederic Eggleston. For four years he had had to deal with Sir Arthur Robinson who had seen his task as being to shield the Commission from political difficulties. Eggleston, also a lawyer and a Nationalist, had very different ideas from Robinson's on political control of the S.E.C. Moreover, having been a member of the select committees of 1920 and 1922, he was well informed, suspected that the Commission was in serious trouble and was concealing it, and was himself under political pressure. He was on close terms with Swinburne (whose biography he was eventually to write) and knew that he was having disagreements with the other Commissioners, though Swinburne was too honourable to tell him what his specific worries were. One of Eggleston's first actions as minister was to veto an ambitious scheme which had been approved by the Prendergast Labor government (in office from July to November 1924) for the Commission to buy out the Metropolitan Gas Company.

Towards the end of 1924 Swinburne had a breakdown and planned a long overseas trip. He wanted to retire from the Commission but was persuaded to stay on and report on the brown coal industry in Germany. On 19 January, while on board ship, he wrote an alarming letter to his fellow Commissioners:

> We cannot blink our eyes to the fact that the details on which our fundamental work was founded are not coming out in accordance with our expectations.
> (a) The Moisture of the Coal.
> (b) The most economical and effective way of burning same for Steam Raising.
> (c) the economical production of Briquettes.
> (d) The proper use in all our Boilers and Plants of *all* the coal we produce.

The basic trouble was that Monash was not spending nearly enough time at Yallourn in co-ordinating coal supply, the powerhouse and briquette manufacture; the same applied to other senior staff, the S.E.C. was 'top heavy'. 'We are up against it and I cannot split hairs.' He concluded with an account of some of his observations, on his last trip to Yallourn, of inefficiency, indiscipline and idleness, and a remark that there was far too much pipe-smoking round Head Office. It was a cranky letter. Monash, Gibson and Lyle decided not to answer for the moment. When Monash did eventually reply after six months, he explained that the letter had 'caused considerable consternation to us all, and a very extreme vexation to myself personally', that he had wanted to cool off while 'labouring under a sense of injury and embarrassment', and that they knew and were highly alarmed by the fact that Swinburne had been talking to Eggleston before he left. Their experience of Eggleston had been that he was 'a carping critic, accepting our explanations with obvious reservations, instead of as a helpful coadjutor, fighting our battles in Cabinet, in Parliament, and in the Press'. Monash's letter of nearly 4000 words was not so much a reply as a general defence of his management, and illustrated his sensitivity to criticism and the tone of injured innocence with which he would reply to it. He hit hard, but without making an irreparable breach: 'I feel quite sure that you will permit me to be equally candid and frank, and that our discussion of these matters will in no way impair our friendship or cordial personal relations'.

Monash was broadly in the right. The interest of his letter lies mainly in his definition of the problems facing the Commission and of correct administrative principles. He defined the chief problems as 'excessive moisture in the coal, the inability of the power-house to burn the fine coal without the loss of boiler efficiency . . .; the indifferent performance of the briquetting boiler plant; the inadequate output of coal from the open cut'. All these problems had been actively in hand, steady improvements were being made and solutions were in sight. Swinburne's main point had been answered by the appointment in 1924 of J. M. Bridge as superintendent and co-ordinator at Yallourn. Local supervision had to be continuous to be any good at all. He was reminded of the contrast between Birdwood 'buzzing about' as Corps commander and his own method:

> I have brought the same conception to bear upon the discharge of my duties with the Commission, i.e. to be and stay, as far as possible, in one place, i.e. my H.Q. office, where everybody knows where to get me, at a moment's notice, for immediate discussion or reference, and rapid decisions; where I can have before me, all the time, a complete and not a partial picture of what is going on, and from which place I can, at all times, reach every responsible subordinate, face to face, or by telephone, with the minimum of delay.

I take leave to describe my method as scientific and efficient, and the other method, i.e. of a great show of personal activity by much travelling about, as dilettante and futile.

Of course occasional visits were essential to keep in touch.

Monash denied that any of the major difficulties were of his making. They all sprang from decisions of the Commission before his time, to wit: 'the original estimates of capital and operating costs'; 'the assumption that the coal deposits south of the river were identical in physical character with those north of the river'; the 'entire disregard' of his Fortuna report; and the contractual engagement of three independent heads of branches in watertight compartments. The worst decision of all had been to employ Clark, whose engagement had just been terminated; the Open Cut was not nearly wide enough, the problem of the rate of coal production was very serious and large expenditure would be necessary. Finally,

It was galling in the extreme to have you "discover" and "rub-in" defects and difficulties which were already patent to everybody concerned, . . . unaccompanied by one word of praise to anybody for anything. There was no coating to the pill.

Swinburne, who was still in Europe, had been greatly impressed in Germany with the possibilities of brown coal development and had regained some faith. Though he wrote a full reply he was wise enough not to send it, recognizing the intensity of Monash's emotion. He did, however, give an assurance that he had been reserved with Eggleston (he had refused to supply him with a copy of his letter to the Commissioners), and, fairly enough, protested his general loyalty. 'You appear satisfied with your military methods and no doubt with reason . . . my business experience [is] that efficiency in civil life is not attained by the chief official sitting at Headquarters.' All would be right if they continued to pull together: 'I am afraid however that is not possible if you maintain the attitude plainly discernible in your letter'.

In the absence of Swinburne and Lyle, who was also on an overseas trip, Professor Sir David Orme Masson had been appointed as a temporary Commissioner. Monash and Gibson had wanted Robinson, but Eggleston would not appoint him. In the face of the political clamour, Monash and Gibson decided in July to take the offensive. They had consulted Clapp who, from his contacts in the government and the Treasury, advised that sooner or later an inquiry would be forced on them. Monash was entirely confident in the long-term economic soundness of the S.E.C., and that any reputable inquiry must be at the very least broadly favourable in its conclusions and thus restore public confidence. There was reason to fear that the government might become so alarmed that it would veto further development. So on

29 July the Commission formally asked Eggleston to appoint an inquiry, especially into the prospect of the S.E.C. paying its way; they could tolerate no longer the constant accusations of ignorance and extravagance. From afar, Lyle agreed and Swinburne disapproved. Eggleston welcomed the proposal and eventually, on Clapp's suggestion, Willits H. Sawyer from Columbus, Ohio, was appointed. Monash had thought it best not to advise on the appointment and was well pleased that the choice had fallen on an expert in the economic aspects of large-scale electrical undertakings who knew little about brown coal.

Sawyer was not appointed until December 1925. Meanwhile the political situation deteriorated. In September, some stupid remarks in the Legislative Council by the minister of forests, agreeing with its ancient enemies that the Commission needed urgent inquiry, brought about a confrontation with the Cabinet, Monash demanding a better understanding and threatening resignation. Gibson was so angry that, to Monash's alarm, he did resign—but was persuaded to withdraw. A meeting with Cabinet on 19 October was peaceful. On 23 December Monash again addressed Parliament in order to get the financial allocation passed and had his way again, giving an absolute assurance that the S.E.C. would be profitable in the very near future. He also informed Parliament that a recent German expert visitor had told him that if the people of Victoria lost faith in the enterprise 'he was prepared to find the capital and buy the whole undertaking'. This was Emil Gaudlitz, very senior in the German brown coal industry, making a private visit. Once Monash had grasped his attitude, he asked him to make a report. Gaudlitz's response was, 'You have a great big deposit and are opening it up as though it was only a tinpot thing'. Overburden should be removed years, not weeks, ahead. The plant was too small, it needed much greater investment and machine power. The moisture content was no longer a problem with modern techniques; despite it, Yallourn's heating power was better than that of any works in Germany. It was a welcome opinion, though Gaudlitz also made some rude remarks about inefficiency.

In December Monash wrote a masterly 'Memorandum on Coal-winning operations at Yallourn'. Gaudlitz's report and the impressions gained in Germany by Swinburne and Bridge made this the right moment for review. Monash concluded that they would need to double coal output over the next three years; previous operations had been hand to mouth. They had to have further specialist advice from Germany on methods and machinery. Bridge had already found the right man, of whom Gaudlitz warmly approved—J. Klitzing, a mine manager (who had been seriously wounded during the war). In January Monash asked Eggleston for permission to engage him and, when no reply came, went ahead. Eggleston rebuked him and complained that he was not being kept well enough informed. Klitzing was a winner: he arrived and had his report drafted within weeks, in mid-April. Monash read it in German and told him he had never 'had the pleasure of reading a report which was so comprehensive, so closely reasoned, so convincing and so constructive'. He arranged for a bonus and for Klitzing's appointment as consulting engineer, and for the next four years wrote to him in Germany regularly and confidentially. His ability to converse in German had helped to make friends and allies of both Gaudlitz and Klitzing.

Asked by Eggleston to comment on a letter of instruction he was sending to Sawyer, Monash persuaded him to modify certain aspects. He himself wrote for Sawyer a temperate 5000-word statement of the S.E.C.'s problems. Soon after Sawyer arrived late in February, Eggleston took him to Monash's office and was soon dismissed: 'Well, Mr Eggleston, there's no occasion to keep you'. Eggleston was convinced that Sawyer did not receive enough frankness from Monash during the inquiry. Just at this time Monash was under some pressure from Lord Burnham to consider advising the British government on electrical development. Sawyer's report after his two-month investigation was only broadly satisfactory to the Commission, for whom the Gaudlitz and Klitzing reports had been very handy. Unequivocally, Sawyer judged the enterprise to be economically sound, and he entirely supported the Commission's claim to take over retail distribution. Of the Commissioners, he remarked: 'I can hardly conceive a higher type of citizenship and personality devoted to public duty'. But he was pessimistic about the possibility of the S.E.C. paying its way for several years. And he gave some very awkward advice: he strongly recommended a mark-time policy on power-plant and briquetting extensions, temporary closure of the New Cut and return to the old mine with its lower moisture content, for the general moisture problem had not been commercially solved. Deliberately or not, Sawyer had given the government what it wanted—authority to cut expenditure and play absolutely safe. Cabinet adopted the report and ordered the Commission to implement it. The *Age* exulted over what it saw as a vindication. The *Argus* considered the government had blundered: the Commission should act on the Sawyer report only to the extent it saw fit.

Sawyer had also been determined to reform the Commission's higher management. He considered Monash was too much in control, 'carrying a load which no man should be called upon to carry'; his proper task was to guide policy, inspire and lead, not to exercise detailed management. What was needed was an electrical engineer executive on the American model, to iron out major technical problems; Sawyer may have been articulating the criticism that Swinburne had been trying to make. He said he had signed the report on the understanding that the Commission had agreed to take on an additional member, to appoint a deputy chairman, and to give greater power to the superintendent at Yallourn. Monash had approached Clements of the Melbourne Electric Supply Co. with the proposition that he either become co-ordinating manager at Yallourn or join the Commission with special responsibility for electrical activities. Monash privately advised the latter: he opposed Sawyer's desire to have a general manager—it would be swapping horses in midstream, would merely shift the load, disrupt routine and antagonize staff. Clements chose to join the Commission and not to go to Yallourn, and on 18 May told Monash that Sawyer and Eggleston were content with the outcome, but that Sawyer forcibly demanded that Clements start with the Commission immediately or 'he would be in a considerable quandary as to how to suitably alter a certain portion of his report'. Clements immediately began sitting with the Commission, worked on something like a half-time basis, proved to be a compatible and able colleague, and eventually succeeded Monash as chairman. He relieved Monash of substantial duties, though it is doubtful if Monash relaxed his authority much. Bridge's powers at Yallourn were built up.*

When he received it, Eggleston made some notes on Sawyer's report which display the depth of his suspicion and misunderstanding. The report, he noted, stated that the economic value of brown coal was unproven. He still believed that the moisture problem was crippling. Monash had to tell him, on Swinburne's advice, that his belief that the Yallourn powerhouse would not be able to generate more than 35 000 kilowatts was nonsense; the load would soon be 45 000. Eggleston accepted Sawyer's judgement that the Commission would not make a profit for years. On all these matters he was grossly mistaken.

Late in June 1926, Eggleston issued his orders. The Commission was to 'proceed with those works and programmes which have been specifically approved or recommended by Mr W. H. Sawyer'; if it departed from his advice it must tell the government its reasons, and if it desired to proceed when Sawyer had advised postponement it must report to the government. Swinburne protested privately to Eggleston: his letters were 'almost an insult to the members of the Commission', could he

---

*In some reminiscences, penned in old age, Eggleston asserted that Sawyer's signing the report was conditional not only on appointment of a new expert executive but also on Monash taking a year's leave. Eggleston's memory was obviously faulty. Gibson, Swinburne and Lyle would never have given this assurance and gone back on it; nor could Monash's pride have possibly allowed him to agree. Monash had, however, been mentioning the possibility of a long holiday in 1927 which may eventually have confused Eggleston. Eggleston also mentioned that Sawyer's 'rather devious' intention was 'the removal of the overriding influence of Monash for the time being'.

not show more cordiality and *savoir faire*? Eggleston replied that he did not see why he should show all the tact, and it was difficult to be cordial when the Commissioners would not give him their confidence. Four months of determined conflict followed. Monash, with the full support of his fellow Commissioners including Swinburne (until he resigned in July on health grounds), replied on the particular issues with assertive arguments bordering on the insulting and concluding 'Yours obediently'. On 1 July Eggleston was given a conclusive reply to his assertion that the boiler plant had basic combustion problems. On 19 August, again on Swinburne's advice, Monash sent a long screed on the history of the moist coal question and the utilization of brown coal in general, requesting its publication as a parliamentary paper. Eggleston replied with many comments and suggested alterations, insisting he knew better. The Commission published the unamended document as part of its annual report.

The chief urgent problem, however, was development of coal production. Monash explained to Klitzing that the government, being weak and unpopular and wanting to curb expenditure, had probably asked Sawyer to recommend a delay in development; and that Eggleston had seized on Klitzing's suggestions for reworking the old mine as a means of deferring his vital plans for development of the New Cut, despite Swinburne's vehement support of Klitzing's recommendations against Sawyer's. The Commission's submission to the minister on 30 July condemned his intention of referring the matter to an advisory power board representing the Commission, the Railways and the Tramways, whose constitution Sawyer had recommended, simply because such a body could not possibly be as expert as the Commission; and it necessarily implied lack of confidence. The matter was very urgent indeed; the Commission knew Sawyer had been wrong and that new German equipment had to be acquired. Monash was becoming highly agitated and on 17 August told Gibson: 'I am getting thoroughly fed up with the position, and don't see how we can carry on much longer, if we have to be continually fighting the Minister on proposals which we know to be essential and unavoidable'. Eggleston kept stalling through conferences, but at last in September cabled Sawyer and Klitzing for advice. Sawyer had nothing to say, Klitzing enthusiastically supported the Commission, so Eggleston at last submitted, allowed purchase of some of the vital machinery, and thus committed the government to the New Cut developments. He was desperately overworked and ill; the government had a majority only of one, and he was perhaps influenced by the Commission's recent impressive financial returns. Early in 1927, after many discussions, he approved expenditure on further equipment and began to consider long-term developments. When in April he lost his seat at the election,

Monash was delighted: it would be 'impossible to get a worse Minister'.*

It was a sad ending, with much rancour on both sides. However prejudiced and ignorant, Eggleston had been full of good will, and eventually reached the theoretical conclusion that a corporation such as the S.E.C. should be free from ministerial supervision. He had been misled by Monash's determined optimism and by his refusal to take him into his confidence, and believed grave matters were being concealed. Sawyer also criticized Monash's policy of presenting the S.E.C.'s achievements in terms of an unqualified success story. Commenting on the annual report for 1925–26, he told Eggleston:

> The facts are, the Commission being human makes mistakes the same as every one else does, and it is about time they told the truth and were frank. . . . I do not see how they can expect confidence until they speak in a different tone.

But there was less propaganda and more truth than Sawyer and Eggleston knew. Eggleston was clumsy and had not the tact or charm to come to terms with Monash. But Monash would not have brooked control by any minister. The only thing to be done with an aggressive and misguided minister was to fight him down. In doing so, he took the Commission far along the road to independence.

Monash had been under tension as he showed in uncharacteristic remarks in June 1926—'An Extraordinary Speech' was the *Age's* headline—in which he referred to fools and idiots criticizing the S.E.C. The Commission succeeded in its defiance because the government was unstable, because the public had been broadly reassured by the Sawyer report, and because it was becoming very clear that their financial situation was steadily improving. Monash's bold offensive had in the end been justified. From now on it was downhill going, the Commission never again had seriously to defend the basis of its operations. For a while yet the *Age* huffed and puffed, but it was beaten. Monash was soon to say one morning: 'I feel quite sorry for *The Age* today: the Commission has just shown a profit!' It hardly mattered now that the *Herald* was no longer an enthusiastic supporter (for Monash had taken Murdoch on and beaten him on the question of

---

*Eggleston concluded in his reminiscences: 'The ruthless egotism of Monash should have been mitigated by the sense of duty of the other members of the Commission—but it was not. . . . The fact was of course that they had not bargained on Monash's fierce resistance to the report, and when they saw his attitude they had not the guts to act'. It would be truer to conclude that the Commissioners knew that Gaudlitz and Klitzing were right and Sawyer wrong.

In 1929, when there was a briquette shortage, Monash publicly blamed Eggleston for the delays he had imposed; Eggleston made a spirited reply. Lyle, Gibson and Clements jointly rebuked Eggleston in a private letter.

building the Shrine of Remembrance). In October 1927 he wrote exultantly to Walter and Lou:

> The position is so good that many people are still disposed to regard it as too good to be true, and the only mutterings one now hears indicate that people are wondering where the catch is, and when and how the collapse will come.... Thus are the critics and croakers being confounded. But no one will ever know the hard fight it has been, both to conquer the stupidity of ignorant Ministers and Parliamentarians, and to flog my organisation into efficient functioning.

And he wrote dead pan to Sawyer to inform him of the latest profitable figures.

Monash attributed much of the S.E.C.'s better performance and certain ultimate success to the adoption of German technology:

> The solution of nearly all my problems has lain in the direction of the whole-hearted adoption—in nearly every stage—of German methods, policies and machinery. You can imagine the degree of hostility and opposition engendered by such a course of action. Nothing but my war prestige would have sufficed to justify the purity of my motives, and I doubt if any one else could have battled through such a line of action.

It is true that the R.S.L., Labor and the manufacturing lobby all remained hostile to German influence and imported machinery; *Smith's Weekly* in 1927 remarked on the Commission's 'pro-German bias that has been marked throughout its history'. Certainly Monash's prestige was very important, but by about 1925 the public hostility to everything German was fast declining and German methods, important though they were, perhaps were not quite as significant as he asserted. But there is little doubt that the Gaudlitz and Klitzing advice, at a critical stage, had galvanizing effects. In 1930 Monash described how Bridge and his staff had brought about 'a startling reduction in operation costs, due to the introduction of large scale coal-winning land dredgers and large scale electric railway haulages; a heavy reduction in maintenance charges, and an almost entire elimination of annoying breakdowns and stoppages to coal supply'. Officers were regularly sent to Germany; the superintendent of the briquetting factory had returned with full knowledge, among other things, of how to introduce the electrolytic process of dust collection.

Labour relations in the S.E.C. were on the whole harmonious. Monash was influenced by the 'national efficiency' stream of thought which, reinforced by his military experience, inclined him towards enlightened, scientific management which would increase productivity by means of humane and conciliatory treatment of the workforce. The policy from the first, according to the Commission's industrial officer, was to try to 'do the fair thing' and to be generous in cases of real doubt. Throughout, Monash got on excellently with the Melbourne Trades Hall Council, partly because of his diplomacy no doubt, but also because the union movement was eager on ideological grounds to help a state enterprise to succeed. In their experience Monash was proving to be a good employer, they recognized the potential importance of the S.E.C. in promoting higher employment through industrialization, and by dealing directly with Monash they could gain greater control over the unionists at Yallourn. As early as September 1921 the disputes committee of the T.H.C. was conferring with him over a threatened stoppage.

But the conditions at Yallourn in the pioneering days were harsh, and from 1924 the local branch of the Australian Workers' Union became increasingly militant and won concessions through strike action, sometimes with the ultimate sanction of the Arbitration Court. The demand for a 44-hour week was a major issue which came to a head in November–December 1926. After the court largely rejected the union case, nearly one thousand men from the open cuts struck. The confrontation lasted three weeks and was settled just when severe power restrictions on Melbourne were about to be imposed. Monash had been conferring with representatives of the T.H.C. and the A.W.U. and agreed to do without some work on Saturdays. The Melbourne union officials persuaded the Yallourn men to return to arbitration, but when the verdict yielded them little there was much bitterness.

A conflict in March 1927 arose from the bad relations between men in the powerhouse and a foreman who was alleged to bully and abuse them. After an inquiry he was reinstated, whereupon the whole workforce struck, demanding his dismissal; much of Melbourne was without power for three days. Having consulted Monash, E. J. Holloway, secretary of the Trades Hall disputes committee, and the State officials of the relevant unions tried to persuade the men to return to work on the promise of a conference, but they at first voted unanimously against. Monash refused to proceed under duress and the men eventually agreed after three days, on Holloway's urging, to return to work and to accept the judgment of an immediate inquiry by the Commissioners themselves. The men were stingingly condemned in the judgment and the foreman declared not guilty, but he was to be transferred—on grounds of expediency, Monash frankly said. The *Argus* and numerous indignant correspondents were outraged at this 'Victory for Wrong'. Monash believed that his co-operation with the Trades Hall, their increased control over the Yallourn unionists, and the undertaking, after a showdown, that future disputes must be subject to agreed channels for resolution, justified his concession. The incident concluded with a private exchange with Holloway. Monash wrote:

> I have to a large extent pledged my future prestige and the public confidence in me upon the assurance that steps will now be taken by all concerned to... greatly reduce the probability of sudden interference with public services. I have said publicly that such a result would far overshadow any detailed aspect of the recent dispute and its settlement. I have got to make good that pronouncement, or I shall suffer in the public esteem.

In reply Holloway assured him that

> we all appreciated the way you handled some very ignorant and hostile criticism from people who ought to have known better and who certainly proved themselves to be very small Australians; however, it is good to know there are some men who can play the game and forget self and act and speak like a *real* citizen.

The incident cleared the air and no major conflicts followed. The young union organizer, P. J. Kennelly, later recalled that 'You could talk to Monash', though not to Gibson. But Monash had taken the precaution of drawing up an emergency plan for keeping Yallourn going by volunteer labour in a serious strike situation. Ted Holloway, a future distinguished Federal minister and no fool, remained a devoted admirer. Monash was 'one of the greatest men I ever met.... the really great men were those who could spare time and inclination to do little human acts which others would brush aside'. And he cited a case where two young girls, part-time kitchen-hands at the Naval and Military Club, were charged with pilfering food. Holloway rang Monash about it, Monash investigated and had the charges withdrawn. Holloway rang to thank him. 'Forget it', he replied, 'I got quite a kick out of it'. No doubt Monash exercised his charm on Holloway, who had found a hero, but it was also, in Holloway's view, a matter of being prepared to go half-way and doing the right thing. The important point is that in the late 1920s, a period of industrial strife, and long after, the S.E.C.'s paternalism became highly popular with its employees.

Monash got on very well with Ned Hogan, the Labor premier from May 1927 to November 1928, and with Tom Tunnecliffe, his minister. Hogan was far more astute than his predecessor, Allan. Tunnecliffe lacked Eggleston's analytical ability, but was intelligent and level headed. The government agreed happily to the Commission's request late in 1927 to reappoint Monash for five years, but refused to raise his salary. Hogan often spoke warmly in his support in Parliament. Tunnecliffe was concerned to persuade Monash that it was high time he had a proper holiday for a few months. The Trades Hall Council invited him in August 1928 to chair a conference with employers on industrial peace; he had to refuse. W. J. Duggan, president of the Australasian Council of Trade Unions, referred to him as an excellent arbitrator; unionists knew they would get 'a fair and open go from him'. The Labor government did clash with the Commission by insisting on giving local preference for construction of a turbo-generator; when he presented the facts to the Tariff Board, Monash ran into stiff criticism from the protectionist Sydney *Bulletin*. But a year later the government gave way in a similar case because of the almost double cost involved. Late in 1929, when Labor took office again, Monash wrote privately: 'I am bound to say that the affairs of the Electricity Commission always prosper better under a Labor Government than otherwise. They have always accorded me a free hand and have abstained from embarrassing interference'. Monash and the Labor Party met cheerfully in defence of Victorian 'state socialism'. In his frequent addresses to S.E.C. staff on comradeship, teamwork, being employees and servants of the people and all being workers for the state, Monash was, not entirely consciously, in harmony with Labor philosophy.

In 1927, after full allowance for interest payment and depreciation, the S.E.C. showed a profit. Publicity began to be triumphant. Sawyer's conclusions that there would be no surplus until 1929 and that the Commission had outbuilt immediate demand had been quickly disproved. Parliamentary opposition died away as it came to be realized that the Commission had thoroughly justified itself. Most politicians admitted the charge when early in 1929 Hogan stated: 'This State enterprise has come out of the shadows in which it was staggering for years [when it] deserved the sympathy and consideration of the government and parliament, but did not get much of either'. Monash's strength had given the S.E.C. a degree of independence which had never been intended; in later years it had a hard battle to preserve it.

Monash would not, or could not, relax. In January 1929 he wrote to Rosenhain:

> This success has brought with it the necessity for expansion, and we are all again immersed in the huge task of launching a programme of new development, which amounts to almost a complete duplication of the original programme . . . to carry us on until about 1935. . . . we have Governments and Parliaments composed of men of low intellectual calibre, and timorous and narrow vision. So—there is always a fight on, at almost every stage of the business—and there is never a time when I have not to direct a campaign of publicity,

education and persuasion, in order to advance and stabilize each successive step.

The battles with various municipalities continued. In 1927 Monash waged a sustained campaign against inner Melbourne councils concerned to protect their electrical enterprises and once addressed a combined meeting of the Labor central executive and Labor councillors on the question. Conflict with Ballarat and Bendigo continued for years before his polite bullying brought about their agreement to eventual absorption into the S.E.C. network. A revival of the movement for a uniform State-wide tariff had to be beaten off in 1928. The serious Commonwealth proposal to grant a bounty on New South Wales coal exports to Victoria had to be derided. The Depression from 1929 did not greatly disturb development, though the drying up of loan funds delayed the duplication scheme and Monash had the 'very disagreeable task' of sacking hundreds of men. Entry into the field of manufacturing and selling electrical appliances on easy time-payment terms opened a battle which continued long after Monash's death and brought immediate vilification from the interests affected. And always the Commission was subject to political opportunism: in April 1930 Monash remarked that 'another epidemic of petty and spiteful criticism has broken out among the "outs", and I find myself almost daily dancing attendance upon Ministers in order to fortify the "ins" in protecting us from these attacks'. But he was getting on well with his Labor minister, John Cain.

The initial job had been done. The S.E.C. grid covered almost all Victoria, and Albury and Corowa in New South Wales; over the decade electricity consumption had immensely increased and the basis for future industrial development had been laid; Sugarloaf–Rubicon, the first hydro-electric scheme, had been operating since April 1929; briquettes had become the standard industrial and a very popular household fuel; the rural population delighted in its access to electricity; and the Commission was financially unassailable. The Yallourn scheme was 'the greatest of its kind in the world', the journalists were saying. Power was not so very cheap, perhaps; difficulties throughout had raised costs, then with the Depression the government left the Commission to finance its own future development. But, overall, the S.E.C. was established as a highly successful state enterprise.

To what degree was Monash the Commission? Gibson, Swinburne, Lyle and Clements were unusually able men (and always dead on time for meetings). In general, he used them as a sounding-board. He could not simply have imposed himself on them, though he probably persuaded them sometimes, against their better judgement, to allow him his head. Apart from Swinburne's period of dissent, they seem to have been a very good team indeed—Monash out front, but certainly not a lone policy-maker. As executive officer, his political skills and ability to get his own way drove the Commission through difficulties which would probably have overwhelmed lesser men. Eggleston recalled that 'When we had any trouble in Parliament he used to say to me: "Get the members into a committee room and I will speak to them," and he was unusually successful in convincing them and in time the critics stayed away'. R. G. Menzies, a junior member of the McPherson Nationalist ministry of 1928-29, recalled in old age, no doubt with some exaggeration, what happened when Cabinet rejected the Commission's proposed allocation: Monash invaded the Cabinet room and

> we all stood up instinctively, we all stood up, we were all in the presence of a man we knew was a greater man than we would ever be. . . . He looked around towards the Premier and he said 'Well Mr. Premier, I gather that the Cabinet has rejected my proposal.' 'Well, yes, yes, I think that's right, Sir John.' 'Well', he said, 'that can only be because they've utterly failed to understand it. I will now explain it.' And he sat there, with that rock-like look, and he explained it, and one by one we shrivelled in our places, one by one we became convinced, or at any rate, felt we were convinced, of the error of our ways. And for half an hour he went on; he explained the thing step by step. And we were left silent. . . . And that settled it, there was no more, not another word came out and so Sir John said, looking at the Premier, 'Well, sir, I take it that your decision is reversed. Indeed, anticipating your approval of my proposal, and so that there will be no delay, I have brought with me (and he pulled it out of his breast pocket) the Order-in-Council that will be necessary for this purpose.' And he passed it around and it was signed, and he went out.

State politicians—who after all, by any realistic comparative test, were little more than local government politicians, despite their absurd parliamentary trappings—could not withstand his power of lucid argument, his negotiating skill and his forceful personality. As has been remarked, he dealt with 'recalcitrant cabinets in the manner of Napoleon with the Directory'.

Before, as well as after, his death Monash was a legendary figure to S.E.C. employees. Applying his experience of military leadership and organization though lacking the sanctions of military discipline, he had to rely on personality and intellectual authority. As in the A.I.F. he displayed his gift both of exacting their best from his colleagues and of making them his personal friends. He led and did not drive, his senior officers agreed. He made the most of their considerable abilities. Herman was a man after his own heart, but Monash never quite hit it off with H. R. Harper, the other senior officer. The secretary to the Commission, Roy Liddelow, recalled that 'his office was a place strictly for business and his day was so planned that he got through the work of two ordinary men'. There was the same attention to and involvement in detail, once the main decisions had been taken, as in his military career, without obsession with doing everything himself. 'What's the use of having a dog unless you let it bark for you?' was one of his common sayings. (But he did do far too much himself, nevertheless.) He went to the *root* of problems, Bridge recalled, no man gave decisions more quickly and definitely: 'There was never anything spectacular, no sabre rattling, just peaceful penetration and common sense in a marked degree until the objective was reached'. Liddelow described how 'If his decision on a complex problem was needed, he would sit silent at his desk while all sides of the question were put to him. Then with a breath he blew away the chaff and gave a decision that everyone knew was right'. In every committee, S.E.C. or not, chairman or not, he shrewdly practised the rule of committeemanship of waiting to be the last speaker, summing up and carrying the meeting. Bridge recalled especially his dynamic personality, his infectious optimism, and his 'charity in his judging of his co-workers who were not so liberally endowed as he'. Elizabeth Taylor, his private secretary, worshipped him: 'Nothing can rob me of those eleven years I spent in his service'. W. J. Price, who was assistant secretary in the 1920s, forty years later gave a vivid account of Monash's policy-forming methods. He gave much of his leadership in draft memoranda: quite often he would not arrive at the office until 10 o'clock or later, which was extraordinary in those days, but he would then produce those 'blue colored quarto sheet drafts—then you would know it was on'. The draft would go close to a decision, but it demanded advice and contradiction from senior personnel, he was not bound by it, he was known to be highly approachable and open to argument. He often opened a memorandum on a policy question with phrases such as, 'In order to crystallize a discussion upon these matters, I set out hereunder certain views'. He was not the sort of executive who pressed a button and called for a report: if it was important enough, he took the initiative.

At Yallourn Monash constantly asked, 'What can I do to help?', and he often inquired about progress of community activities and development of the public and private gardens. He was known, at least by a sense of his direct leadership and personal kindness, to all there down to day-labourers. One of his 'bright young men' recalled how he would sit and talk with anybody, S.E.C. man or not, in the train down: he 'was the sort of man who would encourage anybody; ... you could talk to him as though he was your father. He was a very good listener; gave you the impression that you were a most important person'. He talked to you as one bloke to another, many of the Commission men agreed. A future chairman of Commissioners remembered how he would say, 'G'day Hunt', and quiz him: there was nothing he didn't know about what was going on. He was a boss you could approach 'without fear or trepidation'. One youth leaping down the office stairs was appalled to realize Monash was on the corner, but he stood aside with a smile and a friendly remark. Elizabeth Taylor and the commissionaire outside used to refer to him to each other as 'Poppa'—he rather liked it. He made personal donations to the Yallourn sub-branch of the R.S.L. and other town societies, just as he wrote private letters of good wishes to staff members getting married, and attended productions by the S.E.C. Drama Club.*

Herman, his closest professional associate, must have the last word:

He was a great leader—the only *real* leader I have encountered in 37 years of continuous work—and a genius in getting to the heart of any problem and finding its solution; nothing was too big for him to confront when the necessity arose, and nothing was too small to engage him to the full if his personal attention to detail was essential; he was considerate and understanding to the humblest of his staff. When occasions for the exercise of discipline arose, his first thought was to find a way out for the offender without sacrificing control of his men. I have always believed that I was his friend as well as his officer—more, I am sure of it.

The S.E.C. legend cannot be gainsaid: the creativity, loyalty and affection he inspired seem to have few or no parallels in any other large Australian corporation. He was such a superb champion, battling in the full glare of publicity against the sour men of little faith, a champion who saw the S.E.C. through to an unusual position of public pride and acclaim for a State instrumentality. His inspirational quality continued long after his death. As for himself, he was so totally committed to the task, delighting in overcoming its sheer difficulty, that, even from about 1927 when the war really had been won, he gave up his ambitions to travel or to devote himself to scholarship or to his many hobbies, in order to see it through.

---

* There is one other general aspect: in a period when the public service was riddled by conflicts between the Masons and the 'Micks', the S.E.C. may have set a rare example. Monash once apologized for a subordinate who, in interviewing a prospective employee, demanded to know what his religion was. 'The Commission has never made, nor ever authorised anyone to make, any discrimination whatsoever in the matter of religion, and does not and will not countenance any enquiries in this sense by any officer with the objective of in any way influencing the selection of applicants for appointments.'

16

A National Possession
1920–1929

THE SERVICES were stripped to the bone after the war. Early in 1920 Monash had taken part in a conference of senior army officers which made detailed recommendations on defence and military organization which were largely ignored. Pearce still hoped that Monash could be employed part time, and he revived the advisory Council of Defence to which Monash was appointed early in 1921, in the hope that he might become its executive officer. As it turned out, the Council 'more or less existed only on paper' and met rarely. After the Washington treaties of February 1922, which for the moment calmed lurking fears of Japan, the government swung the axe. Though compulsory military training continued, Chauvel as inspector-general and White as chief of the general staff had to preside over wholesale dismissals and resignations from the Army.

On 30 July 1923 Sir Hugh Denison's Sydney evening *Sun* called for Monash to reorganize Australia's skeleton army. Brigadier-General H. W. Lloyd wrote to Monash enclosing the cutting and made a plea:

> General Sir John Monash is a man of outstanding brilliance and proven capacity for clarity of thought; commands universal respect; and is our foremost organizer. . . .
> The military condition of Australia never needed so acutely before the touch of a master hand. Our people and government are blind to their danger. . . . It is felt they will not lend the same ear to anyone else. . . .
> I hope, sir, you will pardon my candour but our ship of defence is perilously near the shoals and a storm is brewing—there is no one else for the helm.

Monash put him off: 'It would be a very thankless job. . . . Nothing can be done without money'. The *Sun* continued its futile campaign for Monash as commander-in-chief.

With the private backing of the service chiefs, Monash eventually, in November 1923, came out with a scathing denunciation of the starvation of the forces. The Air Force was a sham. There was only enough ammunition to last the Artillery for a few hours and, so far as he knew, there were no Mills bombs and not a single tank in the country. He was a great supporter of the League of Nations but to assume it would prevent future wars and thus make defence unnecessary was 'like deciding that we will have no more burglaries and then dismissing the police force'. The speech created a mild sensation and the acting prime minister, Dr Earle Page, and the minister for defence were forced to plead that Monash was unduly pessimistic. Monash gave evidence several times to the Parliamentary Joint Committee on Public Accounts on defence expenditure, vehemently defending the Royal Military College, Duntroon, whose existence was threatened. 'If the College is destroyed, we destroy also what hope Australia has of defending herself.' He also supported the desperate action of June 1924 by the chiefs of staff, who requested the minister to make public their opinion that defence spending was totally inadequate. A week later Prime Minister Bruce announced a five-year defence programme which slightly mollified them. He also asked Monash in July to review the conflicting advice from the Navy and the Shipping Board on the cost of building a 10 000-ton cruiser in Australia. In his report Monash was inconclusive in the absence of detailed plans, but in criticizing the Navy's excessive estimates seemed to lean towards construction in Australia. Cabinet was divided, Labor strongly supported local enterprise—it was briefly a major political issue. The government eventually decided to have the cruiser built in England.

Monash's last active military work was in September 1925 when Chauvel asked him for a week to Duntroon to take part in a Staff Tour for Senior Officers conducted by Blamey. Monash was greatly interested and could not refrain from boasting to Bertha:

> I soon found myself quite at home in the work, and although feeling at first a little rusty, have found no difficulty in speedily taking a position of authority, and laying down vital principles. Chauvel is deplorably slow, weak and hesitating, and carries no weight. He soon deferred to me, and let me take the leading role in the discussions. Most of the others . . . come to me for advice, guidance and help. So I feel quite at ease, and in no sense a back number.

In 1921 Monash celebrated the 8th of August with a dinner at Iona. He asked the eight most senior officers of the Corps living in Melbourne and their wives and Lady Bridges and his sister Mat; Bertha was hostess. Dinner jackets were worn, without decorations. Monash sent telegrams to the other generals round Australia and read out the return greetings. On Armistice Day Gellibrand organized a return function. Monash did not hold another such dinner until 1925 when he asked about twenty officers—without their wives. Gellibrand in Hobart held a similar dinner at which the three toasts were: the King, Fallen Comrades and 'Our Leader and the Men he Led'. Thereafter Monash presided at what became a sentimental and emotional annual occasion. They drank a potent rum and brandy punch, became merry and sang. Gellibrand, when he could attend, found it 'the pleasantest and most interesting gathering I know in Australia'. White enthused year after year:

> By your goodness our storehouse of recollections has yet another recollection. . . . Your annual gatherings are something more than splendid hospitality; they are a potent (mark the word!) means of cementing ties, and of preserving a fellowship which I venture to say is the outstanding achievement of the A.I.F.

Annually from the West, Hobbs wrote warmly-felt and neatly-turned compliments. Monash also sometimes entertained old comrades on the anniversary of Hamel.

These gatherings eased surviving strains in personal relationships, notably in the case of Gellibrand. Chauvel remained on good terms. Once, when arriving at a formal function he said to his wife, 'There's old John, looking like a prize Shorthorn!' One of his orders was dangling down; Lady Chauvel adjusted it. When Chauvel retired, Monash was glad to write an effusive tribute in the *Herald* and remarked to Bruche: 'I hope this will dissipate the current belief that there is or has ever been any strain or jealousy between us'. In 1929 Monash wrote a letter of great humanity to Elliott, whose resentment at not having been allowed a divisional command during the war was destroying him.

In 1923–24 Monash's reputation both as a great war leader and unchallenged spokesman for returned soldiers was consolidated. The R.S.L., whose membership was numerically weak and which had fallen out with the Federal government over its aggressive methods of promoting soldier preference, again tried to capture him as national president. In 1920 he had accepted nomination by three State branches, but when he found that the other State branches had nominated Captain Gilbert Dyett and that he was involved in a faction fight, he refused to stand. Next year he refused Rosenthal's request to him to stand against Dyett: it was out of the question for it was nearly a full-time job, the State government would not tolerate it, he 'would never dream of' contesting an election. Ernest Turnbull, president of the Victorian branch, also brought pressure to bear. Monash remarked that it was not as great a compliment as it seemed for the League was turning to him when it was 'in danger of decay, owing to the defective leadership'. He continued to advise both Dyett and Turnbull.

Rosenthal, Morshead and a group of 3rd Division officers were constantly imploring Monash to visit Sydney so that his many friends and admirers could honour him. He could not decently go on putting them off. The occasion he chose was an invitation to open the Jewish War Memorial Hall in November 1923. He pleaded with his hosts not to let the engagement become widely known, as he was weary of publicity and adulation. So he was in one mood, but in another he welcomed it as his due. A large crowd and a battery of press photographers met him at Central Station and the *Sydney Morning Herald* wrote a eulogistic leader:

> To find a parallel to the military career of men like Sir John Monash it is necessary to go back to the American Civil War, or . . . to those illustrious Puritan captains who turned the course of British history so sharply at Marston Moor and Naseby.

But his visit did not attract much notice until he began to attack defence policy. He was banqueted by the Jewish community, and given a parliamentary lunch by the premier and a citizen's reception at the Town Hall. Military officers entertained him at a dinner at which, he told Rosenthal, he wore uniform for the first time for more than three years, he inspected ex-A.I.F. police, and was entertained by the University Club. Everywhere he was lavishly praised.

In July 1923 the Victorian branch of the R.S.L. at its annual conference resolved unanimously 'that the matter of suitably recognising the services to Australia of Sir John Monash be the first business of the incoming State Council'. The council decided to give him a soldiers' banquet, and the New South Wales branch endorsed its action. A dining club, which met at Scott's Hotel, had actually been founded in protest at the lack of appreciation of Monash, who occasionally attended. The *Returned Sailors and Soldiers' Annual* bitterly attacked the Commonwealth government for not treating him with 'ordinary decency'. The R.S.L. took the Town Hall on Anzac Day 1924. Turnbull, E. A. Drake-Brockman, McGlinn, representatives of the political parties, and S. Fowler, a 'digger spokesman', not one of them a permanent soldier, eulogized him. Turnbull claimed that every trade, profession and calling and every shade of political and religious opinion was represented that night. Fowler brought down the house when he said:

> The standard by which they judged him was personal efficiency, character and integrity. . . . mass opinion was almost always an infallible index of a man's true worth. . . . The secret of his popularity lay in the fact that he possessed that rare and indefinable quality which entitled the man to be regarded in the 'digger's' eyes as 'dinkum'.

Turnbull presented an illuminated address; it had been suggested by Jacka, V.C., who in proposing it had said: 'As a soldier he's like one of ourselves, and doesn't like swank. I think he'd like an address from us better than anything else'.

Monash rose to reply visibly moved amid a tumultuous ovation. He claimed it was the most severe ordeal he had ever faced. He had never been a man to seek praise: the greatest reward was 'the consciousness of having unselfishly tried to do one's job'; the best thing in life was *service*. He had no grievance about inadequate recognition; he had never hoped for more than the esteem of his comrades on active service. All his honours were as a representative of the A.I.F.: all the glory was theirs. He had always regretted he was so little known personally among the troops. He went on to speak of the meaning of Anzac Day, the significance of the Gallipoli campaign and the nature of the A.I.F. 'It was difficult for a former soldier to talk about defence, because he laid himself open to the charge that he was a militarist, a fire-eater, a jingo. The war was rotten, no soldier wanted another, and it was for that reason that he was anxious.' Finally, the R.S.L. must subdue its internal strife: its great task was to teach the traditions of the A.I.F. He shook hands with all seven hundred present.

The press waxed enthusiastic on behalf of 'Australia's Greatest Soldier' or 'Mighty Monash'. H. S. Gullett of the *Herald* remarked: 'Nothing has become the hero of the last 100 days of the war more than his modest bearing since he cast off his uniform. There he has been a pattern to every returned man . . . no Digger of the ranks walks about with less self advertisement'.

In November 1923, 'at a word', as Monash put it, 'the A.I.F. sprang to life again, in their thousands, both horse and foot', and as special constables protected the citizenry of Melbourne during the police strike. On appallingly low pay and harried by special supervisors, more than half the metropolitan force went on strike from Friday 2 November and were automatically dismissed. That day the lord mayor elect, W. Brunton, formed a Citizens' Protection Committee, with Sir Robert Gibson as vice-chairman and Monash and Elliott as members. It met next morning and began to plan enrolment of special constables who would serve under the Chief Commissioner of Police, Alexander Nicholson. That night the mob invaded the city, looting and brawling; about two hundred people were injured.

Monash's account of his day's activities is as follows:

> Before we separated [in the morning] I got the following organization going. I told Elliott to go to the Town Hall and organize the specials, then being enrolled, into "squads" under competent leaders. I told Forsyth . . . to act as the connecting link (liaison) between Elliott and Nicholson. . . . Nicholson did nothing whatever.

When the looting started, Forsyth, after waiting for police co-operation, acted upon the orders of Sir Robert Gibson, and sent out the specials on duty into the streets. I arrived on the scene after the street trouble was over. Realizing the paralysis of the police organization, I decided there and then (I would not have been justified in doing so in the forenoon) to create an organization *independent* of the Police. [I] got hold of Elliott and instructed him to commence the organization of a Headquarters and a fighting and feeding staff, on military lines. This was about midnight.

He was relying on the authority given him by Brunton and Robinson, the attorney-general.

Early on Sunday morning Monash was at the Town Hall organizing. McCay rang offering to help. Monash put him in over Elliott (whom he relegated to 'outside commander') and settled with him the principles of the organization of mounted, foot and motor constabulary on a five-battalion basis. He sent out messages to dozens of his former commanders and when they arrived they saw 'he had the whole of Melbourne and suburbs laid out on a map before him with coloured pins and the whole situation well under control'. He joined State Cabinet, presided over by the arch-conservative Robinson, later that morning, when it was resolved that no striker would be re-employed. Many hundred specials were enrolled that day and the next, under Monash as commander of the Special Constabulary Force; Cabinet had authorized recruitment of up to five thousand men. Though there was unfounded fear that the unions would come out in support of the police, order had been restored. Monash warned the public to keep out of the city at night; after dark now, in fact, the city and suburbs were being policed as never before by ferocious marching patrols. However, on the Tuesday a crowd of 125 000 at Flemington cheered the favourite winning the Melbourne Cup.

Before leaving for Sydney on Friday the 9th, Monash handed over the Constabulary to McCay and sent an advisory memo to Gibson. The situation was well in hand. The most urgent need was to appoint a new chief commissioner of police, such as Jess, Lloyd or McNicoll. The special constabulary should be reduced to one thousand men but put on a proper footing with regard to pay and conditions; as police recruits were enlisted and trained, the constables could be released and the force go out of existence in less than six months (as was to happen).

It was a notable demonstration of the effectiveness of the ex-service middle classes when organized again. Major-General George Johnston wrote to Monash to suggest that it would be a great pity to disband the constables, 'a wonderfully fine body of men'. If made permanent, under Monash's leadership, though non-military and non-political, they could act as strike-breakers, protecting loyalist workers. Friends at the Athenaeum Club had enthusiastically welcomed the idea. Little can be deduced from Monash's reply which, as so often, gave his correspondent the impression that he agreed, though with reservations. He told Johnston that the suggestion was in line with a world-wide movement of which the Italian Fascists and the Ku-Klux-Klan were examples. The difficulty was that no government could countenance such a movement as it would be hostile to the unions and would be regarded as purely political; he himself obviously, in his position, could have nothing to do with it. Nevertheless, he would discuss the proposal 'with one or two influential friends'. The secret 'White Guard' may have derived from Johnston's suggestion but, though he must have known of its activities, Monash was not involved.

Within a fortnight of the strike, reflecting widespread feeling that the police had been grossly exploited by the government, there were calls for a royal commission under Monash, who would be acceptable to all parties. The Labor Party, and especially its parliamentary leader, George Prendergast, was very sympathetic to the cause of reinstating the strikers, and when eventually in July 1924 Labor came to office Prendergast appointed a commission under Monash. Proceedings opened on 8 September and lasted for three months. Monash quickly wrote most of the fairly short report himself. It was released on 4 February 1925 and contained no surprises: the strikers were condemned but the government was criticized for lack of attention to grievances. It was realistic of the commission to oppose reinstatement of the strikers: the middle-class reaction had been callous and vindictive, the Allan coalition ministry now in office would never accept it and the police force would be divided into hostile camps of strikers and scabs—but Monash in any case could never have forgiven the strikers' refusal of duty. His chief concern was to bring about appointment of an able chief commissioner on a decent salary and he eventually had much to do with persuading Blamey to accept the post in July.

The Anzac Day march was established as an annual event from 1925 when 25 April was a Saturday. There had been small marches from 1917 to 1920 and a major one in 1921 in which Monash took no part for reasons unknown. There was no march in the next three years. Monash favoured a march on the nearest Sunday to Anzac Day, for men could not be expected to forgo a day's wages. From 1922 to 1924 he attended 4th Brigade and other reunions and spoke to the University students. In 1925 Elliott was chief organizer of the march for the R.S.L. On 16 April Monash was asked to lead it together with Chauvel and official Naval and Air Force representatives, but the Service authorities disapproved and refused to be sponsors. The invitation to Monash crossed with a letter he had written to the R.S.L.: 'I am most anxious to take part in the Anzac Day march, but just as anxious not to take any prominent position, but merely to assemble with the "Diggers" and be one of them, in a quite unobtrusive manner'. His letter was released to the press by the organizers and won much favourable comment. He was almost certainly dissembling. Someone had to lead. Who, if not he? But he preferred to march in mufti. Monash did in fact lead, carrying an umbrella beneath his arm, in a line of four, with two aides and a representative of the R.S.L. Only about five thousand marched. The crowd broke into applause when he entered the Exhibition Building for the commemorative service at which the governor-general and the prime minister spoke. He was soon asked to preside over the Anzac Day Commemorative Council and, as usual, took charge. This council and the R.S.L. persuaded the government to pass an Act which not only made Anzac Day a public holiday but required the closing of all hotels and places of entertainment. Victoria long continued—unlike the rest of Australia—to keep it a close holiday. Monash entirely approved of the R.S.L. view that it should be a sacred day, with no relaxation—'*our* Good Friday', as one soldier said.

In 1926 about twelve thousand veterans marched, despite heavy rain. Under strong pressure Monash gave way on the uniform question; he turned out in full rig with sword, orders, decorations and medals, wearing a peaked cap and not the digger hat, marching at the head with Blamey and an aide close behind. This time he presided at the Exhibition, and spoke first, followed by the lieutenant-governor and prime minister. He had had a brush with the Catholics whose priests demanded that they fall out at Albert Street and make their way to St Patrick's Cathedral: it was a forerunner of many subsequent disputes about the conduct of Anzac Day rites. Monash was content with the vaguely Protestant service: 'All People that on Earth Do Dwell', 'Nearer my God to Thee', the Lord's Prayer, Kipling's 'Recessional' and Chopin's 'Funeral March', even though Catholics and orthodox Jews could not attend.

1927 was the test, for the Day coincided with the visit of the Duke of York (George VI). Monash and his men organized intensively for a huge turnout. He proudly predicted to Birdwood that twenty-five thousand would march and that a million people would line the route. He was not so very far out: it was one of the greatest Anzac Day marches ever. Monash, alone at the head, led twenty-five to thirty thousand men, and the crowd was at least half a million, possibly the largest yet in Australian history. He fell out to join the Duke at the temporary cenotaph in front of Parliament House, to take the salute. At the Exhibition Building only he and the Duke made addresses.

Then Sir John Monash begins to speak. At once a cheer starts to rumble its way up to the rafters, but he checks it with uplifted hand. A short, thoughtful speech, the keynote of which is that, as the men in France were spurred to finer effort by the slogan "Remember Gallipoli!" so the people should face their titanic task of nation-building with that slogan ever ringing in their ears.

Brudenell White wrote: 'I never expect to see again in my lifetime such an impressive ceremony. . . . I offer you my sincere and warm congratulations upon a remarkable achievement'.

Subsequent marches could not possibly be so impressive, but Melbourne's annual commemoration of Anzac Day was another Monash triumph. The R.S.L. in Sydney tried to persuade him to organize Anzac Day there; when at the dinner on Anzac Eve 1927 a New South Wales V.C. threatened to capture him, there were roars of 'No you don't, he's ours'. He was annually invited to lead the march in Sydney but, although he gave advice and almost consented in 1930, it did not come off. Monash did accept the honour paid him by the government of New South Wales in inviting him to take a major part in the unveiling of the cenotaph in Martin Place in February 1929 before a huge crowd. He had a rousing reception when he arrived, and sprang to attention and saluted when ex-diggers gave him three cheers.

The cause closest to his heart in his last years was the building of the Shrine of Remembrance. The movement had a chequered history. A State advisory committee on war memorials in 1920 recommended an arch of victory over St Kilda Road. The lord mayor, J. W. Swanson, called a public meeting on 4 August 1921, and an executive committee was formed, of which Monash was a member. The meeting resolved that the memorial should be non-utilitarian, a monument; the proposal for a triumphal arch gained little support. Monash joined the site sub-committee together with representatives of the State government and city council; after reviewing about twenty locations, they had agreed by March 1922 on the site. The terms of an architectural competition were drafted and agreed on with the Royal Australian Institute of Architects. Monash was appointed chairman of the assessors, who gave first place to the design for a shrine of remembrance, a 'visible manifestation of the people's grief', by the young Melbourne architects and old diggers, P. B. Hudson and J. H. Wardrop. Monash was delighted with the conception, a monument on an awesome scale, which derived from the Mausoleum of Halicarnassus. The announcement of the winners in December 1923 was, however, disastrous: Murdoch of the *Herald* launched a virulent campaign to damn the winning entry, and innumerable ideas, especially hospitals and war widows' homes, were canvassed afresh. It was enough for the Lawson–Allan government to go cold. The Allan–Peacock ministry eventually agreed to honour

Lawson's promise of funds, but most of the members of the war memorial committee had lost enthusiasm.

Monash was wary about appearing to promote the Shrine too prominently, and indeed told Rosenhain he had 'refused, both on personal and ethical grounds', to lead the movement. Among other things, the *Herald* was a staunch supporter of the S.E.C., which needed all its friends. Early in 1926 a conference between representatives of the war memorial committee and of Cabinet decided to abandon the scheme. Against Monash's opposition the proposal for a city square with a cenotaph, Anzac Square, at the top of Bourke Street, was adopted, to the delight of the *Herald*, and the city council and the R.S.L. committed themselves to support. The proposal envisaged a square extending west at least half-way to Exhibition Street.

But Monash fought and won the battle. Young enthusiasts in Melbourne Legacy like A. N. Kemsley and W. D. Joynt, V.C., had encouraged him, and had the strong support of the Institute of Architects which was adamant that the judgement of the competition must not be upset. At the R.S.L. dinner on Anzac Eve 1927, Monash came out strongly for the Shrine proposal, whereupon by arrangement Kemsley and his friends, scattered through the gathering, jumped up to applaud, and carried the house. Then on 26 April Monash issued a forceful statement which was backed by Grimwade, Coxen, Elliott and other senior officers. It was a striking example of his authority: the R.S.L. swung back, Legacy was with him, and the *Age* and *Argus* fell in behind. The phenomenal success of the Anzac Day march had made it possible.

Monash's basic attitude was that the memorial must be for remembrance and not a celebration of triumph or might. Anything utilitarian, such as a city-beautification scheme like the proposal for a square, was not a memorial. Commenting on Murdoch's opinion that the Shrine design was 'too severe, stiff and heavy, that there is no grace or beauty about it and that it is a tomb of gloom', he told Lawson that Murdoch was 'merely childish'. The Shrine design was

> a beautiful conception, dignified, noble, appealing, and eminently suited as a memorial of great service and sacrifice, without that ridiculous note of victory and conquest which characterized the memorials of the barbarian past....
>
> There are no structures in the world more impressive than Napoleon's tomb in Paris, and Grant's tomb on the Hudson, and the same note is struck by the Shrine.
>
> Added to all this, it is a magnificent piece of architectural design, which will constitute one of the most beautiful buildings in the world.

But the *Herald* fought it out in strong language, speciously claiming

...ading the Anzac Day march, 1927

Inspecting New South Wales ex-servicemen police, 1923

Using the dictaphone: Monash and his S.E.C. secretary, Elizabeth Taylor

that 'the People had spoken'. The initiative lay with a sub-committee of the war memorial executive committee of which Monash was a member, which considered, as well as the Shrine on St Kilda Road and the Anzac Square, possible adaptation of the Shrine to a Spring Street site (now the headquarters of the Royal Australasian College of Surgeons). In recommending the Shrine on St Kilda Road, the sub-committee dismissed the Anzac Square proposal largely on grounds of cost. On 20 May, with one dissentient, the full committee adopted the report. It was now a matter of convincing the Hogan Labor government, which took office that day. Hogan and his party were inclined to favour a hospital as a war memorial, but eventually gave way in view of the commitments made by previous governments. On Armistice Day the governor set the foundation stone of the Shrine. Murdoch conceded defeat: in line with his constant policy of making peace once he had won, Monash wrote to thank him for his 'very broad-minded and sportsmanlike attitude'.

Monash took over construction of the Shrine, having been appointed deputy chairman under the lord mayor. He conducted negotiations with governments, supervised the public appeal for funds which in 1928 was very successful, and wrote personally to wealthy men and berated the Victoria Racing Club for its mean donation. He employed Fairway and the Reinforced Concrete Co. both for old time's sake and for economy, worked on calculations of quantities, and attended every quarterly meeting of the committee for three years. In reply to R.S.L. complaints that employment on the Shrine works was not confined to returned soldiers, he explained that some Italians were being used exclusively for carving and stone-cutting. He opposed the suggestion of burial of an unknown soldier: it had become hackneyed and, though possibly suitable for a national shrine, was inappropriate for a State memorial. He vehemently rejected a proposal that he, Chauvel and White should be commemorated by statues or busts.

He was perturbed early in 1930 to find that the inscription Hudson had recommended for the west wall was 'a garbled and plagiarized version of a poem by Simonides and a speech by Pericles'. He consulted the classicist Professor T. G. Tucker and, with advice from the poet Bernard O'Dowd and Felix Meyer, rewrote the inscription himself, to read: LET ALL MEN KNOW THAT THIS IS HOLY GROUND. THIS SHRINE ESTABLISHED IN THE HEARTS OF MEN AS ON THE SOLID EARTH COMMEMORATES A PEOPLE'S FORTITUDE AND SACRIFICE. YE THEREFORE THAT COME AFTER GIVE REMEMBRANCE. As the historian Ken Inglis first remarked, the words are of neither Christian nor Jewish origin but, as elsewhere in Australian war memorials, in the tradition of stoic patriotism. The Shrine was not dedicated until November 1934, three years after Monash's death.

In the 1920s the breakdown of the brave new world, unemployment, class conflict and failure of soldier settlement made for sour disillusion. The belief had even grown that the war had been a terrible mistake; millions of soldiers had died and millions more had gone through purgatory—for what end? Monash was driven to intensify his efforts to commemorate Anzac Day and make the Shrine a worthy memorial. In lecturing, writing and in interviews, he reiterated that Gallipoli was 'the greatest event in the history of this young nation': it had

> created a great tradition, not only to uphold the A.I.F. throughout the long following years of effort, sacrifice and suffering, but also to stimulate the manhood and womanhood of Australia to the noblest ideals of patriotism, and the highest manifestation of good citizenship.

Loyalty to a common cause, courage, comradeship and mutual co-operation were part of a tradition which might inspire all Australians. So it might. But Monash did not adequately understand the deep grievances of Irish Catholics and the mainstream of the labour movement arising from the war years, and failed sufficiently to shape his exposition of the admirable A.I.F. ideal to contribute much to healing the deep divisions in Australian society. Perhaps no one could have done so; Bean made a brave try over the years. Similarly Monash's R.S.L. successors, before and after World War II, never had the eloquence or the understanding of their critics' position to carry conviction that they were not glorifying achievement in war but rather commemorating noble sacrifice and pleading for a higher comradeship. The R.S.L. was generally a minority movement, never properly represented the A.I.F and fell under right-wing control. It thereby distorted the image of the A.I.F. and hindered acceptance of its achievements as part of the nation's glory. And a very large minority of the soldiers wanted only to forget the war and everything to do with it.

Monash had to go on reminding the public of the A.I.F.'s great achievements, playing down his own role. 'Who would dare to claim for himself any of the credit of the A.I.F.! We were all one great team.'

> Leadership counts for something, of course, but it cannot succeed without the spirit, élan and morale of those led. Therefore I count myself the most fortunate of men in having been placed at the head of the finest fighting machine the world has ever known.

Occasionally, however, he could not resist saying:

> No man can rob me of this, that I won the confidence of the men I led, and have retained that confidence today. Hardly a military leader of the war has escaped criticism, but I am happy in the knowledge that I have never had to meet any criticism of my tactical leadership of the Australian field army.

This is almost true: he had never had to meet any substantial criticism, in print at least. He could also write excellently about the war, with exaggerated but not unreasonable assessments of the Australian contribution, as when the editor of the *Argus* persuaded him to contribute on the tenth anniversaries of the outbreak of war and the August 1918 offensive.

Throughout the 1920s his authority over the returned men grew, as their unchallenged spokesman. But he had his troubles with the press. He had constantly to tread that fine line of making his standard proud claims for A.I.F. achievements without making disparaging statements of the worth of British troops. Inevitably, sometimes he was caught not knowing he was being reported, or he perhaps went a little too far, or his remarks were garbled and quoted out of context. British ex-servicemen in Australia sometimes protested at the mild comparisons he did make. In one shameful incident in 1927 he and Bean were almost entirely innocent. The Melbourne *Herald* and *Sun* printed a story that in the proofs of a Gallipoli volume of the official British war history there were contemptuous references to the Anzacs as an 'ill-trained, ill-led, disorganised rabble'. Monash knew the report was false—he had seen the proofs and admired the work, but in his interview with the *Herald* his sceptical remarks were buried in the final two sentences of a long report. The headlines were: 'SLIGHTS IN BRITISH OFFICIAL HISTORY ASTOUND LEADERS' and 'MONASH, JEALOUS OF DIGGERS' HONOR, WANTS FULL INQUIRY'. He had been unwise enough to state the undoubted truth: that the Dominion armies had a very poor opinion of the British troops at Gallipoli, apart from the magnificent 29th Division. And he had referred to the story as just another of 'those deprecations of the Australian soldier which appear every two or three months in England'. These remarks and an invention that Bean was calling a conference of generals to refute the allegations were flashed around the world. The incident was quickly exposed as a mare's nest but the newspapers then attempted to work up a supposed disagreement between Monash and Bean. Monash summed up the Australian press as for the most part 'unspeakably unfair and mischievous' and believed that the 'unprincipled newspaper proprietary' had 'concocted the original misreport'.

These encounters were difficult to avoid: if the press was determined to run a story, he could hardly in his position refuse to comment when asked. Apropos of Robert Graves's *Good-bye to All That*, he told Bruche:

> Late one evening I was rung up at my house. 'Age speaking. Is there any truth in the story that Australians murdered prisoners at Morlancourt', etc etc etc. Nobody in my position would have failed to seize the opportunity to deny such an allegation emphatically. It was not until next day that my very few remarks, in a greatly

expanded form, were published in the form of a criticism of Graves' book, of which I had not previously heard. . . . What the newspapers *did not* publish were my emphatic remarks to the effect that it was about time the Australian press gave up taking notice of every stupid calumny that was uttered about Australian soldiers, and gave up pestering me to make public denials of these calumnies.

The Monash–Bean relationship remained uneasy. Both were inclined to forgive and forget, and perhaps Monash had it in mind that his ultimate reputation would depend very much on Bean's judgement. When the first volume of the *Official History* was published in 1921, he read it immediately and wrote to the author fulsomely. No evidence survives of his reactions to Bean's second Gallipoli volume except that in writing to the official British historian in 1929, Monash remarked that Bean often went 'wrong in his judgment of men and events through lack of technical knowledge'.

The letters of adulation from old soldiers flowed in.

> It must be a proud memory to you to know that your great victories, in contrast with other great military leaders, were gained with so little loss of life and your diggers know that these results were brought about by your genius. You knew the Digger—trusted him—supported him—and knew how to lead him—one of them now says shake!!

Innumerable requests to visit and speak interstate and in the country had to be refused. When he agreed to address the Geelong branch of the R.S.L. he was promised a welcome 'such as only the "digger" can give to one whom he loves and admires'. After a visit to the Seymour branch, when hundreds of returned men from miles around rolled up, he was told that 'you have a place in our hearts and affections of which you cannot fail to be deeply conscious'. Two or three diggers even won his permission to name their sons after him.

The miscellaneous duties in support of the R.S.L. never ended: opening State conferences; appealing for funds for Anzac House; moving a motion to appoint a returned man as city engineer at a Prahran public meeting; administering the fund created by Paderewski's concerts in aid of war orphans; attempting with the governor, Lord Somers, to arbitrate a bitter conflict between the R.S.L. and migrant ex-servicemen. He was a patron of Legacy, but could not be active. He was as helpful as possible to the Australian War Memorial in gathering records and pledged to it his own collection of semi-official papers. To the end of his life he made no attempt to lay down the burden.

Monash was elected vice-chancellor (part-time) of the University of Melbourne in 1923. His central educational beliefs came to be, in some part, explanations of his own career: 'Intellectual giants are not born. They are made by exercise of the mind'. There is 'no such thing as effortless genius—no such thing as undeserved success. For success rests solely upon industry and self-denial all along the line'. Remaining true to the German tradition in which he had grown up and against all the trends of the twentieth century, he fought a losing campaign:

> The greatest mistake in life is to specialise education too early. Nothing is more absurd than for a boy of 14 years to decide what calling he shall pursue. The first essential is to be an educated man. When such foundations have been laid it is time enough to select a walk in life.
> We should have a knowledge of the laws of Nature, of the history of civilisation, and of art, music and literature. To whatever extent we lack these things, to that extent is our vision and outlook limited and cramped.

The professions in Australia were dominated by narrow, poorly educated men without cultural background. Nevertheless there were examples of self-made men who had reached the top in politics, industry and commerce because they had taken the democratic opportunity of undertaking higher education and thereby made the most of their talents. His view of the function of a university was devastatingly simple:

> Ours is the game of life, but most of us do not understand the rules governing either our physical, mental or moral welfare. Most of us are actuated by our emotions and prejudices, instead of by an intelligent understanding of the laws which govern human conduct and human affairs. These laws it is the business of the University to teach.

Basic research was almost equally important:

> the discoveries of abstract science, at first apparently wholly unserviceable and purposeless, have led, over and over again, in ways entirely unforeseen, to the enlargement of the scope and practice of the engineer, and to the production of practical results of the most unexpected, yet profoundly important character.

The general aim of education was to encourage

> the capacity to think clearly, to express oneself lucidly in the written and spoken word, to reason infallibly, to memorize tenaciously—in short to train the mind to be not merely a storehouse of relevant knowledge, but also a finely-tempered and efficient thinking-machine.

His grasp of fundamentals fitted him well for university administration.

In a statement seeking electoral support from graduates for election to council, Monash did not act the demagogue. The main objective was to increase the annual State grants. The council should not act on educational questions without full academic advice. Research was essential, but much past research had been of poor quality; the primary function of a university was to teach, hence teaching ability should be the chief criterion for appointment. Extension and postgraduate work should be developed. The 'crying need' of the University was for 'active interest of its graduates in its welfare'.

Sir John Grice, vice-chancellor since 1918, had resigned because of poor health. Sir John MacFarland, chancellor since 1918, was now seventy-two: his eventual successor was very much in mind. Monash's rival was the unpopular Sir James Barrett, the busybody promoting dozens of good causes. He got on well with Barrett: in 1915 he had remarked to Vic how strange it was that 'in spite of his great capabilities, and industry and splendid work' he 'always continues to antagonise people'. He had announced his support for Barrett, but the swell of opposition led him to change his mind. As usual, however, he was fearful of fighting and losing an election, but told MacFarland he would hold himself 'ready to respond to any clear and definite demand'. MacFarland arranged a private meeting of council and took an informal vote; Monash had the numbers (only just, according to the *Argus*) and Barrett withdrew from the contest. Some councillors had been perturbed about the nature of Monash's domestic arrangements.

Early in the century Monash and Barrett had been successful leaders of a University reform movement. Twenty years later they and MacFarland were seen by most of the staff as a conservative clique ruling with an iron hand. The University was expanding fast, from 2366 students in 1920 to 3256 in 1930. Much was achieved: new buildings for Arts, Anatomy, Agriculture and Botany and new chairs such as Commerce, Metallurgy, Obstetrics and Dentistry. But the State grants remained pitifully low, and progress was bought at the cost of petty economies and gross exploitation of lesser staff, academic and non-academic.

Monash became vice-chancellor while amendments to the University Act were at last going through Parliament. They derived from a pre-war internal inquiry which had recommended an enlarged council with greater representation of academic staff and of the government. Monash won an immediate great victory: he interviewed Sir William McPherson, the treasurer, who was unwilling to increase the annual grant of £30 000 to more than £40 000, 'but I pegged away for another half-hour', and the result was £45 000. Monash deplored the enlargement of academic membership of the council—'a bad, bad business which Parliament forced on us . . . as the price we had to pay for a decent increase in our grant'. His main effectiveness was in fundraising. Nobody else could have been remotely as forceful on the frequent deputations to the government: he dwelt on the overcrowded classrooms, overworked professoriat, grossly underpaid teaching staff and disgraceful library. He persuaded the Commonwealth government to maintain Walter Bassett's aerodynamical laboratory; he spoke on the wireless in 1923 in support of the Conservatorium building fund; he persuaded the Commonwealth Bank through Sir Robert Gibson to make a small grant. At a dinner in 1926 at Menzies Hotel, given by eighty graduates to eighty wealthy citizens, he made the principal speech, which brought tangible results: among other things he was aiming for ten men to provide a library fund of £20 000, and for the Melbourne City Council to take over maintenance of the grounds and thus make another chair possible. He campaigned unsuccessfully for annual State grants of something like £110 000.

He bore much of the brunt of professorial assertiveness, especially when he was acting chancellor for twelve months from March 1925 while MacFarland was on leave. He soon confided that 'the University is about as difficult to manage—if not more so—than an army'. He had a horror of the academic staff having a voice in financial decisions, especially on salaries, and strongly opposed any professor being a member of the finance committee, even without voting power. In his view the seven staff members on council formed a solid block and made meetings 'extremely disagreeable' and 'acrimonious'. Professors Berry, Skeats and Harrison Moore were 'a nuisance, pressing all sorts of proposals in the interests of the staff quite regardless of financial considerations'. Reform of the council's committee system was one burning issue. D. K. Picken, Master of Ormond College, warned Monash that 'no amount of mere politeness can cover the feeling re employer–employee relationship'. Minor issues were over the location of council meetings—at the Town Hall or at the University—and the professorial board's decision to endorse custom and not to insist on daily wearing of gowns by students. Monash was affronted: 'From time immemorial all university men have worn gowns, and I have heard no cogent argument against the continuance of the custom'.

As vice-chancellor he had to adjudicate on squabbles over allocation of the pitifully small research fund and moderate disputes within the Physics, Botany and other departments. Primed by his son-in-law, he was effective in establishing the school of Dentistry and bringing about legislation preventing the registration of dental mechanics as dentists. He examined the distinguished J. J. C. Bradfield for award of a doctorate of Engineering for the University of Sydney. As chairman of the selection committee for the chair of Metallurgy, although he 'adopted every expedient of debate', he was outvoted six to one and J. N. Greenwood was appointed over Rosenhain's candidate. Monash was active in reorganizing the Engineering school when Payne retired. In 1925 he was Melbourne's representative at an inter-university conference which reached agreement on creation of new chairs in innovatory fields and lobbied the prime minister on ways and means of easing entry of graduates to the Commonwealth Public Service. He joined the Rhodes Scholarship Selection Committee and the board of the Walter and Eliza Hall medical research institute.

When in 1923 F. W. Hagelthorn, a constructive senior State politician, inquired whether the University might make a study of local poverty and unemployment, Monash replied that it was not its function to take up such a question in any more than a theoretical fashion; perhaps he feared involvement in party-political issues. But when it was suggested to him that the 'young and indiscreet' Economics professors D. B. Copland and L. F. Giblin should be curbed, as their statements were shaking confidence in the share market, he brusquely replied that University staff were unfettered in their views. In 1929 the Italian consul-general brought strong pressure to bear against Dr Omero Schiassi, temporary part-time lecturer in Italian and a militant anti-Fascist. Monash took the view that Schiassi's political views were of no concern to the University unless he was using his position to help his political activities. If that were so, he should probably not be reappointed.

'If I had nothing else at all to do', Monash told Rosenhain, 'my University duties alone could easily constitute a full-time job, even though wholly honorary'. He relieved the ageing MacFarland of much that the chancellor would normally do. He was almost the last of the part-time vice-chancellors. His final ambition, the chancellorship, was to elude him.

Some of Monash's most revealing remarks on education, his own philosophy and experience, and ambition were dashed off in 1923 in reply to a journalist:

> 1. Many young men, on the threshold of their career, seem to think that they can't get on without the help of influential friends. This is a mistake. To have their paths made easy jeopardises ultimate success. To have to fight, and fight hard, to get a place on the lower rungs of the ladder is a healthy tonic. Early struggles and difficulties tend to a strengthening and refining of character, and a development of a man's best faculties.
>
> 2. While self-confidence is essential, a young man should always be ready to pay heed to the advice of older and more experienced men. What a young man lacks most is experience, which ripens judgment and informs the mind. Endeavour, therefore, to get the fullest benefit from the experience of others, until you have yourself acquired a balanced judgment.

3. When you come into contact with successful men, study them and their methods; try to discover the factors which have led to their success, and model your own methods upon them.

4. Among the qualities necessary for success are Industry and Concentration. Few men inherit genius. They get it by hard work and unswerving application. An orderly mind, and clear thinking, are based on an orderly and rational mode of living. Learn to come to clear and definite decisions on all problems that confront you. Don't chop and change about. Having once made up your mind, stick to it; unless, of course, new considerations alter the case.

5. Avoid extreme views. They are seldom right. The truth generally lies somewhere about the happy mean.

6. There's always plenty of room at the top, in every calling, whether profession, trade or craft. The duffers crowd into the lower ranks and stay there.

7. Strive for a broad education. . . . Knowledge is power. There's no such thing as useless knowledge. . . . Delay coming to a final decision as to the calling which you will select, until circumstances compel you. Until then, seek knowledge in all directions for its own sake. This will also help you to discover the kind of calling for which your particular faculties best suit you.

8. There is no better help to thinking clearly, talking lucidly, and acting with judgment than to read a few books on the elements of jurisprudence and law.

9. Adopt as your fundamental creed that you will equip yourself for life, not solely for your own benefit, but for the benefit of the whole community.

The presidency of the Australasian Association for the Advancement of Science from September 1924 was no light honour, for it involved becoming for two years the official spokesman for science. When Sir Edgeworth David and Sir Baldwin Spencer asked him to accept the post, he reminded them that he was not a scientist in the true sense but an applied scientist. The congress met in Adelaide and his presidential address on 'Power Development' was aimed at the public. His most important contribution was to lobby the Federal government to establish the Council for Scientific and Industrial Research with reasonable funding, and he had a leading say in drawing up its constitution. In 1926 he worked hard to persuade Professor David Rivett—'I used every argument I could think of'—to accept the executive directorship of C.S.I.R., the post which might easily have been his if the timing had been a little different, and for which he was so ideally suited. He was also active during his term in helping to arrange the funding of Australia's first chair of Anthropology, at the University of Sydney. As an elder statesman he stayed on the association's governing body and attended the congresses in 1926 and 1928 at Perth and Hobart. In 1925 he was elected to the Australian National Research

Council, which had some skimpy funds at its disposal, and became vice-president in 1926.

Monash's interest in the professional concerns of engineers continued, though peripherally. He was elected Australian council member of the Institution of Civil Engineers (London) in 1923. He remained a staunch though inactive member of the committee of the Institution of Engineers, Australia, and became chairman in 1924 of the trustees of the allied societies—engineering, architectural, surveying and chemical—which were jointly building Kelvin Hall in Collins Place. He advised and lobbied the government on legislation relating to the engineering and architectural professions and on engineering appointments. Against infuriating delay and quibbling he eventually resolved conflicts over the Kernot Memorial Fund. He was called on to give free advice to the Melbourne Cricket Club about how to increase crowd accommodation: his interesting report suggested how space might be used to enable all of a crowd of seventy-five thousand to get a good view, but his eventual proposal to reduce the playing field to a circle was a confession of ignorance of the requirements of the Melbourne Football Club.

The old bushwalker felt strongly on conservation issues. In 1920 he backed Barrett strongly in his campaign to protect Mallacoota Inlet from exploitation by professional fishermen and hunters. He gave Barrett a letter to use:

> It was a rare spectacle to see the great flights of pelicans, swans, ducks, dabchicks and numerous other native birds, and to contemplate the quiet waters . . . teeming with every kind of aquatic life. . . . Surely we are not always going to take the sordid view? Will you remind the Minister how, a few years ago, a short sighted policy converted several of our most fertile and beautiful river valleys, . . . in the sole interests of a few hundred dredge miners, into a permanent hideous wilderness of desolation? [Could the needs of a few fishermen] justify the surrender of so beautiful a national heritage as Mallacoota still is?

The same year he wrote to the minister to deplore the 'ruthless devastation of the forests' on the Buffalo plateau. Cheap letting of grazing and use of fire without restriction to promote growth of grass should be stopped instantly.

From time to time journalists put out hopeful stories about Monash entering Commonwealth politics: the country needed a leader, he would have immense support if he ran. Late in 1922 he came under pressure to stand. During 1923 Bruce, with whom he was 'on rather good terms', was letting it privately be known that he would like him as a member of his government. Late the following year, after yet another snub at the time of the British Fleet's visit,* Bruce made some sort of considerate gesture to Monash, who replied gratefully. In May 1925 Bruce urged him to stand for the Senate at the election late in the year. Monash, in reply, said he felt committed to see the S.E.C. through its critical years and that he had shaped his course in the belief that his 'services were not wanted in the Federal sphere'; the chance of a political career had been missed in 1919 when Hughes had stood in his way. Bruce in reply understood fully: it was lamentable that he was not employed in the national sphere—'But what is is'. In October 1925 Monash, quite remarkably, was given an individual place by name in the official Commonwealth table of precedence, immediately following the first military member of the Military Board. But his chip remained: he continued occasionally to complain of the Commonwealth's treatment of him. The government did sometimes make use of him. He regularly took part in publicity for Commonwealth loans, he was called on to welcome and entertain officers of the visiting French, British, American and Japanese naval units between 1922 and 1925, and he carried out the cruiser investigation; but he had to refuse requests in 1926 and 1928 to investigate the British Phosphate Commission and to cost the future Hume dam, mainly because the State government was unwilling to release him. In 1926 it was rumoured that he might become high commissioner in London. State governments used him too. Monash became fed up with Lawson ringing him up at night, sometimes waking him up, for 'advice about some trumpery worry a man in his position should be able to settle for himself'. He also occasionally advised premiers of other States on engineering appointments.

Monash's political views were not highly sophisticated. Like most engineers he believed firmly in material progress by means of technological advance in a free enterprise system. He often used a historic definition of engineering as 'the art of directing the great sources of power in Nature for the use and convenience of man'. He had had great hopes of the comradeship of the classes arising from war service, which might 'do much to maintain industrial and political peace'. He was no exploiter of labour: all classes should share the fruits of progress and a good worker deserved a high wage—he often gave a rise to those he noticed. It would be convenient if extremist elements—Communists and die-hard employers—could be suppressed. 'There were extremists

* This time both Percy Deane, secretary of the Prime Minister's Department, and Chauvel assured him he had been invited to everything, that they had taken special care. Still the invitations did not arrive. It was becoming farcical. In January 1926, almost unbelievably, it happened again: Monash was not summoned to welcome Lord Allenby when he arrived at Spencer Street station and returned soldiers and the press made the most of it. Next year, however, the invitation to meet the Duke and Duchess of York on St Kilda Pier arrived safely.

everywhere, but [they] were seldom right. He had formed in the war a great respect for the virtue of compromise'; and for the need for give and take among people of differing political and economic creeds. British institutions were as civilized as anything the world had seen; there was no better system than parliamentary democracy; but all governments were more or less incompetent and by and large politicians were a sorry tribe. No party had a monopoly of good ideas or good men. The Labor Party was of course instilled with foolish and dangerous notions, but with regard to his own work he came to recognize that he got on better with Labor governments. He approved of the White Australia policy and, while in principle a free trader, believed that in Australian circumstances moderate protectionism was justifiable. He was pessimistic about the future of humankind, about the possibilty of improving men and women by Act of Parliament, and in particular about current Australian trends. He confessed to Rosenhain in 1923:

> I do not know whether. . . there is any real change in the Australian atmosphere, but I cannot help feeling that . . . we are drifting into a less and less satisfactory state. There is less culture, less art, less music, less scientific achievement, and more of everything that is sordid and unpalatable in life. While our population is increasing, and our prosperity is increasing, so is our vulgarity and our sordidness, our want of discipline, and our criticism of each other. I do not find it nearly as pleasant a place to live in as it was before the war. . . . I do not know how much of this outlook is due to a change in myself, and how much to a real change in the community.

If only it were 'possible to get people interested in the things that really matter, instead of in sport, jazz and the passing sensation', and cure Australia of its isolationist tendencies. His campaigning for defence preparedness was based more on the general necessity to keep a nucleus of naval and military forces and equipment than on any discernible threat. Having met the officers of a visiting Japanese squadron, he was satisfied that 'the Japanese people entertain nothing but the most cordial friendship for Great Britain and Australia'. The Japanese consul subsequently made great efforts to cultivate his acquaintance. When in 1925 Hindenburg was elected president of Germany Monash commented: 'I feel certain that the fears of a revival of a warlike spirit in Germany are grossly exaggerated. The work of the Disarmament Commission has been thoroughly done, and Germany is militarily powerless for the next quarter of a century'. In 1930 he decried the possible importance of the aeroplane in future warfare. Like everyone else, however wise and well informed, he had no inkling of what was in store.

Monash perhaps missed working in reinforced concrete and occasionally fought old battles in trying to convince people of its virtues for building. He went out of his way, when he heard that the steel interests were using the same old propaganda, to advise the Royal Automobile Club of Victoria to build in concrete. When Fairway and Lynch consulted him about troublesome aspects of Walter Burley Griffin's design for the Capitol Theatre, he suggested some modifications, drawing on the back of a matchbox in the train home to Heyington. The Reinforced Concrete Co. paid him out in February 1923 and the South Australian company was finally liquidated in 1925. For some years Humes tried to work him quite hard for his fat director's fee, usually of £350 a year, but the connexion sometimes placed him in awkward conflicts of interest. The S.E.C. made some use of concrete pipes in its extensive works and might well have used more. Monash was convinced of their utility—he knew he knew best on the question—and it would be ridiculous if the S.E.C. avoided using them because of his position. But he had to take special care not to influence his subordinates' advice. In 1923 when Nettlefold complained to him of prejudice in the S.E.C. against Hume pipes, he would do no more than forward his engineer's report justifying his advice, and tell Nettlefold that his position as chairman of the S.E.C. made it difficult rather than easy for him to help the company's interests. Nettlefold remained bitter about lack of business with the S.E.C. A more cautious man would have resigned the directorship, but Monash was too sure of his own rectitude to acknowledge the danger fully. He urged Gibson to hurry to conclude the arrangement to pay him out of the Reinforced Concrete Co. so that no accusations could be made against him, but meanwhile he was determined that the company should have its proper share, as the obvious first contender, of S.E.C. reinforced concrete buildings.

He retained his directorships of Humes, Atlas Insurance and Luna Park until his death. He remained chairman of Luna Park throughout, but rarely attended directors' or annual meetings, though he was occasionally active on particular problems. Monash's agreement with Lawson remains obscure. He said more than once that a condition of his employment was that he took no other paid work but that he was permitted to retain one or two directorships until such time as he could conveniently break free. It may be that Lawson had connived at retention of the directorships because he felt it was not politically possible to offer Monash more than £3000 a year; perhaps Monash had confined himself to a general assurance or had fudged the issue. Yet in 1922 he accepted another directorship with an insurance company (but resigned when Atlas protested). In 1923 he joined the board of Saddler's Citizens and Graziers' Assurance Co., but retreated hastily when he was warned that questions would be asked in Parliament. Moreover, when he became vice-chancellor later that year, Labor members were disturbed at his use of his time and he was warned again. He then resigned as chairman and director of the Maria Island Co. The threatening storms blew away and his outside activities were never again seriously queried.

A large part of Monash's capital had been invested pre-war in suburban houses. After the war he dabbled in buying tenements and selling the houses singly, but from 1922 he systematically sold his properties in the belief that their values would decline and that they were troublesome to manage. He had also become aware that well-known landlords were subject to bad publicity; some ex-diggers protested at a rent rise—'I am poor and you are rich', one wrote to him, and later an activist group of Richmond tenants condemned him for exploitation. He often used rent-purchase agreements as a method of mid-term sale (having made a full analysis of the advantages—'Rent purchase algebraically considered').

He was a shrewd, but not a very shrewd, investor. He made it a rule never to invest in gold-mining. He still liked to dabble; he joined syndicates promoting a non-puncturable resilient tyre and a diamond-digging venture in New South Wales; he was deceived by a film promoter; he backed old diggers and advised them in a salt-manufacturing enterprise which went bust; he had an interest in Kelvinator refrigerators and recorded the performance of his own model; he made good and bad investments in New Zealand and Tasmanian tree-planting ventures. After bitter experience of reproaches, he refused to allow his name to appear as an investor: 'Perhaps when your friends are told of this condition, they will not be so ready as they appear to be to, practically, make me a present of 200 shares', he once wrote . He lost nearly £700 he had lent to Josh Anderson—whether for old times' sake or from feeling that he owed him something—when he went bankrupt in 1926. And he lost £300 when Rosenthal, to his great shame, could not repay him and became insolvent. Monash knew very well that these and many smaller loans to friends were often money thrown away.

From about 1922 he systematically transferred his assets to Bertha in order to avoid eventual probate duty. His childhood friend Victor Wischer was now his solicitor. 1924 was the year of his greatest worth (£63 000) and 1922 the year of highest income (£6665), though in 1930 it was still as high as £5360 including his £3000 salary. The detail of his annual and running calculations leaves no remote possibility of inaccuracy. In 1922 he bought several acres near Olinda in Bertha's name; they planned a nine-bedroom country house with gardener's cottage and tennis court, and peacocks, pheasants and swans on the lawns. He also bought and subdivided in her name land at Heathmont.

As late as 1926 he was hoping still to build at Olinda, but there was never time to spare. He joined the Ranelagh Club at Mt Eliza and bought land, but was irritated when his name was used to attract other purchasers. Eventually Bertha and Gershon decided to buy a house at Long Island, Frankston.

Accusations of profit arising from S.E.C. extensions to land privately owned could not easily be avoided. In December 1922 an inimical contributed paragraph to the *Australian Financial Gazette* drew attention to Monash's landholdings in the Dandenongs which the power lines were expected to traverse. George Meudell, who had an interest in the journal and who regarded Monash as 'the greatest Australian', was horrified and wrote to apologize. Monash assured the editor: 'I have not invested a sixpenny piece in any land in the Dandenong Ranges, nor is it true that the power from Morwell will pass through those ranges'. This was a deception, for the Olinda property had been bought that year in Bertha's name. He was prepared to take the calculated risk that his denial would carry the day, as it did. The *Gazette* made an abject withdrawal, but it would have sufficed to say that the site of the land was irrelevant to S.E.C. plans. In 1926 he warned one of his officers to take especial care that the case for imminent extension of power to Heathmont was watertight.

On Monash's return from the war the Jewish community looked to its most famous member to take the lead on communal questions and represent it as a spokesman. Although only a 'cultural Jew', he could not refuse requests without seeming to reject his origins. So early in 1921 he chaired the committee making arrangements for the Victorian section of the visit to Australia of the chief rabbi of the British Empire, J. H. Hertz, and presided over the public meeting of welcome; they both received demonstrative receptions. He unveiled the military honour boards in the Melbourne, East Melbourne and St Kilda synagogues and, in 1924, the memorial in the Melbourne General Cemetery to Jewish servicemen. On request he supplied a New Year message for the *Australian Jewish Herald* in which he denied any contradiction between being patriotic and loyal to the Empire and being a good Jew. When the unstable 'Pompey' Elliott referred in the Senate to Lieut-Colonel Margolin, D.S.O., as 'an illiterate Polish Jew', Monash sprang to his defence in a letter to the *Argus*. The community continued to delight in honouring him. In 1926 he was called on to open the communal hall in Carlton sponsored by the Judaean League; that it was to be named Monash House was kept a secret from him.

Rabbi Abrahams of the Melbourne Hebrew Congregation had conducted Vic's funeral ceremony. Two months later Monash joined the board of management of the St Kilda congregation and was soon presenting the prizes at its Sabbath school. He respected the Reverend Jacob Danglow and was his friend, but warned him there was little chance of attending meetings regularly. In April 1921 Danglow married Bertha and Gershon. A most painful row followed with the acting rabbi (Abrahams had retired) of the Melbourne congregation who was insulted by receiving from Monash two guineas, which he returned, for supplying an inscription, which had not been used, for Vic's grave; and he resented being superseded for the wedding. Monash was justly indignant and wrote to the president of the congregation to resign his membership. Having received apologies, he withdrew his resignation with good grace and promised to attend Melbourne on the Day of Atonement. In 1923 Monash attempted to resign from the St Kilda board of management; after an urgent plea to reconsider, he withdrew, but rejected an offer to make him president of the congregation. In 1925 he advised on the arch of the new St Kilda synagogue, and two years later at its opening celebrations proposed the toast to Danglow.

He was taking his religion with some, perhaps only a little, seriousness. From 1920 he kept Yom Kippur (the Day of Atonement) at least to the extent of staying home from the office, though he did not fast. But from 1925 at least, borrowing a prayer book, he attended synagogue that day, although he did not accept the invitation in 1927 to be Chosan Torah ('Bridegroom of the Law' at the conclusion of the High Holidays). In 1929 he wrote frankly to Danglow to ask which was the correct prayer book for Yom Kippur; he had had the greatest difficulty, when he attended, in following the service. He was asked to be Chosan Torah that year, but he refused as he expected to be on holiday. In 1930 he took a ceremonial part in the consecration of the new Toorak Road synagogue of the Melbourne congregation; he opened the Ark and placed the scrolls inside. And that year, when asked to interest himself in the formation of a liberal congregation (Temple Beth Israel), he wrote in reply:

> However much the new movement may claim no desire of antagonism to existing Congregations, it would be inevitable that any public association of myself with such a movement would be resented by some of the more orthodox members. . . . Please bear in mind that I am now getting on in years, and while I might in my younger days have welcomed and taken up such a modernizing movement with some enthusiasm, I feel that this work is for a younger generation.

But he offered to advise and assist. When, about this time, he was considering economies he might have to make, he included in the list his membership of the St Kilda and Melbourne congregations. Monash was a very private man—no one, perhaps, was in his confidence on this matter. However, the uncertain indications are that in his late years he was coming round, if no more, to take some comfort in religious ceremonies which he had hardly ever attended since he was a boy; and that he sympathized with the liberal Jewish position.

He had also adopted moderate Zionism and, in doing so, made himself an important exception to the influential Jews of the time. After the 1917 Balfour declaration of intent by the British government to encourage recognition of Palestine as the Jewish homeland, the League of Nations approved a British mandate to this end. Migration proceeded slowly with little substantial Arab opposition until 1928–29. As early as August 1920 Monash had presided over a public meeting at which the visiting Israel Cohen had whipped up support for the cause, and had pledged himself to give £100 a year for five years. He was influenced by Zionist friends such as Dr Leon Jona and Margolin and by Lizette Bentwitch whose cousin was (Professor Sir) Norman Bentwich, then attorney-general in the Mandatory government in Palestine.

In 1922 Monash refused an invitation to preside over a recruiting meeting for Zionist supporters—he was simply too busy. Late in 1924 he did chair a meeting of the Palestine Welfare League of Victoria which aimed at purchasing 250 acres for £5000 to settle fifty families. On this or another occasion, Alec Masel, a leading figure in the Zionist movement, recalls approaching Monash in trepidation (possibly with the young rabbi, Israel Brodie), remembering his links with the English anti-Zionists, and being delighted with his promised unswerving support. In October 1927 Monash became national president of the Australian Zionist Federation on the understanding that he could give no time at all and would be a figure-head. Next July a letter to all Australian Jews, seeking recruits, was sent under his name. Late in the year he exercised a restraining influence on a Zionist meeting in Melbourne about conflicts at the Wailing Wall in Jerusalem. He wrote to Brodie:

> While I, in common with every Jew, have the utmost sympathy with the unfortunate sufferers, it is quite another matter for me to be associated, however indirectly, with any action of any body of British citizens which seeks to express publicly any sentiments critical of or hostile to the British authorities.

Until a few months before, General Lord Plumer, whom he greatly admired, had been the British High Commissioner in Palestine; in 1925 Monash had again been spoken of as a possible appointee. The proposed resolutions were watered down, but not enough for the Jewish Advisory Board, the official representative body, which dissociated itself from the meeting. In September 1929, after Arab massacres of settlers, many Zionists wanted to make emphatic protests against British administration. In Melbourne the community came together: Monash presided at a Town Hall meeting of some two thousand. The chief emphasis was on organizing for funds. Monash had set the tone of the meeting: it was an occasion of unspeakable sadness, they had a right to be bitter, but it was no use passing resolutions critical of the administration. They relied on Britain to carry out its obligations under the mandate: 'Every Jew who had made his home in the British Empire owes it unbounded gratitude, complete loyalty, and profound allegiance'. A few weeks later when Bentwich was nearly assassinated, Monash again restrained some of the local militants. And when in October 1930 Sydney Zionists asked him to support their protest against a British White Paper, which was to lead to further restrictions on Jewish immigration, he wrote some weeks later to apologize for mislaying their letter. He had given full support to the local Friends of the Hebrew University of Jerusalem.

An indication of how limited and mild anti-Semitism was at this time is that Monash, as a community leader, never had to speak out in protest about any major local incident. Moreover his own life seems to have been singularly free from anti-Semitic insult or discrimination. There was, of course, a quite widespread and openly expressed mild hostility to Jews, based on their alleged business cleverness and on the ancient religious prejudice against 'the Christ-killers'; such discrimination as there was seems to have been largely confined to a few social and sporting clubs. But Australia was a pluralist society, the Jews were less than 1 per cent of the population and, as the historian Israel Getzler has remarked, 'If sceptical Australians ever had an ideology it has been the liberal democratic-egalitarian creed, a "fair go" for all'. And the hard-pressed small shopkeepers, the ruling class under threat and the academic exponents of racial hatred, who classically in Europe attempted to use Jews as scapegoats, have not emerged in Australia. There was possibly more anti-Semitism in Melbourne, where most of the Jews were of central European origin and thus a more conspicuous minority, than in Sydney where British Jews, further from the ghetto tradition and socially almost entirely assimilated, were dominant. Monash's standing policy, which he was fortunate never to have to modify, was to proclaim that anti-Semitism in Australia did not exist. In contrast Sir Isaac Isaacs fought any hint of anti-Semitism he found. The fame of these two great Australians greatly raised Jewish morale. *Smith's Weekly* and the *Bulletin*, where the current of anti-Semitism ran strongest, were to some extent nobbled, revering Monash as they did. Even when Isaacs became chief justice and then governor-general in 1930, Monash's fame and popularity remained much greater: apart from his military prowess, he had moved much more widely in the community, had incomparably more friends and acquaintances, and his friendly conversational style and objective thinking were far more attractive than Isaacs's tendency to emotional dogmatism. Monash and Isaacs never came to know each other very well—surprisingly given the similarity of their religious scepticism and interest in Jewish scholarship, history and culture; moreover Isaacs had not yet taken up an anti-Zionist position. The conclusive retort— 'What about Monash?'—to someone sounding off about 'the bloody Jews' in pub or club surely happened thousands of times. As the author Colin McInnes has remarked: 'Monash, by the simple fact of his presence and prestige, made anti-Semitism, as a "respectable" attitude, impossible in Australia'. He had often heard old soldiers begin to attack Jews, but when Monash was mentioned, 'they spoke with reverence. . . . And worshipping him as they did (and through him, their own youth and courage), they could never publicly deny the hero they themselves had freely followed: nor could they deny his people'.

Monash's reputation as a great man was unchallengeable. Yet there was a sorry, trivial incident late in 1922 which showed that his sensitivity about his origins, which for so long he had entirely controlled, still remained. His old friend Dr Springthorpe was now elderly and rather deaf. Entertaining a visiting Adelaide author at the Naval and Military Club, he remarked, rather loudly in the smoke-room, that the club premises had previously been those of the German Club, that Monash the president was of German descent, and that it had been rumoured in Egypt he had been shot as a spy. An outraged member informed Monash, who wrote to Springthorpe:

> I never believe in harbouring a grievance, and therefore take the course of writing to frankly tell you how greatly I regret and resent your conduct at the Naval and Military Club yesterday. . . . I think I am right in questioning the good taste of such remarks under any circumstances, but particularly in the precincts of a club of which I am President, and in which my name is held in respect. I do know that your conversation was much resented by other members.

In reply Springthorpe explained that the context of his remarks was 'the stupidity of popular clamour' against those of German descent, and denied that his remarks were in bad taste. Monash then went far—but not far enough—to accept Springthorpe's explanation, recognizing that the account he had received was exaggerated and acquitting him of 'any unfriendly motive'. Springthorpe wrote a dignified letter in reply regretting that Monash had taken the attitude of a judge rather than a friend. Perhaps Monash had hurried his reply, and he certainly healed the breach by a phone call or at next meeting with an apology or explanation.

As Paddy McGlinn remarked, 'Sir John Monash became a national possession, so that all could avail themselves of his time and talents'. He refused presidencies and vice-presidencies galore. He accepted invitations to speak, usually on the war and its lessons, about once a month—to the Victoria League, the Commercial Travellers' Association, the Boobooks, the Wesleyan Pleasant Sunday Afternoon, the Chamber of Manufactures, the Bendigo Chamber of Commerce, to name some almost at random. He had to refuse many more than he accepted: 'In view of so cordially worded an invitation, it must seem ungracious to you that I feel unable to comply. . . .' Soldiers' widows asked his advice on the education of their children, deserted wives implored him to find their husbands. Piteous letters came from incapacitated ex-servicemen and from acquaintances of the distant past who were in distress. Unemployed diggers implored him to find them jobs: 'I have applied for 16 different jobs during the last few weeks and nothing doing. Who did we fight for? The man with money and property!' Politicians, old girl friends on behalf of their husbands, even the governor, likewise asked him to use his influence—one politician pleading for a constituent received a savage reply and was sorry he had asked. Monash did try to help some of the large number who were far beyond his capacities: he wiped out the remainder of a loan to an incapacitated soldier; he got an old gunner a job on the trams; he left money with the Charity Organisation Society for aid in extreme cases; he gave a few pounds to a fellow-founder of the University Union who was an invalid pensioner; he charitably recognized he had been professionally bitten by an old soldier. And always there were references to write for scores of soldiers, some of them for great men of the future like Generals Mackay, Morshead and Vasey, and Lord Casey. When they were close friends he would go to great lengths: in support of the successful appointment of McGlinn to the Commonwealth Public Service Board, he lobbied Bruce twice, as well as several other members of the government.

He was called on to write forewords to war books, battalion histories, epic poems on Gallipoli and volumes of verse; messages, not only for Anzac, Armistice and Empire Days, but in support of thrift or Commonwealth loans, or as the representative Australian sending a recorded message of gratitude to Thomas Edison on his seventy-fifth birthday. At least once annually he had to present the prizes at school speech-nights. Scotch College made special demands; he often followed the boat race in a launch with the headmaster W. S. Littlejohn and Robinson, and he gave the motto to the house named after him: 'Mak Siccar' ('Make Sure'). He competed in the St Vincent's Hospital's Ugly Man competition to help its funds. As a Grand Officer of the French Order of the Legion of Honour, he had to bestow a lesser honour of the order on a local recipient. He joined the Victorian Society for the Protection of Animals, the National Geographical Society, the Royal Colonial Institute, the Big Brother Movement, the Society of Australian Authors, the Egypt Exploration Society and other movements without hope of being an active member. Sometimes he was testy about unreasonable demands. One society lady was put in her place:

> I have discovered, to my cost, that the way the public has of expressing its gratitude for services . . . to the State . . . is to make exorbitant demands upon its willing servant, so as to deprive him of every moment of leisure, and . . . to require explanations why its many demands upon his time, energy and health cannot always be met.

But he would reply at length to a schoolgirl inquiring about the uses of electricity.

He had Scouting obligations to meet. He had to take special interest in the two troops named after him, visit the camps at Anglesea, and make occasional public affirmation of his belief in Scouting as admirable for character-building and as training for good citizenship. He also became president and patron of the Lord Somers Camps.

He was a very ready speaker, but he still prepared his more important speeches carefully in full, memorized as much as he could, and reduced his draft to skeleton notes. Lesser speeches became routine, often a repetition of remarks made a dozen times before but, unless under great pressure, he would still carefully jot down the headings and main points. He wrote out four sentences of gratitude beforehand when the Council of the University elected him vice-chancellor. But he became fairly skilful in varying his speeches according to the mood of his audience and what previous speakers had said. He was weary of mouthing the same conventional sentiments over and over, as he had to do, comforting himself that many in his audience liked to hear platitudes and that some were perhaps hearing them for the first time. Some people thought him a fine orator. This seems unlikely: he constructed his speeches well, could speak forcefully, was of course masterly when expounding a subject, and could raise a laugh, but he was essentially a conventional and moralistic speaker who was a little heavy-handed. He did not use much oratorical emphasis and probably was lacking in the essential histrionic quality and sense of timing. His greatest virtue was that he did not ramble at length. It is not an area in which Australians have excelled, especially in his generation, and he was certainly a good speaker by contemporary standards.

Monash remained faithful, or almost so, to Lizette Bentwitch until he died. On her arrival in Melbourne in September 1920, *Punch* described her as bringing 'a very English accent, trunks full of fascinating fripperies that have a Continental flavour, and reminiscences of social London'. Even Vic, however, had told John that her taste in dress was showy. She was a miniature-painter of some skill. Though she had a good figure, Lizzie was rather unprepossessing in appearance—what *does* he see in her? was a frequent comment—but intelligent, voluble, with a photographic memory, slightly 'scatty'. She resided in turn at the Windsor, Cliveden Mansions and the Oriental. Melbourne, being Melbourne, gasped with the gossip but, apart from the wowsers, there was more amusement than spite in it. In official circles, however, there was resentment at the irregularity—which may even explain attempts to exclude him from official occasions. At the theatre and at concerts there was a hush, then a buzz as they came in to take their seats. They were often seen lunching at Menzies, then walking up Collins Street in animated conversation. He referred to her as 'Ell' in his diaries and may have so addressed her.

He didn't give a damn for public opinion. He often demanded an invitation for her on formal occasions such as the opening of Parliament or a Government House garden party; she accompanied him to Naval and Military Club balls, though not in the official party when Bertha was hostess; she went with him to Perth, Hobart, Buffalo, and eventually to India. However, he let it be understood that she would not accompany him at private functions. He had arranged with the *Argus* that she would be mentioned with him as present on formal occasions and that they would never suffer from derogatory comment. They had to put up with the convention that a gentleman on his own might talk to them, but that a gentleman, if his wife was with him, would avoid them so as not to give recognition to people living irregularly. According to unreliable folk-memory, parasol up, Lizette floated off Frankston (or St Kilda) pier one day, and Monash presented her rescuer with £5. He constantly sent her books. In 1925 and 1926 they and Bertha suffered from reports in the gutter press, which pretended to wonder why he did not marry the 'pleasant-faced Jewess who sits behind a large ostrich fan' at the theatre, and cited the 'troublesome' daughter as the difficulty. Bertha indeed had no time for 'That woman'.

He had kept in touch with Annie Gabriel, the 'love of his life'. Fred Gabriel was employed as an inquiry agent by the Commonwealth Customs and he and Annie spent some time in Melbourne. In 1912 she was ill in hospital in Sydney and, presumably unable to write to her clandestinely, Monash wrote frequently to her son, asking him to pass on messages of sympathy. John visited Annie and Fred in Sydney in November 1914 and when next month they moved to Melbourne Annie wrote in distress on hearing John was sailing, arranging to meet: 'Will you write to St. Kilda P.O. the same name as usual. ... It is awful to think you have to go'. Two or three years later Mat wrote to John about running across Annie. She did not know if he was interested, Annie was still youthful-looking, as mercurial as ever in jumping from subject to subject, but most of her thoughts centered round a subject that was not at all in Mat's line; she had a 'somewhat undignified frivolous bearing', in short she was 'cheap'. After the war the Gabriels returned to Sydney. Monash lent her money. They met again when he was in Sydney in 1929, and had twenty-four hours together. After returning home he sent her his photograph, and he saw her again in Melbourne early in 1930.

Living arrangements at Iona worked out happily. Monash had the highest opinion of his son-in-law: Gershon Bennett's integrity, personality, sincerity and moral code were admirable. The birth of grandchildren—John Monash 1922, David Monash 1924, Elizabeth Monash 1926—added a new dimension to his life. The boys were the sons he had never had and recompense for the dying of his name. He soon began to spend half an hour a day, usually after breakfast, with Baby John. The reading of stories to his grandchildren perched on his knees would be punctuated with giggles and shrieks of laughter; he would romp and crawl around, giving piggy-backs, pretending to chase. He told funny stories and revived his conjuring skills (very enjoyable but 'never of a very high order', according to Gershon); he even enjoyed giving the baby its bottle. When Bertha and Gershon went on holiday, he supervised the nurse and sent daily reassuring telegrams such as, 'Family splendidly noisy. Trust you having good time. Love. Dad'. He learned phonetics and the latest teaching methods and taught the boys to read by the time they were five; he was playing draughts with John when he was six; he coached them in tending silkworms; he treasured their first written exercises and letters. He took them on excursions, including the turning of the first sod at the Shrine works. They became the most important part of his life. He had a great gift with children and should have had a dozen of his own.

He remained the calm centre of his wider family's affairs. Mat, who visited him most Sundays, wrote to him in 1922: 'My dear big John, I can never thank you enough for all you have done and all you do do for me. . . . but for you I should have gone under long ago'. But he could not heal the renewed breach, though he earnestly tried, between her and Lou, who was going through a disturbed time. 'All this is ridiculously petty and childish', he wrote to Walter,'—but what *is* to be done? To women, with their narrow outlook, such matters may loom very large. Personally, I can't understand it'. He kept in touch with his much-loved Rosenhain nieces and helped to pay for their education. He continued to keep the Roths in comfort and gave his cousins holiday trips. Tante Ulrike said he had always treated her like an eldest son, had never failed her. Sa Simonson died in 1923.

He eased the path for his widowed sister-in-law Belle through troubled days of sickness, and aided his Moss and Simonson nephews and nieces with their problems. He was troubled by relatives in Germany and elsewhere, with whom he had long been out of touch, and various cousins' sons-in-law asking for financial help. His chief contact was his first cousin Berthold Monasch, an able engineer and patent attorney, who not only guided him in giving help especially to the older generation but was a kindred spirit; but, to his shame, Monash had to neglect most of these remoter family obligations, including his American relatives. Some of his happiest associations were with Bertha's friends, at least two of whom made him godfather to their children and looked on him as something like a father to themselves.

He had no time and little inclination to make Iona a centre of hospitality, apart from the Bennetts' Sunday tennis parties followed by a convivial evening tea. The annual 8th of August dinners were exceptional. In the early twenties he had the governor to dine with the S.E.C. Commissioners and Clapp, and their wives; he gave a dinner for Frank Tate on his departure on an overseas trip, and another for his old friend Lee Murray, visiting from London, to meet fellow engineering students from long ago. Occasionally he had to return the hospitality of hostesses like Angela Thirkell ('that Burnsey-Jonesey woman') who had managed to lure him to a private dinner party. He kept a modest cellar, almost entirely of Australian wines, of which he kept a careful inventory. He enjoyed his wine, though he did not drink it regularly; when home for dinner, he usually had a whisky beforehand with Gershon. He almost never drank beer, was a steady tea- and an irregular coffee-drinker. The normal staff at Iona was a chauffeur, gardener, cook and maid. He advised his pre-war chauffeur, Monty Carroll, at length on the business aspects of running a farm. He sent Dyer, his crippled gardener, to Dr Sewell and paid the bills and arranged for his old-age pension; 'I must say you are the best friend I ever met with', wrote Dyer. He helped his successor through problems relating to his wife's death, paying Wischer to handle the estate. Patrick Dwyer, chauffeur from 1924, became a family institution and regarded Monash as a marvellous boss.

Despite all his unavoidable commitments, Monash used his supreme powers of organization to keep a large proportion of evenings free for music, the theatre and domestic relaxation. He became a masterly avoider of purely social engagements. Bertha and Gershon enjoyed, as Vic rarely had, evenings of reading aloud. Dickens was his lasting love, and *David Copperfield* the most loved of all. He usually arranged a couple of evenings a week between 1922 and 1925 reading much of Dickens, Thackeray, George Eliot, Lytton, Meredith, Disraeli, Scott and the like, but branching out to works of travel, biography, poetry, drama and modern fiction. But after ten he regularly did his basic thinking and planned the next day's work.

The soothing Sunday routine of record-keeping and collecting continued. He made synopses of weekly accounts and reviewed his finances in close detail. He did use office assistance in indexing his correspondence. His detailed temperature readings of the electric hot-water system were relevant to his professional concerns. Listing his collections of photographs and war souvenirs was of practical use. But his cataloguing of his albums of mementoes, the many inventories of his tools, annual lists of functions not attended and meticulous analyses of motor trips in terms of time, distance and speed, were purely compulsive. Every few months he overhauled his clothes for moths. Annually he had to sign the governor-general's, governor's and lord mayor's visiting books.

In 1919 in London Monash had been brooding on how to enlarge his library of about four thousand volumes, and ordering new book cases. One of his main diversions came to be expanding his collection, and classifying and rearranging it. He managed to slip in regularly to Cole's Book Arcade and A. H. Spencer's and Ellis Bird's shops, and ordered extensively from overseas catalogues. He did not much care whether editions were rare or valuable—his books were for reading. His purchases display his catholic taste in literature, science and history—especially Jewish and military. His main purpose was to fill the gaps in his holdings of the standard ancient classics and English, French and German literature and also his collection of plays. So he added Voltaire, Balzac and Anatole France; Dante; Bunyan, Pepys, Stevenson and Wilde, to give a few examples. He bought and read Emil Ludwig's biographies in German. He seized on reminiscences and histories of the war: all of Liddell Hart and Churchill, Robertson, Fuller, Maurice—and *Good Soldier Schweik* and *Her Privates We*. Although he was of too early a generation to be in touch with the modernism of Freud, Proust, Cézanne or Schönberg, his current reading was wide. Bernard Shaw was a top priority—there is a special urgency in his orders—and he read Pirandello's *Six Characters*, delighted in H. L. Mencken, considered Keynes's *Economic Consequences of the Peace* an important work, at least purchased Maurois' *Disraeli* and Durant's *Story of Philosophy*. He was advanced enough to buy Aldous Huxley's *Crome Yellow*, Michael Arlen's *The Green Hat*, Sinclair Lewis's *Babbitt* and Cabell's *Jurgen*. He seriously believed the novels of the fashionable William de Morgan rivalled Dickens's, and enjoyed Leacock, Wodehouse, A. P. Herbert, Conan Doyle, the Baroness Orczy, Edgar Wallace and Ellery Queen. He remarked that in fifty years he had lost only one book of those he had lent.

He had a small collection of Australiana and kept up with current publications: the *Australian Encyclopaedia*, Murdoch's *Deakin*, Selby's *Memorial History of Melbourne*, Martin Boyd's *The Montforts*, the early publications of Melbourne University Press including Myra Willard's *White Australia Policy* and S. H. Roberts's *History of Australian Land Settlement*; and *The Art of George Lambert*. His periodicals included *John o' London's Weekly, Foreign Affairs* (U.S.A.) and *Homes and Gardens*. And he immediately bought Fowler's *Modern English Usage* and Herbert Read's *English Prose Style*. When he presented the prizes at an annual meeting of the Shakespeare Society, he called on the Federal government to subsidize Shakespearian productions. He also became vice-president of the new Sydney branch of the English Association, and pleaded in the *Argus* for better use by public men of 'the most expressive, the most elastic, and the most appealing language in the world'.

Monash had a mania for having his books autographed by authors, and carried on an extensive correspondence to this end; as a second-best he would paste in a snipped-out signature or the letter itself. A red sticker on the back of the book meant the autograph had been won. Pattie Deakin supplied Alfred's signature; Hamilton cheerfully complied for his *Gallipoli Diary*—'How jolly of you to write to me'; Foott, having been assured that future history would not suffer, tore off General Bridges's signature from an official document. Mrs Aeneas Gunn was told that she was the first Australian author in his collection to be published in German. He also prized his autograph book which contained about five hundred signatures of Australian and British generals, leading British politicians and many eminent Frenchmen. The King had taken the book away in 1918 and returned it with many of the signatures of his family. Foch, though besieged by society ladies in London embracing and kissing him, had made a shaky signature; Billy Hughes's was almost the most illegible of all. Monash would not purchase any autographs: all who signed had to be known to him.

Like many collectors, Monash had a standard section of sexology and erotica in his library. It included the works of Havelock Ellis and other students of sex, books on the erotic in literature, studies of phallic worship and flagellation, the *Kama-sutra*, Casanova, de Sade, etc. He also had a collection of photographs of nudes and 'indecent' photographs, and occasionally acquired examples of cheap pornography. From before the war he usually ordered from overseas catalogues or, under an assumed name, from Sydney, and once was interviewed by a Customs officer who eventually destroyed the parcel. Like poets and painters in all ages he tried his hand at licentious writing and drawing; in 1930 he completed a substantial work, based on experiences in London in 1917–19, which he referred to in his indexes as the 'Gulston' narrative (which does not survive), and versified in the manner of Jack Lindsay in *Fauns and Ladies*. Most of his contemporaries would have been horrified if they had known of this secret interest. Later generations for the most part would regard it as nothing out of the way. Whether his interest in erotica and pornography was primarily scientific curiosity, or amused observation of the foibles of mankind, or gave play to deeper needs, is a matter for surmise.

He displayed his war trophies in the hall and main passage of Iona. They included his collection of shoulder-straps from about two hundred German regiments; a bottle containing earth from Gallipoli, scraped up at the last moment before leaving; a German light machine-gun which he had dismantled and transported to Walter via officers going on leave; a scrap of the propeller from von Richthofen's plane; a box of iron crosses captured on 8 August; and models of a tank and of a bridge constructed over the Somme presented to him by relevant units.

He had no time to play the piano now, but music remained his great love. He attended nearly all the seventeen first nights of the Grand Opera season of 1924, and the eight Kreisler concerts of 1925. 'After all the violin is the King of Instruments', he remarked. He had developed a late passion for Wagner, bought all the scores from Germany and collected books on him. Monash had helped to form the guarantee fund for the visits from Sydney of the Verbrugghen orchestra and supported the movement to establish a permanent Melbourne orchestra. At concerts he often had the score on his knee. In 1926 he was among the first to buy a wireless with loud-speakers, mainly in order to listen to music. His collection of gramophone records was almost entirely of Wagner, Beethoven, Mozart, Mendelssohn, Haydn and Chopin. According to Gershon Bennett, 'From music he seemed to emerge like a giant refreshed to deal with the workaday world'.

Monash knew Longstaff and Streeton well from the war years and was friendly with Tom Roberts and George Bell. For Streeton, one of the great honours of his life had been dining in the Corps mess at Le Cateau in November 1918; Monash had put him on his left hand and told him not to rise for anyone. He watched Web Gilbert several times at work on his memorial to the 2nd Division which was to go to Mont St Quentin, and on his Broken Hill war memorial. He bought one of the bronzes of *The Bomber*, having noticed and corrected a mistaken position of the hand in the first modelling. In his opinion 'a man should buy pictures because they please himself, not because they please his friends'. He was relatively uneducated in art and did not pose as a connoisseur. In the 1920s he bought paintings by Roberts, Walter Withers, A. E. Newbury (*The Edge of the Lake* was 'a little gem'), Dora Meeson, Esther Paterson, Thea Proctor and Jessie Traill, and Norman Lindsay etchings and Lionel Lindsay woodcuts. He took up a minor Jewish portrait-painter, Percy White, presented White's portrait of himself to Monash House, and arranged other commissions (Isaacs, Blamey and MacFarland) for him. He still occasionally sketched on holidays.

There was no chance of keeping up his pre-war habit of attending every first night at the theatre. His memories of George Coppin, the Bland Holts and the Brough-Boucicault company remained green. Nellie Stewart was still appearing. He continued to be a patron of Gregan McMahon's Melbourne Repertory Theatre Society and of Allan Wilkie's Shakespearian company. In 1928 he welcomed the star of *The Maid of the Mountains*, Gladys Moncrieff, to a lunch in her honour at the Windsor. Next year he backed Phil Finkelstein's production of *Journey's End*, writing publicity and giving a press conference to boost it. He admired Sherriff's play for its reality in depicting how little glory there was in war, the omnipresence of fear and the suppressed sentiment, and in 1931 went to see the film version.

Late in 1923 Monash had developed a new interest: he joined the Astronomical Society, bought an 80 mm Zeiss telescope and had a platform built in the back garden. He told Associate Professor Hercus:

> It is not so much the actual location and identification of the heavenly objects which interest me, as the algebraical and mathematical processes which their location involves. There is no relaxation that I know of . . . more pleasing than to dabble in algebraical and trigonometrical formulae, and to perform computations which can be verified by actual observation.

It was infuriating when evenings were spoiled by cloud. When in Canberra in 1925, he made a point of visiting the newly-opened Mount Stromlo observatory. After 1925 his interest declined and he preferred to spend nearly all his free evenings reading. In 1927 he bought a microscope, but used it little. He still played with arithmetical puzzles and re-examined the uses of logarithms, listing examples where their use was either essential or the easiest method. He became a devotee of the *Herald* crossword, and took the trouble to find out who the author was in order to compliment him.

His interest in his garden had revived in 1921 when he captured Dyer, the head gardener from Stonnington, State Government House, who worked a transformation. Dyer's friendship with the curator at the Botanic Gardens brought supplies of dahlia tubers and surplus plants and seeds. Monash began to grow eucalypts in pots, but his pergola and orderly ranks of roses were his chief pleasure. The development of the garden, like everything else, was subject to strict record-keeping and his obsession with tidiness. 'To him the garden was lovely when every blade of grass was in its place and every dead twig satisfactorily disposed of', Gershon Bennett recalled. From about 1926 he spent more time in his workshop. Item 9 of his 'Workshop Instructions' reads: 'Keep the tool box locked and hide the key'.

Monash was no longer interested in being a club-man in the sense of using any club regularly for dining or as a major centre of social life—he wanted to get home early as often as possible. But at the Naval and Military he was enveloped with admiration and affection and could regularly meet old cronies. His duties as president were fairly burdensome: he had to attend many social functions, entertain visitors and club-guests, visit deathbeds, and soothe indignant members during the small crises which beset any such institution. The annual club ball, at which he was said to be the perfect host, was revived in 1924. He retained membership of the Yorick, University and Old Scotch Collegians' clubs, but hardly ever entered their doors. However, he had an 'extraordinarily enthusiastic reception' when he attended in 1928 the sixtieth anniversary of the Yorick Club's foundation. He was a founding member of Melbourne Rotary in 1921 and was coerced into becoming president for a year in 1922; a group led by Professor W. A. Osborne, the founding president, wanted him to stand out against a commercial clique and put the movement on a sound basis. Monash unwillingly accepted, had to preside weekly and carry out the 'somewhat difficult ritual'. His attendance record in the early years was better than all but the secretary's; it was a handy means of meeting civic leaders, developing contacts and settling small matters. In 1926 he addressed the sons of Melbourne Rotarians on 'Patriotism' and he was involved in preparations for the Australasian Rotary Conference in Melbourne; even in 1931 he was chairman of the movement's international service committee. Two clubs which Monash really enjoyed were the Wallaby and Beefsteak. Every month in the weekend the Wallabies, a small group of professional men, several of them Jewish, patrolled the nearer foothills of Melbourne, in suits and ties, deep in converse. He had been elected annual president in 1920, had Chauvel as a guest to speak, and conducted a party to Buffalo over the Cup weekend. In 1924 he attempted to call the club to greater order: our

> outings are, I am afraid, being robbed of much of their former enjoyment and 'sociableness' by some lack of organization, and indiscipline among the members. We are falling into the bad habit of separating into small groups, following different routes....
> A little more leadership on the part of the President, a little more exhortation to members to keep together, and obey the orders as to routes and halts, and a little more definiteness as to routes and times and distances, and the thing will right itself.

His rebuking of members for unpunctuality gave him a reputation for having 'some traits of the autocrat', according to the club historian, but the stick he had sent from Gallipoli remained the club's prize emblem. Through Meyer, in 1923 he joined the Beefsteaks, a dining club of about twenty members who were mainly professors and medicos. In 1925 he offered to resign as he could so rarely attend, but in 1926 and 1929 hosted the club at Iona and gave carefully prepared papers on 'Leadership in war' and 'The development of the physical sciences and engineering over the last century'. The latter was a masterly summary of the achievements of science and engineering with regard to material welfare, which concluded, for discussion: 'Human nature appears to have remained precisely where it was, and the soul of man has not changed'. Worse: 'As the war has proved, the engineer and the chemist have put into man's unchecked and careless hand a monstrous potentiality of ruin and self-destruction. What are we going to do about it?' In 1927 he accepted the presidency of the Old Scotch Collegians' Association, but resigned next year when he found that he could spare no time for it. 'I have entirely failed', he confessed, which was 'extremely disagreeable' to have to admit. He kept up membership of the Royal Automobile Club of Victoria and occasionally attended a hill-climb. He took his car several times for outings of inmates of the Children's Hospital and other handicapped children to the beach and elsewhere, organized by Rotary or the R.A.C.V. He made little use of his membership of the Melbourne Cricket Club but attended a Test match for a few hours at New Year 1929. His remaining club was the Metropolitan Golf to which John Gibson had introduced him in 1921. He did not raise any serious enthusiasm for the game, though the company was pleasant and the surroundings beautiful, but in 1930 he became interested again, bought Ivo Whitton's instructional book and filed a report of a device to teach the perfect swing. This was one theoretical problem far beyond his capacity.

Monash was not a creatively witty man, ready in conversational riposte. But he enjoyed stories and anecdotes and appreciated wit and, slightly laboriously perhaps, he would recount the latest. He appreciated the conventional 'dirty story', so common in his generation. He was a long-time reader of London and Melbourne *Punch*, filed anecdotes in his Commonplace Book, and had a liking for the pun; one of his better ones was, on seeing a workman loading a truck with briquettes, 'The age of shovelry is not yet dead'.

From 1921, following some reaction to the war and his wife's death, Monash's health had picked up. Early in 1923 he told Walter that 'hard work and long hours do not seem to affect me at all', he had thrown off his digestive troubles and lumbago, and colds seemed to pass him by; he had for a long time hardly lost an hour's working time from indisposition. He showered in the mornings—always cold, sometimes hot as well—and exercised before breakfast according to Bjelke-

Petersen routines. He had simple tastes in food—his daughter remembered porridge, boiled mutton and caper sauce, and soused herrings as among his favourites—and he drank moderately. He remained a fairly heavy smoker—usually a pipe, sometimes cigarettes or cigars. From the mid-1920s he began to refer to stress, nerve strain, desperate tiredness and recurring lumbago (especially after he ricked his back in settling a washing-machine into place). In 1924 he wrote to his doctor of nausea and gastric disturbance and sought help to tide him over the ordeal of the science congress. Then in the next few months, in addition to his S.E.C. work, the Science presidency, the vice-chancellorship and all his other commitments, he carried out the cruiser investigation and the long-running commission into the police. Late that year he was constantly weary. He struggled to 'lead a more obscure and quieter life', but his defences against importunity were weak. He did not take proper holiday spells. A pleasant week at Broken Hill in 1922 with Saddler, chairman of the Silverton Tramway Co., included an unexpected welcome from a large crowd, a civic reception, an evening with the local R.S.L. and an interview with the *Barrier Miner*, but also much interesting clambering round the mines. He returned in 1925 to unveil the war memorial. The 1926 trip to Perth and back by railway for the science congress he found wonderfully interesting. In January 1928 he did take a spell in Tasmania after the science congress and in October had a fortnight at Buffalo. And he made occasional short holiday motoring trips.

From 1927 high blood pressure became the most alarming symptom in his consultations with Sidney Sewell and Alan Newton. From early 1921 to early 1924 his weight had risen from 12½ to 13½ stone; he then brought it down a little, before in 1925 eliminating carbohydrates from his diet and reducing to little more than 11 stone early in 1926, when he felt more 'buoyant and elastic' than for many years. In 1927 he told his sister Lou that he had become very placid and phlegmatic and regularly had seven hours or more unbroken sleep each night. His weight crept up to about 13 stone again in 1929. All the ominous signs were there, but though in 1928 he seriously planned overseas leave for most of 1929 he did not take it.

In January 1929 Monash confessed to the Rosenhains that he had at last come fully to realize that he had to 'give up all hope, for the rest of my days, of any real privacy or leisure'. He was becoming even further involved in public commitments and he could not abandon the S.E.C. at its current stage of development. In the last twelve months, almost all his leisure had disappeared; he had had to jettison all his hobbies.

My main waking pre-occupation has become a continuous struggle to find the time to do the most urgent things of the moment. Now you will be thinking all the time how foolish of me all this is. Why don't I withdraw myself from most of these activities—why don't I learn to say, 'no', more frequently. ... I can assure you that these very questions have constituted for me a major problem for a long time past—a problem to which I greatly fear there is only one solution, and that is, for me to retire into absolute obscurity. There are no half measures possible.... Such a day of retirement is bound to come, through physical and mental inability to carry on. But to one whose whole life has been one of strenuous endeavour to reach objectives and to achieve ambitions, it is not so easy voluntarily to give up the status, the prestige, the public confidence and acclaim, which come with successful endeavour—so long at any rate as one is able to pay the heavy price of 'hanging on' to what one has won.

With his eyes open, he made the decision to go on. Dr Johnson's words are perhaps apposite: 'Men have a solicitude about fame, and the greater share they have of it, the more afraid they are of losing it'.

In 1924 C. Brunsden Fletcher, editor of the *Sydney Morning Herald*, met Monash at Yallourn. From what he had heard of him, he imagined him to be the type of a strong military man, the one who had laid down the law to Hughes.

> Sir John is nothing like the man of my imagination. He is neither tall nor physically impressive. He is a Jew at first glance, and typical in face and feature. A short, thick-set man, he does not carry any of the advantages which one associates with fine soldierly presence. ... But one knew that here was no boaster.... Perhaps it was the contrast between the ordinary set speech of the political leader seeking to impress an audience, and Sir John's simple exposition as he led us from one point of vantage to another, that first held my attention. But the man grew upon me. He was masterful.... one began to study his hands. They were so strangely out of harmony with his body, but so curiously expressive of the soul within him. I could see his forbears of more than two thousand years back, as prophets and Jewish leaders of the Maccabean type, hold up just such hands in adjuration or command—the hands of a man of genius, shapely and strong, but eloquent of mind and imagination. ... Now that I have seen him and spoken with him, have asked questions and received answers, have watched him with his subordinates, and have studied his ways with ordinary folk, I am quite satisfied. Australian problems on the largest scale have at least one man capable of solving them; and his energy and resource ought to be our greatest immediate asset.

His presence was certainly not soldierly, his figure was fleshy, bulky, thick-set, slightly stooped but square-shouldered. He did not

a University garden party in 1930 with J. G. Latham

anting a tree near the Shrine, 1930

A photographic portrait by Spencer Shier

Leaving Iona for the office

dress smartly, except on formal occasions, usually wearing rather ordinary suits and a grey felt hat or occasionally a bowler. His head was large and powerful with a high-domed forehead; his face was strong and full of character, heavily wrinkled and curiously calm. His hair and bushy eyebrows and moustache were brown, his complexion reddish-brown and a little florid. The jaws were powerful. The eyes were large and brown—shining, piercing, probing. The hands were indeed highly expressive. He had a peculiar way of standing, observing or in conversation, with chin thrust forward and head hunched. The voice was normally quiet and contained, the accent neutral—if anything, educated Australian rather than educated English.

His charm was powerful and his manner highly courteous. He was socially unassertive, seeming at first reserved and dignified. But all say he was warm, genial, homely, unassuming, approachable, human, decent, gentle—perhaps a little gruff at first until a cheery smile set the nervous at ease—modest in bearing, not condescending in manner. He gave an impression of simplicity. He was a good listener who did not interrupt or dominate a conversation, was skilled at leading people to talk on their areas of special ability, ready to discuss matters with those inferior in knowledge. He displayed no false humility, did not lay down the law but argued his cases. He was considerate to his drivers, to reporters, and to the young. Minor encounters are revealing. A former sergeant talking to him at a Canberra function was brushed aside by a bigwig; as soon as possible Monash broke off, 'like the thorough gentleman he was', to resume the conversation. The Western Australian journalist and politician, Sir John Kirwan, recalled meeting him on a train, not knowing who he was; with gentlemanly reticence they did not introduce themselves but conversed pleasantly for hours without mention of the war. Only next day at the Canberra Hotel did Kirwan realize who his companion had been.

At the same time, on formal occasions he expected punctilious respect to be paid to him and his office of the moment. Ernest Scott wrote to his wife from Perth in 1926, describing a Government House party at which Monash, as retiring president of the science congress, fretted because the governor did not seek him out:

> It is astonishing that a man of John Monash's quality should be so sensitive about recognition by people who, as persons, are so clearly inferior to him. But I believe that some deliberate slights have been put upon him, and he is apt to sniff deliberation in any apparent failure to notice him when he has all his stars and ribbons on.

But if as a double outsider Monash was always sensitive to a possible slight, there were few who decried him on these grounds. It was impossible for him entirely to forget the disadvantages of his origins: he enjoyed his popularity and sense of achievement all the more.

His contemporaries struggled to define where precisely his greatness lay. H. I. Cohen explained the 'magnetism of his personality' as the product of a 'rare alliance of great force of intellect with great power of character'. Scott singled out his 'sharp, decisive coming to the point, and his way of illuminating the matter under discussion with a flood of accurate knowledge and the clearest of understanding', together with 'his extreme gentleness and his beautiful courtesy'. Similarly, his colleagues in the Institution of Engineers recalled especially his 'remarkable clarity of expression and his faculty for eliminating the non-essentials in any problem brought before him', his 'wonderful memory', approachability, and 'his invariable tact, courtesy, and kindness'.

An extraordinary range of contemporaries revered him. The entrepreneur W. S. Robinson, sharpest of men, was proud of his friendship with 'the greatest fighting man Australia has produced', with a great Jew, acquisitive—for knowledge of every kind. John Curtin acknowledged him as 'Australia's greatest military genius'. Sir Robert Menzies recalled his 'immense virtuosity', his 'utter integrity of mind and force of personality which conveyed with everything that he said the stamp of truth and of conviction'. He was 'the greatest advocate I ever listened to'. C. J. Dennis admired no living Australian more. Walter Murdoch, from personal knowledge, 'had a great admiration for him as a man'. Arthur Streeton judged he was 'undoubtedly the greatest brain in Australia, and enclosed within such a simple, sincere nature almost hiding his great gifts: as though he had been just one of us, an ordinary citizen'; and he ranked him among his contemporaries with Smuts and Einstein. His S.E.C. colleague Herman simply described him as 'the ablest, biggest-minded and biggest-hearted man I have ever known'.

Eric Simonson, his nephew and aide, in 1939 wrote for broadcasting a lengthy estimate of the man, which though eulogistic was acute. Of his character he said:

> He always remained a student, and in the spirit of the student and of the experienced man of affairs, he had a quietism that, in general, pervaded his thoughts and his actions. He was without caprice. In deliberation and in counsel he had a calm serenity and a patience that was impressive. He listened to the opinion of others, at all times with a complete courtesy. Faced with pompous ignorance, he was curt; with deceit, he was brusque, but to honest endeavour, lacking in knowledge, as with the young he was patient and encouraging. By the asking of pertinent questions he often led others to clarify their own ideas. To all men he was just. In everything his decision

was incisive and firm.... He ruled his own life by reason, and with Socratic wisdom he led others to do the same. Faced with opposition, he sought its basis; standing firm or compromising as expedience suggested or circumstances dictated.... He developed an uncanny faculty of sensing when others might be in difficulties and of the best way of helping or of strengthening them when they required it.... His integrity was instinctive and unassailable.... His simple sanity, his obvious sagacity and his disinterested firmness won him respect, loyalty, admiration and affection.

If Monash was a genius it was his 'infinite capacity for taking pains' which made him so. He was not a polymath, but a man of very broad knowledge; he himself always denied that his mental endowment was unusual. None of his learning was profound. His mathematics were not brilliant; his engineering was sound and wide-ranging but he had little opportunity to show great distinction; his practice of law was limited to minor specialisms; his knowledge of literature and music was wide but did not run deep; he wrote very well indeed, but not superlatively. Even as a soldier he never had opportunity to excel at the highest level of generalship. He did not have a powerfully original mind.

He achieved greatness, essentially as an administrator, by cultivating to a super-pitch of excellence the ordinary talents and virtues: a retentive memory, energy and capacity for hard work, concentration, orderliness, common sense, power of logical analysis, attention to detail, fine judgement—and a temperament and constitution which enabled him always to work harmoniously with colleagues and to stand heavy strain. Associates like Josh Anderson and McCay may have been more brilliant but fell far behind because they lacked his stability.

Monash's own view of what made for success was quite clear: it was a matter primarily of concentration, of study and hard work, not genius. One must be thorough master of one's self, know one's own mind and be courageous enough to formulate what one wants. Character, personality and the capacity to inspire were necessary: pick the right men and impress your views on them. Be indifferent to praise or blame, admit it when you are wrong; yet be confident enough to carry on independently of criticism. Those who played to the gallery or lost heart in the face of criticism were useless. Of all studies, logic and law gave the best training. Studying while young to understand and practise clear and accurate thinking should be part of everyone's education. Of all legal studies, the law of evidence was the most useful, but constitutional law and legal history also built strong foundations. The study and practice of engineering had taught him precision, the study of law essentially how to marshal facts.

When asked how he found 'time for everyone and everything',

Monash usually answered: 'By rigid adherence to method and routine'. He used to rebuke those who refused tasks because they were too busy: 'You can always find time to do one thing more'. Planning was everything. At the close of the day's work at the S.E.C. and last thing at night he would make his agenda for the morrow, major and trivial tasks both. Every task undertaken was carried through to completion if possible, and the document or calculation checked. 'A statement written, it was invariably re-read, the tees were crossed and the i's were dotted. Obscurities and ambiguities were searched for and eliminated, all loose ends were tightened.' Each day was time-tabled, rigidly but for a few minutes allowed for making up leeway or for relaxation. He had, supremely, the gift of turning instantly from one task to the next. Planning, once the main purpose had been settled, extended to the smallest detail. Unpunctuality by others, who upset his time-table, distressed him; he was constantly checking his watch. The telephone was for business, not chatter. Although he was obsessive in his record-keeping, his habits stopped short of the neurotic and were turned to good account in his meticulously detailed conduct of all his military and business affairs.

The staggering amount of work he got through can be explained only on the assumption that he gave little more than half his working time to the S.E.C. No one in Australia's history, perhaps, has crammed so much work, and so much effective work, into a life. Yet he did not normally work more than a 60-hour week; he had become very clever at making regular time for his grandchildren, his private records, reading, the theatre, the garden and other hobbies, and for Lizette. Work was the best thing in life, he often said. He had early acquired the habit, it alleviated his early professional and marital disappointments, and when he began to make his mark it gave abiding satisfaction in demonstrating his sheer capacity. In his last decade without necessary contradiction he would continue to accept responsibilities both as a means of repaying his debt to the community which had made him great and in order to sustain the sense of his own distinction. Yet his work by no means excluded other aspects of life and was not a drastic solace for that quiet desperation which perhaps the mass of men and women feel: he enjoyed what leisure he had, even though he filled much of it with a kind of private work, and did not often feel that his remaining time was only a matter of enduring a crazy world.

Almost his greatest gift was to be a teacher. His clarity of mind and of exposition was his strength above all others. To define the heart of a problem and reduce it to the simplest terms was his central quality of leadership: 'With a breath he blew away the chaff'. In his early days of teaching his sisters and coaching, he had learned patience and the ability to translate technicalities to the simplest possible terms.

Monash seems to have made few enemies. Apart from some military associates like Bean and Gellibrand who had reservations about his qualities as a soldier and as a man, and McInerney and Ozanne and their friends, hardly anyone in the last two decades of his life emerges as a hostile critic. Eggleston was one: he did not like Monash and, while recognizing his ability, left several references in his private papers to his 'ruthless egotism' and also accused him of intellectual dishonesty. (There may be simple reasons for the dislike: Eggleston resented Monash's high-handed relationship with him as his minister, and considered he had once been rude to his wife.) The egotism was real and ruthless enough, and part of his strength. It was another aspect of his confidence in his own ability, his sensitivity to criticism, his need for recognition, the limelight, honours, and for praise, especially by women. Monash had to win and keep on winning. Yet he struggled successfully to control his drives, his ambitions were almost satisfied, he mellowed. Few traces remained of the lapses of his earlier years into self-pity. The dominant side of his nature to which nearly all attested—the honesty, the simplicity, fairness, kindliness and gentleness—had conquered the baser instincts. In his later years he no longer was impelled to establish personal dominance over an associate, by reason, charm, or mere assertiveness, except occasionally in his work. If ancient injustices still rankled, his composed front was rarely disturbed.

He could be a fairly devious man, who in minor ways was not above slightly bending the truth, elaborating on the facts, or telling only part of a story in order to promote the most favourable impression. If caught out, he could trust to his power of argument to carry conviction that there had been a misunderstanding or that he was acting for the best. This is a common human weakness. What is slightly surprising is his occasional practice of such minor deceptions in matters of insignificant importance—perhaps indicating a chronic unwillingness to admit less than perfection of achievement. Often however, they were merely 'white lies', excuses to avoid unreasonable demands on his time, or attempts to cut off futile time-wasting argument.

Two of his deviations from the truth are of special interest. One was a sustained leg-pull. Irritated by worshipping men and women who would ask 'What was the greatest moment of your life, Sir John?', he would reply: 'The day Ned Kelly told me to hold his horse in Jerilderie' or 'The day Ned Kelly gave me good advice', to which he usually added the accidental meeting of Allied war leaders on 11 August 1918. The Kelly encounter almost certainly had never happened, but he did not mind his remarks appearing in the press. (He did not necessarily sympathize with the Kellys, but he was genuinely interested in the bushrangers and ruminated over what great soldiers they might have made.) The other is rather strange. He more than once told the story, which was published, of when leaving Gallipoli on the last night he realized he had left behind his despatch-case containing his diary-letter and the evacuation orders which he was souveniring, and hurrying (or running) back a mile and a half to retrieve it. It was not true: he *had* left it behind but he had sent an aide to pick it up. Was his unnecessary retailing of the story an attempt to demonstrate that he too was a volunteer digger who would not always obey Army rules?

If it had been possible to conduct a proper survey of public opinion on who was the greatest living Australian, Monash would have won comfortably. In 1924 the Sydney journal *The Home* sought to compile a list of the seven greatest by asking the views of those prominent in journalism and the arts. Monash was included in all but one of fourteen responses and far outpolled anyone else. Without being asked to rank their choices, Desbrowe Annear, the architect, and H. H. Champion, the left-wing littérateur, nominated him as their first choice. The journalist Adam McCay described him as 'the perfect brain, endowed with a boldness, not of adventure, but founded on knowledge and faultless calculation'. In 1928 the Melbourne *Herald* set out on a similar quest for the twelve greatest living Australians. The limited number of opinions sought were unanimous only in naming Monash, Hughes and Melba in their lists. Fred Johns, editor of *Who's Who in Australia*, gave Monash the longest entry in the 1927 edition and in his *Australian Biographical Dictionary* of 1934 more space than any other of the dead.

Australia had had few national heroes. Twentieth century candidates like Mannix, Melba, Victor Trumper and Les Darcy were only sectional in appeal. No politician could span the bitter post-war divide: Hughes was probably hated more than he was loved. Monash came nearest to a hero-figure in the 1920s. The soldiers had to have a hero and, when it came to the point, there was no competitor. Whether or not Chauvel and White were comparable in generalship, neither had led the Corps, neither had a strong public image, and they were professional soldiers: the hero of a volunteer army had to be a civilian, not a 'pukka soldier'. The people had to have a hero, a representative of the warriors who, by their achievements, had made Australia a nation at last. Even the most irreverent and sceptical Australian, suspicious of all heroes or bitter about the war, was usually prepared to acknowledge the suffering and achievement of the soldiers. Perhaps the conservative Imperial-minded middle classes were more inclined to laud a supreme general than to give full credit to the rank and file. Monash was broadly acceptable to the labour movement and the working class and even to such leftist intellectuals as there were: he was an outsider who had come from nowhere, it was popularly believed that the Establishment and the conservative politicians were against him, and he didn't put on side. The public trusted him more than any politician. The popular belief formed that he was a decent unpretentious bloke. It seemed that power had not corrupted him. He was one tall poppy who was not cut down. Admittedly his fame in Victoria and Melbourne, where he was constantly in the public glare, was far greater than elsewhere. Though soldiers all over Australia, especially in Sydney, revered him, outside Victoria many people nevertheless wondered what had become of him. However, his fame and popularity seemed to grow through the 1920s. Currie and Russell, the parallel Canadian and New Zealand leaders, great soldiers who had contributed significantly to the growth of national pride, did not attract any comparable respect.

An acknowledged great man is subject constantly to being closely observed, recognized by most of those who pass in the street, gossiped about, consulted by politicians and press on grave affairs of state and on shoes and ships and sealing-wax. Much of the time he has to act a part, to accentuate a protective affability as part of a public personality, and to be stoically resigned to having to be an actor. Privacy becomes all the more important. It is also a matter of recognizing and enjoying the nonsense of it all: Monash's ironic inner eye was still usually though not always observing himself, he could see through the pretensions of power and place when he chose to, and—nearly all passion spent and ambitions achieved—his dominant agreeable outlook did not require much adjustment to the acting role.

17

A Very Tired Man
1929–1931

IN 1927 Tante Ulrike, last of the elder generation of the family, died. So next year did Field Marshal Earl Haig, Swinburne, Colonel Hall and Monash's sister-in-law Belle. John Gibson died in 1929, and in 1930 Jim McCay with whom he had walked neighbouring paths for fifty years.

In March 1929 Monash was stricken by the sudden death from a rare influenza virus of his elder grandson, John Monash Bennett—'the torch-bearer of my name'. He had only just begun at Scotch College. Monash wrote to Walter:

> No one will ever know how much I had built upon this boy. He had been my constant companion since his birth. . . . While in no sense a prodigy, he was an exceptionally talented lad, and extraordinarily lovable. . . .

He gathered the scraps of his first writings and sums, and set himself to compose a brief memoir of his life, which he could not bring himself to carry out. He endowed a school prize and provided a drinking fountain in his memory. In the following months he built an elaborate and intricate dolls' house for Betty Bennett, 'a two storey house in miniature, made to scale from working drawings . . . complete even down to electric light, bathroom fittings, and staircase'. He confessed that for months the stuffing had been knocked out of him. This family sorrow contributed to his decision to abandon his proposed tour overseas. But there was solace in the birth in August of another grandson, John Colin Monash Bennett.

That winter he was delighted to welcome his niece Nancy Rosenhain on an extended visit. She was a talented exponent of Dalcroze eurhythmic dancing; he introduced her to Education Department officials and presided at a demonstration. Nancy stayed in Melbourne until early 1931 when her elder sister Mona died—not yet thirty—and she returned to England. Mona's death was another bitter blow. Meanwhile he had been teaching six-year-old David running writing, simple sums, the order of the months and their number of days, the vowels and consonants, the oceans and continents and the alphabet in reverse. He also showed Charlie Chaplin films to David and Betty.

Monash was now very tender to old friends. He wrote to Billie (Card) Bowater in California, recalling how often they had danced together, and asked her to reply soon. He was glad to meet Vida Goldstein again when she interviewed him for the *Christian Science Monitor*. He sent a message to William Elliott, if still alive: 'Give him my very kindest regards and tell him that I keep very green the memory of my boyhood in Jerilderie'. In December 1929 he made a few notes for the memoirs he intended to write.

The Depression hit a man like Monash hard in that the engineer, as the agent of progress, was so nullified. The S.E.C. was not so very badly hit, but professionally and personally he was highly exposed to cases of distress. He became treasurer of an R.S.L. appeal for unemployed diggers, but confessed he was 'quite at a loss to know how to deal with' the innumerable individual pleas for employment. He had no solution except that of the orthodox financiers: it was quite beyond the power of the country to maintain the workingman's standard of living. Casting around desperately, J. E. Fenton, acting prime minister during J. H. Scullin's absence in Britain, invited Monash to a secret meeting with members of the government and sent members of the Development and Migration Commission to consult him. He advised them that it was urgent to reduce the basic wage and pensions in line with the fall in the cost of living.

About August 1930 Monash drew up a plan for personal economies which indicates how panicky he had become and that he was even recalling the long striving for financial security by his grandfather and father: surely he would not, after all, end his life little better off than they had been? His income had declined from £5360 in 1929–30 to £4336 in 1930–31. He had no superannuation, but had given to his daughter his life assurance policies which were about to mature. He was facing a cut in salary and his tax on income had risen to almost £1000. He planned extreme reductions in expenditure for the year of £1468. Substantial economies could be made in spending on furniture, clothing, wine, and even tobacco, on private presents and on charity; he cancelled subscriptions to a dozen societies.

The Hogan Labor ministry was determined that the judges and the highest-paid functionaries like Clapp and Monash be seen to suffer more substantial reductions in salary than the general 10 per cent wage reduction. Monash and the Commission acknowledged that 10 per cent was reasonable but 20 per cent would be 'savage and vindictive', and it also involved the S.E.C.'s independence. Moreover in Monash's view it was bound in with the broken promise to raise his salary, once profitability had been assured, and with the Commonwealth's failure to display any practical gratitude for his services. The pity of it was that he came to regard Hogan as an enemy. He determined to fight the matter politically and was in close touch with Nationalist politicians. He pleaded that his negotiation of the purchase of the Melbourne Electric Supply Co. had profited the State by nearly £700 000 and that his salary was irrelevant to the budget. The government gave way to the Legislative Council for the moment, but in 1931 passed legislation imposing a 27 per cent salary cut on S.E.C. Commissioners and others. By then, however, Monash had realized that his financial position was secure enough.

In November 1929 Birdwood, who had long looked forward to the honour, was rumoured as likely to be the next governor-general. According to Sir Robert Garran (no other evidence has come to light) in the following February or March the Scullin Labor cabinet considered Isaacs and Monash for the appointment and chose the former. It seems that Monash had not been sounded out. If he ever considered the matter, he could not have taken it seriously: he was not married and had a breath of scandal about him. Late in March the *Herald* and *Sun* tipped the chief justice of the High Court, Sir Adrian Knox, and mentioned Monash and Chauvel among other possibilities. When eventually Scullin had won his long battle with King George V to have Isaacs accepted (Birdwood being the Palace candidate), Monash wrote to tell Isaacs how greatly he rejoiced at 'this culmination of a great career.

Two most welcome honours were bestowed, the highest his profession could offer. In December 1929 the Institution of Engineers, Australia, awarded Monash the Peter Nicol Russell Memorial Medal; the presentation was broadcast over a national link-up. And in June 1931 he was awarded the Kernot Memorial Medal—recompense indeed for the effort he had made in providing for it over many years.

On Armistice Day 1929 Scullin announced the promotion of Monash and Chauvel to the rank of general. Chauvel was about to retire as chief of the general staff and inspector-general. Monash explained to a friend that his own promotion had

> been urged upon every Commonwealth Government since the Armistice, but each Government [had] declined to take action for fear of its political inexpediency in relation to its then Opposition. It remained for the present Labour Government, immediately on taking office, to brush aside questions of political expediency in favour of the discharge by the Commonwealth of its undoubted obligation to Chauvel and myself.

Letters and telegrams of congratulations poured in. Promotion of

Monash and Chauvel to field marshal had first been recommended by an anonymous senior officer in a letter to the *Age* in 1928. Some R.S.L. sub-branches and at least one politician in 1930 agitated for this further promotion for Monash, but the campaign never quite took off. He replied to one supporter: 'It has been the rule of my life never actively to seek any preferment in any direction whatsoever. All my advancement in my career—both civil and military—has come to me entirely unsought'. He was deceiving himself to some extent, but he was broadly correct: though he had firmly pressed his rights, he had not, since his younger days, crawled to his superior officers or sought to use political influence, as many of his military colleagues had.

Monash was touched when Scullin wrote to him on the eve of his sixty-fifth birthday and retirement from the active list: 'Your letter is the very first of its kind sent to me by any previous Prime Minister, either in his personal or representative capacity'. Scullin also allowed him to remain on the Council of Defence. When the Labor government had abolished compulsory military training Monash and White had jointly asked Scullin to make it clear that the Council of Defence had not been consulted. During the current hard times Monash considered it useless to make a public protest; the only thing to do was to help to re-create the volunteer militia. The Council of Defence was eventually summoned to advise and Monash and White had some success in retaining essential elements of military organization. Monash supported the League of Nations disarmament conference of 1931 and the Women's International League for Peace and Freedom's Disarmament Declaration.

In November 1928 he had declined the federal presidency of the R.S.L. Subsequently three State branches approached him again. Dyett was widely unpopular, but even when the New South Wales president told Monash that 'universally the returned soldiers have looked up to you as "the father of the A.I.F." ', he replied that he had the highest opinion of Dyett. He would still have liked the honour and to have fought for R.S.L. objectives, but he did not have the time, he was too old, and didn't want to be merely a figure-head. In 1931 he again suffered embarrassing public and private entreaties from Perth to stand for the presidency, and told the Western Australian president that he was 'a very tired man', that the league had preferred to manage its affairs without interference from the 'brass hats', and that he had regarded the matter as closed years before.

In February 1930 Monash let it be known that he would not march again on Anzac Day, for last time it had stressed him 'very seriously, both physically and psychologically'; he would retain nominal command but take a car to the saluting base. A few weeks later he changed his mind. Blamey had offered him a horse, but he would not ride, as other senior officers did, since it would only indicate to the politicians that he was too old for his job. So he marched again and 'finished the day in a thoroughly exhausted and nervous condition'. The stress was increased by a reunion next day of the soldier members of the Commercial Travellers' Association, at which he spoke unusually emotionally. In 1931 he rode for the first time, and the theme of his address in the Exhibition Building again was that the surest way for the Australian people to lift themselves out of their troubles was to emulate the comradeship of the A.I.F.

In March–April 1930 he for once made a serious misjudgement. *Smith's Weekly* persuaded him to agree to publish a series of articles under his name, defending the digger from attacks in various war books. Monash got on well with the journalist, Eric Baume, during two long interviews. He perhaps saw it as an opportunity to humanize himself to the diggers and reinforce his popularity—or perhaps simply to try to convey his respect and affection. The result was disastrous—vulgar bombast in the *Smith's* style, even though Monash had considerably toned down Baume's drafts. No doubt he had been as busy as usual, but he miscalculated in not vetoing the articles. *Smith's* exaggerated the impact by sensational headings and illustrations. Monash did indeed receive many grateful letters, applauding his defence of the diggers, but he also had a letter from Bean:

> If I might presume to do so, I would advise you to let it be known that the articles ... were not from your pen. I think they went down with a certain number of the more or less unthinking and less well-educated members of the A.I.F., but I could hardly tell you how many ex-soldiers and officers of the other sort have spoken to me about them and expressed themselves as puzzled or astonished that this style of thing should have come from a great commander of the A.I.F. The basis of knowledge and erudition in them was evidently so slight and the generalisations so empty, that I felt sure they were not your considered work, but what hurt more than anything was the sort of implicit assumption (though it does appeal to one class of Australian) that there was nothing worthy outside the A.I.F. ... I know very well that you do not believe this stupid, vain myth, but ... it makes one feel as though the name of the A.I.F. ... was being dragged through the mud. ... if they are read abroad they will do to our reputation the very damage which they are intended to avert. I would urge you, for the sake of your own reputation, to be cautious in your interviews with the press, and, when you do speak, to give them something that we can all feel is really worthy of your great calibre of mind and of the very great position which you occupied.
>
> ... I hope you will realize that this ... is written in the spirit of entire goodwill towards yourself, and solely from care of that

precious thing which you and I and some others have to some extent in our keeping—the great name of the A.I.F.

There was nothing to be done but to bluff his way out of it. Monash distributed a statement to senior officers, and secretaries of the R.S.L. and service clubs in each State, requesting that his 'disclaimer of the language and many of the sentiments' in the articles be made widely known. And, not to put too fine a point on it, in letters to worried friends like Bruche he lied his way out of the mess. Needled by *Truth's* jibing at an 'amazing hoax', however, *Smith's* refuted his disclaimer by printing photographs of his editorial amendments to the manuscript. Later in the year *Smith's* featured a condemnation of the Shrine of Remembrance as 'a hollow and specious monument to one man's egotism'.

The jumble of Monash's strenuous life had continued through 1930. He lobbied to have Blamey reappointed as chief commissioner of police; was at least partly responsible for the University of Melbourne granting Bean an honorary doctorate; spoke in support of a Commonwealth conversion loan (they had their backs to the wall as in 1918); read Major Douglas's book in order to find out what Douglas Credit was; refused an invitation to inquire into the South Australian railways, and brushed aside speculation in the Sydney press that he would become city administrator or controller of the northern coalfields; welcomed Amy Johnson when she flew into Melbourne; judged prize essays on 'Peace'; wired the prime minister in protest at the proposal to tax the import and sale of books; and endured a sweltering trip to Benalla where he had to make speeches and suffer many in his praise.

Monash knew very well that, as he remarked in 1926, citing the police strike and the Anzac Day march, he 'had only to put up his little finger to call the A.I.F. back to life'. But he resisted all attempts to ensnare him in secret organizations, or in the Depression years to place himself at the head of some movement to challenge or overthrow the Scullin Labor government, and always advised constitutional procedures. Yet, as with the clandestine White Guard, he must have known of the League of National Security and the Order of Silent Knights and argued with their members; many senior officers and members of the Naval and Military Club were involved.

Throughout the 1920s there had been sporadic cries that Monash and the A.I.F. would rule the country far better than the awful politicians. In 1927 two appeals came from Sydney. One group, the Imperial Patriots, saw him as a potential Mussolini. The other, the Warringah Constitutional Club, wanted him to head a political movement that would represent the diggers against the two 'big machines' of capital and labour. Less seriously, Monty Grover, the journalist, proposed his ideal form of government, under which Monash would be Organizer-General; the Chief of Imagination—someone like C. J. De Garis or Hugh D. McIntosh—would put up schemes which would have to pass the test of Monash's 'cool, business-like logic'. But there were frequent hints from old diggers: 'I hold you in great esteem as our Leader, and if you ever want a willing follower I am yours to command', wrote Colonel Field of Castlemaine in February 1929. In June that year C. Leslie Cother of East Malvern tried to interest Monash in his plan for the Knights of the Empire, a secret body governed by the Supreme Council of King Arthur, consisting of Knights (men), Squires and Men-at-arms (lads), and Pages (boys). It would be 'an effective secret service, a mobilisation of trained men for defence and an effective answer to communistic propaganda'.

In 1930, as the Depression deepened, the pleas became more urgent. Monash was called on to lead an Empire Loyalty League to combat the 'foreign-Irish-Catholic' attempt to impose an Australian governor-general. A Miss Sadleir-Forster pestered him to become Dictator— 'Napoleon, Mussolini, Yourself!' A Hobart priest telegraphed: 'Assume dictatorship do not fear save Australia as Mussolini saved Italy'. A speaker at an Adelaide Rotary lunch brought down the house when he recounted:

> I had a dream the other night. It seemed that the returned soldiers, with Sir John Monash at their head, were in control of the government of Australia and were to be there for five years. All State and Federal politicians had been paid off. Then I woke up and found it was only a dream. I said "Damn".

More ominously, 'Old Digger' wrote to the *Bulletin*:

> There is only one man who can save Australia, and that is John Monash. . . . Put Australia under semi-military rule. . . . General Monash is one of the greatest organisers the world has ever seen, and with the advice of financiers, backed up by drumhead court-martials, he would save Australia within three years.

These were unimportant manifestations. But an approach by the prominent businessman Robert Knox, Kingsley Henderson the architect, and L. N. Roach of Bank House in November 1930, on behalf of 'certain gentlemen', was much more serious. Monash and Sir Robert Gibson were being asked to lead some kind of movement. Supported by Gibson, Monash replied:

> as a public officer, I should feel myself absolutely precluded from any public action or any public declaration of my views which could conceivably place me in antagonism with any section of public opinion and by doing so would jeopardise the important public

interests committed to our respective charges. [Moreover] the strenuous work which I have had to undertake during the last 16 years has greatly sapped my vigour and mental elasticity and has, to a large extent, destroyed my capacity for assuming at my time of life very grave and far-reaching public responsibilities beyond those which I at present carry.

Knox and Henderson were prominent in January in arranging for the subversion of Joe Lyons, the Labor minister who became United Australia Party prime minister.*

When in December 1930 Monash accepted the government's invitation to represent Australia at the Durbar for the opening of New Delhi, the right wing suspected a plot to get him out of the way. Major-General Grimwade wrote: 'My friends ... view your selection very gravely, and think there are sinister motives behind it'. Monash replied that the requests to him not to leave Australia had totally different and contradictory objectives.

> One group consider that I should remain in Australia for the purpose, in the near future, of leading a revolution, to constitute myself Dictator, and oust the present constitutional system, including Vice-Regal representatives, etc. etc. This is, of course, merely hot air. If ever the time should come that an English-speaking community alters its system of government and abandons the present democracy, I feel convinced that this would come about by constitutional means and not by the methods of violence so familiar in Latin countries.
>
> The other group of people want me to stay here in order to suppress the revolution which they evidently expect will be instigated by the communists and red-raggers. In other words, they want me to be here in order to uphold the present constitutional system of government, which is the direct antithesis of what the other group are clamouring for.
>
> As to this, I am inclined greatly to discount the existence of any serious danger of an upheaval. . . .
>
> To suggest that the Commonwealth Government made this appointment in order to get me out of the country is, of course, sheer nonsense.

A man from Sydney, H. C. Swain, flew down to urge him not to go, and later wrote:

> *you* and *you alone* in possessing the qualifications and the earnest respect of all decent members of the community, could save Australia from the disastrous economic and social calamity impend-

---

* Monash mysteriously entered in his diary, 12/1/31: 'Record warning. 1. A rash policy. 2. War Record. 3. Jew'.

ing. . . . Obviously an immediate change in form of Government is essential. . . . My services are at your disposal.

Monash sent a bare acknowledgement. A day or so later he had a letter from C. Barclay Smith:

A number of Sydney business men, who sit among the ruins of their businesses, view your departure for India with great misgiving. . . . Your name is on the lips of every sane man in this State. . . . For God's sake, Sir John, abandon all idea of leaving your country when it needs you most.

This time he blew up:

What do you and your friends want me to do? To lead a movement to upset the Constitution, oust the jurisdiction of Parliament, and usurp the governmental power? If so, I have no ambition to embark on High Treason, which any such action would amount to.

What would you say if a similar proposal were made by the Communists and Socialists to seize political power for the benefit of the proletariat and the extinction of the bourgeoisie, as they have done in Russia? Would you not call that Revolution and Treason to the Crown and Constitution?

Depend upon it, the only hope for Australia is the ballot-box, and an educated electorate. You and your people should get busy and form an organization as efficient, as widespread, and as powerful as that of the Labor Party. . . .

If it be true that many people in Sydney are prepared to trust to my leadership, they should be prepared also to trust my judgement.

Representing Australia at New Delhi was the kind of official occasion Monash much enjoyed, India would be highly interesting and he badly needed a long break. He was restored to the active list and Keith Officer of the Prime Minister's Department briefed him and supplied him with official reading. F. J. McKenna of the Prime Minister's Department was appointed as his secretary. Someone warned Monash over the phone that Gandhi had ordered him to be poisoned.

A large crowd saw him off at Spencer Street station on 14 January 1931. He sailed from Adelaide; Lizette, with a friend, was on board and was to accompany him throughout, except to official functions—and of course she was not officially accommodated. In Perth, Hobbs, Jess, C. P. Smith and other old associates met him and saw him through a civic reception where he had to endure eight speeches before replying; they moved on to an R.S.L. lunch. The voyage across the Indian Ocean was peaceful and Monash was drowsy much of the way. After two days at Government House, Bombay, he had three days at Agra where he responded conventionally to the Taj Mahal by moonlight. The holy city of Benares was anything but pleasant: the palace was tawdry and its officers uncouth; the temples and priests made a 'disgusting spectacle'; the idolatry, the filth, the stench displayed 'civilisation at its lowest'. 'There is nothing beautiful or artistic about a Hindu temple, so unlike the noble mosques of the Mohammedans.' At New Delhi he stayed for six days in the Viceroy's palace with Lord and Lady Irwin, in company with Currie from Canada and other Empire representatives. Next day he did his job, making a pithy speech at the opening of the Dominion columns. The Viceroy took him for a long walk to discuss grave Imperial matters; Sir Edwin Lutyens, the great architect, turned out to be an 'elderly buffoon', but Monash was overwhelmed by the grandeur of his creation.

He moved on to the north-west frontier and had a 'wonderful day' being conducted through the Khyber Pass, without attention from snipers, and stepping over the Afghan border. He enjoyed meeting the senior officers, including Colonel Wylly, his old 3rd Division staffer; they were honoured to entertain a great soldier. The Government of India insisted that he extend his tour, so he had two additional weeks in the south; the comfortable trains helped him to endure the clammy heat. Again there were great contrasts, as between the Nizam of Hyderabad, a 'dirty little miser', and the eminent Maharajah of Mysore, whom he described vividly. Mysore was 'an eye-opener', a wonderful city and state, 'a proof that the Indians are fully capable of modern government by a benevolent bureaucracy for the benefit of the people as a whole, both urban and rural. . . . There is an air of culture, art and refinement everywhere'. He proceeded through Madras to Ceylon, spending five days cooling off in the hills, and sailed for home on 21 March.

As usual Monash had made his work-associate a good friend—in this case a quite intimate one. McKenna was an experienced and sophisticated public servant, and a devout Catholic. Monash was royally treated everywhere, McKenna recalled, but he remained 'very simple and unpretentious, and noticeably courteous to everyone'. A few months later he wrote no ordinary obituary:

> Could one resist a personality at once so strong and forceful, yet so simple and lovable; a man whose humility and modesty combined with a strength of character almost colossal made him dear to all who knew him? His broad-minded, tolerant and fearless outlook . . . giant intellect . . . total disregard for self-interest. . . .

He recalled him making a gift of sufficient money to an enthusiastic guide to see him through his medical course. When they got home, McKenna sent him a recording of a song in which Monash had delighted, 'Barnacle Bill the Sailor'.

On arrival home on 5 April Monash reported his impressions of India in at least eight talks to clubs and societies, as well as in the press. He was sensibly cautious: his impressions were necessarily superficial, there were 'a thousand Indias'. He stressed to Officer the interest of having been there just when Gandhi had been released from gaol and a truce had been arranged with the Viceroy; the opposition of the provincial governments to the Viceroy's conciliatory policy, and the fierce attitude of Englishwomen especially; the relative absence of Indian notabilities at vice-regal functions; the spirited participation of the Delhi populace in the celebrations; and the unnecessary display of force by the Army on the frontier. In his public utterances he tended to be pessimistic, though interlacing comments of praise and wonder. 'The whole thing was in a terrible mess, and how the problems could be satisfactorily solved was beyond his comprehension.' He was not sure that Gandhi was not a humbug. 'Everything in social life and religion tends to *degeneracy* of man and beast.' Home Rule had to be opposed, it was premature: a potential enemy on Australia's trade route could not be tolerated. Yet his Indian experiences had moved and disturbed him.

On his return late in March, speakers at a civic reception in Perth had encouraged him to save the nation. Monash replied that 'he had no desire whatever to upset the position of the constitution of Australia and find himself up against a brick wall'. He may not fully have known that in February the inchoate movement for handing Australia over to him, in the *Bulletin* and elsewhere, had peaked. One Melbourne correspondent to the *Herald* had called for an 'emergency governing body' of Monash, Gibson and Lyons; Arthur Streeton recommended a take-over by men like Monash, Gibson, Clapp, Sidney Myer and Blamey, and putting politicians on the land. To J. M. Prentice, a prominent Sydney journalist and radio commentator, Monash was 'the one man in Australia . . . I could have accepted and gladly served under . . . as a DICTATOR'. A militant member of the Flying Corps Association in Western Australia recommended that 'several thousand picked Australian ex-soldiers should take Canberra, overthrow Parliament, and establish a dictatorship under General Monash'. The appeals died away in 1931, although the Scullin government was still staggering on. In New South Wales at least, the New Guard had organized to a point far beyond vague hopes of a leader like Monash taking over. It was now known he was no Hindenburg, devoted to saving his country. But he was the only national figure who could have played such a role.

Photographs of him in 1931 display his tiredness and ageing. Since mid-1929 his doctors' warnings, especially about his blood pressure, had become urgent. He had taken only a little notice and did not much reduce his speaking and other outside engagements, though in 1930 he again reduced his weight by a stone. There were signs that he was beginning to fail, such as the *Smith's* episode; and when in December 1930 he sent Rosenthal a brief outline of his life for use in a projected biographical study of war leaders, his memory, especially for dates, was uncertain. Three months absence from the S.E.C. produced a heavy backlog of work. Nellie Melba and Annie Gabriel had died in February; 'Pompey' Elliott had suicided in March. Late in May Monash

> began to notice a disposition—steadily getting worse—to fatigue under quite moderate physical exertion—such as after a walk of a mile or so, or pottering about in my workshop, or climbing stairs and the like. I was soon out of breath and puffing, and would have to lie down feeling more or less exhausted. [Sewell] speedily diagnosed the *immediate* cause of this, as irregularity of heart action, some dilation, and some valvular leakage. He prescribed digitalis and stimulating massage, and periodical detailed examinations.

He drastically reduced his engagements, rested much more and did not hold his 8th of August dinner but, among other commitments, he was guest of honour and speaker at the opening of the new Kernot Engineering school at the Working Men's College and was examining a doctoral thesis in Engineering. He saw Sewell on 20 August and Sewell and Sir Richard Stawell together on the 28th, and on 1 September wrote to Walter:

> I feel it my duty to advise you and Lou of certain developments in regard to my health, which may, possibly, preclude my writing to you again. . . . a sense of duty impels me to write now, while I am able to do so.

After detailing his heart condition he went on to say that his doctors had grave suspicions that he had a growth in the abdomen, but that they would not operate because his heart was not sound enough.

> This has caused me to do all in my power to put my affairs in order. . . . I feel, of course, rather cast down. I have still much work that I should . . . enjoy doing, but I feel that I ought to shape my course to be ready for any emergency.
>   Love to you both and to Nancy and Peggy
>   Yours affectionately
>   John Monash

He continued to carry out his S.E.C. duties, though he made a bee-line for home every evening. He had two pleasant sunny days at Yallourn and told Sewell that he was daily feeling better.

On 29 August he had written a memo for himself, headed 'Emergency Action'. It was a two-stage list of papers to be burned—first, erotica and a packet entitled 'A closed chapter' (possibly Annie's letters), and second, mainly Lizzie's letters.

He attended the University council meeting on 7 September and chaired the Shrine committee on the 11th; every agenda item was ticked through. He was at the Beefsteaks' dinner on the 12th; Tate quoted Henry V's rallying speech before Harfleur—Monash looked it up and had a copy typed. He took a cutting from the *Argus* which discussed the frequency of high blood pressure as the 'price of success'. He ordered copies of *Straight and Crooked Thinking* by Thouless and Angela Thirkell's first book. He probably did not go to synagogue on the Day of Atonement. Two days later, on the 23rd, he attended the 6th Battalion reunion and spoke briefly:

> I came to you tonight, not only because I love to be with you again, but because I feel that I will never attend another reunion. . . .
>
> One bitter regret, as the closing period of one's life draws near, is that although the spirit of patriotism has not perished among the community, political and governmental authorities offer so little stimulus to the young men of today to follow the example of those of the past generation.

He wrote his last letters on the 28th and 29th. He told Sir Arthur Robinson he would not be able to keep a speaking engagement in mid-October; the slightest physical or mental stress was prostrating him. He apologized to Coxen for not having been able to attend his retirement function. He arranged to dispatch a carcase of lamb to Walter and Lou for Christmas and sent a cheque to Mat to see her through till the end of the year.

He had a slight heart attack at Iona on the evening of the 29th and a major one three or four days later. Others followed, and pneumonia carried him off at 10.55 a.m. on 8 October. He was sixty-six. Sewell, in making his announcement to the press, said that Monash had told him he preferred to wear out than rust out, and that beyond doubt war strain had contributed largely to his death. Those close to him who mourned came to realize that it was just as well: for such a Titan to have lingered on, crippled, would have been grievous indeed. Unlike so many great Australians, he had been spared all sense of failure and frustration at the end of his career. Birdwood and all the senior Australian generals long outlived him.

The impact of his death that day was profound. Returned soldiers and the S.E.C. were in a state of shock. At Caulfield Military Hospital 'a wave of grief and consternation swept through the wards'. Federal and State parliaments adjourned after dozens of members had paid their clumsy tributes. The impact was a measure of the effects of the war on Australia and Monash's identification as the leader of the A.I.F.

Only the kindest sentiments are to be expected in obituaries and letters of condolence, but the striking aspect of the hundreds of tributes paid was the emphasis on his personal qualities rather than his achievements. Again and again people stressed his kindliness, courtesy, considerateness and fairness.

His political chief, John Cain, was eloquent: 'The history of Australia will contain no nobler record. I feel a sense of great personal loss, ... especially as he passed away in the full vigour of his amazing and versatile faculties. His life was an inspiration; his death leaves us with a sense of irretrievable loss'. His comrade Julius Bruche summed him up as 'a genius who was singularly tolerant and broadminded, bore no malice, and always looked for the good in everything'. Bruche had just been appointed chief of the general staff and was looking forward to consulting Monash: almost his first duty on arrival in Melbourne was to be a pallbearer. Frank Tate wrote: 'I shall always think of him as supremely able in whatever he undertook, and, as a man and a friend, a simple sincere soul'. The Seymour branch of the R.S.L. doubted 'if any General at any time has ever been so near and dear to the hearts of his men'. His son-in-law remembered above all 'his love of children, his simplicity and his gentleness—for his was the gentlest soul that I have ever known. ... This man was very human, and, therefore, not without fault, but [his] overwhelming gentleness placed him amongst those who light a beacon fire for us poor mortals to look up to'. Gladstone's eulogy on the death of Wellington was quoted in the press. So was Tennyson's verse on the same occasion:

> Mourn for the man of amplest influence,
> Yet clearest of ambitious crime,
> Our greatest yet with least pretence,
> Great in council and great in war,
> Foremost captain of his time,
> Rich in saving common-sense,
> And, as the greatest only are,
> In his simplicity sublime.

In Sydney Rabbi Cohen preached on the text: 'Know ye not that there is a prince and a great man fallen this day in Israel?' Years later, most appropriately of all, Rabbi Danglow quoted Carlyle on Napoleon:

> He had a certain instinctive and ineradicable feeling for reality and did base himself upon fact. He saw through all entanglements the practical heart of a matter. He drove straight towards that. He had an eye to see and a soul to dare and do.

C. J. Dennis, Enid Derham and Alan Moyle wrote funerary poems (which are best not revived). And, having just received his warning letter, his sister Lou remarked that it was 'written by a brave and courageous man, who never I think shirked an unpleasant job in his life'.

The funeral was the most impressive and largely attended Australia had known. If the King had died, he could not have been shown more respect than that given to the boy from Richmond and Jerilderie of Jewish-Prussian parentage. The Commonwealth arranged a state funeral on Sunday the 11th. A move to have him buried at the Shrine was thwarted, for he had said, 'The Shrine should be no man's tomb'. The body lay in state, with a military guard, in the Queen's Hall, Parliament House, from 5 p.m. on Friday the 9th. Hour after hour a steady stream shuffled in and around the bier, including many wounded diggers and bereaved wives and mothers, leaving their wreaths or bunches of home-grown flowers. 'Comrade and friend, farewell', was the message from the boys at Caulfield. Till 3 in the morning they came, 'workers whose duties held them late in the city; police from their beats; solitary figures who might be kinsmen of soldiers lost. . . .' At 7 a tramwayman headed the queue of workingmen, followed by many young shop assistants. By mid-morning there were

> City business men. Clerks and assistants. The squatter and the farmer. The wife of the rich. The wife of the poor. Elegance and beauty of dress. Sombreness and shabbiness. Many folk of the Jewish race. Returned soldiers. Police constables. Members of the Salvation Army. Schoolboys and schoolgirls. Parents and little children.

There was mourning in the synagogues. That afternoon at the football grand final between Richmond and Geelong the teams, wearing black armbands, lined up and, as not always on such occasions, the crowd of sixty thousand observed a 'remarkable hush'. Many cricket matches were abandoned.

At 12.30 on Sunday Rabbi Danglow conducted a private service in the Queen's Hall; Chauvel gave the address. The body was carried down the steps and placed on the gun-carriage. For nearly an hour, in grey chilly weather, some fifteen thousand returned soldiers, sailors, airmen and nurses marched past. About 2 the procession began— returned soldiers leading; the official military escort, detachments of the Scotch College Cadet Corps and the Melbourne University Rifles; the gun-carriage, farewelled by the plaintive chants of the rabbis. Monash's charger followed, boots reversed in the stirrups; then, on foot, chief mourners, general officers, representatives of the governor-general, governor and Federal and State governments. Outside the Windsor Hotel, Lizette was grieving uncontrollably. Right, round the corner into Collins Street, the opposite route to Anzac Day's, to the mournful beat of muffled drums, the tinkling of medals distinct in the hush, returned men and soldiers awkwardly tried to master the slow march, between the pressing crowds. Never, perhaps, had Melbourne seen so many flags, at half-mast but stiff in the breeze. Down beautiful old Collins Street in leafy spring, past the Naval and Military (the old German) Club, left into Swanston Street opposite the Town Hall, scene of so many balls, receptions, University council meetings and confrontations with the civic fathers. Approaching St Paul's the M.U.R. band broke into 'The Dead March in Saul'. Past Flinders Street station whence he had travelled many thousand times—home to Richmond, Hawthorn and Heyington; to Gippsland for walking tours and bridge-building; again and again to Yallourn. Over Princes Bridge which he had helped to build forty-five years before. He was departing the city, whose most famous citizen he had been. On past the bluestone Barracks where he had never been quite at home. Aero Club and R.A.A.F. Moths and Wapitis were escorting overhead. Then to the scaffolded Shrine whose dedication he had desperately wanted to live to hear. The official escort and the main body of ex-servicemen turned off for a service at which Chauvel, G. W. Holland of the R.S.L. and 'Fighting Mac', Chaplain McKenzie of the Salvation Army, gave addresses; 'Lead Kindly Light', 'Nearer my God' and 'Oh God our Help in Ages Past' were sung.

The cortège moved on down St Kilda Road followed by hundreds of cars and thousands walking, determined to follow all the nine miles to Brighton cemetery. The crowd remained deep; blinds on the route were drawn. At Gardenvale another naval and military escort joined. A huge assemblage was waiting on North Road, as minute-guns sounded out. Eight Jewish ex-servicemen carried the coffin to the chapel where Rabbis Danglow and Brodie conducted the first part of the service. Later, as the body was lowered to the grave, next to his wife, the Last Post sounded, followed by a 17-gun salute and the Reveille. The police estimated that the crowd had numbered 300 000, 250 000 at least;* fifty thousand had been at Brighton. The funeral had been broadcast. Services and ceremonies were held all over Australia and in London at Hampstead synagogue; that Sunday afternoon at the University of Sydney hundreds of people stood bareheaded as Chopin's Funeral March rang out from the war memorial carillon. In the following days patriots objected to the inappropriate Union Jack shrouding the coffin and flying over Parliament House. The *Age*'s special writer found a Kipling association: Monash had 'acquired an extraordinary Imperial prestige without favor and without fawning. [There had been] unfathomable respect to one who had talked with crowds and kept his virtue; had walked with kings nor lost the common touch'.

* The estimate for Field Marshal Blamey's funeral, twenty years later, was also about 300 000.

In the following week, of all the eulogies at various commemorations, two stand out. Addressing Melbourne Legacy, Brudenell White said:

> His ambition . . . was certainly not a predominant factor in his career although it had its influence. Sir John was a simple man and to my mind his simplicity was his most marked and perhaps his most charming characteristic. Had you asked him from what sources he rceived most gratification—from tasks well fulfilled, from honour, from power, from pride of place or from the plaudits of the crowd, I think he would have replied that from all these he received less pleasure than from the greeting at the end of the day accorded him by a devoted grandchild. . . . There seems to be for us a great lesson in this simplicity which we will do well to take to heart. . . .
>
> Ambition, of course, he possessed but the ambition which seeks power, authority or riches is scarcely worth the name. The only ambition for which I have any regard is that which comes from an impelling will to make a job of any task undertaken. That is the ambition which your patron had in a marked degree. Any task which he essayed had perforce, by reason of the character of the man, to be performed in a completely effective manner. . . .
>
> . . . the three great contributors to success will be found to be integrity, even-mindedness or wisdom, and untiring industry. [To these qualities] he himself would have ascribed most of his achievement. Apart from his right mindedness which was natural, he possessed a calmness of judgment and a tolerance which made reference for his advice a pleasure. . . .
>
> With each promotion Sir John developed a greater and greater capacity for handling his fellow men and evidenced in greater degree as he advanced that firm but human touch which engenders fellowship. This is unusual and it is passing strange how the power grew with him. He realised its value too, for after his long association with it he understood that the great power behind the A.I.F. was the fellowship within it.

At Temple Beth Israel, Gershon Bennett's cousin, Henry Isaac Cohen, who over the previous decade had grown close to Monash, surpassed himself in his oration. Was there any parallel, he asked, to the way in which a great military leader won a warmer and warmer place in the hearts of his countrymen, culminating in a funeral tribute likely to remain unparalleled? He was

> patient and gentle, full of worldly wisdom, simple in his tastes, temperate in his habits; a true father in Israel. . . . He has died just as he would have wished—in harness; in the plenitude of his great mental powers; in the height of his fame; beloved of his kith and kin; with the affectionate regard of his race and people; with an

unsullied name honoured throughout the whole civilised world. . . . First in war, first in peace, first in the hearts of his Countrymen.

Numerous memorials were raised at Yallourn, Scotch College and elsewhere; eventually, in 1950, an equestrian statue near Government House gates was unveiled. Before and after his death the name was used for innumerable streets, many buildings, prizes, an Israeli communal settlement, a South Australian soldier-settlement township, a ship, a Tasmanian mountain, and eventually a Canberra suburb. And in 1958 the second Victorian university was named after him, perpetuating his name again as a household word, however ignorant staff, students and the public have been of its significance; that he was the first choice as a great Victorian Australian, before Deakin, is some indication of his surviving reputation. He would have liked the University's motto: 'Ancora Imparo'—'I am still learning'.

Annually from 1933 to 1975 a pilgrimage was made to his grave or statue. Perhaps Adam Lindsay Gordon and Henry Lawson are the only Australians to have been annually commemorated for a longer term. Soon after Monash's death Gershon Bennett laboured to bring out an edition of the war letters home: the excerpts appeared in 1934 with Cutlack, who wrote the important foreword, named as editor. In the longer term, the major assessment of Monash as a soldier was Bean's in volume 6 of the *Official History*, published in 1942. No other substantial published study was made until Smithers' military biography of 1973, although several eulogistic biographical articles, essays and pamphlets had appeared. The Jewish community has revered him as their greatest Australian and perhaps second only to Joshua as a Jewish warrior. The S.E.C. and the R.S.L. have also kept his memory green.

Otherwise Monash's name has faded from memory. No outstanding twentieth-century Australian leader—none of Deakin, Hughes, Monash, Blamey, Bruce, Curtin, Chifley, Menzies—has retained full living acknowledgement as a great man. Australians are not given to praising famous men or making legendary heroes of many other than bushrangers and sportsmen. But perhaps it was no ordinary nation which allowed Monash to lead in a time of uncommon stress.

APPENDIX I

Post-1931

A year after Monash's death a memorial to him in Yallourn Town Hall Square and a bronze tablet at Monash House, Carlton, were unveiled. Scotch College built memorial gates. The federal congress of the R.S.L. resolved to support building of a memorial in Canberra (some delegates wanted a replica in each capital) but the movement came to nothing. The Melbourne movement for a memorial, launched in December 1931, had a chequered history. It was agreed that it would take the form of an equestrian statue, but there was immediate protest against this conventional response: Russell Grimwade, supported by Daryl Lindsay, suggested instead a memorial column surmounted by a figure on a hilltop at Berwick or elsewhere on the road to Yallourn. An appeal for funds for the statue was opened at a public meeting in April 1932; McGlinn was appointed organizer and Blamey deputy chairman to the mayor. But it was a difficult period in which to raise money and it took two years to find the £5000 which was almost enough. A competition for the statue, open to all of British nationality, was held, but the winning design was so unpopular that the result was upset and a local sculptor, W. L. Bowles, was given the commission. The National War Memorial Committee and the State government had agreed that the statue should be within the precincts of the Shrine; but the new Shrine trustees, although they had agreed to a statue of King George V, refused to comply; public opinion strongly opposed any individual statue there. Eventually, in May 1937, the City Council decided on a site away from the Shrine, near the entrance to Government House. The war held up completion of the statue, which had been sent to England for casting in 1939. In 1951 a memorial in the Jewish War Memorial, Darlinghurst, Sydney, was unveiled.

Blamey, T. W. White and Grimwade were the speakers on the anniversary of Monash's death from 1933 to 1935, usually to a crowd of about three thousand. McGlinn and Stewart were the organizers, the R.S.L. and S.E.C. aiding. From 1936 until 1943 Jewish university graduates and students sponsored another annual oration; in 1937 Isaacs gave a notable eulogy which claimed that Australia's 'proud equality in the British Commonwealth of Nations' was established at Mont St Quentin. From 1951 the venue of the annual pilgrimage and commemorative address was moved from the grave to the statue in the Domain. From 1965 the ceremony was held near the anniversary of Monash's birth. On the centenary of his birth Sir Robert Menzies gave the address at the statue, there were lectures at the University of Melbourne and elsewhere, commemorative dinners were organized by Monash University and the St Kilda Hebrew Congregation, and a centenary stamp was issued—but there was little public awareness.

During his lifetime Monash's name had been used for streets, a branch of the British Legion of Ex-Servicemen, scout troops, houses at Scotch College and other schools, a cavern at Mount Buffalo, an avenue of trees on the Creswick road from Ballarat—even for a horserace and a racehorse. Soon after his death, there were fruitless proposals to rename Yallourn, St Kilda Road, and the Anderson Street bridge after him. But prizes were established at the University and by the Melbourne division of the Institution of Engineers, Australia, and the Australian Zionist Federation sponsored a forest of eucalypts in his name. In 1946 Kfar Monash, the 203rd communal settlement under the Jewish National Fund, largely financed from Australia, was established in Israel; it has a Monash Memorial Museum and a surrounding Monash Grove. In 1967 the new head office of the S.E.C. was named Monash House.

Oddly his fame may have been perpetuated most, shortly after his death, by a crude representation in the American Ripley's 'Believe It or Not!' strip, in which Monash was featured (all in capitals) as 'The Man who Defeated Germany. Hindenburg and Ludendorff Testified that General Sir John Monash (a non-professional soldier), Commander of the Australian Forces, Won the War by Breaking through in the decisive 2nd Battle of the Marne'.

The family immediately considered bringing out a biography; Felix Meyer was the chief, inadequate adviser and J. B. Lewis was suggested as a possible author. Few reviewers in Britain or Australia had much of interest to say about the *War Letters*. One exception was Edmund Blunden:

> I should not be surprised if these letters gained the reputation of being the best penned by any soldier of similar rank and sphere. Monash was able to think of the war not only as a problem for the intellect but also as a destiny that was shaking the chateau windows and shattering the face of things.

There was surprised comment at Monash's evident breaches of security and regret at his invidious comparisons of Australian with other troops. In his defence it was said that the letters were not written for publication and that he would have edited out unpleasant aspersions and misleading exaggerations written to boost morale at home. The book was a modest success in Australia, and in England was chosen as the Book Society book of the month.

Under his will Monash left all his estate of some £27 000 to Bertha apart from annuities to Lizette (£200 a year), Mathilde and the Roth sisters, and small bequests to other relations and friends and to Jewish charities. Until her death in 1954 Lizette annually on 8 October placed an 'In Memoriam' notice in the *Argus*.

His sister Mat died in 1939, Lou Rosenhain in 1942, Walter in 1934. Gershon Bennett had a distinguished career in dentistry and in the army in World War II; some years after his death in 1955 Iona was sold and pulled down. Bertha died in 1979 after a life of widespread public service. Of their children David served in the 2/23rd Battalion, A.I.F., as a private, took an honours degree in History and a diploma in Education and became a Labor Party candidate, headmaster of a progressive school and one of Her Majesty's Education Commissioners; Betty graduated in Science and Education and became a tertiary teacher of chemistry; Colin, especially as noted critic for the *Age*, has played a leading part in the revival and development of the Australian film industry. There are seven great-grandchildren.

APPENDIX II

Major Allanson and Robert Rhodes James

Rhodes James first published the Allanson statement as a 'confidential unpublished account . . . made available to me'. I have not been able to establish the source or date. However in 1935 Allanson was angered when he read Monash's war letters: the one written on 16 August 1915 included an exaggerated account, for home consumption, of 4th Brigade's advance in the early morning of the 7th and a passing remark that 'the Indian Brigade came up on our right, but did not do nearly so well'. According to John North, author of *Gallipoli, the Fading Vision* (1936), Allanson's revelation of Monash's behaviour 'was only forthcoming' because of his resentment at this remark. In his published diary Allanson stated only that after going to 4th Brigade, 'finding it impossible to get on we swung to the right'. When Bean interviewed him a week or two after the event, he made no record of any criticism of Monash. Nearly fifty years later, Field Marshal Lord Slim, who served with Allanson in this very action, recalled that he was an unreliable witness, prone to exaggerate. Allanson admitted a general dislike for Australians.

It is possible that any encounter between Monash and Allanson was witnessed only by members of Monash's staff, who would have been anxious to protect his reputation and 'hush up' the incident.

It should be said that overall Rhodes James's *Gallipoli* is a brilliantly written work. In his judgement of Monash and 4th Brigade Rhodes James was following in the footsteps of John North, whom he personally consulted. Rhodes James did not accept the advice of H. V. Howe, the Australian military historian who had visited 4th Brigade a few days after the action, that Allanson's account was untrue, and that his proposed treatment of Monash was ludicrous and would expose him to ridicule. Some of the evidence he uses is almost worthless. For example, the New Zealander Malone's diary note that in the first weeks 4th Brigade was 'the least effective of all the Anzac units' is absurd in view of the brigade's holding of the most difficult sector, Bean's judgement that this was one of the four finest feats of the A.I.F. (see p. 252 above), its superior record of decorations, its MG unit, etc. Rhodes James quotes a British officer writing of Monash at the end of April. It was Major Jerram of the Marines writing of 3 May—in that context his mild criticism has no force. Monash was not 'physically and mentally exhausted' in August. Rhodes James's interpretation of the situation on 7 August neglects the evidence: no troops could possibly have reached 4th Brigade's objective; the Turks were not 'completely encircled'. This is not to say that victory could not have been won, but 4th Brigade could not have taken any leading part.

APPENDIX III

Monash Portraits

OILS

Sir John Longstaff, as official war artist, painted four portraits (1918-19). Two are held by the Australian War Memorial, one by Monash University, and one (with battlefield background) by the Art Gallery of New South Wales.

James Quinn, as official war artist, painted two portraits (1918-19). One is held by the Australian War Memorial, the other by the Bennett family.

Isaac Cohen's portrait (1919?) is held by the National Gallery of Victoria and in 1982 is at Government House, Melbourne.

A portrait by Percy White (late 1920s) is at Monash House (S.E.C.).

Monash sat in 1919 for Solomon J. Solomon. The whereabouts of any resulting portrait is unknown.

STATUE

The equestrian statue by W. L. Bowles is in The Domain, Melbourne.

BUSTS

Bronze castings of the bust by Paul Montford (1928) are held by the Australian War Memorial, Monash University and the S.E.C.

W. L. Bowles made a small bust (*c*. 1932-34) for reproduction and sale by the Australian War Memorial.

OTHER

Deriving from the group portrait of generals in the National Portrait Gallery, London, J. Singer Sargent made a crayon sketch which is held by the National Gallery of Victoria, and two pencil sketches which are in the Monash Papers.

In 1919 Leopold Pilichowski made a pencil sketch (whereabouts unknown).

In 1919 Dora Ohlfsen produced a medallion and/or a plaque cast in bronze (whereabouts unknown).

In the 1920s Agnes Paterson painted a miniature and a double miniature of Monash and Lizette Bentwitch (whereabouts unknown).

A posthumous pencil drawing by Noel Counihan (*c.* 1962) is reproduced in *On Lips of Living Men* (ed. J. Thompson).

Notes

ABBREVIATIONS

AA	Australian Archives
ADB	*Australian Dictionary of Biography*
AG	Annie Gabriel
AWM	Australian War Memorial
AV	*The Australian Victories in France in 1918*
BB	Bertha (Monash) Bennett
BM	Bertha Monash
D	Diary
GF	George Farlow
Herald	Melbourne *Herald*
ID	Intimate Diary
JM	John Monash
LB	Lizette Bentwitch
LM	Louis Monash
LR	Louise (Monash) Rosenhain
M & A	Monash & Anderson
MM	Mathilde Monash
MP	Monash Papers
MP (AWM)	Monash Papers (Australian War Memorial)
S.E.C.	State Electricity Commission of Victoria
SMH	*Sydney Morning Herald*
Sun	*Sun-News Pictorial* (Melbourne)
VM	Victoria (Moss) Monash
WR	Walter Rosenhain
WS	Will Steele

Page

1-2. Pages 1-2 are largely based on 'The Life, Labours, Joys and Sorrows of B. L. Monasch bookbinder, printer, publisher and inn-keeper of Krotoschin in the province of Posen', translated by Peter Fraenkel, typescript roneoed, MP. Excerpts are published in *Year Book XXIV of the Leo Baeck Institute,* London, 1979; note Fraenkel's introduction, pp. 195-6. The *Encyclopedia Judaica* (1971), v.10, has a summary history of Krotoschin. JM made notes on his family tree, 10 Jan. 1923. MM to JM, 23 Aug. 1915, and JM to Culleton, 6 Aug. 1918, discuss possible derivation from Manasseh. 'Sudfeld family-tree documented by Alfred Sudfeld and Max Nordau', MP, documents the Nordau connexion.

3. A. Behrend's Reminiscences, MP, and family letters indicate the nature of Louis' business.

3-6. Family letters, especially between Louis and Bertha, are the sources for the courtship. 'You may feel': 29 July. 'What do I care': 16 Sept.
6. *Age*, 6 June 1864, mentions the number of passengers. 'on our calling': Behrend's Reminiscences.
6-7. Family letters, especially those from Graetz, indicate the chain of migration.
7. Mathilde's Notes and Bradford to JM, 30 June 1917, are the chief sources on baby John.
JM's list, 'Striking Events of my Childhood', includes the Deniliquin stay. Mathilde's Notes mention his playing for his father.
7-8. 'pronouncing the gutturals': JM to WS, 24 July 1884. Mathilde cites Dethridge in her Notes. The headmaster was R. A. Armstrong.
8. The evidence on when they moved to Jerilderie is inconclusive, but see LM to BM, 14 Oct. 1874; JM to Adolph Monasch, 1 Dec. 1874; JM's 'Various Notes'.
9. Crossroads like a station: *Sun*, 2 Dec. 1926. The beginning of JM's first 'yarn' describes a township like Jerilderie. G. L. Buxton, *The Riverina 1861-1891*, Melbourne, 1967, pp. 172-3, remarks on the Jerilderie Show. McIntyre to JM, 9 Aug. 1918, comments on Bertha's popularity.
Mathilde's Notes describe Elliott. He wrote to JM on 23 Sept. 1885, also 2 Apr. 1881, 27 Apr. 1892, 12 June 1922. 'composing acrostics': JM to Latham, 20 June 1922.
9-10. Mathilde's Notes and her interview in the *Herald*, 17 Oct. 1931, are the main sources on Jerilderie. 'happy recollections': JM to Elliott, 27 May 1892. The map is in MP. 'miserable set': JM to Leo Monash, Aug. 1882.
10. Recollections of goats and bottles are in a *Sun* interview, 2 Dec. 1926. Mathilde's Notes describe the companionship and pranks. A note on the unlikelihood of the Kelly story is in my first draft, MP.
For Kane, see *ADB* 2.
10-11. Behrend to BM, 6 May 1876, indicates her possible unhappiness.
11. 'I had always': Elliott to JM, 23 Sept. 1885. 'the foundation': JM to Elliott, 6 June 1922.
For Scotch College, Annual Reports; *History of Scotch College Melbourne 1851-1925*, Melbourne, 1926; G. H. Nicholson (ed.), *First Hundred Years. Scotch College, Melbourne, 1851-1951*, Melbourne, 1952; *Young Victoria*; advice from Dr E. L. French and Mr G. W. Noble.
12. The careers of the post-matriculation class are indicated in JM to Littlejohn, 2 June 1906; Armstrong to JM, 19 June 1918.
Of three letters from JM to LM, one is undated, the second is dated 16 Jan. 1877 (1878) and the third is 3 Feb. 1878. 'was so enthralled': Mathilde's Notes.
12-13. The account of Bertha's training is from Mathilde's Notes.
13. 'Monday, getting up 7': undated letter.
Sladen's comment in the footnote is from his *My Long Life. Anecdotes and adventures*, London, 1939, p. 299.
13-14. JM described his bar mitzvah to LM, 10 July 1878. 'thoughts and ideas': D, 30 Dec. 1882.
14. LM wrote to JM on 23 July. Behrend's epistle is dated 13 July. 'used to hate': JM to WR, 27 Mar. 1911.
'Our old relationship': JM to Pulver, 8 Sept. 1885.
14-15. These remarks on the Jewish community are based on the works by Getzler, Goldman and Medding listed in the bibliography and on C. A. Price, *Jewish Settlers in Australia*, Canberra, 1964.
15-16. M. C. Davis, *History of the East Melbourne Hebrew Congregation . . .*, Melbourne, n.d., is relevant.
16. My *The Rush to be Rich . . .*, Melbourne, 1971, ch. 9, has much on Melbourne of the period. 'a Renaissance gone wrong': J. M. Freeland, *The Australian Pub*, Melbourne, 1966, p. 148.
18. Of Louis' few surviving letters, the ones used here are 23 July, 8 Oct. 1878, 20 Jan. 1880. His father slightly cold: JM to AG, 10 July 1889.

18-19. Louis a mild and gentle man: MM to JM, 5 June 1918. Bertha's conviction about Johnny: MM to JM, 14 Nov. 1915; LR to MM, 14 Oct. 1931. 'loved and honoured': Bradford to JM, 30 June 1917. Tireless energy: JM to Aunt Henrietta, 20 Feb. 1886.

19. The scrappy information on Bertha is found in Behrend's Reminiscences; JM to Leo Monash, 10 Apr. 1887; MM to JM, 1 Feb. 1899, 14 Nov. 1915; C. Deakin to JM, 27 June 1886; Burke to MM, 29 June 1933; F. Meyer, *Herald*, 10 Oct. 1931. For Catherine Deakin see J. A. La Nauze, *Alfred Deakin. A biography*, Melbourne, 1965; C. Deakin to JM, 15 Sept. 1880; JM to LM, 19 Sept. 1880.

Not particularly Jewish-looking: MM to JM, 6 Apr. 1915. Bertha's letters were of 26 Jan. and 1 Feb.

19-20. The essays on the explorers, Milton and *Macbeth* are in MP.

20. 'in German I read': JM to LM, 18 Mar. 1880.

20-1. Farlow's Notes are in MP.

21. Re Wischer: JM to LM, 3 Feb. 1878; Wischer to MM, 1 July 1933. Re Jackson: Jackson to JM, 8 Jan. 1880; D, 11 Jan. 1887. Re Hyde: Mathilde's Notes; JM to WS, 15 Apr. 1883; Hyde to JM, 9 July 1882; M. de F. Bishop, *One Man in his Time. Edward Bishop master builder 1844-1902*, Hawthorn, 1979, ch. V.

21-2. JM's early writings are in Souvenirs Book 1 and in a notebook. The *Sun*, 21 June 1924, 2 Dec. 1926, mentions Cole's Book Arcade.

22. Mathilde's Notes record her memories of parties. 'a born teacher': *Herald*, 17 Oct. 1931.

'My dear Monash': Morrison to JM, 5 Jan. 1881. Louis was persuaded: JM to LM, 9, 20 Jan., 6 Feb. 1881. 'had a lot of fun': JM to LM, 28 Jan.

22-3. Souvenirs Book 1 contains the time-table. For Aucher and Mueller, JM to Littlejohn, 2 June 1906.

23. With regard to the *Macbeth* essay, I follow closely comments by Professor David Bradley of Monash University. Monash's source was the New Variorum edition (New York, 1873) in which the relevant commentaries derive from *Notes and Queries*, 11 Sept., 2 Oct. and 13 Nov. 1869.

24. 'from everywhere': BM to JM, 26 Jan. 1882, also 1 Feb. The paragraph is based on JM to Leo Monash, 15 Feb. 1882.

25. LM's letters to JM are of 15 July 1881, 28 Feb., 6, 26 Mar., 13 Apr. 1882; JM to LM, 26 July 1882.

25-6. Various notebooks contain his collecting intentions.

26. 'studying closely': ID, 22 May; a Commonplace book contains transcriptions and notes.

26-7. D records his doings at the Wesleyan society. JM to Pulver, 8 Sept. 1885, records his influence.

27. 'Yesterday (Sunday)': ID. For Walker, *ADB* 6.

28. 'first spoke to Mr Deakin': ID, 6 Mar. 1882. 'most beautiful woman': JM to WS, 15 Apr. 1883. Sanders' ball: ID and D, 24 June. Mathilde's Notes refer to astronomy. Remarks on sailing and fishing are in D, Feb. and Sept.

28-9. 'I cannot understand': ID, 13 Aug. 1882.

29-30. D records his exam failures and movements. Admitting infatuation with theatre: D, 11 Aug. 1889.

30-1. A cuttings book contains his newspaper writings.

31. The manuscripts of his stories are in MP.

'my first venture': JM to WS, 13 Feb. 1883.

31-2. 'generally miserable': JM to Hyde, 9 Jan. 1883. His reports on work and exams are to WS, 13 Feb., and Hyde, 28 Feb.

32. 'in these days': JM to WS, 16 Mar. 1883.

32-3. 'I have seldom felt': JM to WS, 16 Mar. 1883. Hyde's letters were of 14 Mar. and 30 Apr. 'a burden to those around me': JM to WS, 16 Mar.

33. 'If ever I needed': ID, 8 May 1883. 'Various Notes' for his time-tables, etc.

33-4. Hyde's letter was of 28 Mar. 1883.

34. *'your "mother-tongue"'*: JM to Leo Monash, 9 May 1883.
34-5. JM's version of Victorian history is in the same letter to Leo. 'We have often been twitted': JM to Leo Monash, July 1887.
35. This correspondence about free thinking consists of: Leo Monash to JM, 1 Mar., 21 June 1883; JM to Leo Monash, 9 May; JM to WS, 15 Apr.
35-6. 'I was left to myself': JM to Eva Blashki, 26 July 1886. 'a man can live happily': JM to WS, 15 Apr. 1883. 'Everything that I see': D, 21 Aug. 1883. Monash was reading *The Martyrdom of Man* in 1916 (notebook, 4 Oct.) and recommended it in a letter to Mrs Berry, 10 Apr. 1924. See F. B. Smith, 'Three Neglected Masterpieces . . .', *Meanjin Quarterly*, Mar. 1973, on Reade's book, and his Religion and Freethought in Melbourne, M.A. thesis, Univ. Melbourne, 1960.
36-7. For the additions to his library: JM to WS, 15 Apr. 1883. 'I find myself': JM to Leo Monash, 9 May 1883. Some of his pencil sketches are in Souvenirs Book 1. The discouragement from diary-keeping is noted in D, 26 July 1883.
37. 'had a complete breakdown': D, 20 Aug. 1883. The remarks on the Improvement Society are in D, 11, 14 Sept.
37-8. The comments on working on physics and reading Scott are in D, especially 2, 22 Sept., 2 Oct., and to WS, 24 July 1883.
38. Scott's and Blainey's histories are the main sources for the University in the 1880s.
38-9. On 13 Feb. 1883 JM discussed the possibility of a club in a letter to WS. 'the Union took its birth': JM to Sweet, 20 Mar. 1913. For the conversazione proceedings and JM's speech, *Argus*, 15 Aug. 1883.
39. The first issue of the *Melbourne University Review* has an account of the Union's foundation and objects; see also M.U.U. committee minute-book (Archives, Univ. Melb.)
39-40. JM to WS, 24 July 1884, has comments on support for the Union. 'respected the secrecy': Lewis's Notes, MP; see also Lewis in *Melbourne University Magazine*, July 1920.
40. 'a dark youth': Lewis's Notes.
40-1. The dates of swearing and of commencement of service are from records in MP. 'In the storm of enthusiasm': JM to Leo Monash, 27 June 1887. Farlow's Notes and *Melb. Univ. Review*, Aug. 1884, give further details. My *Rush to be Rich*, pp. 201-3, outlines Victoria's defence policy.
42-3. 'Our University has made great strides': JM to Pulver, 8 Sept. 1885. D, 10 Aug. 1884, has comments on his course.
43. JM described his part in composing the anthem to O. Behrend, 1 Mar. 1909. JM comments on the lectures, D, Aug.-Oct.
43-4. 'complimented and thanked': D, 13 Sept. 1885. JM's letters to Lewis contain much about the *Review*.
44. Some of the happy moments are recorded in D, 19 June, 20 July 1885. Deakin wrote on 25 July and 6 Aug.
44-5. 'Certainly the acquisition': D, 5 Feb. 1885. For the rumour, O'Hara to JM, 18 Feb.
45. His diary relates his military experiences. 'I have scored a great triumph': D, 1 Sept. 1885.
45-6. C. H. Chomley, *British Australasian*, 31 July 1919, recalled his efficiency. The other quotations are from D, Sept.-Oct. 1885.
46-7. 'I should much like to perfect myself': D, 7 Feb. 1885. The diary has much on chess and the piano in 1885.
47-8. 'If any nice-looking girls': Farlow's Notes. 'smilingly stopped': Kate Lewis's Notes, MP.
49-50. D, 19 June and 13 Sept. had comments on neglect of work. The diary entries for 15 June and 6 Sept. are from ID, the others from D.
50. A letter to Elliott of 20 Sept. 1885 is revealing about his ambition. He wrote to Leo on 26 Feb. 1886. The Blake quotation is from his *Disraeli*, London, 1966, p. 9.

51. 'lingered in great pain': JM to Lewis, 25 Oct. 1885; Kate Lewis's and Lewis's Notes, MP. 'the darkest recollection': D, 19 June 1885. 'watch over and cherish':, JM to VM, 7 Dec. 1890.
'I have lost': JM to R. Blashki, 7 Dec. 1885. Steele's inquiry: WS to JM, 20 May 1888; JM to WS, 28 May.
51-2. For Mrs Lewis, M. B. Lewis, *Don John of Balaclava*, Melbourne, 1977, passim.
52. For father, JM to Leo Monash, 11 Jan. 1887, 29 Nov. 1889.
For Evergood, *ADB* 8.
52-3. 'Eva I find is': D, 19 June 1885. 'Eva I find to be': D, 5 Aug. 1885. 'The girls, I can perceive': D, 9 Aug. 1885. 'This evening': D, 4 Sept. 1885. 'I am now of an age': ID, 6 Sept. 1885. 'The comedy is': ID, 16 Sept. 1885.
53. 'the thousand tongued chorus': JM to E. Blashki, 2 Nov. 1885.
54-5. 'I have told you often': JM to J. Blashki, 4 June 1886. Mat reminding him: MM to JM, 3 Nov. 1918. No position to marry: JM to J. Blashki, 23 Dec. 1886. 'it be very clearly understood': JM to Stockfeld, 19 Dec. 1886. 'Jeanette was there': D, 21 Apr. 1887. 'I would know now': D, 23 Dec. 1887. 'most indiscreet': D, 13 Jan. 1889. 'spiteful, tearful': D, 11 Aug. 1889.
55-6. JM wrote at length to Eva Blashki on 26 July 1886.
56-7. 'No sane man': JM to R. Blashki, 14 Feb. 1886. 'People are born': JM to E. Blashki, 7 Oct. 1885.
'the nothingness': Commonplace Book. 'meaningless form': D, 25 Jan. 1887, 23 June 1889.
57-8. 'Withdraw yourself': JM to E. Blashki, 2 Nov. 1885. 'Hence I may take': JM to E. Blashki, 7 Oct. 1885. Man's 'first duty': JM to E. Blashki, 2 Nov. 1885. The following quotations are from letters to J. Blashki, 17 May 1886; R. Blashki, 7 Dec. 1885; and E. Blashki, 7 Oct. 1885.
58. 'I have had much': JM to Leo Monash, 13 May 1888.
Setting up with Lewis: D, 16 Sept. 1885; JM to Leo Monash, 11 Jan. 1887. Terms of employment: JM to Lewis, 25 Oct., 24 Nov. 1885; Lewis to JM, 31 Oct., 22 Nov.
58-9. For Munro, *ADB* 5. 'was in great fear': D, 28 July 1886. 'his restless energy': Lewis's Notes. 'you may be sure': JM to Leo Monash, 11 Jan. 1887; also D, 12 Sept. 1887.
59-60. Fillips to pride: D, 29 July, 26 Aug. 1886, 8 May, 7 July, 2 Sept. 1887. 'deeply hurt': D, 10 Sept. 1886. For the picnic, D, 8, 15 Feb., 27 Mar., 27 Apr., 8 May 1887.
60. Each new stage: D, Apr.-Aug., passim. Accidents: D, 27 July, 3, 21 Aug. 1887. Relations with Lewis and Higgins: D, 2, 18 Sept., 6 Oct., 30 Nov., 6 Dec. 1887. 'strangely unsympathetic': D, 13 Jan. 1888. Warm relationships: from S. Anderson, 27 Oct. 1890; from Woods, 26 June 1889, 29 May 1919.
'so elated': D, 23, 26 Oct. 1887, 20 Jan. 1889. Other work: D, 29 Sept., 16 Oct., 30 Nov. 1887, 24 Jan. 1888.
61. foresaw no difficulty: D, 28 July 1886. 'most miserable time': D, 29 Nov. 1886; see also D, 10 Sept. Reading: D, 16, 30 Jan. 1887; JM to Farlow, 14 Dec. 1886; JM to WS, 16 Feb. 1887. Flagged again: D, 6, 13, 20 Feb. 1887. 'any better prepared': D, 6 Mar. 1887; also D, 5, 14 Mar. and to O'Hara, 5 Dec. 1886.
61-2. 'at the spree which followed': D, 17 Apr. 1887. 'I am well received': D, 19 July, 11 Aug. 1887. Working for last few weeks: D, 14, 19, 30 Sept., 4, 16, 26 Oct., 6 Nov. 1887. 'As if by inspiration': D, 15, 20 Nov. 1887. 'Thus three old friends': D, 1 Dec. 1887.
62-3. Asking O'Hara: JM to O'Hara, 11 Dec. 1887; D, 23 Nov. 'the wonderful process': JM to WS, 16 Sept. 1888. 'severe admonition': D, 23 Feb. 1888.
63. 'wretched business': JM to GF, 26 July 1886. 'The matter which': D, 18 Aug. 1886; also letters to Miller, 13 Aug. and to Leo Monash, 27 June 1887. 'unfit for work': D, 25 Feb. 1887.
63-4. Attached to battery: *Vic. Govt Gazette*, 7 Apr. 1887. Bach's descendant: *Sun*,

NOTES (pages 64–77)

10 Feb. 1933. 'The undercurrent of my thought': D, 6 Mar. 1887. 'At last after many a weary': D, 6 Apr. 1887. Early fantasies: JM to Stockfeld, 12 Mar. 1887.
64. 'sneers and reproaches': *Daily Sketch* (London), 14 July 1919. Professional military career: JM to Leo Monash, 13 May 1888.
   'I displayed an utter want': D, 17 Apr. 1887. 'You are not yet popular': GF to JM, 6 June 1887. 'began to realise': D, 17 June 1887. 'partly deservedly': D, 24 June. 'All my fears': D, 17 May. 'amongst most men': D, 24 July.
64-5. Successive diary entries on Goldstein and Stanley cover Mar.-Oct. 1887.
65. Working into duties: D, 11, 15 May 1887. June parade: D, 27 June. Shooting: D, 20 Mar., 16 Oct. 1887, 29 Jan. 1888. Lecturing: 11 Sept., 6, 18 Dec. 1888. 'at last I may feel safe': D, 9 Nov. 1887. On Goldstein: D, 18 Dec. 1887, 13 Jan., 5 Feb. 1888. On Appleton: D, 13 Jan. 1888.
65-6. Sources for this incident are: D, 19, 23 Feb. 1888; JM to Stanley, 15 Feb.; JM to WS, 19 Feb.; news cutting, Souvenirs Book.
66. 'to the time when': D, 28 Mar. 1888. D, 5 Apr., covers events of the camp. On 5 Apr. JM wrote to Lowe who replied on 9 Apr. 'a very firm footing': JM to GF, 22 July 1888.
66-7. For the picnics, D, 6 Feb. 1887, 24 Jan. 1888. For the Kaiser's dinner, D, 27 Jan. 1889. 'not much influence': JM to E. Corrie, 25 Sept. 1889.
67. 'I came out strongly': D, 1 Oct. 1886. 'toady enough': D, 26 Oct. 1887.
67-8. 'made a choice': D, 2 Aug. 1886. 'When once you have mastered': JM to E. Blashki, 26 Oct. 1885. Diary references to piano are 2, 26 Aug., 12 Sept. 1886, 16 Jan., 21 Apr., 11 May, 24 July, 2, 17, 21 Aug. 1887, 8 Mar. 1888.
68. 'I often feel': D, 10 July 1887. 'I have fortunate capacity': D, 13 Sept. 1885. 'I can find enjoyment': D, 28 Apr. 1889.
   'Another showy accomplishment': D, 12 Sept. 1886. 'I am no judge': D, 12 Nov. 1887.
   'That man can be': JM to J. Blashki, 4 June 1886. 'my initiation': D, 21 Aug. 1887. 'thoroughly disgusted': D, 20 Mar. 1887. Discussions with Hyde and Steele: D, 1 May, 14 Sept., 6 Oct., 20, 30 Nov. 1887.
69. Conversations with Fredman: D, 5 Sept. 1886. Fink's lecture: D, 3, 30 Aug. 1887. 'Perhaps some day': D, 30 Aug. 1887. Graetz symposium: D, 30 Nov. 1887. 'the great desirability': D, 23 June 1889. 'Nothing more': D, 11 Aug. 1889; the lecture is in MP. For Goldstein's lecture, Goldman, *The Jews in Victoria*, p. 322.
69-70. 'strolled thru the country': JM to Stockfeld, 29 Dec. 1886; D, same date. 'On all our trips': Farlow's Notes. 'very best walking trim': JM to VM, 3 Sept. 1891.
70. Accounts of the trips are in the diaries. 'feelings of awe': JM to VM, 23 Aug. 1891. Farlow's amusement: GF to JM, 2 Dec. 1892.
70-1. Diary notes of encounters with girls are: Rennick, 26 Aug. 1886; Daley, 1 June 1887; Murphy, 16 July, 27 Nov. 1887, 12 Aug. 1888; Robinson, 15 Dec. 1886; Goldstein, 12 Oct. 1887; Huntsman, 23 June 1888. The Bendigo account is at 17 Aug. 1887. 'devote myself solely': D, 5 Sept. 1886.
71-2. 'against any false slip': ID, 1 Jan. 1887.
72. 'had an interesting flirtation': JM to Stockfeld, 10 Feb. 1887; D, 6, 7, 8 Feb. 1887; Souvenirs Book.
72-3. 'Standing in the crowd': D, 23 Feb. 1887. 'Returning to my office': D, 14 Mar. 1887. 'I did meet her': D, 20 Mar; D, passim, until end July.
73-4. The more important diary entries on Rosie are: 5 Sept. 1886, 21 Aug., 26, 30 Sept., 10 Oct., 29 Dec. 1887, 29 Apr. 1888.
74. Respectable girls: D, 13 Jan., 5 Feb. 1888.
74-6. 'honest account': D, 18 Nov. 1888. 'Not only is my diary': JM to E. Blashki, 13 Sept. 1885. 'A diary is just whatever': JM to E. Blashki, 2 Nov. 1885. 'somehow I have never yet': JM to WS, 8 Dec. 1888. 'I feel it like a burden': JM to VM, 2 Jan. 1890; also D, 30 Jan. 1887, 6 Jan, 15 June 1889.
76-7. 'to sum up for myself': JM to R. Blashki, 7 Dec. 1885. 'I am very satisfied': ID. 'I have . . . developed': ID, 8 May 1887. 'I am mostly disliked': ID, 1 Jan.

NOTES (pages 77-94)

1887. 'Sam Ewing': D, 12 Nov. 1887. 'bustling activity': JM to WS, 15 Jan. 1888.
77. For Social Darwinism, C. D. W. Goodwin, *Economic Enquiry in Australia*, Durham, N. C., 1968, ch. 10. 'devote himself to the good': D, 4 Sept. 1885. 'especial business': D, 4 Sept. 1885.
78. 'fit of depression': D, 3 Aug. 1887; also 23 Oct. 1887, 29 Jan. 1888.
78-9. avoiding company: D, 20 Jan., 10 Feb., 1 Mar. 1888. 'getting drunk': D, 23 Mar., 18 Apr. 'salvation from much misery': JM to WS, 29 Apr. 1888. 'I am developing a faculty': D, 29 Apr. 1888. 'I have got myself': JM to WS, 3 Feb. 1889.
79-80. JM replied to WS on 28 May, WS replied on 5 June.
80. Lewis's suggestion: D, 17 Mar. 1888. 'I have been so indiscreet': D, 23, 28 Mar. 'at one leap': JM to GF, 14 Apr.; D, 5 Apr.; ID, 14 Apr. Terms: JM to Graham & Wadick, 6 Apr. JM to Munro, 5 Apr.; Munro to JM, 7 Apr.
80-1. Could not help wondering: JM to Leo Monash, 13 May 1888. 'if you aim': Kernot to JM, 10 Apr.; JM to Kernot, 14 Apr.
81. For the Outer Circle railway, see G. Blainey, *A History of Camberwell*, Melbourne, 1964, pp. 50-4.
81-2. 'with much hesitation': JM to Leo Monash, 29 Nov. 1889. Asserting himself: JM to WS, 24 June 1889. 'I appear to have': D, 2 June, also 13 May 1888. Graham & Wadick satisfied: D, 13 May, 18 June 1888. Revelling in dignity: D, 8 July, also 30 Sept. 1888.
82-3. 'the arts of organization': JM to Leo Monash, 29 Nov. 1889. 'at the greatest pressure': D, 18 Apr., 2 May 1888. Irritability: JM to WS, 13 May 1888. 'some cause for gratification': JM to WS, 29 Apr.; WS to JM, 20 May. 'In the old days': JM to WS, 13 May, 31 Aug., 16 Sept. 1888.
83-4. 'goes on the false doctrine': JM to WS, 8, 13 Dec. 1888; but see also his description of the navvy to Mary Card, 21 Sept. 1891, printed in *Labour History*, no. 40, May 1981.
Relations with employers: D, 22 Sept., 18, 25 Nov. 1888, 7 Apr. 1889.
frightening escape: JM to AG, 1 Aug. 1889.
84-5. 'the sight of the heavy engines': JM to VM, 14 Nov. 1890.
85-6. Diary entries about the lecture are at 19, 20, 22 Aug. 1890. The paper was published as a pamphlet (copy in MP). Work diaries and other records relating to the contract are in MP and the Reinforced Concrete Co. papers (Univ. Melb.)
87. JM's diary, May-Aug. 1888, and his letters to AG are the sources for the developing relationship.
The first sentence of the description of Annie is based on JM to K. Roth, 26 Sept. 1889.
88. D, Sept.-Nov. and letters carry on the story. 'Bitterly I repented': D, 2 Sept. 1888.
88-9. 'I little realized': D, 18 Nov. 'An interesting phase': D, 25 Nov., 2 Dec. 1888. 'What have I to live for': JM to AG, mid-Nov., undated.
89-90. D, Dec. 1888-Mar. 1889 and letters continue the story. The quotations are from letters of 8 Dec., 24 Nov., c. 30 Dec. 1888, 13 Jan. 1889. See also letters between JM and WS, Mar.-Aug. 1889.
90. Inevitable crisis: D, 17 Mar. 1889; JM to Hill, 21 Mar.; JM to AG, 24 Mar. D, 7 Apr., for Fred's approach.
90-1. 'would sooner abandon': ID, 24 Apr. 1889.
91-2. 'a poem in white muslin': D, 26 Sept. 1886. D, June-Nov. 1888, contains much re the Corrie sisters.
92. 'No one can see much of you': D, 7 Apr. 1889. Evie's compact and the consequences: D, 19 May, 10 June, 20 July 1889; Evie to JM, 17 July. 'At last we approached': D, 6 July.
92-3. The 'touching, mournful letter' was of 18 July. His ID and D show that he did not contemplate suicide.
93. 'my attention': D, 23 June. 'I bespoke her': D, 20 July. 'Vic. is clearly': D, 11 Aug.
93-4. Father's illness: JM to WS, 20 Aug. 'there came to me': D, 20 Aug. JM wrote to Evie on 21 and 25 Aug.

94-5. 'her sudden offer': D, 23 Aug. 'I cannot gauge': D, 25 Aug. 'Her final decision': D, 28 Aug.
95-6. 'I went forth': D, 2 Sept.
96-7. 'an *incubus*': D, 16 Sept. 'My great longing': D, 22 Sept., misdated for 18th. JM to AG, 26 Sept; JM to K.Roth, 22, 26 Sept.
97. 'No time to think back': D, 21 Sept. Eva Blashki's wedding: D, 18, 19 Sept.
97-8. 'You do not seem to me': JM to VM, 29 Sept. Evie 'completely unreserved': D, 30 Sept. 'I am not yet very sure': D, 3 Oct.
98-9. MM's letter was of 13 Oct. 'The forthcoming round': D, 11 Oct. D, 17-23 Oct. covers the subsequent embarrassments. Footnote: see E. (Corrie) Whitfield to JM, 9 Oct. 1893, 11, 24 Apr. 1907. Information from Mrs W. Birman, Perth.
99. JM's descriptions of Vic are in letters to Hyde, 11 Jan. 1890; Leo Monash, 29 Nov. 1889; WS, 23 Nov. 1889; A. Behrend, 18 Dec. 1890; see also, D, 21 Oct., 14, 28 Nov., 11 Dec. 1889.
  'she became of a sudden': D, 5, 6 Nov. 1889. The calculation of number of letters is at the front of letter-book 3.
99-100. 'I took occasion': D, 18 Nov. 1889. 'I am not a saint': JM to VM, 3 Mar. 1890; cf. D, 26 Mar. 'I have again fallen': ID, 26 Jan. 1890.
100. 'I told her my plans plainly': D, 13 Apr. 1890. Offer to release: D, 13, 14 July.
100-1. 'You seek *any* form': JM to VM, 8 Aug. 1890. 'I was irritable': D, 23 Aug. 'I could not help admiring': D, 6 Sept. The offer to Vic is in a letter of 7 Sept. 'She did not flinch': D, 7 Sept. 'Your promises show me': VM to JM, 7 Sept. The rows are described in D, late Oct.-early Nov. In town with another man: D, 12 Dec. 1890; cf. Firman to VM, 10 Mar. 1890, at back of letter-book 3. JM replied to Behrend on 18 Dec. 'If ever I needed your help': JM to VM, 14 Dec. 1890.
101-2. Father aloof: JM to AG, 10 July 1889. Falling out with Mat: D, 11 Aug., 18 Nov., 22, 31 Dec. 1889. Loan to Uncle Roth: JM to Roth, 24 Jan. 1891; to VM, 3 Feb. Loan to K. Roth: JM to K. Roth, 26 Feb., 30 May 1891, 30 Jan. 1892.
102-3. Kernot's timely spur: D, 22 Aug. 1890. 'very confident': JM to VM, 13, 15 Oct., 24 Nov., 7 Dec. 1890. 'Attended my last subject': D, 27 Feb. 1891.
103. 'idea of being a premature genius': ID, 14 July 1889. 'the best efforts of my life': JM to AG, 1 Mar. 1889. Confidence oscillating: D, 28 Apr., 19 May 1889. 'Sometimes I sit brooding': JM to AG, 31 July 1889. 'I have a strange knack': JM to VM, 21 Sept. 1889. Listing acquaintances: Souvenirs Book 2. Catalogue of 'prenuptial friends': notebook. 'I don't want *money*': JM to AG, 1 May 1889. 'The accumulation of money': ID, 24 Apr. 1889. 'I had not the heart': D, 20 July 1889.
103-4. 'I have lost my buoyancy': ID, 5 Jan. 1891. Quarrels before wedding: D, Feb.-Apr.
104-5. .The account of the honeymoon is based on D, 8-28 Apr. 1891 and JM to MM, 12 Apr.
106. There is much correspondence with Lewis in these years; note Lewis to JM, 27 June 1892, and D, 21 Sept. 1889, 5 Oct. 1891.
  The letters from and to Moss are of 17 June and 3 Aug. 1891. 'I want you to understand': JM to VM, 16 Sept. 1891.
106-7. His diary for 1891 records his various applications. 'a fever of excitement': D, 3 Sept. 1891.
107. 'the dead level inaction': JM to Lewis, 10 Jan. 1892.
  'The risk is great': D, 11 June 1890; also 2 July, 18, 20 Aug., 19 Sept. 1891; correspondence with Chalmers, 1890-92.
  'told her'; D, 29 June 1891.
107-8. 'right and duty': cf. JM to MM, 11 Aug. 1916. The incidents are related in the diary.
108. Vic's finances: D, 6 Jan., 28 Feb., 5 July 1892. Father's debts: D, 23, 29 Aug. 1892. The major crisis was at the end of April. His New Year summing-up was in ID. Naming his daughter: D, 15 Feb. 1893.

546 NOTES (pages 108–122)

'severe moral twinge': D, 13 Feb. 1892.
108-9. 'be for many years': JM to Leo Monash, 9 Sept. 1893; JM to WS, 13 Mar., 22 May 1892; JM to Elliott, 27 May 1892; Lewis's Notes. Law exams: D, 19, 24, 25 Oct.; JM to WS, 25 Oct. 1892, 28 Oct. 1893.
109-10. 'Strange isn't it': JM to VM, 14 Sept. 1891.
110. 'The commission is': JM to GF, 17 Apr. 1889; for other details, D, 12 Aug. 1888, 11 Aug., 13 Dec. 1889, 25 Sept. 1890.
    The formal submission to O.C., North Melb. Battery, was on 20 June 1889. 'master of my subject': D, 2, 22 Sept. 1889. 'The moment when': D, 29 Sept. 1889, also D, 24 Sept., and to VM, 25 Sept.
110-11. 'the *amour propre*': JM to Stanley, 2 Oct. 1889. Competition between batteries: D, 31 Jan., 7 Mar. 1891.
111. Relations with fellow officers: D, 11, 18 Nov. 1888, 24 Apr., 10 June 1889, 4, 19 Apr., 10 Nov. 1890, 8 Apr., 24 July 1891.
    'On the way home': D, 7 Apr. 1889; also 22 July 1888, 13 Jan., 6 July 1889; JM to GF, 17 Apr. 1889.
111-12. There is much about the gun in his correspondence and in his diary, especially July 1889-Apr. 1890. On Outtrim: D, 1 Apr., 1 July, 19, 26 Aug. 1890, 28 May 1892, 14 Nov. 1893.
112. 'a first-rate style': *Argus*, 23 Dec. 1893. Diary comments on lectures are on 3 Oct., 14 Nov., 22 Dec. 1893, 1 Feb., 8 Oct. 1894. Most of the lecture notes are in MP. Science Club lecture: D, 20-22 Aug. 1893.
112-13. Monash's fulsome letter to Outtrim was of 5 Aug. 1893; Outtrim to JM, 24 July, 2, 3 Aug. 1893. Goldstein's flattery: D, 25 Nov., 22 Dec. 1893. Shoeburyness proposal: D, 24 Mar., 7 Apr. 1894.
113. Saltwater swing-bridge: D, 11, 13 Feb. 1892. 'content at negotiating the storm': D, 21 Feb. 1892. His diary records the other events.
113-14. Arbitrator's admiration: D, 2 June 1892. Strain and anxiety: D, 1-9 June 1892. 'Equity' letters: *Argus*, 29 Nov. 1892, 3 Feb. 1893. Walking the lines: D, 10, 24, 26, 27 Aug. 1893. Extravagance: memo for Mr Moir, MP; JM to Gillett & Co., 13 July 1894; JM to Shaw, 9 Sept. 1893; JM to Wheeler, 26 Aug. 1893. For the case, D, 5, 6 Sept. 1893; *Argus*, 9 Nov. 1929.
114. JM wrote a description of the situation for engineers to Gardiner, 24 Dec. 1893. 'when each individual': JM to Leo Monash, 9 Sept. 1893. His letter to Karl Roth, 25 May 1893, was a masterly call to duty.
114-15. His diary tells much of the Harbor Trust episode; also JM to Zox, 1 June 1893, 20 Mar. 1894; JM to Thornley, 24 July 1894; JM to chairman Harbor Trust, 20 Mar., 29, 31 May 1894.
115. Correspondence Apr.-June 1894 covers these forlorn hopes.
116. Comments on Anderson: D, 20 Jan., 8 Feb., 15 Nov. 1892. Formation of partnership: D, 15-19 June 1894; JM to Anderson, 19 June.
116-17. 'Having come to realise': ID, 1 Jan. 1893. The other quotations are from D.
117. Mat identified his 'pet failing' in a letter of 15 Feb. 1893. The anonymous letter is in Souvenirs Book 3. The rest of the paragraph is based on the diaries.
117-18. D for Sept.-Nov. tells the story. 'we went to Mr Simonson's house': JM to GF, 14 Oct.; GF to JM, 17 Oct. 1894.
118-19. 'Vic having held out': D, 24 Oct; JM to Moss, 26 Oct., Moss to JM, 7 Dec. 1894. 'The statements which you have made': JM to VM, 9 Dec. 'An act of marital authority': JM to K. Roth, 2 Dec. 1894.
119. Father's death: D, 15-21 Dec. 1894. A statement of assets and liabilities and a cashbook in MP indicate his problems; also JM to GF, 12 Dec. 1895, 16 June 1896; JM to Elliott, 20 June 1896, 5 Sept. 1897.
119-20. The diaries tell the story.
121. M & A letter-books display the early work of the partnership. Letters to *Age*, e.g. 30 Apr., 13, 21 May 1895.
121-2. JM commented on Anderson, D, 26 July, 1 Aug. 1894, 4, 12 Mar. 1895. He

recorded the possibility of breaking the partnership, D, 22, 27 Dec. 1894.
122. The Landys contract is largely displayed in the M & A letter-books, July 1895-Sept. 1896; see also JM to MM, 6 Dec. 1896; *Argus, Age,* 8 Sept. 1896; income tax return, M & A letter-book, 19 May 1898.
122-3. M & A letter-books, Feb. 1896-Jan. 1897, tell the story.
123-4. Again the letter-books are the major source. JM to Formby, 4 Jan. 1896, describing the state of the profession, was generous advice to an unemployed engineer.
124. The more illuminating D entries are on 23, 24 Feb., 5 Mar., 2 Apr., 14, 28 May, 11 June 1895. JM's suggestion of a conversazione was in a memo of 1 Dec. 1894. JM to Hall, 8 Feb. 1895, was his plan. For its success, D, 2, 3 May 1895; C. Holled Smith to Templeton, 16 May, Souvenirs Book 3; *Argus,* 3 May; *Australasian,* 11 May 1895.
124-5. This paragraph is based on correspondence late in 1895 and early 1896 with Hall, Outtrim, Farlow and Stanley. The culmination was in JM to Outtrim, 29 July, and Outtrim to JM, 29 July 1896.
125. 'some have supposed': JM to Hall, *c.* 4 Oct.; Hall to JM, 5 Oct. 1896.
'Poor old Outtrim': JM to Wheeler, 7 Nov. 1896; D, 24 Oct. 'My success here': D, 10 Nov. 1896.
126. JM wrote to VM about the Portland case on 2 Oct. 1897. Eggleston's remark is from his 'Confidential Notes'.
Monash's diary is the major source for the Queensland trip together with his letters to VM of 28 Sept. and to Anderson of 28 Sept. and 1 Oct.
126-7. D and letters to VM are similarly the sources for his health.
127. The more important letters are to VM, 19 Dec., and to Anderson, 21 Nov.
128. A transcript of the case is in MP.
There is much material on his irrigation work of which letters to VM and Anderson are the most important; also P. McCaughey, *Samuel McCaughey,* Sydney, 1955; JM to McKinney, 11 Dec. 1899; *Herald,* 25 Jan. 1905; Adelaide *Register,* 26 June 1906. Riverina Creeks Preservation League Papers (Mitchell Library, Sydney, MSS 46) contain transcripts of the 1898 cases.
129. 'I spent the greater part': JM to VM, 3 Nov. 1897.
130. Anderson's letters were of 2 and 4 Feb. 'It leaked out': JM to VM, 9 Feb.
130-1. 'With so many responsibilities': JM to Behrend, 20 May 1898. 'I don't grudge you': JM to Anderson, 29 Jan. 1898. 'I am not good': JM to Anderson, 11 Sept. 1898. M & A letter-books and the partners' letters to each other are the major sources on the firm.
131. JM to Anderson, 26 Mar. 1898, describes the coaching. Anderson's subsequent letters to JM in W.A. outline relations with Carter, Gummow.
JM's letters to VM are the chief source for his W.A. period.
131-2. The account of the Forrests' dinner is dated 10 Aug. 1898. 'the reason why': JM to VM, 29 Aug.
132. These reports of business opportunities are in letters to VM, July-Nov. 1898.
132-3. The quarry episode is covered in letters between JM and Anderson, July-Sept. and in letters between JM and Shaw, 1899-1901.
133. JM's letters to MM are an additional source, e.g. 10 Aug., 5 Sept., re Ada, and 9 Jan. 1899, re Vic in Perth society. The report of her dress is from an unidentified cutting.
134. Letters to MM, 18, 31 Jan., 9, 14 Feb. 1899, and to Anderson, 24 Nov. 1898, give progress reports. For O'Connor, see M. Tauman, *The Chief. C. Y. O'Connor,* Perth, 1978, especially p. 196.
134-5. JM to VM, 6 Nov. 1898, and Anderson to JM, 7 Dec. 1898, are illuminating on the partners' relationship. The bridge's testing on 20 July 1899 was extensively described in the newspapers.
135. JM described the Monier process to Behrend, 27 June 1899. Examples of his letters to Baltzer are 15, 22 Aug. 1901. M & A letter-books are the source for the pipe-factory negotiations.

135-6. The letter-books cover a range of minor work which is not mentioned here. 'Inaugurate general retrenchment': D, 22 Oct. 1900. M & A to Gummow, 6 Oct. 1900, is an example of a pleading letter.
136. M & A letter-books, Oct. 1897-May 1900, contain the story.
June 1898-Feb. 1901 is the relevant period in the letter-books for the Wheelers Creek bridge. 'to err on the side of extravagance': JM to Anderson, 19 Sept. 1900.
137-8. 'is "punded" closely': *Bendigo Independent*, 24 Nov. 1900. 'Things are pretty bad': JM to MM, 17 May 1901. Kernot's opinion is in a letter to M & A, 12 June 1901.
138. The report of the inquiry into the M.M.B.W. is in *Victorian Parliamentary Papers*, 1901, no. 7. JM to Gummow, 21 Nov. 1899, and JM to Behrend, 1 May 1900, give his motives for joining the inquiry. JM wrote to VM from Tasmania on 22, 27, 29 Dec. 1901.
138-9. For the formation of the company, M & A to Gummow, Forrest, 5, 14 Aug., 13 Nov. 1901, and to Mitchell, 30 July 1901. The agreements with Gummow are in MP.
139-40. JM reassured Gummow in a letter of 14 Jan. 1903.
For negotiations with the shires, see M & A to Taylor, 12 Oct., 14 Nov. 1900. Newspaper reports of the cases and judgments are on 17-28 June 1901, 2-13 Feb., 25-26 Sept. 1902. See also Reinforced Concrete Co. records, item 685; Cussen's opinion, MP; JM to WR, 7 Oct. 1902; *Herald*, 26 Sept. 1902.
140. 'to face the position': JM to Gummow, 17 Aug. 1903. 'between an insolvency': JM to LR, 5 May 1906. D, Sept. 1902-May 1903 and JM to Gibson, 7 Jan. 1903, are also relevant for financial considerations.
141. 'You will soon find out': JM to LR, 18 Nov. 1902. Bertha's letter during the war was of 1 Aug. 1916; her further remarks were made to the author.
141-2. 'After some years': JM to WR, 8 Jan. 1918.
142-3. 'when men get rotund': JM to Leo Monash, 1 July 1898. Cf. JM to VM, 4 Sept. 1898, on setting little store by social functions.
143. 'a complete cinematograph view': JM to MM, 15 Aug. 1897.
143-4. JM wrote to MM on 5 Sept. and 21 Nov., MM to JM on 15 Nov. 1898.
144. Among JM's letters to LR were those of 15 Dec. 1901 and 18 Nov. 1902.
Particularly relevant letters include MM to JM, 28 May, 18 Oct. 1905; JM to LR, 18 Nov. 1902, 5 May 1906.
144-5. The correspondence contains the stories.
145. Skimpy diary entries are useful on his club activities. His handwritten founding motion of the University Club is in Souvenirs Book 5.
145-6. 'A most delightful evening': D, 13 Dec. 1902.
146. 'Music I never touch': JM to LR, 18 Nov. 1902. 'While, in a sense': JM to Bruno Monasch, c. 17 Nov. 1905.
146-7. 'a crowd of Jews': D, 18 Nov. 1889, 24 July 1890.
147. His diary and Souvenirs Books are the sources for this paragraph.
147-8. The comments on the Chinese are in letters to VM, 7 Oct. 1897, 28 Aug. 1891.
148. The article was in the Aug. 1898 issue of *Alma Mater*. The diaries and correspondence are useful on the movement for reform. His analysis of finances is in a letter to Gibson, 25 Sept. 1902.
149. The correspondence is informative on his university teaching.
150-1. 'I am beginning to feel': JM to Behrend, 1 May 1900. 'The adverse experiences': JM to LR, 21 Jan. 1902. 'The Monash of that day': *Smith's Weekly*, 10 June 1933.
151. 'I have come to the conclusion': JM to Behrend, 1 May 1900.
151-2. 'He came to the Court': 'Monash Oration'. Cf. P. Jacobs, *A Lawyer Tells*, Melbourne, 1949, pp. 18-19. Menzies cited Cussen in his memorial address, 1965, MP. For the Kannaluik case, cuttings books, MP; Reinforced Concrete Co. records (item 306). For Masson's opinion, *Argus*, 23 Apr. 1902.
152-3. M & A letter-books give the story, Apr. 1902-Oct. 1904; *Kerang New Times*, 11 Oct. 1904, for the opening.

NOTES (pages 153–166) 549

153. Examples of Monash's theoretical interest are M & A to Baltzer, 22 Dec. 1902, and JM to Gibson, c. 10 Jan. 1903. A file of his correspondence with Austrian and German experts is in MP. His reports to the Victorian Institute of Engineers are in its *Procs*, May 1905, June 1906. Examples of letters to Gummow and Baltzer are 11 Feb., 2 Mar., 26 June, 10 July 1905. For his brush with Emperger, JM to Gummow, 17 Feb. 1906.
154. Beaten to the punch: JM to Gummow, 15 July 1903. Information on the progress of the pipe factory is widely scattered in the M & A letter-books.
 The Reinforced Concrete Co. records cover Raveloe (item 399), Chastleton (item 418), the Bank Place building (item 557) and the Aust. Mortgage Land & Finance building (item 566). For Bank Place, see also JM to Gummow, 8 Apr. 1904, 26 May 1905, and *Age*, 5 Mar. 1906.
154-5. The agreements on the founding of the company are in MP; correspondence in the Reinforced Concrete Co. records enlarges on the agreements. Monash's accounting, 16 Apr. 1905, of his and Anderson's interests is in MP; see also JM to Anderson, 17 May 1906, 19 June 1907; JM to Gummow, 19 June 1904; JM to Jack Anderson, 25 May 1904.
155. 'latterly it is all I can do': JM to LR, 18 Nov. 1902. For the irate client, see the Galopin correspondence (M & A), July 1903-Feb. 1905. Christensen and Jack Anderson enliven the M & A correspondence.
155-6. The advice to his cousins was to K. Roth, 28 June 1900, and to Behrend, 27 June 1898. The Bendigo engineer was Richardson, to whom JM wrote on 22 Jan. and 6 May 1902.
156. 'every *inch* tells': M & A to Jack Anderson, 5 July 1902.
157-8. 'His orders were models': Farlow's Notes. 'I have a board': JM to GF, 7 Jan. 1897.
158-9. *Argus*, 6-8, 12 Nov. 1895 and D, 31 Oct. 1895, are revealing on the Templeton viewpoint. Terraine quotes Roberts in his biography of Haig, p. 42. Monash's chafing at incompetence: JM to Goldstein, 4 Mar. 1893; to Stanley, 26 June 1896; to Miller, 18 Apr. 1895. The *Argus* report was 21 Oct. 1895. 'I don't object': JM to Hall, 8 Sept. 1897.
159. Hall's reassurance was dated 13 Nov. 1897. 'they are not only very lenient': JM to Lawes, 20 May 1898; also to GF, 11 Dec.; to Hall, 6 Nov., 4 Dec.; to VM, 19 Dec. 'I will have to choose': JM to VM, 18 Oct. 1898. JM to Hall, 5 July 1899; Hall to JM, 8 July. The correspondence with Farlow is extensive in this period.
159-60. On the new command: JM to VM, 13 Sept. 1898, 4 Apr. 1899; to Lawes, 20 May 1898. Shooting: *Argus*, 3 Apr. 1899; JM to VM, 4 Apr. 1899.
160. 'misfortune not to be chosen': *Herald*, 11 Apr. 1930. 'This is certainly not an occasion': JM to Bevan, c. 25 Sept. 1899, in reply to 24 Sept.
160-1. 'I have had to almost entirely neglect': JM to LR, 30 June 1903. 'Battery going to the Devil': D, 24 July 1903; cf. 12 Sept. 1903. For Hutton's reforms, see E. W. Perry, 'Military Reforms of Sir Edward Hutton . . .', *Victorian Historical Magazine*, no. 113, Feb. 1959.
161-2. 'Having, for very many years': JM to C.O., Aust. Garrison Artillery, 25 June 1907. Referring to has-been: JM to Stanley, 2 Aug. 1906; to Hanby, 29 Dec. 1906.
163. The remarks on his financial situation are in letters to MM, 29 June 1907, 22 Feb., 29 June 1908, and to LR, 5 May 1906.
163-4. The extensive records of the Reinforced Concrete Co. are the basis of this paragraph.
164. Some records relating to the S.A. company are in MP.
 'deeply grieved': JM to Gibson, 20 May 1916. Gibson's letter was of 4 Oct. 1907, JM's of 1 Feb. 1909. VM to JM, 5 Oct. 1917, has a comment on Lynch's devotion.
165. The papers to the institutes are listed in the bibliography. 'nothing talks so strongly': JM to WR, 5 May 1906.
165-6. Complaints about the Preston contract: *Age*, 20-26 Mar. 1908. The text of the

arbitration proceedings is in MP. See also Reinforced Concrete Co. records, item 796; *Building*, Nov.-Dec. 1908; JM to Calder, 13 Oct. 1908; *Argus*, 1, 15 June 1910.

166. D. A. L. Saunders tells much of the story in *Architectural Science Review*, vol. 2, no. 1, Mar. 1959. See also, *Building*, Feb.-Apr. 1909; *La Trobe Library Journal*, no. 6, Oct. 1970; JM to Reay, 23 Feb. 1909; Peebles to JM, 25 May; JM to Peebles, 23 Sept. 1909. Gibson to JM, 30 Jan. 1918, and Fairway to JM, 19 July 1918, describe the structural defects. Reinforced Concrete Co. records, items 705 and 890, are helpful on the patents situation.

Mackey's request was on 14 Dec.

167. The letters to and from LR are of 5 May and 20 June 1906.

167-9. The more important items in this correspondence are MM to JM, 21 Mar., 15 Apr. 1907, 8 Jan., 2 Apr., 10 May, 30 July, 3 Sept., 2 Oct. 1908; JM to MM, 22 Feb., 29 June 1907; LR to JM, 8 Oct. 1908. 'Frankly, I have always': JM to MM, 23 Mar. 1908.

169. JM wrote to McCay on 7 Dec. 1907.

Hollingworth's letter was of 20 Dec. 1907; JM to Hanby, 15 Jan., 11 Apr. 1908; JM to Hall, 28 Mar. 'a splendid send-off': JM to MM, 1 June 1908; farewell dinner, *Age*, 18 July 1908.

169-70. Coulthard-Clark is the authority.

171. 'looks just lovely': VM to JM, 13 Jan. 1910. The Kitchener scheme is covered in Bean, *Two Men I Knew*, pp. 8-16; Hill, *Chauvel of the Light Horse*, pp. 39-40; Scott, *Australia during the War*, pp. 194-5.

JM to Bruche, 12 Jan. 1909, is a good example of easing into staff work. For the Hall-Williams contest, *Herald*, 9 Oct. 1931.

171-2. 'the one real live'; JM to Mackey, 14 Dec. 1907. 'Do you remember': Bruche to JM, 21 Feb. 1914.

172. *Wangaratta Chronicle*, 21 Nov. 1908, has an account of the exploration; Wears to JM, 8 Nov. 1906; Peebles to JM, 22 Sept. 1909.

172-3. JM wrote to Sandow on 24 Dec. 1908.

173. *Punch's* jibe was on 5 Aug. 1909.

Some of the letters seeking advice were to the Rosenhains, 2 Aug., 8 Dec., and to Leo Monash, 16 Aug. 1909, 8 Jan. 1910.

173-4. There is a file on the trip in MP.

174. The account of their travels is taken from his letters to MM. 'I must confess': JM to MM, 24 July 1910. Conviction war imminent: biographical notes for Rosenthal, 4 Dec. 1930.

174-5. Relations with the Rosenhains are covered in LR to JM, 10 Mar., 8 Sept., 19 Oct. 1910; JM to MM, 6 June, 13 Sept. 1910; JM to LR, 21 Nov. 1910; JM to WR, 2 Jan., 22 Mar. 1911; WR to JM, 8 Sept. 1910, 5 Jan. 1911.

176. 'The great secret': JM to Oliver, 1 Jan. 1911.

176-7. The remarks on return to Melbourne are in notes for a talk, 14 Nov. 1910. 'America was a most fascinating': JM to LR, 21 Nov. 1910. 'I say that a visit': JM to WR, 2 Jan. 1911.

177. Remarks on use of electric power are in *Herald*, 6 Dec. 1910; *Argus*, 12, 15 Apr. 1911.

For his private finances, JM to MM, 30, 31 Oct. 1910. 'The outlook is very unsatisfactory': JM to WR, 2 Jan. 1911.

177-9. There is scattered material on the Reinforced Concrete Co. in MP; see also item 890 in the company records.

179. The letter to LR is of 8 July 1911.

179-80. Company records and JM's letters to Gibson are the main sources. For Collins House, JM to WR, 30 Mar. 1912. Higgins's house still stands at 4 Ray St, Beaumaris; cf. *Beaumaris Newsletter*, July 1965 (Beaumaris Historical Trust Collection, La Trobe Lib.); cf. J. M. Freeland, *Architecture in Australia*, Melbourne, 1968, p. 221.

180. Settling wage claim: JM to Gibson, 14 May 1912. Gas co. case: Reinforced

Concrete Co. records, item 930. 'a rooted objection': JM to WR, 21 Apr. 1914. Evidence to Legislative Council, *Herald*, 21 Dec. 1911. 'hope that the Government': JM to Leo Monash, 6 June 1912.
180-1. Investment files, MP, indicate his flutters. The material on Luna Park is from his letter-book with the Reinforced Concrete Co. records.
181. Of several letters to Schultze, that of 30 July 1911 is the most rewarding.
181-2. 'our inability to entertain': JM to WR, 15 Sept. 1911. JM described the house to MM, 22 June 1912.
182. Description of alterations and domestic details have been drawn from the 1912-14 correspondence, especially JM to MM.
183. 'I have come to the conclusion': VM to JM, 26 May 1913.
183-4. 'steady conscientious work': JM to E. Simonson, 8 Jan. 1910.
184. 'If they had the bad manners': JM to Caldwell, 14 Mar. 1906.
184-5. 'all is right': JM to MM, 13 May 1912, and to LR, 31 May 1912. 'I returned home': JM to WR, 27 Mar. 1911. There is a file on diet in MP.
185. The letter to the deputy postmaster-general was of 29 Aug. 1912; to Thomas Cook, 14 Nov. 1910.
185-6. The records of the Melb. Univ. Graduates' Association are in the M.U. archives; *Argus*, 1, 24 May, 24 Oct. 1911; JM to WR, 15 Sept. 1911, 21 Apr. 1912; Sweet to JM, 3 July 1912.
186. The soundings in 1908 were to Theodore Fink, 20 Oct. There is much correspondence in MP in Mar. 1912 about his successful candidature. 'I am already greatly indebted': JM to Higgins, 20 Mar. 1912. JM to MM, 13 May 1912; Lewis to JM, 11 Apr.; JM to Lewis, 16 Apr. 1912.
186-7. There are revealing letters to MM, 11 Sept., 15 Dec. 1912, about his university work. Bassett's recollection is in the S.E.C. archives (Historian's files). The correspondence, 1912-14, in MP is rich on university matters. See also Univ. Council and Senate minutes; Scott's *History*, pp. 214-15; *Argus*, 7 July 1914; JM to VM, 10 Sept. 1915.
187. 'I strongly favour': JM to J. A. Smith, 26 July 1909; JM to Hoadley, 15 May 1909.
187-8. Correspondence on the V.I.E. is thick in MP, 1911-14. His notes for replying to a toast at the conference of the Institute of Mining Engineers, 23 May 1914, are illuminating.
188. The editorial was in the Dec. 1913 issue of the *Varsity Engineer*.
188-9. This important address is in the Institute's *Procs* (see bibliography).
189. The *Age* editorial was on 7 Mar. 1913. Gummow wrote on 21 Apr. There is much more in MP relating to the V.I.E. For Monash's successful campaign to re-establish an Industrial and Technological Museum within the Science Museum of Victoria, see E. W. Perry, *The Science Museum of Victoria. A history of its first hundred years*, Melbourne, 1972; corresp., MP, especially JM to Mackey, 11 Apr. 1913; JM to Swinburne, 14 May 1914; *Argus*, 25 Nov. 1912.
189-90. For his Boy Scouts involvement, see *Age*, 8 Feb. 1911; JM to WR, 27 Mar. 1911; JM to Madden, 20 Mar., 12 Oct. 1912; D. M. Benn, The Origins and Development of the Boy Scout Movement in Victoria (1908-1940), B.A. Hons. thesis, Monash Univ., 1972; address to 1914 rally, MP.
190. 'My corps has had to do': JM to WR, 27 Mar. 1911. On high-level administration: JM to WR, 27 Mar., 15 Sept. 1911. Foott was cited by A. W. Bazley in *Reveille*, 1 May 1937.
190-1. Perry's remarks are in *Victorian Historical Magazine*, no. 109, pp. 30-1; cf. J. M. A. Durrant to Black, *c*. 14 Apr. 1937, Bean Papers, box 276.
192. He wrote to McCay on 12 Nov. and to Mrs McCay on 25 Nov. 1912. McCay's reply was on 18 Dec.
192-3. JM's comment on the draft order is dated 18 Nov. 1912; White replied on 26 Nov.
193. 'the training of our officers': JM to Dooley, 28 Mar. 1924; cf. JM to Sellheim, 26 Jan. 1910. Coulthard-Clark quotes Stanley, p. 43. The journalist's assertion was in *Punch*, 24 Sept. 1914.

Bruche's recollection of the appointment is in Thompson (ed.), *On Lips of Living Men*, p. 35. See also JM to Bruche, 9 July 1913, and to LR, 26 June. He reported progress to Bruche, 14 Aug.

193-5. 'My impression is': JM to Price-Weir, 11 Sept. 1913. The brush with Bruche is in JM to Bruche, 9 July, 14 Aug., 6 Sept. 1913; Bruche to JM, 15 July, 21, 23 Aug. 1913.

195. Much of the correspondence about dress is in a letter-book with Reinforced Concrete Co. records. 'condition of close tutelage': JM to Hughes, 17 Nov. 1913, MP.

195-6. He described the brigade to WR, 6 Jan. 1914. The notes for the lecture on 10 Oct. 1913 are in MP. The '3 principles' note is dated 9 Nov. 1913. The rocket was addressed to Redmond, 24 Mar. 1909.

196-7. Williams's remark is in his *These are Facts*, Melbourne, 1977, p. 19. The lecture notes are dated 11 Feb. 'I was prepared': *Gallipoli Diary*, i, pp. 249-50; Hamilton is also quoted in *Herald*, 9 Oct. 1931. There are many press reports of the day's proceedings; JM to Bruche, 26 Mar. 1914, for his own views.

197. Hamilton's remarks are in a letter to JM, 14 Feb. 1929. The gunner was Cox-Taylor, to JM, 17 Feb. 1914.

Some of the *Age* attacks were on 18 Feb., 5 Mar., 2 Apr. 1914. Monash's defence is to Bruche, 26 Mar.

197-8. 'as a disloyalist': JM to MM, 2 Oct. 1915. The controversy is largely covered in *Argus*, 30 Mar., 6, 8, 9 May, 4 July 1914.

198-9. 'I am a little too old': JM to WR, 27 Mar. 1911. 'The days and weeks': JM to LR, 26 June 1913.

199-200. The *Punch* profile was on 24 Sept. 1914.

200. 'There is no satisfaction': JM to VM, 6 Dec. 1915.

201. 'Germany clanked obstinately': W. Churchill, *The World Crisis 1911-1914*, Sydney, 1923, i, p. 13.

202. 'to help the Empire': JM to K. Roth, 26 Sept. 1914. 'It may cause you': JM to G. Monash, 19 Oct. 1914.

Scott, *Australia during the War*, pp. 31-5, has a good account of the problems associated with the congress.

202-3. He replied to McCay the same day. Monash's principles of censorship are in MP (AWM), box 79, 22 Aug. Ch. 3 of Scott's *Australia during the War* is on the Censorship. JM's warning to MM was on 20 Aug. For a conflict of authority with the minister for defence, see Munro Ferguson to Sec. of State for the Colonies, 1 Sept. 1914, PRO CO 616/3/88, cited by K. Fewster, Expression and Suppression: Military Censorship in Australia during the Great War, Ph.D. thesis, Univ. N.S.W., 1980, p. 25.

203-4. 'I have not volunteered': AIF 13/2/12, AA. Legge's recommendation is to be found in Bean Papers, folder 138.

204. Semmens and Wanliss were the battalion commanders in letters of 15 and 13 Sept.

'I started this job': JM to Bruche, 1 Oct. 1914. In general his letters to Bruche are revealing. MP (AWM), box 79, have much on the organization of the brigade.

204-5. *Table Talk*, 3 Dec. 1914, has some details of the whispering campaign. JM mentions many A.I.F. officers of German origin to MM, 2 Oct. 1915, and to Cunningham, 24 July 1915. For hostility to Bruche, MM to JM, 24 June 1916, and to Sellheim, Mrs Sellheim to JM, 27 Aug. 1918 and 23 Apr. 1930, also *Argus*, 27 Aug. 1918. The Defence Department report on Monash is in Pearce Papers, bundle 7, item 2. 'If I had listened': G. F. Pearce, *Carpenter to Cabinet*, London, 1951, pp. 124-5. The *Argus* correspondence was on 20-27 Oct. 'It puzzled him completely': *Argus*, 22 Dec. Monash commented on 'the McInerney clique' to MM, 2 Oct. 1915.

205-6. Munro Ferguson wrote to JM on 17 Dec. For the Collins House send-off, *Argus*, 22 Dec.

206. JM described the departure to VM, 30 Dec., and events at Albany to Dodds, 28 Dec., Legge, 30 Dec., Bruche, 31 Dec. 1914, and Hall, 11 Jan. 1915.
206-7. Monash noted the obsession with falling overboard, D, 6 Jan. 1915. 'The fleet at sea': JM to VM, n.d. His letters to VM and his D describe events on board ship. 'His powerful personality': *Argus*, 4 Feb. 1915.
207. Monash covers happenings at Colombo to VM, 18 Jan., to Pearce, 13 Mar., and to Birdwood, 17 Mar.
207-8. This paragraph is based on JM to VM, 19 Jan., also 26 Jan.
208. JM described the progress through the canal to VM, 29, 30 Jan.; cf. *Argus*, 10 Mar.
208-9. 'a small, thin man': JM to VM, 13 Feb. 'an exceptionally able man': Birdwood to Munro Ferguson, 25 Feb., Novar Papers. Birdwood consulting Ryan: JM to VM, 29 May 1916. The footnote derives from Gellibrand's annotations of *Australian Victories in France*, AWM.
209. 'elegant, graceful': JM to VM, 13 Feb. 'a very energetic': Godley to Pearce, 30 Mar., also 16 Apr., Pearce Papers. JM's comments on Birdwood's and Godley's staffs were to VM, 13, 27 Feb.
209-10. 'I am afraid the First Division': JM to VM, 25 Mar. For the attempt to assert independence, JM to Chaytor, 30 Mar. 1915, and Butler, *Official Medical History*, i, 63n.
210. JM reported Godley's comment to VM on 13 Feb. The reports of 12 and 15 Feb. are from D. 'in saddle from 7.50': D, 3 Mar. On divisional training: JM to VM, 13, 16, 27 Mar. Notes for his address to the battalions are in MP (AWM), box 80. The diary of C.Q.M.S. Guppy (AWM) records how inspiring it was. Letters to VM, 22, 30 Mar. record praise of reviews.
211. Monash's comments on Egypt and the deputation were to VM, 10, 27 Feb. Smith loving him as a father: Smith to VM, 11 June 1917; cf. Smith to JM, 1 Apr. 1915. 'McGlinn and all the other Paddies': JM to VM, 25 Mar. For the Luxor trip, D, 26 Mar., JM to VM, 30 Mar.
211-12. For the meeting with Hughes, VM to JM, 11, 23 Jan. 1915. On his health: JM to VM, 13, 30 Mar. 'In the middle of a busy Cairo street': JM to VM, 8 Apr.; cf. to VM, 24 Dec. 1914. Birdwood's letters to his wife are in the Birdwood Papers, AWM.
212. 'our Australian relatives': JM to Pearce, 13 Mar., Pearce Papers. 'exceedingly interesting': Gov.-Gen's Military Sec. to Pearce, 26 Apr., Pearce Papers. On VD, Butler, *Official Medical History*, i, pp. 77-8.
212-13. JM wrote to VM about the inquiry, 5 Apr.; see also S. Brugger, *Australians and Egypt 1914-1919*, Melbourne, 1980, pp. 145-7.
213. 'final overhaul of kits': JM to VM, 13 Apr. 'The men are in the highest spirits': JM to VM, 11 Apr.
213-14. The farewell letters and some of the pencil sketches are in MP (AWM), box 80. There are several letters to VM, 13-24 Apr. The lieutenant's diary-note is the dedication to K. T. Henderson, *Khaki and Cassock*, Melbourne, 1919.
214. For the Gallipoli campaign and its origins, *Official History*, i; Rhodes James, *Gallipoli*; Moorehead, *Gallipoli*; North, *Gallipoli: the fading vision*. 'a strong feint': quoted by North, p. 208.
214-15. 'My only feelings': JM to VM, 25 Apr.
215-16. 'You have got through the difficult business': quoted by Rhodes James, *Gallipoli*, p. 130. For this chapter the *Official History*, i-ii, may be assumed as a continual reference.
216. This paragraph is based on D, Locke's war diary, MP (AWM), box 81, and battalion histories. 'to collect the scattered fragments': D. The brigade medical officer was Beeston, writing to JM, 7 Feb. 1917, 20 Dec. 1918.
218-19. MP (AWM), box 81, contains much of relevance. 'it needed a lot of nerve': JM to VM, 18 July 1915.
219-20. Monash's report on the action is in an official letter-book, MP. His own diary

and Locke's are useful, as is Bean's D7. Jess sent an extract from his diary to JM, 20 Mar. 1919. See also Aspinall-Oglander, *Military Operations*, i, pp. 310-12; White, *The "Fighting Thirteenth"*, ch. 5.
220. JM's letter to Godley is in MP (AWM), box 81.
220-1. 'the disastrous attack': *Official History*, ii, p. 205. Item 891 in the Bean Papers is also relevant. 'the worst stunt': *Reveille*, Apr. 1955.
221. Hamilton's order is cited in *Official History*, ii, p. 291; pp. 98-116 cover this action. Monash's report of 12 May is in the official letter-book in MP. 'Our Brigadier Monash': F. T. Makinson diary, 11 May (Mitchell Library).
221-2. Chauvel described the headquarters, *Australasian*, 27 Apr. 1935. JM's comment on Godley's futile raid is in his notebook. 'I am living cheek by jowl': quoted by Hill, *Chauvel*, pp. 54-5. 'I shall never forget': Chauvel to JM, 1 June 1922.
222-4. 'those first three weeks': JM to Bertha, 7 June. 'We have been amusing ourselves': JM to VM, 16 May. 'We have got our battle procedure': JM to VM, 30 May. 'are as docile': JM to VM, 16 May, and to Bertha, 7 June.
224. The jokes are in letters to VM of 8, 14 June. His letter to Masson was on 14 June.

JM describes the casualties in his and McCay's staffs in letters to VM, 16, 20 May, 8 June. 'There was no courage' and the following quotation are from *Sun*, 22 Aug. 1925.
224-5. 'all my people exercising' and following quotation: JM to VM, 18 July. 'everlasting tramping': to Bertha, 7 June. Pride in not skulking and insensitivity about 'nerves': JM to VM, 8 June, 30 May, 9 Sept.
225-6. 'instantly from all over the place': JM to Bertha, 6 June. C. Smith, Narrative of Experiences (MS, AWM), p. 41, and White, *The "Fighting Thirteenth"* are also relevant. See also D, 21 May. 'we noticed a Turk': JM to Bertha, 6 June. Plan for taking Baby 700: D, 24 May. 'well able to push forward': JM to VM, 14 June.
226. 'Nothing could more adequately tell': JM to VM, 21 May. Hamilton's recollection, *Herald*, 9 Oct. 1931. JM described his spell to VM on 27, 30 May.
226-7. JM described the Quinn's affray to VM on 30 May; see also Hill, *Chauvel*, pp. 55-7; White, *The "Fighting Thirteenth"*; *Official History*, ch. 7.
227. 'then called for three cheers': JM to C. P. Smith, 3 June.
227-8. JM gave his opinion of Bean in letters to VM, 30 June, and MM, 18 July. His summary of the brigade's activities is in MP (AWM), box 81. 'One ought not to hide': JM to VM, 31 May, 3 June. VM wrote about placing his letters in the press on 9 July and 31 Oct. and Bertha on 16 Nov; JM replied on 5, 25 Sept.
228-9. Monash and Chauvel exchanged letters on the Legge issue on 14 June; *Official History*, ii, pp. 417-18, 423.
229-30. WR told MM of Burnage's report on 3 Nov. and on 20 Oct. of the lying reports. MM told JM on 20 Oct. of the returned man's assertion. 'You are positively': Bertha to JM, 24 Aug., also MM to JM, 23 Aug. Other relevant letters are JM to VM, 4 July, 14 Aug., 10 Sept.; JM to MM, 2 Oct, 18 May 1916. Writing to MM on 19 Feb. 1920, Minnie Behrend is illuminating on hostility to Monash within the Jewish community. 'It may surprise you': Cunningham to JM, 24 July 1915, also 2 Aug. 'openly and deliberately': JM to O. Behrend, 18 Feb. 1916. In general, for persecution of German-Australians, McKernan, *The Australian People and the Great War*, ch. 7.
230. D covers much of this material. 'An exceptionally thrilling': JM to VM, 20 June. He mentions the flies to VM on 18 July.

JM described his birthday to VM on 27, 30 June.
231. 'I guess that you are just the same': B. Card to JM, 5 Oct.

'You ask about Dawson': JM to VM, 6 Dec. 1915.
231-2. Romantic illusions: *Official History*, ii, pp. 424-9. 'We have dropped': JM to VM, 18 July.
232-4. Monash's diary and Cox's (AWM) provide details on the preliminary days. 'strolled round to Reserve Gully: Bean in Sunday *Sun* (Sydney), 11 Oct. 1931.

'What do you think': interview with G. H. Knox, 1978. A typed shorthand account of the address is in MP (AWM), box 82. 'It meant some effort': JM to VM, 25 Nov.
234. 'a wild tangle': *Official History*, ii, p. 461; see also pp. 583-4.
234-5. 'It was like walking out': JM to VM, 16 Aug.
235. 'I found Overton': JM to Bean, 4 May 1931. 'yelling and swearing': JM to VM, 16 Aug. 1915. 'I heard a slight movement': ibid; see also Pope's diary, Bean Papers.
236. Monash says in his diary, 'Cox supports me that men are done.' Cf. JM to Bean, 4 May 1931; but cf. also Bean, D 11.
236-7. Allanson's account is quoted by Rhodes James, *Gallipoli*, p. 272. Cf. Smithers, *Sir John Monash*, p. 119. See appendix II and annotation.
237. Monash unsuccessful in persuading Wiltshires: Bean, D 10. Godley's order is in *Official History*, ii, pp. 654-5.
238. The Official Historian's judgement on Monash's position is at ii, p. 661; his opinion of the machine-gunners is at p. 662. The medical arrangements: Butler, Official Medical History, i, pp. 302-3. Bean's D 15 has much on that morning's action. The following are the major sources for 7-8 Aug.: *Official History*, ii, ch. XXIII; Aspinall-Oglander, ii, pp. 191-211; Chataway, *History of the 15th Battalion*, ch. 4; Bean's D 15, his Sari Bair Operations file, and letter to Edmonds, 17 June 1931 and enclosures; Howe to Rhodes James, 7 Nov. 1964, Bazley Papers, AWM; C. Smith, Narrative of Experiences, ch. 5, AWM.
  Crossing the Asma Dere: cf. *Official History*, ii, p. 664.
238-9. MP (AWM), box 82, has much relevant material.
239. 4th Brigade being cut up: JM to VM, 4 Oct. Higher planning a muddle: JM to Aspinall-Oglander, 22 Sept. 1931. Aspinall-Oglander criticizes Birdwood in *Military Operations*, ii, pp. 191, 200. 'the attainment of Hill 971': *Official History*, ii, p. 664; but cf. Bean's view at the time in D 11. 'covered with deep ravines': Birdwood to his wife, 4 Aug., Birdwood Papers.
239-40. Godley's report is in Pearce Papers. 'magnificent night march': Birdwood, *Khaki and Gown*, London, 1941, p. 275. Cox's letter, Cox Papers. JM made his claims in letters to VM of 16 Aug., 9, 10 Oct., 6 Dec. Murdoch gave his absolution on 23 Sept. to Fisher, Murdoch Papers. Bean recorded Glasgow's opinion in his D 10.
240. 'swept by a wave': Butler, Official Medical History, i, p. 228; also pp. 252-3. The criticism of Monash was in Chataway, *History of the 15th Battalion*, p. 65.
240-1. The two medical officers are quoted by Butler, Official Medical History, i, pp. 351, 321.
241. 'The great essential': JM to VM, 9, 10 Oct. 'Letters from Australia': JM to WR, 17 Oct.
241-2. Showing seniors over the line: D, Birdwood to Hamilton, 17 Oct., and Godley's report, MP (AWM), box 82.
242. For this engagement, Bean, D 15; *Official History*, ii, pp. 723-45; Aspinall-Oglander, ii, pp. 355 ff.; Wanliss, *History of the 14th Battalion*, ch. 12.
  'everybody got rattled': lecture to officers, Oct. 1916, MP (AWM), box 86; MS., Leadership in War, p. 23. Controversy with Godley: JM to Godley, 24 Aug. 1915 (twice); Godley to JM, 24 Aug., MP (AWM), box 86.
242-3. 'For connoisseurs of military futility': Rhodes James, *Gallipoli*, p. 309; 'a rotten, badly organized show': D, 27 Aug.; also *Official History*, ii, pp. 746-52; Wanliss, pp. 72-4; MP (AWM), box 83. 'would be better for him': JM to Godley, 28 Aug., official letter-book, MP. Row with Cox: Hamilton to Birdwood, 21 Aug., Hamilton Papers, Liddell Hart collection; Cox to JM, 28, 29 Aug., JM to Cox, 29 Aug., official letter-book; D, 28 Aug., 3 Sept.
243. sleeping out: D, 31 Aug. 1 Sept. Medical condition: Butler, i, p. 348; D, 28 Aug.
243-4. 'the poor quality': JM to VM, 5 Sept.; also 16 Aug. 'we give the Turks': JM to WR, 25 Sept. 'The real army': JM to VM, 15 Jan. 1916.
244. D and letters to VM of 4 Oct. and 10 Nov. 1915 and to Bertha, 2 Oct., are the basis of this paragraph.

NOTES (pages 244–253)

JM was amusing in writing to VM on 20 Sept. on the glory of being a general. His diary and letter to Chaytor of 3 Oct. illustrate his difficulties in camp. He attacked the base officers in a letter to VM of 25 Sept.

244-5. He told VM of his worries about the brigade on 4 Oct. Concerts and lectures: JM to VM, 4 Oct.; Hughes to JM, 30 Apr. 1930; Chataway, p. 97.

245. D and letters to VM, 19, 24, 28 Oct., 1 Nov., cover period in Egypt.

On honours: JM to VM, 19, 28 Oct., 10 Nov., 6 Dec.; JM to McCay, 11 Nov.; Pope to JM, 11 Jan. 1916. 'all a gamble': JM to WR, 14 Mar. 1916.

246. Most of the correspondence on the seniority question is in MP (AWM), box 84; some is in the official letter-book, MP, including the draft to Chauvel of 14 Nov. Birdwood's rebuke was on 25 Nov. Cf. also JM to McKenna, 4 June 1931, re origins of Chauvel's seniority.

D, 8, 9 Nov., and *Official History*, ii, p. 823, cover the 'Hackney Wick' affair. Kitchener's visit: D, 13 Nov.; JM to Bertha, 13 Nov.

246-7. The Bauchop's Hill period is covered in D, MP (AWM), box 84, especially JM to COs, 14 Nov.; JM to VM, 25 Nov., 1, 6 Dec.; JM to WR, 25 Nov.

247. Monash gave his opinion of Murdoch's report to Wagstaff, 9 Nov. 1927; cf. Bean to Hetherington, 6 May 1958, Bean Papers.

Conviction nothing to rumours: JM to Meikle, 5 Dec.; JM to VM, 6 Dec. The following pages are drawn almost entirely from the Evacuation diary-letter to VM.

247-8. 'Every man knew': White, *The "Fighting Thirteenth"*, p. 55.

248-9. Worst strain he had experienced: Springthorpe, *Age*, 1 Feb. 1916. Leaving for beach: D, 19 Dec. Forgetting portfolio: D, 19 Dec.; JM to Campbell, 19 Apr. 1929.

249-50. On the transport: see also D, 20 Dec.; to Locke, Treloar, 19 May 1922.

250. 'First came the band': Rule, *Jacka's Mob*, p. 28; cf. Makinson diary.

250-1. Reception of the diary-letter: VM to JM, 28 Feb., 13 Mar. 1916; MM to JM, 19, 26 Mar.; Bertha to JM, 22 Feb., 6 Mar., 31 Oct. 1916. Springthorpe's account was published, *Age*, 1 Feb. JM stated his hope of having the letter published to VM, 1 Jan., 22 Apr.; cf. also 16 Sept. His reference to 'smuggling' was to Campbell, 19 Apr. 1929. Leaving nearly five hours before the last: D, 19 Dec.; *Official History*, ii, pp. 876-8. Bean holding it against him: Bean Papers, folder 42.

251. North quotes Churchill in *Gallipoli: the fading vision*, pp. 278, 77. For Monash's long-term view, *Argus*, 2 Aug. 1924, and speech to Melb. Rotary, 1929, MS, MP; cf. also JM to McGlinn, 6 Nov. 1918, and to Hamilton, 28 Nov. 1928. 'one of the most famous events': JM to VM, 26 Jan. 1917.

Alleged mediocre performance: e.g., Birdwood to Bean, 21 Apr. 1922, White to Bean, 27 Feb. 1931, Bean Papers. 'Monash was a leader': *Official History*, ii, pp. 588-9. 'defects in leadership': ibid., vi, p. 205; cf. Bean, *Two Men I Knew*, p. 171.

251-2. 'like every one': Bean, D 43, 2 May 1916. 'want of success': Bean, D 15, 21 Aug. 1915. 'Sleepy old John Monash': Bean, D 10, 30 Aug. 1915. One of four greatest achievements: *Official History*, iv, p. 488n. Absolving 4th Brigade: ibid., ii, p. 644. 4th Brigade every bit as good: Bean to Edmonds, 17 June 1931, Bean Papers. Howe's view: Howe to Rhodes James, loc. cit.

252. White's opinion: *Herald*, 9 Oct. 1931.

252-3. Hamilton's remark: *Gallipoli Diary*, ii, pp. 249-50. 'Monash has, I think': Birdwood to Munro Ferguson, 26 Nov. 1915, Birdwood Papers. Godley's views: Godley to Pearce, 18 Nov. 1915, Godley Papers; Godley to Hutton, 1 Dec. 1915, Hutton Papers, British Library. McGlinn's views: McGlinn to JM, 2 July 1918, 12 Sept. 1917.

253. Chauvel's views: Chauvel to JM, 22 Oct. 1915; Hill, *Chauvel*, p. 157. 'very proud': Johnston to JM, 13 Nov. 1915. 'I knew General Monash': *Daily Telegraph* (London), 30 Sept. 1935. McGlinn's opinion: VM to JM, 25 July 1915; also MP (AWM), box 84, Feb. 1916. Also Burnage to JM, 12 Jan. 1916; Adams to JM, 18 Oct. 1915; Eastwood to JM, 6 Apr. 1916.

NOTES (pages 253–264)   557

253-4. The Rosenhains' reports were in WR to MM, 20 Oct., 1 Dec. 1915; cf. B. H. Perry to P. Pedersen, Nov. 1980 (privately held). 'He saved some of our battalions': J. F. McGlinn to VM, 30 July 1916.
254. 'It was averred': *Official History*, vi, p. 205. Perry's remarks were in *Stand-to*, Oct.-Nov. 1950.
 'fighting commander': *Official History*, ii, p. 589.
255. The Christmas memory was in *Green Room*, 10 Oct. 1923. Monash describes the movement to VM, 23, 30 Dec. 1915.
255-6. MP (AWM), box 84, contains much on training in Egypt. 'all staffs exist to help units': quoted by J. H. Moore, *Morshead*, Sydney, 1976, p. 36. 'it is the same rush': JM to VM, 15 Jan. 1916. Rumours: JM to WR, 30 Jan.
256. 'refitting and recruiting': JM to B. Card, c. 27 Jan.
256-7. The family correspondence in MP is plentiful.
257-8. A letter from JM to Bank of Australasia, 23 Nov. 1914, relates to Concrete Constructions Co. Letters from Gibson, 10, 31 Aug., 19 Oct. 1915 and from Taylor, 4 Aug., described the situation. JM's rebuke was on 8 Sept. Fink's news: VM to JM, 25 Feb. 1916; MM relayed praise on 5 Feb. and 11 Sept. Creswell wrote on 22 Feb. VM passed on Madden's and Smith's remarks on 25 June and 1 Aug. 1916.
258. A.I.F. reorganization: *Official History*, iii, ch. II. D, 14-17 Feb., notes the farewells. His comments on Russell were to VM, 15 Jan., and to McCay, 11 Feb. (not sent). 'Godley always': JM to VM, 15 Jan.
258-9. 'Surely Australia': JM to McCay, 11 Feb. 'scandal that Australia': JM to WR, 12 Feb., also 14 Mar. Cf. JM to Andrew Fisher, 25 Jan. 1916. 'far and away the ablest soldier': JM to VM, 22 Apr. He commented on his own prospects and applauded McCay's promotion to VM on 15 Jan. and 24 Feb.
259. Pearce's request to Birdwood was on 4 Feb., Pearce Papers. Birdwood's reply of 24 Mar. is in Bean Papers, folder 67. Birdwood's letters of 11 Feb. and 24 Mar. to Munro Ferguson, Novar Papers, are also relevant.
259-60. 'I am not at all sure': JM to VM, 5 Mar., also 8, 22 Apr., 29 May. His advice to cultivate Hughes was on 15 Jan.
260. Recruitment of officers: *Official History*, iii, p. 54n. 'the most powerful weapon': JM to Bernard, 9 July 1916.
 The main sources for the march are: *Official History*, iii, pp. 288-91; D, 26-28 Mar.; Rule, *Jacka's Mob*, pp. 36-7; White, *The "Fighting Thirteenth"*, p. 59; Chataway, *History of the 15th Battalion*, p. 105; JM to VM, 29 Mar.
261. He described the conditions to VM, 29 Mar., 8 Apr., and to WR, 12 May. Khamseen: to VM, 29 Mar., also for his attack on the postmen.
261-2. 'I turned out': JM to VM, 26 Apr. 'Birdwood brought him': JM to VM, 29 Mar, also 22 Apr.
262. JM wrote to McGlinn on 20 May after Godley's inspection. 'anything but a picnic': JM to WR, 12 May. He wrote later to Fitchett, 23 Dec. 1920 and 6 Jan. 1921.
 'One of those crochetty': JM to Bertha, 8 May. 'putting Australian troops': JM to McGlinn, 19 Apr., also 30 Apr.; JM to McCay, 28 Apr., 10 May; Cox to JM, 3 May. Cox recommended JM to Birdwood on 3 May, Birdwood Papers. Godley supported him on 20 May, ibid.; his letter to Pearce is in Godley Papers. Birdwood wrote to Pearce and Munro Ferguson on 6 June, recommending Monash.
263. 'I shall be more than content': JM to Leo Monash, 18 May. Address to battalions, dated 21 May, MP (AWM), box 85. March past: Cox to JM, 29 May.
 'the people here': JM to LR, 20 June. 'war in France': JM to VM, 18 July.
263-4. 'he is a real good fellow': JM to McGlinn, 18 June. The chief sources for the raid are MP (AWM), box 85; *Official History*, iii, pp. 300-4; JM to WR, 3 July; Wanliss, *History of the Fourteenth Battalion*, ch. 18.

264-5. D records the news. 'You know without': McCay to JM, 19 June. 'While I know': JM to VM, 6 Nov. McGlinn exulted to VM, 27 Aug. Garcia sent his doggerel on 30 Aug. 'altho' I know': Goldstein to JM, 16 July.
265. This paragraph is based on letters to VM, 16, 18, 22 July, 16 Oct.
265-6. 'a very mixed': JM to VM, 30 July. Uncharacteristic admission: JM to VM, 16 Sept. 'equal in every way': JM to Birdwood, 27 July; cf. to Griffiths, 24 July. 'Most of them are men of standing': JM to VM, 22, 30 July; cf. JM to Locke, 28 Aug. Dismissal of brigadier: D, 7, 9, 12 Aug; JM to Rankin, 1 Aug.; Rankin to JM, 9 Aug. MP (AWM), box 85, have relevant material. Re Pope: Pope to JM, 2, 5 Aug.; JM to Pope, 3 Aug.; JM to McGlinn, 2, 17 Aug.
266-7. The Farmars: JM to VM, 30 July; Mrs Farmar to VM, 26 Sept.; interviews with Susan Scammell and Hugh Farmar, June 1979.
267. JM described his transition to VM on 16, 22 Aug. On Colman: JM to VM, 30 July, 21 Nov.
The correspondence is: JM to White, 28 July, 2, 10 Aug.; White to JM, 4 Aug.; JM to Moore, 2 Aug.; Birdwood to Pearce, 3 July, Birdwood Papers; JM to VM, 10, 16 Sept.
267-8. Attempt to break up the division: *Official History*, iii, pp. 862-8. Examples of Monash's protest campaign are letters to McGlinn, 17 Aug.; King-King, 8 Sept.; White, 22 Aug.; Bruche, 8, 19 Sept.; Birdwood, 16, 26, 30 Aug., 22 Sept.; Griffiths, 10 Sept. Birdwood replied on 19 Aug., 4 Oct., and White on 26 Aug. Note also Bean, D 67, 9 Dec. 1916, and Fitzhardinge, *The Little Digger*, pp. 182-5.
268. Referendum: JM to A.I.F. Administrative Headquarters, 16 Oct.; JM to Miller, 17 Oct.; Miller to JM, 19 Oct.
268-9. JM to VM, 27 Oct., records his support of conscription. Agnes Murphy wrote on 9 Jan. 1917 and he replied on 5 May. 'it was the way Hughes': Wilson's diary, 11 Aug. 1918, Imperial War Museum. The embarrassing Minnie Behrend: MM to JM, 2 Jan. 1917, 28 Feb. 1919. His misconception about the A.I.F. vote is in a letter to VM, 2 Jan. 1917.
269. 'No single brigade had met': JM to VM, 26 Oct. He commented on the long training period to White, 22 Aug.
269-70. Bean, D 67, 7 Dec. 1916, describes 3rd Division's training. See also D; JM to Foster, 7 May 1917; JM to Durrant, 2 Oct. 1916; McNicol, *The Thirty-Seventh*, p. 22. 'early this morning': JM to VM, 6 Nov., also WR to VM, 29 Nov., Bruche in Thompson, *On Lips of Living Men*, p. 135, and D, 17 Nov.
270-1. On the hat question, Monash had a sharp exchange with C. H. Chomley, editor of the *British Australasian*: JM to Chomley, 19, 22, 27 Aug.; Chomley to JM, 21, 24 Aug. Bean commented in *Official History*, iv, p. 563, and v, p. 13n. Birdwood wrote to Monash on 15 Nov.; the reply was on the 18th. On this question I largely rely on an interview with Brigadier D. A. Whitehead, 5 Jan. 1981.
271-2. The transcript of this address is in MP (AWM), box 86.
272. This paragraph is based on Farmar's Reminiscences. The remark about 'The Guards' is taken from McNicol, *The Thirty-Seventh*, p. 119.
Brand wrote on 3 Sept. and Durrant on 20 Aug; JM replied to Brand on 8 Sept.
272-3. JM described these visits to VM on 6, 11 Aug., 10, 16 Sept. Relevant material is also in MP (AWM), box 85. 'We are being inspected': JM to WR, 9 Sept. Birdwood reported to Pearce on 16 Oct., Pearce Papers.
273-5. JM reported French's promise to VM on 16 Sept. His diary from 22 Sept. records his preparations. He reported the King's inspection to VM on 30 Sept. JM exulted to Durrant in a letter of 2 Oct. The late Leonard Mann emphasized some of the troops' disgruntlement to me in an interview on 7 Apr. 1976.
275. Springthorpe's report appeared in *Age* on 13 Nov. JM reported his investiture to VM on 23 Oct.
D and a letter to VM on 10 Oct. record his leave. JM to VM, 6 Nov., covers his weekend at Surrenden.

275-6. On the delay, JM to WR, 9 Sept., and Bean, D 67, 7 Dec. JM recorded the scale of war production to VM, 16 Sept. 'the best-trained Division': JM to VM, 21 Nov. Artillery: JM to VM, 27 Oct.; JM to Birdwood, 27 Oct.; Birdwood to JM, 1 Nov. The last march: JM to VM, 15 Nov.; JM to C.O., 43rd Battalion, 21 Nov.
276. 'You should have just heard': JM to VM, 21 Nov., and see D.
277-8. Bean's D 67, 1 Dec. 1916, includes remarks on feeling against 3rd Division. 'in every way': Godley to Pearce, 11 Dec., Pearce Papers. Birdwood also wrote to Pearce on 24 Dec. and to Munro Ferguson on 31 Dec., Birdwood Papers. McNicol, *The Thirty-Seventh*, p. 44, indicates the unpopularity of the parade. Haig's gesture: JM to VM, 21 Dec.
278. JM commented on his health in letters to VM, 6 Nov. 1916, 26 Apr., 6 Aug., 24 Sept., 14 Nov., 28 Dec. 1917, also to MM, 17 Mar. 1918, and in D, 2 Jan. 1917.; see also back of this diary.

Mme Plouvier: JM to VM, 9 Dec. 1916, 2 May 1918; also a letter from her nephew to JM, 23 Apr. 1926. Croix du Bac: JM to VM, 2 Feb., 15 May 1917, and D.
278-9. JM described his front to VM, 21 Dec. 1916; also *Official History*, iv, pp. 564-5. The instructions on trench feet were issued on 11 Dec. He described troops' entertainment to VM, 11 Jan. 1917.
279-80. *Official History*, iv, pp. 563-9, and D cover these operations. Monash's report to Godley was on 31 Jan. His letter to WR was on 4 Mar.; also, JM to White, 27 Feb., MP (AWM), box 86.
280. Monash's remarks on his men were to MacFarland, 29 Jan.; Foster, 7 May; White, 27 Apr.; Brand, 18 Apr.; Locke, 4 May; VM, 15 May. 'but I can assure you': JM to Godley, 11 Dec. 1916, also 7 Mar. 1917. Dering's departure: Birdwood to JM, 4 June; Dering to JM, 29 July; JM to VM, 19 July 1917.
281. There is much evidence on the Ozanne case. See my long version with my first draft, MP; P. Hardy's Review of the Evidence, MP; B. McKinlay, 'The Case of Gunner A. T. Ozanne', *Recorder*, no. 57, Apr. 1972.
281-2. JM's opinion of McNicoll was given to VM, 15 Jan., and Foster, 7 May 1917; of Grimwade, to VM, 1 Oct.; to Foster, 7 May. Jobson: JM to Foster, 7 May. Some of Monash's letters to Jobson were on 24 Apr., 9 June; see Jobson to JM, 10 June. The letter asking for resignation was on 30 July, MP (AWM), box 87; also JM to Birdwood, 1 Aug. Rosenthal's account of taking up his command, *Reveille*, Oct. 1931. 'how *all* my Commanders': JM to VM, 1 Oct.
282. The urgent letter to McCay was on 15 Apr. Monash gave reasons for dismissals to Foster on 7 May. Sacking of C.O.s of 37th and 44th Battalions: MP (AWM), box 86. 'As you know': JM to Cannan, 20 Jan. 1917. Dismissing an officer: e.g., to HQ, 2nd A & NZ Army Corps, 22 Jan. 1917; but cf. to Summerhayes, 15 Dec. 1917. Persuading McNicoll: JM to McNicoll, 18 Aug. 1917. Officers abusing soldiers: JM to Lyons, 26 Apr. 1917. Conduct of sergeant-majors: MP (AWM), box 87, 14 July 1917. Story's protest is in MP (AWM), box 86. Scientific approach: cf. JM to Plumer, 8 Feb. 1917. D records Plumer's visits.
282-4. On Legge: JM to VM, 26 Apr. 1917. 'declared he has become': JM to VM, 26 July 1917. Congratulating Hobbs: JM to Hobbs, 7 Jan. 1917; Hobbs to JM, 12 Jan. Changes in divisional commands: *Official History*, iv, pp. 23-5. 'A respect for you': White to JM, 12 Jan. 1917. On Chauvel's promotion: JM to VM, 15 May 1917. Brush with Holmes: Holmes to JM, 26, 27 June; JM to Holmes, 27 June. On MacLagan: JM to VM, 26 July.
284. White's explanation was in a letter of 30 Jan.; cf. JM to VM, 2 Feb. 'You can't have it both ways': Godley to JM, 22 June, in reply to a letter of same date. Monash pointed out the errors to Dodds, 12 July, 2 Aug.

JM described his leave to VM, 14, 26 Mar., and advised Cannan, 10, 17 Sept.
284-5. 'It is perfectly wonderful': JM to VM, 2 Feb.; cf. his teasing, 30 May. 'You can hardly imagine': JM to VM, 5 Feb. 'I hate the business of war': JM to VM, 16 Mar.

285-6. Reassurance about Gibson: JM to VM, 16 Mar., 25 Apr. '[War] is not a business': JM to Gibson, 29 Apr.
286. Working like a well-oiled machine: JM to VM, 4 Mar., 25 Apr. Godley's praise: JM to VM, 4 Mar. Sick-rate: JM to Godley, 12 Apr. German raids: *Official History*, iv, pp. 569-70; McNicoll to JM, 1 May, MP (AWM), box 86.
286-7. 'I need not say, my dear madam': JM to Mrs Urquhart, 6 Apr. 1917. Influence to bear: e.g., from and to Lady Doughty, 30 Aug., 14 Sept.
Official History, iv, chs I-XIII, describes the course of events.
287-9. Monash described the adjustment of position to VM, 26 Mar., to WR, 24 Apr., and his movements to VM, 26 Apr.; see also D. Harington's comment was to Edmonds, 27 Jan. 1932, AWM. 'there was concentrated': *Official History*, iv, pp. 576, 578; cf. JM to Bean, 17 Mar. 1930. D, 8 May, and JM to VM, 26 Apr., 15 May, cover meetings with the Canadians.
289-90. 'for weeks past': JM to VM, 19 May. MP (AWM), box 86, include the notes for company commanders dated 13 May, and his letter to Godley of 4 May. His diary lists the conferences. Jackson told Liddell Hart of his comments, on 4 Oct. 1935, Liddell Hart Papers, LH 1/516. 'The attack always had': JM to VM, 19 May. He recorded in D his inability to sleep.
290. 'The northern corps': *Official History*, iv, p. 560. Terraine, *The Road to Passchendaele*, p. 119, records the number of shells. The plan is described in *Official History*, pp. 571-87.
290-1. E. M. Brissenden's diary, 28 Apr. 1917 (AWM), has remarks on gas-training. JM's description to WR, including the long quotation, was on 16 June.
Official History, iv, chs XV-XVI, covers the battle of Messines.
291-2. 'the most perfect attack': C. E. Carrington, *Soldier from the Wars Returning*, London, 1965, p. 147. 'I am the greatest possible believer': JM to WR, 14 June.
292. Godley's letters to Pearce of 12 June and 8 July, Godley Papers, contain high praise of the division. The Official Historian's judgements are in iv, pp. 679, 681. JM wrote to Birdwood on 27 June. The papers relating to the 37th Battalion are in MP (AWM), box 86. 'apotheosis of banality': JM to VM, 24 Sept.
JM described the evacuation of Nieppe to VM on 20 June and his visit to the Tanks on 19 July. The yarn with Plumer was noted in D, 23 June.
292-3. He described his leave to VM on 11 July.
293. *Official History*, iv, pp. 712-21, covers the Warneton assault. MP (AWM), box 86, and D add detail. The 'Mr Monash' joke is from Farmar's Reminiscences.
293-4. D and letters to VM, 6, 16 Aug., 1, 10 Sept., cover the break out of action.
294. 'A brilliant success': JM to VM, 24 Sept.
294-5. Bean noted Harington's praise in *Official History*, iv, p. 836n., and his own meeting with 11th Brigade, p. 840. Broodseinde and its preparation are described in ch. XX.
295. JM's description of Ypres was to VM on 1 Oct. The delay in evacuating the wounded: *Official History*, pp. 839-40
295-6. Swarms of prisoners: *Official History*, p. 856. 'perhaps the most complete': p. 866.
296. MP (AWM), box 88, have comparative casualty statistics. 'All the enemy's manifestations': JM to WR, 6 Oct.
296-7. Terraine's justification: *The Road to Passchendaele*, pp. 336 ff., and *The Western Front*, pp. 151 ff. Cf. *Official History*, pp. 938-46.
297-8. Monash pleading for delay: JM to WR, 15 Oct. Other sources for Passchendaele: *Official History*, pp. 909-26; JM's report of 12 Oct., MP (AWM), box 87; JM to Godley, 14 Oct.; Bean, D 89-90; F. C. Green, *The Fortieth*, Hobart, 1922, ch. 14.
298. Monash's reports: to Godley, 14 Oct., 1 Nov.; to WR, 15 Oct.; cf. to VM, 18 Oct.
298-9. D notes encounters with McNicoll and Russell. MP (AWM), box 87, have the 'poem'. *Official History*, pp. 932-3, for the gassing.

299. The request to White was on 28 Jan. 1917. Birdwood's ambition: Birdwood to Hutton, 30 Sept. 1916, Hutton Papers, British Library.
299-300. *Official History*, v, pp. 5-12 describes the Australianization campaign and Murdoch's part. Murdoch's letters to Hughes, 22, 26, 30 Aug., Murdoch Papers, are crucial.
300-1. 'I am almost convinced': JM to VM, 6 Aug.; cf. JM to WR, 11 Sept. 'I dined with him': JM to VM, 24 Sept.; cf. JM to WR, 23 Sept. Haig's remark to Simonson: VM to JM, 24 Nov. My remarks on Haig are based on Terraine's biography and an interview with Mr D. W. King, May 1979.
301. 'Monash for an Australian Commander': Bean, D 91, c. 18 Oct.; cf. D 94, 3 Dec., and D 90 re Haig having Monash to dine.
301-2. Some of the more important documents are: Birdwood to Murdoch, 26 Oct., Murdoch Papers; Fisher to Hughes, 26 Oct., Hughes Papers; Murdoch's letters to Hughes, Murdoch Papers. Rearrangement of the Corps: *Official History*, v, pp. 2-5, 11-15; Birdwood to divisional commanders, 3, 9 Nov.
302. 'universally regarded': JM to VM, 14 Nov. 'in ordinary fairness': Birdwood to Murdoch, 15 July, Murdoch Papers. 'Birdwood will try': Murdoch to Hughes, 23 Dec. (?), Murdoch Papers.
302-3. Murdoch's despatch to the *Herald* was published 18 Aug. 1917. Monash's views on rum are in a letter to Carruthers of 4 Jan. 1918. Miss Butler wrote about the rest centre on 28 Jan. 1918; also JM to VM, 18 Mar. 1918. 'Those fellows knew': Fennessy to JM, 8 Jan. 1918. 'rousing and prolonged cheering': C. R. Cuttriss, *"Over the Top" with the Third Australian Division*, London, 1917?, p. 112. Letters relating to his popularity are from Devine, 17 Sept. 1917, Mrs Farmar, 26 Aug. 1917, Sugden, 12 Jan. 1918, 'Your old trumpeter', 4 Mar. 1918; see also Teesdale-Smith to VM, 31 Jan. 1917; Perth *Mirror*, 10 Oct. 1931.
303. Letters to VM of 16 Sept., 9, 21 Dec. 1917, are examples of indiscretion. Documents to WR: JM to WR, 3, 22 June 1918; WR to JM, 11 July 1918.
303-4. 'General Monash as a leader': Farmar to Sellheim, quoted VM to JM, 7 Aug. 1917. Farmar's Reminiscences are the source for the rest of the paragraph. Cf. also Farmar's farewell letter to JM, 5 Sept. 1917.
304. Jackson's revealing letter was of 23 Jan. 1918.
His letter to Liddell Hart was of 4 Oct. 1935, Liddell Hart Papers, LH 1/516.
305. Leaving Godley: JM to VM, 14 Nov., also 18 Oct. 1917. 'Of all this you and I': White to JM, 5 Dec. 1917. Mentions of other brushes with Corps are in D; Rosenthal diary (Mitchell Lib.), 25 Dec. 1917; JM to Gwynn, 6 Jan. 1918; *Official History*, v, pp. 34, 90.
305-6. JM told VM on 18 Oct. that Dodds had tipped him off. MM wrote on 3 Jan. 1918. For Birdwood's remark, JM to VM, 12 Jan. 1918.
306-7. JM's letters to VM on the subject are on 13 Jan., 15 Mar. (long quotations), 4 Apr.; hers are of 4 Jan., 10 Feb., 7 May, 5 July 1918.
307-8. Monash describes the situation in *Australian Victories*, pp. 1-3. For the raids on 30 Nov., JM to Farmar, 1 Dec.; *Official History*, v, p. 689.
308. For the Feb.-Mar. raids, *Official History*, v, pp. 43-4, 47-8, 690. Notes for pep talks are in MP (AWM), box 87. 'definitely established': JM to VM, 15 Mar. 1918. The draft plan for Warneton is in MP (AWM), dated 22 Feb.
308-9. MP (AWM) have much material for this period. On machine-gun tactics, JM to Jackson, 28 Feb. Guidance of MG battalion commander: JM to Blacklow, 4 Mar. 26 Feb. conference: Notes 3 Division Conference, AWM 213/1/1, and MP (AWM), box 87. Drake-Brockman's comments are from his *The Turning Wheel*, Perth, 1960, p. 117.
309-10. 'A Division is such a big affair': JM to VM, 15 Mar. 1918. Officers of German descent: JM to VM, 15 Mar. 1918. His comments on Coxen were to VM, 16 Mar. Abbott's diary (Univ. New England) for 14 Feb.-1 Mar. is of interest; P. P. Abbott, *ADB* 7; JM to VM, 3 Mar. 1918. Plumer and 3rd Division: JM to VM, 12 Jan. 1918.

310. 'other divisional commanders': JM to VM, 15 Mar. Holiday: JM to VM, 17 Mar., 2 Apr.; JM to MM, 17 Mar.; Rosenthal's diary, 22 Mar.
   This paragraph is based largely on *AV*, pp. 6-8; JM to Birdwood, 28 Mar.; JM to VM, 2 Apr.
311-13. 'I found them sitting': JM to VM, 2 Apr.; the other accounts are in *AV*, pp. 9-10; to Birdwood, 28 Mar.; to Chauvel, 14 Apr.; to O'Donnell, 24 Apr.; and in 'Leadership in War'. 'At four o'clock: *AV*, p. 9. 'It was already 1 a.m.': *AV*, p. 10. 'It was really a question': JM to VM, 2 Apr. 'momentarily expecting': JM to WR, 31 Mar., MP (AWM), box 88. 'on that crisp, clear': *AV*, p. 11. Bean's account: *Official History*, v, pp. 174-92; Monash's famous orders are appendix 3. Consultations with Congreve: JM to Birdwood, 28 Mar.
313-14. 'With what strength': *Official History*, v, p. 215; pp. 212-26 cover the engagement. Monash was reticent in *AV*, p. 15.
314. *Official History*, v, pp. 229-35, and JM to Birdwood, 30 Mar., cover events of 29-30 Mar.
314-15. D and letters to Birdwood, 30 Mar., and to VM, 2 Apr., and White to JM, 31 Mar., are the sources for much of this paragraph. Monash quotes Mullens's letter, *AV*, p. 15. Picnic atmosphere: *Official History*, pp. 188-92, and 192n. for the salvage operation.
315. 'These Tommy divisions': JM to VM, 4 Apr.; also JM to WR, 5 Apr.
315-16. 'almost a debacle': JM to Fairway, 14 Apr., but cf. JM in *Herald*, 8 Sept. 1920. Interpretation in this paragraph is largely based on *Official History*, v, pp. 284-97, 672-4. The title of W. D. Joynt's *Saving the Channel Ports 1918*, Melbourne, 1975, is more exaggerated than the text.
316. Monash's letters to VM of 12, 16 Apr., 2, 31 May, are revealing with regard to A.I.F. recognition.
316-17. 'good commanders': Rawlinson's diary, 14 Apr. The 11 Apr. message is in MP (AWM). 'It is hard, sometimes': JM to VM, 12 Apr. Recapture of Villers-Bretonneux: JM in *Age*, 19 Feb., 13 Apr. 1920. On von Richthofen: JM to VM, 23 Apr.; to Blake, 19 July; to Cannan, 23 July; to Treloar, 30 July.
317. *Official History*, vi, pp. 32-6, 45-8, and *AV*, pp. 21-2, describe peaceful penetration.
317-18. The Morlancourt minor battles are covered in *Official History*, pp. 61-94.
318. Jess's recollections were in a letter to JM, 25 July 1921. Re attacking south of the Somme: *Official History*, vi, pp. 529-30; Bean, *Two Men I Knew*, pp. 141-3; *AV*, pp. 22-3; Corps Conference, 10 Apr. 1918, MP (AWM).
   On relations with the French and his new headquarters: JM to VM, 4 June. Bean's comment is in D 113, 31 May. Monash's departure: D and *AV*, p. 24n.
318-19. 'McCay has coolly asked': JM to VM, 12 Jan. The other letters are in MP. Monash replied to Jackson on 29 Mar. D records Birdwood's news.
319. Bean recorded White's views on Birdwood in his D 113, 31 May 1918. Monash's comment on Birdwood was in his 'Leadership in War'. Elliott's views on Birdwood are plain in his letters to his wife (AWM); Gellibrand's diary, 11 Nov. 1918, is also illuminating. Many of the senior officers used to mock Birdwood's constant scoutmasterly addressing of the troops as 'Boys', e.g. McGlinn to JM, 2 July 1918.
319-20. Birdwood wrote to Pearce, 12 Mar., Birdwood and Pearce Papers. 'He has commanded': Birdwood to Pearce, 13 May, Pearce Papers.
320. White stated his view to Bean, 14 Oct. 1938, White Papers.
320-1. JM stated his reactions to VM, 14, 31 May, 4 June. He replied to WR's letter of 7 June on 12 June.
321. JM reassured VM, 4 June, and WR, 1 June. Smyth wrote on 23 May, Hobbs on 30 May, McCay on 27 May, Cannan on 30 May, McGlinn on 2 July. Elliott wrote to his wife on 1 June. VM reported on home reactions on 11, 19, 27 June, 14 July, and Belle Grant on 27 June. Sir R. McC. Anderson wrote on 2 Jan. 1919 to the 'mere militia man'. Fink wrote to Murdoch, 29 May, 19 June, Murdoch Papers. Cf. A. D. Ellis, *The Story of the Fifth Australian Division*, London, 1919?, p. 308.

321-2. Monash's note about disaffected brigadiers is dated 6 June, MP (AWM), box 88. 'There was immediately': Bean, D 111, 17 May, and D 109.
322. Murdoch's cables were on 20 and 21 May. MP (AWM), box 92, contain most of this material. Hughes's cable to Pearce is mentioned by Bean, D 198.
322-3. Murdoch's letters of 21, 25 May, 3 June, are in Birdwood Papers. Birdwood wrote to Munro Ferguson on 27 May, Novar Papers. A copy of Dodds's undated letter to Pearce is in MP (AWM), box 92. Bean's note of his letter to Dodds and his marginal addition are in his D 111, 1 June.
323. Murdoch wrote to Monash on 21 May and Monash replied on 24, 25 May. His opinion of Murdoch is in JM to VM, 31 May.
  'free from intrigue or cabal': JM to Hughes, 2 June.
323-4. 'though a lucid thinker': *Official History*, vi, pp. 195-6. McGlinn's letter was of 2 July. Bean's letter to White was of 26 June, Bean Papers, folder 60; cf. his letter to Murdoch of 5 July, ibid.
324. Murdoch's letter of 6 June is also in the Murdoch Papers. JM replied on 11 June. 'It is a poor compliment': draft to Birdwood (not sent). 'You and your friends': draft (not sent), MP (AWM), box 92. JM had a 'long and important' talk with Howse, D.
324-5. Monash wrote to Bean on 11 June. Bean commented in his D 109, 15 June. 'Monash is a man': D 115, 16 June. Birdwood's letter to Murdoch is reported in Bean's D 109, 10 June; cf. Birdwood to Battarbee, 10 June, Walter Long Papers, Wiltshire Record Office, 947/534. On 24 June JM made a note of his conference with Birdwood, MP (AWM), box 92. The remark about a pogrom is in JM to VM, 25 June; letters to WR of 12 June and to LR of 30 June are relevant.
325. Latham's menu notes are in his Papers (National Library), series 20, folder 17. Bean's memo of 25 June is in Hughes Papers. Bean recorded Murdoch's powers of argument in D 114, 13 June. Copies of Birdwood's letters to Hughes, Pearce, and Munro Ferguson of 21 June, 15 June and 15 June are in his Papers. Copies of JM's and Hobbs's letters to Pearce of 21 and 27 June are in MP. Rawlinson's opinion of Murdoch is in a letter to Birdwood of 27 June, Birdwood Papers. Bean wrote to White on 26 June and White replied on 4 July, Bean Papers, folder 60. JM wrote to McGlinn on 27 June; cf. to LR, 30 June.
326. JM wrote to Birdwood on 29 June and again, describing Hughes's visit, on 2 July, Birdwood Papers.
  Bean records Hughes's reaction in D 116, 14 July. Long told Birdwood of his efforts on 2 July, Birdwood Papers. The Monash-White correspondence is in MP (AWM), box 92. Note also Cutlack to Bean, 4 May 1958, Bean Papers, folder 475.
326-7. 'there is no doubt': Bean D 116, 14 July. Murdoch reported White's rebuke to Bean in a letter of 12 July, Murdoch Papers. The hint of the generals' meeting is in a scrappy note by Bean, based on information from Gellibrand, in his Notebook 94A. Bean's desperate letter to White was of 10 July, Bean Papers, folder 195. The Murdoch-Monash exchange was on 12 and 17 July. JM's letters to WR of 13 July and to Gibson of 20 July are revealing. He relied on the advice of Henry Noyes, a close friend of Walter Long: Noyes to JM, 24, 29 July. Relevant correspondence about the end of July was to Murdoch, 27, 31 July; from Murdoch, 25, 27 July; to Hughes, 27 July, to Birdwood, 1 Aug. 'White does not impress him': Murdoch to Bean, 21 July, Bean Papers, folder 195. Cf. also Murdoch to Bean, 24, 31 July, Bean Papers, folder 60; Bean to Murdoch, 27 July, Murdoch Papers.
328. *Official History*, vi, pp. 212-14, covers the question of the future of the command. Chauvel to Birdwood, 12 Aug., 5 Sept., Birdwood Papers, and Hill, *Chauvel*, pp. 157-8, for Chauvel's intervention. For Murdoch's despatch, *Herald*, 8 Aug., 9 Aug. editorial; Munro Ferguson to Birdwood, 12 Sept., Birdwood Papers; MM to JM, 15 Sept.
  'our high-intentioned': *Two Men I Knew*, p. 173.

329. Discussions with Birdwood: JM to VM, 4 June 1918. Bean wrote the entry on Gellibrand for the British *Dictionary of National Biography*. July recommendation: JM to Birdwood, 14 July.

There is much on the Gellibrand–McNicoll relationship in MP (AWM), box 88; MP, June correspondence; Gellibrand Papers, box 188; McNicoll to Elliott, 25 Apr. 1921, Elliott Papers; JM to Birdwood, 23 Sept.

329-30. 'stupid in the extreme': JM to WR, 12 July; JM to Bruche, 20 May. 'personal staff': *Official History*, vi, p. 208.

330. JM described Bertangles to VM, 31 May and 25 June. Interviews with Sir Alfred Kemsley and Messrs Hunter Rogers, J. T. Smith and H. C. Thomas contributed to my view of the atmosphere at Corps.

330-1. An interview with Monash in the *Herald*, 27 July 1918, is relevant. 'incorrigibly civilian': *Official History*, vi, p. 5. Break-up of battalions: JM to 3 Div brigadiers, 2 Apr. 1918; JM to Rawlinson, 22 June; JM to Murdoch, 15 Apr. 1919.

331. Hobbs's demonstration: Rosenthal diary; JM to VM, 18 June. JM's Notes for Divisional Commanders' Conference are in MP (AWM), box 88. Narrow escape: D, and JM to Bruche, 31 Dec. 1929.

Rawlinson's orders: D, 12-14 June; *AV*, pp. 25-6. Aggressive raiding: *Official History*, vi, pp. 218-42.

331-2. 'Taking it all in all': JM to LR, 30 June.

332. Terraine, *To Win a War*, pp. 75, 87, is excellent on the tactical reasons for Hamel. 'It was high time': *AV*, p. 27. The main documentation of the plan is in MP (AWM), box 88; *AV*, pp. 27-9. Footnote: see F. Maurice, *The Life of General Lord Rawlinson of Trent*, London, 1928, pp. 221-4; J. Smyth, *Leadership in Battle*, London, 1975.

332-3. 'pirouetting': *AV*, p. 31. For use of the tanks, Blamey, *Herald*, 2 Aug. 1930; H. G. Viney, *Mufti*, 1 Mar. 1939.

333. 'asked for about 2000 men': *Official History*, vi, p. 262. 'affability, courtesy': JM to VM, 5 July. See Haig's diary for 1 July and Birdwood to Pearce, 8 July, Pearce Papers. Rawlinson's doubts were entered in his diary.

333-4. 'meeting full of tense situations': *AV*, pp. 35-6. 'Do you want me': *Official History*, p. 274. Hamel plan: *Official History*, ch. VIII; *AV*, pp. 26-38; D; Bean, D 116; 'Leadership in War', p. 24.

335. 'the main barrage crashed down': *Official History*, pp. 284-5. 'Not even Messines': *AV*, p. 38; J. F. L. Fuller, *Memoirs of an Unconventional Soldier*, London, 1936, pp. 289-90. 'A war-winning combination': Essame, *The Battle for Europe*, p. 104. 'It wasn't a battle': A. C. Taylour to author, 13 Apr. 1976. In general for the battle: *Official History*, ch. IX; *AV*, pp. 38-43; D. Orgill, *The Tank: Studies in the Development and Use of a Weapon*, London, 1970, ch. 4; R. A. Beaumont, 'Hamel, 1918—A Study in Military-Political Interaction', *Military Affairs*, Spring 1967.

335-6. 'the first modern battle': Smithers, *Sir John Monash*, p. 212. One of the more interesting inquiries about Hamel was from Currie of the Canadians, 13 July. 'All England is talking about it': JM to VM, 15 July. The orders were published as *Operations by the Australian Corps against Hamel* (S.S. No. 218). Clemenceau's visit: *Official History*, pp. 334-5; *AV*, p. 44.

336. JM described the lunch in Amiens and the visit of the mission to VM, 15, 19 July; also JM to Smart, 1 July; Métin to JM, 21 July.

336-7. Post-Hamel activities: MP (AWM), box 86; *AV*, pp. 46-8; *Official History*, ch. X. Brand warned JM on 8 July. *Official History*, pp. 487-8, notes his visits to brigades. Smithers, *Sir John Monash*, pp. 274-5, movingly criticizes his lack of appreciation of the British war effort, but the matter is difficult to judge.

337. 'the first offensive operation': *AV*, p. 45; cf. JM to Steele, 26 Aug. 1930.

337-8. A commonplace: e.g. A. Dawes, *Sun*, 11 Oct. 1947; cf. Ellis, *Story of the Fifth Division*, pp. 321-2. Blamey's claim: *Herald*, 2 Aug. 1930; cf. Cannan to JM, 2 Aug. 1928. 'Men like Monash': *Reveille*, Oct. 1931; Cutlack, *SMH*, 9 Aug. 1920; cf. E. A. Drake-Brockman, *Commonwealth Parl. Debates*, 13 July 1922.

NOTES (pages 338–355) 565

338. The relevant Bean diary is 116. 'I expressed the readiness': *AV*, pp. 49-50. JM's letter to Blamey was dated 18 Aug. The letter to the AWM was of 18 June 1928.
339-40. Rawlinson's diary entries are important; *Official History*, pp. 479-80, 524-5, and ch. XIII in general. 'the great stroke was made': *Herald*, 8 Oct. 1931.
340. The early part of this paragraph is based on correspondence between Bean and White in June 1935, White Papers; cf. *Official History*, p. 525n. Monash's beliefs were stated to Bruche, 10 Oct. 1919, and to Steele, 26 Aug. 1930.
340. Arguing for an extended objective: Fuller, op. cit., p. 299; cf. *Official History*, pp. 494-5; JM to Bruche, 10 Oct., 1919. Memo on details: MP (AWM), box 88. 'a destroyer would stand by': JM to VM, 2 Aug., 17 Dec.
340-1. 'Spent the whole': Blamey to Black, 12 Apr. 1937, Bean Papers, box 276. Haig's visit: Haig's D and Bean D 116. Monash given an entirely free hand: JM to Bruche, 10 Oct. 1919. Rawlinson's comments are in his diary.
341. This paragraph is based on *Official History*, pp. 505-6; Bean's D 116; and folder 59, Bean Papers.
341-2. 'enormously increasing the labour': JM to Bruche, 22 Oct. 1919. Gellibrand objected to the leap-frogging arrangements; see his annotations of *AV*, AWM.
342. 'It was inspiriting': *AV*, p. 93. As well as *AV*, chs 5-6, see *Official History*, ch. XIII.
343. Warning MacLagan: cf. Bean Papers, folder 59. The message is in *AV*, pp. 99-100. 'the men felt': *Official History*, p. 525; cf. A. Dean and E. W. Gutteridge, *The Seventh Battalion A.I.F.,* Melbourne, 1933, p. 119.
343-4. 'A strange and ominous quiet': *AV*, pp. 100-1.
344-6. 'Sir, this is a most wonderful day': Thompson, *On Lips of Living Men*, p. 142. Blamey with feet up: H. Lilya to author, 15 Jan. 1980. 'The advance was the most bloodless': *Official History*, p. 544. Panorama when the mist broke: C.E. Montague, *Disenchantment*, London, 1940, pp. 194-8; Leonard Mann, *Flesh in Armour*, Melbourne, 1944, chs 37-8. 'the discipline': Rawlinson to Wigram et al., 28 Aug., Rawlinson Papers, National Military Museum, London. 'The Huns never knew': Cutlack, *SMH*, 9 Aug. 1920. For 8 Aug. in general, *Official History*, ch. XIV; *AV*, pp. 101-11.
346-7. 'the main responsibility': *Official History*, p. 606. Bruche's account is in *On Lips of Living Men*, p. 143.
347. Monash quoted Hindenburg in the *Age*, 12 Apr. 1920; Ludendorff is quoted in *Official History*, p. 1045. Bean angry: D 116, 9 Aug.; *Official History*, pp. 598-604. 'had no idea how far-reaching': JM to LB, 5 Sept. Disappointed: *AV*, pp. 112-13.
347-8. This paragraph is based on *Official History*, pp. 617-49.
348. Ibid., pp. 649-84; *AV*, pp. 118-19; Bean, D 116, 10 Aug.
348-9. 'had so strongly desired': *AV*, p. 115. Herring's account is in *Reveille*, 1 Nov. 1937. Condemned the unnamed general: McNicol, *The Thirty-Seventh*, p. 222. Cf. Monash's account; *AV*, pp. 115-18. Cf. *Official History*, pp. 685-712.
349-50. 'Quite early I had a call': JM to VM, 11 Aug.; cf. Haig, D. 'uttered a few words': Hetherington, *Blamey*, p. 47.
350. Birdwood wrote to JM, 10 Aug. JM described the ceremony to VM, 14 Aug.
351. My account is coloured by an interview with H. C. Thomas, 21 Aug. 1980. Bean's comments are in his D 116, 11, 12, 17 Aug.
   'the possibility': *AV*, p. 119. Currie wrote on 28 Aug. *Official History*, pp. 713-17, covers the rearrangements. Brand's protest of 12 Aug. is in MP (AWM), box 92. See also JM to Hughes, 16 Aug.: *AV*, pp. 121-2; *Official History*, p. 733.
351-2. Bean noted the mutinous stirrings, D 116, 18, 19 Aug. 'The decisions which had to be given': *AV*, p. 124, also pp. 180-1.
352-3. Chuignes is described in *Official History*, pp. 724-60 and *AV*, pp. 126-37.
353. Orders too late: *Official History*, pp. 765, 767. Felt intuitively: *AV*, p. 143.
353-4. 'a merry and exciting three days': *AV*, p. 148, and in general pp. 147-52.
354. 'And so you think': *AV*, p. 158.
354-5. 'The strategic object in view': *AV*, p. 154. The junior officer is Sir Alfred Kemsley.

355. 'according to text-book principles': J. M. A. Durrant, 'Mont St Quentin', *Army Quarterly*, v. 31, no. 1, Oct. 1935. 'could hardly believe': *Official History*, p. 815.
'on the top of Mont St Quentin' (footnote): letters from Phillips to JM of 19, 28 Oct., and from JM to Phillips of 24 Oct. are illuminating. 'You spoiled a damn good battle': Liddell Hart, *Daily Telegraph* (London), 9 Oct. 1931. Cf. *Official History*, p.815.
'I was compelled to harden my heart': *AV*, p.170.
356. Monash and Blamey upset: Bean, D 116. For Mont St Quentin in general: *Official History*, ch. XVIII; *AV*, ch. 11; Terraine, *To Win a War*, pp. 128-9.
356-7. 'In the absence of properly co-ordinated action': *AV*, pp. 164-5. 'By this bold': Rawlinson to Allenby et al., 14 Nov. 1918; Essame, *The Battle for Europe*, p. 149, agrees with Rawlinson. Cf. Lord Lytton, *Argus*, 30 Apr. 1921. 'Within Australian experience': *Official History*, p. 873. 'If one is tempted': Smithers, *Sir John Monash*, p. 251. 'reminiscent of some of the surprise tactics': JM to McCay, 6 Sept. Footnote: B. Pitt, *1918. The Last Act*, London, 1962, pp. 215-18. Colonel Repington, the *Times* military authority, at the time judged it to be 'a most brilliant and remarkable feat' (*The First World War 1914-18*, London, 1920, ii, p. 366).
357. JM described the chase in letters to McCay on 6 Sept. and to Dodds on 7 Sept. See also *AV*, pp. 175-82, 199. Prestige of the Corps: JM to Springthorpe, Notes, 4 Oct. MP (AWM), box 92.
357-8. Monash describes the Hindenburg line in *AV*, pp. 182-3, 191-5. 'the Australian teas': Montgomery to JM, 7 Nov. 1919. 'by this time': *AV*, p. 200. Planning of Hargicourt: *Official History*, pp. 890-914; *AV*, pp. 198-203, 209.
358-9. '256 Vickers guns': Smithers, *Sir John Monash*, p. 261. 'about a record': Rawlinson to JM, 19 Sept. The Bean quotations are from his D 116, 17, 18 Sept. For Hargicourt, *Official History*, pp. 914-32; *AV*, pp. 209-10; Terraine, *To Win a War*, p. 150.
359. Bean's views are in *Official History*, pp. 876-7, and in D, 18, 28 Aug. 'by nature and intellect': JM to VM, 11 Sept. Hughes 'rather a handful': JM to LB, 17 Sept. Cf, *AV*, pp. 185-7. 'The men were great': A. Conan Doyle, *The British Campaign in Europe, 1914-1918*, London, 1928, p. 205. 'somewhat rugged': *Weekly Despatch* (London), 16 June 1918. Examples of favourable publicity are *Illustrated Sunday Herald*, 22 Sept., *Observer*, 22 Sept., *Daily News*, 25 Sept., *Morning Post*, 28 Sept.
359-60. 'demurred that the needs': *Official History*, p. 879. W. F. Whyte, *William Morris Hughes. His Life and Times*, Sydney, 1957, pp. 369-70, has a highly imaginative version. Monash and Rawlinson agreeing: *AV*, p. 245. 'was chasing me round': *Smith's Weekly*, 17 May 1930.
360-1. JM protested to Birdwood on 15 Sept. His letter to Fourth Army was on 17 Sept. *Official History*, pp. 895-6, and Scott, *Australia during the War*, pp. 745-6, cover the incident.
361. Bean covers the mutiny in *Official History*, pp. 932-4, 940, and in D 117, 27 Sept.; cf. *Australian*, 28-29 July 1979. Footnote: see Bean's note on disbandment of the battalions in his Notebook 94 B.
'I welcome any pretext': Bean, D 116, 8 Sept. JM's request for discretion was to Dodds, 7 Sept.
362. 'I have done a thing unprecedented': McNicol, *The Thirty-Seventh*, p. 252. His notes of the meeting are in MP (AWM), box 89.
JM's claim to Murdoch was on 15 Apr. 1919. Cf. *Official History*, pp. 935-40; *AV*, pp. 245-8; D, 25 Sept.; JM to Dodds, 26 Sept.; Gellibrand to JM, 22 Sept.; Bean, D 117, 27 Sept.
'The last thing': JM to generals, 3 Oct. 'with as little fuss': JM to Birdwood, 28 Oct. 'I was taking a chance': JM to Blamey, 18 Oct. Stalling and arguing: JM to Birdwood, 13 Nov.
362-3. He wrote to Springthorpe on 2 Oct. Blamey's recollections were in *Reveille*, Oct. 1931. 'I often have to carry on': JM to Meyer, 1 Apr.
364. 'more a matter of engineering': Notes, 29 Sept.-2 Oct. 1918, Gellibrand Papers, box 190a. 'with blackboard and chalk': *AV*, p. 223.

NOTES (pages 364–376)

364-5. Rawlinson noted JM's request in his D. 'It was contrary to the policy': *AV*, pp. 226, 228.
365-6. JM and the war correspondents: Bean, D 117, 28, 30 Sept. Blamey swearing: interview with J. T. Smith, Apr. 1976. 'the most brilliant battle-plan': *Official History*, p. 994; cf. Gellibrand's annotation of *AV*.
366. The note of the conversation is in Phone messages, 29 Sept., Gellibrand Papers, box 190a.
366-7. 'a day of intense effort': *AV*, p. 242. 'time and again': Gellibrand's annotation to *AV*. Gellibrand's Notes, 29 Sept.-2 Oct. 1918 are illuminating; cf. *Official History*, p. 1009.
367. 'You Australians are all bluff': *Official History*, p. 1021. 'an astonishing performance': *AV*, p. 251.
'General Rawlinson desired me': *AV*, p. 252. Bean's D 117, 9 Oct., and marginal note is illuminating.
In general, for the Hindenburg line operations: *Official History*, ch. XX; *AV*, chs 14-16; Essame, *The Battle for Europe*, pp. 182-91.
367-8. 'In that war of "bloodbaths"': Terraine, *To Win a War*, p. 187. 'it was the least costly period': *AV*, p. 262. 'the losses of his brigade': *Official History*, vi, p. 209. Casualty figures are to be found in the *Official History*, especially vi, p. 1044n., and the Official Medical History, ii, appendix 1, and iii, statistical appendices, especially table 26.
368-70. 'It may be that hereafter': *AV*, p. 263. 59th Battalion mutiny: *Official History*, pp. 875-6. 'Drunk with success': J. G. McLean, *War and its Glories*, Melbourne, 1920, p. 82. 'We always knew': White, *The "Fighting Thirteenth"*, p. 157. 'the everlasting contradiction': Geoffrey Hutton, *Age*, 26 Nov. 1977. Bean's suspicions: e.g., D 116, 4 Sept. 'In this decisive fighting': *Official History*, p. 940. 'Some critics have declared': *Herald*, 21 July 1923. *AV*, p. 249, gives his reasons for withdrawal of the Corps. The figures in the footnote are taken from Official Medical History, iii, statistical appendices, table 10.
370. Monash's prediction was in *Argus*, 23 Sept.; he wrote to Pearce on 3 Oct.
'the performance of my five Divisions': JM to Pearce, 5 Nov. The tabulation of achievement is from *AV*, pp. 257-9. Terraine's remarks are from *The Smoke and the Fire*, p. 190.
370-1. Birdwood wrote on 3 Oct.; JM wrote to Dodds on 2 Oct. 'had spoken for nearly an hour': JM to VM, 3 Nov. D has details of his leave, also JM to VM, 3 Nov.
371-2. Blamey's reply to Rawlinson is in MP (AWM), box 89. Hobbs and Blamey wrote to JM on 20, 22 Oct., JM to Hughes on 21 Oct. Wilson's diary (Imperial War Museum) has a note of the meeting and Rawlinson records JM's view in his diary. Slanted casualty statistics: *Official History*, p. 1049n. Other relevant letters are Birdwood to JM, 31 Oct., and JM to Dodds and Blamey, 31 Oct. Wanting to be in at the death: JM to McGlinn, 6 Nov.
372. JM described the chateau and his plans to VM on 12 Nov.
372-3. Uncertainty if offered G.O.C.: JM to VM, 23 Aug., 27 Sept. Pressing for decision: White to JM, 5 Oct.; JM to Birdwood, 12 Oct.
373. 'Monash is a far more capable': Bean, D 116, 13 Oct. Informed Birdwood: JM to Birdwood, 13 Nov.; Birdwood to JM, 16 Nov.
'Sitting down on the Rhine': JM to VM, 20 Nov.
Bean is the only source of information: D 117 and *Two Men I Knew*, p. 180.
375-6. Blamey, Coxen, Hobbs, Grimwade, Durrant and Foott wrote about Monash to Black in Apr. 1937, Bean Papers, box 276. Foott wrote to Mrs Beresford, 12 Oct. 1931, Foott Papers, AWM. Glasgow wrote in *The Whiz-Bang*, Dec. 1931. Hobbs wrote to JM on 8 Nov. 1918. Cf. J. W. Springthorpe, diary, 5, 9 Nov. 1918 (La Trobe Lib.). Elliott often wrote admiringly of Monash to his wife, Elliott Papers. Cannan was quoted by Colonel A. Argent in a letter to P. Pedersen, 19 Nov.1980. 'had a staff in which': Jess to JM, 25 July 1921. Morshead wrote to JM on 1 Jan. 1919. Jacka's view was stated in a letter by B. H. Perry to P. Pedersen, Nov. 1980.

376. Terraine's remark is in *Haig, the Educated Soldier*, p. 215. Hamilton's comment is in *United Empire*, May 1923. Bean quoted Congreve in *Official History*, vi, p. 190. Rawlinson's anti-Semitism: Rawlinson to Montgomery, 8 May, 9 Sept. 1920, Montgomery-Massingberd Papers, Liddell Hart Collection. Repington's remark is in his *The First World War 1914-1918*, London, 1920, ii, p. 512. Note also Major-General Sir Charles Gwynn's views in *Reveille*, 31 Mar. 1931.

376-7. WR to JM, 7 June 1918, and VM to JM, 20 Jan. 1919, report Long's and others' views. J. D. Rogers records the Oct. rumour in his MS. 'Say not the Struggle' (held by Rogers family). The *Smith's* report was on 7 Aug. 1920. Beach Thomas was reported in *Herald*, 26 Apr. 1923. Cf. Glasgow in *The Whiz-Bang*.

377. Liddell Hart's *Daily Telegraph* obituary was reprinted in his *Through the Fog of War*, London, 1938. Cf. *Daily Telegraph*, 11 Feb., 7 June 1930; a comment in the *Times*, 1936, quoted by Scott, *History of the University*, p. 196; Liddell Hart to Walter Murdoch, 14 Apr. 1941, Liddell Hart Papers.

377-8. Lloyd George's remarks are from *War Memoirs*, pp. 3368, 3382, 3424. S. Roskill, in his *Hankey: Man of Secrets*, 3 v., London, 1970-74, pp. 484, 521, and Bean, Bean Papers, file 130, are illuminating on the problem of the commander-in-chief.

378. Liddell Hart's opinion is in his 'The Problem of quickening Manoeuvre', Lloyd George Papers, House of Lords, G 9/3/85. My discussion owes something to Terraine's *The Smoke and the Fire*, ch. 13, Smithers, *Sir John Monash*, pp. 290-1; and to a letter from Ronald Lewin, 29 Aug. 1979.

378-9. 'was considered in 1918': F. K. Norris, *No Memory for Pain*, Melbourne, 1970, p. 306; cf. *Australian*, 23 Aug. 1979. Taylor gave his view in *The First World War. An Illustrated History*, London, 1963, p. 179; Eden in *Another World 1897-1917*, London, 1976, pp. 120-1 (cf. his *Places in the Sun*, London, 1926, p. 65); Montgomery in his *History of Warfare*, London, 1968, p. 494; Essame in his *The Battle for Europe*, pp. 116-18; Terraine in *The Smoke and the Fire*, ch. 13; and Toland in his *No Man's Land. The Story of 1918*, London, 1980.

379-80. JM wrote to Wootten on 15 May 1923. An example of his stress on preparation for war is his letter to Innes, 14 Mar. 1928. 'In the regular Army': 'Leadership in War'; cf. *Age*, 9, 13 Jan. 1920. The comment on Haig is from Terraine's *Haig*, p. 52. Wavell on robustness: *Generals and Generalship*, London, 1941, p. 15.

380-1. 'a perfected modern battle plan': *AV*, p. 38. 'Engineering is a mode': Sir H. Barraclough, *J. Institution Engineers, Australia*, Oct. 1931, p. 363.

381. The staff brigadier was Rogers: 'Say Not the Struggle'. 'The most affectionate': Blamey, *Reveille*, Oct. 1931. 'a good story': Durrant to Black, loc. cit.

381-2. Surviving pencil drafts: e.g., MP (AWM), box 89. Praise of Blamey: *AV*, pp. 268-9; cf. H. Lilya to author, 15 Jan. 1980. 'I cannot express': Blamey to JM, 10 Apr. 1920; JM to Blamey, 12 Apr. 'Officers of his headquarters staff': *SMH*, 27 Dec. 1919.

382-3. 'to secure complete domination': Notes for Springthorpe, 4 Oct. 1918, MP (AWM), box 92; cf. speech to Eccentrics Club, 23 Apr. 1919, MP.

383. 'A passive defence': 'Leadership in War'. An 'energetic offensive policy': *AV*, p. 263.

383-4. The 1924 interview was in *Gossip* (Adelaide), 4 Sept. Satisfying Bean: *Official History*, vi, p. 940. 'He was the only general': Thompson, *On Lips of Living Men*, p. 141.

384. 'once a plan had been crystallized': 'Leadership in War'. 'recuperative effect': ibid.

384-5. Blamey made some remarks on battle conferences in *Reveille*, Oct. 1931. 'proved a powerful instrument': *AV*, pp. 128-9. 'With us, the written orders': 'Leadership in War'. Bruche's recollections are in Thompson, *On Lips of Living Men*, p. 144.

385-6. 'Opportunism defeated itself': *The Smoke and the Fire*, pp. 179-80. 'Birdwood and White': Elliott to Bean, June 1929, Elliott Papers; cf. his preface to W. H. Downing, *To the Last Ridge*, Melbourne, 1920. 'his subordinate commanders':

SMH, 27 Dec. 1919. 'those whom Monash trusted': Foott to Black, 3 Apr. 1937, loc. cit.

386. 'in relation to the machines': Orgill, *The Tank*, p. 64. 'one can easily see': Smithers, *Sir John Monash*, pp. 274-5, 291.

386-7. 'I had formed the theory': *AV*, pp. 75-6. 'Australian troops were the first': 'Leadership in War'. A standard battle drill: my brother, R. P. Serle, made this formulation.

387. 'a brilliant meticulous organiser': *J. Royal United Services Institute for Defence Studies*, v. 122, June 1977, p. 66. 'It is only necessary': 'Leadership in War'. 'In a well-planned battle': *AV*, p. 204.

387-8. JM wrote in gratitude to Foster on 10 Sept. 1918. White's fascination: address to Legacy, Oct. 1931, MP. Haig's peculiar views on discipline: 'Themes', 15 Sept. 1919, MP. 'Haig was, technically speaking': 'Leadership in War'. 'great moral strength': Blamey, *Reveille*, Oct. 1931. Cf. Eric Simonson, Monash — the Man and his Methods, radio broadcast, 1939, MP, p. 8.

388-9. Useful comments on his attitude are in *Herald*, 22 Apr. 1922; *Punch*, 14 May 1925; Adelaide *Advertiser*, 2 Nov. 1934. 'was always "buzzing about"': JM to Swinburne, 2 July 1925, S.E.C. Archives. 'A force which finds itself': 'Leadership in War'. Wavell's view is expressed in *Generals and Generalship*, pp. 33-4. Smithers makes useful comments in *Sir John Monash*, pp. 207-8.

389-90. 'There was never any sign': *Official History*, vi, p. 208. 'it is quite futile': JM to WR, 20 June 1916. 'I never got him nearer': Jackson to Liddell Hart, 4 Oct. 1935, Liddell Hart Papers, LH 1/516. Liddell Hart replied on 9 Oct.

390. 'something undefinable': W. Kent Hughes, 1947 memorial address, MP. 'great architect of the universe': S. Storer, *The War to end War*, p. 3. Storer quotes an unnamed war correspondent.

'He said in the friendliest way': Lilya to author, 24 Dec. 1979. 'Sit down and light your pipe': *Argus*, 23 Oct. 1937. 'Do you understand?': interview with Hunter Rogers, 23 Sept. 1980. Beaurepaire wrote on 27 June 1918; cf. letters from Laloe, 19 Dec. 1918, Purdy, 6 July 1918, Law, 1 Sept. 1925. 'the absolute antithesis': *Bulletin*, 10 Jan. 1924.

391. 'I am nothing but': Sydney *Sun*, 1 Apr. 1918. Docking at Alexandria: *Reveille*, Oct.1931. The outstanding advocate: *Herald*, 3 Feb. 1932. On presenting decorations: McInnes, *England — Half English*, p. 188.

391-2. 'The detailed explanation': J. M. A. Durrant, *Leadership*, Brisbane, 1941. 'The democratic institutions': *AV*, pp. 263-5. 'While you could distinguish': interview with O'Connor, 13 Feb. 1919, Speeches, MP. Cf. *Christian Science Monitor*, 3 July 1919.

392. 'Try as one will': JM to Springthorpe, 13 Jan. 1918.

392-3. 'Very much and stupid comment': *AV*, p. 265. 'the barrack-room discipline': *Morning Post* (London), 24 Aug. 1927. 'We release the individual's intelligence': *Herald*, 19 Sept. 1918. 'does not mean lip service': *AV*, p. 265. 'It is more expedient': 'Leadership in War'.

393-4. 'From almost the earliest days': *AV*, p. 266. Battle with Cox: *Smith's Weekly*, 12 Apr. 1929. 'There was thus no officer caste': *AV*, p. 267. 'If the Australians hate anything': *Everylady's Journal*, 6 Feb. 1920; cf. *Argus*, 15 Nov. 1919.

394. 'It is because we do not consider': JM to Meyer, 1 Apr. 1918; cf. JM to Foster, 14 Sept. 1918. One had to judge: *Jewish Chronicle* (London), 2 May 1919. 'his somewhat shallow interpretations': *Herald*, 28 Feb. 1919. I disagree with Smithers' comment, *Sir John Monash*, pp. 274-5.

394-5. His letter to Carruthers was on 12 May 1918.

395. Some of the relevant correspondence is JM to Birdwood, 14 July; Birdwood to JM, 16 July; Godley to JM, 28 July 1917; cf. *Official History*, v, pp. 25-32.

395-6. Birdwood's memo was dated 11 Dec. 1917. An example of Monash's considerateness is his letter to Howse of 27 Oct. 1917. A memo by Hobbs of 17 July 1918 is in MP (AWM), box 87; cf. *Official History*, vi, pp. 486-7. For the later

stages of the war see JM to Divisional commanders, 8 Sept. 1918; also *Herald*, 3 Dec. 1932.
396. 'I do frankly': Notes for Springthorpe, 4 Oct. 1918. 'no army has ever': G. F. R. Henderson, *Stonewall Jackson and the American Civil War*, London, 1911, ii, p. 338. 'With such an army': e.g., *Jewish Chronicle* (London), 2 May 1919. Something like primitive Christianity: cf. McKernan, *Australian Churches at War*, pp. 137 ff.
396-7. 'Every day was filled': *AV*, p. 270. No consolation: cf. McKernan, p. 110. Letters from distressed relatives of 24 Feb., 1 July, 13 Sept. 1918 are examples of the burden. His letter to Dodds was of 4 May 1918; Dodds replied next day.
397. 'incorrigibly civilian': *Official History*, vi, p. 5. 'neither careful nor careless': *Reveille*, Oct. 1931.
397-8. For Bean, *ADB* 7. At loggerheads in 1918: e.g. Bean, D, 21 Aug., 2, 6, 11, 13, 16, 17 Sept. 1918; cf. *Table Talk*, 15 Oct. 1931. Monash believing the most attractive story: e.g., Bean, D, 21 Aug, 16 Sept. 1915, 3 Dec. 1917. Files 42 and 138 in Bean Papers, and Bean to Murdoch, 27 July 1918, Murdoch Papers, are also relevant.
398. 'as a leader': *Herald*, 8 Oct. 1931. 'greatest military leader': *SMH*, 10 Oct. 1927. 'neither a hero': Bean to G. Long, 6 July 1930 (privately held). Bean's account in *Official History*, vi, is on pp. 198-211. Note Bean's labelled comment on his diaries that the contents were 'what the writer at the moment believed to be true'.
398-9. White's comments are in his letter to Black, 7 Apr. 1937, loc. cit.
399. Cutlack's affection for Monash is also shown in his letter to Bean, 30 June 1959, Bean Papers, folder 475.
400. The annotated copy of *AV* is in AWM. Note also Gellibrand to Bean, 4 July 1935; undated comments on draft *Official History*, vi, Bean Papers, folder 71; 6 Jan. 1943 and 26 Apr. 1943, folder 74.
400-1. Elliott's letter to Bean of June 1929, Elliott Papers, box 38/9, is also relevant.
401-2. 'The more one studies': Roskill, *The Art of Leadership*, London, 1964, p. 9. Birdwood recognizing the goods were there: Bean, *Two Men I Knew*, p. 171n. Monash and photographers: Bean, D 116, 21 July 1918. Monash and press publicity: Cutlack's foreword to *War Letters*, pp. xii-xiii. Pestering Birdwood: Birdwood to Pearce, 18 Sept. 1918, Birdwood Papers. Bazley's summing-up: *Reveille*, May 1937. Examples of Monash's exaggerations: Goulburn *Evening Post*, 22 Apr. 1922; JM to Chauvel, 14 Apr. 1918; JM to O'Donnell, 24 Apr. 1918.
402-3. 'able inarticulate' was J. A. Spender's description, quoted by Terraine, *The Western Front*, p. 70.
403. 'could fail to see in him': *Reveille*, May 1937. 'tradition of orderly thinking': Brain's memorial address, 1945, MP.
404. JM described these functions in letters to VM, 13, 17, 28 Dec. For his anticipation of the hollowness of fame, see p. 58 above.
404-5. 'Having started': Carruthers to JM, 16 Oct. 1918. JM prompted Read on 24 Dec.; cf. JM to Birdwood, 2 Oct., and Pershing to JM, 31 Jan. 1919. He commented on his G.C.M.G. to MM, 21 Jan. 1919. He described the coat-of-arms to VM on 23 Aug., 5 Dec. 1918, and to MM, 21 Jan. 1919. He wrote to Wallington, 14 Feb. 1919, and to Wears, 31 Dec. 1918.
405. Blamey wrote to JM, 8, 15, 30 Jan.; JM to Blamey, 2, 13 Jan.; JM wrote on 2 Jan. to Rawlinson who replied on the 14th. JM lobbied Birdwood by letter on 21, 25, 28 July and 14 Oct. 1919.

The full text of JM's address to senior officers is in MP (AWM), box 89. 'I thought I knew': Ryan to Pearce, 5 Dec. 1918, Pearce Papers; see also Ryan to VM, 5 Dec.; JM to Ryan, 19 Dec.
406-7. Fitzhardinge states Hughes's views in *The Little Digger*, pp. 351-2. Examples of Murdoch's despatches to the *Herald* are 28 Feb., 11 Mar. 1919; cf. JM to Murdoch, 15 Apr., Murdoch to JM, 20 Apr.; and Fink to Murdoch, 2 Apr.,

NOTES (pages 407–415)

Murdoch Papers. 'Mr Hughes not really responsible': 'Themes on which to Write', 12 Sept. 1919, MP. JM made notes on his interview with Hughes of the 20th, MP (AWM), box 92. 'Government surrenders': *Herald*, 28 Feb. 1919. 'Details of Masterly Scheme': *Herald*, 1 Mar. 'I seek to give Australia': Sydney *Sun*, 27 Feb.

407. D, 26-28 Mar. records Pearce's review.

JM's letter to Bruche of 3 Jan. is revealing. 'tumultuous and difficult days': JM to Noyes, 8 May; cf. to Hobbs, 2, 16 Jan.; to Watt, 16 May; to MM, 21 Jan., 11 Mar.

JM wrote to Chauvel, 9 Dec. 1918. Examples of letters to Hobbs are 14, 16, 23 Jan. 1919.

407-8. For the 3rd Division Artillery trouble, see Grimwade to JM, 6 Jan.; Hobbs to JM, 7 Jan.; JM to Hobbs, 14 Jan.; file in Gellibrand Papers, box 188. 'were examples': Aurousseau to author, 27 Feb. 1980. Entirely tolerant: JM to Hobbs, 14 Jan. 'Be strict': MP (AWM), box 90. 'They were to be treated': *Everylady's Journal*, 6 Feb. 1920.

408. *Official History*, vi, pp. 1056-62, summarizes the organization.

409. Reports of the conferences of 27 May and 10 June 1918 are in MP (AWM), box 92. Bringing Hughes and Long together: Note of interview with Hughes, 18 Dec. 1918, MP (AWM), box 92, and JM to Birdwood, 5 Dec. For the scheme in general: *Official History*, pp. 1062-72; cf. Sir Hugh Brain in *On Lips of Living Men*, p. 149.

409-10. Re shipping, note W. S. Robinson's advice to JM, 17 Mar. 1919. 'It has been a tough': JM to Murdoch, 15 Apr. 1919; cf. JM to Parker, 17 Feb., 3 Mar.; also T. Waters, *Much besides Music*, Melbourne, 1951, and Pearce, *Carpenter to Cabinet*, London, 1951, pp. 149-50.

410. For the fierce campaign, JM to Hobbs, 23 Jan., to Whitham, 29 Jan., to White, 30 Jan. JM's crushing reply and White's comments are in the Demobilization correspondence, MP, 22 Jan.; he wrote to the secretary of the Defence Department on 25 Feb.

The polite letter was to Travers Clarke on 7 Mar. 'carrier of an infectious disease': JM to Cohen, 11 Dec. 1918. The brush with Cook: Cook to JM, 4, 11 Mar.; JM to Cook, 7, 13 Mar. His reply to Bruce was on 7 Apr. His apology to Gunner McAdam was on 14 May.

411. Rate of repatriation: see his message to the A.I.F., 17 Mar. Preening himself: JM to Watt, 16 May; to Noyes, 8 May; to MM, 31 Mar., 10 May, 10 June. Bullying Pearce: JM to McCay, 13 Aug. *Waimana* incident: Proceedings court of inquiry, MP; JM, letter to the *Times*, 3 Nov.; Mrs K. D. Johnstone to author, 26 Mar. 1976. Blessedly uneventful: reports from O.C.s troopships, MP; but cf. Angela Thirkell ('Leslie Parker'), *Trooper to the Southern Cross*, London, 1934. The official account was 'The History of the Department of Repatriation and Demobilisation A.I.F.', MP (AWM). Speed of demobilization: note Scott, *Australia during the War*, p. 822n., and Foott to Black, 3 Apr. 1937, Bean Papers, box 276.

411-12. Fletcher's story was in *SMH*, 3 May 1924. 'behaved in a most discourteous': JM to Beardsmore, 20 Sept. 1920; cf. to Currie, 26 Oct.

412. JM's letters to MM and his D are the main sources for his social life in mid-1919.

413. 'our modern Judas Maccabaeus': *Jewish Chronicle*, 17 Jan. 1919. MM's letter was of 1 Feb.

413-14. 'Jewish influence': JM to NZ & A. Division, 22 Nov. 1915, and subsequent correspondence in Jan. 'Remember you are a Jew': Woods Lloyd, Q.C., recalled this story. 'Most people I hear': VM to JM, 30 Nov. 1918.

414. Margolin wrote on 9 Feb. Zangwill was reported in *Daily Sketch*, 24 Jan. JM told VM of the late 1918 report on 3 Nov.; cf. Springthorpe's diary (La Trobe Lib.), 4, 9 Nov. 1918. JM's letter to MM was on 10 May 1919.

415. 'In Australia': Speeches, MP, 2 Mar. 1919. 'In Australia we have no Jewish question': *Jewish Chronicle*, 2 May 1919.

The *Morning Post* letter was on 23 Apr. JM's later disclaimer was to Dr J. L. Jona, quoted *West Australian*, 26 Nov. 1948.

415-16. The *Jewish Guardian* report was on 8 Nov. 1919 and the *Jewish Herald* reprint on 9 Jan. 1920.

416. 'It is only four miles': *Evening News*, 26 Apr., and instructions to Rosenthal, 16 Apr. The quotations are from news cuttings in MP.

416-17. The *Manchester Guardian* letter was on 6 May, that to the *Times* on 30 Apr.; cf. 3 May. 'with the single': *Sunday Chronicle*, 27 Apr.

417. The Overseas Club speech was reported in the *Times*, 27 Mar. 'I've been the greatest': *West Australian*, 20 Dec. For an example of his tributes to British troops, *Christian Science Monitor*, 3 July.

418. For the motivation of writing *AV*, see his correspondence with Sladen; Waters, *Much besides Music*, p. 179; his letter to Murdoch of 24 Sept.; and his letter to MM of 22 Sept. 'Not for thirty': R. H. Croll, *I Recall*, Melbourne, 1939, p. 32. See correspondence with Hutchinson's, Ellis, Bruche and Rosenhain. Bean's judgement was in *Anzac to Amiens*, 1961 ed., p. 536n.

419. 'vivid and simply told chronicle': H. Barraclough, *J. Institution of Engineers, Australia*, Oct. 1931. See 1920s correspondence about selling the book.

419. For Legge's warning: VM to JM, 5 Jan. 1919.

JM's letters to McCay of 13 Aug. and to Pearce of 8 Aug. and 1 Sept. reveal his grievances; but cf. his further letter to McCay of 10 Oct.

419-20 Birdwood's letter to Munro Ferguson of 6 Dec. 1918 is in Birdwood Papers; another of 8 July criticizing JM is in Novar Papers. Munro Ferguson's comments are in a letter to Birdwood of 2 May 1919. 'thinks he won the war': Birdwood to Stonehaven, 21 July 1925, Stonehaven Papers, National Library, 2127/1/1. 'too optimistic': D, 8 July.

420. 'Entertain strong': JM to Barrett, 22 Apr. 1919. 'No! It's tempting': Waters, *Much besides Music*, p. 178. His main letter to Barrett was on 22 Apr. He wrote to Watt on 16 May. Noyes was advising Monash, writing on 8 July; cf. JM to Noyes, 20 Oct., to Springthorpe, 19 Sept., to Fairway, 8 Oct. He mentioned Dorman Long, D, 14 Aug.

420-1. He gave Springthorpe his views on standing for the Senate on 19 Sept.; Springthorpe replied on 29 Dec.

421. Monash's diary entries are the chief source on his marital situation.

'Frankly I would sooner': JM to McCay, 10 Oct. 1919. The *Times* sub-leader was on 15 Nov. *Evening Standard*, 8 Nov., is a good example of his interviews. Farmar wrote on 13 Nov.

422. JM wrote to WR on 6 Dec. His D is illuminating, especially for Vic's health for which see also JM to MM, 22 Sept., 14 Dec.

West Australian, 20 Dec., describes the reception.

422-3. *Herald*, 26 Dec., *Age* and *Argus*, 27 Dec., and *Table Talk*, 1 Jan. 1920, reported the homecoming.

423. MM's letters were of 30 Dec. and 19 Nov.

423-4. Scott wrote on 26 Dec., Wears on the 26th, Latham on the 24th, C. P. Smith on the 29th, Barrett on the 19th and Foott on the 22nd. The *Age* gave praise on the 26th and 27th, the *Herald* leader was on the 19th.

424. *Age* reported the Town Hall welcome on 13 Jan. 1920. 'obliterating monuments': Speeches, 25 Jan. 1920, MP; also *Argus*, 26 Jan., 11 Feb.; correspondence with I. Selby, Dec.-Jan.; JM to Leo Monash, 15 Feb. 1882.

The anonymous letter was on 17 Feb. The Andersons wrote on 29 Feb. JM's letters to WR of 18 Feb. and 3 Mar. reveal a little of his emotions.

424-5. JM's correspondence illustrates the demands on him. 'I think we soldiers': JM to White, 21 Feb. 1921.

425-6. 'I have not swerved': JM to Gibson, 7 Oct. 1919, also his letters to Gibson of 20 July and 23 Dec. 1918; cf. Gibson to JM of 22 Nov. 1918. Fairway's letters to JM of 27 June, 12 Oct. 1917, 19 July 1918 and 17 Mar. 1919 are revealing

NOTES (pages 426–433) 573

on the business. 'a satisfactory livelihood': JM to WR, 22 Mar., 11 May 1920.
426. His views on future military occupation are in letters to Sir R. Anderson, 8 Mar. 1920, Currie, 26 Oct. 1920, Jackson, 25 Jan. 1922. Letters to WR, 22 Mar. 1920, and to Watt, 1 Sept. 1920, outline negotiations.
Relevant letters are to WR, 11 May, 14 July; to McBeath, 4 Mar., 21, 29 Apr.; from McBeath, 6 Mar.; to Greene, 19 Mar., 29 Apr.; to Pearce, 7, 14 May; from Pearce, 12 May. See also G. Currie and J. Graham, *The Origins of CSIRO*, Melbourne, 1966, ch. 5.
426-7. 'Every day that passes': JM to WR, 14 July 1920.
427. Correspondence in MP about the Hume takeover includes W. R. Hume to JM, 14 Nov. 1918; JM to Hume, 11, 18 Nov. 1919, 11 June, 26 July 1920; JM to WR, 14 July 1920; JM to Robertson, 14 Sept. 1922. See also G. D. Snooks, 'Innovation and the Growth of the Firm. Hume Enterprises 1910-40', *Aust. Economic History Review*, vol. 13, no. 1, Mar. 1973.
427-8. JM recorded McBeath's approach in D. The Robinson reference is to *If I Remember Rightly*, Melbourne, 1967, p. 107. 'There is nothing': Swinburne to JM, 30 July 1920. JM recorded the agreement with Lawson to WR on 12 Aug. JM recalled the promise of a salary increase in a letter to H. I. Cohen of 17 Oct. 1930. *Smith's Weekly* stated its view on 13 Dec. 1919, 7 Aug., 1920, 14 June 1924, 31 July 1926.
428. JM to Gibson, 13 Dec. 1920, and Gibson to JM, 9 May 1921, are the important letters. McBeath gave his advice on 2 Aug. 1920.
428-9. Currie wrote on 24 Aug. 1920. Rosenthal wrote about Birdwood on 8 Apr. The *Nation* commented in its Feb. issue, *Smith's* on 7 Aug. JM complained to Pearce on 11 Mar. and commented to Rosenthal on 1 Mar. White's remark was passed on to me in an interview with C. Meeking, 1980. The *Herald* urged special thanks on 7 Jan. 1920 and reported the circulating document on 6 May. Parliamentary moves were reported in *Argus* on 31 Mar. and elsewhere on 1 May, news cuttings, MP. JM commented to WR on 11 May. JM wrote bitterly to Watt on 1 Sept.
429. JM's remark on Hughes was to Mrs Farmar, 9 Jan. 1923.
429-30. 'I am very indisposed': JM to Bainbridge, 10 June 1920. JM wrote to White about the matter on 26 June; White replied on the 30th. 'A plush rope': *Bulletin*, 10 June. Rosenthal and Bruche wrote on 8 July and 13 Sept.; JM replied to Bruche on 15 Sept. Re the anniversaries, JM wrote to Bruche on 5 July and 9 Aug. He made other expressions of his resentment at the government's ingratitude to Morshead on 1 June and to Russell on 7 Oct. 1921.
430. 'The jealous and petty treatment': Morshead to JM, 29 May 1921; cf. G. Meudell, *The Pleasant Career of a Spendthrift*, London, n.d., p. 230. Drake-Brockman's remarks are in *Commonwealth Parl. Debates*, 13 July 1922.
431. JM's private admission about the honorary degree was in a letter to Jenkinson, 13 July 1923. Barraclough's comment was in *J. Institution of Engineers, Australia*, Oct. 1931, p. 363.
431-2. The correspondence on appointment of the Police Commissioner is: JM to Lawson, 19 May, to Baird, 26 July, to Bruche, 11 Aug. On the Herz case: Zarkin to JM, 26 Mar., 23 Apr. 1920; JM to Garran, 22 June; see also J. Clarke, *Dr Max Herz Surgeon*, Sydney, 1976, pt 7. Hirschfeld case: 'You must be perfectly well aware': JM to Maddock, 2 July 1926; also JM to Garran, 19 Apr. 1920 and to Bruce, 23 July 1923; Saddler to JM, 26 July 1923; Mrs Hirschfeld to JM, 27 June, 22 Nov. 1926; White to JM, 7 Aug. 1926.
432. 'I have always been loyal to you': Wright to JM, 11 Sept.; JM to Wright, 13 Sept. 1920; cf. JM to Butler, 2 Feb. 1926.
432-3. 'could not give the club': unidentified American report in cuttings book, MP. Sir John Grice's diary, Univ. Melb. Archives, establishes that Monash attended the dinner. 'My boy, you surely don't think': interview with N. Rosenthal. A dozen interviewees volunteered the story of the blackballing. A letter from the Melbourne Club Archivist to the author, 9 May 1980, establishes the existence

NOTES (pages 433-444)

of Jewish members and the absence of any information in the records about Monash. Sir F. W. Eggleston recounts a story about the Australian Club in his 'Confidential Notes'. Cf. *Farrago* (Univ. Melb.), 15 Oct. 1931, for the virility of the myth.

433-4. The Rosenhain letters were on 2 Sept. 1920, 18, 23 Feb. 1921; one of JM's replies was on 7 Dec. 1920. The *Bulletin* reports were on 2, 25 Dec. 1920; JM wrote in protest on 14 Dec.

434. Barrett wrote on 23 Mar. 1920. Fearing a breakdown: JM to Nettlefold, 20 Dec. 1920. 'a chronic state': JM to LR, 10 Apr. 1921. 'by a course of medicine': to LR, 30 Sept. 1921. 'doctor's orders': e.g. to Treloar, 20 Sept. 1921; to T. W. White, 14 Oct. 1921.

435. Cecil Edwards's *Brown Power*, A. D. Spaull's thesis and article, Jean Holmes's article and Eggleston's *State Socialism in Victoria*, pp. 160-73, (see bibliography) provide a basis for this chapter.

Lenin's remark was made to the 8th All-Russian Congress of Soviets, Dec. 1920.

Monash wrote to Rosenhain on 12 Aug. 1920.

435-6. Edwards, pp. 15-53, gives the background of the Commission's foundation.

436. Monash's correspondence with McBride is the main source for the Fortuna operation.

437. 'a big and strenuous job': JM to Rawlinson, 14 Mar. 1922. He described the conflict with Clapp to Rosenhain, 18 Jan. 1921.

437-8. His address to Parliament was reported, *Age*, 15 Dec. 'Monash was a brainy Hercules': Eggleston, 'Confidential Notes'. Rupturing of friendships: JM to Merz, 18 Jan. 1921. The *Argus* reported the conference on 20 Apr. 'senseless hydraulic works': *Herald*, 19 Apr.

438-9. 'imbued with a profound hatred': JM to McKinstrey, 18 Mar. 1930.

439. Edwards, pp. 61-2, and the reminiscences of many S.E.C. men (S.E.C. Archives) are the basis for JM at Yallourn.

439-40. The chief sources of the German question are JM to Morshead, 6 Mar. 1922; JM to Eichelgrun, 17 July; JM to WR, 28 Dec.; Spaull, Origins and Rise, ch. 9.

440. Eggleston made these remarks in his *George Swinburne. A Biography*, Sydney, 1931, pp. 438, 442. JM's letter to Herman was on 6 Dec. 1922 (S.E.C.). Robinson's frank statement: *Vic. Parl. Debates*, v. 165, pp. 2231 ff.

440-1. Edwards, pp. 65-6, 83, 101-03, and Spaull, Origins and Rise, pp. 120-32, cover the moisture problem. The S.E.C.'s Annual Report for 1925-26 was the formal admission of trouble.

441. JM's letters to WR of 18 Jan. 1921 and 28 Dec. 1922 comment on the distribution problem.

441-2. JM's key letter to Robinson was on 24 Aug. 1922. Edwards, pp. 64-5, 69-72, and Holmes, p. 242, deal with the political problem.

442. Battle with the M.C.C. and the Electrical Defence Committee: Report and Evidence of the Select Committee on Electricity Supply, *Vic. Parl. Papers*, 1922; JM to Robinson, 25, 28 Oct. 1922 (S.E.C.); Edwards, pp. 72-3, 75-81; Holmes, p. 243; Eggleston, *State Socialism*, p. 167. 'towards the middle of December': JM to WR, 28 Dec. 1922.

442-3. JM's notes on the bill (S.E.C.) are illuminating. Clements wrote on 20 Dec.; cf. Frank Clarke to JM, 3 Dec. For Ballarat and Bendigo, Edwards, pp. 88-9, *Age*, 30 Aug. 1923.

443. Town of Yallourn, Some Notes (S.E.C.) outlines Monash's views. 'It is the architect': Chairman to Secretary, 2 Oct. 1923 (S.E.C.). 'a model industrial town': JM to Mona Rosenhain, 11 Nov. 1924. Growth of vegetation: Chairman to Acting General Superintendent, 15 Aug. 1923 (S.E.C.); JM to McKinstrey: 28 May 1930.

444. *Herald*, 21 Sept. 1921, and *Industrial Mining Standard*, 16 Feb. 1922, provide good examples of his public addresses. His correspondence (S.E.C.) is rich in persuasive argument to politicians and journalists.

NOTES (pages 444–455) 575

444-5. *Sun*, 17 June 1924, has a good description of the 'turning on'. For the trial, Robertson to Nave, 3 June 1978 (S.E.C.) Robinson wrote on 2 Oct. Edwards describes the briquettes, p. 86.
445. For *Age*'s criticisms, 28 Sept.-4 Oct. 1923, 10 Nov. 1924, 5 Feb. 1926, are outstanding examples. 'Just his stamp of mind': *SMH*, 4, 5 Dec. 1924.
446. The *J. of Chemical Engineering* attacked on 5 Jan. 1925. JM wrote to LR, 16 July 1925.
446-7. 'a very nasty squabble': JM to BB, 19, 20 Feb. 1924. There is much correspondence in S.E.C. Archives over Swinburne's worries.
447. Examples of Robinson's help are his letters to JM of 21 Sept. 1923 and 11 July 1924 (S.E.C.). Swinburne too honourable: Swinburne to Eggleston, 26 Jan. 1925, Eggleston Papers. JM to Prendergast, 23 Sept. 1924, and JM to Eggleston, 19 Nov. (S.E.C.), illustrate the Gas Co. proposal.
447-9. Swinburne's letter of 19 Jan., JM's reply of 20 July and Swinburne's further reply of 2 Sept. are in the S.E.C. Archives.
450. The minister, H. F. Richardson, spoke as reported in *Vic. Parl. Debates*, v. 169, pp. 756-7; cf. JM to Barrett, 7 Sept. 1925. Gibson wrote to Eggleston on 3 Sept., Eggleston replied on 5 Sept., Eggleston Papers. Gibson wrote to JM on 3 Sept., Monash replied on 4 Sept. Cf. JM to Eggleston, 2 Sept., and Report of Interview between the Electricity Commission and Cabinet, 19/10/25, by JM (S.E.C.). 'he was prepared to find the capital': *Argus*, 23 Dec. 1925. 'you have a great big deposit': Monash's Memo. on Coal-winning Operations at Yallourn (S.E.C.).
450-1. JM wrote to Eggleston on 25 Jan. 1926; Eggleston replied on 11 Feb. (S.E.C.). Klitzing's Report on Coalwinning Operations at Yallourn was published in *Vic. Parl. Papers*, no. 6 of 1926. JM commented on it to Klitzing on 19 Apr.; their subsequent correspondence is at S.E.C.
451. JM wrote about the letter of instruction to Eggleston on 11 Jan. 1926 (S.E.C.). 'Well, Mr Eggleston': 'Confidential Notes'. Advising British government: L. S. Amery to JM, 21 May; Burnham to JM, 25 May 1926. Sawyer's Report on the Status and Affairs of the State Electricity Commission of Victoria is in *Vic. Parl. Papers*, no. 2 of 1926. *Argus* commented on it, 21 May, *Age* on 22 May.
451-2. Monash's interview with Clements, 1 May (S.E.C.), is revealing; see also JM to Clements, 1, 10 May; Clements to JM, 6 May (S.E.C.). Footnote: Eggleston's 'Confidential Notes'.
452. Notes on Sawyer Report are in Eggleston Papers, MS 423/7. JM disabused him re the power house's capacity on 13 May (S.E.C.).
452-3. JM reproduced the orders in replying to Eggleston, 30 June (S.E.C.). Swinburne protested on 4 July and Eggleston replied on the 6th, Eggleston Papers.
453-4. JM wrote to Klitzing on 14 June, 20 Sept., 27 Oct. 1926. Swinburne's vehement support: Swinburne to Allan, 20 June, Eggleston Papers, 7/224. JM's letter to Gibson is in S.E.C. Archives. Eggleston giving way: JM to Eggleston, 16 Nov.; Eggleston to JM, 17 Nov.; JM to Klitzing, 6 Dec. 1926, 1 Mar., 12 Apr. 1927. Footnote: 'Confidential Notes'; *Argus*, 5, 8, 9 July 1929; Eggleston to Lyle, 9 July (S.E.C.); the joint letter was of 12 July, Eggleston Papers.
454. Eggleston's theoretical conclusion: *State Socialism*, p. 50. 'The facts are': Sawyer to Eggleston, 1 Feb. 1927, Eggleston Papers. For Eggleston, W. Osmond, *F. W. Eggleston (1875-1954): Portrait of an Australian Intellectual*, Ph.D. thesis, Univ. Sydney, 1980.
454-5. 'I feel quite sorry': R. H. Croll, *I Recall. Collections and Recollections*, Melbourne, 1939, p. 93. 'the position is so good': to WR, 21 Oct. 1927, 6 Jan. 1928.
 In general for the Sawyer Report and its aftermath see S.E.C. Annual Report for 1925-26; Chairman's Correspondence (S.E.C.); Edwards, pp. 92-103; Spaull, *Origins and Rise*, ch. 10; Holmes, pp. 244-7.
455. 'The solution of nearly all my problems': JM to WR, 21 Oct. 1927. The *Smith's* remark was on 26 Feb. 'a startling reduction': JM to McKinstrey, 18 Mar., also 28 May 1930.

455-6. Doing the fair thing: H. A. L. Binder interview (S.E.C.).
456-7. This account of the strikes is based on an unpublished paper by Dr A. D. Spaull, The Pattern of Industrial Conflict at the Yallourn Brown Coalmines. 'I have to a large extent': JM to Holloway, 30 Mar. 1927; Holloway to JM, 1 Apr.
457. Kennelly told D. M. Bennett this. 'one of the greatest men I ever met': *Age*, 27 Mar. 1963.
457-8. 'I am bound to say': JM to Thompson, 16 Dec. 1929. An address to S.E.C. officers, 25 June 1929, is in MP.
458. 'This State enterprise': *Vic. Parl. Debates*, v. 178, p. 3402.
458-9. 'This success has brought with it': JM to WR, 3 Jan. 1929. 'another epidemic': JM to Goodman, 28 Apr. 1930.
459. 'the greatest of its kind': e.g., *Herald*, 25 Apr. 1930.
459-60. Monash commented to McKinstrey on the harmony among the Commissioners in a letter of 18 Mar. 1930. 'When we had any trouble': 'Confidential Notes'. 'we all stood up': Menzies' 1965 memorial address. 'recalcitrant cabinets': S. Encel, *Cabinet Government*, Melbourne, 1962, p. 311.
460-1. 'his office was a place': *Sun*, 13 Nov. 1950. Bridge wrote 'Monash — An Appreciation of his work for the S.E.C.', MP. 'Nothing can rob me': Taylor to Meyer, 11 Oct. 1931, MP. An interview with Price is in S.E.C. Archives.
461-2. This paragraph is based on W. E. Gower, R. A. Hunt, F. J. Richardson and Rigby interviews (S.E.C.); also Richardson to Nave, 3 June 1978. Footnote: JM to Matthews, 11 May 1926 (S.E.C.).
462. 'he was a great leader': Herman to BB, 9 Oct. 1931.
463. JM described the early 1920 conference to WR, 18 Feb., and to Currie, 26 Oct. Letters about appointment to the Council of Defence are JM to Lawson, 4 Feb. 1921; Lawson to JM, 10 Feb.; JM to Russell, 7 Oct. and to WR, 29 Apr. For the Council of Defence, see J. McCarthy, *Australia and Imperial Defence 1918-39*, Brisbane, 1976, passim. On the condition of the Army, JM to Birdwood, 2 Aug. 1922, and Hill, *Chauvel*, pp. 200-4.

Lloyd wrote to JM on 31 July; JM replied on 6 Aug.; Morshead supported Lloyd to JM on 7 Aug.
463-4. JM's 1923 attack was reported, *SMH*, 13 Nov. JM wrote to Page, 15 Nov. JM to White, 26 Apr., 15 May 1924, illustrate agitation re defence. Hill, *Chauvel*, pp. 212-13, covers the June 1924 action; cf. *Smith's Weekly*, 14 June. There is much on the cruiser question in correspondence and news cuttings in MP for July-Aug.
464. 'I soon found myself': JM to BB, 16 Sept. 1925; also JM to Godley, 22 Sept.
464-5. Gellibrand wrote about the Tasmanian gathering on 14 Aug. 1925. 'The pleasantest': Gellibrand to JM, 16 July 1928, also 16 Aug. 1927. 'By your goodness': White to JM, 9 Aug. 1927.
465. A. J. Hill passed on the 'prize Shorthorn' story from the Chauvel family. JM's tribute to Chauvel was reported, *Herald*, 11 Apr. 1930; cf. JM to Bruche, 29 Apr. JM wrote to Elliott on 16 Sept. 1929.

Argus, 17, 19 Apr. 1920, and G. L. Kristianson, *The Politics of Patriotism. The Pressure Group Activities of the Returned Servicemen's League*, Canberra, 1966, p. 36, cover the 1920 attempt to capture JM as president. Rosenthal wrote on 25 May 1921; JM replied on 30 May. 'in danger of decay': JM to A. Robinson, 31 Aug. 1923; cf. JM to Turnbull, 5 Sept. 1923.
466. The *SMH* eulogy was on 12 Nov. Correspondence with J. J. Cohen, Aug.-Oct., Rosenthal to JM, 25 Sept., JM to Rosenthal, 20 Oct., dealt with arrangements for the visit; see also *Bulletin*, 25 Oct.
466-7. 'The matter of suitably recognising': *Herald*, 25 July 1923; *Age*, 31 Aug. 1923, 23 Feb. 1924. *Sun*, 2 Sept. 1949, recalls the dining club. *Argus*, 26 Apr. 1924, reports the banquet and speeches. 'As a soldier': *Age*, 23 Feb. 1924.
467. 'Nothing has become the hero': *Sunday Times*, 4 May 1924.
'the A.I.F. sprang to life': JM to Shelton, 26 Nov. 1923.
467-8. 'Before we separated': JM to A. Robinson, 9 Nov.

NOTES (pages 468-478) 577

468-9. Johnston wrote on 13 Nov. and JM replied on the 16th.
469. *Herald*, 10 Nov., is an example of the call for a commission. JM wrote to Argyle, the chief secretary, on 10 Feb. and 27 July about the need for an able commissioner and Blamey's suitability. The Report of the Royal Commission on the Victorian Police Force is in *Vic. Parl. Papers*, 1925, no. 5. MP contain the transcript of evidence, cuttings, notes, etc. Two important accounts of the strike are E. W. Perry, 'The Police Strike in Melbourne', *Vic. Historical Mag.*, no. 169, Aug. 1972, and Jacqueline Templeton, 'The Melbourne Police Strike of 1923', *Strikes*, ed. Iremonger et al., Sydney, 1973.
469-70. Service authorities disapproving: Annual Report of the R.S.L. (Vic.) for 1925. Accounts of the marches are largely from news cuttings, MP.
470. JM to Fr Clack, 14 Apr. 1926, and Clack's reply of the 16th illustrate the clash with the Catholics.
470-1. JM's letter to Birdwood was on 5 Apr. 1927. 'Then Sir John Monash begins': unidentified cutting, MP. White wrote on 26 Apr.
471. 'No you don't': *Herald*, 25 Apr. 1927. News cuttings, MP, are the source for the N.S.W. attempts to persuade him to lead the march in Sydney and for his 1929 visit. A good source for Anzac Day ceremonies is C. Ansell, Some Aspects of the Celebration of Anzac Day in Victoria up to 1939, 4th-year honours thesis, Monash Univ., 1975.
471-2. 'a visible manifestation' is a quotation from Ansell. The *Herald* campaign was centred on Jan.-Mar. 1924; see especially, 12 Feb., 5 Mar.
472. 'refused, both on personal': JM to WR, Mar. 1927.
I have benefited from Sir Alfred Kemsley's private account to me; note Joynt's letter to the *Age*, 23 Aug. 1926.
472-3. 'too severe, stiff and heavy': Lawson to JM, 30 July 1927. 'a beautiful conception': JM to Lawson, 1 Aug. 1927. 'very broad-minded': JM to Murdoch, 23 Mar. 1928.
473. One key-letter of Monash's was to Luxton, 25 Mar. 1929.
473-4. JM's letter to Tucker of 17 Feb. 1930 is valuable evidence. Inglis's remark is in 'The Anzac Tradition', *Meanjin Quarterly*, xxiv, no. 1, 1965, p. 42. The foregoing account has been based on the mass of correspondence in MP, and on Russell, *We Will Remember Them*.
474. 'Created a great tradition': Anzac Day message, 15 Apr. 1921.
474-5. 'Who would dare': *Aust. Jewish Herald*, 21 Oct. 1926. 'Leadership counts for something' and 'No man can rob me of this': *Argus*, 15 Mar. 1927. *Argus* contributions: 2 Aug. 1924, 4 Aug. 1928.
475. The *Herald* and *Sun* reports were on 7 Oct. 1927; JM to Bean, 11, 14 Oct.; Bean to JM, 11 Oct.; JM to Birdwood, 12 Oct. 'unspeakably unfair': JM to LR, 21 Oct. 1927.
475-6. 'Late one evening': JM to Bruche, 20 Mar. 1930.
476. JM wrote to Bean on 7 Nov. 1921 and to Aspinall-Oglander on 20 Aug. 1929.
'It must be a proud memory': Rush to JM, 1 Dec. 1928. 'You knew the Digger': Collett to JM, 10 Jan. 1924. The secretary of the Geelong R.S.L. wrote on 25 June 1928.
These examples are selected from a vast correspondence in the 1920s. An example of help to the AWM is JM to Pearce, 26 Sept. 1924.
476-7. 'intellectual giants are not born': *Herald*, 27 Sept. 1930. 'no such thing as effortless genius': Scotch College speech night address, 1928, MP. 'The greatest mistake in life': *Argus*, 15 Sept. 1923; cf. to F. Paton, 13 Oct. 1922. 'We should have a knowledge': JM to Mrs Hammond, 17 June 1930. Too many narrow men: *Geelong Advertiser*, 15 Dec. 1920. Examples of self-made men: *Herald*, 12 Apr. 1924. 'Ours is the game of life': *Herald*, 27 Sept. 1930. 'the discoveries of abstract science': talk to Beefsteaks, 1929, MP. 'The capacity to think clearly': JM to R. Campbell, 11 Apr. 1928.
478. 'Short Statement of Views on University Matters', 1923, MP, was for graduates.

NOTES (pages 478–487)

JM's letter to VM about Barrett was on 10 Sept. 1915. 'ready to respond': JM to MacFarland, 2 May. Further correspondence includes: JM to WR, 6 June; MacFarland to JM, 3 May; JM to Barrett, 20 June; Barrett to JM, 21 June; Picken to JM, 16 June; JM to Picken, 18 June; note *Argus*, 23 June.
Scott's and Blainey's histories of the University are relevant here.

478-9. 'but I pegged away': JM to MacFarland, 27 July. 'a bad, bad business': JM to LR, 16 July 1925. A speech of 18 Sept. 1922, MP, is a good example of his protests at penury; see also the printed proceedings of a deputation to the premier in 1922, MP. JM to WR, 25 Dec. 1926, described the dinner, and JM to Bainbridge, 15 Mar. 1927, the approach to the M.C.C.

479. 'the University is about as difficult': JM to Jenkinson, 13 July 1923. Disagreeable meetings: JM to WR, 18 Nov. 1925. Correspondence with Barrett and Picken in 1925 is illuminating. Blainey quotes the remark on gowns, p. 171.

479-80. There is much correspondence in 1923 about crises in the physics and botany departments. On dental matters see especially his letters to Argyle, 29 Nov. 1923, and to WR, 25 Dec. 1926. He reported on the metallurgy chair to WR on 7 Dec. 1923.

480. Hagelthorn wrote on 30 Oct. and JM replied on 2 Nov. George Meudell wrote in protest at Copland and Giblin on 1 Oct. 1930 and JM replied on 6 Oct. JM wrote about Schiassi to Carosi on 14 Aug. and to MacFarland on 16 Aug.
'If I had nothing else': JM to WR, Mar. 1927.

480-1. He made these remarks in a letter to Dixon, 3 Aug. 1923.

481-2. JM wrote to Spencer on 22 Jan. 1924. 'I used every argument': JM to Julius, 29 Mar. 1926. G. Currie and Graham, *The Origins of CSIRO*, Melbourne, 1966, pp. 129, 141, cover his work on C.S.I.R.'s foundation.

482. His reports to the M.C.C. were on 16 May and 28 June 1921 and his eventual suggestion was made to Mackey on 6 Jan. 1923.
'It was a rare spectacle': JM to Barrett, 6 July 1920. 'ruthless devastation': JM to Clarke, 15 Nov. 1920. JM also battled for Melbourne's parklands, e.g., *Herald*, 4 Nov. 1922.

482-3. *Sun*, 6 Feb. 1923, is one example of a call for the leader. JM to WR, 28 Dec. 1922, records the pressure to stand. Farmar to JM, 16 Dec. 1923, mentions Bruce's hopes. Snub over British Fleet visit: correspondence with Deane and Chauvel, 12-20 Mar. 1924. Bruce's gesture: JM to Bruce, 20 Oct. 1924. JM replied to Bruce on 5 May 1925, Bruce in turn on the 8th. Monash's place in the order of precedence was gazetted on 15 Oct.; cf. JM to McKenna, 4 June 1931. 'advice about some trumpery worry': Waters, *Much besides Music*, p. 179.

483-4. JM's hopes of comradeship: e.g., *Daily Telegraph* (London), 30 July 1919; *Age*, 27 Jan. 1920. Civilized British institutions: *Age*, 27 Dec. 1919. 'I do not know': JM to WR, 7 Dec. 1923. 'possible to get people': JM to Ohlfsen, 3 Mar. 1925. 'the Japanese people': JM to Sladen, 16 Nov. 1925. 'I feel certain': *Herald*, 28 Apr. 1925. Deriding aeroplanes: JM to Miss Isaacs, 12 Feb. 1930.

485. Advising on Capitol theatre: Fairway to JM, 12 Dec. 1921; JM to Fairway, 8 Dec. Reinforced Concrete Co. Paying him out: J. Gibson to JM, 21 Feb. 1923. There is scattered correspondence with Humes in MP. JM wrote to Nettlefold on 26 Nov. 1921, 3 Mar., 18 Apr. 1923, Nettlefold to JM on 20 Feb., 6, 14 Apr. 1923, 25 Oct. 1929. Urging Gibson: JM to Gibson, 10, 12 May 1921, 3 Jan. 1923.

485-6. Agreement with Lawson: JM to Fink, 30 Mar. 1921, to Skipper, 3 Nov. 1923, to Saddler, 5 July 1923.

486. Protests at his landlordism: JM to Haynes, 22 May 1922; *Sun*, 1 Nov. 1923.
Correspondence in 1922-23 reveals much of his investment dabbling. 'Perhaps when your friends': JM to Goodman, 29 Apr. 1931; cf. 3 Mar. 1930.

486-7. Files on private finances in MP provide exhaustive detail.

487. Meudell's letter was of 31 Jan. 1923. JM wrote to Howlett Ross on 5, 7 Feb. 1923; he replied on 6 Feb. Cf. *Australian Financial Gazette*, 28 Dec. 1922, 25 Feb. 1923. The 1926 warning was to Bate, 31 May.

NOTES (pages 487–503)

Age and *Argus*, 24 Mar. 1921, cover the Hertz meeting. New Year message for *Aust. Jewish Herald* was on 13 Sept. 1921. The letter to the *Argus* was on 6 May 1921; cf. JM to Margolin, 7 May. Opening of Monash House, *Aust. Jewish Herald*, 21 Oct. 1926.

487-8. JM wrote to Danglow on 3 May 1920. Row with acting rabbi: Solomon to JM, 5, 17 Apr., 1 June 1921; JM to Solomon, 6, 13 Apr., 7 June; JM to Joseph, 28 Apr., 7 June; Joseph to JM, 3 May, 1 June.

488-9. His diary-appointment books reveal his position. His letter to Danglow was on 17 June 1929. Michaelis asked him to be Chosan Torah on 24 Sept. 'However much the new movement': JM to Levinson, 28 Aug. 1930.

489. I. Cohen, *The Journal of a British Traveller*, London, 1925, pp. 50-2, describes his contacts with JM. Pledged himself: JM to Zeltner, 10 Aug. 1920.

489-90. The speech to the Palestine Welfare League was on 22 Dec. 1924, MP. The letter to Brodie was on 30 Nov. 1928. *Jewish Herald*, 12 Sept. 1929, reports the Town Hall meeting. There is a fair amount of correspondence in MP on all these events.

490-1. 'If sceptical Australians': Getzler, *Neither Toleration*, p. 120. The *Bulletin*, 10 Dec. 1925, remarks on the differences between Melbourne and Sydney Jews. Monash's standing policy: e.g., interview for a Polish newspaper, 25 Mar. 1930, news cuttings, MP. 'Monash, by the simple fact': McInnes, *England — Half English*, p. 187.

491. JM wrote to Springthorpe on 28, 30 Nov. 1922; Springthorpe replied on 29 Nov., 1 Dec.

492. Correspondence of Apr.-June 1923 covers McGlinn's appointment.

492-3. 'I have discovered to my cost': JM to Lady Masson, 10 June 1929.

493. The files of JM's speeches are the main source of these comments. Note also VM to JM, 14 Jan. 1917; JM to Bell, 26 May 1926.

493-4. 'a very English accent': *Punch*, 30 Sept. 1920. Springthorpe has some interesting comments in his diary (La Trobe Lib.), 14 Jan. 1926. Eggleston's remarks in his 'Confidential Notes' are curious.

494. The gutter-press: *Truth*, 29 Aug. 1925; *Smith's Weekly*, 20 Mar. 1926. Innumerable people have spoken to me about Lizzie.

495. JM's letters to the Rosenhains are the chief source on him with the children.

495-6. 'My dear big John': MM to JM, 18 Oct. 1922. 'All this is ridiculously petty': JM to WR, 5 May 1924.

496. The 'Parties' file, MP, is useful. Gershon Bennett's Sir John Monash Memorial Oration, 1936, MP, and Bertha Bennett's recollections to me were very helpful on his private social life; also JM to LR, 14 July 1925.

496-7. Thinking late at night: *Herald*, 29 June 1929.

497. His indexes, library and 'General to sort' files, correspondence with booksellers, and *Argus*, 15 Sept. 1923, provide the evidence on his library. 'the most expressive': *Argus*, 25 May 1927.

499. Nearly all the war trophies are with MP (AWM).
    'From music he seemed to emerge': G. Bennett's memorial oration.

499-500. Great honour of Streeton's life: Streeton to Meyer, 11 Oct. 1931, MP.

500. 'It is not so much': JM to Hercus, 3 Oct. 1924. There are astronomical files in MP; note also JM to WR, 18 Nov. 1925.

501-2. Re Rotary, see Osborne to JM, 6 Apr. 1922; JM to Osborne, 7 Apr.; JM to WR, 28 Dec. 'outings are': JM to Robertson, 26 May 1924. 'some traits of the autocrat': A. Hart, *History of the Wallaby Club*, Melbourne, 1944, p. 56. The papers to the Beefsteaks are in MP. 'I have entirely failed': JM to Oehr, 4 Oct. 1928.

502-3. 'hard work and long hours': JM to WR, 26 Feb. 1923. The 1924 letter was to Newton on 11 Aug.

503. Some revealing letters about his health are to WR, 18 Nov. 1925, 6 Jan. 1928; to LR, 16 July 1925, 21 Oct. 1927; to MM, 26 July 1931; see also Indexes — diagrams of my weight, MP.

504-5. 'Sir John is nothing like': *SMH*, 3 May 1924.
505. These impressions are based on a huge number of sources. Some which are especially revealing are: Sir Hugh Brain, memorial address, 1945; Sproule to G. Bennett, Oct. 1931, MP; A.C.D., *The Duckboard*, 1 Feb. 1924; *Herald*, 8 Nov. 1931; *Reveille*, Oct. 1931; Mrs Willox to author, 3 Mar. 1976; J. Kirwan, *My Life's Adventure*, London, 1936, p. 254.
505-6. 'It is astonishing': E. Scott to Mrs Scott, 26 Aug. 1926, Scott Papers, National Lib.
506. H. I. Cohen gave the memorial address to Temple Beth Israel, MP. Scott wrote to G. Bennett on 9 Oct. 1931. The formal minute of the Institution of Engineers, Australia, was recorded in its *Journal*, Oct. 1931.

'The greatest fighting man': W. S. Robinson, *If I Remember Rightly*, Melbourne, 1967, pp. 106-7, 109. Curtin was quoted in *Argus*, 7 Dec. 1929. Menzies made these remarks in his 1965 memorial address. Walter Murdoch wrote in these terms to Liddell Hart, 19 Oct. 1940. Dennis wrote to JM, 14 June 1922; Streeton to Meyer, 11 Oct. 1931; Herman to BB, 9 Oct. 1931.
506-7. Eric Simonson's 'Monash — the Man and his Method', a radio broadcast of 1939, is in MP.
507. Some of Monash's views on what makes for success are drawn from Simonson and from his own remarks in *The Motor Truck & Business Transport Monthly*, Oct. 1926, and *Everylady's Journal*, 6 Feb. 1920.
507-8. 'By rigid adherence': *Argus*, 15 Sept. 1923. 'A statement written': Simonson's broadcast.
509. Eggleston's criticisms are mainly in his 'Confidential Notes'. On obsession and neurosis, see Ross Day to author, 27 Oct. 1981.
509-10. An example of his recounting his meeting with Ned is in *Table Talk*, 18 Apr. 1929; also JM to N. Campbell, 19 Apr. 1929.

Of many who knew Monash with whom I conversed, I owe much to Kelvin and R. B. Lewis, Sir Alfred Kemsley, A. Masel, and the late J. S. Gawler, G. E. Knox and Eric Wilson. Useful press interview reports not previously mentioned include *The Home*, 1 Dec. 1920; *Gossip* (Adelaide), 4 Sept. 1924; H. S. Gullett, *Herald*, 21 July 1923; R. L. Curthoys, *Argus*, 15 Sept. 1923.
510. The *Herald's* survey was on 8 Sept. 1928. Brian Fitzpatrick reflects this general view in *The Australian Commonwealth. A Picture of the Community 1901-1955*, Melbourne, 1956, pp. 208-9.
510-11. *Bulletin*, 14 Oct. 1931, is interesting in its explanation of Monash's popularity as a volunteer soldier.
512. 'No one will ever know': JM to WR, 3 Feb. 1929. Letters to Littlejohn of 13 Mar. and 22 Oct. outline his endowments. The plans for the doll's house are in the Iona file, MP.
513. JM wrote to Bowater on 20 May and to Vida Goldstein on 15 May 1930; I have not been able to trace any interview in the *Monitor*. His message for Elliott was in a letter to Bruche of 10 July 1930.

His views on financial policy are in a letter to Bruche, 27 Sept. 1930. He told Murdoch on 9 Sept. of the secret meeting. 'I argued strongly': JM to BB, 30 Sept.

As well as his list of economies, see his Federal Income Tax file and letter to BB, 3 Oct. 1930.
513-14. Some relevant letters are: JM to Argyle, 20 Nov.; Argyle to JM, 22 Nov.; to H. I. Cohen, 17 Oct.; Cohen to JM, 8 Dec.; to Edgar, 21 Nov.; to H. E. Cohen, 5 Dec. 1930; see also *Vic. Parl. Debates*, Dec. 1930.
514. Garran's assertion is in his *Prosper the Commonwealth*, p. 322. The *Herald* and *Sun* items were on 24 and 25 Mar. JM wrote to Isaacs on 3 Dec. 1930. The best account of Isaacs's appointment is by Cowen, *Isaac Isaacs*, ch. 8.

Monash's speech at the presentation of the Russell medal is in MP.
514-15. 'been urged upon every': JM to Cowen, 14 Nov. The anonymous letter to the *Age* was published on 28 June 1928. Campaign for further promotion:

H. E. Williams to JM, Nov. 1929; W. H. Edgar, *Sun*, 11 Dec. 1930; Castlemaine R.S.L. to JM, 22 June 1930. 'it has been the rule of my life': JM to Field, 24 June 1930.

515. Monash thanked Scullin in a letter of 25 June 1930. Council of Defence: JM to Shepherd, 17 Apr.; Shepherd to JM, 15 May 1930. Monash's and White's joint letter to Scullin was of 13 Nov. 1929. 'White and I made a fight': JM to Bruche, 31 Dec. 1929. Cf. JM to Bruche, 20 Jan. and 27 Sept. 1930, and other letters between them.

'I decline presidency': D, 20 Nov. 1928; letters to R.S.L. officials, 29 Nov. 1928, 31 July, 2 Aug. 1929, 23, 26 May 1930; JM to Collett, 23 Apr., 2 June 1931; Collett to JM, 2 June 1931.

515-16. JM wrote to Stewart on 12 Feb. 1930. Letters by JM of 1, 3, 29 Apr. 1930 reveal his feelings. *Australian Traveller*, 10 May 1930, reports the Commercial Travellers' reception.

516-17. Bean's letter was of 21 May. See *Smith's Weekly*, Apr.-June, especially 21 June; *Truth*, 15 June; correspondence with Baume, Apr.-May; JM to Bean, 19, 27 May; JM to Bruche, 27 Sept.; Chapman to JM, 13 May; JM to Chapman, 15 May; F. E. Baume, *I Lived these Years*, London, 1941, p. 133. *Smith's* attacked JM over the Shrine on 27 Dec. 1930.

517. 'had only to put up his little finger': *Age*, 21 July 1926.

517-18. Sporadic cries: e.g., *Herald*, 28 July 1923. Two appeals: Llewellyn to JM, 27 Apr.; Warringah Constitutional Club, 7 May 1927. Grover wrote in *Adam and Eve*, 1 Feb. 1927. Field wrote on 24 Feb. 1929; cf. 6 Oct. 1931. Knights of the Empire: Cother to JM, 8 June 1929.

518-19. Empire Loyalty League: Johnston to JM, 30 Apr. 1930. Cf. correspondence with a Goulburn Valley movement: Stewart to JM, 24 July, 9 Aug.; JM to Stewart, 31 July, 15 Aug. 1930; and B. Fitzpatrick to JM, 27 Sept. 1930; JM to Fitzpatrick, 30 Sept. Miss Sadlier-Forster wrote on 24 Nov., 5, 14 Dec. 1930.Fr Graham telegraphed on 17 Mar. 1931. For the Rotary speaker, *Advertiser* (Adelaide), 6 Dec. 1930. 'There is only one man': *Bulletin*, 3 Dec. 1930. 'as a public officer': JM to Knox, 12 Nov. 1930; Roach to JM, 12 Nov.

519-20. Grimwade wrote on 16 Dec. and JM replied next day. Swain wrote on 22 Dec. and Barclay on the 19th. JM replied on 23 Dec. 1930.

520-1. JM's letters to BB, D and files in MP are the chief sources for the Indian trip. A letter to Rosenthal, 9 Sept. 1931, sums up his frontier experience.

521. McKenna wrote his obituary in the *Angelus*, Nov. 1931; cf. McKenna to JM, 1 May 1931; Bean Papers, folder 64.

522. Monash reported to Officer on 1 May 1931. Some of his comments on India were reported in *Sun*, 1, 6 Apr., 11 Aug. 1931; of his speeches, see especially to Beefsteaks, MP.

'he had no desire whatever': *Age*, 1 Apr. 1931. The *Herald* correspondent was published on 10 Feb., Streeton in *Argus*, 9 Feb., 'Mungana Mike' in *Bulletin*, 11 Feb. Prentice's views are in *Reveille*, Dec. 1931. For the W.A. Flying Corps Association, *West Australian*, 14 Mar. Cf. *SMH*, 20 Feb.; *Bulletin* ed., 25 Feb. 1931; Sir Henry Barraclough in *J. Institution Engineers, Australia*, Oct. 1931; Cullen to JM, 21 Apr. 1931.

522-3. His biographical account to Rosenthal was dated 4 Dec. 1930. A letter to Harold Cohen of 15 May 1931 well demonstrates his declining powers. 'began to notice a disposition': JM to WR, 1 Sept. 1931.

524. *Sun* reported his address to the 6th Battalion reunion on 24 Sept., 6, 9 Oct. Sewell was reported in *Herald*, 8 Oct.

524-7. The account of reactions to the death and of the funeral is largely taken from the cuttings book in MP. Tate wrote for the Beefsteaks to BB, 24 Nov. Gershon Bennett's remarks are from his Sir John Monash Memorial Oration, 1936. Danglow's quotation of Carlyle is from his 1962 memorial address. LR wrote to BB on 13 Oct.

526-7. Lizette's grief: oral evidence from an unimpeachable witness, Ian Mair.

528-9. Brudenell White's and H. I. Cohen's addresses are in MP.
529. J. M. Swan, later a professor at Monash University, was the first to suggest the name of the University.
531-3. MP contain much material on commemoration of Monash. Blunden's review of the *War Letters* was in *Book Society News* (London), Oct. 1935.
534-5. 'confidential unpublished account': *Gallipoli*, p. 272. The letter of 16 Aug. is in *War Letters of General Monash*, pp. 62-3. The North Papers (Liddell Hart Centre for Military Archives) contain a letter from North to Bean, 9 June 1936, and a letter from Allanson to North, 18 Dec. 1935 (file 1/3, items 76, 28). A copy of *Personal Diary kept in the field by Lt. Col. C. Allanson, commanding 1/6 GR, 20 July-3 December 1915, Gallipoli Campaign* (n.p., n.d.) is in the National Army Museum, London. Rhodes James told North of Slim's opinion in a letter of 28 Feb. 1964 (North Papers, file 1/3, item 402). Allanson stated his dislike for Australians in a letter to North, 18 Dec. 1935, loc. cit.

I am grateful to Mr A. J. Hill for advice on the possibility of the incident having occurred.

Rhodes James's letter to North is cited above. Howe's letter to Rhodes James, dated 7 Nov. 1964, is in the Bazley Papers, AWM. Malone's diary note is cited in *Gallipoli*, p. 271. Jerram's remark is in The Life of Lt-Col. Charles Frederic Jerram, ch. 13 (Royal Marines Museum, Southend, ACQ 23/80 (c) Arch 9/2/J). 'physically and mentally exhausted': *Gallipoli*, p. 272. 'completely encircled': *Gallipoli*, p. 273.

Select Bibliography

The Monash Papers

1. The *Monash Papers proper* were under the control of the family for fifty years and have now been deposited in the National Library of Australia. They comprise possibly the most extensive collection of private papers to have survived in this country. They include:
    (i) Diaries. After some false starts they become substantial early in 1883. Gaps follow, but from July 1886 to 1890 they are rich and full. They then taper off until they end in July 1896. The brief 'Intimate Diary' contains irregular entries between 1882 and 1898. Diary-appointment-books are included for the years 1895–1931, except for 1904–13 and 1924–25. During the war years Monash occasionally made brief valuable comments in them. It is possible that he kept some kind of diary, other than appointment books, in the 1920s; if so, it has not survived.
    (ii) Correspondence, amounting to about 70 000 to 75 000 inwards and outwards letters, including almost all the Monash & Anderson letter-books, 1894–1906. From 1883 Monash began to press-copy his more important letters and from 1885 all his letters. From about 1900 much of his general correspondence was typed by secretaries but he continued to write by hand and press-copy most of his private letters. His L series of out-letters runs from 1-14, from January 1883 to March 1913. Two 'PB' volumes run from May 1906 to July 1912; other 'PB' books are in the Reinforced Concrete Co. records (and one, from July 1901 to March 1902, is held privately by Mr A. G. Lynch of Toorak). During the war much of his family and other private correspondence continued to be by hand, with carbon copies in field-service books. Much wartime military correspondence remains. After the war he resumed press-copying some of his family and other private letters. The general 1920s correspondence is voluminous. The correspondence includes family letters 1850s-1870s, his semi-official correspondence in 1919 about demobilization, and letters relating to him after his death.
    (iii) Military records, including correspondence, pre-war and post-war.
    (iv) Notes for and transcripts of lectures and speeches and manuscripts of writings, such as his address on 'Leadership in War' to the Beefsteaks.

(v) Subject-files relating to private finances; engineering, S.E.C., University and Shrine affairs; and to clubs and societies, Jewish movements, royal commissions, boards of inquiry and arbitration cases.
  (vi) School and University notebooks and essays, engineering and other notebooks.
  (vii) Personal records.
  (viii) Souvenirs.
  (ix) Commonplace books.
  (x) Press-cuttings.
  (xi) Pamphlets.
  (xii) Photographs.
  (xiii) Indexes.
  (xiv) Memorials: addresses, obituaries, press-cuttings, broadcasts.

In the last weeks of his life Monash destroyed small sections of his papers including his letters from Annie Gabriel and Lizette Bentwitch. Gershon Bennett subsequently destroyed nearly all his letters to Lizette and possibly earlier isolated items. The Papers remain an extraordinary near-complete record of an adult life.

I have added to the Papers a typescript of my first draft which is 70 000 words longer than the final product. (I shall be happy to supply to any student annotation of excised material.)

I have also included some of my correspondence with veterans of the First A.I.F. and military historians.

2. The *Monash Papers, Australian War Memorial*, Canberra, were selected by Sir John Monash for deposit in the AWM but were not transferred until 1949. The most important section comprises personal files, August 1914-December 1919, including correspondence, orders, reports, narratives, notes on conferences and other material which are in boxes 79-94a, AWM. The collection also includes demobilization papers, maps, photographs, manuals, books, pamphlets, newspapers, weapons and other souvenirs. Much official and semi-official correspondence is not included and remains in the Monash Papers proper. In the author's opinion, whether Monash suppressed or destroyed any evidence to his detriment remains an open question.

3. The records of the *Reinforced Concrete and Monier Pipe Construction Co. Pty Ltd* in the University of Melbourne Archives include material relating to the Monash & Anderson partnership and before. Boxes 1 and 2 contain records of Monash's work on the Outer Circle railway and for the Harbor Trust. Series 2/1, 2/2, 2/3 (March 1902–May 1906) and 2/6, 2/7 (July 1913–October 1914), five PB volumes, comprise letter-books which include personal and military as well as business material. Boxes 3-123, files 17-1084, cover the Monash & Anderson period as well as the company's work in Monash's time.

4. *State Electricity Commission of Victoria: Archives.* The Chairman's Correspondence and Papers contain the essential Monash material.

5. The *La Trobe Collection, State Library of Victoria*, contains a few minor items.

Other Manuscript Sources

Bean, C. E. W. Papers, AWM.
  (This great collection consists mainly of Bean's wartime diaries and note-

books, but also contains a mass of correspondence. Bean in later life was very worried about releasing his diaries and notebooks and carefully labelled each with a note that his statements therein were 'what the writer at the moment believed to be true'. As the collection was only recently released and was not comprehensively indexed at the time I consulted it, I am likely to have missed relevant material.)
Birdwood, Field-Marshal Lord. Papers, AWM.
Cox, General Sir H. V. Papers, AWM.
Eggleston, Sir F. W. 'Confidential Notes', III, Menzies Library, Australian National University.
  Papers, NL.
Elliott, Major-General H. E. Papers, AWM.
Farmar, Colonel H. M. Reminiscences (held by the Farmar family).
Gellibrand, Major-General Sir J. Papers, AWM.
Godley, General Sir A. J. Papers, AWM.
Haig, Field-Marshal Earl. Papers, National Library of Scotland.
Hughes, W. M. Papers, NL.
Liddell Hart, Captain Sir B. H. Papers, Liddell Hart Centre for Military Archives, King's College, University of London.
Murdoch, Sir K. A. Papers, NL.
Novar, Viscount. Papers, NL.
Pearce, Sir G. F. Papers, AWM.
Rawlinson, General Lord. Diaries, Churchill College, University of Cambridge.
  Papers, National Military Museum, London.
White, Lieut-General Sir C. B. B. Papers, NL

Official Sources

(i) Australian War Memorial, Canberra

The voluminous military archives have rarely been thoroughly explored. The author made soundings at vital points in the War Diaries of formations and units, orders and reports.

(ii) Australian Archives, Melbourne

The records of the Departments of Defence and the Army, before and during the 1914-18 war, contain marginal information relating to Monash, but the author discovered nothing of significance relating to Monash not covered in MP and MP (AWM).

(iii) Commonwealth of Australia

Parliamentary Papers and Parliamentary Debates contain much relating to defence and the 1914-18 war and scattered references to Monash.

(iv) Victoria

Parliamentary Papers and Parliamentary Debates contain much relating to the State Electricity Commission.

Select List of Writings by Monash

Books

The Australian Victories in France in 1918. Hutchinson, London, 1920; Lothian, Melbourne, 1923, revised; Angus & Robertson, Sydney, 1936.

War Letters of General Monash, ed. F. M. Cutlack. Sydney, 1934.

Articles and Pamphlets

(i) Military

'The Evolution of Modern Weapons'. United Service Institution of Victoria, *Journal*, October 1894.

'Lessons of the Wilderness Campaign 1864'. *Commonwealth Military Journal*, April 1912.

'Retrospect of the War'. *Argus*, 2 August 1924.

'Seven Years Ago — and now'. Melbourne *Herald*, 11 November 1925.

'The Decisive Battle — ten years ago'. *Argus*, 4 August 1928.

'How Kitchener Landed'. *Reveille*, March 1930.

'Were Aussies Barred?'. *Reveille*, May 1930.

Monash also wrote official military orders and pamphlets such as: New Zealand and Australian Division. Fourth (Australian Infantry) Brigade. *Operation Standing Orders*. By Col. J. Monash, Cairo, 1915; and *Demobilisation of the A.I.F.: things which Australian soldiers ought to know*. London, 1919. I have not seen a copy of his *100 Hints for Company Commanders* (1913 or 1914, reissued to 1916).

He also wrote forewords or introductions to at least ten battalion histories and other war books.

(ii) Engineering

The Superintendence of Contracts. Carlton, 1890.

'Reinforced Concrete in Building Construction'. Royal Victorian Institute of Architects, *Journal*, July 1904.

'Notes on Tests of Reinforced Concrete Beams'. Victorian Institute of Engineers, *Proceedings*, vi, 1905.

'Notes on a Contemporary Example of a Reinforced Concrete Structure and Further Tests of Reinforced Concrete Beams'. *Ibid.*, vii, 1906.

'Notes on Modern Building Construction'. *Ibid.*, viii, 1907.

'Notes on Modern Building Construction'. *Building, Lighting, Engineering*, January, February, March 1908.

'Concrete Construction'. Royal Victorian Institute of Architects, *Journal*, May 1908.

'Notes on some recent Structures in Reinforced Concrete'. Victorian Institute of Engineers, *Proceedings*, xiii, 1912.

'The Engineering Profession in Australia'. *Ibid.*, xiv, 1913.

'Machine Foundations'. *Scientific Australian*, March 1914.

'Public Works in Victoria'. *Handbook to Victoria*, ed. A. M. Laughton and T. S. Hall. Melbourne, 1914.

'The State Electricity Scheme'. *Monthly Journal of the Melbourne Chamber of Commerce*, June 1924.

'Power Development'. *Report of the Seventeenth Meeting of the Australasian Association for the Advancement of Science 1924.* Adelaide, 1926.
'Electric Light and Power'. London *Times*, 9 May 1927.
'Engineering as a Profession'. *Scotch Collegian*, May 1928.
'Electrical Advance in Australia'. *Electrical Review*, 19 October 1928.
'Electrifying a State'. *Argus*, 20 November 1929.

(iii) Other

'Melbourne Gossip' by 'Nectabanus'. *Jerilderie Herald*, 21 October, 25 November 1882.
'Statement of an Eye Witness'. *Bendigo Independent*, 5 December 1882.
Melbourne University Review. Articles certainly written by Monash are 'Ourselves', July 1884; 'A Question of Identity', August 1884; 'Reformed Spelling', September 1884; 'Going to the Play', September 1884; 'Our Smoking Room and what we say in it', December 1884, March 1885.
'Some Impressions of Travel'. Victorian Institute of Engineers, *Proceedings*, xii, 1911.
'Work of the University – Problem of Finance'. Melbourne *Herald*, 19 November 1925.
'If I were Czar of Radio'. *Australian Popular Radio Monthly*, August 1928.
'The "Help-you" Spirit in Public Service'. *Victorian Railways Magazine*, October 1928.
'Memories in an Autograph Book'. *Argus*, 9 November 1929.
'The University in the present Crisis'. *Herald*, 29 September 1930.
'What I Saw in India'. *Herald*, 7 April 1931.

Writings on Monash

Brasch, Rabbi R. 'Sir John Monash'. *Journal & Proceedings, Royal Australian Historical Society*, vol. 45, pt 4, 1959.
Edwards, Cecil. *John Monash*, Melbourne, 1970.
Falkus, M. 'Monash', *The War Lords*, M. Carver (ed.). London, 1976.
Gammage, W. 'Sir John Monash: a military review'. *Historical Studies*, vol. 16, no. 62, April 1974.
Hetherington, J. *John Monash.* Melbourne, 1962.
Holmes, Jean. 'Administrative Style and Sir John Monash'. *Public Administration*, xxvii, June-September 1969.
Isaacs, Sir Isaac. 'The Monash oration – 1937'. Printed in Max Gordon, *Sir Isaac Isaacs. A Life of Service.* Melbourne, 1963.
McInnes, Colin. 'Joshua Reborn', *England – Half English.* London, 1961.
Northwood, V. R. *Monash.* Melbourne, 1961.
Palmer, Vance. 'The Soldier', *National Portraits.* Sydney, 1940.
Perry, E. W. 'The Military Life of General Sir John Monash'. *Victorian Historical Magazine*, xxviii, December 1957.
—— 'General Sir John Monash, Scholar, Engineer and Soldier'. *Journal of the Australian Jewish Historical Society*, vol. 4, pt 6, 1957.
Smithers, A. J. *Sir John Monash.* London and Sydney, 1973.
Spaull, A. D. 'Sir John Monash – a Vanishing Hero? A Bibliographical Commentary'. *Journal & Proceedings, Royal Australian Historical Society*, vol. 56, pt 3, 1970.

Spaull, A. D. 'Sir John Monash and the State Electricity Commission of Victoria 1920-31'. *Public Administration*, xxiv, September 1970.
Storer, S. *The War to end War and General Monash*. Swan Hill, 1977.
Terraine, John. 'Monash: Australian Commander'. *History Today*, January 1966.
Thompson, John (ed.). *On Lips of Living Men*. Melbourne, 1962.

Newspapers

The main Melbourne newspapers — the *Age, Argus* and *Herald* — have been extensively used. Other newspaper references have largely been drawn from the cuttings books in MP.

Books, articles and theses

Adam-Smith, Patsy. *The Anzacs*. Melbourne, 1978.
Aspinall-Oglander, C. F. *Military Operations; Gallipoli* (Official British History). 2 v., London, 1929, 1932.
Bean, C. E. W. *Anzac to Amiens: a shorter history of the Australian fighting services in the first world war*. Canberra, 1946.
—— *The Official History of Australia in the War of 1914-18*, vols 1-6. Sydney, 1921-42.
—— *Two Men I Knew: William Bridges and Brudenell White. Founders of the A.I.F.* Sydney, 1957.
Blainey, Geoffrey. *Centenary History of the University of Melbourne*. Melbourne, 1957.
Butler, A. G. *Official History of the Australian Army Medical Services 1914-18*. 3 v., Sydney, 1930-43.
Chataway, C. P. *History of the 15th Battalion, Australian Imperial Forces*. Brisbane, 1948.
Coulthard-Clark, C. D. *The Citizen General Staff. The Australian Intelligence Corps 1907-1914*. Canberra, 1976.
Cowen, Zelman. *Isaac Isaacs*. Melbourne, 1967.
Dixon, Norman. *The Psychology of Military Incompetence*. London, 1976.
Edmonds, J. E. (ed.) *Military Operations; France and Belgium, 1918* (Official British History). 4 v., London, 1935-47.
Edwards, Cecil. *Brown Power. A jubilee history of the State Electricity Commission of Victoria*. Melbourne, 1969.
Eggleston, F. W. *State Socialism in Victoria*. London, 1932.
Essame, H. *The Battle for Europe 1918*. London, 1972.
Fussell, Paul. *The Great War and Modern Memory*. New York and London, 1975.
Fitzhardinge, L. F. *The Little Digger 1914-1952. William Morris Hughes. A political biography*, vol. 2. Sydney, 1979.
Gammage, Bill. *The Broken Years: Australian soldiers in the Great War*. Canberra, 1974.
Garran, R. R. *Prosper the Commonwealth*. Sydney, 1958.
Getzler, I. *Neither Toleration nor Favour. The Australian chapter of Jewish emancipation*. Melbourne, 1970.

Goldman, L. M. *The Jews in Victoria in the Nineteenth Century*. Melbourne, 1954.
Hamilton, Sir Ian. *Gallipoli Diary*. 2 v., London, 1920.
Hetherington, John. *Blamey. Controversial Soldier. A biography of Field Marshal Sir Thomas Blamey, GBE, KCB, CMG, DSO, ED*. Canberra, 1973.
Hill, A. J. *Chauvel of the Light Horse. A biography of General Sir Harry Chauvel, G.C.M.G., K.C.B.* Melbourne, 1978.
Inglis, K. S. 'The Australians at Gallipoli', *Historical Studies*, nos 54-55, 1970.
James, Robert Rhodes. *Gallipoli*. London and Sydney, 1965.
Lloyd George, David. *War Memoirs*. 6 v., London, 1933-36.
Longmore, C. *The Old Sixteenth: being a record of the 16th Battalion, A.I.F., during the Great War, 1914-1918*. Perth, 1929.
McKernan, Michael. *Australian Churches at War*. Sydney, 1980.
—— *The Australian People and the Great War*. Melbourne, 1980.
McNicol, N. G. *The Thirty-Seventh: history of the Thirty-Seventh Battalion A.I.F.* Melbourne, 1936.
Medding, P. Y. *From Assimilation to Group Survival. A political and sociological study of an Australian Jewish community*. Melbourne, 1968.
Moorehead, Alan. *Gallipoli*. London, 1956.
North, John. *Gallipoli: the fading vision*. London, 1936.
Robson, L. L. *The First A.I.F. A study of its recruitment 1914-1918*. Melbourne, 1970.
Ross, Jane Stewart. Militarism in the Australian Army. Ph.D. thesis, University of Sydney, 1973.
Rule, E. J. *Jacka's Mob*. Sydney, 1933.
Russell, W. B. *We Will Remember Them. The Story of the Shrine of Remembrance*. Melbourne, 1980.
Scott, Ernest. *Australia during the War. Official History of Australia in the War of 1914-18*, vol. xi. Sydney, 1936.
—— *A History of the University of Melbourne*. Melbourne, 1936.
Spaull, A. D. The Origins and Rise of the Victorian Brown Coal Industry 1835-1935. M.Comm. thesis, University of Melbourne, 1968.
Sugden, E. H. and Eggleston, F. W. *George Swinburne. A biography*. Sydney, 1931.
Terraine, John. *Haig, the Educated Soldier*. London, 1963.
—— *The Road to Passchendaele*. London, 1977.
—— *The Smoke and the Fire*. London, 1980.
—— *The Western Front 1914-1918*. London, 1964.
—— *To Win a War. 1918, the year of victory*. London, 1978.
Wanliss, Newton. *The History of the Fourteenth Battalion, A.I.F.* Melbourne, 1929.
White, T. A. *The "Fighting Thirteenth": the history of the Thirteenth Battalion, A.I.F.* Sydney, 1924.
Woolf, Leon. *In Flanders Fields. The 1917 Campaign*. London, 1960.

Index

Nearly all military formations and units are under the headings Australian Imperial Force and British Army. Ranks of officers are those attained at the end of their careers.

Abdel Rahman ridge, 236, 238
Abrahams, Rabbi J., 104, 118, 487-8
Adams, Lieut-Colonel J., 242, 253
Aerial League of Australia, 170, 190
Age (Melbourne), 59, 113, 121, 147, 181, 189, 197, 198, 250, 370, 400, 423, 424, 445, 446, 451, 454, 472, 475, 527, 533
Albert, 310, 311, 352
Allan, John, 446, 457, 469, 471
Allanson, Major C. J. L., 236-7, 534-5
American Army, 315, 333-5, 360-1, 363-7, 417
Amiens, 311, 316, 330, 336, 348, 350, 353; battle of, 343ff.
Ancre River, 311, 317
Anderson, Ellen, 116, 424
Anderson, Jack, 138, 155
Anderson, J. T. N., 108, 116, 121-4, 130-40, 155, 156, 424, 486, 507, 584
Anderson Street bridge, 134-5
Andrew, Prof. H. M., 33, 37, 42, 45
Anti-Semitism, 16, 147, 325, 415, 490-1
Anzac Cove, 214-15
Anzac Day, 261, 416, 467, 469-71, 474, 515-16
Architects, Royal Victorian Institute of, 154, 165
Argus (Melbourne), 103, 112, 113, 114, 124, 125, 147, 181, 198, 205, 207, 227, 250, 445, 451, 456, 472, 475, 487, 494, 498
Armentières, 263, 277, 278, 280, 308, 316
Armistice, 362
Armstrong, E. La T., 12, 38n., 109, 166
Asma Dere, 238
astronomy, 500
Atlas Assurance Co., 427, 485
Australasian Association for the Advancement of Science, 481
Australia Valley, 234
Australian Imperial Force: chs 8-13; formation, 203; reorganization 1916, 258; Headquarters, London, 265, 266, 281; publicity for, 359, 417; casualties, 367-70; achievement, 368, 370, 474-6; qualities, 391-4, 396; fellowship, 396, 474
Australian Corps, 299, 316, 317, 319-28, ch. 12, 416
1st Division, 203, 209, 210, 214, 215, 251, 258, 260, 283, 295, 316, 329, 330, 342, 348, 352, 353, 357, 358-9, 361, 372
2nd Division, 260, 263, 283, 295, 297, 318, 329, 331, 337, 342, 348, 353, 354, 355, 357, 367
3rd Division, 260, 264-318, 319, 327, 329, 342, 352, 353, 354, 355, 357, 365-7, 376, 390, 392, 393, 394, 408, 410
4th Division, 259, 260, 271, 283, 284, 293, 297, 301, 310, 313, 315, 333, 336, 342, 352, 353, 357, 358-9, 361, 372
5th Division, 260, 283, 314, 317, 319, 342, 348, 353, 354, 355, 357, 365-7
4th Brigade, ch. 8, 272, 302, 336, 352, 376, 382, 384, 393, 535
9th Brigade, 266, 279, 290, 291, 293, 297, 310, 312, 313, 314, 315, 317-18, 352
10th Brigade, 266, 279, 279-80, 290, 291, 297, 310, 312, 313, 329, 354
11th Brigade, 266, 279, 293, 312, 313, 314, 317, 318
1st Light Horse Brigade, 208, 221-2
13th Battalion, 204, 215, 216, 218, 219, 220, 221, 227, 234, 235, 238, 242, 248, 258, 260, 263, 369
14th Battalion, 204, 215, 216, 219, 221, 225, 228, 230, 234, 235, 238, 242, 258, 263
15th Battalion, 204, 215, 216, 219, 220, 221, 222, 225, 226, 234, 235, 238, 240, 240-1, 247, 258, 260

591

16th Battalion, 204, 215, 216, 219, 220, 221, 228, 234, 235, 238, 258
33rd Battalion, 279, 291, 317
34th Battalion, 317
37th Battalion, 270, 279, 291, 292, 295, 302, 308, 349
38th Battalion, 279, 295, 297, 308, 313
39th Battalion, 279, 296, 307
40th Battalion, 279, 296, 307, 314
41st Battalion, 296, 314
42nd Battalion, 295, 314
43rd Battalion, 276, 295, 314
44th Battalion, 279, 291, 296
Australian Intelligence Corps, 169-72, 173, 190-3
Australian Labor Party, 173, 198, 201, 281, 446, 447, 455, 457-9, 469, 473, 484, 514, 520
Australian Natives' Association, 34, 147
Australian Victories in France in 1918, 304, 337, 338, 342n., 368, 370, 381, 394, 396, 400, 420, 431; writing of, 418-19
Australian War Memorial, 338, 476

Baby 700, 218, 219, 226, 232
Bailleul, 263, 278, 292
Baillieu, W. L., 179, 427
Balfour, A. J. (Lord), 414, 489
Baltzer, W. G., 135, 154
Barrett, Sir J. W., 148, 187, 420, 424, 434, 478, 482
Bassett, (Sir) W. E., 187, 479
Bauchop's Hill, 243, 246
Baxter & Saddler, 126-8, 131-4, 134, 135
Bazley, A. W., 401, 403
Bean, C. E. W., 211, 220, 227, 233-4, 238, 251-2, 254, 270, 292, 295, 299-300, 301, 312-13, 318, 329, 338, 339-40, 347, 351, 358-9, 359, 361n., 365-6, 368, 373, 383, 388, 390, 392, 394, 396, 397, 399, 400, 401, 402, 418-19, 475, 476, 509, 516-17, 517, 529, 535, 584-5; judgement of Monash, 397-8; *Official History* cited, 239, 254, 260, 264, 279, 286, 287, 292, 296, 313-14, 330, 334, 339, 343, 346, 347, 348, 355, 356, 360, 369, 389; plots with Murdoch 1918, 321-8
Beaurepaire, (Sir) F., 279, 390
Beefsteaks, 382, 501-2, 524
Behrend, A., 3, 6, 13-14, 19, 36, 47, 66, 67, 68, 77, 78, 101, 102, 119, 130, 145, 150, 183
Behrend, Minnie, 52, 55, 68, 102, 229, 269
Behrend family, 127, 205, 229
Bellicourt, 364-5
Benjamin, Ada, *see* Krakowski, Ada
Bennett, Bertha, *see* Monash, Bertha
Bennett, David M., 495, 512-13, 533
Bennett, Elizabeth M., 495, 512-13, 533
Bennett, Gershon, 257, 294, 413, 433, 479, 487, 488, 495, 496, 499, 500, 528, 529, 533, 584
Bennett, John Colin M., 512, 533
Bennett, John M., 495, 512

Bentwitch, Elizabeth, 265, 421, 433-4, 489, 493-4, 508, 520, 524, 526, 533
Bertangles chateau, 316, 330, 331, 344, 346, 350-1
Bevan, D., 157, 160, 172
Birdwood, Field Marshal (Lord) W., 208-77, 283, 292-319, 329, 330, 339, 341, 350, 361, 362, 368n., 395-408, 412, 415-33, 448, 470, 514, 524; and Bean–Murdoch plot, 319-28; qualities, 319
Blamey, Field Marshal (Sir) T. A., 220, 329, 332, 333, 337, 338, 340, 346, 350, 354, 356, 357, 362, 363, 366, 371, 375, 379, 382-3, 384, 388, 389, 396, 397, 405, 444, 464, 469, 470, 500, 515, 517, 522, 527n., 529, 531
Blashki, Eva, 52-5, 57, 97
Blashki, Jeanette, 54-5, 94, 98
Blashki, Minnie, *see* Behrend, Minnie
Blashki, Rose, 53, 54, 245
Blashki family, 48, 52-5, 70
Boer War, *see* South African War
Bony, 366, 367
Boulogne, 293, 310
Boy Scout movement, 189-90, 425, 493
Boyd, J. A., 146, 147
Brahe family, 15, 31, 36
Brand, Major-General C. H., 264, 272, 329, 336, 351, 389, 422
Brandt, Moritz and Hilda, 7, 13, 24
Bray, 311, 352, 353
Breslau (Wroclaw), 1, 174
Bridge, J. M., 448, 450, 452, 455, 461
Bridges, Major-General Sir W. T., 169-70, 202, 203, 209n., 210, 215, 216, 217, 219, 224, 305, 400
Briggs, C. T., 440
British Army: chs 8-13, passim
 First Army, 353
 Second Army, 293, 294
 Third Army, 313, 316, 352, 353, 358
 Fourth Army, 316, ch. 12
 Fifth Army, 313, 316, 319
 Australian and New Zealand Army Corps, 208
 I Anzac Corps, 294, 300
 II Anzac Corps, 277, 290, 292, 294, 305
 III British Corps, 339, 341, 343, 346, 352, 353, 357, 361, 364
 VII British Corps, 311
 IX British Corps, 357
 32nd Division, 352, 353, 354
 35th Division, 311, 313, 314
 46th Division, 365
 N.Z. and Australian Division, 208ff.
 Tank Corps, 332-7, 340-2, 348, 349, 363-5
British Association for the Advancement of Science, 198, 202
Broodseinde, 294, 295-6, 302, 354, 385
Bruce, (Viscount) S. M., 410, 431, 464, 482-3, 492
Bruche, Major-General (Sir) J. H., 161, 170, 171-2, 193, 194-5, 197, 199, 204, 268, 330,

INDEX

332n., 339, 342, 347, 385, 387, 407, 430, 431, 432, 465, 517, 525
Brunton, (Sir) W., 467-8
Buffalo, Mount, 70, 141, 157, 166, 172, 183, 205, 423, 482, 503, 532
Bullecourt, 221, 252, 290, 299, 317, 400
Bulletin (Sydney), 31, 390, 429, 430, 434, 458, 518
Burnage, Lieut-Colonel G. F., 227, 229, 253
Burnham, Lord (H. L. W. Levy-Lawson), 404, 412, 418, 451
Butler, Lieut-General (Sir) R. H. K., 339, 341, 343, 361
Byng, Field Marshal (Viscount), 349, 352

Cain, John, 459, 525
Canadian Expeditionary Force, 289, 299, 300, 330, 338, 339, 341, 342, 346, 347, 348, 350, 351, 387, 389, 409
Canberra, 180, 187
Cannan, Major-General J. H., 221, 227, 236, 253, 281, 282, 293, 296, 312, 313, 317, 321, 376
Card (Bowater), Billie, 231, 256, 513
Card family, 68, 119, 146, 176, 199, 231
Carruthers, Brigadier-General R. A., 329-30, 394, 404
Catani, C. G. D. E., 134, 137
Cathie family, 181
Celtic Club, 198
Chaulnes, 341, 351
Chauvel, General Sir H. G., 169, 208, 209, 221-2, 226-7, 228, 246, 251, 252, 253, 259, 283, 305, 306, 328, 375, 400, 407, 413, 416, 425, 429, 433, 463, 464, 465, 469, 473, 483n., 501, 510, 514, 514-15, 526
chess, 46-7, 119, 231
Chipilly, 343, 346, 348, 419
Christensen, C., 123, 137, 153, 155
Chuignes, battle of, 352-3
Chunuk Bair, 233, 239
Churchill, (Sir) W. S., 201, 232, 251, 349, 404, 497
Clapp, (Sir) H. W., 437, 449, 496, 513, 522
Clark, L., 38n., 439, 449
Clemenceau, G., 336, 350
Clements, F. W., 436, 443, 452, 453n., 459
coal-mining, 121, ch. 15
Cohen, H. E., 390
Cohen, H. I., 443, 506, 528
Cole's Book Arcade, 22, 28, 497
Collins House, 179, 205, 206, 427
Concrete Constructions, 257, 426, 427
Congreve, General (Sir) W. N., 311-14, 376
conscription, 202, 268-9, 299
contracting, 80-6, 108, 113, 156, 168
Cook, Sir J., 201, 202, 326, 404, 407, 410, 411
Corrie, Evie, 91-2, 94, 97, 98
Country Party, 438, 441, 446
Courage, Brigadier-General A., 332, 333, 363

Courtney's Post, 216, 218, 225, 226, 227, 230, 233
Cox, General (Sir) H. V., 233-42, 262, 263, 264, 271, 283, 302, 393
Coxen, Major-General W. A., 309, 330, 333, 376, 381, 407, 472, 524
Creswell, Vice-Admiral Sir W. R., 180, 258
Currie, General (Sir) A. W., 289, 299, 339, 341, 348, 350, 351, 369, 377, 412, 428, 511, 521
Cussen, (Sir) L., 38n., 109, 139-40, 148, 151, 186, 187
Cutlack, F. M., 338, 382, 385, 399, 401, 529
Cuttriss, Rev. C. P., 299, 303

dancing and balls, 67, 71, 142-3
Danglow, Rabbi J., 230, 414, 488, 525, 526, 527
Dare, Lieut-Colonel C. M. M., 253, 302
David, Sir T. W. E., 436, 481
Dawson, Private, 231, 408
Deakin, A., 19, 28, 38, 44, 107, 114, 115, 147, 151, 171, 250, 498, 529
Deakin, Catherine, 19, 24, 28, 250, 423
Deakin family, 28, 34
Dean-Pitt, Colonel, 110, 113, 158
defence: pre-war, 41, 160, 169-71; post-war, 463-4, 484
Defence, Council of, 426, 463, 515
Dennis, C. J., 261, 412, 506, 525
Depression: 1890s, 106, 114; 1929-, 459, 513-14, 518
Dering, Major Sir H., 275, 280
Dernancourt, 313, 315
Deutscher Verein von Victoria, *see* German Club
Dickens, Charles, 13, 26, 30, 107, 182, 496
Dixon, Dr N., 402
Dodds, Major-General T. H., 206, 305, 323, 370, 372, 373, 405
Dorman, Long & Co., 135, 420
Douellens, 310, 311
Drake-Brockman, Major-General E. A., 318, 430, 466
Drake-Brockman, Major G., 309
Durrant, Major-General J. M. A., 260, 263, 272, 321, 376, 381, 391, 405, 407
Dyett, (Sir) G., 465, 515

East Melbourne synagogue, 1, 13, 15
Eastwood, Lieut-Colonel T. R., 232, 234, 238
Eggleston, (Sir) F. W., 126, 438, 440, 447-54, 457, 460, 509
Egypt, 206, 208-13, 229, 245, 251, 256-63, 421
electricity, 177, ch. 15
Eliot, George, 13, 30, 68, 496
Elliott, Major-General H. E., 230, 314, 315, 319, 321, 329, 348, 376, 385, 394, 400-1, 421, 465, 467-8, 469, 472, 487, 523
Elliott, W., 9-11, 30, 513

594 INDEX

Engineering Students' Society, 85-6, 102, 117
Essame, Major-General H., 335

Fairway, C. T., 164, 166, 173, 178, 257, 286, 426, 428, 473, 485
Farlow, G., 20-1, 33, 45, 47, 61, 62, 69-70, 77, 80, 90, 103, 104, 108, 109, 110, 118, 140, 145, 157, 159, 169, 172
Farmar, Colonel H. M., 266, 266-7, 272, 274, 278, 282, 303-4, 421
Fink, T., 69, 187, 222, 257, 321
Fisher, A., 201, 299, 325
Fletcher, C. B., 411, 445, 504
Foch, Marshal F., 313, 331, 337, 338, 339, 341, 349, 350, 363, 372, 378, 379, 498
Foott, Brigadier-General C. H., 190, 330, 376, 381, 386, 405, 407, 424
Fortuna mine, 436, 439, 449
Foster, Brigadier-General H. J., 170, 191, 265, 387
Fraser, Brigadier-General L. D., 330, 381
French, Field Marshal Lord, 273, 372, 404
French Army, 293, 308, 313, 318, 339, 358
Fuller, Major-General J. F. C., 335, 340, 376, 377, 378, 497
Fyansford bridge, 131, 134, 135, 136, 139-40, 152, 155

Gabriel, Annie, 87-97, 99, 103, 206, 494-5, 523, 524
Gabriel, Fred, 87-97, 105
Gabriel, G., 87, 257
Gallipoli campaign, 215-54, 272, 368n., 384, 389, 390, 413, 467, 474, 475, 476; landing, 215-16; evacuation, 247-51
Garran, Sir R. R., 199, 302, 370, 431, 514
Garrison Artillery, 21, 63-6, 110-13, 124-5, 156-62, 169
gassing, 290, 292, 299, 317, 318, 331, 332, 342, 353, 365
Gaudlitz, E., 450-1, 454n.
Gellibrand, Major-General Sir J., 209, 319, 321, 327, 329, 332, 348, 349, 352, 353, 355, 364, 366-7, 375, 385, 389, 394, 397, 400, 405, 408, 431, 464-5, 509
German brown-coal technology, 439, 440, 449, 455
German Club, 66-7, 69, 93, 98
Germania Cottage, 7, 19
Germans in Melbourne, 15-16, 19, 34, 46, 66-7, 205
Gibbon, Edward, 23, 26, 52, 109
Gibson, John, 121, 127, 135, 138, 139, 154, 155, 164, 166, 167, 172, 173, 177-9, 180, 184, 187, 199, 206, 211, 256, 257, 286, 425-6, 427, 428, 502, 512
Gibson, Sir Robert, 164, 167, 427, 436, 446-54, 457, 459, 467-8, 479, 518, 522
Gippsland, 69, 70, 121-3
Glasgow, Major-General Sir T. W., 239, 315, 321, 327, 329, 352, 357, 361n., 375, 376, 395, 405
Godley, General Sir A. J., 208-10, 216-64, 277-305, 350, 357, 413
Goldstein, Lieut-Colonel J. R. Y., 63-5, 69, 107, 110, 111, 113, 119
Goldstein, Vida, 71, 513
Graetz, H., 2, 13, 36, 69
Graham & Wadick, 81-4, 86, 106, 107, 113, 123
Grimwade, Major-General H. W., 266, 271, 274, 275, 281, 309, 329, 376, 408, 472, 519, 531
Gullett, (Sir) H. S., 369, 467
Gummow, F. M., 131, 134, 135, 136, 138, 139, 140, 153, 154, 155, 164, 168, 179, 189
Gurkhas, 233, 235, 236

Haig, Field Marshal (Viscount), 268, 275, 277, 280, 284, 289, 292-324, 332-41, 347-80, 388, 390, 395, 397, 402, 404, 412, 416, 429, 512
Hall, G. W. L. M., see Marshall-Hall
Hall, Colonel W. H., 124, 125, 157-61, 169, 171, 203, 212, 250, 512
Hamel, 303, 315, 318, 326, 337, 338, 340, 342, 352, 363, 375, 384, 385, 386, 413, 416, 465; battle of, 332-6
Hamilton, General Sir I., 196-7, 203, 212, 213, 214, 216, 221, 226, 232, 241, 247, 252, 259, 376, 404, 498
Hanby, Lieut-Colonel, 161, 169
Harbor Trust, Melbourne, 107, 108, 112, 113-15
Hargicourt, battle of, 357-9, 360, 361, 363
Harington, General (Sir) C. H., 282, 287, 295, 296, 297, 376, 388, 392
Harper, H. R., 436, 461
Hart, (Sir) B. Liddell, 304, 377, 378, 379, 389-90, 497
Healesville, 70, 122, 123, 130
Henderson, G. F. R., 191, 379, 396
Herald (Melbourne), 140, 302, 328, 406, 418, 420, 424, 429, 444, 445, 454, 467, 471-2, 475, 500, 510, 514
Herman, H., 436, 439, 440, 460, 462, 506
Herz, Dr M., 431
Higgins, G., 59-60, 62, 117, 149, 179, 186, 187
Higgins, H. B., 38, 43, 180
Hill, John, 87, 90
Hill 60, 237, 241, 242, 254
Hill 971, 233, 236, 239
Hindenburg, Field Marshal P. von, 317, 347, 370, 484, 522, 532
Hindenburg line, 354, 356, 357, 358, 363-7, 370
Hirschfeld, Dr E., 431-2
Hoad, Major-General J. C., 124, 170
Hobbs, Lieut-General Sir J. J. T., 283, 294, 305, 316, 317-18, 320, 321, 325, 331, 336, 337, 353, 355, 361, 371, 373, 374, 375, 376,

INDEX 595

395-6, 405, 407, 412, 416, 432, 465, 520
Hodgson, Tom, 25, 28, 45
Hodgson family, 19, 26, 28, 36
Hogan, E. J., 457, 458, 473, 513-14
Holloway, E., 456-7
Holmes, Oliver Wendell, 57, 68
Holmes, Brigadier-General W., 246, 253, 259, 263, 283, 283-4, 395, 400
Howe, Captain H. V., 238, 252, 534
Hudson, P. B., 471, 473
Hughes, W. M., 211, 260, 265, 268, 269, 281, 299-302, 320-7, 333, 340, 353, 359-61, 369-73, 378, 383-4, 404-12, 413, 416, 420-1, 422, 426, 429, 430, 440, 483, 498, 504, 510, 529
Hume Pipe Co. (Aust.) Ltd, 426, 427, 485
Huntsman family, 28, 67
Hutton, Lieut-General Sir E. T. H., 160, 170, 253
Hyde, A., 13, 21, 22, 31, 32, 33, 68, 146, 199
hydro-electricity, 436, 437-8, 441, 459

Imperial Federation League, 147-8
Industrial Workers of the World, 269, 410
Institute of Science and Industry, 426-8
Institution of Civil Engineers, London, 107, 121, 124, 140, 164, 186, 482
Institution of Engineers, Australia, 187, 431, 482
Iona, 181-2, 208, 244, 285, 287, 433
Isaacs, Sir I. A., 38, 139, 147, 151-2, 490-1, 500, 514, 519, 520-2, 532

Jacka, Captain A., 225, 233, 283, 376, 467
Jackson, Major-General G. H. N., 263, 265, 266, 274, 278, 290, 295, 303, 304, 305, 309, 315, 319, 389-90
Jackson, Stonewall, 254, 356-7
James, R. R., 237, 242, 534-5
Jerilderie, 8-10, 12, 31, 119, 128, 513
Jess, Lieut-General (Sir) C. H., 204, 210, 220, 309, 318, 468, 520
Jewish community: at Krotoschin, 1-3; in Australia, 6, 13-15, 23, 34, 69, 415-16, 466, 487-91, 529; in England, 414-15
Jobson, Brigadier-General A., 266, 279, 281-2, 293, 321
Johnston, Major-General G. J., 253, 321, 468-9

Kellett, Matron, 294, 318
Kelly gang, 10, 509-10
Kemsley, (Sir) A. N., 472
Kernot, Professor W. C., 33, 38, 42, 43, 59, 80, 81, 102, 107, 113, 115, 116, 119, 137, 149, 153, 185, 187, 189, 482, 514, 523
King George V, 211, 273-5, 350-1, 379, 404, 413, 498, 514
Kitchener, Field Marshal Lord, 170-1, 204, 209, 211, 232, 246, 263, 319, 402n.
Klitzing, J., 450-1, 453, 454n.
Knox, R., 518-19

Koch, J. A. B., 24, 31
Koondrook bridge, 152-3
Krakowski, Ada, 73, 119, 133, 231
Krakowski family, 67, 119
Krotoschin (Krotoszyn), 1-2, 174

Latham, Lieut-Commander (Sir) J. G., 185, 325, 423, 431
Lawson, (Sir) H. W., 427, 428, 431, 436, 438, 441, 471-2, 483, 485
League of National Security, 517
League of Nations, 464, 489, 515
Le Cateau, 372, 405, 406, 499
Legge, Lieut-General J. G., 204, 206, 210, 228, 230, 246, 259, 263, 283, 321, 419
Lemnos, 213, 214, 244, 255
Lessing, G. E., 20, 23, 26, 36, 57
Lewis, J. B., 40, 43, 46, 47, 58-60, 80, 102, 116, 146, 199, 213, 316, 532
Lewis, Mrs, 51-2, 68, 423
library, 26, 146, 182, 497-9
Liddell Hart, (Sir) B., *see* Hart
Liedertafel, Metropolitan, 67, 143
Lilydale, 196-7, 212, 226, 252
Lloyd, Brigadier-General H. W., 463, 468
Lloyd George, D. (Earl), 299, 300, 308, 325, 359, 360, 377-8, 379, 404
Locke, Major-General W. J. M., 210, 216, 232, 238, 244, 245, 302, 321, 376
Lone Pine, 232, 234, 251, 252
Long, Bishop G. M., 326, 409
Longstaff, (Sir) J., 318, 412, 413, 499, 536
Ludendorff, General E., 208n., 346, 347, 370, 385, 532
Luna Park, 206, 426, 485
Lyle, Professor Sir T. R., 427, 436, 446-54, 459
Lynch, A., 138, 139, 164, 177, 178, 426, 485
Lyons, J. A., 519, 522
Lytton, Bulwer, 13, 26, 30, 36, 182, 496

Macaulay, T. B. (Lord), 20, 26
McBeath, Sir W. G., 407, 426, 427, 428
Macbeth essay, 26
McCaughey, D. and (Sir) S., 128-9
McCay, Lieut-General Sir J. W., 12, 20, 169-70, 173, 179, 192, 193, 202, 203, 204, 209, 224, 228, 245, 246, 251, 253, 258, 260, 262, 264, 266, 282, 283, 300, 302, 305-6, 319, 320, 321, 324, 329, 387, 398-9, 400, 407, 413, 421, 468, 507, 512
McCulloch, Sir J., 12, 20
Macdonald, D., 124, 125
MacFarland, Sir J., 42, 205, 478, 479, 480, 500
McGlinn, Brigadier-General J. P., 204, 210, 211, 216, 221, 225, 234, 248, 250, 253, 260, 265, 321, 324, 325, 405, 432, 492, 531
McInerney, Major, 198, 205, 211, 509
McKenna, F. J., 520-1
Mackey, (Sir) J. E., 40, 109, 117, 138, 146, 147, 150, 166, 186
MacLagan, Major-General E. G. Sinclair,

216, 252, 259, 284, 293, 302, 310, 311, 321, 327, 331, 332, 333, 336, 346, 348, 357, 358, 364, 366, 371, 375, 405
MacLaurin, Colonel H. N., 216, 217, 224
McMahon, Gregan, 183, 500
McNicoll, Brigadier-General (Sir) W. R., 266, 281, 282, 296, 298, 310, 312, 313, 314, 329, 348, 349, 376, 405, 431, 468
McPherson, Sir W., 460, 478
Madden, Sir J., 28, 143, 184, 258
Maloney, Dr W. R. N., 198, 281
Manasse family, 3-6, 15
Margolin, Lieut-Colonel E. L., 414, 487, 489
Maria Island Land & Development Co., 426, 486
Marshall-Hall, Professor G. W. L., 107, 143, 148, 187, 231
Martin, L., 2, 3, 6
Masson, Professor Sir D. O., 152, 186, 224, 449
Master Builders' Association, 165-6, 177
Meier family, 28
Melba (Dame) Nellie, 13n., 47, 139, 143, 510, 523
Melbourne & Metropolitan Board of Works, 106-7, 135, 138, 139, 154, 165-6, 179, 445
Melbourne City Council, 442, 479
Melbourne Club, 432-3
Melbourne Cup, 70, 91, 99, 101, 129, 143
Melbourne Electricity Supply Co., 441, 442-3, 447, 452, 514
Melbourne Hebrew Congregation, 119, 146-7, 487-8
Melbourne Hotels Ltd, 427, 428
Melbourne University Graduates' Association, 185-6, 187
Melbourne University Review, 39-41, 43-4, 49
Melbourne University Union, 38-9, 43-4, 47, 49
Menzies (Sir) R. G., 151, 460, 506, 529
Menton, 284, 310
Meredith, George, 174, 182, 496
Messines, 293, 295, 302, 303, 305, 307, 316, 335, 341, 354, 385, 387, 388; battle of, 282, 287, 289-92
Metropolitan Gas Co., 180, 447
Meyer, Felix, 174, 184, 231, 321, 363, 394, 473, 502, 532
Michell, A. G. M., 164, 187, 438
Miller, Dr (Captain) J., 21, 63, 88, 107, 111, 112, 115, 119, 124, 146, 158
Mitchell, D., 13, 121, 135, 138, 139, 140, 154, 155, 164, 177-9
Moir, G., 136, 151
Monasch, B.-L., 1-3
Monasch, Berthold, 496
Monasch, Bruno, 146, 183-4
Monasch, Julius, 3, 6, 7, 8
Monasch family, 1-7, 174
Monash, Bertha, née Manasse, ch. 1, 27, 28, 49, 51, 52, 53, 58, 101, 104, 109, 163

Monash, Bertha, 108, 117-20, 133, 141, 143, 172, 173, 175, 181, 182, 211, 212, 213, 228, 229, 257, 265, 374, 412-13, 424, 433, 434, 486-7, 488, 494, 495, 496, 533
MONASH, General Sir John:
chronological: family background, 6-7; boyhood, 7-24; speech and accent, 7-8, 20; education, school, 8-12, 18-24; bar mitzvah, 13-14; early literary ambitions, 21, 29, 30-1, 34; *Macbeth* essay, 23; university student, ch. 2 passim, 61-3, 102-3, 108-10; editor *Melb. University Review*, 39-41, 43-4, 49; engineering student, 31, 33, 37, 42, 102-3, 109-10; University Company, 41, 44-6; mother's death, 51-2; work on Princes Bridge, 58-60; joins Nth Melb. Battery, 63; social life, 66-77; Outer Circle works, 80-6; Annie Gabriel *affaire*, 87-97; courtship and engagement, 93-9; wedding 104-5; studies law, 108-9; with Harbor Trust, 107, 113-15; Monash & Anderson founded, 116, 121-4; temporary marital break and father's death, 117-20; promoted captain and major and to command Nth Melb. Battery, 124-5; works in Queensland, N.S.W. and W.A., 126-34; begins Monier work, 134; Fyansford disaster, 136, 139-40; Monier Pipe Co. formed, 138; formation Reinforced Concrete Co., 155; prosperity, 163-7; promoted lieut-colonel in A.I.C., 169; overseas trip, 173-7; buys Iona, 181-2; joins University Council, 186; president Victorian Institute of Engineers, 187; commanding 13th Infantry Brigade, 193-7; appointed to command 4th Brigade, A.I.F., 203; in Egypt, 208-13; Gallipoli campaign, 213-54; April-May fighting, 215-27; promoted brigadier-general, 228; battle of Sari Bair, 232-41; evacuation and diary-letter, 247-51; promoted major-general commanding 3rd Division, 264-7; training 3rd Division, 265-76; battle of Messines, 287-91; Broodseinde, 294-6; Passchendaele, 296-8; knighted, 305; defending Amiens, 310-16; promoted lieut-general and corps commander, 318-20; resisting the plot, 321-8; Hamel, 332-6; origins of 8 August, 337-40; 8 August offensive, 341-7; Mont St Quentin, 354-7; Hargicourt, 357-9; Hindenburg line, 363-7; Director-General of Repatriation, 404-11; hailed as famous Jew, 413-16; returns home and death of Vic, 422-4; chairman of S.E.C., ch. 15; Anzac Day and the Shrine, 469-73; vice-chancellor, 476-80; Jewish leader and Zionist, 488-91; urged to be Dictator, 517-20, 522; in India, 520-2; death and funeral, 524-7

military: in militia, 41, 44-6, 63-6, 76, 78, 82, 110-13, 124-5, 156-62, 169-72, 181, 190-7, 202; South African War, 160; military historian, 190-2; military censorship, 212, 213, 250-1, 303; tank tactics, 386; psychology, 394-5; on Australian soldier, 391-3, 396; military theory and methods, 195-6, 241, 271-2, 379-81, 382-7, 389-90, 448-9; reputation, ch. 13, 474-5

general: as administrator, 81-3, 448, 507-9; ambition, 29, 30, 37, 41, 42, 49, 50, 58, 76, 77-8, 79-80, 86, 90, 91, 103, 116, 127, 150, 199, 306-7, 504, 511, 528; appearance and manner, 40, 50, 150, 278, 359, 363, 504-5; assessment, 504-11; business interests, minor, 180-1, 485-6; clubs, 119, 145, 184, 501-2; collecting, 26, 75, 149, 173-4, 182, 433, 497; diary-keeping, 20, 24, 25, 37, 74-6, 117, 142, 149, 182; diet, 141, 185, 278; drawing, 13, 68, 146, 213, 305, 363; drinking habits, 46, 79, 102, 119, 126, 185, 496; as engineer, 58-60, 80-6, 106-9, 113-16, 121-4, 130-1, 134-40, 151-6, 163-6, 168-9, 176-80, 181, 185-7, 187-9, 247, 380-1, ch. 15, 483, 484, 507; German background, 7-8, 19, 23, 34, 46, 66-7, 99, 146, 174, 181, 202, 203-4, 204-5, 229-30, 259, 281, 321, 491; health, 78, 94, 126-7, 141, 172-3, 179, 185, 211, 241, 244, 247, 252, 278, 363, 370, 434, 502-3, 522-3; and honours, 229, 245, 284, 305-6, 404-5; Jewish background and activities, 13-14, 20, 34, 35-6, 69, 146-7, 167, 181, 211, 245, 321, 325, 402, 413-16, 432-3, 487-91; languages, 7-8, 23-4, 34, 42, 174, 336, 372; legal practice, 113-14, 123, 126-34, 151-2, 164; library, 26, 146, 182, 497-9; mathematics, 9, 19-20, 23-4, 25, 29, 37, 42-3, 61-2, 109, 381, 507; music, 7, 13, 18, 20, 30, 31, 36, 37, 47, 67-8, 78-9, 97, 116, 133, 142, 146, 183, 265, 284, 310, 499; personal finances, 25, 50, 52, 58, 106, 107, 108, 117, 119, 124, 132, 140-1, 150, 163, 167, 177-81, 285, 486, 513; political views, 34-5, 147, 482-4; religious views, 15, 27, 35-6, 53, 55-8, 146-7, 488-9; as speaker and lecturer, 27, 37, 39, 69, 97, 110, 112, 116, 149, 195-6, 245, 271-2, 308-9, 493, 504; sport, 21, 31, 46, 67, 70, 502; success, views on qualities making for, 188, 480-1; as teacher, 9, 10, 22, 25, 33, 50, 110, 112, 113, 185, 187, 508-9; work, 79, 508; work methods, 81-3, 85-6

Monash, Leo, 24, 33, 34, 35, 41, 50, 58, 176
Monash, Louis, ch. 1, 25, 29, 31, 55, 73, 94, 98, 101, 117-18, 119
Monash, Louise, *see* Rosenhain, Louise
Monash, Mathilde, 7, 10, 11, 19, 22, 25, 31, 33, 37, 46, 47, 48, 52, 54, 93, 94, 98, 101-2, 117, 118, 119, 121, 140, 141, 143-4, 167-8, 175, 183, 203, 229, 230, 250, 305, 328, 413, 423, 464, 494-5, 533
Monash, Max, 3, 6, 7, 8, 12, 13, 24, 184
Monash, Vic, 93-108, 110, 116, 117-21, 126, 129-30, 133, 135, 141-3, 146, 159, 161, 171, 172, 173-6, 179, 180, 181, 183, 200, 211-12, 213, 222, 228, 229, 230, 256-7, 260, 264, 265, 267, 269, 284-5, 286, 306, 320-1, 374, 412-13, 414, 421-4, 488, 494, 496
Monash & Anderson, 116, 121-4, 130-40, 152, 154-5
Monash University, 529, 532
Monash Valley, 216, 218, 219
Monier concrete construction, 131, 134-9, 151-5; *see also* Reinforced Concrete & Monier Pipe Construction Co.
Monier Pipe Co. Pty Ltd, 138, 154
Mont St Quentin, battle of, 354-7, 369, 375, 385, 387, 532
Montbrehain, 367, 384
Montgomery, Field Marshal Lord, 379, 389, 402n.
Montgomery (Field Marshal Sir A. A. Montgomery-Massingberd), 330, 332, 337, 338, 339, 340, 354, 357, 366, 388
Moore, Professor (Sir) H., 109, 186, 479
Morlancourt, 312, 313, 317, 331, 337, 342, 475
Morrison, Dr A., 12, 22, 29
Morrison, R., 11, 29
Morshead, Lieut-General (Sir) L. J., 291, 376, 405, 430, 466, 492
Morwell, 428, 436, 438, 439
Moses, M., 11, 23, 36
Moss, A., 257, 330, 351, 405
Moss (Grant), Belle, 94, 107, 496, 512
Moss, D., 106, 118
Moss, Vic, *see* Monash, Vic
motoring, 181, 183, 433
Munro, David, 58-60, 80
Munro Ferguson, Sir R. (Lord Novar), 197, 206, 212, 277, 321, 322, 325, 328, 420, 423, 424, 429, 430
Murdoch, (Sir) K. A., 239, 247, 281, 294, 299, 300, 301, 302, 321, 338, 351, 359, 360, 362, 373, 394, 397, 406, 409, 418, 444, 454; plots with Bean, 322-8; and Shrine, 471-3
Murdoch, Walter, 498, 506
Murphy, Agnes, 70-1, 268
Murray, Lieut-Colonel H. W., 220-1, 283, 422
Murray, Lee, 38n., 412, 496
Mustapha Kemal, 216
Myers, Rabbi I., 13, 36, 69

Nanson, Professor E. J., 25, 42
Napoleon, 277, 379, 398, 413, 460, 472, 525
Narrandera 8, 9, 24, 29, 148
National Party, 420, 426, 446, 460, 483

598 INDEX

Naval and Military Club, 110, 119, 145, 160, 184, 226, 432, 457, 491, 494, 501, 517, 527
Nek, The, 218, 219, 251, 400
Nettlefold, (Sir) T. S., 427, 485
New Zealand Forces: Brigade, 208, 214, 219, 232, 234, 236, 242, 258, 260; Division, 290, 291, 292, 295, 297, 298, 330, 378
Newbigin, E. A., 138, 178
North Melbourne Battery, Metropolitan Brigade, Garrison Artillery, 63-6, 110-13, 124-5, 156-62, 169, 422

O'Connor, C. Y., 131, 134
Officer, (Sir) F. K., 520, 522
Official Historian, *see* Bean
Official Medical Historian, 240-1
O'Hara, J. B., 40, 42, 61, 62, 68
Old Scotch Collegians Association, 502
Old Scotch Collegians Club, 145, 502
Ormond College, 42
Outer Circle Railway works, 80-6, 106, 113-14, 123
Outtrim, Major F. L., 112, 113, 115, 124, 125
Ozanne, Quartermaster-sergeant A. T., 281, 509

Paris, 174, 284, 303, 310, 421
Passchendaele, 292, 293, 301, 302, 377, 400; battle of, 296-8
patents work, 124, 151, 155
Payne, Professor H., 185, 186, 431, 436, 480
peaceful penetration, 317, 336, 339
Pearce, (Sir) G. F., 204, 205, 212, 230, 239, 246, 253, 259, 262, 265, 277, 284, 319, 322, 323, 325, 327, 370, 405, 407, 409, 411, 420, 421, 426, 429, 463
Peebles, N. G., 166, 172
Péronne, 353, 354, 355, 356, 369
Perry, E. W., 190, 254
Pershing, General J. J., 333, 412
Ploegsteert, 305, 308
Ploegsteert Wood, 287, 290, 316
Plumer, Field Marshal (Viscount) H., 277, 282, 286, 289, 291, 292, 293, 294, 296, 297, 305, 309, 325, 376, 388, 392, 402, 489
police strike, 467-9; royal commission, 447, 469
Pope, Lieut-Colonel H., 235, 236, 238, 242, 253, 260, 266, 302, 321
Pope's Hill, 216, 218, 219, 221, 226, 233, 265
Prendergast, G. M., 447, 469
Presbyterian Ladies' College, Melbourne, 13n., 19, 52, 141, 144
Preston reservoir, 163, 165-6
Prince of Wales (Edward VIII), 261-2, 372, 416, 429-30
Princes Bridge, 58-60
Public Library, Melbourne, 16, 26, 27, 35, 36, 102, 165, 166
Pulver, L., 14, 15, 19, 24, 27, 36
Punch (London), 12, 309, 363
Punch (Melbourne), 173, 181, 199, 493-4, 502

Püttmann family, 15, 24, 28, 31, 36, 46, 48, 67, 68

Queensland, 126-8
Quinn, James, 412, 536
Quinn's Post, 216, 218, 219, 221, 225, 226, 227, 230, 233, 254, 265

raids, 263-4, 279, 286, 307-8
railways, 123, 138, 139, 177, 420, 435, 445, 453; *see also* Outer Circle Railway works
Rawlinson, Field Marshal (Lord) H., 316, 318, 325, 330-72 passim, 376, 384, 388, 390, 405, 412, 413
Read, Major-General G. W., 363-4
Reed, J. B. A., 152-3
Reinforced Concrete & Monier Pipe Construction Co., 155, 163-7, 177-80, 184, 257, 286, 426, 427, 428, 437, 473, 485; *see also* Monier concrete construction
Returned Sailors' and Soldiers' Imperial League of Australia (R.S.L.), 321, 337, 419, 425, 430, 431-2, 439, 455, 465-76, 513, 515, 517, 520, 525, 529, 531
Ritchie, E. G., 165-6
Riverina, 7, 8-10, 24, 128-9
Robinson, Sir A., 146, 179, 427n., 436, 437, 440, 441, 442, 444, 447, 449, 468, 492, 524
Robinson, Gerald, 179, 205
Robinson, Jess, 71, 74
Robinson, W. S., 179, 322, 427n., 506
Rosenhain, Louise, 7, 52, 118, 121, 140, 141, 143-4, 167-8, 174-5, 183, 198, 231, 253, 265, 275, 293, 340, 434, 495, 525-6, 533
Rosenhain, Mona and Nancy, 175, 512
Rosenhain, W., 142, 144, 165, 167-8, 171, 174-5, 196, 198, 204, 253, 265, 275, 303, 310, 340, 418, 422, 427, 432, 434, 435, 440, 480, 503-4, 523, 524, 533
Rosenhain family, 67, 202, 205
Rosenthal, Major-General Sir C., 204, 282, 301, 310, 312, 314, 317, 321, 329, 337, 353, 354, 367, 375, 376, 385, 405, 430, 432, 465, 466, 486, 523
Roth, Herman, 144-5, 155
Roth, Karl, 7, 14, 33, 68, 97, 102, 119, 144, 183, 202, 257
Roth, Louis, 136, 144-5
Roth, Max, 6, 114
Roth (Monasch), Ulrike, 6, 13, 114, 119, 130, 144-5, 183, 205, 423, 495, 512
Roth family, 7, 12, 16, 29, 68, 102, 114, 140, 144-5, 167, 183, 495, 533
Rotary, 501
Royal Air Force, 335, 342
Royal Military College, Duntroon, 171, 172, 204, 331, 464
Russell, Major-General Sir A. H., 216, 230, 241-2, 245, 247, 253, 258, 263, 290, 293, 298, 301, 376, 511
Ryan, Surgeon-General Sir C., 209, 371

INDEX

Saddler, V. J., 126-8, 131, 132, 135, 138, 140, 152, 155, 431, 485, 503
St Kilda Hebrew Congregation, 487-8, 532
St Quentin Canal, 357, 363-7
Salisbury Plain, 265-76
Sander family, 28, 31
Sandow, Eugen, 172-3
Sargood, Lieut-Colonel Sir F. T., 112, 147
Sari Bair, battle of, 234-42, 252, 254
Sawyer, W. H., 450-5, 458
Schild, Rosie, 73-4, 78, 92, 94, 97
Sclater, Lieut-General (Sir) H., 272, 273, 276
Scotch College, Melbourne, 12-13, 16, 19-21, 22-4, 40, 171, 184, 203, 425, 492, 529, 531, 532
Scott, Professor (Sir) E., 423, 505, 506
Scott, (Sir) Walter, 13, 24, 30, 37, 107, 423, 496
Scullin, J. H., 513, 514, 515, 517, 522
Serapeum, 260, 261, 262
Sewell, (Sir) S. V., 434, 496, 503, 523, 524
Shaw, A. G., 152, 164
Shaw, George Bernard, 182, 310, 497
Shaw, W. B., 84, 132
Shrine of Remembrance, 455, 471-3, 474, 495, 517, 524, 527, 531
Simonson, Eric, 245, 257, 265, 274, 278, 292, 310, 405, 506-7
Simonson, Max, 98, 104, 108, 117, 118, 183
Simonson, Paul, 257, 278, 282, 301, 310, 312, 330, 351, 374, 405
Simonson, Sarah, 98, 118, 130, 142, 183, 257, 495
Sinclair-MacLagan, *see* MacLagan
Skelsey, Major F. W., 218, 251
Sladen, D. B. W., 13, 418
Smith, C. P., 207, 211, 227, 230, 258, 423, 520
Smith, J. A., 186, 187, 188
Smith's Weekly, 377, 428, 430, 455, 516-17
Smithers, A. J., 356, 386, 529
Smyth, Major-General Sir N. M., 283, 294, 302, 329
Somme, River, 263, 264, 310-18, 331-57 passim, 377
South African War, 160, 170
South Australian Reinforced Concrete Co. Ltd, 164, 180, 257, 426, 428, 485
Speight, R., 113-14, 131
Springthorpe, Dr J. W., 44, 248, 250, 257, 275, 362, 370, 372, 383, 396, 420-1, 491
Stanley, Major-General J., 65-6, 110, 111-12, 172, 193, 371
Stanley-Monash practice gun, 111-12
State Electricity Commission of Victoria, 425, 427-8, ch. 15, 472, 483, 485, 486, 496, 503, 508, 513-14, 523, 524, 529, 531, 532
Steele, W., 33, 35, 41, 48, 51, 54, 61-2, 66, 68, 76, 79-80, 82, 84, 90, 95, 97, 102, 108, 119, 145-6, 149, 199
Steenwerck, 278, 287, 305
Stettin (Szczecin), 3, 4, 174

Steward, (Sir) G., 229-30
Stewart, Brigadier-General J. C., 355, 531
Stockfeld, Clara, 47-8, 321
Story, Lieut-Colonel C. B., 282, 362
Streeton, (Sir) A., 499, 506, 522
Suez Canal, 208, 261
Sun (Sydney), 418, 463
Sun-News Pictorial (Melbourne), 475, 514
Suvla Bay, 230, 232, 233, 236, 239, 241, 242
Swanson, (Sir) J. W., 442, 471
Swinburne, G., 427-8, 436, 447-53, 459, 512
Sydney Morning Herald, 411, 445, 466, 504
Syme, D., 113-14

Tate, F., 231, 425, 496, 524, 525
Taylor, Elizabeth, 461-2
Taylor, R., 136, 137, 140, 154, 177, 231, 257
Terraine, J., 297, 368, 370, 376, 379, 385, 387
Tilney, Lieut-Colonel L. E., 234, 262
trade unions and Yallourn, 455-8
Troedel family, 12, 15
Turnbull, E., 465, 466-7
Turnverein (Melbourne), 25, 47, 146

United Service Institution, 112, 124, 161, 170
University Club, 145, 147, 184, 185, 186, 501
University of Melbourne, 20, 22, ch. 2, 61-3, 77-9, 85-6, 102-3, 107, 108-10, 113, 144, 148-9, 163, 184, 185-7, 199, 306, 418, 431, 476-80, 493, 517, 532

Victoria Police, 166, 171, *see also* police strike
Victoria Racing Club, 184, 473
Victorian Institute of Engineers, 140, 153, 165, 184, 185, 187-8
Victorian Railways, *see* Railways
Villers-Bretonneux, 315, 316, 317, 318, 337, 349-50, 425

Wagner, Richard, 310, 499
Walhalla, 70, 122-3
Walker, Lieut-General Sir H. B., 216, 219, 245, 246, 251, 252, 253, 283, 294, 305, 329, 400
Walker, T., 27, 31
walking trips, 69-70
Wallaby Club, 184, 206, 260, 501-2
Warneton and Warneton line, 291, 293, 308
Warren, Professor W. H., 127, 153
Watt, W. A., 406, 410, 420, 426, 429
Wavell, (Lord) A. P., 380, 389
Wazzir, battle of, 213
Wears, W. L., 172, 189-90, 231, 405, 423
Wesley Church Mutual Improvement Society, 26-7, 31, 37
Western Australia, 107, 122, 131-4, 206
White, General Sir C. B. B., 169, 192, 197, 230, 250, 252, 253, 259, 263, 265, 267, 269, 283, 284, 294, 299, 300, 301, 305, 308, 315, 317-18, 319, 320-7, 329, 330, 339, 372, 373, 375, 385, 387, 388, 389, 396, 397, 398-9,

400, 401, 402, 405, 407, 413, 415, 425, 429, 444, 463, 465, 471, 473, 510, 515, 528
White Guard, 469, 517
Williamson's, J. C., 12, 143, 183
Williamstown Rifle Range, 45, 65-6
Wilson, Field Marshal Sir H., 269, 325, 350, 359, 371
Wiltshires, 181, 426, 428
Wischer, V., 13, 21, 27, 486
Wischer family, 12, 28, 31
Wootten, Major-General (Sir) G. F., 266, 282, 379

Wright, C. E., 119, 172, 182, 432
Wylly, Colonel G. G. E., 265, 521

Yallourn, ch. 15 passim, 529, 531, 532
Yorick Club, 65, 119, 125, 145, 432, 501
Ypres (and battles of), 290, 293, 294, 295, 298, 310, 330, 337, 341

Zichy-Woinarski, C. J., 40, 42, 43
Zionism, 154, 414, 415, 416, 489-90
Zox, E. L., 15, 115

WITHDRAWN